Barcode in Back

HANDBOOK OF MANAGERIAL BEHAVIOR AND OCCUPATIONAL HEALTH

NEW HORIZONS IN MANAGEMENT

Series Editor: Cary L. Cooper, CBE, *Distinguished Professor of Organizational Psychology and Health, Lancaster University, UK.*

This important series makes a significant contribution to the development of management thought. This field has expanded dramatically in recent years and the series provides an invaluable forum for the publication of high quality work in management science, human resource management, organizational behaviour, marketing, management information systems, operations management, business ethics, strategic management and international management.

The main emphasis of the series is on the development and application of new original ideas. International in its approach, it will include some of the best theoretical and empirical work from both well-established researchers and the new generation of scholars.

Titles in the series include:

Handbook of Managerial Behavior and Occupational Health

Edited by

Alexander-Stamatios G. Antoniou

Lecturer in Psychology, University of Athens, Greece and Consultant in Organizational Psychology and Behavior

Cary L. Cooper, CBE

Distinguished Professor of Organizational Psychology and Health, Lancaster University, UK

George P. Chrousos

Professor of Pediatrics and Chairman, First Department of Pediatrics, University of Athens Medical School, Greece

Charles D. Spielberger

Distinguished Research Professor of Psychology and Director, Center for Research in Behavioral Medicine and Health Psychology, University of South Florida, USA

Michael William Eysenck

Professor, Psychology Department, Royal Holloway, University of London, UK

NEW HORIZONS IN MANAGEMENT

Edward Elgar
Cheltenham, UK • Northampton, MA, USA

Published by
Edward Elgar Publishing Limited
The Lypiatts
15 Lansdown Road
Cheltenham
Glos GL50 2JA
UK

Edward Elgar Publishing, Inc.
William Pratt House
9 Dewey Court
Northampton
Massachusetts 01060
USA

A catalogue record for this book
is available from the British Library

Library of Congress Control Number: 2008939766

PEFC/16-33-111
CATG-PEFC-052
www.pefc.org

ISBN 978 1 84844 095 1

Printed and bound in Great Britain by MPG Books Group, UK

Contents

Contributors

Alexander-Stamatios G. Antoniou   University of Athens, Greece.

Alicia Arenas   University of Salamanca, Spain.

Terry A. Beehr   Central Michigan University, Mount Pleasant, MI, USA.

Wolfgang P. Beiglböck   Faculty of Psychology, University of Vienna, Austria.

Rabi S. Bhagat   University of Memphis, TN, USA.

Richard E. Boyatzis   Case Western Reserve University, Cleveland, OH, USA.

Denise M. Breaux   Florida State University, Talahassee, FL, USA.

Elena Briones   University of Salamanca, Spain.

Chris Brotherton   School of Life Sciences, Heriot-Watt University, Edinburgh, Scotland, UK.

Wendy J. Casper   University of Texas at Arlington, TX, USA.

George P. Chrousos   University of Athens, Greece.

Roman Cieslak   Trauma, Health, and Hazards Center, University of Colorado at Colorado Springs, CO, USA and Department of Psychology, Warsaw School of Psychology, Poland.

Cary L. Cooper   Lancaster University, UK.

Sarah E. Crozier   Manchester Business School, University of Manchester, UK.

Marina Dalla   School of Philosophy, National and Kapodistrian University of Athens, Greece.

Marilyn J. Davidson   Manchester Business School, University of Manchester, UK.

Charlotte A. Davis   University of Memphis, TN, USA.

Carolyn Deighan   School of Life Sciences, Heriot-Watt University, Edinburgh, Scotland, UK.

Philip Dewe   Department of Organizational Psychology, Birkbeck, University of London, UK.

Michael William Eysenck   University of London, UK.

Senta Feselmayer   Faculty of Psychology, University of Vienna, Austria.

Rhona Flin   Industrial Psychology Research Centre, University of Aberdeen, UK.

Adrian Furnham   Department of Psychology, University College London, UK.

Santiago Gascón   Faculty of Medicine, University of Zaragoza, Spain.

Simone I. Grebner   Central Michigan University, Mount Pleasant, MI, USA.

David Holman   Institute of Work Psychology, University of Sheffield, UK.

Brian M. Hughes   Centre for Research on Occupational and Life Stress, Department of Psychology, National University of Ireland, Galway, Ireland.

Ellen Kenner   University of Maryland, College Park, MD, USA.

Bruce Kirkcaldy   International Centre for the Study of Occupational and Mental Health, Düsseldorf, Germany.

Vladimirn Kuznetsov   Northern State Medical University, Arkhangelsk, Russia.

Terry Lansdown   School of Life Sciences, Heriot-Watt University, Edinburgh, Scotland, UK.

Michael P. Leiter   Centre for Organizational Research and Development Acadia University, Wolfville, NS, Canada.

Edwin A. Locke   University of Maryland, College Park, MD, USA.

Manuel L. London   State University of New York at Stony Brook, NY, USA.

Marilyn Macik-Frey   Nicholls State University, Thibodaux, LA, USA.

Begoña Martínez-Jarreta   Faculty of Medicine, University of Zaragoza, Spain.

Katerina Matsa   State Psychiatry Hospital of Attica, Drug Dependence Unit, Athens, Greece.

Cristina Menni   Centro Studi Patologie Cronico Degenerative, Monza, Italy.

Timothy P. Munyon   Florida State University, Talahassee, FL, USA.

Debra L. Nelson   Department of Management, Oklahoma State University, Stillwater, OK, USA.

Karen Niven   Institute of Work Psychology, University of Sheffield, UK.

Alicia Omar   National University of Rosario, Argentina.

Pamela L. Perrewé   Florida State University, Talahassee, FL, USA.

Ayala Malach Pines   Ben-Gurion University, Beer-Sheva, Israel.

James Campbell Quick   University of Texas at Arlington and Lancaster University, Management School, Arlington, TX, USA.

Jonathan D. Quick   Management Sciences for Health, Cambridge, MA, USA.

Klaus-Helmut Schmidt   Institut für Arbeitsphysiologie an der Universität Dortmund, Germany.

Georg Siefen   Westfalia Clinic for Child and Adolescent Psychiatry and Psychotherapy, Marl-Sinsen, Germany.

Johannes Siegrist Department of Medical Sociology, University of Düsseldorf, Germany.

Charles D. Spielberger University of South Florida, Tampa, FL, USA.

Herman Steensma Leiden University, The Netherlands.

Jennifer E. Swanberg University of Kentucky, Lexington, KY, USA.

Carmen Tabernero University of Córdoba, Spain.

Peter Totterdell Institute of Work Psychology, University of Sheffield, UK.

Jürgen Wegge Technische Universität Dresden, Germany.

Ashley Weinberg University of Salford, UK.

Moshe Zeidner Faculty of Education – Human Development and Counselling Department, University of Haifa, Israel.

Foreword

The *Handbook of Managerial Behavior and Occupational Health* is the most recent addition to two impressive lists of management and of occupational health books offered by Edward Elgar, this time combining these two research areas in a handbook that focuses on the implications of managerial behavior for occupational health. As such the volume is a must have addition to the library of managers, scholars and students of these two fields of theory, practice and research. The volume starts with a theoretical framework that includes chapters on occupational health psychology, stress, leadership development, addiction to work and coping. The chapters for this introductory part, as well as the six other parts of the volume, are written by an international and interdisciplinary group of scholars. The other six parts include chapters on such important topics as organizational psychology, occupational stress, burnout, immigration, and the roles of emotions at work and social support; all of them topics of great theoretical importance that also have practical implications for today's rapidly changing work environment.

Ayala Malach Pines

Professor and Chair
Department of Business Administration
School of Management
Ben-Gurion University

Preface

Over the past decades the nature of work has changed dramatically around the world. The introduction of new technologies in the workplace, followed by a huge shift towards globalization, has resulted in marked changes in business organizations, management structures and employment relationships. Organizations in countries hit by recession have been forced to downsize in an effort to survive. There has been a noticeable rise in short-term contracts, possibly as a result of the deregulation of fixed-term contracts and the limited requirements on permanent employment in many countries (OECD, 2006). Other changes include new work patterns, such as self-regulated work and team work, and a shift towards a more flexible workforce, including the number of employees along with their skills and functions (Sparks et al., 2001).

The combination of globalization and technological changes has helped to create a new labour force varied greatly by ethnicity, gender and age. The United Nations estimates that in 2005, 3% of the world's population – about 191 million people – were people who had migrated, with 33% of these having moved from a developing to a developed country, 33% having migrated between developing nations, and a further 33% having moved from one developed country to another developed nation (UN Department of Economic and Social Affairs, 2006). Furthermore, the steadily increasing rate of female participation in the labor force, combined with decreasing male rates, has brought the labour force close to a gender balance (BLS, 2007). The rise in female participation rates holds for married women and single women alike. In the workforce, the trend toward greater age balance is strong, increasing labour force participation among mature and older workers.

As the workplace has transformed, research reported in organizational psychology publications has had an impact on both the individual employee and organizational levels. This *Handbook* focuses on theory and research, concentrating on seven major areas: occupational health psychology, specific issues in organization psychology, managing occupational stress and increasing well-being, professional burnout, migration and health, emotional intelligence and work related support.

Part I: Conceptualization and theoretical framework
This section provides the foundation material for occupational health psychology and managerial behavior. Occupational health psychology reinforces the importance of psychological health in the workplace, why this is important, and levels of theory and practice (individual, group and organizational). One of the chapters provides evidence for the type of leadership and behaviours that are more effective in a complexity perspective. The remaining chapters demonstrate how stress can be harmful and how to identify appraisal patterns associated with different coping strategies.

Part II: Specific issues in organization psychology
The focus of this section is work–life diversity and professional development policies. The first three chapters discuss the influence of age on group performance and health, the work–life issues of single employees without children and latent motivation associated

with social frustration among Russian managers. The other chapters expand on the understanding of factors that enhance occupational safety and interpersonal justice in the workplace. Included in this section are discussions on unhealthy relationships at work and emerging ethical issues.

Part III: Occupational stress, well-being and health

The stress experienced as a direct result of a person's occupation has an adverse effect on the health of individuals and organizations. The aim of this section is to understand the issue of occupational stress in the context of social inequality, facing the temporary workforce and in small- and medium-sized companies. Various chapters explore relationships between several personal and interpersonal variables, such as altruism, affect and stress, and demonstrate the way that stress depletes employees' emotional resources, making them more vulnerable to mental health problems.

Part IV: Professional burnout, coping and prevention

Professional burnout can have serious consequences on an individual's health. This section focuses on the role of person-organization value congruence on the experience of burnout in different countries and the concept of burnout among health professionals. Moreover, it covers certain coping strategies that seem to affect levels of burnout and distress, and suggests training programs for burnout prevention and for helping people to cope with demanding work situations.

Part V: Immigration, acculturation and health

The health of individuals and organizations is determined by a range of social, economic and environmental factors. Some conditions that affect population health – such as employment, living and working conditions and social support – can be especially challenging for immigrant groups in many countries. This section explores the health of immigrants as well as certain acculturation factors related to their mental health problems.

Part VI: Emotion at work

Recent research has begun to focus on the role of emotions in the workplace and the relation between cognition and emotions. This section has been attributed to new research around the construct of Emotional Intelligence (EI) and the role EI may play in occupational stress. The second chapter examines the relation between the psychological contract and emotional labour at work, together with the implications for psychological well-being and organization functioning.

Part VII: Social support aspects

The final section concerns the impact of a perceived support network and availability of functional support on stress. Longitudinal data are reported on the relations between social support from co-workers and supervisors and work strain characteristics such as job demands and job control.

At this point, we would like to express our sincere thanks to all contributors to this new volume who very enthusiastically participated in this project and provided original and in-depth insights on current issues of working life. It is an honour for us to welcome such an international team of over 50 experts, academics and professionals from many universities and research centers worldwide. In conclusion, credits go to Edward Elgar's staff for their assistance throughout the stages of this project. Their professionalism made this effort possible.

References

Bureau of Labor Statistics (BLS) (2007), 'Women in labor force: a databook', Report 1002, United States Department of Labor, www.bls.gov/cps/wlf-databook2007.htm.
Cooper, C.L. and S. Jackson (1997), *Creating Tomorrow's Organizations: A Handbook for Future Research in Organizational Behaviour*, Chichester, UK: Wiley.
OECD (2006), *OECD Factbook 2006: Economics, Environmental, and Social Statistics*, Paris: OECD.
Sparks, K., B. Faragher, and C.L. Cooper (2001), 'Well-being and occupational health in the 21st century workplace', *Journal of Occupational and Organizational Psychology*, **74**, 489–509.
UN Department of Economic and Social Affairs (2006), 'International migration 2006', New York: United Nation Publication, retrieved on January 20, 2009, www.un.org/esa/population/publications/2006Migration_Chart/Migration2006.pdf.

PART I

CONCEPTUALIZATION AND THEORETICAL FRAMEWORK

1 Occupational health psychology: from preventive medicine to psychologically healthy workplaces

Marilyn Macik-Frey, Jonathan D. Quick, James Campbell Quick and Debra L. Nelson

Introduction

Our approach in this chapter is to trace the origins of occupational health psychology (OHP) from preventive medicine, psychology, and engineering to its foundation in an organizational context. From there we examine OHP's future directions in the form of positive advances and new horizons, finishing with a focus on psychologically healthy workplaces. Our aim is to provide such a resource for OHP scholars, researchers, and practitioners alike. Raymond et al. (1990) conceptualized and defined OHP as an interdisciplinary specialty of overlapping theory and research from psychology, management, public health, preventive medicine, industrial engineering, epidemiology, and occupational medicine and nursing. The interlocking interests and collaborations between the American Psychological Association, the National Institute for Occupational Safety and Health, and the Academy of Management helped to anchor and extend this emerging specialized area of OHP. Key objectives for OHP include the prevention of occupational injuries, diseases, and disorders coupled with the enhancement and advancement of occupational health and vitality.

The foundational publications include the *Journal of Occupational Health Psychology*, whose three editors encourage research in exciting new areas such as positive health and preventive intervention studies, and the *Handbook of Occupational Health Psychology* (Quick & Tetrick, 2003). OHP is truly interdisciplinary and draws on medicine, management, psychology and supporting disciplines. This chapter has four major sections on: the emergence of OHP; the burden of suffering for poor occupational health; future directions in OHP; and psychologically healthy workplaces.

The emergence of occupational health psychology

OHP emerged from a set of interdisciplinary scientific contributions from medicine, psychology, and engineering in an organizational context. Figure 1.1 shows these scientific origins, the current convergence and foundation of OHP, and the future directions of OHP. Macik-Frey et al. (2007) previously reviewed the broader context of occupational health. Although the scientific origins date back well over a century and provide a backdrop to the current focus on the past two decades, our key concerns are the present of OHP and the future. Within the preventive medicine and public health tradition, our concern is for the burden of suffering and for the creation of psychologically healthy workplaces.

The modern science and practice of preventive medicine emerged from the study of disease epidemics during the 1800s. Properly labeled 'epidemiology', it is the basic science and fundamental practice of public health and preventive medicine (Wallace & Doebbeling, 1998). The origins of epidemiology are Greek (*epi* – upon + *demos* – people), with roots in the writings of Hippocrates (see Smith, 1994, which is a translation

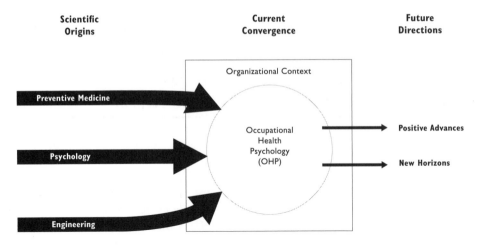

Figure 1.1   Occupational health psychology

of Hippocrates' writings on disease epidemics) as well as the Holy Bible (see Leviticus, Chapter 11, 1952, which includes dietary laws for safe food consumption). However, when the famous Hungarian physician Ignace Semmelweis discovered in the mid-1800s that the incidence of puerperal fever could be drastically cut by setting handwashing standards in obstetrical clinics, the foundations for the germ theory of disease were set.

Public sanitation and personal hygiene emerged in the US during the late 1800s, and Milton J. Rosenau (1913) was the first medical doctor to organize this emerging science and practice into the now classic handbook (Wallace & Doebbeling, 1998). The many editions of *Preventive Medicine and Hygiene* led to later editions after 1950 titled *Public Health and Preventive Medicine*.

The science of psychology closely followed preventive medicine in its concern for human well-being. In the same year that Rosenau published his classic *Preventive Medicine and Hygiene*, Hugo Münsterberg (1913) published his classic volume *Psychology and Industrial Efficiency*. Münsterberg was concerned with industrial accidents such as in steel manufacturing and railroad injuries, a relatively common feature of the early years of the industrial revolution. While Münsterberg's book focused on workers, Colgate psychologist Laird's book (1929) focused on executives. Laird was the first psychologist to be concerned with executive health and his theme was 'every executive his own psychologist' (Laird, 1929: 13).

Engineering, the applied science of physics, matter, and motion, is a third stream contributing to the current framework and practice of OHP. Frederick Winslow Taylor's (1911) classic work in scientific management aimed initially at translating engineering principles into human work systems to be applied on the shop floor. Taylor (1912) later saw the heart of scientific management as a transformation of the labor–management relationship from a competitive to a cooperative one. Subsequent engineers, especially industrial engineers, used these principles to transform work environments into more anthropocentric ones (see Lucak, 1992 in Nelson & Quick, 2006: 478). Figure 1.1 shows preventive medicine, psychology, and engineering converging in an organizational context to create a foundation for OHP.

Preventive medicine in an organizational context

Employee mental health and well-being has a long history (see Elkind, 1931). Public health and preventive medicine have been key foundations for the dramatic rise in human life expectancies, as much as 50% to 100% increases in various population groups around the world (Quick et al., 2003a). In the 14th edition of *Public Health and Preventive Medicine*, Wallace and Doebbeling (1998) expanded the scope to include such OHP hazards as noise, musculoskeletal disorders, and industrial accidents as well as behavioral factors affecting health, such as social relationships, violence, and substance abuse. Sickness absence continues as a key outcome (Ihlebaek et al., 2007).

The three key concerns of public health and preventive medicine are: (i) active and passive surveillance mechanisms that lead to early identification of health problems or disorders (Halperin et al., 2001); (ii) the identification of health risk factors (Last & Tyler, 1998); and (iii) the development of intervention and treatment strategies for those who are suffering especially through preventive stress management, including primary, secondary, and tertiary prevention (VandenBos, 2007).

Occupational stress

Stress on the job is associated with accidents both on and off the job and job-site. Since 1991, work stress, distress, coping and/or the negative consequences of work stress have been central to the emergence of OHP. Perrewé and Ganster's *Research in Occupational Stress and Well Being* series (2002–06) brings important managerial and organizational connections to the concerns of OHP. For example, even positive racial stereotypes can have negative effects on people at work (Cocchiara & Quick, 2004). The American Orthopaedic Association is concerned with the adverse effects of stress and burnout on the profession's leaders (Quick et al., 2006). A review of PsychArticles and PsychInfo databases conducted on 13 March 2007 resulted in 127,108 citations when using the key words 'work stress' and 'job stress'. Thus, the 'stress' theme continues to be a powerful rubric within OHP.

Organizational health psychology

The origins of OHP are reviewed elsewhere (see Sauter et al., 1990; Barling & Griffith, 2003). Adkins (1999) applied these OHP concepts and pioneered the concept of an organizational health center to create an organizational venue. She did this in the Air Force Materiel Command, a Fortune 100 industrial organization with five air logistics and maintenance depots and over 100,000 employees, the vast majority of whom were federal civil servants and a small minority were military personnel. Her organizational health center reported directly to the commanding general officer of the depot.

Adkins (1999) developed the concept for use in major industrial restructuring and downsizing initiatives in the early to mid-1990s. However, the concept can be equally applied well in growing, dynamic, and world-class organizational contexts (Adkins et al., 2000). One evaluation in the former context found savings in terms of the prevention of suicides and workplace violence as well as cost avoidance, in one depot amounting to $33 million in costs avoided (Quick et al., 2003b).

The *Journal of Occupational Health Psychology* (JOHP) is a key theory, science, and practice journal for OHP articles, which since 2000 fall into seven categories: stress, to include physical and emotional; burnout; work–family; aggression, violence, and harassment; safety; employment issues; and health issues. A search using PsychArticles,

Table 1.1   Incidence of OHP topics in the Journal of Occupational Health Psychology

Topics	Years of publication		
	1996	1997–2001	2002–2006
Stress (coping, social support, demand, control)	11	24	30
Burnout	0	7	8
Work–family	2	14	14
Violence/aggression/discrimination	2	11	18
Safety	1	12	7
Health and well-being	1	0	8
Employment/unemployment	0	2	14
Job insecurity	0	5	4
Substance abuse	0	1	4
Work design and environment	3	1	5
Gender	2	3	3
Conflict	0	4	2
Recovery	0	1	1
Leadership	1	2	3
Aging	1	0	2
Justice	0	4	0
Workaholism	0	0	1
Psychological contract	0	0	0
POB	0	1	2

PsychInfo and Psychology and Behavioral Sciences Collection databases from 1988 to the present resulted in only 328 citations matching the search for 'occupational health psychology', of which 322 were JOHP articles. Table 1.1 shows the incidence rates for OHP topics in JOHP since its inaugural publication in 1996.

The burden of suffering

One of the rationales for the emergence of OHP is the existence of a burden of suffering in organizations and working populations. A concept originally used within the public health community, it is highly relevant in an organizational context too. The burden of suffering captures both morbidity and mortality. Morbidity rates refer to either the incidence rate (number of new cases) or the prevalence rate (total number of cases) of a particular health problem in a population group. Mortality refers to the number of deaths in the group. Epidemiology and the burden of suffering help estimate, for example, the costs of unintentional and violent injuries (Doll et al., 2007).

The burden of suffering concept includes both the economic costs and the humanitarian concerns in the organizational context. There are difficulties in calculating the costs and effects in each case. The US Bureau of Labor Statistics, the International Labor Organization in Geneva, Switzerland, the US Center for Disease Control and Prevention, the American Institute of Stress, and the National Safety Council track some of these economic costs. From a humanitarian perspective, the difficulty in developing a valuation of pain and suffering relates to the complications in quantifying, for example, emotions. How do we measure emotion? What is the value of a human life?

In his presidential remarks to the American College of Occupational and Environmental Medicine, Bernacki (2002) focused on the employers' perspective in the valuation of morbidity and mortality, suggesting that such valuation includes:

- direct costs of diagnosis and treatment of occupational and non-occupational conditions;
- disability costs;
- higher wage costs;
- lost production;
- idle assets;
- employee turnover;
- planned overstaffing; and
- indirect business taxes and non-tax liabilities.

He estimated that the direct cost to US business of worker ill health adds up to approximately 7% of labor costs.

Occupational fatal injury costs
Biddle et al. (2005) tested an accurate, timely, and readily available state-based estimate of the costs associated with fatal occupational injuries. A key challenge in developing a cost calculator for fatal injuries is the competing cost assessment methods, the willingness-to-pay method and the cost-of-illness method. The International Labour Office (ILO) reported at the 17th World Congress on Safety and Health at Work in September 2005 that 2.2 million people die of work-related accidents and diseases each year, though this may be vastly underestimated.

Work loss and productivity
Mortality is one component for Berger et al. (2001) in examining the indirect costs (that is, work loss and productivity costs). Two others are morbidity and reduced productivity. Here again we encounter differing perspectives and alternative valuations. For example, the American Heart Association in 1999 used the traditional societal perspective to estimate the indirect costs of coronary heart disease (CHD), the leading cause of death in the US, to be $46.7 billion, of which $6.9 billion is related to morbidity and $39.8 billion (81%) to mortality. The estimates may be quite different if one uses the employer's perspective for CHD.

Presenteeism   The lost productivity costs of occupational health may exceed the direct medical costs. While most evaluations of occupational health outcomes examine only the medical costs, a broader view should consider absences and presenteeism (diminished productivity resulting from health issues while at work). Does presenteeism really exist? Collins et al. (2005) pay particular attention to chronic health conditions, which diminish employee productivity even when they are physically present on the job. Ricci et al. (2007) estimate that fatigued workers cost employers $136.4 billion annually in health-related lost productive time, an excess of $101.0 billion compared with workers without fatigue.

Workplace bullying   Rayner et al. (2001) and Einarsen et al. (2003) have drawn attention to the negative effects of workplace bullying and emotional abuse on the health of the workplace. Workplace bullying is a form of emotional abuse and harassment that has a huge impact on a company's bottom line. Urbanski (2002) estimated a sum of $180 million in lost time and productivity due to bullying.

Health insurance trends and costs
Health insurance costs are an increasingly important concern in America for employers and employees alike. From a consumer or employee perspective, Langer (2004) found that 78% of respondents are dissatisfied with the cost of the nation's healthcare system, including 54% who were very dissatisfied. Employers continue to be concerned with tracking and understanding their companies' insurance healthcare costs. Healthcare costs for employees not borne in an organizational context are borne by society. While the US has the best medical system in the world that can treat the sick, it does not have the best health system in the world that emphasizes prevention. Two alternative models are the 100% reimbursement model in Switzerland and the National Health Service model in the UK. The US follows neither model, leaving 40 million uninsured.

Intrinsic value: a matter of virtue
Our discussion so far in this section is related to the utilitarian value of a man or woman. However, we began by pointing out that the burden of suffering bridges both economic costs and humanitarian concerns. For us to consider the latter, we must bring focus to the intrinsic value of a man or a woman. Kant's (1958) metaphysic of morals may be one of the best pathways for helping us understand human intrinsic value. We suggest that it is a matter of virtue, and character.

Kant's first categorical imperative is this: act only on that maxim through which you can at the same time will that it should become a universal principle. He takes a subjective maxim and moves it to a universal law in human behavior. Then Kant moves to his practical imperative: act in such a way that you always treat humanity, whether in your own person or in the person of any other, never simply as a means, but *always* at the same time as an end (1958, p. 96 emphasis added). Men and women are ends in and of themselves. Therefore, we should be concerned as employers, fellow employees, and all with whom we labor. To do otherwise, in Lee Iacocca's words (1984), turns the company into a labor camp.

Organizations need not be labor camps. For example, in one case study of a major industrial restructuring and closure process, the chief executive placed the care and well-being of all employees as a top priority, a very close second to the mission of the organization (Quick et al., 2003b). Over the six-year process affecting 13,000 employees, there was not a single fatality (either suicide or homicide), not a single incidence of workplace violence, and over $33 million in cost avoidance.

Future directions in occupational health psychology
Figure 1.1 shows two sets of future directions for occupational health psychology, one of these being positive advances and the other being new horizons. In this section we develop each of these categories of future directions. Within each we see four sets of forces at work. A more in-depth treatment of these positive advances and new horizons may be found in Macik-Frey et al.'s (2007) review article.

Toward a more positive future

The four positive advances that we envision emerging from the present work in OHP are: a greater emphasis on positive health, the emergence of positive forms of leadership, a renewed interest in mood and emotion, and a push for preventive interventions. The four positive advances are already unfolding.

Positive health   The philosophical roots of positive health might be traced to Aristotle, who described eudemonia as the realization of one's true potential (Aristotle, 2000). Ryff and Singer (1998, 2002) noted that researchers and health practitioners alike tended to define health as the absence of negative states as opposed to the presence of positive states. In their integrative scheme, psychological well-being encompasses six components: autonomy, personal growth, mastery of the environment, positive relationships with others, purpose in life, and self-acceptance (Ryff & Singer, 2001; Ryff et al., 2004). Psychology has seen the emergence of positive psychology, the science of positive subjective experience (Seligman & Csikszentmihalyi, 2000). Included in positive psychology's mission is the need to focus on both human strengths and positive institutions. Extending the ideas of positive health and positive psychology, Luthans (2002a, b) called for positive organizational behavior (POB), building human strengths at work. Wright and Cropanzano (2000a, b) build upon Luthans's foundational work with attention to psychological well-being. More recently, Nelson and Cooper (2007) offer a broader and more inclusive view of POB.

Leadership   According to some (see Hogan & Kaiser, 2005), leadership is the most important issue in the human sciences. Leadership research often focuses on traditionally studied outcomes such as productivity, but leaders can influence outcomes such as health and happiness at work (Quick & Quick, 2004). Part of the leader's role, in essence, is encouraging employee well-being, as well as creating and sustaining healthy organizations. Avolio and Gardner (2005) in particular have drawn attention to the positive forms of leadership development. A key here is authentic leadership, a process that results in self-awareness and self-regulated positive behaviors that are demonstrated by both leaders and followers (Luthans & Avolio, 2003). Authentic leaders express their true selves and display hope, optimism, and confidence. Authentic leaders influence followers through many pathways, such as unconditional trust on the part of the follower, positive emotions engendered by the leader, and self-determination as fostered by the leader, who places a premium on follower development (Ilies et al., 2005). Studies of leadership in military settings have shown that supportive leader behavior was associated with increased job engagement and buffered soldiers from the adverse health effects of extremely stressful environments (Britt et al., 2004).

Mood and emotions   Both mood and emotions are playing a more focal role in OHP. Positive mood, for example, has been linked with better immune system functioning (Stone et al., 1987; Stone et al., 1994) and with higher performance at work (Erez & Isen, 2002). Negative mood has been related to self-reported ill health, while positive mood was related to better subjective health (Benyamini et al., 2000). Perceived organizational politics were positively related to depressed mood at work among workers from a wide array of occupations (Byrne et al., 2005). A daily diary study of human resource employees demonstrated that individuals who believe that work demands thwart their work performance or that work demands lead to bad moods were more likely to experience unpleasant moods on the same day (Harris & Daniels, 2005). Emotional labor, or emotion work, is managing emotions for a wage (Hochschild, 1983). Grandey (2000) presented a model in which emotional regulation, including deep acting and surface acting, was linked with individual well-being (burnout and job satisfaction) as well as organizational well-being (performance and withdrawal behavior). Emotional intelligence, or emotional competence, has been introduced as an integrated set of affect-related skills at work (see Mayer et al., 2000). Emotional competence served as a buffer in the relationship between emotional labor and employee well-being.

Preventive interventions   The public health notions of prevention has been a powerful engine in advancing health and well-being, both in general populations and also with working populations in organizations. Despite calls for well-designed prevention and intervention studies, few have emerged, and there have been some disappointments. Health promotion programs, along with other occupational health and safety interventions as a whole, have not demonstrated sustained changes in employee behaviors (Heaney, 2003). Researchers face challenges in studying interventions and prevention in particular. Interventions evolve and change once they are implemented. Consider, for example, the history of health circles used in Germany (Aust & Ducki, 2004). Adapted from quality circles and other employee participation approaches, health circles operate on the assumption that employees are in the best position to improve their own job conditions (Brandenburg & Slesina, 1994). A review of research evidence indicated that reliable indications of the success of health circles were absent, due in large part to the weaknesses of the methods used in the studies (Aust & Ducki, 2004). As the definition of health becomes more holistic and positive, interventions should target the enhancement of individual strengths that promote overall well-being, and individual states that promote health.

Expanding the vision of OHP
As occupational health continues to evolve as a field of study, we believe that several new topics hold high potential. These new horizons for OHP are signaled in Figure 1.1 and deal with the need to address the changing nature of organizations and workers and how these changes relate to health. We address technology, virtual work, globalization and the aging of the workforce as four significant new horizons. We deal with these in even greater depth elsewhere (Macik-Frey et al., 2007).

Technology   The rapid pace of technological changes has resulted in many unexpected and potentially problematic outcomes. The growing dependence on information technology with long hours spent behind computer terminals and with decreasing amounts of human interaction are key factors to investigate (Sparks et al., 2001). Negative physical and psychological health concequences of working with technology have been shown (e.g., Ekberg et al., 1995; Dillon & Emurian, 1996; Aaras et al., 2000; Sparks et al., 2001). The ever-increasing rate and quantity of information that workers must manage and the elimination of time and space barriers present high potential for stress and its negative outcomes. With technology we have a loss of a specific 'workday' and 'workplace', leaving workers with a 24-hour workday that can be accomplished in any location.

Demands for worker accessibility anytime and anywhere result in emails being sent from home at 3:00 a.m. and addictions to devices such as the Blackberry (aka 'Crackberry'). Incredible changes in the way people work and how this impacts on health is a key area of study for the future.

Virtual work   Although the benefits of virtual work are well documented both from the employer's and the employees' perspectives (Harpaz, 2002), virtual work may also present its own unique set of challenges from an occupational health perspective. Lynch (2000) suggested that the manner of communication inherent in virtual work lacks the interpersonal connectedness that humans require for health and well-being. Virtual work thus increases the risks of social isolation and loneliness, which are important risk factors for cardiovascular health. Other researchers agree that social isolation and loneliness are associated with negative psychological and physical outcomes (see Pennebaker, 1990). Although the research on the impact of isolation on health is fairly consistent and compelling, the research on the prevalence and impact of isolation on virtual workers is less so. Virtual work may enhance rather than hinder effective social support and relationship development (Walther, 1995) and adaptation to alternative forms of communication may be possible that allows for similar relational capacity as traditional communication forms (Townsend & DeMarie, 1998). Potential moderators of the relationship between virtual work and social isolation might include individual differences in coping, communication technologies, type and patterns of communication interactions, early trust development, and presence of other social networks (Macik-Frey, 2006). From an OHP perspective, virtual work appears to be an area ripe for discovery.

Globalization   As the workplace becomes increasingly global, there are interesting areas to explore related for OHP. Spielberger and Reheiser (2005) note that health and well-being of the worker is not simply a US issue. There is a growing interest in the need to protect the health, safety and general welfare of the global workforce (WHO, 2000). This globalization of OHP leads to interesting questions. What impact do cultural differences have on health, stressors, and the ability to overcome health and safety issues? Are there universal principles related to the safety and health of workers? Spector et al. (2002), for example, found that the positive relationship of work locus of control with physical well-being that is characteristic of the US was not consistent across the 24 cultures they studied. Other globalization topics include the implications of cultural differences related to work values, dress code, language, religion, training needs and leadership attitudes toward diversity (Sparks et al., 2001). Worker selection across cultures has been limited (Ployhart, 2006), though selection may have a huge impact on individual and organizational success. The International Commission on Occupational Health (ICOH) is a 90-country, multidisciplinary organization that has as its mission the promotion of occupational health at an international level. The ICOH has expressed the need to re-orient its activities to address new technologies and the globalization of the economy. Members advocate a 'transcultural' approach to the problems of occupational health (Caillard, 1999).

Aging   The aging of the population in the US and throughout the world is a challenge for many organizations (US Census Bureau, 1995; World Bank, 1999; Bovbjerg, 2001;

Peterson, 2002; Spiezia, 2002; Holtz-Eakin et al., 2004; Rice & Fineman, 2004). Peterson (2002) described this worldwide phenomenon as a transformation – even a revolution – with few parallels in humanity's past. This 'age wave' referred to as the 'demographic transition' (Holtz-Eakin et al., 2004) describes the rapid aging of the developed and increasingly the less developed worlds' populations. Along with aging, the population is living healthier lives and the expectation is that the average age of the workforce will continue to increase. Two disturbing trends worthy of exploration are early retirement and agism. First, older workers, although living longer and healthier lives, are exiting the workforce earlier even though this is not always in their best economic or psychosocial interests (Spiezia, 2002). There appears to be a discontinuity in the trend for older workers to leave the workforce earlier. How this paradoxical situation impacts on OHP is a key area for study. Second, longstanding stereotypes regarding aging include the perception that older workers have decreased performance, decreased stamina, are difficult to train, are inflexible, are greater safety risks and have less capacity to work. Along with these beliefs is the assumption that these are 'natural' outcomes of getting older. Research has systematically shown that these assumptions for the most part are false, but are responsible for ongoing discrimination against older workers (Johnson, & Neumark, 1997). One possibility to explore in future research is whether job performance changes considered a result of the 'normal' declines of aging may be confused with the effects of limiting the human capital investment in older workers that might enhance skill retention and development.

The future is now: psychologically healthy workplaces
As we have seen, OHP emerged from preventive medicine, psychology, and engineering with the aim of either preventing health problems in organizations or helping to repair the damage, some of which inevitably occurs. However, prevention and treatment (that is, repairing damage) are only two of the missions of psychology. The emergent third mission is to build upon strength factors; hence, the positive psychology movement. In this vein, the psychologically healthy workplace initiatives in the US emerged from the cooperative agreement between the National Institute for Occupational Safety and Health and the American Psychological Association. Grawitch et al. (2006) conducted a critical review of the research literature to examine the links between health workplace practices, employee well-being, and organizational improvements. Their review synthesized much of the research since 1990, linking healthy workplace practices in organizations to employee well-being and organizational improvements. They adopt the four guiding principles of organizational health set forth by Adkins et al. (2000):

1.   Health exists on a continuum of mortality to vibrant well-being.
2.   Organizational health is a continuous process, not an obtainable state.
3.   Health is systemic in nature and results from interconnections of multiple factors.
4.   Organizational health relies on fulfilling relationships that are achieved through communication, collaboration, and relationship building actions.

From these guiding principles for healthy organizations and the literature review, Grawitch et al. (2006) set forth a PATH (Practices for Achievement of Total Health) model, which we review. We follow that review in this section with a number of case examples of award-winning organizations.

Practices for Achievement of Total Health (PATH)
The PATH model originates in healthy workplace practices, which are proposed to positively impact on both employee well-being and organizational improvements (ibid.). The model provides for the interaction of employee well-being and organizational improvements, the two outcome variables.

Healthy workplace practices The PATH model identifies five categories of healthy workplace practices: work–life balance, employee growth and development, health and safety, recognition, and employee involvement. The authors briefly explore each of these categories, which are designed to have a specific and varied positive impact upon employee well-being and organizational improvement.

Employee well-being Employee well-being represents the physical, mental, and emotional facets of employee health, though there is no general agreement on the best indicators of it. The authors provide an array of indicators in their PATH model: physical health, mental health, stress, motivation, commitment, job satisfaction, morale, and climate.

Organizational improvements The PATH model proposes specific organizational improvement outcomes that result from healthy organizations. The authors note eight illustrative organizational improvements in this statement of the model: competitive advantage; performance and productivity; reduced absenteeism and turnover; reduced accident and injury rates; increased cost savings; hiring selectivity; improved service and product quality; and better customer service and satisfaction.

2006 APA national award winning organizations
The American Psychological Association (APA) recognizes state-level psychologically healthy workplace awards and best practices honors, and these winners may be nominated for national awards. The APA national award winners are systematically evaluated on the five categories of healthy workplace practices included in the PATH model (APA, 2006). There is not a single pathway to this level of recognition. During 2006, the APA recognized six national award winners, each for different strengths and excellence (APA, 2006). We draw attention to three of these that illustrate different aspect of occupational health psychology at work. These organizations are in telecommunication, healthcare, and research.

Multiple channels of communication The Comporium Group is a medium-sized, for-profit organization located in South Carolina whose business is telecommunication services. The company supports a variety of civic and non-profit organizations in addition to its core business of enhancing the quality of life for its residential and commercial customers. This family-owned group of companies places great emphasis on the health and well-being of its employees, resulting in a work environment that feels more like a family unit than a workplace. The average employee tenure is 10 years and the voluntary turnover rate is a low 2.3%. A key feature of the group of companies is its multifaceted internal communication program.

A prescription for success   Great River Health Systems (GRHS) is a not-for-profit healthcare employer of choice with strong commitment to patient care and customer service along with its dedication to helping employees maintain good health. GRHS's employee-centered culture fosters a positive work environment that acknowledges and celebrates both individual and group successes. One of the key success indicators for GRHS is the dramatic increase in patient satisfaction with the quality of care and services they received. Located in Iowa, GRHS's turnover rate is 12.8%, compared to a statewide average of 18% and a national average of 17%.

Global well-being   IBM's T.J. Watson Research Center is the headquarters for the largest industrial research organization in the world. Because of the competitive pressures of the technology industry, the Watson Center places particular emphasis on creative solutions that enable employees to achieve greater work–life balance. A large for-profit organization headquartered in New York, IBM maintains an extensive menu of employee wellness resources that include online tools, classes on a variety of health-related topics, and access to a workout center, sports, and recreation facilities. Between 2005 and 2006, the company found reductions in employee health risks and savings from disease management efforts that grew to $36 million.

2007 APA national award winning organizations
Award winners and honorees in the 2007 competition included the Good Samaritan Hospital of Maryland, the Houston Texans National Football League franchise, the National Institute for People with Disabilities Network, and more (APA, 2007). We review a newspaper, a social service organization, and a medical center.

Una gran familia de empleados   The most widely read newspaper in Puerto Rico is El Nuevo Dia, an organization that prides itself on being a great place to work. Evidence for this assertion comes from employee survey results that indicate 85% of the workforce rate the benefits as superior and almost 90% are satisfied. A low turnover rate of 3% had led to over 50% of the workforce with more than 10 years of tenure. Excellence on the job is recognized and rewarded with awards, such as for creative photography and article writing.

Together they make it happen   Koinonia Homes is a medium-sized, not-for-profit social service organization in Ohio that provides residential and vocational services to individuals with developmental disabilities. The organization gives evidence to its claim to building effective relationships and partnerships based on its 20–40% below industry average turnover rate. 'Lunchroom chats with the CEO' enable direct support workers and front-line supervisors to share ideas and concerns with the big boss. Current and former employees refer many job applicants, with longevity achieving a high average of five years for direct support staff.

Prevention is the best medicine   The DuBois Regional Medical Center (DRMC) uses health education, motivation, friendly competition and incentives to positively affect employees' lives and the medical center's financial bottom line. To achieve these positive outcomes, this Pennsylvania-based medical center implemented a 'Health Quest' program that has ultimately reduced sick time utilization, led to cost savings from DRMC's health insurance provider while at the same time improving morale and communication. The participation rate in Health Quest is about 40%.

We see in these case examples that there is no one best way to achieve employee well-being or to improve organizational health (APA, 2006, 2007). There are a variety of pathways and specific practices within the PATH model framework of five categories of healthy workplace practices. Employees and organizations that are inspired by these cases, rather than intent on copying them, are likely to profit in psychological, medical, and financial terms.

Conclusion

This chapter has reviewed the foundations of OHP, primarily from its inception circa 1990. Figure 1.1 traced the roots of OHP in preventive medicine, psychology, and engineering. We are intrigued by what we imagine the future holds. First, the general notion of health in the traditional, medical sense will be obsolete. Issues such as absenteeism, burnout, strain, depression, cardiovascular disease, despair, and withdrawal will fade to notions of engagement, purpose, thriving, hope, vigor and optimism. 'Health' will be less about overcoming deficiencies and illness and much more about learning the secrets of the self-actualized person. Organizations will address the 'health' of their workers from this more holistic paradigm providing increased respite, opportunities for autonomy, challenging and meaningful goals, and social support. It will be commonplace for organizations to work to create mutual purpose with their employees, not just because it is the right thing to do for the individual, but because the benefits to the organization are becoming realized. No longer are these premises practiced as only a benefit to the individual, but because research and time demonstrates that the 'healthy' worker is the best worker and the business that promotes this new sense of health is good business.

Along this line, 'zest' will emerge as a positive trait among people at work, which is characterized by anticipation, energy, and excitement (Peterson et al., 2008). In their large-scale study of over 9,800 working adults, Peterson et al. found that zest predicted an orientation to work as a calling, to the experience of work satisfaction, and to the experience of general life satisfaction. All these are positive outcomes. However, the health risk of cardiovascular disease as the leading cause of death for men and women continues. Wright et al. (in press) found that psychological well-being was predictive of composite cardiovascular health as measured by pulse product, a new way of looking at cardiovascular health. Beyond the individual man and woman, we all need to help to build psychologically healthy workplaces, a model for which and case examples of which we included in the final section of the chapter.

Acknowledgements

The authors thank Cary L. Cooper, Lennart Levi, Ronald C. Kessler, Larry Murphy, Paul Rosch, and Lois Tetrick for comments and suggestions in the authors' major review of occupational health in *Journal of Management*, December 2007 Review Issue. We thank Joel A. Quintans for his graphic expertise, Carol Byrne for her IT expertise, and Alankrita Pandey, Jesika McKenzie, and Deeti Chudgar for the research assistance support each provided in preparation of this chapter.

References

Aaras, A., Horgen, G. & Ro, O. (2000), 'Work with the visual display unit: health consequences', *International Journal of Human–Computer Interaction*, **12**: 107–34.

Adkins, J.A. (1999), 'Promoting organizational health: the evolving practice of occupational health psychology', *Professional Psychology: Research and Practice*, **30**: 129–37.

Adkins, J.A., Quick, J.C. & Moe, K.O. (2000), 'Building world class performance in changing times', in L.R. Murphy & C.L. Cooper (eds), *Healthy and Productive Work: An International Perspective*, Philadelphia, PA: Taylor & Francis, pp. 107–32.

American Psychological Association (APA) (2006), 'Psychologically Healthy Workplace Awards and Best Practice Honors', Psychologically Healthy Workplace Program, Washington, DC.

American Psychological Association (APA) (2007), 'Psychologically Healthy Workplace Awards and Best Practice Honors', Psychologically Healthy Workplace Program, Washington, DC.

Aristotle (2000), *The Nicomachean Ethics*, trans. R. Crisp, Cambridge: Cambridge University Press.

Aust, B. & Ducki, A. (2004), 'Comprehensive health promotion interventions at the workplace: experiences with health circles in Germany', *Journal of Occupational Health Psychology*, **9**: 258–70.

Avolio, B.J. & Gardner, W.L. (2005), 'Authentic leadership development: getting to the root of positive forms of leadership', *Leadership Quarterly*, **16**: 315–38.

Barling, J. & Griffiths, A. (2003), 'A history of occupational health psychology', in J.C. Quick & L.E. Tetrick (eds), *Handbook of Occupational Health Psychology*, Washington, DC: American Psychological Association, pp. 19–33.

Benyamini, Y., Idler, E.L., Leventhal, H. & Leventhal, E.A. (2000), 'Positive affect and function as influences on self-assessment of health: expanding our view beyond illness and disability', *Journal of Gerontology*, **55B**: 107–16.

Berger, M.L., Murray, J.F., Xu, J. & Pauly, M. (2001), 'Alternative valuations of work loss and productivity', *Journal of Occupational and Environmental Medicine*, **43**: 18–24.

Bernacki, E.J. (2002), 'Presidential remarks', American College of Occupational and Environmental Medicine annual meeting, Chicago, IL, 18 August.

Biddle, E., Hartley, D., Starkey, S., Fabrega, V. & Richardson, S. (2005), 'Deriving occupational fatal injury costs: a state pilot study', Washington, DC: Bureau of Labor Statistics.

Bovbjerg, B.D. (2001), 'Older workers – demographic trends pose challenges for employers and workers', FDCH Government Report, 16 November.

Brandenburg, U. & Slesina, W. (1994), 'Health promotion circles: a new approach to health promotion at worksite', *Homeostasis in Health and Disease*, **35**: 43–8.

Britt, T.W., Davison, J. & Bliese, P.D. (2004), 'How leaders can influence the impact that stressors have on soldiers', *Military Medicine*, **169**: 541–5.

Byrne, Z.S., Kacmar, C., Stoner, J. & Hochwarter, W.A. (2005), 'The relationship between perceptions of politics and depressed mood at work: unique moderators across three levels', *Journal of Occupational Health Psychology*, **10**: 330–43.

Caillard, J.-F. (1999), 'Introduction to the special section on psychological and behavior approaches to occupational health', *Journal of Occupational Health Psychology*, **4**: 84–6.

Cocchiara, F.K. & Quick, J.C. (2004), 'The negative effects of positive stereotypes: ethnicity-related stressors and implications on organizational health', *Journal of Organizational Behavior*, **25**: 781–5.

Collins, J.J., Baase, C.M., Sharda, C.E., Ozminkowski, R.J., Nicholson, S., Billotti, G.M., Gurpin, R.S., Olson, M., Turpin, O. & Berger, M.L. (2005), 'The assessment of chronic health conditional on work performance, absence and total economic impact for employers', *Journal of Occupational and Environmental Medicine*, **47**: 547–57.

Dillon, T.W. & Emurian, H.H. (1996), 'Some factors affecting reports of visual fatigue resulting from use of a VDU', *Computers in Human Behavior*, **12**: 49–59.

Doll, L.S., Bonzo, S.E., Sleet, D.A. & Mercy, J.A. (2007), *Handbook of Injury and Violence Prevention*, New York: Springer.

Einarsen, S., Hoel, H., Cooper, C.L. & Zapf, D. (2003), *Bullying and Emotional Abuse in the Workplace*, London: Taylor & Francis.

Ekberg, K., Eklund, J., Tuvesson, M., Oetengren, R., Odenrick, P. & Ericson, M. (1995), 'Psychological stress and muscle activity during data entry at visual display units', *Work and Stress*, **9**: 475–90.

Elkind, H.B. (ed.) (1931), *Preventive Management: Mental Hygiene in Industry*, New York: B.C. Forbes.

Erez, A. & Isen, A. (2002), 'The influence of positive affect on the components of expectancy motivation', *Journal of Applied Psychology*, **87**: 1055–67.

Grandey, A. (2000), 'Emotional regulation in the workplace: a new way to conceptualize emotional labor', *Journal of Occupational Health Psychology*, **5**: 95–110.

Grawitch, M.J., Gottschalk, M. & Munz, D.C. (2006), 'The path to a healthy workplace: a critical review linking healthy workplace practices, employee well-being, and organizational improvements', *Consulting Psychology Journal*, **58**, 129–47.

Halperin, W., Monson, R.R. & Baker, E.L. (2001), *Public Health Surveillance*, New York: John Wiley.

Harpaz, I. (2002), 'Advantages and disadvantages of telecommuting for the individual, organization and society', *Work Study*, **51**: 74–80.

Harris, C. & Daniels, K. (2005), 'Daily affect and daily beliefs', *Journal of Occupational Health Psychology*, **10**: 415–28.

Heaney, C.A. (2003), 'Worksite health interventions: targets for change and strategies for attaining them', in Quick & Tetrick (eds), pp. 305–23.

Hochschild, A.R. (1983), *The Managed Heart*, Berkeley, CA: University of California Press.

Hogan R. & Kaiser, R.B. (2005), 'What we know about leadership', *Review of General Psychology*, **9**: 169–80.

Holtz-Eakin, K.D., Lovely, M.E. & Tosun, M.S. (2004), 'Generational conflict, fiscal policy, and economic growth', *Journal of Macroeconomics*, **26**, 1–23.

Iacocca, L. (1984), *Iacocca: An Autobiography*, New York: Bantam Books.

Ihlebaek, C., Brage, S. & Eriksen, H.R. (2007), 'Health complaints and sickness absence in Norway, 1996–2003', *Occupational Medicine*, **57**: 43–9.

Ilies, R., Morgeson, F.P. & Nahrgang, J.D. (2005), 'Authentic leadership and eudaemonic well-being: understanding leader–follower outcomes', *Leadership Quarterly*, **16**: 373–94.

Johnson, R.W. & Neumark, D. (1997), 'Age discrimination, job separations, and employment status of older workers: evidence from self reports', *Journal of Human Resources*, **32**: 779–811.

Kant, I. (1958), *Groundwork of the Metaphysic of Morals*, trans. and analysed by H.J. Paton, New York: Harper & Row.

Laird, D. (1929), *Psychology and Profits*, New York: B.C. Forbes.

Langer, G. (2004), 'Health care pains: growing health care concerns fuel cautious support for change', ABC News.com, http//abcnews.go.com/sections/living/ US/healthcare031020_poll.html.

Last, J.M. & Tyler, C.W., Jr. (eds) (1998), 'Public health methods', in Wallace and Doebbeling (eds), pp. 1–66.

Leviticus, Chapter 11 (1952), *The Holy Bible*, Toronto, New York, Edinburgh: Thomas Nelson & Sons.

Luthans, F. (2002a), 'The need for and meaning of positive organizational behavior', *Journal of Organizational Behavior*, **23**: 695–706.

Luthans, F. (2002b), 'Positive organizational behavior: developing and managing psychological strengths', *Academy of Management Executive*, **16**: 57–72.

Luthans, F. & Avolio, B. (2003), 'Authentic leadership: a positive development approach', in K. Cameron, J. Dutton & R. Quinn (eds), *Positive Organizational Scholarship*, San Francisco, CA: Berrett-Koewer, pp. 241–58.

Lynch, J.J. (2000), *A Cry Unheard: New Insights into the Medical Consequences of Loneliness*, Baltimore, MD: Bancroft.

Macik-Frey, M. (2006), 'Virtual work: loneliness, isolation, and health outcomes', paper presented at the Academy of Management Meeting, Atlanta, GA, August 15.

Macik-Frey, M., Quick, J.C. & Nelson, D.L. (2007), 'Advances in occupational health: from a stressful beginning to a positive future', *Journal of Management*, **33**: 809–40.

Mayer, J.D., Caruso, D.R. & Salovey, P. (2000), 'Emotional intelligence meets traditional standards for intelligence', *Intelligence*, **27**: 267–98.

Münsterberg, H. (1913), *Psychology and Industrial Efficiency*, Boston, MA: Houghton-Mifflin.

Nelson, D.L. & Cooper, C.L. (2007), 'Positive organizational behavior: an inclusive view', in Nelson & Cooper (eds), *Positive Organizational Behavior*, London: Sage, pp. 3–8.

Nelson, D.L. & Quick, J.C. (2006), *Organizational Behavior: Foundations, Realities and Challenges*, 5th edn, Mason, OH: Southwestern/Thomson.

Pennebaker, J.W. (1990), *Opening Up: The Healing Power of Confiding in Others*, New York: Morrow.

Perrewé, P.L. & Ganster, D.C. (2002–06), *Research in Occupational Stress and Well Being*, Amsterdam: Elsevier/JAI.

Peterson, P.G. (2002), 'The shape of things to come: global aging in the twenty-first century', *Journal of International Affairs*, **56**: 189–99.

Peterson, C., Park, N., Hall, N. & Seligman, M.E.P. (2008), 'Zest and work', *Journal of Organizational Behavior*, (December).

Ployhart, R.E. (2006), 'Staffing in the 21st century: new challenges and strategic opportunities', *Journal of Management*, **32**: 868–97.

Quick, J.C., Cooper, C.L., Nelson, D.L., Quick, J.D. & Gavin, J.H. (2003a), 'Stress, health, and well-being at work', in J. Greenberg (ed.), *Organizational Behavior: The State of the Science*, 2nd edn, Mahwah, NJ and London: Lawrence Erlbaum, pp. 53–89.

Quick, J.C. & Quick, J.D. (2004), 'Healthy, happy, productive work: a leadership challenge', *Organizational Dynamics*, **33**: 329–37.

Quick, J.C., Saleh, K.J., Sime, W.E., Martin, W., Cooper, C.L., Quick, J.D. & Mont, M.A. (2006), 'Stress management skills for strong leadership: is it worth dying for?', *Journal of Bone and Joint Surgery*, **88-A** (1): 217–25.

Quick, J.C. & Tetrick, L.E. (eds) (2003), *Handbook of Occupational Health Psychology*, Washington, DC: American Psychological Association.

Quick, J.C., Tetrick, L.E., Adkins, J.A. & Klunder, C. (2003b), 'Occupational health psychology', in I. Weiner (ed.), *Comprehensive Handbook of Psychology*, New York: John Wiley, pp. 569–89.

Raymond, J.S., Wood, D.W. & Patrick, W.D. (1990), 'Psychology training in work and health', *American Psychologist*, **45**: 1159–61.

Rayner, C., Hoel, H. & Cooper, C.L. (2001), *Workplace Bullying*, London: Taylor & Francis.

Ricci, J.A., Chee, E., Lorandeau, A.L. & Berger, J. (2007), 'Fatigue in the U.S. workforce: prevalence and implications for lost productive work time', *Journal of Occupational and Environmental Medicine*, **49**(1): 1–10.

Rice, D.P. & Fineman, N. (2004), 'Economic implications of increased longevity in the United States', *Annual Review of Public Health*, **25**: 457–73.

Rosenau, M.J. (1913), *Preventive Medicine and Hygiene*, New York: D. Appleton.

Ryff, C.D. & Singer, B. (1998), 'The contours of positive human health', *Psychological Inquiry*, **9**: 1–28.

Ryff, C.D. & Singer, B.H. (2001), *Emotion, Social Relationships, and Health*, Oxford and New York: Oxford University Press.

Ryff, C.D. & Singer, B. (2002), 'From social structures to biology: integrative science in pursuit of human health and well-being', in C.R. Snyder & S.J. Lopez (eds), *Handbook of Positive Psychology*, Oxford and New York: Oxford University Press, pp. 541–55.

Ryff, C.D., Singer, B.H. & Love, G.D. (2004), 'Positive health: connecting well-being with biology', *Philosophical Transactions of the Royal Society of London*, **359**: 1383–94.

Sauter, S.L., Murphy, L.K. & Hurrell, J.J. Jr (1990), 'Prevention of work related psychological distress: a national strategy proposed by the National Institute of Occupational Safety and Health', *American Psychologist*, **45**: 1146–58.

Seligman, M. & Csikszentmihalyi, M. (2000), 'Positive psychology: an introduction', *American Psychologist*, **55**: 5–14.

Smith, W.D. (ed./trans) (1994), *Hippocrates, Volume VII: Epidemics 2, 4–7* (Loeb Classical Library), Cambridge, MA: Harvard University Press.

Sparks, K., Faragher, B. & Cooper, C.L. (2001), 'Well-being and occupational health in the 21st century workplace', *Journal of Occupational and Organizational Psychology*, **74**: 489–509.

Spector, P.E., Cooper, C.L., Sanchez, J.I., O'Driscoll, M., Sparks, K., Bernin, P., Bussing, A., Dewe, P., Hart, P. Luo, L., Miller, K., deMoraes, L.R., Ostrognay, G., Pagon, M., Pitariu, H., Poelmans, S., Radhakrishnan, P., Russinova, V., Salamatov, V. & Salgado, J. (2002), 'Locus of control and well-being at work: how generalizable are western findings?', *Academy of Management Journal*, **45**: 453–66.

Spielberger, C.D. & Reheiser, E. (2005), 'Occupational stress and health', in A.-S.G. Antoniou & C.L. Cooper (eds), *Research Companion to Organizational Health Psychology*, Cheltenham, UK and Northampton, MA, USA: Edward Elgar, pp. 441–54.

Spiezia, V. (2002), 'The graying population: a wasted human capital or just a social liability?', *International Labour Review*, **141**(1–2): 70–113.

Stone, A.A., Cox, D.S., Vladimarsdottier, H. & Jandorf, L. (1987), 'Evidence that secretory IgA antibody is associated with daily mood', *Journal of Personality and Social Psychology*, **52**: 988–93.

Stone, A.A., Neale, J.M., Cox, D.S. & Napoli, A. (1994), 'Daily events are associated with a secretory immune response to an oral antigen in men', *Health Psychology*, **13**: 400–418.

Taylor, F.W. (1911), *The Principles of Scientific Management*, New York: W.W. Norton.

Taylor, F.W. (1912), 'Testimony before Special Committee of the House of Representatives to Investigate the Taylor and Other Systems of Shop Management Under Authority of House Resolution 90', Vol. III, pp. 1377–508. The document contained Dr. Taylor's testimony before the committee from Thursday, January 25 through Tuesday, January 30.

Townsend, A.M. & DeMarie, S.M. (1998), 'Virtual teams: technology and the workplace of the future', *Academy of Management Executive*, **12**: 17–30.

Urbanski, L. (2002), 'Workplace bullying's high cost: $180M in lost time, productivity', *Orlando Business Journal*, 18 March.

US Census Bureau (1995), *Bureau of Census Statistical Brief: Sixty-five plus in the United States*, Washington, DC: US Census Bureau, http://www.census.gov/socdemo/.

VandenBos, G. (ed.), (2007), *APA Dictionary of Psychology*, Washington, DC: American Psychological Association.

Wallace, R.B. & Doebbeling, B.N. (1998), *Maxcy–Rosenau–Last Public Health and Preventive Medicine*, 14th edn, Stamford, CN: Appleton & Lange.

Walther, J.B. (1995), 'Relational aspects of computer-mediated communication: experimental observation over time', *Organizational Science*, **6**(2): 186–203.

World Bank (1999), *World Development Indicators*, Washington, DC: World Bank.

World Health Organization (WHO) (2000) (URL), www.who.int/oeh/OCHweb/OCHweb/OSHpages/ OSHdocuments/Global/Strategy/GlobalStrategyonOccupationalHealth.htm.

Wright, T.A. & Cropanzano, R. (2000a), 'The role of organizational behavior in occupational health psychology: a view as we approach the millennium', *Journal of Occupational Health Psychology*, **5**: 5–10.

Wright, T.A. & Cropanzano, R. (2000b), 'Psychological well-being and job satisfaction as predictors of job performance', *Journal of Occupational Health Psychology*, **5**: 84–94.

Wright, T.A., Cropanzano, R., Bonett, D.G. & Diamond, W.J. (in press), 'The role of employee well-being in cardiovascular health: when the twain shall meet', *Journal of Organizational Behavior*.

2 When stress is less (harmful)

Terry A. Beehr and Simone I. Grebner

This chapter is dedicated to a good colleague and friend, Joseph E. McGrath, who recently passed away after a long and productive career, studying psychological aspects of stress, groups, research methods, and time.

Introduction

Occupational stress occurs when stressors in the workplace, that is 'stress producing environmental circumstances' or 'stress producing events and conditions' (SPECs; McGrath & Beehr, 1990; Beehr & McGrath, 1992, 1996; Semmer et al., 2005), lead to distress or strain reactions in the person. These SPECs are characteristics of the work environment that are usually considered harmful, because for most people and most of the time, people's reactions are deemed indicators of harm to themselves. The strain reactions to these SPECs can include both psychological reactions such as depression, anxiety, mental illness (Stanley & Burrows, 2005), and burnout (Maslach & Leiter, 2005), and physical reactions such as increased blood pressure and risk for cardiovascular disease (Theorell, 2005), headaches, and the development of infectious disease (although evidence about effects on immunity is mainly for non-occupational stressors; e.g., see review by Stetler et al., 2005).

Several prominent theories explain procedures and mechanisms that may explain occupational stress effects, including role theory (e.g., Kahn et al., 1964; Beehr & Glazer, 2005), conservation of resources theory (Hobfoll, 1998), person–environment fit theory (French et al., 1982), and demand–control theory (Karasek, 1979). The details of each of these theories is beyond the scope of the present chapter, but as applied to stress in the workplace they have in common the general idea that stress involves some pressure (SPECs) in the form of expectations, demands, or threats, or loss to which the person responds. Although SPECs are expected to cause strains, sometimes this causal effect is weak or missing, and that is the theme of the present chapter. By definition and as shown by much research, therefore, stress should be a bad thing, but there might be exceptions to this rule-by-definition. Exceptions come in three forms:

1. some SPECs, although leading to harmful strains, are actually valued positively by the person;
2. some SPECs can lead to good outcomes as well as strains or bad outcomes; and
3. under some conditions, the SPECs may not lead to strains.

Furthermore, occupational stress is sometimes related to occupational success, and the worker's perception of his or her own success at work can be a resource that helps facilitate each of the three exceptions, above. SPECs of certain types can lead to success experiences (see 2 above), which make the SPECs valued by the person (see 1 above), and the success can be viewed as a resource that strengthens the person so they will be less susceptible to SPECs (see 3 above). Such subjective success is discussed more in detail after an explanation of the three basic exceptions above.

SPECs that are valued by the employee

Thus, stress may be less harmful if the cause is enjoyed or appreciated by the stressed person, if some favorable outcomes result from it (as well as some unfavorable ones), and/or if co-occurring conditions render the effects of the SPEC harmless. SPECs that are examples of the first exception, that the source of stress is itself valued positively, are quite simple. They include receiving a promotion to a new job with more responsibility or being chosen to make a presentation to important people in one's company. These events are honors that often would be seen as positive and desirable by many employees, but they might be stressful nonetheless; that is, they might result in harmful strains for the individual in spite of the desirability. The second situation above occurs when the SPEC results in strains but also results in some good outcomes for the person; the SPEC itself is not necessarily valued positively by the person, however. The third situation refers to moderator effects; again, the SPEC is not necessarily valued positively by the person, but in this case the SPEC that usually would lead to strains does not do so because of the existence of specific personal or environmental variables that alter or alleviate the effects that the SPEC has on the person. This is commonly called a 'moderator effect'.

Good outcomes from stress

This chapter focuses primarily on exceptions 2 and 3 above, that is, on stressful situations in which the employee's reactions or outcomes might not be bad, and might even be good. The general idea of good outcomes from stressful experiences invokes the concept of 'eustress' proposed by Selye (e.g., 1976), although his discussion of it tended to be a bit sparse and more philosophical than empirical. A few modern writers also have promoted the idea of searching for less negative and even positive outcomes of stress (e.g., Le Fevre et al., 2003; Nelson & Simmons, 2005; Simmons & Nelson, 2007). This trend is probably encouraged by a broad, current push for a more positive psychology (e.g., Seligman & Csikszentmihalyi, 2000). As will be discussed later, however, there might be a relationship between some of these favorable outcomes of stress and exception 1, above, because the way that people evaluate the SPEC may be related to the way they react to it (as in stress appraisal theories; e.g., Lazarus & Folkman, 1984). In fact, it seems almost certain that, as time goes on during a stress process, if there are some good outcomes, the person is more likely to positively value the experience. Therefore, in some cases, exceptions 2 and 3 above might lead people to re-evaluate the SPEC, post hoc, as having been a positive experience.

It should be noted that the definition of occupational stress used here (SPECs lead to strains) focuses on employees' reactions or outcomes that are important mainly to the person rather than to the employing organization. These outcomes or strain reactions are often categorized into three types: psychological, physical, and behavioral (Beehr & Newman, 1978; Cooper & Dewe, 2004). We can therefore ask what aversive psychological, physical, and behavioral reactions to potential SPECs are primarily important to the person.

The stressed person's own psychological reactions are of course important to him or her. For example, being anxious, depressed, or burned out would be aversive psychological states that can stem from occupational stress, and increased risk of cardiovascular illnesses and infectious diseases could matter a great deal to him or her. Harmful behaviors that are due to SPECs and would be classified as strains (i.e., as immediately harmful to the person) are less clear. Many writers list all behaviors resulting from SPECs as strains, including turnover, absenteeism, and changes in job performance. Although such behaviors are important, they are a poor fit for the definition of strains, because in most jobs they are more relevant to the organization than to the person (Beehr & Newman, 1978; Beehr & Bhagat, 1985; Beehr, 1995). For some jobs there are possible exceptions in which very poor performance is monitored and punished quickly or very good performance is monitored and rewarded quickly, making performance quite relevant to the person. In most circumstances, however, the potential consequences of these behaviors (e.g., performance) to the person tend not to be very immediate. Even so, we shall subsequently describe instances in which subjective occupational success is associated with SPECs. Behaviors that are harmful to one's self and that result from occupational stress would better fit the definition of strain; these might include licit and illicit drug use including smoking and drinking behaviors, stress eating, and suicide attempts. The empirical research on these behavioral strains is quite sparse compared to many other potential stress outcomes, however.

Theories about good stress outcomes

But what are the possible good outcomes from occupational stress? Even though they do not help to define stress, some good reactions might occur when experiencing stress. One set of positive outcomes for the person would be positive feelings such as job satisfaction. At least three long-standing theories have implied there can be good outcomes from stress. Selye's concept of eustress was already noted, above, as one. Another is the original demand–control theory (Karasek, 1979) of occupational stress, which argued that stressful demands (probably a subset of SPECs) would be associated with job satisfaction under some conditions (especially when the right amount of control was present). A third theory implying potentially good outcomes from stressful situations is Lazarus's (Lazarus, 1966; Lazarus & Folkman, 1984) cognitive appraisal theory. Some situations that would potentially be stressful and harmful can be appraised as less threatening, and so they might not be harmful to the person. According to that theory, stressors can be appraised initially as harm/loss, threat, or challenge. Any of these could lead to aversive outcomes if the person cannot or thinks he or she cannot cope with them. Nelson and Simmons (2005; Simmons & Nelson, 2007) recently argued, however, that when SPECs are appraised as challenges, they can lead to positive outcomes for the person. Using Selye's term 'eustress', they further argue that the presence of positive psychological states accompanying SPECs indicates or defines eustress.

Positive psychological states that can occur during stressful conditions include hope, trust and general positive affect (Nelson & Simmons, 2005); and also feelings of pride, accomplishment, and (job) satisfaction. There is little speculation about stress leading to better physical health, however. It must therefore be asked whether people can feel good about a stressful situation even when it is harming them physically. Do a healthy mind and a healthy body have to go together, or can they be independent?

Good outcomes of SPECs

Obtaining good outcomes of stress is partially an oxymoron for some definitions of stress. That is, one traditional way to define stress is by its (bad) outcomes, for example, role stressors are characteristics of role expectations that are likely to result in adverse outcomes for most people or most of the time (Kahn & Quinn, 1970). This kind of circular definition seems to make bad outcomes of stress highly likely and good outcomes less likely. Apart from occupational stress, physical exercise would be considered stressful in some ways (e.g., bodily responses to it resemble some parts of autonomic nervous system arousal), and yet it can result in good outcomes such as better mood and greater physical fitness (e.g., Emery et al., 2003; Atlantis et al., 2006; Henry et al., 2006). Few jobs are designed in ways that result in good aerobic exercise, however, but it is possible that physical exertion required in some jobs, which should be stressful, might also result in physical fitness and therefore better health. One recent study showed that even if people think the physical activity required in their jobs is only of aerobic quality, it can result in better physical fitness (Crum & Langer, 2007). Can it be possible for workplace SPECs to make people more healthy or at least more physically fit?

Aside from physiological benefits, psychological benefits might also be possible when SPECs are experienced. In a study of a task force consisting of high-level managers and professionals working on a demanding task, two SPECs (monitoring demands and time demands) were positively related to greater job satisfaction, even though they were also related to more aversive psychological strain (Beehr et al., 2001). For these people and in this situation, it could be argued that the demands were challenging and that meeting the challenge resulted in higher satisfaction. Another study of managers reported that experienced 'stress' was related to satisfaction (Cavanaugh et al., 2000). It has been argued that a challenge appraisal, which was considered mainly a negative appraisal by Lazarus and Folkman (1984) could be a considered a positive appraisal resulting in positive emotions (Simmons & Nelson, 2007). This would be consistent with the research showing that job characteristics such as variety and autonomy, which could be present in a challenging job, often result in favorable psychological reactions (Hackman & Oldham, 1980). Furthermore, we could speculate that it was no accident that these results were found with samples of highly educated, skilled people in jobs offering some control or autonomy. It is possible for SPECs to harm people psychologically (being related to greater psychological strain) even while those people become more satisfied. A chance to achieve challenging (but stressful) goals might explain this phenomenon.

In a completely different type of stressful work situation, some American soldiers deployed to Bosnia for a peacekeeping mission were exposed to stressful events such as seeing the results of genocidal warfare and being exposed to life-threatening dangers themselves (Britt et al., 2001). To the extent that they perceived their work in Bosnia to be important and meaningful, they reported actually receiving some psychological benefit from the experience. The measure of benefit was primarily composed of items suggesting that they have achieved a new perspective on life and an ability to deal with stress. People who experience SPECs, therefore, might become stronger and more stress resistant because of the stress – a good outcome of SPECs. There was no clear stressor measure in that study, but in a similar situation (deployment on a peacekeeping mission to Kosovo), a set of three SPECs (personal costs of deployment, exposure to life-threatening situations and seeing the plight of others in a war zone) were weakly but negatively related to benefits (Britt et al., 2007). As in the first study, perceptions of meaningful work were positively related to perceived benefits. Taken together, these two studies suggest that in the context of a stressful situation, people might believe that they have become better people if they also believe that their work is meaningful, but that the SPECs themselves are unlikely to have actually led to such benefits. The SPECs were positively related to strains, but were negatively related to benefits.

Job satisfaction might be a good outcome that can be positively affected by SPECs, however. Among white-collar workers in a manufacturing organization, one SPEC based on demand–control theory (Karasek, 1979) was positively related to psychological strains but was also weakly but positively related to job satisfaction (Beehr et al., 2001). The demand stressor, time demands, appeared to have both good (job satisfaction) and bad (psychological strain) effects on the employees. Two other presumed SPECs, monitoring and problem-solving demands, did not have this type of mixed good and bad outcomes, however. Instead monitoring demands were positively related to job satisfaction and unrelated to strains, while problem-solving demands were positively related to strains and unrelated to job satisfaction. Thus, two of the three demands that are ordinarily assumed to be SPECs, time and problem-solving demands, might have been promoting greater satisfaction among these employees. The results for time demands were especially intriguing, suggesting the possibility that a SPEC could simultaneously lead to both bad effects (psychological strains) and good (job satisfaction).

Thus, SPECs can lead to good psychological or physical well-being in addition to or instead of leading to strains.

Moderator effects

Under some conditions, SPECs may not lead to strains. That is, workplace environmental conditions or events that are considered stressors because they usually lead to strains have little relationship to strains if certain conditions are met. This is the essence of a moderator effect, and moderator variables are frequently proposed in occupational stress theories and empirical research. From the beginning of serious research on occupational stress, some theories explicitly proposed moderators (e.g., see models by Kahn et al., 1964; Beehr & Newman, 1978; Karasek, 1979). Moderator variables can occur in either the environment or the person.

Person characteristics as moderators

Person moderator variables proposed to weaken the relationship between occupational stressors and strains include Type B behavior (opposite of Type A behavior), rigidity (lack of flexibility), and hardiness.

Type A behavior consists of a chronic sense of time urgency and competitive drive (Friedman & Rosenman, 1974), and it was shown to be related to coronary heart disease, but some research suggests that the key component is hostility (Laungani, 2005). Type B people, the focus here, are the opposite of Type As, being more easygoing. Type B was originally conceived as behavior, but it is sometimes treated as a personality characteristic. In addition to Type B person characteristics being less susceptible to coronary heart disease (strain) directly, research has often examined it as a moderator of SPEC → strain relationships. Among a group of police and firefighters, for example, relationships between SPECs and cardiovascular disease seven years later were actually negative for Type Bs even though they were positive for Type A people (Schaubroeck et al., 1994). Thus, Type Bs may be a set of people for whom SPECs do not lead to strains.

Flexibility might also be a personal characteristic moderating relationships between

SPECs and strains. People who are more flexible would seem to adapt to changing situations; they are other-directed and open-minded (Kahn et al., 1964). Kahn et al. proposed flexibility–rigidity as a moderator over 40 years ago, but it has seldom been tested in research. Although flexibility intuitively sounds like a favorable trait, as a stress moderator, it was proposed to have a negative effect. Flexible people had a strong positive relationship between role conflict and psychological strain, but for rigid people there was no relationship. Thus, rigidity is a useful concept, because rigid people might feel less need to communicate with others (under conditions of SPECs or any other time) and thereby give others less power over them. For rigid people, SPECs may not lead to strains.

A third example of a potential individual difference moderator is hardiness. A hardy personality, as can be construed by its very label, is supposed to be one that allows the person to withstand SPECs without incurring serious strains. Hardiness consists of belief that one has control over one's own life events, being committed to one's life activities, and viewing change as challenging rather than threatening (Beehr & Bowling, 2005). Hardiness has been found to alleviate the relationship between SPECs (life stressors, but not necessarily work stressors) and strains (Kobasa 1979; Kobasa et al., 1982). Thus, for hardy people, SPECs may not lead to strains.

Although research has found that people with certain personalities can be stress resistant, there are also ample studies not finding moderating results for personality. Thus more needs to be learned about this inconsistency. Nevertheless, there is reason to believe that for some people, SPECs may not lead to strains.

Situation characteristics as moderators
In addition to characteristics of the person, some characteristics of the situation have also been posited as potential moderators of the SPEC → strain relationship. Prominent among these in the occupational stress literature are control and social support.

Demand–control theory positions job control as a prominent element in occupational stress (Karasek, 1979). In that theory, control consists of discretion or authority over doing the job's tasks. It could consist of control specifically over decision making (Hurrell & McLaney, 1988), scheduling or timing (Jackson et al., 1993; Wall et al., 1996; Sargent & Terry, 1998), and methods (Jackson et al., 1993; Wall et al., 1996), for example. According to the theory, demands or SPECs may not lead to strains for employees whose jobs provide them with sufficient control over their situation.

Social support is a second situational characteristic that can help alleviate the stressful effects of SPECs at work. Interpersonal relations were suggested as a moderator by Kahn et al. (1964) in their early study of occupational stress. Social support has been defined vaguely and differently over the decades (House, 1981; Beehr, 1985). In occupational stress research, however, it is usually operationalized as social interactions characterized as performing one of two types of functions: emotional or instrumental. Emotional support consists of providing emotional comfort and sympathy to the stressed person, and instrumental support is the provision of more tangible help in dealing with problems in the workplace (e.g., helping to get work done during a period of overload or giving instructions or information the stressed person is lacking). Some research has found that social support can buffer or moderate the relationship between SPECs and strains (e.g., see meta-analysis by Viswesvaran et al., 1999). Therefore, social support from others may form a condition under which SPECs do not result in strains.

It must be acknowledged that although some research has found work situation characteristics such as control and social support to moderate the SPEC → strains relationship, the results have thus far been inconsistent. As with the person or individual difference moderators, there is reason to believe that the environment can moderate this relationship, but more research is needed.

Subjective occupational success and occupational stress
Even though the vast majority of empirical studies in occupational stress research focus on negative conditions or events such as chronic stressors and daily hassles (Semmer et al., 2005), many studies also have examined work-related resources such as social support (e.g., Beehr, 1995; Visweswaran et al., 1999) and job control (e.g., Karasek & Theorell, 1990; Terry & Jimmieson, 1999) on well-being and health. In current psychological research there is 'a call for a more balanced, comprehensive assessment of positive as well as negative aspects of the person and the environment' (Lopez & Snyder, 2003, p. 461; see also Antonovsky, 1991; Seligman & Csikszentmihalyi, 2000; Nelson & Simmons, 2005), and subjective success can be such a positive outcome. Subjective success can plausibly be conceptualized as a resource in the organizational stress process (Grebner et al., 2006a,b, 2007a,b; Grebner, in preparation). Goal attainment is related to general positive affect (Harris et al., 2003) and also has been shown to be positively related to well-being outside the work domain (e.g., Emmons, 1986; Carver & Scheier, 1990; Brunstein, 1993; Diener & Lucas, 1999; Elliot et al., 1997) and in work-related research (e.g., Locke & Latham, 1990, 2002, 2004; Maier & Brunstein, 2001; Wiese & Freund, 2005). Subjective success, along with social support, control, hardiness, and several other variables discussed previously, can be a work-related resource that might be important for employee well-being and health. We argue, therefore, that subjective occupational success as a resource needs to be studied more in organizational stress research.

Definition, measurement, and dimensionality of subjective occupational success
There may be two reasons why not many studies focus on subjective success at work as an antecedent of well-being and health or as a consequence of work-related resources or SPECs. First, in the available literature subjective success has frequently been equated with indicators of well-being or simple positive attitudes such as job and career satisfaction (e.g., Dette et al., 2004; Ng et al., 2005). However, although job and career satisfaction might covary with success (even causally), they are not the same as success experiences (e.g., Locke & Latham, 1990, 2002, 2004; Sonnentag, 2002). Therefore, a definition of subjective success is required that distinguishes subjective success from possible consequences on the individual level.

A second reason for the disregard of subjective success in research on organizational stress might be that a well-established instrument that allows us to measure subjective success is not available so far. Hence, Grebner et al. (2007a,b) recently developed and validated an instrument in a series of qualitative and quantitative studies that assesses work-related subjective occupational success experiences. They define subjective occupational success as positive experiences at work that are goal related and salient for the individual in terms of subjective goal attainment or reasonable movement toward a goal. They assume that subjective occupational success can be represented by reaching milestones of processes, or results in terms of actions, outcomes, and long-term consequences that are related to one's own work behavior (see also Sonnentag, 2002). Subjective occupational success is multidimensional, consisting of goal attainment, pro-social success, positive feedback, and career success.

Goal attainment   Grebner et al. (2007a,b) conceptualize subjective goal attainment as the core dimension of subjective success (e.g., attaining or exceeding goals, goal attainment despite adverse conditions, and acting for one's own interests/ideas). Goal attainment can be related to task performance such as meeting or exceeding organizational goals, respectively, goals that are assigned by one's supervisor. In addition, successful coping with SPECs is often experienced as success (e.g., Holahan & Moos, 1990; Perrez & Reicherts, 1992; Thoits, 1994; Grebner et al., 2004) and therefore can be considered as one facet of goal attainment. Moreover, subjective success includes also attainment of personal goals (e.g., Maier & Brunstein, 2001) that need not necessarily be relevant for the organization (e.g., making business contacts that help to find another job). This is important, because feelings of nonwork success can be an ego-strengthening resource that can make one more resilient in the face of work-related SPECs.

Most importantly, subjective work-related goal progress and attainment are important predictors of job satisfaction and organizational commitment (e.g., Locke & Latham, 1990, 2002; Maier & Brunstein, 2001; Wiese & Freund, 2005), and positive affect (Harris et al., 2003). However, it is less well understood what role goal attainment plays for a broader range of well-being indicators, including strains resulting from work-related SPECs.

Pro-social success   Pro-social success represents a second dimension of subjective occupational success (Grebner et al., 2007a,b). Pro-social success includes supporting other people (cf. helping behavior, Organ et al., 2006), solving conflicts, preventing negative outcomes for others/causing positive outcomes for others, and being asked for advice. It includes successful engagement in organizational citizenship behavior toward other individuals in the workplace (Podsakoff et al., 2000). Moreover, pro-social success can be related to task fulfillment, for instance when a manager successfully supports a subordinate by providing advice that helps get the work done.

Positive feedback   A third dimension of subjective occupational success is positive feedback from others (e.g., supervisor, co-workers, subordinates; Grebner et al., 2007a,b). Positive feedback is a possible positive consequence of attaining or exceeding one's goals (e.g., Locke & Latham, 1990; London, 2003). Moreover, it is plausible that positive feedback can also be a consequence of pro-social success. Of course, positive feedback does not follow automatically when goals are attained or pro-social success is experienced, but rather it depends on specific circumstances. For feedback to be given, successes must be apparent for others, and others must be willing to provide positive feedback. Furthermore, the norms of group or organizational cultures may encourage or discourage providing feedback to one's co-workers. The importance of positive feedback has frequently been emphasized for a number of purposes (e.g., Locke & Latham, 1990; Kluger & DeNisi, 1996; London, 2003) and the association of positive feedback with positive emotions is well known (e.g., Taylor et al., 1984; Kluger & DeNisi, 1996; London, 2003). More research is needed, however, examining positive feedback as a facet of subjective success.

Career success   The fourth dimension of subjective occupational success is career success, a possible long-term consequence of goal attainment, pro-social success, and positive feedback – in particular positive feedback from the supervisor (Grebner et al., 2007a,b). Some studies operationally equated subjective career success with career or job satisfaction (e.g., Ng et al., 2005). Grebner et al. (2007a,b) define subjective career success as subjectively significant career moves (e.g., promotion, acquiring new projects) or career-related events (e.g., outperforming others, making important work contacts) which can be long-term consequences of accumulated immediate successes. Subjective career success does not follow automatically from cumulative goal attainment, but it also depends on other circumstances (e.g., career opportunities in a given organization or career, leader–member exchange, and organizational politics).

Antecedents of subjective occupational success
Many situational factors may influence subjective occupational success. For instance, goal attainment can depend on macro-level factors (e.g., market situation), meso-level factors (e.g., organizational politics), and micro-level factors such as task characteristics (e.g., job control, time pressure), social conditions (e.g., social support, conflicts), and attributes of goals such as goal difficulty (Locke & Latham, 1990, 2002; Latham & Locke, 1991; Seijts et al., 2004). In particular, work-related resources can promote goal attainment and may facilitate subjective success in general. Job control may facilitate goal attainment and pro-social success because it implies that an employee can either define task-related or contextual goals or choose between predefined task-related goals. Moreover, job control might help to avoid or cope with barriers to goal attainment (i.e., SPECs) (e.g., Frese & Zapf, 1994).

Having adequate social support at hand when needed also might be useful for goal attainment. For instance, others can provide necessary information or tangible help which is especially important when tasks are novel or high in complexity (Sonnentag, 2002). Moreover, emotional support can help to calm down and to return to task-relevant thinking and actions after a experiencing a SPEC at work (e.g., Dahlen & Ryan, 2005), which in turn can facilitate further goal attainment.

Beyond characteristics of the work situation, characteristics of the individual also can determine whether success is experienced. In particular, self-efficacy (Stajkovic & Luthans, 1998) can play an important role for success. For instance, people who perceive themselves as highly efficacious tend to invest sufficient effort and are less likely to cease their efforts prematurely despite the presence of SPECs (Bandura, 1982). Furthermore, people high in self-efficacy perceive stressful situations as less threatening in the first place (e.g., Jex & Bliese, 1999; Sonnentag, 2002), 'set higher goals, are more committed to assigned goals, and find and use better task strategies to attain the goals' (Locke & Latham, 2002, p. 706).

Particular types of work-related SPECs might even be beneficial, at least to a certain degree, to subjective success experiences (e.g., time pressure might increase frequency of goal attainment). So-called 'challenge stressors' are thought to be 'obstacles that are to be overcome in order to learn and achieve', and they have been found in a meta-analysis to correlate positively with performance (LePine et al., 2005, p. 765). However, hindrance stressors, such as role ambiguity, role conflict, organizational constraints–problems of work organization, work interruptions, and social stressors, job insecurity, and organizational politics might be detrimental to the experience of success (hindrance stressors, ibid.). These SPECs unnecessarily thwart personal growth and goal attainment (e.g., ibid.; see also Frese & Zapf, 1994). For example, frequency of goal attainment might be reduced by increasing role ambiguity, because when roles are not clear employees are uncertain what the goals actually are. Moreover, in particular hindrance stressors might tend to elicit task-irrelevant cognitions such as worries or rumination (Brosschot et al., 2005), which in turn can use personal resources that could otherwise be used for task accomplishment.

Consequences of subjective occupational success
Subjective success can be beneficial in terms of affective states (e.g., positive emotions such as joy and pride, see Fineman, 2000; Ashkanasy et al., 2002; Lord et al., 2002), momentary well-being (e.g., tension) and more stable indicators of well-being such as psychosomatic complaints and job-related well-being (e.g., job satisfaction, feelings of resentment). Aside from its potential to affect the individual's strains, however, it also may contribute positively to performance in terms of meeting organizational goals. Moreover, subjective success might encourage or strengthen some of the individual's other personal resources (e.g., optimism, positive affectivity, numbers of socially supportive others, e.g., Park et al., 1996). In general, people tend to raise their goals and increase their persistence (and self-efficacy) following success experiences (e.g., Audia et al., 2000).

The four dimensions of subjective success are positively related to various indicators of well-being (e.g., Locke & Latham, 1990, 2002; Harris et al., 2003; Wiese & Freund, 2005). Current work in progress (Grebner et al., 2007b), suggests also that work engagement is related to the four subjective success indicators, and engagement has been found to predict work performance (Salanova et al., 2005). Moreover, the dimension of pro-social success was positively related to affective commitment, which is also in line with the literature (e.g., Locke & Latham, 1990, 2002). Furthermore, in-progress work suggests negative associations of the core success dimension of goal attainment with resigned attitude toward one's job, which is defensive, resentful maladaptation to suboptimal working conditions (Semmer, 2003) and to exhaustion. Whether success ameliorates the harmful effects of SPECs on well-being in terms of buffer effects is important to investigate in future studies. One may hypothesize that offenses by co-workers may stop when an employee attains or exceeds his or her goals and receives publicly positive feedback by the supervisor.

In addition, it is plausible that subjective success might also be beneficial in terms of physiological stress responses. For instance, successful coping can lead to faster recovery of physiological stress parameters (e.g., Haynes et al., 1991) compared to unsuccessful or inadequate coping (e.g., in terms of persevering negative cognitions after termination of the stressful situation (Brosschot et al., 2005)). Moreover, it is conceivable that when a goal is attained, employees can better switch off their minds after work compared to situations when goal attainment is difficult or many obstacles have to be removed.

Overall, we conclude that it is important to examine antecedents and consequences of subjective occupational success, because subjective success might be a resource that is understudied in occupational health psychology. Goal attainment, pro-social success, positive feedback, and career, together, comprise subjective success. Theoretically, subjective success can be considered as a personal resource, because success is beneficial for employee well-being in terms of direct effects (Grebner, 2007a,b). Furthermore, future research should also focus on possible buffer effects of subjective success on relationships between work-related SPECs and strains.

Conclusions

SPECs (McGrath & Beehr, 1990; Beehr & McGrath, 1992, 1996; Semmer et al., 2005) in the work environment can lead to strain reactions in the person. SPECs often represent expectations, demands, threats, or loss related to an employee's job. However, SPECs do not always lead to stress reactions by the individual. This might occur when (i) SPECs are valued positively, although they lead to harmful strains, or when (ii) SPECs lead to good outcomes as well as strains, or when (iii) SPECs do not lead to strain at all. Moreover, we argue that under certain circumstances, job stress might be related to occupational success which can in turn be considered as a resource in the stress process because it is positively related to well-being (Grebner et al., 2007a,b; Grebner, in preparation). An example of a valued SPEC is the increased responsibility related to a promotion that is considered as a (subjective) career success. An example of a SPEC that can lead to a good outcome might be role overload that is positively related to performance that in turn leads to positive feedback by others. Finally, a SPEC that does not lead to strain at all might be a conflict with a co-worker whose detrimental effects are buffered by emotional support by the supervisor. Therefore, it is important to ask whether employees can have positive feelings during a SPEC or as a consequence of a SPEC, even when it is harming them at the same time. This might, for instance, be the case when people can achieve challenging but stressful goals, that is when employees are successful. In general, we assume that SPECs are sometimes related to different types of occupational success (i.e., goal attainment, pro-social success, positive feedback, and career success) that in turn can have beneficial effects on employee well-being and buffer detrimental effects of SPECS on employee strains (Grebner et al., 2007a,b; Grebner, in preparation). Therefore, it is important to examine antecedents and consequences of occupational success that can be considered as resources in the occupational stress process (Grebner et al., 2007a,b; Grebner, in preparation). Moreover, it is crucial to investigate how frequently success or a good outcome is tied to the experience of stress and to what extent this has effects on employee well-being and health in the long term. There can be a positive psychology even in relation to occupational stress.

References

Antonovsky, A. (1991), 'The structural sources of salutogenic strengths', in C.L. Cooper & R. Payne (eds), *Personality and Stress: Individual Differences in the Stress Process*, Chichester: Wiley, pp. 67–104.

Ashkanasy, N.M., Zerbe, W.J. & Härtel, C.E.J. (2002), *Managing Emotions in the Workplace*, Armonk, NY: M.E. Sharpe.

Atlantis, E., Chow, C., Kirby, A. & Singh, M.A.F. (2006), 'Worksite intervention effects on physical health: a randomized controlled trial', *Health Promotion International*, **21**, 191–200.

Audia, P.G., Locke, E.A. & Smith, K.G. (2000), 'The paradox of success: an archival and a laboratory study of strategic persistence following radical environmental change', *Academy of Management Journal*, **43**, 837–53.

Bandura, A. (1982), 'Self-efficacy mechanisms in human agency', *American Psychologist*, **37**, 122–47.

Beehr, T.A. (1985), 'The role of social support in coping with organizational stress', in Beehr & Bhagat (eds), *Human Stress and Cognition in Organizations: An Integrated Perspective*, New York: John Wiley, pp. 375–98.

Beehr, T.A. (1995), *Psychological Stress in the Workplace*, New York: Routledge.

Beehr, T.A. & Bhagat, R.S. (1985), 'Introduction to human stress and cognition in organizations', in Beehr & Bhagat (eds), *Human Stress and Cognition in Organizations: An Integrated Perspective*, New York: John Wiley, pp. 3–19.

Beehr, T.A. & Bowling, N.A. (2005), 'Hardy personality, stress, and health', in C.L. Cooper (ed.), *Handbook of Stress Medicine and Health*, 2nd edn, London: CRC Press, pp. 194–211.

Beehr, T.A., Glaser, K.M., Canali, K.G. & Wallwey, D.A. (2001), 'Back to basics: re-examination of demand-control theory of occupational stress', *Work and Stress*, **15**, 115–30.

Beehr, T.A. & Glazer, S. (2005), 'Organizational role stress', in J. Barling, E.K. Kelloway & M.R. Frone (eds), *Handbook of Work Stress*, Thousand Oaks, CA: Sage, pp. 7–33.

Beehr, T.A. & McGrath, J.E. (1992), 'Social support, occupational stress and anxiety', *Anxiety, Stress, and Coping*, **5**, 7–19.

Beehr, T.A. & McGrath, J.E. (1996), 'The methodology of research on coping: conceptual, strategic, and operational-level issues', in M. Zeidner & N.S. Endler (eds), *Handbook of Coping: Theory, Research, Applications*, New York: John Wiley, pp. 65–82.

Beehr, T.A. & Newman, J.E. (1978), 'Job stress, employee health, and organizational effectiveness: a facet analysis, model, and literature review', *Personnel Psychology*, **31**, 665–99.

Britt, T.W., Adler, A.B. & Bartone, P.T. (2001), 'Deriving benefits from stessful events: the role of engagement in meaningful work and hardiness', *Journal of Occupational Health Psychology*, **6**, 53–63.

Britt, T.W., Dickinson, J.M., Castro, C.A., Moore, D. & Adler, A.B. (2007), 'Correlates and consequences of morale versus depression under stressful conditions', *Journal of Occupational Health Psychology*, **12**, 34–47.

Brosschot, J.F., Pieper, S. & Thayer, J.F. (2005), 'Expanding stress theory: prolonged activitation and perseverative cognition', *Psychoneuroendocrinology*, **30**, 1043–9.

Brunstein, J.C. (1993), 'Personal goals and subjective well-being: a longitudinal study', *Journal of Personality and Social Psychology*, **65**, 1061–70.

Carver, C.S. & Scheier, M.F. (1990), 'Principles of self-regulation: action and emotion', in E.T. Higgins & R.M. Sorrentino (eds), *Handbook of Motivation and Social Behavior*, New York: Guilford, pp. 3–52.

Cavanaugh, M.A., Boswell, W.R., Roehling, M.V. & Boudreau, J.W. (2000), 'An empirical examination of self-reported work stress among US managers', *Journal of Applied Psychology*, **85**, 65–74.

Cooper, C.L. & Dewe, P. (2004), *Stress: A Brief History*, Oxford: Blackwell.

Crum, A.J. & Langer, E.J. (2007), 'Mind-set matters: exercise and the placebo effect', *Psychological Science*, **18**, 165–71.

Dahlen, E.R. & Ryan, M.C. (2005), 'The experience expression and control of anger in perceived social support', *Personality and Individual Differences*, **39**, 391–401.

Dette, D.E., Abele, A.E. & Renner, O. (2004), 'Zur Definition und Messung von Berufserfolg' (Definition and measurement of occupational success), *Zeitschrift für Personalpsychologie*, **3**, 170–83.

Diener, E. & Lucas, R.E. (1999), 'Personality and subjective well-being', in D. Kahneman, E. Diener & N. Schwarz (eds), *Well-being: The Foundations of Hedonic Psychology*, New York: Russell Sage Foundation, pp. 213–29.

Elliot, A.J., Sheldon, K.M. & Church, M.A. (1997), 'Avoidance personal goals and subjective well-being', *Personality and Social Psychology Bulletin*, **51**, 1058–68.

Emery, C.F., Shermer, R.L., Hauck, E.R., Hsiao, E.T. & MacIntyre, N.R. (2003), 'Cognitive and psychological outcomes of exercise in a 1-year follow-up study of patients with chronic obstructive pulmonary disease', *Health Psychology*, **22**, 598–604.

Emmons, R.A. (1986), 'Personal strivings: an approach to personality and subjective well-being', *Journal of Personality and Social Psychology*, **51**, 1058–68.

Fineman, S. (2000), *Emotion in Organizations*, 2nd edn, London: Sage.

French, J.R.P., Jr., Caplan, R.D. & Harrison, R.V. (1982), *The Mechanisms of Job Stress and Strain*, London: Wiley.

Frese, M. & Zapf, D. (1994), 'Action as the core of work psychology: a German approach', in M.D. Dunnette, L.M. Hough & H.C. Triandis (eds), *Handbook of Industrial and Organizational Psychology*, Vol. 4, Palo Alto, CA: Consulting Psychologists Press, pp. 271–340.

Friedman, M. & Rosenman, R.H. (1974), *Type A Behavior and Your Heart*, New York: Alfred A. Knopf.

Grebner, S. (in preparation), 'Subjective occupational success as a resource', in S. McIntyre & J. Houdmont (eds), *Occupational Health Psychology: European Perspectives on Research, Education and Practice*, (Vol. 2), Maia, Portugal: ISMAI Publishing.

Grebner, S., Elfering, A., Achermann, E., Knecht, R. & Semmer, N.K. (2006a), 'Subjective success: a resource in the stress process?', paper presented at the 27th Stress and Anxiety Research Conference, Rethymnon, Greece, July.

Grebner, S., Elfering, A., Achermann, E., Knecht, R. & Semmer, N.K. (2006b), 'Subjektive berufliche erfolgserlebnisse und befinden' (Subjective occupational success experiences and well-being), paper presented at the 45th Congress of the German Society for Psychology, Nürnberg, Germany, September.

Grebner, S., Elfering, A., Achermann, E., Knecht, R. & Semmer, N.K. (2007a), 'Subjective occupational success as a resource in the stress process: development and validation of a new multidimensional instrument', paper presented at the 13th European Congress on Work and Organizational Psychology, Stockholm, Sweden, May.

Grebner, S., Elfering, A., Achermann, E., Knecht, R. & Semmer, N.K. (2007b), 'Subjective occupational success as a resource: development and validation of a multidimensional instrument', manuscript submitted for publication, University of Bern, Switzerland.

Grebner, S., Elfering, A., Semmer, N., Kaiser-Probst, C. & Schlapbach, M.L. (2004), 'Stressful situations at work and in private life among young workers: an event sampling approach', *Social Indicators Research*, **67**, 11–49.

Hackman, J.R. & Oldham, G.R. (1980), *Work Redesign*, Reading, MA: Addison-Wesley.

Harris, C., Daniels, K. & Briner, R.B. (2003), 'A daily diary study of goals and affective well-being at work', *Journal of Occupational and Organizational Psychology*, **76**, 401–10.

Haynes, S.N., Gannon, L.R., Orimoto, L., O'Brien W.H. & Brandt, M. (1991), 'Psychophysiological assessment of poststress recovery', *Psychological Assessment: A Journal of Consulting and Clinical Psychology*, **3**, 356–65.

Henry, R.N., Anshel, M.H. & Michael, T. (2006), 'Effects of aerobic and circuit training on fitness and body image among women', *Journal of Sport Behavior*, **29**, 281–303.

Hobfoll, S.E. (1998), *Stress, Culture, and Community: The Psychology and Philosophy of Stress*, New York: Plenum.

Holahan, C.J. & Moos, R.H. (1990), 'Life stressors, resistance factors, and improved psychological functioning: an extension of the stress resistance paradigm', *Journal of Personality and Social Psychology*, **58**, 909–17.

House, J.S. (1981), *Work Stress and Social Support*, Reading, MA: Addison-Wesley.

Hurrell, J.J. & McLaney, M.A. (1988), 'Exposure to job stress: a new psychometric instrument', *Scandinavian Journal of Work, Environment, and Health*, **14**, 27–8.

Jackson, P.R., Wall, T.D., Martin, R. & Davids, K. (1993), 'New measures of job control, cognitive demand and production responsibility', *Journal of Applied Psychology*, **78**, 753–62.

Jex, S.M. & Bliese, P.D. (1999), 'Efficacy beliefs as a moderator of the effects of work-related stressors: a multilevel study', *Journal of Applied Psychology*, **84**, 349–51.

Kahn, R.L. & Quinn, R.P. (1970), 'Role stress: a framework for anlaysis', in A. McLean (ed.), *Mental Health and Work Organizations*, Chicago: Rand-McNally, pp. 60–115.

Kahn, R.L., Wolfe, D.M., Quinn, R.P., Snoek, J.D. & Rosenthal, R.A. (1964), *Organizational Stress: Studies in Role Conflict and Ambiguity*, New York: John Wiley.

Karasek, R.A. (1979), 'Job demands, job decision latitude, and mental strain: implications for job redesign', *Administrative Science Quarterly*, **24**, 285–308.

Karasek, R.A. & Theorell, T. (1990), *Healthy Work: Stress, Productivity, and the Reconstruction of Working Life*, New York: Basic Books.

Kluger, A.N. & DeNisi, A. (1996), 'The effects of feedback interventions on performance: historical review, a meta-analysis and a preliminary feedback intervention theory', *Psychological Bulletin*, **119**, 254–84.

Kobasa, S.C. (1979), 'Stressful life events, personality and health: an inquiry into hardiness', *Journal of Personality and Social Psychology*, **37**, 1–11.

Kobasa, S.C., Maddi, S.R. & Kahn, S. (1982), 'Hardiness and health: a prospective study', *Journal of Personality and Social Psychology*, **42**, 168–77.

Latham G.P. & Locke, E.A. (1991), 'Self-regulation through goal setting', *Organizational Behavior and Human Decision Processes*, **50**, 212–47.

Laungani, P. (2005), 'Stress, culture, and personality', in C.L. Cooper (ed.), *Handbook of Stress Medicine and Health*, 2nd edn, London: CRC Press, pp. 213–31.

Lazarus, R.S. (1966), *Psychological Stress and the Coping Process*, New York: McGraw-Hill.

Lazarus, R.S. & Folkman, S. (1984), *Stress, Appraisal, and Coping*, New York: Springer.

LeFevre, M., Matheny, J. & Kolt, G.S. (2003), 'Eustress, distress and interpretation in occupational stress', *Journal of Managerial Psychology*, **18**, 726–44.

LePine, J.A., Podsakoff, N.P. & LePine, M.A. (2005), 'A meta-analytic test of the challenge stressor–hindrance stressor framework: an explanation for inconsistent relationships among stressors and performance', *Academy of Management Journal*, **48**, 764–75.

Locke, E.A. & Latham, G.P. (1990), *A Theory of Goal Setting and Task Performance*, Englewood Cliffs, NJ: Prentice-Hall.

Locke, E.A. & Latham, G.P. (2002), 'Building a practically useful theory of goal setting and task motivation', *American Psychologist*, **57**, 705–17.

Locke, E.A. & Latham, G.P. (2004), 'What should we do about motivation theory?', *Academy of Management Review*, **29**, 388–403.

London, M. (2003), *Job Feedback. Giving, Seeking, and Using Feedback for Performance Improvement*, Mahwah, NJ: Lawrence Erlbaum.

Lopez, S.J. & Snyder, C.R. (2003), 'The future of positive psychological assessment. Making a difference', in Lopez & Snyder (eds), *Positive Psychological Assessment: A Handbook of Models and Measures*, Washington, DC: American Psychological Association, pp. 461–8.

Lord, R.G., Klimoski, R.J. & Kanfer, R. (2000), *Emotions in the Workplace*, San Francisco, CA: Jossey-Bass.

Maier, G.W. & Brunstein, J.C. (2001), 'The role of personal work goals in newcomers' job satisfaction and organizational commitment: a longitudinal analysis', *Journal of Applied Psychology*, **86**, 1034–42.

Maslach, C. & Leiter, M. (2005), 'Stress and burnout: the critical research', in C.L. Cooper (ed.), *Stress Medicine and Health*, 2nd edn, New York: CRC Press, pp. 155–72.

McGrath, J.E. & Beehr, T.A. (1990), 'Time and the stress process: some temporal issues in the conceptualization and measurement of stress', *Stress Medicine*, **6**, 93–104.

Nelson, D.L. & Simmons, B.L. (2005), 'Eustress and attitudes at work: a positive approach', in A.-S.G. Antoniou & C.L. Cooper (eds), *Research Companion to Occupational Health Psychology*, Cheltenham, UK and Northampton, MA, USA: Edward Elgar, pp. 102–10.

Ng, T.W.H., Eby, L.T., Sorensen, K.L. & Feldman, D.C. (2005), 'Predictors of objective and subjective career success: a meta-analysis', *Personnel Psychology*, **58**, 367–408.

Organ, D.W., Podsakoff, P.M. & MacKenzie, S.B. (2006), *Organizational Citizenship Behaviour: Its Nature, Antecedents, and Consequences*, Thousand Oaks, CA: Sage.

Park, C.L., Cohen, L.H. & Murch, R.L. (1996), 'Assessment and prediction of stress-related growth', *Journal of Personality*, **64**, 71–105.

Perrez, M. & Reicherts, M. (1992), *Stress, Coping, and Health: A Situation Behavior Approach: Theory, Methods, Applications*, Bern: Hogrefe & Huber.

Podsakoff, P.M., McKenzie, S.B., Paine, J.B. & Bachrach, D.G. (2000), 'Organization citizenship behaviors: a critical review of the theoretical and empirical literature and suggestions for future research', *Journal of Management*, **26**, 513–63.

Salanova, M., Agut, S. & Peiro, J.M. (2005), 'Linking organizational resources and work engagement to employee performance and customer loyalty: the mediation of service climate', *Journal of Applied Psychology*, **90**, 1217–27.

Sargent, L.D. & Terry, D.J. (1998), 'The effects of work control and job demands on employee adjustment and work performance', *Journal of Occupational and Organizational Psychology*, **71**, 219–36.

Schaubroeck, J., Ganster, D.C. & Kemerer, B.E. (1994), 'Job complexity, "type A" behavior, and cardiovascular disorder: a prospective study', *Academy of Management Journal*, **37**, 426–39.

Seijts, G.H., Latham, G.P., Tasa, K. & Latham, B.W. (2004), 'Goal setting and goal orientation: an integration of two different yet related literatures', *Academy of Management Journal*, **47**, 227–39.

Seligman, M.E.P. & Csikszentmihalyi, M. (2000), 'Positive psychology', *American Psychologist*, **55**, 5–14.

Selye, H. (1976), *The Stress of Life*, New York: McGraw-Hill.

Semmer, N.K. (2003), 'Individual differences, work stress, and health', in M.J. Schabracq, J.A.M. Winnubst & C.L. Cooper (eds), *Handbook of Work and Health Psychology*, 2nd edn, Chichester: Wiley, pp. 83–120.

Semmer, N.K., McGrath, J.E. & Beehr, T.A. (2005), 'Conceptual issues in research on stress and health', in C.L. Cooper (ed.), *Handbook of Stress Medicine and Health*, 2nd edn, New York: CRC Press, pp. 1–43.

Simmons, B.L. & Nelson, D.L. (2007), 'Eustress at work: extending the holistic stress model', in Nelson & C.L. Cooper (eds), *Positive Organizational Behavior*, London: Sage, pp. 40–54.

Sonnentag, S. (2002), 'Performance, well-being, and self-regulation', in Sonnentag (ed.), *Psychological Management of Individual Performance*, Chichester: Wiley, pp. 405–23.

Stajkovic, A.D. & Luthans, F. (1998), 'Self-efficacy and work-related performance: a meta-analysis', *Psychological Bulletin*, **124**, 240–61.

Stanley, R.O. & Burrows, G.D. (2005), 'The role of stress in mental illness: the practice', in C.L. Cooper (ed.), *Handbook of Stress Medicine and Health*, 2nd edn, New York: CRC Press, pp. 87–100.

Stetler, C., Murali, R., Chen, E. & Miller, G.E. (2005), 'Stress, immunity, and disease', in C.L. Cooper (ed.), *Handbook of Stress Medicine and Health*, 2nd edn, New York: CRC Press, pp. 132–54.

Taylor, S.M., Fisher, C.D. & Ilgen, D.R. (1984), 'Individuals' reactions to performance feedback in organizations: a control theory perspective', in K.M. Rowland & G.R. Ferris (eds), *Research in Personnel and Human Resources Management*, **2**, 81–124.

Terry, D.J. & Jimmieson, N.L. (1999), 'Work control and employee well-being: a decade review', *International Review of Industrial and Organizational Psychology*, Vol. 14, Chichester: Wiley, pp. 95–148.

Theorell, T. (2005), 'Stress and prevention of cardiovascular disease', in C.L. Cooper (ed.), *Handbook of Stress Medicine and Health*, 2nd edn, New York: CRC Press, pp. 71–85.

Thoits, P. (1994), 'Stressors and problem-solving: the individual as psychological activist', *Journal of Health and Social Behavior*, **35**, 143–60.

Viswesvaran, C., Sanchez, J. & Fisher, J. (1999), 'The role of social support in the process of work stress', *Journal of Vocational Behavior*, **54**, 314–34.

Wall, T.D., Jackson, P.R., Mullarky, S. & Parker, S.R. (1996), 'The demand–control model of job strain: a more specific test', *Journal of Occupational and Organizational Psychology*, **69**, 153–66.

Wiese, B.S. & Freund, A. (2005), 'Goal progress makes one happy, or does it? Longitudinal findings from the work domain', *Journal of Occupational and Organizational Psychology*, **78**, 287–304.

3 Leadership development from a complexity perspective
Richard E. Boyatzis

Introduction

While there is a developing literature of multi-level theories of leadership (Hunt, 1991; Schneider & Somers, 2006), little work of this nature has been done on leadership development. From a complexity perspective, leadership development requires more than helping a person who is, or wants to be, a leader. It also requires development of the dyadic relationships, teams and organization of which the person is a part. In other words, you cannot help a person's development as a leader to be sustainable without also working on the systems and relationships that constitute their context – the situations in which that person will express their leadership.

Considering all of the time, effort, and money invested in attempts to develop leaders through education, training, and coaching, there are few theories that help us to understand the change process. Other than McClelland (1965) and Prochaska et al. (1992), the actual process of change is like a mysterious black box.

One of the reasons for this paucity of good theory is that the underlying paradigm on which theories are conceptualized is lacking in credibility. The idea of smooth, continuous change does not fit with the reality that most of us experience. This chapter will describe a theory of leadership development that has produced demonstrable results at the individual level and explains the multi-level causality needed for sustainable development. Once concepts from complexity theory are applied, it then becomes possible to explain sustainable change at all levels of human and social organization, not just leadership development. In addition to development of leadership as the focus of the change effort, leadership will also be examined as a critical component providing communication of thoughts and feelings across the multiple levels involved in any sustainable change.

Complex systems

The three features of complex systems and complexity theory that will be explored are: (i) non-linear and discontinuous dynamical systems, including tipping points and catastrophic change; (ii) self-organizing into patterns of equilibrium or disequilibrium in which emergent events start a new dynamic process through the pull of specific attractors; and (iii) multi-levelness (the application of this theory at all levels of social organization) and the interaction among these levels through leadership and reference groups.

A complex system is a multi-level combination of systems that may behave independently of any one of the component systems.[1] It is more than a simple system (at a single level) or a complicated system, such as non-linear dynamics within a simple system.

Specifically, to be a complex system, it must have three properties. One is *scale* (Eric Baer articulated this concept in the Complexity Forum). Scale refers to the multiple levels of systems that are mirror images of or comparable to each other (Casti, 1994). For example, to observe a team's sustained development, change must occur in the behavior of individual team members, as well as within the organization that manages or owns the team. A second property is *interaction*. That is, identification of the factors that provide interaction among the levels – and description of how they do it. The third property is *function* – a description of how the components of the system function or affect each other.

Desired, sustainable change
Sustained, desired change can be described by intentional change theory (ICT) (Boyatzis, 2006a). 'Desired change' is something that a person would like to occur. It is not accidental or the result of acts of nature, such as earthquakes. It is not inevitable, like the effect of aging on the loss of elasticity of muscle tissue.

The change is 'sustainable' in that it endures over time. It has a feature of self-perpetuation, repeated re-invention, or replication. Sustainable, in this definition, means that the components do not atrophy or exhaust during the change process. A desirable, sustainable change requires intentionality for it to occur or to maintain a current desirable state, relationship, or habit. Knowing that things can atrophy or drift into a less desired state, the desire to maintain the current state requires deliberate investment of energy in this maintenance.

Desired sustainable changes in an organization's leadership or within people who are leaders are changes in the nature of the relationships between the leader and the people around him/her, changes in their own behavior, thought patterns, beliefs, attitudes, feelings, perceptions, purpose, roles taken, and identity. Such changes are, on the whole, discontinuous. That is, they appear as an emergent or catastrophic change, which is a property of complex systems (Casti, 1994). The experience of these changes is one of surprise or discovery (Boyatzis, 2006a). Self-awareness or mindfulness (of self and context, both social and natural) is often inversely proportionate to the degree of surprise.

The dynamics of emergence often result in the changes being non-linear. For example, a linear relationship between a leader's behavior and performance would mean that each meeting with colleagues would show increased effectiveness and rapport or the opposite – steadily decreasing relationships. Any executive knows that you may see no improvement over several meetings and then, in the fourth, it all comes together and they begin to build a new relationship. Gersick (1991) called this discontinuity, 'punctuated equilibrium' – moments of discontinuous, revolutionary change interspersed with periods of equilibrium-seeking behavior. Therefore, leadership development is often a non-linear and discontinuous, emergent phenomenon appearing or being experienced as a set of discoveries. ICT attempts to isolate not merely *when* these differences emerge, but *why* they occur.

The discontinuities occur at tipping points (Holland, 1995), like the emergence of a consensus toward a new strategy in an organization. Malcolm Gladwell popularized this idea with his book *The Tipping Point* (2000), but McClelland (1998) and Boyatzis (2006b) showed that up to a certain point, the relationship between people's abilities and their performance as a leader may not appear to exist. Once a specific point is reached, the effect of a small incremental increase in their behavior produces a dramatic increase in their leadership. Effective use of a tipping point in organizations is often expected when hiring a 'star' leader. But often, this expectation is disappointed, and frustrating to all.

Leadership development as intentional change

At the individual level for development of a leader, ICT describes the essential components and process of desirable, sustainable change in one's behavior, thoughts, feelings, and perceptions related to leadership effectiveness (Boyatzis, 2001, 2006a). The 'change' may be in people's actions, habits or competencies. It may be in their dreams or aspirations. It may be in the way they feel in certain situations or around certain people. It may be a change in how they look at events at work or in life. In this sense, ICT may be said to describe and explain learning as a form of this desired adaptation or evaluation. Indeed, for many years the theory was called 'self-directed learning' (Kolb & Boyatzis, 1970; Boyatzis, 2001; Goleman et al., 2002). Although it may apply to younger people, the work cited here and the focus of its development over the last 38 years has been on adults in or preparing for leadership and management roles.

A desirable, sustainable change may also include the desire to maintain a current desirable state, relationship, or habit. But knowing that things can atrophy or drift into a less desired state, the desire to maintain the current state requires investment of energy in this maintenance while external (or internal) forces may naturally provoke a change.

In this way, desired, sustainable change can be explained and described through ICT. In this sense, the changes must be intentional in pursuit of being an effective leader. This is in contrast to those who are pushed into leadership, are coerced because of the social desirability, or just assume that they should move 'up' to get ahead in their career. In these cases, people drift into considering being a leader, but give little thought to being an effective leader or why they may want to be one.

When there is the lack of intentionality for a change, knowledge or skills, even if acquired temporarily (i.e., for a test), are soon forgotten (Specht & Sandlin, 1991). Students, children, patients, clients, and subordinates may act as if they care about learning something, go through the motions, but they proceed to disregard it or forget it – unless it is something that they want to learn. This does not include changes induced, willingly or not, by chemical or hormonal changes in one's body. But even in such situations, the interpretation of the changes and behavioral comportment following it will be affected by the person's will, values, and motivations. In this way, it appears that most, if not all, sustainable behavioral change is intentional. The dilemma with leadership development is that a person may want to be a leader, but may not want to invest the energy and time needed to develop the competencies needed to be an effective leader. The process of intentional change is graphically shown in Figure 3.1 (Boyatzis, 2001, 2006a; Goleman et al., 2002).

Since this desire seems important, it may not be in their consciousness or even within the scope of their self-awareness. Wake-up calls, or moments and events that awaken people to the need for consideration of a change, may be required to bring them to the process of desired, intentional change (Boyatzis et al., 2002; Boyatzis & McKee, 2005; McKee et al., 2008). Before we get into the details, let us step back and ask why we believe that this is a sound theory of leadership development.

How do we know it works?

Decades of research on the effects of psychotherapy (Hubble et. al., 1999), self-help programs (Kanfer & Goldstein, 1991), cognitive behavior therapy (Barlow, 1988),

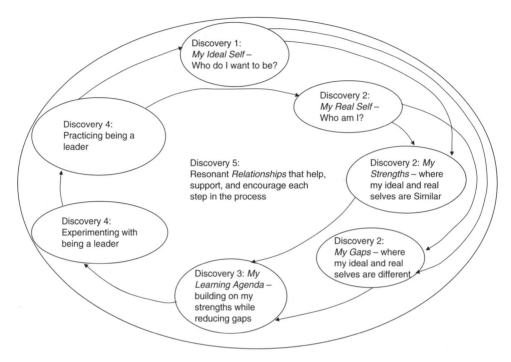

Figure 3.1   Intentional change theory

training programs (Morrow et al., 1997), and education (Winter et al., 1981; Pascarella & Terenzini, 1991) have shown that people can change their behavior, moods, and self-image. But most of the studies focused on a single characteristic, such as maintenance of sobriety, reduction in a specific anxiety, or a set of characteristics often determined by the assessment instrument, such as the scales of the MMPI (i.e., Minnesota Multiphasic Personality Inventory). As was said earlier, there are few models or theories of how individuals change and develop in sustainable ways (McClelland, 1965; Prochaska et al., 1992).

The intent of much of the training in organizations or MBA programs is to produce leaders or at least people who can act in the ways that effective leaders act. This often means producing value added and development on the emotional, social and cognitive intelligence competencies that have been shown to predict effective leadership (Bray et al., 1974; Boyatzis, 1982; Howard & Bray, 1988; Luthans et al., 1988; Spencer & Spencer, 1993; Goleman et al., 2002).

The 'honeymoon effect' of typical training programs might start with improvement immediately following the program, but within months it drops precipitously (Campbell et al., 1970). Only 15 programs were found in a global search of the literature by the Consortium on Research on Emotional Intelligence in Organizations to improve emotional intelligence. Most of them showed an impact on job outcomes, such as number of new businesses started, or life outcomes, such as finding a job or satisfaction (Cherniss & Adler, 2000), which are the ultimate purpose of development efforts. But showing an impact on outcomes, while desired, may also blur *how* the change actually occurs.

Furthermore, when a change has been noted, a question about the sustainability of the changes is raised because of the relatively short time periods studied.

The few published studies examining improvement of more than one of these competencies show an overall improvement of about 11% in emotional and social intelligence competencies 3–18 months following training (Hand et al., 1973; Wexley & Memeroff, 1975; Latham & Saari, 1979; Noe & Schmitt, 1986; Young & Dixon, 1996). More recent meta-analytic studies and utility analyses confirm that significant changes can and do occur. But they do not have either the impact that the level of investment would lead us to expect or many types of training (Burke & Day, 1986; Baldwin & Ford, 1988; Morrow et al., 1997). There are, undoubtedly, other studies that were not found and reviewed, or not available through journals and books and, therefore, overlooked.

The results appear no better than standard MBA programs, when there is often no attempt to enhance emotional intelligence competencies. The best data here come from a research project by the American Assembly of Collegiate Schools of Business (AACSB). They found that the behavior of graduating students from two highly ranked business schools, compared to their levels when they began their MBA training, showed only improvements of 2% in the skills of emotional intelligence (DDI, 1985). In fact, when students from four other high-ranking MBA programs were assessed on a range of tests and direct behavioral measures, they showed a gain of 4% in self-awareness and self-management abilities, but a *decrease* of 3% in social awareness and relationship management (Boyatzis & Sokol, 1982; Boyatzis et al., 1995).

The honeymoon effect is often the cause for practitioners and scholars to overlook the 'sleeper effect'. The sleeper effect is that a sustainable change in a person's behavior, thoughts patterns or emotional reactions to events does not appear until 6–12 months following completion of the change effort (McClelland, 1985). Since it appears disconnected to the timing of the intervention, it is a discontinuous effect and easily overlooked or wrongly attributed to other factors. Here again, the use of concepts from complexity theory help us notice effects that were overlooked.

A series of longitudinal studies underway at the Weatherhead School of Management (WSOM) of Case Western Reserve University have shown that people can change on this complex set of competencies (emotional and social intelligence) that distinguish outstanding leaders. A required course was designed with ICT to help MBAs develop their leadership competencies. It worked, and the improvement lasted for years. A visual comparison of the percentage improvement in behavioral measures of emotional and social intelligence from different samples is shown in Figure 3.2.

MBA students, averaging 27 years old at entry into the program, showed dramatic changes on videotaped and audiotaped behavioral samples and questionnaire measures of these competencies as a result of the competency-based, outcome-oriented MBA program implemented in 1990 (Boyatzis et al., 1996; Boyatzis et al., 2002; Boyatzis & Saatcioglu, 2008). Four cadres of full-time MBA students graduating in 1992, 1993, 1994, and 1995 showed 47% improvement on self-awareness competencies such as self-confidence and on self-management competencies such as the drive to achieve and adaptability in the one to two years to graduation compared to when they first entered. When it came to social awareness and relationship management skills, improvements were even greater: 75% on competencies such as empathy and team leadership.

Meanwhile with the part-time MBA students graduating in 1994, 1995, and 1996, who

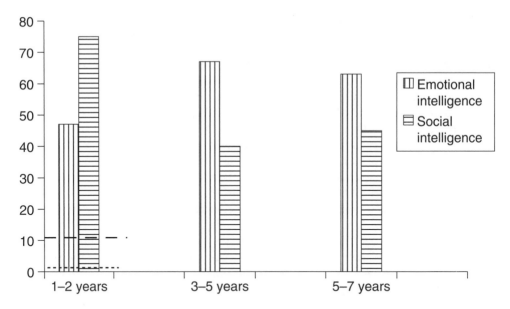

Indicates impact of company and government training programs 3–18 months after training on multiple emotional intelligence competencies

Indicates impact of a variety of above-average MBA programs

Figure 3.2   Percentage improvement of emotional and social intelligence competencies of different groups of MBA graduates taking the intentional change course

were working full-time while attending classes, the dramatic improvement was found again, in these students who typically take three to five years to graduate. These groups showed 67% improvement in self-awareness and self-management competencies and 40% improvement in social awareness and social skills competencies by the end of their MBA program.

Furthermore, Jane Wheeler (1999) tracked down groups of these part-timers two years *after* they had graduated. Even after all that time, they still showed improvements in the same range: 63% on the self-awareness and self-management competencies, and 45% on the social awareness and relationship management competencies. This is in contrast to MBA graduates of the WSOM of the 1988 and 1989 traditional full-time and part-time programs who showed improvement in substantially fewer of the competencies. These studies showed that competencies related to leadership effectiveness can be developed in adults. While it is difficult to claim that work was also done on the other levels within which they worked, we know that the full-time MBAs were working on improving their own competencies while working on team competencies (Druskat & Kayes, 2000).

The positive effects of this program were not limited to MBAs. In a longitudinal study of four classes completing the Professional Fellows Program (i.e., an executive education program at the WSOM), Ballou et al. (1999) showed that these 45–55-year-old professionals and executives improved on self-confidence, leadership, helping, goal setting, and action skills. These were 67% of the emotional intelligence competencies assessed in this study. The intervention, or course in this case, on which these dramatic results were based was designed with ICT. This describes the process as designed in a required course and the elements of the MBA and executive programs implemented in 1990 at the WSOM. Experimentation and research into the various components have resulted in refinement of these components and the theory as discussed in this chapter. For a detailed description of the course, see Boyatzis (1994).

For development in context, Van Oosten (2006) and Boyatzis et al. (2003) reported results from a leadership development program conducted while working simultaneously at the organization level. While the emotional and social intelligence competency program was going on, managers and executives also engaged in appreciative inquiry to develop the culture and organizational systems. For now, let us return to the discoveries that constitute ICT to understand how these changes can occur and why complexity concepts are so critical.

The five discoveries of intentional change theory
This brings us to the next feature of ICT as a complex system. Leadership development involves a sequence of discontinuities, called 'discoveries', which function as an iterative cycle in producing the sustainable change at the individual level. These are: (i) the ideal self and a personal vision; (ii) the real self and its comparison to the ideal self resulting in an assessment of one's strengths and weaknesses of those characteristics related to effective leadership, in a sense a personal balance sheet; (iii) a learning agenda and plan; (iv) experimentation and practice with the new behavior, thoughts, feelings, or perceptions of effective leaders; and (v) trusting, or resonant relationships that enable a person to experience and process each discovery in the process.

The first discovery: catching your dreams, engaging your passion
The first discontinuity and potential starting-point for the process of leadership development is the discovery of who you want to be. Our ideal self is an image of the person we want to be. It appears to have three major components that drive the development of this image: (i) an image of a desired future; (ii) hope that one can attain it; and (iii) aspects of one's core identity, which includes enduring strengths, on which a person builds his desired future (Boyatzis & Akrivou, 2006). It emerges from our ego ideal, dreams, and aspirations. The last 20 years have revealed literature supporting the power of positive imaging or visioning in sports psychology, meditation and biofeedback research, and other psycho-physiological research. It is believed that the potency of focusing one's thoughts on the desired end state of condition is driven by the emotional components of the brain (Goleman, 1995; Boyatzis & McKee, 2005).

This research indicates that we can access and engage deep emotional commitment and psychic energy if we engage our passions and conceptually catch our dreams in our ideal self-image. It is an anomaly that we know the importance of consideration of the ideal self, and yet often, when engaged in a change or learning process we skip over the clear formulation or articulation of that image. If a parent, spouse, boss, or teacher, tells us something that should be different, they are telling us about the person *they* want us to be. As adults, we often allow ourselves to be anesthetized to our dreams and lose sight of our deeply felt ideal self.

It is also clear from this framework that 'strengths-based' approaches to development will probably work better than current methods but will fall short of what the person can achieve (Roberts et al., 2005). In focusing on the person's established strengths, such approaches develop the core identity component of the ideal self as a driver of change, but fail to capture the energy inherent in dreams of the future and new possibilities as well as the emotional driver of hope. Because they are based on what the person has done in the past, they do not adequately engage a person's dreams of the future or consideration of possibilities.

The second discovery: how do I come across to others?
The awareness of the current self, the person that others see and with whom they interact, is elusive. For healthy reasons, the human psyche protects itself from the automatic 'intake' and conscious realization of all information about ourselves. These ego-defense mechanisms serve to protect us. They also conspire to delude us into an image of who we are that feeds on itself, becomes self-perpetuating, and eventually may become dysfunctional (Goleman, 1985).

Several factors contribute to deluding us regarding our real self. First, people around you may not let you see a change. They may not give you feedback or information about how they see it. Also, they may be victims of such self-delusions themselves, as they adjust their perception on a daily basis. Second, enablers, those forgiving the change, frightened of it, or who do not care, may allow it to pass unnoticed.

For people to truly consider changing a part of themselves, they must have a sense of what they value and want to keep. These areas in which the real self and the ideal self are consistent or congruent can be considered strengths. Likewise, to consider what people want to preserve about themselves involves admitting to personal aspects that they wish to change or adapt in some manner. Areas where the real self and the ideal self are not consistent can be considered as gaps, or weaknesses.

All too often, people explore growth or development by focusing on such gaps, or deficiencies. Organization-based leadership training programs and managers conducting annual reviews often make the same mistake. There is an assumption that we can 'leave well enough alone' and get to the areas that need work. It is no wonder that many of these programs or procedures intended to help a person develop, result in the individual feeling battered, beleaguered and bruised, not helped, encouraged, motivated, or guided.

The third discovery: mindfulness through a learning agenda
The third discontinuity in intentional change is development of an agenda and focusing on the desired future that can be approached with joy and excitement, not with the dulling effect of a 'to do' list. While performance at work or happiness in life may be the eventual consequence of our efforts, a learning agenda focuses on development. A learning orientation arouses a positive belief in one's capability and the hope of improvement. This results in people setting personal standards of performance, rather than 'normative' standards that merely mimic what others have done (Beaubien & Payne, 1999). Meanwhile, a performance orientation evokes anxiety and doubts about whether or not we can change (Chen et al., 2000).

As part of one of the longitudinal studies at the WSOM, Leonard (1996) showed that MBAs who set goals desiring to change on certain competencies, changed significantly on those competencies as compared to other MBAs. Previous goal-setting literature had shown how goals affected certain changes on specific competencies (Locke & Latham, 1990), but had not established evidence of behavioral change on a comprehensive set of competencies that constitute emotional intelligence.

Self-organizing and the pull of two attractors
Leadership development produces sustainable, desirable changes as an iterative, cyclical process. As a complex system, development of a leader engages the cycle of change or the lack of it through two self-organizing properties of the human organism. Two attractors, the positive emotional attractor and the negative emotional attractor, determine the context of the self-organizing process and whether it is an adaptation to existing conditions or adaptation to new, emergent conditions. Just like the properties in a closed system moving toward maximum entropy over time as predicted from the second law of thermodynamics, dissonance occurs in the human and our social organizations unless there is intentional investment. In other words, adaptations and adjustments based on Argyris's (1985) concept of single-loop learning will result in a self-sustaining system of a person, his/her life and performance. But over time, even with these properties of self-organization, deterioration will occur.

This is because the human organism is not a fully closed system. Among other things, we need social interaction to allow our 'open-loop' emotional system to function (Goleman et al., 2002). Even more dramatic in its destabilizing effect is the advent of one's life and career cycles. Whether these are the traditional 'seven-year itch' cycles or those of varying periodicity described by Levinson (1978), Erikson (1985) or Sheehy (1995), a person occasionally looks for a change. These are moments of invitation for what Argyris (1985) called 'double loop learning'. This helps to explain why double-loop learning is so difficult and so relatively infrequent. It is inherently destabilizing and must fight against the self-organizing property inherent in a person.

ICT offers an explanation as to how the disequilibrium occurs and then the force that drives a new self-organizing system. An attractor becomes the destabilizing force. We call this the 'positive emotional attractor' (PEA). It pulls people toward their ideal self. In the process of focusing people on future possibilities and filling them with hope, it arouses the parasympathetic nervous system (PSNS) (Boyatzis et al., 2006). Once the PSNS is aroused, people have access to more of their neural circuits, find themselves in a calmer, if not elated state in which their immune system is functioning well and their body is sustained. They are able, in this state, to experience neurogenesis (i.e., the conversion of hippocampal stem cells into new neurons) and the new degrees and extent of learning that becomes possible. It is even suggested that the formation of learning-oriented goals arouses this attractor and results in more successful change (Howard, 2006).

But another attractor is also at play in the system – the negative emotional attractor (NEA). In an analogous manner, it aroused the sympathetic nervous system (SNS) which helps people to deal with stress and threat and protect themselves. Within the threatened environment and state, the NEA pulls a person toward defensive protection. In this arousal, the body shunts blood to the large muscle groups, closes down non-essential neural circuits, suspends the immune system, and produces cortisol – important for protection under threat (Sapolsky, 2004). But cortisol inhibits or even stops neurogenesis and overexcites older neurons, rendering them useless (Boyatzis et al., 2006).

If a person's adaptation is self-organizing, then desired change not already part of this system is only possible when it is intentional. We would add that because of the difficulty in sustaining the effort, it also must be driven by a powerful force. This is where the ideal self activates the energy of the PEA and the two attractors become 'a limit cycle' for the person (Casti, 1994). This also helps us to understand why there is a need for more positivity than negativity in change efforts, but there are upper limits to the effectiveness of positivity as well (Fredrickson & Losada, 2005).

The process of desired, sustainable change requires behavioral freedom and permission to try something new and see what happens. This 'permission' comes from interaction with others as we shall see in the fourth and fifth discoveries in the process.

The fourth discovery: metamorphosis
The fourth discovery is to experiment and practice desired changes. Acting on the plan and toward the goals involves numerous activities. These are often made in the context of experimenting with new behavior. Typically following a period of experimentation, people practice the new behaviors in actual settings within which they wish to use them, such as at work or at home. During this part of the process, intentional change looks like a 'continuous improvement' process.

To develop or learn new behavior, the person must find ways to learn more from current, or ongoing experiences. That is, the experimentation and practice does not always require attending 'courses' or a new activity. It may involve trying something different in a current setting, reflecting on what occurs, and experimenting further in this setting. Sometimes, this part of the process requires finding and using opportunities to learn and change. People may not even think that they have changed until they have tried new behavior in a work or 'real-world' setting.

Dreyfus (1990) studied managers of scientists and engineers who were considered superior performers. Once she had documented that they used considerably more of certain abilities than their less effective counterparts, she pursued how they developed some of those abilities. One of the distinguishing abilities was group management, also called 'team building'. She found that many of these middle-aged managers had first experimented with team-building skills in high school and college, in sports, clubs, and living groups (i.e. fraternities, dormatories). Later, when they became 'bench scientists and engineers' working on problems in relative isolation, they still used and practiced this ability in activities outside of work. They practiced team building and group management in social and community organizations, such as 4-H Clubs,[2] and professional associations in planning conferences and such.

The experimentation and practice are most effective when they occur in conditions in which the person feels safe (Kolb & Boyatzis, 1970). This sense of psychological safety creates an atmosphere in which the person can try new behavior, perceptions, and thoughts with relatively less risk of shame, embarrassment, or serious consequences of failure.

The fifth discontinuity: relationships that enable us to learn
Our relationships are an essential part of our environment. The most crucial relationships are often as part of groups that have particular importance to us. These relationships and groups give us a sense of identity, guide us as to what is appropriate and 'good' behavior, and provide feedback on our behavior. In sociology, they are called 'reference groups'.

These relationships create a 'context' within which we interpret our progress on desired changes, the utility of new learning, and even contribute significant input to formulation of the ideal (Kram, 1996).

In this sense, our relationships are mediators, moderators, interpreters, sources of feedback, sources of support and permission of change and learning. They may also be the most important source of protection from relapses or returning to our earlier forms of behavior. Wheeler (1999) analyzed the extent to which the MBA graduates worked on their goals in multiple 'life spheres' (i.e., work, family, recreational groups, etc.). In a two-year follow-up study of two of the graduating classes of part-time MBA students, she found that those who worked on their goals and plans in multiple sets of relationships improved the most and more than those working on goals in only one setting, such as work or within one relationship.

In a study of the impact of the year-long executive development program for doctors, lawyers, professors, engineers, and other professionals mentioned earlier, Ballou et al. (1999) found that participants gained self-confidence during the program. Even at the beginning of the program, others would say that these participants were very high in self-confidence. It was a curious finding. The best explanation came from follow-up questions to the graduates of the program. They explained the evident increase in self-confidence as an increase in the confidence to change. Their existing reference groups (i.e., family, groups at work, professional groups, community groups) all had an investment in them staying the same, while the person wanted to change. The Professional Fellows Program allowed them to develop a new reference group that encouraged change.

Based on social identity, reference group, and now relational theories, our relationships both mediate and moderate our sense of who we are and who we want to be. From these contexts we: develop or elaborate our ideal self; label and interpret our real self; interpret and value strengths (i.e., aspects considered our core that we wish to preserve); and interpret and value gaps (i.e., aspects considered weaknesses or things we wish to change).

Multi-levels and interaction among the levels
Now we come to the aspect of ICT that makes it a true complex system – its multi-levelness. According to the theory, sustainable change occurs at any level of human and social organization through the same ICT. In this sense, these other levels are fractals of ICT at the individual level. In other words, desired, sustainable change within a family, team or small group occurs through the cyclical iteration of the group through what can be called the 'group-level definition' of the five discoveries. In this case, the ideal self becomes a shared vision of the future of the group. What does the group want to be, what can it be in the future? Similarly, desired, sustainable organizational change occurs through ICT's five discoveries at the organizational level, and so on at the community, country, and global levels. And the theory would predict that development and change is only sustainable when levels above and below are also engaged in a change process.

These other levels are, listed in order of increasing social size:

1. individual;
2, dyad or couple;
3. team, group, family, coalition;
4. organization;

5. community;
6. country/culture; and
7. global.

Boyatzis (in press) examined ICT at the group or team level. Among other observations is that no sports team can succeed in sustainable performance improvement without a resonant leader within the team. The team captain is often the emotional glue that keeps people working together. He/she is the link between the individual and the team change. Meanwhile, the coach is the person who links the team and organization level (i.e., team management and ownership). The team owner or general manager has to move in between the organization and the community, managing public relations, fans, and the political community.

Since bi-directionality of information is necessary within levels of a complex system, there must be an agent that carries the contagion of emotional and other messages back and forth among the levels. While ICT predicts that it is leadership, and resonant leadership in particular, that does this among the individual, dyad, team and organization levels (Boyatzis, 2006a), for interaction with greater levels (such as community, country and global), sustained, desired change, resonant leadership *and* reference or social identity groups (often in the form of coalitions) are also needed.

In this way, leadership affects desired, sustainable change in three distinct ways. First, leaders can help to promote and facilitate change within a level of a complex system, such as within a management team. Second, resonant leadership is also the key to interaction among the many levels. It enables interaction among the levels and that interaction produces adaptive or emergent behavior. The first degree of interaction between and among the individual, small group, and organization levels of ICT is resonant leadership. The second degree of interaction, which in addition to resonant leadership, allows interaction among all levels of ICT is through the formation and use of reference groups. And third, development of effective leadership is, itself, a complex system.

Without leadership there does not seem to be the emergence of desired, sustainable change. Many of the organizational or small group conditions may have been present for a long time, but when a capable or effective leader appears, magic happens – or more accurately, ICT happens (Howard & Coombe, 2006; Van Oosten, 2006). Similarly, a leader may enable individuals to consider intentional change while a small group (or team or family) or their organization undergoes intentional change.

But once the social organization gets larger than the number of people who can comfortably sit around a table, campfire, or circle, coalitions begin to play a critical role. The specific coalitions are those formed around a theme. This theme is often defined in terms of values (what is good or bad) and becomes an identity-forming group. Literature since the 1980s has departed from calling these 'reference groups' and now uses terms such as 'social identity groups', or 'groups representing anticipatory socialization'. In much the same way a coalition government brings together ministers elected to represent a variety of political parties (each representing a different issue) to join together and form a government – elect a prime minister; reference groups enable large social organizations to engage in the discoveries of ICT. It is then up to the leadership (again the first degree of interaction appears critical) to synthesize these into the needed experience for most of the people in the social group at that level (Smith, 2006).

Concluding thought

People can become leaders and more effective leaders. They can change in desired ways but not without intentional efforts. Teams, organizations, communities, and even countries can change in desired ways. But again, without intentional efforts, the changes are slow, result in worse unintentional consequences than the original desire, and arouse a shared hopelessness about the future and diminish the human spirit.

Through ICT, we can understand leadership development, how individuals, groups, organizations, and whole communities can bring about desired changes in a sustainable way, and the critical role of leaders. But to understand intentional change, we must use a variety of concepts from complexity theory. It is through these at times elusive but enlightening concepts that we can guide and reignite individual and collective will to make the world a better place.

Similarly, leadership development cannot be effective or sustainable without using concepts from complexity theory and engaging multiple levels of human and social organization in the change process.

Notes

1. Many of these advances in definitions and understanding complex system came from a three-year faculty seminar called the Complexity Forum (2001–03) at Case Western Reserve University. It was chaired by Professor Mihajlo Mesarovic, with Professors Alexander, Aron, Baer, Barmish, Beer, Boyatzis, Carlsson, Greenspan, Hutton, Kahana, Koonce, Loparo, McHale, Satry, Singer, Solow, Sreenath, Strange, Tabib-Asar, Taylor, and Voltz.
2. 4-H Clubs are community-based groups in which young people do a service for others in the community. They are typical in any US town or village. They are more of a rural or exurban (rather than urban or suburban) organization.

References

Argyris, C. (1985), *Strategy, Change, and Defensive Routines*, Boston, MA: Pitman.

Baldwin, T. & Ford, J.K. (1988), 'Transfer of training: a review and directions for future research', *Personnel Psychology*, **41**: 63–105.

Ballou, R., Bowers, D., Boyatzis, R.E. & Kolb, D.A. (1999), 'Fellowship in lifelong learning: an executive development program for advanced professionals', *Journal of Management Education*, **23**(4): 338–54.

Barlow, D.H. (1988), *Anxiety and Disorders: The Nature and Treatment of Anxiety and Panic*, New York: Guilford Press.

Beaubien, J.M. & Payne, S.C. (1999), 'Individual goal orientation as a predictor of job and academic performance: a meta-analytic review and integration', paper presented at the meeting of the Society for Industrial and Organizational Psychology, Atlanta, GA, April.

Boyatzis, R.E. (1982), *The Competent Manager: A Model for Effective Performance*, New York: John Wiley.

Boyatzis, R.E. (1994), 'Stimulating self-directed change: a required MBA course called Managerial Assessment and Development', *Journal of Management Education*, **18**(3): 304–23.

Boyatzis, R.E. (2001), 'How and why individuals are able to develop emotional intelligence', in C. Cherniss & D. Goleman (eds), *The Emotionally Intelligent Workplace: How to Select For, Measure, and Improve Emotional Intelligence in Individuals, Groups, and Organizations*, San Francisco, CA: Jossey-Bass, pp. 234–53.

Boyatzis, R.E. (2006a), 'Intentional change theory from a complexity perspective', *Journal of Management Development*, **25**(7): 607–23.

Boyatzis, R.E. (2006b), 'Using tipping points of emotional intelligence and cognitive competencies to predict financial performance of leaders', *Psicothema*, **18**: 124–31.

Boyatzis, R.E. (in press), 'Creating sustainable, desired change in teams through application of intentional change and complexity theories', in P. Doherty, M. Kira & R. Shami (eds), *Creating Sustainable Work Systems: Emerging Perspectives and Practices*, 2nd edn, London: Routledge.

Boyatzis, R.E. & Akrivou, K. (2006), 'The ideal self as a driver of change', *Journal of Management Development*, **25**(7): 624–42.

Boyatzis, R.E., Frick, C. & Van Oosten, E. (2003), 'Developing leaders throughout an entire organization by developing emotional intelligence competencies', in L.A. Berger & D.R. Berger (eds), *The Talent*

Management Handbook: Creating Organizational Excellence by Identifying, Developing, and Positioning High-Potential Talent, New York: McGraw Hill, pp. 337–48.

Boyatzis, R.E., Leonard, D., Rhee, K. & Wheeler, J.V. (1996), 'Competencies can be developed, but not the way we thought', *Capability*, **2**(2): 25–41.

Boyatzis, R.E. & McKee, A. (2005), *Resonant Leadership: Renewing Yourself and Connecting with Others Through Mindfulness, Hope, and Compassion*, Boston, MA: Harvard Business School Press.

Boyatzis, R., McKee, A. & Goleman, D. (2002), 'Reawakening your passion for work', *Harvard Business Review*, **80**(4): 86–94.

Boyatzis, R.E., Renio-McKee, A. & Thompson, L. (1995), 'Past accomplishments: establishing the impact and baseline of earlier programs', in Boyatzis, S.S. Cowen & D.A. Kolb (eds), *Innovation in Professional Education: Steps on a Journey from Teaching to Learning*, San Francisco, CA: Jossey-Bass, pp. 167–204.

Boyatzis, R.E. & Saatcioglu, A. (2008), 'A twenty year view of trying to develop emotional, social and cognitive intelligence competencies in graduate management education', *Journal of Management Development*, **27**(3): 92–108.

Boyatzis, R.E., Smith, M. & Blaize, N. (2006), 'Developing sustainable leaders through coaching and compassion', *Academy of Management Journal on Learning and Education*, **5**(1): 8–24.

Boyatzis, R.E. & Sokol, M. (1982), 'A pilot project to assess the feasibility of assessing skills and personal characteristics of students in collegiate business programs', Report to the AACSB, St. Louis, MO.

Boyatzis, R.E., Stubbs, E.C. & Taylor, S.N. (2002), 'Learning cognitive and emotional intelligence competencies through graduate management education', *Academy of Management Journal on Learning and Education*, **1**(2): 150–62.

Bray, D.W., Campbell, R.J. & Grant, D.L. (1974), *Formative Years in Business: A Long Term AT&T Study of Managerial Lives*, New York: John Wiley.

Burke, M.J. & Day, R.R. (1986), 'A cumulative study of the effectiveness of managerial training', *Journal of Applied Psychology*, **71**(2): 232–45.

Campbell, J.P., Dunnette, M.D., Lawler, E.E., III & Weick, K.E. (1970), *Managerial Behavior, Performance, and Effectiveness*, New York: McGraw-Hill.

Casti, J.L. (1994), *Complexification: Explaining a Paradoxical World Through the Science of Surprise*, New York: Harper Collins.

Chen, G., Gully, S.M., Whiteman, J.A. & Kilcullen, R.N. (2000), 'Examination of relationships among trait-like individual differences, state-like individual differences, and learning performance', *Journal of Applied Psychology*, **85**(6): 835–47.

Cherniss, C. & Adler, M. (2000), *Promoting Emotional Intelligence in Organizations: Make Training in Emotional Intelligence Effective*, Washington, DC: American Society of Training and Development.

Complexity Forum (2001–03), Faculty Seminar at Case Western Reserve University, Cleveland, OH. Chaired by Professor Mihajlo D. Mesarovic, with Professors James Alexander, David Aron, Eric Baer, Robert Barmish, Randolph Beer, Richard Boyatzis, Bo Carlsson, Meil Greenspan, Max Hutton, Eva Kahana, Joseph Koonce, Kenneth Loparo, Vincent McHale, Shiva Satry, Kenneth Singer, Daniel Solow, Sree Sreenath, Kurt Strange, Masood Tabib-Asar, Phillip Taylor, and Donal Voltz.

Development Dimensions International (DDI) (1985), *Final Report: Phase III*, Report to the AACSB, St. Louis, MO.

Dreyfus, C. (1990), 'The characteristics of high performing managers of scientists and engineers', unpublished doctoral dissertation, Case Western Reserve University, Cleveland, OH.

Druskat, V.U. & Kayes, D.C. (2000), 'Learning versus performance in short-term project teams', *Small Group Research*, **31**(3): 328–53.

Erikson, E.H. (1985), *The Life Cycle Completed: A Review*, New York: W.W. Norton.

Fredrickson, B. & Losada, M. (2005), 'Positive affect and the complex dynamics of human flourishing', *American Psychologist*, **60**(7): 678–86.

Gersick, C.J. (1991), 'Revolutionary change theories: a multilevel exploration of the punctuated equilibrium paradigm', *Academy of Management Review*, **16**: 274–309.

Gladwell, M. (2000), *The Tipping Point: How Little Things Can Make a Big Difference*, New York: Little Brown.

Goleman, D. (1985), *Vital Lies, Simple Truths: The Psychology of Self-deception*, New York: Simon & Schuster.

Goleman, D. (1995), *Emotional Intelligence*, New York: Bantam Books.

Goleman, D., Boyatzis, R.E. & McKee, A. (2002), *Primal Leadership: Realizing the Power of Emotional Intelligence*, Boston, MA: Harvard Business School Press.

Hand, H.H., Richards, M.D. & Slocum, J.W., Jr (1973), 'Organizational climate and the effectiveness of a human relations training program', *Academy of Management Journal*, **16**(2): 185–246.

Holland, J. (1995), *Hidden Order: How Adaptation Builds Complexity*, Reading, MA: Helix Books.

Howard, A. (2006), 'Positive and negative emotional attractors and intentional change', *Journal of Management Development*, **25**(7): 657–70.

Howard, A. & Bray, D. (1988), *Managerial Lives in Transition: Advancing Age and Changing Times*, New York: Guilford Press.

Howard, A. & Coombe, D. (2006), 'National level intentional change', *Journal of Management Development*, **25**(7): 732–42.

Hubble, M.A., Duncan, B.L. & Miller, S.D. (eds) (1999), *The Heart and Soul of Change: What Works in Therapy*, Washington, DC: American Psychological Association.

Hunt, J.G. (1991), *Leadership: A New Synthesis*, Newbury Park, CA: Sage.

Kanfer, F.H. & Goldstein, A.P. (eds) (1991), *Helping People Change: A Textbook of Methods*, 4th edn, Boston, MA: Allyn & Bacon.

Kolb, D.A. & Boyatzis, R.E. (1970), 'Goal-setting and self -directed behavior change', *Human Relations*, **23**(5): 439–57.

Kram, K.E. (1996), 'A relational approach to careers', in D.T. Hall (ed.), *The Career Is Dead: Long Live the Career*, San Francisco, CA: Jossey-Bass, pp. 132–57.

Latham, G.P. & Saari, L.M. (1979), 'Application of social-learning theory to training supervisors through behavioral modeling', *Journal of Applied Psychology*, **64**(3): 239–46.

Leonard, D. (1996), 'The impact of learning goals on self-directed change in management development and education', doctoral dissertation, Case Western Reserve University, Cleveland, OH.

Levinson, D.J. with Darrow, C.N., Klein, E.B., Levinson, M.H. & McKee, B. (1978), *The Seasons of a Man's Life*, New York: Knopf.

Locke, E.A. & Latham, G.P. (1990), *A Theory of Goal Setting and Task Performance*, Englewood Cliffs, NJ: Prentice-Hall.

Luthans, F., Hodgetts, R.M. & Rosenkrantz, S.A. (1988), *Real Managers*, Cambridge, MA: Ballinger.

McClelland, D.C. (1965), 'Toward a theory of motive acquisition', *American Psychologist*, **20**(5): 321–33.

McClelland, D.C. (1985), *Human Motivation*, Glenview, IL: Scott, Foresman.

McClelland, D.C. (1998), 'Identifying competencies with behavioral event interviews', *Psychological Science*, **9**: 331–9.

McKee, A., Boyatzis, R.E. & Johnston, F. (2008), *Becoming a Resonant Leader*, Boston, MA: Harvard Business School Press.

Morrow, C.C., Jarrett, M.Q. & Rupinski, M.T. (1997), 'An investigation of the effect and economic utility of corporate-wide training', *Personnel Psychology*, **50**: 91–119.

Noe, R.A. & Schmitt, N. (1986), 'The influence of trainee attitudes on training effectiveness: test of a model', *Personnel Psychology*, **39**: 497–523.

Pascarella, E.T. & Terenzini, P.T. (1991), *How College Affects Students: Findings and Insights from Twenty Years of Research*, San Francisco, CA: Jossey-Bass.

Prochaska, J.O., DiClemente, C.C. & Norcross, J.C. (1992), 'In search of how people change: applications to addictive behaviors', *American Psychologist*, **47**(9): 1102–14.

Roberts, L., Dutton, J.E., Spreitzer, G., Heaphy, E. & Quinn, R.E. (2005), 'Composing the reflect best-self portrait: pathways for becoming extraordinary in work organizations', *Academy of Management Review*, **30**(4): 712–36.

Sapolsky, R.M. (2004), *Why Zebras Don't Get Ulcers*, 3rd edn, New York: Harper Collins.

Schneider, M. & Somers, M. (2006), 'Organizations as complex adaptive systems: implications of complexity theory for leadership research', *Leadership Quarterly*, **17**(2): 351–65.

Sheehy, G. (1995), *New Passages: Mapping Your Life across Time*, New York: Ballantine.

Smith, M. (2006), 'Social capital and intentional change: exploring the role of social networks on individual change efforts', *Journal of Management Development*, **25**(7): 718–31.

Specht, L. & Sandlin, P. (1991), 'The differential effects of experiential learning activities and traditional lecture classes in accounting', *Simulations and Gaming*, **22**(2): 196–210.

Spencer, L.M. Jr. & Spencer, S.M. (1993), *Competence at Work: Models for Superior Performance*, New York: John Wiley.

Van Oosten, E. (2006), 'Intentional change theory at the organizational level: a case study', *Journal of Management Development*, **25**(7): 707–17.

Wexley, K.N. & Memeroff, W.F. (1975), 'Effectiveness of positive reinforcement and goal setting as methods of management development', *Journal of Applied Psychology*, **60**(4): 446–50.

Wheeler, J.V. (1999), 'The impact of social environments on self-directed change and learning', unpublished doctoral dissertation, Case Western Reserve University, Cleveland, OH.

Winter, D.G., McClelland, D.C. & Stewart, A.J. (1981), *A New Case for the Liberal Arts: Assessing Institutional Goals and Student Development*, San Francisco, CA: Jossey-Bass.

Young, D.P. & Dixon, N.M. (1996), *Helping Leaders Take EVective Action: A Program Evaluation*, Greensboro, NC: Center for Creative Leadership.

4 Addiction at work: a challenge for occupational health psychology

Wolfgang P. Beiglböck* and Senta Feselmayer**

Introduction

History

Addictive substances at the workplace have been a major issue for a very long time, especially in the military. As far back as the sixteenth century, for instance, regulations were in place in the British Royal Navy governing rum and beer rations which were increased before sailors were sent into battle (Ranft & Hill, 2002). It was not until the nineteenth and early twentieth centuries that alcohol, especially spirits, was recognized as a problematic substance. However, the first preventive measures merely replaced spirits with beer. It was not until later that more 'harmless' substances such as coffee and tea were proposed as substitutes, and working conditions were also recognized as a contributing factor to alcohol abuse at the workplace (Böhmert, 1889; Grotjahn, 1903). The first employee assistance programmes (EAPs), which initially only focused on addiction-related problems, were developed in the 1940s following the example of the Alcoholics Anonymous Movement in the United States, with intervention the preferred approach over prevention. In 1998 a declaration was adopted at the UN General Assembly requesting business to support drug abuse prevention programmes. Earlier, in 1996, the International Labour Organization (ILO) published substance abuse prevention policies for companies. Since then, substance abuse prevention programmes have been widely established not only in companies in the USA and Europe (Beiglböck & Feselmayer, 1998), but also in the Asia-Pacific Region (UNODC, 2007).

Economic fundamentals

Although drugs are more widely used among certain population groups (e.g., criminals or the unemployed) one of the latest household surveys conducted in the USA shows that 70% of all people between 18 and 49 who use illicit drugs (usage within the last 30 days) and 77% of all alcohol abusers (five drinks on five or more days within the last 30 days) are in full-time employment (SAMHSA, 1999). Since many consumers start to use substances on a regular basis around their 20th birthday, their substance-related problems do not become apparent before middle age. A broad study conducted by Mangione et al. (1999) found a close relationship between performance problems (e.g., decreased job performance, absence from the workplace and so on) and moderate to excessive alcohol abuse. Similar results were shown for self-reported marijuana use and the use of prescription drugs for anxiety and depression. Modest alcohol consumption tends to increase productivity (at least in the UK), however, even slightly excessive consumption leads to a significant decline in job performance (Rannia, 2003).

Due to methodological problems, reports differ with regard to the exact financial costs for companies. The widely accepted Stanford Research Institute's rule of thumb which assumes a 25% loss of annual work productivity per employee is only based on estimates. Accidents at the workplace under the influence of alcohol and/or drugs account for 20% of all accidents and up to 5% of all accidents at work, with an intermittent variable as to the general work-related problem behaviour which accompanies substance abuse (Spicer et al., 2003). On the whole, however, it is assumed that alcohol in particular has a significant impact on accidents at the workplace (Lehmann et al., 1993). With regard to annual sick leave, the results show a fivefold alcohol-related increase (Resch & Fuchs, 1998) and a nicotine-related increase of up to one day (Parrot et al., 2000). There are almost no data available for the illicit drug parameters (Cook & Schlenger, 2002) and the hitherto inadequate research on the effects of prescription drugs has precluded their incorporation into relevant programmes. A study conducted at one of the major European drug rehabilitation centres (Schneider, 1991) assumes a 12.5–25% decline in productivity for each alcohol-dependent person in the last year prior to in-patient treatment. These data do not include the consequential loss suffered by companies, as a result of, for example, damaged equipment or claims for damages. For the year 2002, Rannia (2003) estimated that the financial costs for companies in the UK amounted to £1.2–1.8 billion for sick leave and absenteeism. The corresponding figures for nicotine were put at £588 million (if cigarette breaks are included, this figure rises to £5.2 billion).

Original causes
Organizational influences on the one hand and the work environment and personal factors on the other appear to foster the occurrence of addiction among employees. One of the major influencing factors at work is a substance-related work culture, that is, the attitude towards substances at the workplace, the value placed on them, normal drinking behaviour, peer-group pressure, macho ethos and so on. Evidence for such links was found in a number of studies (Ames & Grube, 1999; Mangione et al., 1999).

In this context, social control at work is of particular importance. Professions with little social control (such as, for example, politicians, doctors and to some extent senior executives) seem to face higher risks with regard to substance addiction (Galea & Ghodse, 2005). In addition to these professions there seem to be a number of other high-risk occupations: these include the hospitality and healthcare industries where the easy availability of alcohol and/or prescription drugs undoubtedly plays an important role. Furthermore, shiftwork as well as work-related stress (time constraints, physical danger, financial insecurity etc.) seem to increase the risk potential. Sailors, teachers and journalists are also counted among the high-risk professions, as are people working in security-related jobs, especially members of the armed forces (ibid.).

Personal influence factors generally apply for the whole population – that is, young men with low self-esteem and a family history of substance abuse as well as a forensic history seem to face a particularly high risk (Lehmann & Bennet, 2002). On the other hand, the available data suggest that young girls and/or women are also increasingly affected by substance abuse (Currie et al., 2004). In today's rapidly changing work environment, people who have difficulty adapting to macro or micro workplace changes also appear to be at increasing risk (Ames et al., 2000; Lucas, 2005).

Prevention and intervention
According to Ghodse (2005), a modern and successful workplace prevention programme has to be non-punitive and constructive. It has to include prevention, treatment,

rehabilitation and follow-up measures. It also has to be part of the business development strategy of the company.

A first step is to inquire into the dysfunctional approach to substance-related problems in a company.

Turning a blind eye or acting as a bystander for years are strategies that can be explained by the perplexity and the 'learned helplessness' of executives (Fuchs et al., 1998), but usually will cause the problem to escalate. Dismissals are a short-term solution to the problem, however, as the next alcohol-dependent employee is sure to come. Furthermore, until such a dismissal the employees will be under severe personal stress and management is likely to encounter leadership problems. For instance, it will take between 6 years (for women) and 12 years (for men) for a person to become alcohol dependent (Beiglböck & Feselmayer, 1998).

When an employee's substance-abuse problem can no longer be ignored it is not usually the relevant manager who acts; instead the problem is delegated to the 'respective professionals', that is, occupational doctor, the works council representative and/or the human resources (HR) department. However, that is asking too much of them. The occupational doctor is familiar only with the employee and his/her medical situation but not with any workplace-related problems, the works council is required by its very function to stand by the employee, and at this stage the HR department can only impose severe disciplinary action. As will be seen later on, this precludes an overall approach to the problem. Thus it becomes impossible to provide the employee concerned with effective help.

Another dysfunctional action is to shunt the 'difficult employee' off to more or less officially defined 'social departments'. Thus highly qualified legal experts are eventually reduced to copying and sorting files, and since all employees with substance-abuse problems end up in the same departments, these will house some deplorable drinking habits.

'Co-dependent' behaviour is another inadequate approach. Since this term is widely used in specialist literature we shall also use it here, however, it is not intended to pathologize the behaviour of the people interacting with substance abusers. It is merely a matter of the communicative dynamics which arise out of the interaction with addicts. In most cases this form of interaction is based on an intention to help the employee and save his/her workplace. However, in this context it is often overlooked that this approach will contribute to a further escalation of the alcohol problem. This co-dependent behaviour can take various forms in a company. For instance, a colleague may take on additional work for the addict in order to preserve his/her workplace in the short term. In the long term, however, this prevents the addict from having to face his/her problem. 'As long as somebody is doing my work there is no reason why I should do something that is difficult for me – to do' the addict is unaware of the problems, which cannot therefore be seen and consequently changed.

Ultimately, everybody who lives or works with addicts, who is aware of the problem, but for whatever reason avoids confronting the issue is called a co-dependent. More often than not this is the result of insecurity or one's own addictive behaviour, but quite often also it is done with the best of intentions. The co-dependent tries to help, but goes about it in the wrong way. As a rule co-dependency is defined as follows: a co-dependent is someone who with the best of intentions exhibits too much caring/is too protective towards for an alcoholic, thus preventing the addict from changing his/her drinking habits.

Co-dependents in the workplace environment can be colleagues, supervisors or occupational doctors. We distinguish between three different phases of co-alcoholism, which are characterized by different reactions.

Mothering phase This phase is characterized by forbearance and understanding and one can often hear sentences like: 'He is quite a nice guy, it is a pity he drinks' or 'Maybe he drinks a bit much, but don't we all when we have problems'.

Need to help phase This phase is characterized by certain expectations, misconduct may be tolerated and excused, however, it is also addressed and it is expected that the person concerned will drink less in future. The fellow employee or supervisor becomes involved with the addict's marital or financial problems, so that the original issue – to address the addiction – gets pushed into the background. During this phase the alcoholic makes promises which he/she is unable to keep. Despite sincere efforts nothing will change with regard to the addiction.

This vicious circle of helping, frustration, more helping and still more frustration and so on spirals into the third phase.

Rejection phase Here quite often the only solution is to exclude the employee, the aforementioned frustration now only permits dismissal. However, this development is in the best interests of neither the employer nor the employee.

Although difficult to comprehend, the usually swiftly pronounced prohibition of alcohol is also an inefficient measure if it remains the only method of preventing drug abuse. Removing the beer-vending machines and forbidding alcoholic beverages at company festivities usually only generates massive staff resistance and will encourage secret drinking. This then contributes even more to a denial of the existence of alcohol-related problems and makes an efficient intervention almost impossible. The beer bottles stacked away in the toilet flush tanks are not only well hidden but also well cooled.

Problem analysis and preconditions
Sometimes it is painful to see how companies stand by and do nothing for years and after a dramatic incident (drug- or alcohol-related death of a young employee, accident at work, etc.) demand immediate action. A complete programme should be developed within three weeks and then show immediate results.

However, due to the resistance referred to earlier and the previous ways in which the problem was dealt with, such a speedy implementation guarantees the failure of even the best prevention programme. Effective action needs to be implemented slowly, and will usually take several years.

A first step – as already mentioned above – is the analysis of the previously dysfunctional handling of this problem by the company. Moreover, workplace-related risk factors have to be considered, as does the existing workplace culture with regard to alcohol and drugs (see above).

Raising awareness of this problem at all company levels is an absolute precondition for the implementation of any substance-abuse prevention programme. A concept for the whole company is required which needs to be supported by the entire company and not only by the management board or the works council. This is ensured by a company-wide consistent approach. All actions and decisions should be transparent to the entire workforce.

The following list serves as an example for a problem analysis of the current situation in a company:

- alcohol-dependent fellow workers are protected;
- alcohol problems of fellow workers are downplayed;
- alcohol abuse and above all abuse of illicit drugs is taboo;
- the problem is addressed only after the situation has become hopelessly muddled;
- executives lack insight into the problem;
- executives lack information on alcohol, drugs, early detection and so on;
- no management responsibility is asserted in this field;
- beer-vending machines in the company, despite official alcohol prohibition;
- alcoholic beverages served at external training sessions are paid for by the company;
- co-dependency encourages alcohol dependency;
- no support for executives if they take action; and
- difficult to dismiss alcohol-dependent employees.

Goal definition

Clients often only want to help sick employees. While this is undoubtedly a major task, it is only part of the necessary intervention. When drawing up company-specific subgoals, attention must be paid to the implementation of appropriate primary and secondary prevention programmes. Otherwise addicts will be treated but the original causes will be neglected.

Primary preventive measures are all interventions suited to minimize the manifestation of addiction problems at the workplace. Secondary preventive measures are all interventions designed to recognize existing problems in good time and to take action that will prevent escalation. An efficient prevention programme must therefore cover all three areas.

Mid-term project targets include, for example:

- eliminating taboos;
- early detection;
- integration of prevention programmes into the corporate culture;
- executives dealing with the problem in good time;
- ending the contradiction between alcohol bans and the serving of alcoholic beverages;
- correct leadership dialogue; and
- integrating the procedures to be developed into the management policies.

Implementation phase

Development and implementation of a prevention programme   The most difficult part for a company is the installation of an internal prevention and early detection programme.

As mentioned earlier, such an internal programme can only work if it is supported by the whole company. By that we mean: top management, the works council, middle management and workers. The programme must be consistent and transparent. Experience shows that if even one of these instances is missing or sabotages the programme, the predefined goal will not be reached.

Awareness raising measures   Prior to the installation of any such programme it is essential to raise awareness of the problem at all company levels. This must be done with special care in order to avoid the defensive reactions so often seen in this context. At this stage, company decision makers should already be supported by external consultants. As neutral observers with the respective professional knowledge and the required caution, they are in a position to tread delicately.

In any case, before installing an internal workgroup it is necessary to contact all company decision makers in order to clarify expectations, present feasible and sensible intervention measures, show the impact of the problem on the company (human and financial aspects) and convince them of the necessity for adopting the measures described above. Only after obtaining the agreement in principle of the top management, the HR department and the works council can first measures be drawn up in a project group.

Implementation   Only after the above phase has been completed should a kick-off group be installed. As a matter of common sense the work of such groups should not be limited to addiction problems, and the competence to develop general health promotion programmes should also be included in their remit. This would not only increase employee acceptance of any programme which is then put in place, but it also appears to be important with regard to other psychosocial problems (e.g., psychosomatic disorders) or forms of behaviour which are harmful to health (e.g., malnutrition). Besides, health circles offer a perfect platform for successfully drawing into primary preventive measures employees with addiction problems who otherwise would be impossible to reach (Shain et al., 1986; Shehadeh & Shain, 1990).

This 'project group' should consist of people interested in establishing a company-wide prevention programme, and in addition to representatives from the works council and the medical department should also include representatives from the HR department. It is essential that a member of top management serves as the project mentor, although he/she does not need to belong to the project group. Depending on the company's organizational structure and its activities safety engineers, youth stewards and so on should also be represented in this group. This project group draws up a catalogue of measures and supervises the entire project, which as explained earlier, must cover all three areas of prevention:

1. *Primary preventive measures*   In the field of primary prevention this means, for example: using internal company media (designing and preparing an information folder, regular articles in the company magazine, etc.), regulations governing the use of alcohol and other substances at the company (canteen, festivities, etc.), clarifying workplace conditions and so on. Actions for special target groups, such as vocational trainees, might also be called for. Changing the workplace culture presents a great challenge. In this context, peer-assistance programmes seem a promising, albeit so far little used approach. While this approach is widely used in prevention programmes

in schools, it is almost unknown in workplace environments. The peer assistance approach is based on the premise that co-workers are most qualified to identify the needs of their colleagues (Sonnenstuhl, 1996).

2. *Secondary preventive measures*   While drug-testing programmes are very popular as secondary preventive measures in the security-related professions in particular, 'the evidence of their preventive/deterrent effects is less definitive than generally assumed by industry and the public' (Cook & Schlenger, 2002, pp. 122–41). On the other hand, however, spectacular success has been reported in some cases. For instance, Walsh (1995, cited in Cook & Schlenger, 2002) reports that in 1987, 21% of all railway employees in the United States tested positive in drug usage screenings following accidents; after the introduction of a drug-testing programme this number decreased to about 5%. However, as almost all of the companies that reported such successful figures had implemented comprehensive prevention programmes and drug-testing programmes it is difficult to identify the individual effective factors (Cook & Schlenger, 2002)

Usually drug tests are carried out either during recruitment interviews or after accidents or other work-related incidents. Random testing can cause special ethical problems with regard to almost all procedural details. For instance, giving urine samples under observation can be quite a humiliating experience among colleagues. Apart from unreliable testing methods, a further problem is that it is unclear whether there is a direct causal relationship between the test results and the incident. For instance THC can still be detected several weeks after it was last consumed (see Christofides & Egerton, 2005). Careful thought must therefore be given to the implementation of such measures, and all internal and general legal regulations must be observed. The definition of a chain of custody of drug testing in accordance with the ILO guidelines (1996) is therefore urgently recommended.

More effective secondary preventive measures include the following: installing a crisis group, developing a multi-phase programme and training executives.

As executives and the individuals concerned should turn to the crisis group, it should consist not only of members of the works council and the health department but also of adequately trained executives. The members of the crisis group can act independently of one another, however, they should meet on a regular basis to report and discuss any problems encountered during the implementation of the programme.

A multi-phase programme means linking consistent company policies with support programmes for employees who are at risk. For example, four to six discussions will be held with an employee and the number of participating persons and the consequences for the employee will increase with each meeting. Such multi-phase programmes have a time-frame of about nine months and must be made known to all employees. They need to be adapted to the legal and internal environment. Dismissal is only possible when, despite repeated requests to do so, the employee has refused treatment and will not become abstinent either. These measures are not intended as a disciplinary tool but rather to make the employees concerned consciously aware of the fact that they have a substance-abuse problem.

During this phase of project development it is the external consultant's task to help find individual and customized solutions for the company and to carry out training programmes which should cover at least the following areas (Beiglböck &

Feselmayer, 2000): discrimination; self-reflection; communication; information; and reception of company programmes.

The information and discrimination sections serve to raise general awareness for substance abuse, in particular enabling people to detect and differentiate between use, abuse and addiction. The impact of alcohol consumption on work performance as well as the typical personality changes seen in people at risk and in addicts should be illustrated and discussed in this phase.

Self-reflection depicts one's own drinking behaviour and the company's attitude towards alcohol. *Laissez-faire* in one area and restrictions in another indicate a lack of leadership. Problem-oriented talks lose credibility when employees are requested to abstain from drinking alcohol while management uses alcohol to celebrate winning a contract.

Communication, that is, talking with people who are at risk and addicts, is a particularly difficult task for supervisors with management responsibility. Experience shows that the first problem-oriented talk – the confrontation talk – where special anxiety thresholds must be overcome, is rather difficult. Special training sessions provide answers to the following important questions:

- when to hold such talks;
- who is to participate in such talks;
- how to conduct such talks, for example, which issues should be addressed first and which at a later time;
- when to repeat such talks;
- how to meet the defence strategies of the individuals concerned;
- which consequences are effective.

However, insecurities regarding how to conduct such talks are not the only reason why executives try too late to talk to addicted employees. Based on a study carried out at a German bank, Fuchs et al. (1998) report the following results: asked why confrontation talks were either not conducted at all or conducted too late, 74% of the executives surveyed stated 'insecurity in assessing the situation' and 44% 'lack of proof'; 36% justified their behaviour with 'inhibition and embarrassment', which is about the same figure as for 'fear of the employee's reaction' (34%). The lack of information about alcoholism as a disease also seems to play a major role (28%). With 22%, 'lack of time' – an answer often spontaneously given in workshops – was only in sixth place, and 9% were inhibited by their own alcohol consumption. The fear of hurting an employee (13%) or making oneself unpopular (8%) as well as a lack of support from one's own supervisors (8%) are also factors of some significance. These answers clearly indicate that purely theoretical training of specific talking techniques will not be enough. Since emotional insecurities, but also a feeling of guilt and a lack of information about alcohol dependency, seem to be of major importance, these issues also need to be adequately addressed at appropriate training sessions.

The required skills need to be extensively practised in role plays and by using exemplary cases.

3. *Tertiary preventive measures* In the context of tertiary prevention, this means that the cooperation between the company and the treatment and rehabilitation facilities

needs to be defined, as a multi-phase programme can also provide for the treatment of the employee. The appointment of special contact persons in these facilities, who are known by name to executives and possibly also to the employees concerned, has been favourably received. As a result, inhibitions are overcome more easily and treatment can start more quickly.

However, in order to ensure confidentiality it is vital that the therapist is not the same person as the company's external consultant. This fact needs to be communicated within the company time and again.

In some countries a special representative for the support of addicts has been established within companies. An adequately trained person (frequently a former addict) takes over the care/treatment of a co-worker. In our experience these structures work only in countries with many years of experience in providing non-professional assistance for substance abusers (USA or Germany) or where addiction is not a major taboo. It is therefore necessary to consider these issues before treatment measures are implemented at companies.

Close cooperation between companies and treatment facilities also leads to a better understanding on the company's part of therapeutic processes, and as a result facilitates the re-integration of the employee. For instance, the necessity of long-term non-stationary treatment is better understood and supported and monitored by the company and greater assistance is provided to the patient directly at the workplace (possibly through a change of workplace, for example).

General conditions

In order to ensure an efficient approach to this problem, the following general conditions must be met by companies:

- sufficient time must be given to the project groups and all other guidelines applying to project work must be complied with;
- the necessary financial resources must be provided for the project;
- the established procedures must comply with all employee rights and the applicable company regulations;
- the project group findings must be incorporated into the company policies, that is, line managers are obliged to talk with the employee about his/her problem;
- company procedures must be put into writing, thus defining them as guidelines, or if they have proven effective they should be put into a long-term shopfloor agreement (for examples from different companies, see Ghodse, 2005); and
- on completion of project work, the project group must be transformed into a permanent working group to ensure the continuous implementation of all adopted measures (e.g., training of newly recruited employees and executives, continuing to focus on the issue, continuous adaptation of measures to any changes in the company environment, etc.).

Evaluation

Despite the fact that companies usually attach a great deal of importance to the evaluation of decisions, our experience shows that this is not necessarily true for this particular field. More attention should therefore be given to evaluation in order to ensure continuous optimization. Depending on the defined targets evaluation criteria might include:

1. *Evaluation criteria for primary preventive measures* Awareness of changes in corporate culture with regard to the attitude towards alcohol shown by executives and employees.
2. *Evaluation criteria for secondary preventive measures* (i) number of conducted first talks and/or usage of multi-phase programme; (ii) changes in the number of alcohol-related dismissals and firings; (iii) changes in accident statistics; and (iv) changes in the number of sick leave days – this is applicable only in individual cases, as at the start of the programme an increase in sick leave days should actually be considered a success if it means that employees are undergoing in-patient treatment. Sick leave days are an unreliable indicator since, except in specific cases, it is difficult to distinguish between alcohol-related and other sick leave days.
3. *Evaluation criteria for tertiary preventive measures* (i) number of contacts with occupational doctor and crisis group; (ii) number of employees undergoing treatment; and (iii) anonymous questioning with a questionnaire at longer but regular intervals has proven a suitable method. A further advantage of this method is that 'alcohol at the workplace' will constantly remain on everybody's mind. Permanent awareness of and constant work on this problem are important prerequisites for a programme's success. The financial savings achieved by companies as a result of the implementation of such a programme are difficult to calculate from a methodological point of view, however, it can be assumed that the results will be predominantly positive (Kurtz et al., 1984). A large financial study conducted by the company McDonnell-Douglas from 1985 to 1988 showed that only two years after the introduction of such a programme the benefits outweighed the expenses by 3:1 and this ratio increased further to 4:1 in the following years (Fuchs et al., 1998). And finally, the introduction of such a programme should be mainly determined not by costs but rather by values!

Final remarks
When measures for the prevention of alcohol-related problems at the workplace are more than just cosmetic they prove to be an effective method of addiction prevention. In a closely defined setting they permit the coordination and evaluation of goal-oriented interventions in a personal and situation-related context. Despite the fact that alcohol prevention projects are narrowly defined problem-oriented company healthcare interventions, it cannot be overlooked that the implementation of such programmes will also have an impact on personnel and organizational development.

External consultants need to proceed not only with knowledge of organizational psychology and business administration; they must also be familiar with the organizational procedures in place at the individual company. A narrow, exclusively 'psychotherapeutic' approach to this problem is not only counterproductive for the company, but it will also result in failed projects being seen as further proof that the prevalent nihilistic attitude in this context is the correct one, and decision makers will continue to ignore addiction and even health promotion at the workplace.

Notes

* PhD, University Lecturer, Faculty of Psychology, University of Vienna, Clinical and Health Psychologist, Psychotherapist at the Anton-Proksch-Institut, Vienna, Managing Director of a consulting firm specializing in addiction at the workplace.
** PhD, University Lecturer, Faculty of Psychology, University of Vienna, Clinical and Health Psychologist, Psychotherapist at the Anton-Proksch-Institut, Vienna, Managing Director of a consulting firm specializing in Addiction at the Workplace

References

Ames, G.M. & Grube, J.W. (1999), 'Alcohol availability and workplace drinking. Mixed methods analyses', *Journal of Studies on Alcohol*, **60**, 383–93.

Ames, G.M., Grube, J.W. & Moore, R.S. (2000), 'Social control and workplace drinking norms: a comparison of two organizational cultures', *Journal of Studies on Alcohol*, **61**, 203–19.

Beiglböck, W. & Feselmayer, S. (1998), 'Alcohol in the workplace: attitudes, policies and programmes in Austria', Country Report for the European Commission, DGV F3.

Beiglböck, W. & Feselmayer, S. (2000), 'EAP in Austria', in Masi (ed.), pp. 29–36.

Böhmert, V. (1889), *Der Branntwein in Fabriken* [*Hard Liquor in Factories*], Leipzig: Duncker & Humblot.

Christofides, J. & Egerton, M. (2005), 'Drug screening and detection', in Ghodse (ed.), pp. 151–70.

Cook, R. & Schlenger, W. (2002), 'Prevention of substance abuse in the workplace: review of research on the delivery of services', *Journal of Primary Prevention*, **23** (1), 115–42.

Currie, C., Roberts, C., Morgan, A., Smith, R., Settertobulte, W., Samdal, O. & Rasmussen, V.B. (eds) (2004), 'Young people's health in context. Health Behaviour in School-aged Children (HBSC) study: international report from the 2001/2002 survey', WHO Regional Office for Europe, Copenhagen.

Fuchs, R., Rainer, I. & Rummel, M. (eds) (1998), *Betriebliche Suchtprävention* [*Addiction Prevention in Companies*], Göttingen: Verlag für angewandte Psychologie.

Galea, S. & Ghodse, H. (2005), 'Drug misuse and the work place culture', in Ghodse (ed.), pp. 33–40.

Ghodse, H. (ed.) (2005), *Addiction at Work: Tackling Drug Use and Misuse in the Workplace*, Aldershot, UK and Burlington, VT: Gower.

Grotjahn, A. (1903), *Soll man bei der Arbeit Alkohol genießen?* [*Should Alcohol be Enjoyed During Working Hours?*], Berlin: Mäßigkeits Verlag.

ILO (International Labour Organization) (1996), *Management of Alcohol and Drug-related Problems in the Workplace*, Geneva: ILO, www.ilo.org/public/english/protection/safework/drug/index.htm, 24 June 2007.

Kurtz, N.R., Googins, B. & Howard, W.C. (1984), 'Measuring the success of occupational alcoholism programs', *Journal of Studies on Alcohol*, **45** (1), 33–45.

Lehmann W.E.K. & Bennet, J.B. (2002), 'Job risk and employee substance abuse: the influence of personal backgound and work environment factors', *American Journal of Drug and Alcohol Abuse*, **28** (2), 263–86.

Lehmann, W.E.K., Farabee, D.J., Halcom, M.L. & Simpson, D.D. (1993), 'Employee accidents: influences of personal characteristics, job characteristics and substance use in jobs differing in accident potential', *Journal of Safety Research*, **24**, 205–21.

Lucas, G. (2005), 'Effects and risk of workplace culture', in Ghodse (ed.), pp. 109–26.

Mangione, T., Howland, J., Amick, B., Cote, J., Lee, M., Bell, N. & Levine, S. (1999), 'Employee drinking practices and work performance', *Journal of Studies on Alcohol*, **60**, 261–70.

Masi, D.A. (ed.) (2000), *International Employee Assistance Anthology*, Washington, DC: Dallen Inc.

Parrot, S., Godfrey, C. & Raw, M. (2000), 'Costs of employee smoking in the workplace in Scotland', *Tobacco Control*, **91**, 187–92.

Ranft, B. & Hill, J.R. (eds) (2002), *The Oxford Illustrated History of the Royal Navy*, Oxford: Oxford University Press.

Rannia, L. (2003), *Alcohol Misuse: How Much Does It Cost?*, London: Strategy Unit Labour Office.

Resch, M. & Fuchs, R. (1998), 'Alkohol und Arbeitssicherheit' [*Alcohol and Security at the Workplace*], in Fuchs et al. (eds), pp. 31–49.

SAMHSA (Substance Abuse and Mental Health Services Administration) (1999), Summary of findings from the 1998 National Household Survey on Drug Abuse, SAMHSA, Rockville, MD: Office of Applied Studies, www.workplace.samhsa.gov, 24 June 2007.

Schneider, S. (1991), *Vorteilhaftigkeitsuntersuchung der Alkoholentwöhnungskur im Anton-Proksch-Institut* [*Economical Effects of an In-Patient Detoxification Treatment at the Anton-Proksch-Institute*], Vienna: Unveröffentlichte Diplomarbeit.

Shain, M., Surrvali, H. & Boutilier, M. (1986), *Healthier Workers: Health Promotion and Employee Assistance Programs*, Lexington, MA: Lexington Books.

Shehadeh, V. & Shain, M. (1990), *Influences on Wellness in the Workplace: A Multivariate Approach*, Toronto: Addiction Research Foundation.

Spicer, R.S., Miller, T.R. & Smith, G.S. (2003), 'Worker substance use, workplace problems and the risk of occupational injury: a matched case control study', *Journal of Studies on Alcohol*, **64**, 570–79.

Sonnensthul, W. (1996), *Working Sober: The Transformation of an Occupational Drinking Culture*, Ithaca, NY: Cornell University Press.

SRI (Stanford Research Institute) (1975), Betriebliche Alkoholismus. Programme in US-Firmen. Ein Untersuchungsbericht des Long Range Planning Service [*Alcoholism in Companies. Programs in US-Companies. A Research Report of the Long Range Planning Service*], Menlo Park, CA and London.

United Nations (1998), Special Session of the General Assembly, Guiding Principles of Drug Demand Reduction, IV E 15, New York, 8–10 June.

UNODC (United Nations Office on Drugs and Crime) (2007), *Annual Report* (covering activities in 2006), Vienna: UNODC.

Walsh, J.M. (1995), 'Is workplace drug-testing effective: let's see the data', Guest Editorial in MRO Update, October.

5 Coping and appraisals in a work setting: a closer examination of the relationship
Philip Dewe

Introduction

Coping is generally defined as 'the thoughts and behaviours used to manage the internal and external demands of situations that are appraised as stressful' (Folkman & Moskowitz, 2004, p. 745). Yet despite the 'boundless enthusiasm for coping research' (Somerfield & McCrae, 2000, p. 620), and reviewers acknowledging, at least at the conceptual level, the utility of the concept of appraisal and its relevance in a work setting, the view that the centrepiece 'to understanding coping is the notion of how the person appraises the situation' (Snyder, 1999, p. 9) has 'seemingly been overlooked' (Lowe & Bennett, 2003, p. 393) if not ignored by most work stress researchers. The current study brings together appraisal and coping with the aim of exploring, within a work setting, the relationship between the two. More particularly, using sequential tree analysis, a technique for exploring in this case patterns of appraisals, this study offers a richer description of the coping–appraisal relationship.

The appraisal process as Lazarus (1999) describes it is the mechanism that brings together and links the elements of any stressful encounter – the individual and the environment. There are two kinds of appraisal and 'although they always work interdependently, it is best to discuss then separately' (ibid., p. 75). Primary appraisal has to do with what is at stake (Folkman, 1982). It is where an individual encounter is embued with meaning (Holroyd & Lazarus, 1982). It has to do with the personal significance of an encounter and how relevant it is to one's goals, values, commitments and self-belief (Lazarus, 1999). Stressful encounters are usually appraised in terms of harm/loss, threat and challenge. In addition to these appraisals, 'evaluative judgements' are also made as to what can be done 'to improve' the stressful encounter 'and if so which coping options might work' (Lazarus & Folkman, 1987, p. 146). This process is termed 'secondary appraisal' and involves those efforts taken to manage, resolve or shape the encounter. Secondary appraisal is 'a crucial supplement' (ibid., p. 146) to primary appraisal, the difference between them being not one of timing but of content. One does not operate independently of the other and each should be 'regarded as part of a common process' (Lazarus, 1999, p. 78).

The sheer volume of work stress research leaves no room for doubt that researchers have warmed to the concept of coping. In a work context, coping research can broadly be divided into those studies that are best described as taxonomic with work stress researchers describing, classifying and debating the nature and focus of coping categories that appear common across all work situations, and those studies where the aim is to explore the context within which coping takes place. In relation to coping taxonomies, most researchers agree that the distinction between problem- and emotion-focused coping represents 'a good starting point' (Folkman & Moskowitz, 2004, p. 752). From here, researchers (Ferguson

& Cox, 1997; Burke, 2002; Schwarzer & Taubert, 2002) have gone on to debate the merits of refining this distinction to embrace, for example, avoidance, supportive, proactive, reappraisal and the management of meaning coping. When it comes to exploring the context within which coping takes place, then, despite the contention 'that it is not simply *important* to examine the individual appraisals when studying organizational stress, it is *essential* in order to understand the stress process' (Perrewé & Zellars, 1999, p. 749, original italics) there have been few systematic attempts (i.e., Dewe & Ng, 1999; Lowe & Bennett, 2003) where appraisal and coping emerge as an important focus of work stress research.

There are, argues Schaubroeck, when it comes to concepts like appraisal, 'valid reasons' for work stress researchers 'not placing a priority on them' (1999, p. 754). Two reasons may account for the fact that appraisal has been given a less than complete treatment by work stress researchers. These reasons fall into two not mutually exclusive categories, generally reflecting whether work stress is best measured objectively or subjectively. The first stems from the belief that by focusing on appraisals rather than the 'objective environment', the stress process becomes individualized and such a focus necessarily places limits on the generalizability of any findings (Harris, 1991). This in turn raises concerns about the reliability of such a focus, and more particularly its relevance to management (Schaubroeck, 1999).

The second set of reasons focus around the issue of what holds the greater promise for intervention (ibid.) and the contention that by 'measuring the objective situation we get answers to how we can develop work in such a way to prevent long term psychological damage' (Frese & Zapf, 1999, p. 762). The consequence of focusing on intraindividual processes limits, according to this argument, is the guidance that can be given as to the management of work stress (Harris, 1991) and the ability of work stress researchers to identify those working conditions that 'adversely affect the well-being of *most* workers' and 'ways to alleviate them' (Brief & George, 1991, p. 16, original italics). As is acknowledged (Brief & George, 1991), these reasons and the issues they raise can only be resolved by empirical investigation.

However, while researchers agree that 'current efforts in occupational stress research de-emphasize individual processes in favor of situational variables' (Harris, 1991, p. 21) they also agree that work stress research has much to gain (Brief & George, 1991) from exploring the explanatory potential of concepts such as appraisal. We can, as Frese and Zapf suggest, 'study *all* of the relevant issues of the stress process' (1999, p. 764, original italics) and in this way reflect more carefully on how such processes work. In general however, the distinction between the presence of an event, its evaluation and coping still remains to be fully explored by work stress researchers. Such researchers have, however, considered the issue of how best to represent the concept of appraisal in a work setting. A number of measurement approaches can be identified (Dewe & Ng, 1999) with researchers agreeing that appraisal measures should reflect contemporary theory and capture the thoughtful and purposeful assessment of an encounter. Where the appraisal–coping relationship has been explored, work stress researchers have investigated the association between broad categories of coping and different forms of appraisal (Lowe & Bennett, 2003) and whether this relationship can best be explained by considering the 'sense of congruence' or fit between the appraisal and coping (Dewe & Ng, 1999).

As already noted, coping 'is initiated in response to the individual's appraisal that important goals have been harmed, lost or threatened' (Folkman & Moskowitz, 2004, p. 747). This study extends earlier work by using sequential tree analysis to show patterns of appraisals in relation to different coping strategies. The advantage offered by sequential tree analysis lies in its system of hierarchical ordering. It presents the analysis in a visual display that highlights appraisal patterns in relation to different coping strategies in much the same way as a map offers 'guided paths for visiting various regions' (Li et al., 2000, p. 598). The visual display offered by sequential tree analysis is used as a didactic device to aid and instruct our understanding. The sequential unfolding of appraisals and the patterns formed in relation to particular coping strategies provides a richer context for exploring the congruence between coping and appraisals and the issues involved when attempting to understand the coping–appraisal relationship.

Method

Participants and measures
The population was drawn from individuals working in civic administration in a large provincial city in New Zealand. Respondents worked mainly in clerical, administrative and managerial positions. Functions included corporate and community services, city and regional planning and development, municipal services and human resource management. Questionnaires were distributed to all members of the staff. Those wishing to participate returned the questionnaire by post to the researcher. The 174 who returned questionnaires represented 39% of the sample. The survey was distributed just after the organization had initiated a major restructuring programme. While this was undoubtedly a stressful time, the moderate response rate may well reflect the fact that individual energies may have been more directed towards the issues surrounding the restructuring than completing the questionnaire. Of the respondents, 97 (56.7%) were male and 77 (43.3%) were female. The average age of the sample was 37.4 years and the majority (71.7%) were married or in a relationship. Almost all (93.6%) worked full time, had been in their present jobs for an average of 2.96 years and had worked for the organization for an average of 6.22 years.

Appraisal
A 23-item appraisal measure was used to assess the meanings that individuals gave to a stressful event at work. The appraisal measure was specifically designed for use in a work situation. This measure and its development are fully described in Dewe (1993). Respondents were first asked to think about a situation at work that had been stressful for them and to describe it. Then, thinking about the situation they had just described, respondents were asked to complete the appraisal measure. Respondents used a five-point scale (1 = not at all, to 5 = a great deal) to indicate what the situation involved and meant to them. Examples of the 23 items included: 'failing to meet the expectations of others', 'you appearing difficult to get on with', 'you feeling you would not achieve an important goal', 'you being made to take the blame', and 'you feeling a sense of injustice'. All 23 items were used in the sequential tree analysis. In this way it was possible to provide a richer description of the patterns of appraisals, avoiding the masking of important differences between appraisal items that may arise had the dependent appraisal variables been first analysed into components.

Coping
Coping was measured using the Dewe and Guest (1990) 62-item coping checklist. Respondents were asked to read each item and to indicate using a five-point scale (1 =

did not use, to 5 = used a great deal) the extent to which they used it to deal with the situation they had described. In order to maintain some control over the coping items, the 62 items were subjected to a principle components analysis. The appropriateness of the data for principle components analysis was established using Bartlett's test of sphericity (X^2 = 3538.088; $p \geq 0$) and the Kaiser–Meyer–Oklin measure of sample adequacy (0.55). An examination of the scree plot revealed five components as the most appropriate for this dataset. These five components using a Varimax rotation and explaining 36.57% of the variance are described below:

- Component I (M = 2.59, SD = 0.685, α = 0.81) was made up of 13 items and described *standing back, giving opinions and making people aware*. These included, for example, letting people know where they stand, giving opinions, making sure people are aware you are doing your best.
- Component II (M = 1.76, SD = 0.570, α = 0.82) was made up of 12 items and described *distracting yourself and ignoring the problem until ready to handle it*. These included, for example, take up something unrelated, moving on to other work activities, avoiding the subject of contention.
- Component III (M = 1.79, SD = 0.667, α = 0.76) was made up of eight items and described *expressing irritation and becoming more involved outside work*. These included, for example, getting rid of the tension by expressing irritation to yourself, expressing irritation to other work colleagues just to let off steam, becoming more involved in leisure, deciding to go out with friends.
- Component IV (M = 3.47, SD = 0.659, α = 0.64) was made up of eight items and described *considering options, getting support and advice*. These included, for example, getting advice, drawing on support from your boss, considering a range of plans for dealing with the issue.
- Component V (M = 2.90, SD = 0.722, α = 0.62) was made up of six items and described *facing the problem head on*. These included, for example, taking immediate action, throwing yourself into work and working harder and longer, not trying to solve the problem later.

Analysis
In order to identify coping patterns associated with different appraisals, this research used sequential tree analysis (SPSS: Answer Tree, 1998). It is an exploratory data analysis method used to study the relationship between a dependent variable (coping) and a series of predictor variables (appraisals) that may themselves interact. It produces a data-partitioning tree showing how patterns formed by the predictor variables differentially predict the dependent variable. Sequential tree analysis adopts a parametric approach to divide the sample sequentially into homogeneous groups (nodes). The aim of this technique is to determine whether splitting the sample based on the predictor variables (appraisals) leads to a statistically significant discrimination in the dependent variable. First, using the *F*-statistic, it identifies the best predictor (appraisal) variable of the dependent variable (coping strategy) to form the first branch of the tree. It then merges those scale values of the predictor variable that are judged to be homogeneous into subgroups (nodes). Then, based on other significant predictor variables, it splits each of these nodes into smaller nodes (subgroups).

This sequential process of selecting the best predictor variable and the best grouping of scale values of that variable continues until no more significantly significant predictors can be found. Two user-defined values determine the size of the tree and the sample size in a node. In this case where the significance of F is less than the user-defined value, which was set at the 5% level and where the sample size of a branch was less than 30 and a node was less than 15, then no further splits are made in that branch of the tree. The tree can be read downwards, highlighting in this case, the pattern of appraisals (predictors) associated with the coping strategy (dependent variable). The decision tree format is a didactic device to aid and instruct our understanding of the theory of appraisal and coping. This sequential unfolding of appraisal elements and their patterns achieves a number of outcomes (Dewe & Brook, 2000). It provides a richer description of the relationship between appraisals and coping, it offers insights into the appraisal patterns associated with coping strategies, and it presents a visual display and a way of thinking about appraisals and coping that adds to our understanding of their explanatory potential.

Results

The results of the tree analysis are presented in Figures 5.1–5: one figure for each of the five coping strategies. The initial node at the top of each figure shows the summary statistics (mean; standard deviation) for the whole sample for the coping strategy being measured. The numbers 1 to 5 above the nodes that follow represent the grouping of the appraisal scale points (1 = not at all, to 5 = a great deal) into homogeneous nodes. The appraisal question asked respondents to 'think of the situation they had just written about and indicate on the scale what they believed it involved. The numbers associated with a node represent what respondents believed the situation involved. The figures within the nodes that follow the original node represent the mean coping score, standard deviation and number of subjects. The greater the mean score the more frequently that coping strategy was used. The results are outlined below and are discussed in terms of three findings: first, the appraisals associated with different coping strategies; second, the nature of the appraisal patterns in relation to the frequency with which a coping strategy is used; and finally, what the combination of appraisals tells us in respect of the different coping strategies.

Figure 5.1 presents the tree analysis for the coping strategy 'standing back, giving opinions and making people aware' using these results as an example and, reading the tree downward, it appears that different appraisals are associated with the frequency with which that coping strategy is used. In this case, the more frequent use of this coping strategy involves the appraisal 'you feeling you would lose the respect of someone important to you'. Following on down the left-hand side of the tree, the frequency with which this coping strategy is used is associated with a more complicated pattern of appraisals involving 'you feeling a sense of responsibility' and 'you feeling that you are not getting enough resources'. This finding that different appraisal patterns are associated with the frequency with which different coping strategies are used is common across all the remaining figures, although the appraisal 'feeling a sense of responsibility' plays a role in relation to the frequency with which three coping strategies are used (see Figures 5.1, 5.4 and 5.5).

Staying with the theme that different appraisal patterns are associated with the frequency with which different coping strategies are used and using Figure 5.3 as another example of this theme, then looking at the right-hand side of the tree the more frequent

Standing back, giving opinions and making people aware

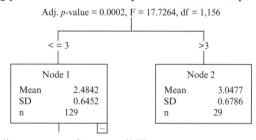

You feeling you would lose the respect of someone important to you

Adj. *p*-value = 0.0002, F = 17.7264, df = 1,156

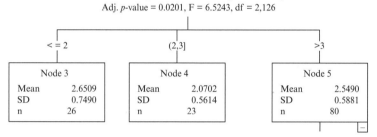

You feeling a sense of responsibility

Adj. *p*-value = 0.0201, F = 6.5243, df = 2,126

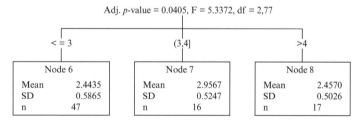

You feeling you are not getting enough resources

Adj. *p*-value = 0.0405, F = 5.3372, df = 2,77

Figure 5.1   *The relationship between the coping strategy 'standing back, giving opinions and making people aware' and appraisals*

use of the coping strategy 'expressing irritation and becoming more involved outside work' is associated with the appraisal 'you feeling intolerant'. When the left-hand side of the tree is examined, it appears more likely to be a combination of 'you feeling intolerant' and 'you being made to take the blame' that is associated with the frequency of use of this coping strategy. In terms of this finding that the frequency with which a coping strategy is used is associated with different appraisals, this may well represent what Lazarus describes as appraisals supporting 'realistic actions' (1999, p. 124) where the frequency with which a coping strategy is used can be distinguished one from the other because

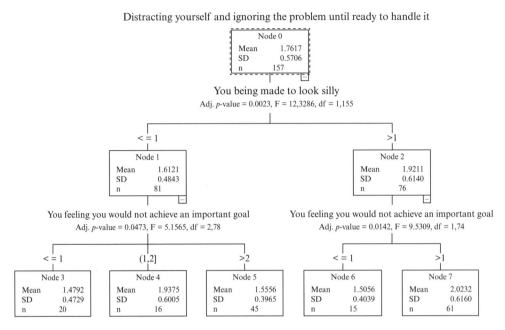

Figure 5.2   The relationship between the coping strategy 'distracting yourself and ignoring the problem until ready to handle it' and appraisals

they reflect 'realistic actions' built around different patterns of appraisal. However, the relationship between appraisals and coping appears more complex than this, as a perusal of the different results suggest. The frequency with which a coping strategy is used also appears to depend, at times, on varying patterns and combinations of appraisals and the intensity with which those appraisals are expressed. It is to this issue that we turn next.

Researchers have for some time been interested in the level of appraisal activity associated with different coping strategies. These results point to a level of appraisal activity that would seem to be influenced by both the number and combination of appraisals and the intensity with which the appraisals are expressed. It is possible to identify a number of appraisal patterns, none of which is mutually exclusive. The first (see the right-hand branch of the tree in Figures 5.1, 5.3 and 5.4) is where one appraisal appears sufficiently intense to influence the frequency with which a coping strategy is used. The second pattern begins to reflect a more complex picture (see the left-hand branch of Figures 5.2–4) where the frequency with which a coping strategy is used appears to depend on both some cumulative additive structure and the level of intensity of the different appraisals. The third pattern is similar to the one just described but here (see the left-hand branch of Figures 5.1, 5.2 and 5.5) while there is a combination of appraisals their cumulative impact does not always depend on their level of intensity. One way to think of these particular appraisal patterns is to consider some sort of 'last straw' effect. Then the added impact of an appraisal may be determined not simply by the absolute level of the intensity of that appraisal but by the intensity of that appraisal in relation to the other appraisals in the pattern.

Finally, at a more thematic level of analysis, there is the issue of the goodness of fit or

Expressing irritation and becoming more involved outside work

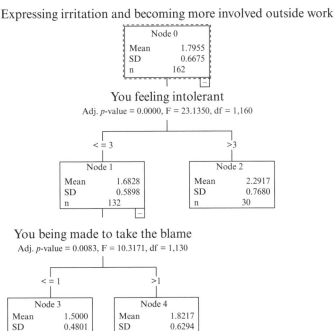

Figure 5.3 *The relationship between the coping strategy 'expressing irritation and becoming more involved outside work' and appraisals*

sense of congruence between coping and appraisals. The idea of 'fit' or a sense of congruence between coping and appraisal follows from the expectation that coping is expected to be consistent with appraisal. Different appraisals will activate different coping strategies. To do this requires that we consider the results in light of Lazarus's (1999) classification of appraisals in terms of their harm/loss ('damage that has already occurred) or threat ('possibility of damage in the future') qualities. The measure of appraisals did not set out to classify the different appraisals in this way. However, by making the distinction between 'being seen as', 'being made to' or 'losing' as *has happened*, and 'feeling a sense of, you appearing as' or 'feeling you may not', as *anticipating*, then the former, using Lazarus's distinction, could be describing harm/loss appraisals and the latter threats.

While exploring these results in terms of the goodness of fit between coping and appraisals needs to be treated somewhat cautiously, they do provide the opportunity to draw attention to this issue. Turning to Figure 5.1 and the left-hand side of the tree, could it be that this pattern of appraisals ('you feeling you would lose the respect of someone important to you', 'you feeling a sense of responsibility' and 'you feeling you are not getting enough resources') reflects more of a sense of threat and wholly consistent with a coping strategy that involves 'standing back, giving opinions and making people aware'. Similar comments could be drawn from an inspection of Figures 5.4 and 5.5. What is clear from these results is that the presumed threat appraisals appear at times to follow from different combinations of appraisals which may account for the way in which they are

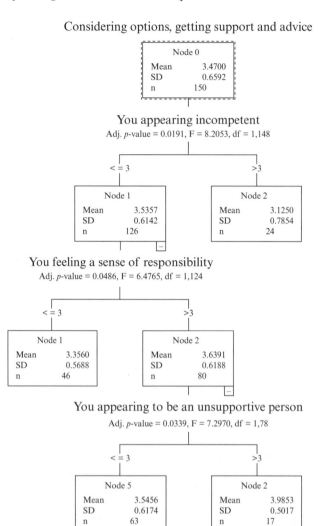

Figure 5.4   The relationship between the coping strategy 'considering options, getting support and advice' and appraisals

associated with different coping strategies, confirming the importance of this association and the need to better understand the relationship.

There is another level of complexity that these results appear to illustrate. It stems from the idea put forward by Lazarus (2001) that harm appraisals which have to do with the past, also have implications for the future so that harm and threat appraisals can occur in the same encounter, although as Lazarus goes on to add 'one or the other usually predominates' (ibid., p. 44). Turning first to Figure 5.2 and the right-hand branch, this appraisal pattern could be interpreted as involving both a *harm* appraisal ('you being made to look silly') and a *threat* appraisal ('you feeling you would not achieve an

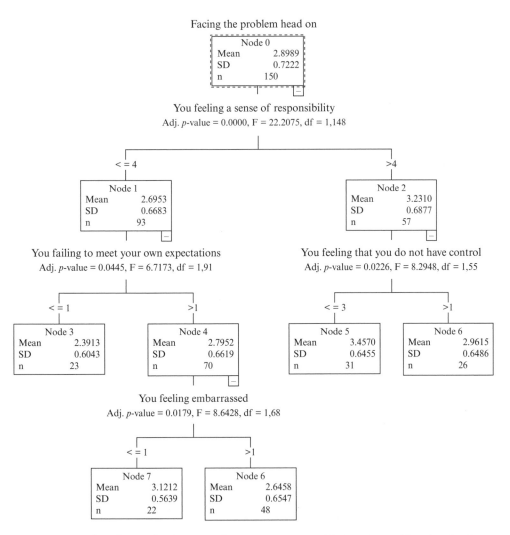

Figure 5.5   *The relationship between the coping strategy 'facing the problem head on' and appraisals*

important goal'). An inspection of the left-hand branch of Figure 5.3 suggests a similar pattern involving both a *harm* appraisal ('you being made to take the blame') and a *threat* appraisal ('you feeling intolerant'). Whether these different appraisals do reflect aspects of harm and threat is of course a moot point. Nevertheless, the patterns of appraisals appear to reflect the type of complexity referred to by Lazarus (2001) and confirm that if we are to understand the relationship between work stress and coping then we need to develop a better understanding of the role of appraisal. Again, as discussed earlier, when considering 'harm–threat' patterns of appraisal the issue of the intensity with which they are expressed and the impact that this has on coping frequency is another facet that needs to be considered when exploring the coping–appraisal relationship.

Discussion

This research set out to explore, using sequential tree analysis, the patterns of appraisal strategies associated with different coping strategies. The results can be discussed at two not mutually exclusive levels. The first is at a thematic level and explores the goodness of fit or sense of congruence between appraisals and coping strategies. The second level is more structural and explores the issues surrounding appraisal patterns, their combination and intensity.

The congruence or fit between coping and appraisals

Turning first to the idea of 'fit' or a sense of congruence between appraisals and coping, coping is expected to be consistent with appraisal. Different appraisals will activate different coping strategies. Yet to draw conclusions regarding the congruence or fit between coping and appraisals requires two types of knowledge: the nature of those appraisals in terms of whether they reflect harm, threat or challenge and the associated type of coping in terms of the coping strategies is problem or emotion focused. Looking first at the issue of consistency, congruence or fit between coping and appraisal, the first step requires a decision about the nature of the appraisal. If, for example, 'feeling you may lose the respect of someone important to you', 'feeling a sense of responsibility' and 'feeling you are not getting enough resources' (Figure 5.1) represent threat appraisals that 'anticipate the actuality of harm' and the 'expectation of whether we can manage it' (Lazarus, 1991, p. 163) then the coping strategy associated with these appraisals ('standing back, giving opinions and making people aware') would appear on the face of it to be congruent with such appraisals. Similarly (see Figure 5.5) if appraisals like 'feeling a sense of responsibility', 'failing to meet your own expectations' and 'feeling embarrassed' reflect threat appraisals, then their association with the coping strategy ('facing the problem head on') would appear to reflect some sort of congruence. Nevertheless in making decisions about congruence or fit, future work stress research will need to continue to investigate what constitutes appraisals such as threat and harm, identifying the components of those appraisals and how those components combine in respect of different coping strategies. If, as Lazarus (1999) suggests, appraisals are made up of a number of psychological components, then the way coping strategies relate to these different components will only be understood when we begin to better understand the way different components form patterns and the nature of the relationship between them.

However, the nature of appraisals is just one part of the decision in determining issues of congruency or fit. Before such a decision about fit can be made it is also necessary to have an understanding or knowledge of the nature of the coping strategy and whether it is problem or emotion focused. When coping strategies are considered within the contest of appraisal, the difficulties of classifying coping strategies emerge and the Lazarus dictum that 'we often end up speaking as if it is easy to decide which thought or action belongs to the problem-or-emotion-focused category' (ibid., p. 123) holds true. Referring back to the examples in the preceding paragraph, determining whether the coping strategies 'standing back, giving opinions and making people aware' and 'facing the problem head on' are problem or emotion focused must be made within the context of appraisal, but even then their focus remains unclear. While, in the examples cited above, it would be possible to argue that in relation to the pattern of appraisals 'standing back, giving opinions and making people aware' could be considered as more emotion focused and 'facing the problem head on' as more problem focused, this still remains a moot issue. When set within the context of appraisal 'we should learn by now that the same [coping] act may have more than one function and usually does' (ibid., p. 123), making any decision about congruence or fit that much more difficult. These results certainly illustrate the need to know more about how a coping strategy is being used and why it is being used in that way before any decision can be made about how we should classify a coping strategy and how we determine its relationship with appraisal.

To conclude this subsection on the question of congruence or fit then, as already indicated, this issue requires a better understanding and expansion of our knowledge of appraisals and coping. However, despite developing our understanding of appraisals and coping, making a decision as to the congruence or fit between the two may be even more complex because of the uncertainty that surrounds whether it is possible to distinguish at times between coping and appraisal and therefore whether 'in any given instance, a stress related thought is an appraisal, a coping process or both' (ibid., p. 78). Adding to the complexity surrounding congruence or fit, researchers (Park & Folkman, 1997) have pointed to what they describe as meaning-focused coping where the emphasis is on finding some sort of meaning or attempting to make sense of events. While 'the concept of meaning in the stress and coping process is theoretically rich and important' (ibid., p. 132), the issue of distinguishing between meaning as appraisal and meaning as coping requires further investigation. In order to answer the questions of what process is occurring, and how best to judge the congruence between coping and appraisal, future work stress research will need to confront how to better understand what is going on in the mind of the individual, the context that gives rise to such thoughts and in what way different thoughts are being focused and used. Because there is always interplay between appraisal and coping, it is more likely to be the case that one cannot be understood unless considered within the context of the other, making the role of appraisal in work stress research an even more important concept to explore.

Structural issues surrounding appraisal

These results present a need to better understand what can be described as 'structural' issues when patterns of appraisal are considered. Such structural issues would include: the number of appraisals associated with the use of a coping strategy, reflecting in some way the level of cognitive activity associated with the use of a coping strategy; the character of the appraisal pattern, including in terms of its composition whether it reflects the more generic themes suggested by Lazarus (1999) of harm, threat or challenge or some combination of these; and finally the level of intensity or potential potency of different appraisals and appraisal patterns. None of these issues is mutually exclusive and each interpretation reflects the downward unfolding of a branch of the tree.

The first issue – the number of appraisals – can be dealt with relatively quickly. This should not be seen as reflecting in any way the view that appraisals are unimportant in terms of our understanding of coping. The reason why this issue can be dealt with reasonably efficiently is simply because these results clearly show that some appraisal patterns seem at least from the tree analysis more cognitively complex than others. For example, Figures 5.1, 5.3 and 5.4 illustrate this by showing that for the coping strategies represented in these figures, the associated appraisals range from just one (right-hand branch of the tree) to more complex patterns (left-hand branch of the tree). These results help to explain why Lazarus uses the term 'cognitive' when referring to appraisal to emphasize 'the complex, judgmental and conscious process that must often be involved in appraising' (2001, p. 51). The difference in the number of appraisals associated with coping may also be explained by what Lazarus refers to as 'short circuiting', where many encounters, because they are frequently recurrences of similar events then, having already experienced similar events, the current event and coping require a less complex pattern of appraisals.

The second issue concerns whether, when taken as a set, appraisal patterns represent some higher-order level of meaning that embraces Lazarus's (2001) view of threat, harm or challenge and therefore whether there is some congruence between this higher-order meaning and coping. Issues surrounding the notion of congruence have been discussed earlier and while any higher-order level of meaning will, as noted, depend on advances in our knowledge of appraisals and coping, it is important when reviewing the different patterns of appraisals to note that harm/loss and threat appraisals are 'apt to be conjoined in the same transaction' and so 'harm appraisals, which have to do with the past, also have implications for the future and, therefore, usually contain elements of threat as well' (Lazarus, 1999, p. 79). In this case, in order to make a decision about the fit or congruence between coping and appraisals, it may be necessary to first determine whether an appraisal is 'harm/loss or threat dominated'. When and how, for example, harm/loss is subordinate to threat in an appraisal and vice versa requires further empirical investigation. However, the idea that appraisals contain elements of both and that at times one may dominate, may help to explain the finding that at different levels of appraisal differently focused coping strategies are used.

The final structural issue concerns whether, in conjunction with different coping strategies, some appraisals are more potent than others. A close examination of the appraisal patterns raises issues about whether the potency of a particular appraisal depends not just on its intensity of expression but also on how it may combine with other appraisals. This in turn raises issues about when different appraisals are combined, what is it about that combination that determines the potency of any particular appraisal, and when in combination, what role different appraisals play. While at one level it is possible to agree that different appraisal combinations seem to express an intuitively reasonable logic in terms of their meaning, at another level the role each appraisal plays and the impact that this has on determining its potency and the frequency with which a coping strategy is used, points again to the complexity of the relationship and the need for further research.

The importance of this research lies in the way sequential tree analysis offers a systematic analysis and visual display of the relationship between coping and appraisals, adding to and instructing our understanding of this relationship. By examining the findings it is possible to identify issues surrounding the coping–appraisal relationship that may be less evident when other more traditional techniques are used. Work stress researchers have debated for some time the use of more 'ecologically sensitive' measures (Coyne & Gottlieb, 1996) and while sequential tree analysis allows the examination of patterns in the data, it is not without its limitations. For example, it is essentially a stepwise method and therefore there is the question of how far to keep splitting a tree. In this respect this research took a cautious approach, setting in relation to the size of the sample a conservative stopping rule that no node be less than 15 in total. So in adopting such statistical rules, the appraisal patterns that emerged are less likely to overcapitalize on chance.

It is also important to note that the issues and questions raised here around the nature and structure of appraisals and their association with coping strategies reflect another debate keenly discussed by work stress researchers. This debate centres on the extent to which self-report data provide an understanding of the complexities surrounding constructs such as coping and appraisals. The call by researchers (Lazarus, 1999) for the use of more qualitative methods and the use of interviews and narrative analysis suggests the direction in which work stress research needs to move if we are to better understand the stress process and explore some of the issues raised here. There is no doubt that the bringing to bear of alternative methods and the development of new, creative ways of exploring these relationships will only add to our understanding. All these issues will continue to be debated, but what should not be lost sight of is that the role of appraisal, its nature and its relationship with different coping strategies is crucial in advancing our understanding of work stress. For work stress researchers to fail to recognize this is to ignore the explanatory potential and power of appraisal and its fundamental role in the stress process.

References

Brief, A.P. & George, J.M. (1991), 'Psychological stress and the workplace: a brief comment on Lazarus' outlook', in P.L. Perrewé (ed.), Handbook on job stress [Special Issue], *Journal of Social Behaviour and Personality*, **6**, 15–20.

Burke, R.J. (2002), 'Work stress and coping in organizations: progress and prospects', in E. Frydenberg (ed.), *Beyond Coping: Meeting Goals, Visions, and Challenges*, Oxford: Oxford University Press, pp. 83–106.

Coyne, J.C. & Gottlieb, B.H. (1996), 'The mismeasure of coping by checklist', *Journal of Personality*, **64**, 959–91.

Dewe, P.J. (1993), 'A closer examination of the patterns when coping with work-related stress: implications for measurement', *Journal of Occupational and Organizational Psychology*, **76**, 517–24.

Dewe, P.J. & Brook, R. (2000), 'Sequential tree analysis of work stressors: exploring score profiles in the context of the stressor–stress relationship', *International Journal of Stress Management*, **7**, 1–18.

Dewe, P. & Guest, D. (1990), 'Methods of coping with stress at work: a conceptual analysis and empirical study of measurement issues', *Journal of Organizational Behavior*, **11**, 135–50.

Dewe, P.J. & Ng, H.A. (1999), 'Exploring the relationship between primary appraisal and coping using a work setting', *Journal of Social Behavior and Personality*, **14**, 397–418.

Ferguson, E. & Cox, T. (1997), 'The functional dimensions of Coping Scale: theory, reliability and validity', *British Journal of Health Psychology*, **2**, 109–29.

Folkman, S. (1982), 'An approach to the measurement of coping', *Journal of Occupational Behaviour*, **3**, 95–107.

Folkman, S. & Moskowitz, J.T. (2004), 'Coping: pitfalls and promise', *Annual Review of Psychology*, **55**, 745–74.

Frese, M. & Zapf, D. (1999), 'On the importance of the objective environment in stress and attribution theory. Counterpoint to Perrewé and Zellars', *Journal of Organizational Behavior*, **20**, 761–5.

Harris, J.R. (1991), 'The utility of the transactional approach for occupational stress research', in P.L. Perrewé (ed.), Handbook on job stress [Special Issue], *Journal of Social Behavior and Personality*, **6**, 21–9.

Holroyd, K.A. & Lazarus, R.S. (1982), 'Stress, coping and somatic adaptation', in L. Goldberger and S. Breznitz (eds), *Handbook of Stress: Theoretical and Clinical Aspects*, New York: Free Press, pp. 21–35.

Lazarus, R.S. (1991), *Emotion and Adaptation*, Oxford and New York: Oxford University Press.

Lazarus, R.S. (1999), *Stress and Emotion: A New Synthesis*, London: Free Association Books.

Lazarus, R.S. (2001), 'Relational meaning and discrete emotions', in K.R. Scherer, A. Schorr & T. Johnstone (eds), *Appraisal Processes in Emotion: Theory, Methods, Research*, Oxford: Oxford University Press, pp. 37–67.

Lazarus, R.S. & Folkman, S. (1987), 'Transactional theory and research on emotions and coping', *European Journal of Personality*, **1**, 141–69.

Li, K.C., Lue, H.H. & Chen, C.H. (2000), Interactive tree-structured regression via principal hessian directions', *Journal of the American Statistical Association*, **95**, 547–60.

Lowe, R. & Bennett, P. (2003), 'Exploring coping reactions to work-stress: application of an appraisal theory', *Journal of Occupational and Organizational Psychology*, **76**, 393–400.

Park, C.L. & Folkman, S. (1997), 'Meaning in the context of stress and coping', *Review of General Psychology*, **2**, 115–44.

Perrewé, P.L. & Zellars, K.L. (1999), 'An examination of attributions and emotions in the transactional approach to the organizational stress process', *Journal of Organizational Behavior*, **20**, 739–52.

Schaubroeck, J. (1999), 'Should the subjective be the objective? On studying mental processes, coping behavior, and actual exposures in organizational stress research', *Journal of Organizational Behavior*, **20**, 753–60.

Schwarzer, R. & Taubert, S. (2002), 'Tenacious goal pursuits and striving toward personal growth: proactive coping', in E. Frydenberg (ed.), *Beyond Coping: Meeting Goals, Visions, and Challenges*, Oxford: Oxford University Press, pp. 19–35.

Snyder, C.R. (1999), *Coping: The Psychology of What Works*, Oxford and New York: Oxford University Press.

Somerfield, M.R. & McCrae, R.R. (2000), 'Stress and coping research: methodological challenges, theoretical advances', *American Psychologist*, **55**, 620–25.

SPSS (1998), Answer Tree (version 2.0.1), SPSS Inc.

PART II

SPECIFIC ISSUES IN ORGANIZATIONAL PSYCHOLOGY

6 The impact of age diversity in teams on group performance, innovation and health
Jürgen Wegge and Klaus-Helmut Schmidt

Introduction

Over the past decade, demographic trends in Europe have focused increasing organizational attention on issues related to the successful management of an aging workforce (de Lange et al., 2006; Hedge et al., 2006; Leibold & Voelpel, 2006; Streb et al., 2008). One aspect that has received rather scant attention in this analysis is the increase in age diversity within workgroups. As employees work into late midlife, not only the number of older employees but also *age diversity* in organizations has increased (Roth et al., 2007). Moreover, prior research on group composition indicates that age diversity in teams is not unproblematic. Age diversity can have both advantages (e.g., utilization of more experience during problem solving) as well as disadvantages (e.g., intensification of conflicts) for team functioning. Thus, the goal of this chapter is to summarize and update what we actually know about these effects. Our synopsis is organized as follows. First, we introduce a general model describing four different paths that link team composition with group productivity. This model is important as it explains why prior diversity research has often found contradicting results. Next, we summarize what is known about the effects of age diversity, and present findings from 16 empirical studies published after the latest state-of-the-art review by Williams and O'Reilly (1998). One striking result of our review is that diversity research produces some insights regarding performance and innovation but totally ignores occupational health. In our view, this is a real gap that has to be addressed in future research. Finally, based on recent findings from our own research, we summarize why age diversity might affect not only team performance, but also occupational health.

General insights regarding effects of team composition

Prior research has revealed that the composition of a team is a very important factor which has to be considered for the design of successful teamwork (Jackson et al., 2003; Wegge, 2003; Gebert, 2004; van Knippenberg et al., 2004). As many personal attributes can be relevant for solving different team tasks (e.g., education, professional experience, physical strength, intelligence, personality), a vast number of studies are available in which team composition effects were investigated. The data for some attributes are already comprehensive and consistent. For example, it was found that isolated talent is wasted talent as the average intelligence of a team is positively correlated with team performance, whereas high diversity in intelligence is not beneficial for team performance (Devine & Philips, 2001). However, for other attributes, that is, personality traits such as extraversion or agreeableness, results are still scarce and rather inconsistent (Kichuk & Wiesner, 1998; Wegge, 2003). Moreover, it was also observed that the impact of the same attribute might differ across team types. Gebert (2004, p. 192) found that diversity

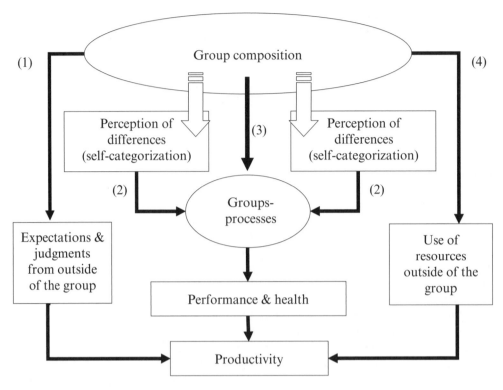

Source: Wegge (2003).

Figure 6.1   Four different ways in which the composition of a group can influence team productivity

in functional backgrounds of team members had no effect in product development teams but was positively associated with the success of top management teams. As Hertel and Scholl (2006) discuss, the inconsistency of findings might also result from differences in the longevity of teams. Rather, homogeneous teams often show better initial performance than heterogeneous teams, while this situation can be reversed over time (Gebert, 2004, pp. 167–72). In a similar vein, the nature of the dependent variable under investigation (e.g., performance or team cohesion) is important. One and the same attribute such as educational diversity can have positive effects in terms of team performance but negative effects on team cohesion. Thus, simple statements claiming that diversity generally has positive or negative effects are unacceptable simplifications. In evaluating the potential effects of a certain team composition, it is always important which *personal attributes*, which *team tasks*, which *time dimensions* and which *dependent variables* are examined.

Another important insight refers to the multitude of ways in which a specific team composition can influence team productivity. Wegge (2003) developed and presented a model that identifies four major ways (see Figure 6.1). According to this model, a certain team composition can lead to high or low productivity because the quality of a specific work outcome (e.g., a problem solution) is based on expectations and judgments regarding the best team composition by persons *outside* of the group (first way). A team decision is often regarded as legitimate, for example, if all relevant interest groups were involved in deriving this decision. The same problem solution, however, might be turned down if one important interest group were not involved in the decision (e.g., a women's representative) or because involved team members were not chosen through a fair election. Thus, independent from the results of teamwork and team processes as such, expectations and judgments regarding an acceptable team composition from outside of the group might affect team productivity.

With regard to the second and third ways, various group processes within the team (e.g., arousal of conflicts, exchange of knowledge, division of work between group members, goal-setting processes, changes in team cohesion) need to be considered for explaining team productivity. The difference between these two ways is based on the activation of 'self-categorization' processes in terms of perceiving team members either as in-group or as out-group members (e.g., man vs. woman, young vs. old persons) within a situation. Self-categorization processes (e.g., 'We are male, they are female') have to be present along the second way while this is not the case along the third way. Higher performance of groups with more male members, for example, might be due to the increasing will-ingness of male team members to demonstrate their physical strength when they define (self-categorize) themselves as male, because gender roles (stereotypes) are more salient in a situation where one gender is in the majority (second way). The good performance of groups with a high proportion of male members, however, might also be due to the fact that male team members typically have more muscle mass, and in tasks requiring physical strength this is an advantage (third way) that promotes good performance independent from male members defining themselves as male. Of course, the activation and salience of gender roles might not only yield advantages. It is also possible that gender salience acti-vates stereotypes that reduce work motivation and/or the willingness to cooperate within the own group (e.g., if the task is perceived as a task where mainly women should be involved, male group members might reduce their efforts). In the same vein, it is possible that some task requirements yield an advantage for women-dominated teams without the activation of self-categorization processes (e.g., because women often show more social support and this is the best predictor for good team performance).

The fourth way by which a specific group composition might have an impact on group productivity is again largely independent from intra-team processes. The team composi-tion can have an influence on team productivity because team members use resources outside of their group which are relevant for the genesis and/or the assessment of their team's performances. The result reported in the study by Gladstein-Ancona and Caldwell (1992) is a good example: In cross-functional teams, team members often have more contacts outside of their group than in functionally homogeneous groups. These outside contacts can be utilized (e.g., by getting the necessary information faster) so that the team's efficiency is increased.

Separating these four ways in diversity research is important as it helps us to under-stand why the same attribute can have effects on team processes and team productiv-ity which – mediated via these ways – are sometimes positive, sometimes negative and sometimes not observable because they probably cancel each other out. Differences in the team members' nationality, to give another example, might at the same time reduce the willingness to cooperate within a group because one does not like working with foreign groups (outgroup, second way) and because a different understanding of hierarchies within cultures complicates communication processes within the team (third way). However, the larger amount of different knowledge available within these teams (third way) or the larger information network outside of the group (fourth way) might lead to finding no general differences in the quality of decisions for groups with high and low cultural diversity. Alternatively, and depending on the intensity of the effects or the specific context of the team, one may also observe that multicultural teams develop particularly bad or good solutions (Stumpf & Thomas, 2003). Thus, differentiating the various ways and the connected processes explains why (i) sometimes no or opposite effects are found and why (ii) there are sometimes conflicting results for the same diversity attribute (e.g., good performance but low team integrity; see also van Knippenberg et al., 2004 for a similar argument).

A closer look at psychological processes underlying diversity effects

Typically, three different theoretical approaches are utilized in diversity research to explain the various effects. Two formulations, namely Byrne's similarity-attraction theory (1971), and Tajfel and Turner's (1986) social identity theory, posit mainly negative effects of group diversity on work outcomes. In contrast, models for information processing and decision making in teams (Kerschreiter et al., 2003; de Dreu, 2006) predict positive effects for diversity on performance.

Byrne's (1971) similarity-attraction theory proposes that humans tend to affiliate with individuals whom they perceive as similar to themselves. Thus, homogeneous workgroups are expected to be characterized by more positive work outcomes, including stronger group cohesion, lower turnover, and improved communication and performance, than workgroups composed of individuals who perceive themselves as dissimilar from one another. This assumption simultaneously provides the basis for the ASA theory which is formulated on the organizational level (Schneider, 1987; Schneider et al., 2001). The theory postulates that different forces (ASA = attraction, selection, attrition) lead to an increasing homogenization of the whole company. However, in extending Byrne's theory, Schneider simultaneously warns of the fact that this not only has the advantages just mentioned but that the innovative ability of the whole company will decline in time. Thus, increasing homogenization might lead to a decrease in heterogeneity of knowledge and reduced questioning of one's own standards, values and approaches. This can be a disadvantage, especially in the case of dynamic environments and high requirements following a change of previous structures and strategies (Keck, 1997).

Consistent with this theory, social identity theory (Tajfel & Turner, 1986) posits that individuals strive for positive self-esteem and that one part of an individual's self-concept, one's social identity, is based on membership in social categories (e.g., according to physical appearance, attitudes). Moreover, individuals strive for positive differentiation between those categories of which they are a member (i.e. their in-groups) and other categories of which they are not a member (i.e., their out-groups). In the case of age, social identity theory predicts that individuals who categorize (define) themselves as a member of a young person age group are likely to evaluate members of their own group (in-group) more positively and similarly compared to members of other age groups (e.g., older people), and to discriminate against members of the out-group, especially when such persons are viewed in competition with a member of the in-group. In addition, the negative effects of self-categorization should also be especially distinctive in cases where the attribute of identification is salient in a situation (i.e., easy recognizable), such as age or gender (see Haslam, 2004). Taken together, similarity-attraction and social identity formulations suggest that in work units that are diverse in salient characteristics such as age, diversity will operate to hamper workgroup processes that contribute to positive work outcomes.

The third line of reasoning – models for information processing and decision making in groups – posits that diverse group composition causes an increase in the information and perspectives available during group discussion, which in turn, may facilitate group decisions and performance (e.g., by a deeper or more elaborate analysis of the problem; Kerschreiter et al., 2003; de Dreu, 2006). Accordingly, diversity is deemed to foster the use of knowledge and the availability of different (unshared) information by intensifying *cognitive conflicts* in teams, thus making better and more innovative decisions possible. This assumption was supported by several studies, although unshared information is often less likely to be mentioned in teams than shared information. Moreover, it has to be considered that heterogeneity of knowledge goes along with higher demands in the processing of contradictory information (West, 2002) and that there are other processes apart from simple availability of knowledge (e.g., conformity pressure, higher credibility of socially validated information) which can prevent a diverse team from making use of its information advantage (Kerschreiter et al., 2003). Nevertheless, the basic assumption of this approach, which is mainly based on lab research, is that the team's diversity, mediated via a higher amount of available information and the increase of cognitive conflicts, can lead to decisions of better quality.

As Wegge (2003) and van Knippenberg et al. (2004) suggest, these three theoretical formulations are not conflicting but address different aspects of the psychological processes by which diversity may influence work unit outcomes. Thus, all three theories are 'true' and it is very likely that – along the various ways described in Figure 6.1 – work unit diversity may exert either positive or negative effects, or both effects *simultaneously.* Depending on various contextual conditions, for example, the specific diversity variable under investigation, the variable's salience in a group, task characteristics, the specific work outcomes that are assessed, we observe negative, null or positive effects. In the following, we focus on what is known about the effects of age diversity.

Empirical findings regarding the effects of age diversity in teams
Based on conclusions from prior review articles (Tsui et al., 1995, p. 203; Williams & O'Reilly, 1998, p. 104) across all available studies, negative effects of age diversity seem to be stronger than positive effects. It was found that teams with high age diversity are often characterized by a bad climate (e.g., less cohesion, lower job satisfaction), have less communication (Zenger & Lawrence, 1989), a higher turnover rate (older people especially leave the group earlier), more problems in decision making (Knight et al., 1999) and lower performance. Although there are several studies which did not prove negative effects of age diversity (O'Reilly et al., 1997), or in which age diversity was even associated with less conflict within teams (Pelled et al., 1999), the overall 'point balance' of previous work on age diversity is clearly *negative.*

According to the more recent review of Jackson et al. (2003), age is still a very prominent criterion in diversity research: 34% of the 63 studies reviewed by these authors examined gender, 31% age, only 19% educational background, and about 13% tenure of team members. To update our knowledge with respect to the impact of age diversity, we decided to scan the new literature starting from the year 1998 in which the often-cited review article of Williams and O'Reilly (1998) was published. In reviewing the new work, we solely focused on those studies that investigated age diversity at the team level. Moreover, we selected performance (regular performance, innovation) and health as dependent variables of interest. Hence, we included only studies in which information on age diversity in groups (isolated or in combination with other demographic characteristics) and information on group performance or health was reported. As all the theoretical models discussed above support the idea that effects of age diversity depend on different context factors (e.g., complexity of group tasks, group longevity, team type), we also examined the particular team form as a potential moderator variable in our synopsis. The results of this analysis are summarized in Table 6.1. All in all, 16 studies that fulfilled the criteria were found: five studies on top management teams, one on product development teams, two on student teams, one on sports teams, and seven on service teams.

Because it is also of interest which variables are examined as potential mediator variables (causal processes) and moderator variables (context factors) in contemporary research on age diversity, information about these variables is presented in Table 6.1. In the following, we briefly describe these 16 studies organized by team type.

Top management teams (TMTs)
In a longitudinal study with 42 TMTs West et al. (1999) found a negative effect of age diversity on subsequent performance (productivity, gains) whereas no correlation was found with prior team performance. A study by Cady and Valentine (1999) was carried out in a division of a high-tech, Fortune 500 company with 50 teams. The effect of diversity in teams (nationality, gender, age, functional background) on innovation was examined. Although a general positive correlation was expected for both categories of innovation (number of ideas, benefits) no significant correlation was found with regard to age diversity. In a study with 57 TMTs of companies which produce electrical products, Simons et al. (1999) again found a negative but not significant effect of age diversity on performance (changes in the profit). Interestingly, three other demographic characteristics (functional background, education, and duration of employment) showed positive effects. The results were interpreted in the following way: age is less relevant for the job than the other three characteristics and for that reason it has no influence on performance. Using 35 simulated business teams with three to five managers, Kilduff et al. (2000) examined the relationship between demographic and cognitive diversity on performance (growth on market share, growth of profit). Age diversity had no significant effect on either cognitive diversity or team performance. Richard and Shelor (2002) considered the effect of age diversity on the company's performance within a large sample of TMTs (4,601 to 1,305 teams) from different industries. Age diversity in TMTs correlated negatively with return on assets (negative linear effect) and positively with sales growth (positive linear effect). The authors also claim that positive effects of age diversity were found solely for low and moderate age diversity levels whereas they were negative for higher levels of age diversity (a reversed U-shaped trend). The documentation of these results, however, is not clear. In addition, some moderator variables were examined: the complexity of the environment (e.g., a high competitive product market with many potential harassments), the innovation climate (e.g., the tendency of the company to deal and cope

Table 6.1 Overview of empirical studies (1998–2007) analyzing effects of age diversity on team performance

Authors	Year	Team form	Number of teams LS CS	Age diversity index	Examined variables DV = Dependent variable Mod = Moderator variable Med = Mediator variable CV = Control variable	Main results

West, Patterson, Dawson & Nickell	1999	TMT Manufacturing	42 LS (Panel) 1990–2000	CoV	1. DV = gains
					2. DV = productivity
					  a. before
					  b. after
						1a. not significant ($r = 0.13$)
						1b. negative correlation ($r = -0.26$, $p < 0.05$)
						2a. not significant ($r = -0.11$)
						2b. negative correlation ($r = -0.30$, $p < 0.05$)

Cady & Valentine	1999	TMT Technical	50 CS	Teachman Index	1. DV = innovation
					  a. number of new ideas
					  b. benefit of new ideas
						1. not significant (number of new ideas, $r = 0.02$, benefit of new ideas, $r = 0.11$)

Simons, Pelled & Smith	1999	TMT Electrical	57 CS	CoV	1. DV = performance (changes in gains)	1. not significant ($r = -0.13$)
Kilduff, Angelmar & Mehra	2000	TMT (Business simulation)	35 CS	CoV	1. DV = cognitive diversity 2. DV = performance (market share gains)	1. not significant ($r = -0.07$ to $r = 0.24$) 2. not significant ($r = 0.16$ to $r = 0.30$)
Richard & Shelor	2002	TMT (all industries)	1305 CS	CoV	1a. DV = return on assets 1b. DV = sales growth 2. Mod = complexity 3. Mod = innovation climate 4. Mod = decentralization CV = size, industry etc.	1a. $r = -0.03$, $p < 0.05$ 1b. $r = 0.07$, $p < 0.001$ various interactions and curvilinear effects are reported (but not clearly described)
Pelled, Eisenhardt & Xin	1999	PDT Electrical	45 CS	CoV	1. DV = performance 2. DV = conflicts	1. not significant ($r = 0.09$) 2. emotional conflicts ($r = -0.45$, $p < 0.05$), cognitive conflicts ($r = -0.27$, $p < 0.05$)

Table 6.1 (continued)

Authors	Year	Team form	Number of teams LS CS	Age diversity index	Examined variables DV = Dependent variable Mod = Moderator variable Med = Mediator variable CV = Control variable	Main results
Polzer, Milton & Swann	2002	StdT 1. semester MBA	83 CS	Demographic Diversity • CoV (age) • Blau's index (others)	1. DV = performance a. creative task performance b. computing power 2. Mod = interpersonal congruency	1a. not significant ($r = 0.05$) 1b. not significant ($r = -0.08$) 2a. at high interpersonal congruency: positive correlation between demographic diversity and creative task performance ($\beta = 0.23$, $p < 0.05$) 2b. at low interpersonal congruency: positive correlation between demographic diversity and computational task performance ($\beta = -0.23$, $p < 0.10$)
Harrison, Price, Gavin & Florey	2002	StdT MBA	144 LS (Trend)	SD	1. DV = grades 2. Mod = team longevity	1. not significant ($r = 0.05$)
Timmerman	2000	SpT 871 Basketball 1082 Baseball	LS (Panel) 1950– 1997	CoV	1. DV = victories 2. DV = ability to work in a team a. Baseball b. Basketball	1a. not significant ($r = 0.03$) 1b. not significant ($r = 0.04$) 2a. not significant ($\beta = 0.00$) 2b. negative correlation ($\beta = -0.11$, $p < 0.01$)
O'Reilly, Williams & Barsade	1998	ST Garment factory	31 CS	CoV	1. DV = innovation a. creativity b. implementation of ideas	1a. not significant ($\beta = -0.16$) 1b. not significant ($\beta = -0.12$) 2. not significant ($\beta = 0.08$)
Williams, O'Reilly & Barsade	1999	ST Garment factory	31 CS	Euclidian distance	2. DV = conflicts 1. DV = team work 2. Mod = relational diversity (minorities vs. majorities)	1. negative correlation ($\beta = -0.29$, $p < 0.10$) 2. if majorities are outnumbered: negative correlation with team work ($\beta = -0.19$, $p < 0.05$)

Authors	Year	Team/Context	N/Design	Measure	Variables	Results

Ely	2004	ST Financial service	486 CS	CoV	1. DV = performance
					  a. customer satisfaction
					  b. sales revenue
					2. Mod = cooperation and team work
					  a. sales revenue
					  b. overall performance
						1. negative correlation
						  a. $r = -0.09, p < 0.05$
						  b. $r = -0.13, p < 0.05$
						2a. at high cooperation, positive correlation with sales volume ($\beta = -4.46, p < 0.01$)
						2b. at lower cooperation, lower correlation with performance ($\beta = -2.38, p < 0.05$)

Leonard, Levine & Joshi	2004	ST retail	700 CS	SD (log (mean))	1. DV = performance (sales figures)	1. negative correlation ($r = -0.16, p < 0.05$)
Hamilton, Nickerson & Owan	2004	ST Garment factory (production)	25 LS (Panel) 1995–1997	SD (log (mean))	1. DV = productivity (time permitted vs. time required)	1. negative correlation [if the ability to work in a team constant, age diverse teams less productive] ($\beta = -0.044, p < 0.05$)
Roth, Wegge, Schmidt & Neubach	2006	ST Local tax office	222 CS	SD	1. DV = performance (process time for requests) 2. Mod = task complexity 3. Med = commitment to the department CV = group size	1. positive correlation ($r = -0.17, p < 0.05$) 2. positive correlation only for high complexity (routine jobs: $r = 0.01$, n.s.; complex tasks: $r = -0.23, p < 0.05$) 3. commitment to the department mediated the correlation for complex tasks ($r = -0.23, p < 0.05$ vs. $r = -0.12$, n.s.; $Z = 2.04, p < 0.05$)
Shemla, Wegge, Haslam, Schmidt & Thies	in prep.	ST Financial service	259 CS	SD	1. DV = performance (commission in %) 2. Mod = tenure differences	1. positive correlation ($r = 0.13, p < 0.05$) 2. in age homogeneous teams comparatively high tenured supervisors are especially effective

Note: TMT = Top management team; PDT = Product development team; StdT = Student team; SpT = Sports team; ST = Service team. LS (longitudinal): Panel = repeated observations of the same research unity, Trend = repeated observations of different research unities; CS = cross-sectional; SD = standard deviation, CoV = coefficient of variation.

with new ideas as well as creative processes), and the degree of decentralization (e.g., how far decisions are delegated top down as well as across organizational levels). Several significant moderator effects were found but unfortunately not documented in detail so that the precise form of these interactions is dubious (the authors state that complex environments, a strong innovation context and high decentralization should be favorable for finding positive effects of age diversity).

Product development teams (PDTs)
In a study of 45 teams of electronic divisions from three big companies, Pelled et al. (1999) examined the correlation between diversity in groups, conflicts, and performance. Age diversity had no direct effect on performance but correlated negatively with the presence of emotional and cognitive conflicts.

Student teams (StdTs)
Polzer et al. (2002) examined the extent to which demographic diversity (age, gender, nationality, and citizenship) influences performance (creative task performance, computational task accomplishment) under the influence of 'interpersonal congruency' as a moderator variable. This variable was defined as the extent to which one's opinion about other team members reflects their own opinion about themselves. The results confirm a positive effect of demographic diversity on creative task performance only under the condition of high interpersonal congruency within the team (median split: low vs. high congruency; beta = -0.12 vs. $+0.21$). On the other hand, if the computational task performance is considered, a reversed effect is found: demographic diversity had a positive effect on computational task performance in groups in which the interpersonal congruency was low (median split: low vs. high congruency; beta = 0.23 vs. -0.29). Thus, effects of diversity obviously might depend on both demands of the task and the congruency of opinions within a group. Harrison et al. (2002) were interested in the difference between 'surface-level diversity' (e.g., difference regarding age and gender) and 'deep-level diversity' (e.g., diversity regarding the importance of success or other values) with regard to collaboration and group performance. In general, age diversity of the 144 MBA teams was no significant predictor of team performance (grades). However, in the course of time, the continuous collaboration among group members weakened the effects of surface-level diversity on group performance but strengthened the deep-level diversity effects. Hence, the authors point out the relevance of 'time' as an important moderator for diversity research.

Sports teams (SpTs)
When we consider that many sportsmen end their career at the age of about 30–40 years, whereas work life ends when the person turns 65 (soon 67 in Germany), it is obvious that in the SpT field, severe range restrictions with respect to age and age diversity are present. Thus, lower correlations might be observed in this field. To our knowledge, only one study with SpTs exists. In a large archive study with 871 American professional basketball teams and 1,082 professional baseball teams over a period of 27 years, Timmerman (2000) found a negative effect of age diversity on basketball performance and no effect for baseball performance. The author assumes that this difference between sports can be explained by differences in task interdependence because effects of age diversity should be stronger in tasks which high interdependency of team members.

Service teams (STs)
O'Reilly et al. (1998) examined the correlation between age diversity and innovation (generating new ideas, implementing ideas) as well as conflicts in 31 project teams, composed of 189 employees from a large garment factory. No significant correlation was found. In another study based on the same sample, Williams et al. (1999) examined the effect of relational diversity (minority and majority in age, tenure, gender, and nationality) on teamwork. Teamwork was measured with the help of the following dimensions: social integration, common goals, promptness, and flexibility in finding decisions as well as the skill to adjust. The results show that with increased age diversity, teamwork becomes worse. In a study of 486 stores with 7,429 jobholders of a large financial services sector, Ely (2004) found that the direct effect of age diversity on performance (customer satisfaction, number of successful customer recommendations) is negative. In addition, two moderator effects regarding the relationship between age diversity and performance (sales revenue, and overall performance) are reported: cooperation and teamwork moderated this relationship as teams which are homogeneous in age benefit most from high cooperation and teamwork. In a study of 700 retail stores, Leonard et al. (2004) also found a negative effect of age diversity on shop performance (sales figures). According to the authors, this can be expected as these tasks require no complex decisions or a broad information basis. Hamilton et al. (2004) examined the influence of diversity (skills, nationality, age) in production teams consisting of six to seven persons in a garment factory. The teams were allowed to compose themselves to a certain degree in a specific period of time. Productivity was measured weekly (e.g., time for specific sewing operations according to complexity, number of pieces per day per person). The results reveal a negative correlation between age diversity and productivity as teams with higher age diversity are less productive. That finding is also consistent with that of Leonard and Levine (2002), who found that age-diverse retail stores are less profitable. However, this analysis was not conducted at the group level. A study by Roth et al. (2006) examined the effects of age diversity in 111 local tax offices. Every tax office has two groups: one team worked on easy tax computations while the other worked on more complex tax declarations. Thus, overall 222 teams with more than 4,500 officers were available for this study. Performance was measured in days required for handling the tax declaration. In general, a negative correlation between age diversity and handling time (indicating a positive performance effect) was found for all teams. When the two groups were analyzed separately, a significant difference was discovered. The positive effect of age diversity on performance could only be found for teams with complex tasks. For teams working on routine jobs, no correlation was found. Furthermore, commitment to the department mediated this effect. In another large field study of a German financial service company, Shemla et al. (2007) examined the effect of age diversity on group performance. As an indicator for performance, average team profits (in percent) were calculated. The results show that age-diverse teams were more successful. As team tasks were rather complex, this effect was expected.

Discussion of recent findings
What do these new results tell us? Is the use of mixed-age teams a good strategy to integrate older employees in the organization? In our view, these findings are quite consistent with the main conclusions of prior review articles on this issue. The 16 recent studies we

found in the literature support both the existence of significant advantages (e.g., Roth et al., 2006 and three further studies) and the somewhat higher possibility of significant disadvantages linked with age diversity in teams (e.g., Ely, 2004 and seven other studies). Moreover, quite often (four studies) no significant effects at all are found or effects are observable only if certain moderator variables are taken into account. Based on the findings summarized in Table 6.1, it seems plausible, for example, that potential positive effects of age diversity are more likely to show up if task requirements are complex (see also Bowers et al., 2000). In view of this overall pattern of findings, a general recommendation for the use of mixed-age workgroups is not appropriate. Negative effects of age diversity are more likely than positive effects and several moderator variables play an important role, in particular task complexity, the quality of team functioning (e.g., cooperation, congruency in attitudes), group longevity and probably also task interdependence.

Another important observation is that most studies on age diversity so far are concentrating on the analyses of TMTs (5 studies) and STs (7 studies). Thus, conclusions for other team forms (e.g., SpTs, PDTs) should be derived with caution. Moreover, it is also clear from these studies that even within one specific team form, correlations might be significantly different depending on other context variables (e.g., type of sport, task complexity) or the specific variables selected to measure team performance (e.g., return on assets or sales growth).

Drawing more precise conclusions based on the results presented here is not warranted in our view as neither the amount of data available nor their quality is sufficient. There is, for example, only one study (Roth et al., 2006) which successfully measured a postulated mediating variable (organizational commitment). Thus, it is not at all clear which processes are really relevant for the observed differences. Moreover, there are only four longitudinal studies available. Interestingly, these studies show quite consistently negative effects of age diversity on team functioning. Finally, even though prior research clearly reveals that some effects of age diversity should only show up if age differences are the basis for the self-definition in teams (following the social identity approach), there have been no recordings of how frequent or salient such differences are within teams (see, however, Schmidt & Wegge, in press, for the presentation of a German scale measuring age salience in teams). In our opinion, all of these limitations are important starting-points for further research activity.

Surprisingly, our literature review also reveals that occupational health is not a topic in age-diversity research. Even though we searched widely through all available media, we found no single study investigating potential links between age diversity and health of employees. Of course, our search was not exhaustive so that it is possible that we missed something here. However, other recent reviewers of the literature have made similar observations (de Lange et al., 2006; Streb et al., 2008). Thus, although health of older employees and potential strategies for the health management of an aging workforce are prominent points in many discussions, research on this issue is scarce, and this is also true when we focus on the link between age diversity and occupational health. Is it possible that there is nothing to discover? Although the potential role of diversity on conflict at work has often been discussed in diversity research (e.g., de Dreu, 2006), the consequences of such conflicts in terms of health problems have rarely been studied. Therefore, we recently started to explore this issue in a new research project.

Age diversity and health

The main goal of the ADIGU project (age heterogeneity of workgroups as a determinant of innovation, group performance, and health) is to analyze the impact of age diversity on measures of work motivation, group performance, and well-being of employees.[1] We reanalyzed available data from a large field study in tax offices (Wegge et al., 2008) and also recently collected new self-reported health data in two other field studies with more than 200 workgroups from public administrations. As this is work in progress, here we present only the basic theoretical assumptions of this project and first findings.

In order to analyze the impact of age diversity on group effectiveness, we rely on the insights from research on group composition that were presented above. Emotional and task conflicts, and communication quality in teams are assessed as potential mediator variables and task complexity, team climate, appreciation of age diversity, and age salience in teams are measured as potential moderator variables. With respect to possible relationships between age diversity and health impairments in teams, we also rely on the theory of Baltes (1997), who describes human development across the life span as a process of selective optimization with compensation (SOC). In other words, successful aging is based on the use of strategies that help the individual to select the most appropriate goals (tasks) that optimize thinking and behavior (energy, time, learning) during goal striving, and that compensate for the potential loss in goal-relevant means (e.g., by increasing effort, time or by the use of external aids). There is considerable empirical evidence to support this formulation. Freund and Baltes (2002) also found that the use of SOC strategies was positively associated with subjective well-being and health. Since complex group decision-making tasks offer much more opportunity to use SOC strategies than simple (routine) group decision-making tasks, it is possible that the health of older workers might also be more positive and stable if they were to work in groups performing complex decision-making tasks that allow for consultation processes within teams. In a similar vein, research on job design has found that high levels of control, skill use and task variety are particularly important for sustaining older workers' health and well-being (Warr, 1997).

Based on these findings, we empirically tested the idea that the relationship between age diversity and health complaints in groups is less positive (attenuated) in groups engaged in complex decision-making tasks than in groups engaged in routine decision-making tasks. This hypothesis was examined using data from 4,597 federal tax employees working in 222 work groups distributed across 111 offices in Germany (Wegge et al., 2008). Age diversity was positively correlated with health complaints but only in the 111 groups working on routine decision-making tasks ($r = 0.21$, $p < 0.01$). As predicted, age diversity was less positively related to self-reported health complaints in complex task groups ($r = -0.07$, n.s.). Thus, in particular, complex tasks might offer opportunities for control, skill utilization and use of SOC strategies that confer a positive, protective function on the subjective health of group members, including older workers.

In our view, this is a very promising finding that deserves more attention in both research and practice as complex task requirements also seem to be a favorable condition for positive effects of age diversity on team performance. Notwithstanding the limitations of the current knowledge on effects of age diversity, we believe that these findings have potentially important implications for practitioners tasked with designing healthy and high-performing teams. In general, these results might suggest that when group task requirements are complex, age diversity confers a positive benefit for performance and self-reported health simultaneously. It remains to be seen whether this assumption can be corroborated in other studies, for other types of tasks and types of teamwork. Nevertheless, the preliminary signs are that designing more-complex group tasks (without severe time pressure) is one promising strategy for the integration of urgently needed older workers in today's organizations. In addition to the various strategies already used in organizations (e.g., interventions focusing on the reduction of age discrimination, the promotion of advanced learning, improving ergonomics for older workers, adaptation of working time, retirement plans and so on, see Roth et al., 2007; Streb et al., 2008), providing more complex group tasks that promote favorable conditions for a successful collaboration of young and old people in teams is promising.

Note

1. See http://www.altersdifferenzierte-arbeitssysteme.de/index.php?option=com_content&task=view&id=2 2&Itemid=.

References

Baltes, P.B. (1997), 'On the incomplete architecture of human ontogeny. Selection, optimization and compensation as foundations of developmental theory', *American Psychologist*, **52**, 366–80.
Bowers, C.A., Pharmer, J.A. & Salas, E. (2000), 'When member homogeneity is needed in work teams: a meta-analysis', *Small Group Research*, **31**, 305–27.
Byrne, D. (1971), *The Attraction Paradigm*, New York: Academic Press.
Cady, S.H. & Valentine, J. (1999), 'Team innovation and perceptions of consideration: what difference does diversity make?', *Small Group Research*, **30**, 730–50.
de Dreu, C.K.W. (2006), 'When too little or too much hurts: evidence for a curvilinear relationship between task conflict and innovation in teams', *Journal of Management*, **32**, 83–107.
de Lange, A., Taris, T.W., Jansen, P.G.W., Smulders, P., Houtman, I.L.D. & Kompier, M.A.J. (2006), 'Age as a factor in the relation between work and mental health: results from the longitudinal TAS survey', in J. Houdmont & S. McIntyre (eds), *Occupational Health Psychology: European Perspectives on Research, Education and Practice*, Vol. 1, Maia, Portugal: ISMAI Publications, pp. 21–45.
Devine, D. & Philips, J.L. (2001), 'Do smarter teams do better: a meta-analysis of cognitive ability and team performance', *Small Group Research*, **32**, 507–32.
Ely, R. (2004), 'A field study of group diversity, participation in diversity education programs, and performance', *Journal of Organizational Behavior*, **25**, 755–80.
Freund, A.M. & Baltes, P.B. (2002), 'Life-management strategies of selection, optimization and compensation: measurement by self-report and construct validity', *Journal of Personality and Social Psychology*, **82**, 642–62.
Gebert, D. (2004), *Innovation durch Teamarbeit*, [*Innovation Through Teamwork: A Critical Analysis*], Stuttgart: Kohlhammer.
Gladstein-Ancona, D.G. & Caldwell, D.F. (1992), 'Demography and design: predictors of new product team performance', *Organization Science*, **3**, 321–41.
Hamilton, B.H., Nickerson, J.A. & Owan, H. (2004), 'Diversity and productivity in production teams', unpublished manuscript, http://www.iza.org/en/webcontent/events/transatlanticpapers_2003/hamilton_nickerson_owan.pdf.
Harrison, D.A., Price, K.H., Gavin, J.H. & Florey, A.T. (2002), 'Time, teams, and task performance: changing effects of surface- and deep-level diversity on group functioning', *Academy of Management Journal*, **45**(5), 1029–45.
Haslam, S.A. (2004), *Psychology in Organizations: The Social Identity Approach*, London: Sage.
Hedge, J.W., Borman, W.C. & Lammlein, S.E. (2006), *The Ageing Workforce. Realities, Myths, and Implications for Organizations*, Washington, DC: American Psychological Association.
Hertel, G. & Scholl, W. (2006), 'Grundlagen kooperativer Arbeit in Gruppen' ['Elements of cooperative work in groups'], in B. Zimolong & U. Konradt (eds), *Enzyklopädie der Psychologie, Ingenieurpsychologie* [*Encyclopedia of Psychology, Engineering Psychology*], Göttingen: Hogrefe, pp. 181–216.
Jackson, S.E., Joshi, A. & Erhardt, N.L. (2003), 'Recent research on team organizational diversity: SWOT-analysis and implications', *Journal of Management*, **29**, 801–30.

Keck, S.L. (1997), 'Top management team structure: differential effects by environmental context', *Organization Science*, **8**, 143–56.

Kerschreiter, R., Mojzisch, A., Schulz-Hardt, S., Brodbeck, F.C. & Frey, D. (2003), 'Informationsaustausch bei Entscheidungsprozessen in Gruppen: Theorie, Empirie und Implikationen für die Praxis' ['Information exchange in decision processes of groups: theory, data and practical implications'], in S. Stumpf & A. Thomas (eds), *Teamarbeit und Teamentwicklung* [*Team Work and Team Development*], Göttingen: Hogrefe, pp. 85–118.

Kichuk, S.L. & Wiesner, W.H. (1998), 'Work teams: selecting members of optimal performance', *Canadian Psychology*, **39**, 23–32.

Kilduff, M., Angelmar, R. & Mehra, A. (2000), 'Top management-team diversity and firm performance: examining the role of cognitions', *Organizational Science*, **11**, 21–34.

Knight, D., Craig, L., Pearce, K., Smith, K.G., Olian, J.D., Sims, H.P., Smith, K.A. & Flood, P. (1999), 'Top management team diversity, group process and strategic consensus', *Strategic Management Journal*, **20**, 445–65.

Leibold, M. & Voelpel, S. (2006), *Managing the Aging Workforce. Challenges and Solutions*, New York: Wiley.

Leonard, J.S. & Levine, D.I. (2002), 'Diversity, discrimination, and performance', mimeo, Haas School of Business, University of California, Berkeley, CA.

Leonard, J.S., Levine, D.I. & Joshi, A. (2004), 'Do birds of a feather shop together? The effects on performance of employees' similarity with one another and with customers', *Journal of Organizational Behavior*, **25**, 731–54.

O'Reilly, C.A., Williams, K.Y. & Barsade, S.G. (1997), 'Group demography and innovation: does diversity help?', in E. Mannix & M. Neale (eds), *Research on Managing Groups and Teams*, Vol. 1, Greenwich, CT: JAI, pp. 183–207.

O'Reilly, C.A., Williams, K.Y. & Barsade, S. (1998), 'Group demography and innovation: does diversity help?', in D. Gruenfield & M.A. Neale (eds), *Research on Managing in Groups and Teams*, Vol. 1, Stamford, CT: JAI, pp. 183–207.

Pelled, L.H., Eisenhardt, K.M. & Xin, K.R. (1999), 'Exploring the black box: an analysis of work group diversity, conflict and performance', *Administrative Science Quarterly*, **44**, 1–28.

Polzer, J.T., Milton, L.P. & Swann, W.B. (2002), 'Capitalizing on diversity: interpersonal congruence in small work groups', *Administrative Science Quarterly*, **47**, 296–324.

Richard, O.C. & Shelor, R.M. (2002), 'Linking top management team age heterogeneity to firm performance: juxtaposing two mid-range theories', *International Journal of Human Resource Management*, **13**, 958–74.

Roth, C., Wegge, J. & Schmidt, K.-H. (2007), 'Konsequenzen des Demographischen Wandels für das Management von Humanressourcen' ['Consequences of demographic changes for the management of human resources'], *Zeitschrift für Personalpsychologie*, **6**, 99–116.

Roth, C., Wegge, J., Schmidt, K.-H. & Neubach, B. (2006), 'Altersheterogenität als Determinante von Leistung in Arbeitsgruppen der öffentlichen Verwaltung' ['Age diversity as a determinant of team performance in a public organization'], *Zeitschrift für Arbeitswissenschaft*, **4**, 266–73.

Schmidt, K.H. & Wegge, J. (in press), 'Altersheterogenität als Determinante von Gruppenleistung und Gesundheit', in N. Schaper, H. Kremer & P. Sloane (eds), *Bildungsperspektiven in alternden Gesellschaften*, Frankfurt: Lang.

Schneider, B. (1987), 'The people make the place', *Personnel Psychology*, **40**, 437–54.

Schneider, B., Smith, D.B. & Paul, M.C. (2001), 'P-E-fit and the attraction–selection–attrition model of organizational functioning: introduction and overview', in M. Erez, U. Kleinbeck & H. Thierry (eds), *Work Motivation in the Context of a Globalizing World*, Mahwah, NJ: Erlbaum, pp. 231–46.

Shemla, M., Wegge, J., Haslam, A., Schmidt, K.-H. & Thies, M. (2007), 'The moderating role of manager tenure on the relationship between group diversity and performance', manuscript in preparation.

Simons, T., Pelled, L.H. & Smith, K.A. (1999), 'Making use of difference: diversity, debate, and decision comprehensiveness in top management teams', *Academy of Management Journal*, **42**, 662–73.

Streb, C.K., Voelpel, S.C. & Leibold, M. (2008), 'Managing the aging workforce: status quo and implications for the advancement of theory and practice', *European Management Journal*, **26**(1): 1–10.

Stumpf, S. & Thomas, A. (2003), *Teamarbeit und Teamentwicklung* [*Teamwork and Team Development*], Göttingen: Hogrefe.

Tajfel, H., & Turner, J.C. (1986), 'The social identity theory of intergroup behaviour', in S. Austin & W.G. Austin (eds), *Psychology of Intergroup Relations*, Chicago, IL: NelsonHall, pp. 7–24.

Timmerman, T.A. (2000), 'Racial diversity, age diversity, interdependence and team performance', *Small Group Research*, **31**, 592–606.

Tsui, A.S., Egan, T.D. & Xin, K.R. (1995), 'Diversity in organizations. Lessons from demography research', in M.M. Chemppers, S. Oskamp & M.A. Costanzo (eds), *Diversity in Organizations: New Perspectives for a Changing Workplace*, London: Sage, pp. 191–219.

van Knippenberg, D., de Dreu, C.K.W. & Homan, A.C. (2004), 'Work group diversity and group performance: an integrative model and research agenda', *Journal of Applied Psychology*, **89**, 1008–22.

Warr, P. (1997), 'Age, work and mental health', in K.W. Schaie & C. Schooler (eds), *The Impact of Work on Older Adults*, New York: Springer, pp. 252–96.

Wegge, J. (2003), 'Heterogenität und Homogenität in Gruppen als Chance und Risiko für die Gruppeneffektivität' ['Heterogeneity and homogeneity in groups as chances and risks for group effectivity'], in S. Stumpf & A. Thomas (eds), *Teamarbeit und Teamentwicklung* [*Teamwork and Team Development*], Göttingen: Hogrefe, pp. 119–41.

Wegge, J., Roth, C., Neubach, B., Schmidt, K.-H. & Kanfer, R. (2008), 'Age and gender diversity as determinants of performance and health in a public organization: the role of task complexity and group size', *Journal of Applied Psychology*.

West, M.A. (2002), 'Sparkling fountains or stagnant ponds: an integrative model of creativity and innovation implementation in work groups', *Applied Psychology: An International Review*, **51**, 355–424.

West, M., Patterson, M., Dawson, J. & Nickell, S. (1999), 'The effectiveness of top management groups in manufacturing organizations', CEP Discussion Papers, Centre for Economic Performance, London School of Economics and Political Science.

Williams, K.Y. & O'Reilly, C.A. (1998), 'Demography and diversity in organizations: a review of 40 years of research', *Research in Organizational Behavior*, **20**, 77–140.

Williams, K., O'Reilly, C.A. & Barsade, S. (1999), 'The impact of relational demography on teamwork: when majorities are in the minority', Research Paper Series, Graduate School of Business, Stanford University.

Zenger, T. & Lawrence, B. (1989), 'Organizational demography: the differential effects of age and tenure distributions on technical communication', *Academy of Management Journal*, **32**, 353–76.

7 Single childfree adults: the work–life stress of an unexpected group*
Wendy J. Casper and Jennifer E. Swanberg

Introduction: Work–life issues of single childfree adults

Recent research suggests that there is increasing diversity in family structures and the personal life responsibilities of today's employees (Rothausen, 1999). A growing and important segment of workers are single adults without dependent children. Single adults make up 42% of the full-time workforce in the United States (Conlin, 2003). This group includes unmarried heterosexual couples who are cohabiting, a group which grew from 523,000 in 1970 to 4 million in 1996 (US Census, 1996), and single adults living alone, estimated at 31.6 million people in the US (Casper & Bryson, 1998). Outside the US, we are also seeing a rise in workers opting out of a traditional family structure. The number of adults choosing to remain childfree is growing dramatically in the European Union (BBC, 2006). In the UK, reporters document growing disquietude at favoritism and supports provided for workers' families and the emergence of the British Childfree Association to advocate for the growing number of workers who are not parents (Goodchild, 2004). In Australia, we have seen the emergence of the World Childfree Association (www.worldchildfree.org) in 2003 to advocate for the concerns of childfree individuals at a global level. The growing increase in workers remaining childfree all over the world has been documented in societies as diverse as Greece, West Germany, Japan, Britain, and Italy (Theil, 2006).

Stress is generally defined as the negative affect and cognitive state related to the occurrence of specific events and/or specific appraisals (Williams & House, 1991; Aneshensel, 1992; Cockerham, 1996). Stress resulting from the interface between work and nonwork roles is an important occupational health issue (Quick & Tetrick, 2003). Substantial research has been conducted through the theoretical perspective of conflict theory (Zedeck & Mosier, 1990; Eby et al., 2005) which asserts that managing multiple roles is stressful because 'role pressures from work and [nonwork] domains are mutually incompatible in some respect' (Greenhaus & Beutell, 1985, p. 77). Research documents numerous deleterious outcomes associated with work–nonwork role stress such as lower job attitudes and increased levels of psychological strain, stress-related physical health concerns, depression, alcohol abuse, and burnout (Kossek & Ozeki, 1998; Allen et al., 2000). However, research exploring the interface between work and nonwork has examined family as the nonwork domain almost exclusively, where family is defined as the presence of a spouse or cohabiting partner and/or dependent children (Young 1996, 1999), and samples used in this research tend to include predominantly married employees with children (Casper et al., 2007). However, given the growing population of single childfree workers around the globe, understanding the stresses these workers experience in managing work and nonwork is important. The current study adopts the perspective of conflict theory to explore how work and nonwork create stress and strain for single childfree employees. Rather than focusing the nonwork domain on family, we define the nonwork domain to include any and all roles that are unrelated to work in paid employment.

Anecdotal accounts in the popular press reveal a variety of stresses encountered by single workers when they are left out of organizations' support programs for children and families. Some accounts suggest that single childfree workers are faced with greater work demands and increased work stress because of the organizational supports provided to their co-workers' families. Specifically, assertions abound that single workers are expected to pick up additional work responsibilities when employees with families need time away from work since their nonwork responsibilities are perceived as less important than those of parents (Scott, 2001). Other accounts suggest that more desirable assignments and clients are given to married employees since they are perceived to have greater financial needs (McCafferty, 2001). Finally, others argue that organizations fail to see that the work stress of some single workers leaves them so exhausted that they do not have time or energy to invest in building the kind of social relationships that they need for support (Bruzzese, 1999). Work stress is a concern for employers given that job burnout can result from such chronic stress, and research suggests that employees with burnout have higher absenteeism and turnover and lower commitment to their organizations (Shirom, 2003) as well as poorer performance and increased levels of accidents and counterproductive work behaviors (Westman & Eden, 1997). Work stress also has important implications for medicine and public health, given that workers with high levels of chronic stress are more susceptible to a variety of health problems including cardiovascular disease, gastrointestinal problems, respiratory disorders, emotional exhaustion, depression, burnout, and violence (Cohen, 1996; Dancey et al., 1998; Epstein, 1998; Landsbergis et al., 2003; Galinsky et al., 2005; Halpern, 2005; Thompson et al., 2005).

Although most of the research examining the link between work and personal life focuses on parents and dual-earner couples, a few prior empirical studies have examined the work–life issues of single adults without dependent children (Young, 1996, 1999). These suggest that these individuals do grapple with work–life issues, such as a tendency to become overly involved in work to compensate for loneliness and isolation, dealing with negative reactions from co-workers about their single status, and discrimination with respect to how seriously their personal needs are taken by their employers. Specific stresses encountered by single adults without dependent children include the requirement to work more hours, the expectations to 'pick up the slack' when co-workers are out of work for family-related reasons, and stress due to resentment about employee benefits programs with greater subsidies and benefits for employees' families (Young, 1999).

Building on conjecture in the popular press (Lafayette, 1994; Murray, 1996; Picard, 1997; Bruzzese, 1999; McCafferty, 2001) and a small amount of past research (Young, 1996, 1999), this study explores the stresses associated with work–life issues among single adults without dependent children. Data were collected by phone interviews, transcribed, and content analyzed. The data collection and content analysis procedures are described in the next section, followed by a discussion of research findings.

Method

Participants
Phone interviews were conducted with 37 single adults without dependent children under the age of 18 living at home. To meet the criteria to participate, singles could be never married, divorced, separated or widowed, could not have children under the age of 18 living at home, and had to work full-time in paid employment. A total of 13 males and 24 females participated in the study, ranging in age from 25 to 59, with a mean age of 37.9 years. All participants identified themselves as heterosexual and 59% were currently not in a dating relationship. Almost half (49%) of participants had never been married, although a substantial portion (38%) were also divorced. Participants were involved in a wide range of different occupations. Some 70% were in managerial or professional jobs, and 68% of participants were employed by a private sector organization.

Participant recruitment began with the snowball recruitment method in which individuals familiar to the researchers were contacted and asked to participate. During this process, a reporter at the local newspaper became aware of the study and wrote an article on the study and topic, which facilitated additional recruitment of participants. In the end, 67% of participants were recruited through this newspaper article and the other 33% were recruited via snowball sampling. All participants lived within the continental United States, with the majority living in northeastern Oklahoma.

Procedures
A semi-structured interview was used to collect the data. The interview protocol was developed by the principal investigator with input from several other researchers. The questions on the protocol were open-ended and included probes to follow up for additional information. Interview questions that form the basis of the data used for this chapter are provided in Appendix 7A. Four graduate students pursuing a Masters or PhD degree in industrial/organizational psychology conducted the interviews after receiving interview training by the principal investigator. Interviews were audio taped and ranged in length from 20 to 70 minutes long. After interviews were completed, they were transcribed and content analyzed.

Coding scheme development
The coding scheme was developed by two researchers with expertise in the work–life literature who were blind to the purpose of the study. These researchers reviewed the data independently and developed coding schemes that they felt would best classify the data and account for the important underlying themes. Next, these two researchers worked together to combine their coding schemes into a single scheme that could be used for content analysis. The final coding scheme was reviewed by the principal investigator, who also had expertise in the work–life literature, and final changes were made in conjunction with the other two work–life experts.

Coding the data
After the coding scheme was finalized, four different graduate students in industrial/organizational psychology were trained in coding data by the principal investigator who was experienced in content analysis. After going through the coding scheme with the

coders, and clarifying points of confusion, the principal investigator and the four graduate researchers independently coded three distinct interviews. Interviews were chosen
that varied in terms of content and tone. After coding each interview independently, the
five researchers met, discussed their ratings, and reached a consensus regarding the 'best'
rating in each case. The coding scheme was clarified and revised as necessary in an iterative process. After conducting this process on three distinct interviews, the five researchers
seemed to be applying the coding scheme in a consistent manner and yielding agreement
in their ratings at least 85% of the time. At this point, the four graduate students were
divided into pairs of two coders to code the rest of the interviews. After conducting independent coding of each interview, the graduate students continued to generate consensus
regarding any rating discrepancies. Overall, coder agreement was high at 85%.

Results

After content analyses were completed, frequencies were run on themes that emerged
from the data. Results revealed a variety of stresses that were reported by single childfree
adults in managing their work and nonwork roles. One of the most common themes
that emerged was a perception of participants that as single people they were subject to
different expectations at work from workers with families. In total, 62% of participants
provided examples of ways in which they felt that they were treated differently from their
co-workers with families. Examples of some of the situations encountered by these single
workers are described by the two participants below:

> It is totally different for those who are single and those who have kids. If a coworker has to miss
> work because they have to take their child to the dentist, that is ok. But, if I have to miss work
> to take my dog to the vet, that is a totally different story. . . . As long as people have children,
> a husband, or family group (a nucleus) there is a lot more tolerance for breaks in the routine.
> When you don't have children or a husband or wife, people assume what's the deal. (55-year-
> old divorced female)

> I have worked in places in the past where if people had children it was ok for them to take off
> to pick up a child or things like that and they weren't required to take personal time off for
> this. This was really the only excuse accepted for being able to leave work early. (43-year-old
> divorced female)

When interviewees were probed to gather more information about the nature of this
differential treatment, several themes emerged. The percentage of participants whose
comments revealed these themes are reported in Table 7.1.

Some 30% of participants described some kind of double standard regarding work
expectations for single and married workers. This double standard was described as
resulting in expectations for single workers to put in longer hours, to volunteer for additional work, and to assume a variety of work activities that were not expected of their
co-workers with spouses and children. This theme was prevalent among both men and
women of varied ages:

> At [my employer's] employee association people ask me to volunteer for more than one event
> because I am single. They think I have nothing else to do, they think I can take off any time I
> want, I tend to resent these remarks, they will make me the chairman of things because I don't
> have kids. (57-year-old divorced male)

Table 7.1   *Examples of supportive and unsupportive actions of organizations with regard to work–life issues for single workers and married workers*

	Supportive incidents	Unsupportive incidents
Singles	Family responsibilities (32%)	Family crises (14%)
	Special events (22%)	Family special events (11%)
	Need time off (24%)	Education (3%)
	Education related (3%)	Social activities/hobbies (16%)
		Long hours (11%)
Married	Daily childcare (38%)	Inflexible maternity leave (3%)
	Personal illness (8%)	Always support married workers (78%)
	Family responsibilities (62%)	

It is assumed that if someone needs to stay late that since I don't have a husband and children that I can stay late because other accountants have to go pick up their children at day care, they have husband to attend to. It is assumed that I am the one that is gonna stay. This is not fair! (33-year-old never married female)

Another common theme that emerged was that single workers felt that their personal concerns were underappreciated and their free time was undervalued compared to their co-workers with spouses and children. Some 35% of participants reported that at their workplaces single people without children were perceived as though they did not have important responsibilities outside of work. Again, comments pertaining to this theme were reported by both men and women, and by participants of varying ages:

I had a mother that was dying and I needed to take her to a friends' funeral and I was told how quickly could I get back to the point where I had to get someone else to take her home from the funeral. Well that was in '97, that's just the kind of subtle pressure you get, not to take the time you need. (59-year-old divorced female)

I am a tutor for after school center, and my boss knows I have to leave at a certain time to make it. I think my boss forgets that I have to go, but he ended up calling me in to talk about a certain issue and he made me miss the tutoring session. (35-year-old never married male)

Recently, one of my dogs died and since I didn't have anybody to help me bury him I requested a day off in the middle of the week to take care of matters and to grieve. I understand there are rules, but I kinda put them to the test, they said they could not give me a death in the family day, so I took a day of vacation. I didn't think that I would have to consume a vacation day. If people lose a spouse they can take a bereavement day and it won't be argued. But I am probably more bereaved about my dog than many people are about their spouse. They challenged me and I did not pursue it. I felt it was not very forward thinking. (55-year-old divorced female)

This generalized perception that many single workers reported that their roles and responsibilities outside of work were not taken seriously by their employers is particularly interesting when contrasted with data on the actual personal responsibilities of these single workers. Study participants reported a vast array of responsibilities to other people with whom they had personal relationships such as extended family members (e.g., parents, siblings), friends, dating partners, members of their church communities, and even an exchange student. Specifically, 65% of the participants were providing some kind of financial assistance to family or friends and 24% were providing some kind of direct caregiving to family or friends. Responsibilities to pets were very common, with 57% reporting having and caring for pets in the home.

Finally, some single workers reported stress due to grappling with the degree to which 'married with children' is perceived as normative in the workplace. Participants reported negative perceptions of those that are single without children and a feeling of being stigmatized and/or socially ostracized from co-workers. Some 19% of participants reported feeling stigmatized because of their single identity and 16% reported that married workers were perceived to be more stable and mature than singles. Several single workers reported stress because they felt that people in their organizations thought that there is something wrong with them because they were single. Specific examples included social pressures to be married, assumptions about their sexual orientation, or social exclusion from work social events that are designed for employees' families. Participants sometimes reported that this subtle social exclusion from work events influenced their well-being and comfort in the workplace. These comments were prevalent among both men and women, both never married and divorced:

> It is funny . . . if you are single you are gay. It is like a big joke around the office. If you are single and don't have a boyfriend, girlfriend or significant other, you are gay. It is just a joke around the office. (28-year-old never married female)

> I don't think they [singles] are looked upon poorly, but I do notice a lot of people, if we have a picnic or Christmas party, if I don't have a girl with me I think they think something is wrong, they are always trying to set me up. It is really just my co-workers, not the management. Everything the company does outside of work is really set up for couples and families. (32-year-old never married male)

> Most people tend to think that the natural state of people is coupled with someone. There are a couple of events a year that are really for married people – like Easter and picnics. I mean a single person is not going to find Easter eggs, it is all for the children and the couples. (55-year-old divorced female)

It is also notable that although specific questions were not asked about the employees' supervisors, many participants appeared to attribute the support they did or did not receive to specific supervisors rather than to the organization at large. This highlights the important role of supervisors in aiding (or thwarting) employees' work–life balance. This is notable in the response of the following participant who, when asked about perceptions of her organization, provided a response which focused on her supervisor's actions and beliefs:

> Interviewer: Do you feel your nonwork responsibilities are perceived similarly to or differently from employees with families?

> Participant: When it comes to family it's similar. Other times I think for me personally I think I have to be more cautious. My previous supervisor I think she did recognize it as similar. If there was something nonwork related that I wanted to do that was important to me she would understand that and be flexible about making arrangements if I needed to change my schedule. (37-year-old never married female)

*Table 7.2   Percentage of supervisors described as supportive and unsupportive of singles'
and married workers' work–life issues*

	Supportive supervisors mentioned (%)	Unsupportive supervisors mentioned (%)
Singles	32	8
Married	41	5

As can be seen in Table 7.2, the frequency data suggests a perceived tendency for super-visors to be more supportive of nonwork issues among married workers. Specifically, although 32% of participants described supervisor actions that were supportive of singles' nonwork issues, 41% described supervisor actions that supported workers with families. Moreover, whereas 8% mentioned unsupportive actions of supervisors toward singles, only 5% discussed a lack of support for married workers.

Finally, in addition to coding individual questions, the entire interviews were coded for the emotional tone conveyed by participants regarding their treatment as a single worker. Participants in 22% of the interviews were classified as reacting to their treatment as a single in an angry or resentful manner.

Discussion

Overall study findings suggest that single working adults without dependent children experience a variety of stresses associated with managing their jobs and their nonwork roles. Specific sources of stress identified included differential treatment and stigmatiza-tion, providing care for others (financial and instrumental), and a lack of support for their nonwork responsibilities. Moreover, participants identified supervisors as playing a critical role in determining the level of support they did or did not receive. In the subsec-tion that follows, we discuss each of these themes in turn and highlight the implications for employee health and wellness as well as for organizations.

Differential treatment and stigmatization

With respect to differential treatment and stigmatization, participants in the interviews repeatedly reported a sense that they were perceived and treated differently from their co-workers with spouses and/or children. Moreover, they characterized this treatment as unfavorable in numerous respects. Specifically, participants often perceived that they were subject to discriminatory behavior with respect to work expectations and stigma-tization due to their single identity. Organizational research has explored discrimina-tion toward a variety of groups in the past including women (Trentham & Larwood, 1998), racial minorities (Dovidio & Gaertner, 2000), workers with disabilities (Dalgin & Gilbride, 2003), and homosexual workers (Horvath & Ryan, 2003). Recent studies suggest that much of today's discrimination at work is subtle and thus, may sometimes be perceived as unimportant by business leaders (Trentham & Larwood, 1998; Brief et al., 2000; Dovidio & Gaertner, 2000). For example, studies have found that race discrimination occurs only under situations in which qualifications are ambiguous (Dovidio & Gaertner, 2000) or in which a business-related reason for discrimination is cited by an authority figure (Brief et al., 2000). Similarly, sex discrimination may also occur more often under conditions in which it was believed to be desirable from a business perspective (Trentham & Larwood, 1998). Interestingly, the discriminatory behavior reported by single adults in this study was also of a more subtle variety. For example, participants reported that their personal needs were overlooked, that social events at their organizations were organized around couples and families, and that they were asked to work late more often than workers with families. However, none of the participants reported more overt forms of discrimination such as differences in pay or promotion opportunities.

It is important to note that the findings reported in this study are based on data collected from working singles, and represent their perception of such discrimination at work. Thus, it is not possible to discern whether the organizations in this study intended to discriminate against single workers or were aware that this perception existed. However, the mere perception of discrimination may have important consequences for the health of individual employees and for their organizations (Rumbaut, 1994; Elmslie & Sedo, 1996; Swim & Stangor, 1998; Meyer, 2003).

Both theory and empirical research suggest that perceiving that one is experiencing discrimination can damage self-esteem. For instance, if single workers perceive discrimination as rejection by their organization or colleagues, the 'looking-glass' approach to the self (Mead, 1934; Cooley, 1956) suggests that they may accept this negative evaluation and have lower self-esteem. Similarly, self-efficacy theory asserts that because self-esteem is built by having a sense of control over one's environment (White, 1959; Bandura, 1997), the helplessness accompanied by discrimination reduces feelings of control and harms self-esteem. Research finds that individuals who experience discrimination at work often have negative psychological outcomes (Elmslie & Sedo, 1996). For example, ethnic discrimination has been found to correlate with depressive symptoms and lower self-esteem (Rumbaut, 1994).

Several theoretical positions also suggest that perceptions of being discriminated against can increase employee stress levels. Meyer (2003) describes minority stress, which is stress that subordinate groups encounter from social settings due to their social status. Single workers may face such minority stress if they work in organizational environments where having a family is normative and they are stigmatized for their single identity. Symbolic interaction theory also suggests that negative evaluations from others leads to negative evaluations of self (Blumer, 1986). Therefore, negative perceptions of single workers (i.e., singles are less mature, there is something wrong with workers because they are single) can lead to stress for single workers who evaluate themselves negatively because of it. Research on race- and sex-based stigmatization finds that members of stigmatized groups internalize this stigma which enhances their stress levels (Swim & Stangor, 1998).

Caregiving demands
One surprising finding was the degree to which single adults without dependent children were engaged in providing both instrumental care and financial support for others in their lives. Although participants, by definition, did not have childcare concerns, many of them were caring for others, which often referred to eldercare. Child- and eldercare differ in important ways that are relevant to the health and wellness of caregivers. Over time, caring for elders becomes more demanding, until the caregiving ends in death, whereas caring for a child ends in the positive experience of the child's increasing independence (Kossek et al., 2001). Moreover, the intensity of the demands of providing eldercare is

often unpredictable, whereas children move through predictable developmental milestones (Swanberg et al., 2006). For instance, an aging relative may need 24-hour care, seven days a week after surgery or during treatment for cancer. Upon recovery, care may no longer be needed. Because of this, providing eldercare is often more difficult and stressful than providing childcare (Braithwaite, 1992). In fact, research finds that those managing eldercare have increased depression and anxiety and poor health outcomes (George & Gwyther, 1986; Strawbridge et al., 1997). Moreover, as the level of involvement in eldercare increases, caregivers exhibit increased levels of psychological strain (Barling et al., 1994) and lower levels of emotional health (Lee et al., 2001). Thus, the nature of the caregiving tasks that single adults without dependent children engage in are those that may be more stressful and difficult than those of their co-workers caring for children.

In addition to providing eldercare, singles may also provide other forms of care to family members and friends that may go unrecognized by colleagues at work. For instance, providing care to family members or friends with cancer contributes to stress among single workers (Swanberg, 2006). Stress levels were even greater among employees who experienced co-workers and supervisors as not supportive of their caregiving responsibilities compared to employees with social support networks at work. Moreover, workplace policies such as the Family and Medical Leave do not recognize singles' friends or dating partners as 'family' and as a result, singles may have to exhaust personal and vacation leave to care for loved ones who are ill, placing additional burdens on single workers.

Supportiveness of employee personal concerns
Finally, single adults in this study consistently reported stress associated with their sense that their personal concerns and responsibilities were not appreciated as important in the same way that the concerns of their colleagues with families were appreciated. Given that caregiving, which often reflected eldercare, was one important responsibility of a substantial number of participants, it is notable that eldercare has not yet received the attention and social support that has been afforded to childcare (Sizemore & Jones, 1990; Wagner & Hunt, 1994). Participants also reported a lack of supportiveness of their organizations with respect to a variety of nonwork concerns. This finding has important implications for employee wellness. Social support has been well-documented as a buffer to the stressor–strain relationship such that employees with social support can handle higher degrees of stress without resulting strain (LaRocco & Jones, 1978; LaRocco et al., 1980; Karasek et al., 1982). If single workers find that their organizations are not supportive of their work–nonwork stresses, it is more likely that this stress will result in deleterious consequences to employee wellness as well as to the organization.

One critical factor affecting employee perceptions of organizational support is the employee's supervisor. Results of the qualitative analysis indicated that when workers discussed support (or lack of it) from their organization, they often referred to their supervisors as the source. This is consistent with the organizational support literature which finds that employees often view actions of their supervisors as indications of organizational support or lack thereof (Levinson, 1965; Eisenberger et al., 1986). Many study participants perceived their supervisors to be more supportive of employees with families than of single workers. Given that perceived supervisor support is related to higher job satisfaction (Griffin et al., 2001) and lower turnover (Eisenberger et al., 2002), organizations have good reason to encourage supervisors to support all employees' nonwork needs, regardless of their personal situations. Supervisor support also has important implications for employee wellness, given research findings that employees with more supervisor support exhibit lower levels of mental strain and that this supervisor support also buffers the stressor–mental strain relationship (Karasek et al., 1982; Perrucci et al., 2007; Breaugh & Frye, 2007).

Limitations and directions for future research

Although this study makes an important contribution by investigating work–nonwork stress among an understudied population, limitations exist to be addressed in future studies. Given the dearth of research on work–nonwork issues among single workers, this study was qualitative and exploratory in nature. Thus, future hypothesis testing studies examining a larger and more generalizable sample are warranted. Moreover, since convenience sampling procedures were used, future research should use more rigorous sampling procedures and seek more diverse samples, including examining workers from outside of North America. Future studies might examine how varying levels of work–nonwork stress relate to strain outcomes such as mental wellness, physical health ailments, burnout, and job attitudes. Such studies are clearly the next step and would provide additional evidence for the contention that work–nonwork role conflict is an important stressor among single adults without dependent children.

Conclusions

In short, this study suggests that single adults without dependent children do indeed experience a variety of stresses at work due to managing their work–nonwork interface and their single identity at work. Given the growing number of workers who fall into this demographic group, the stresses of this group could represent a major public health issue if supports are not provided to help them cope with this stress. Organizations that are successful in providing the support that single workers need to handle their concerns outside of work should benefit by facilitating the health and productivity of this segment of their workforce.

Note

* An earlier version of this chapter was presented at the 2003 Academy of Management conference in Seattle, WA.

References

Allen, T.D., Herst, D.E.L., Bruck, C.S. & Sutton, M. (2000), 'Consequences associated with work-to-family conflict: a review and agenda for future research', *Journal of Occupational Health Psychology*, **5**, 278–308.
Aneshensel, C. (1992), 'Social stress: theory and research', *Annual Review of Sociology*, **15**, 18–38.
Bandura, A. (1997), *Self-efficacy: The Exercise of Control*, New York: Freeman.
Barling, J., MacEwen, K.E., Kelloway, E.K. & Higginbottom, S.F. (1994), 'Predictors and outcomes of elder-care-based interrole conflict', *Psychology and Aging*, **9**, 391–7.
BBC News (2006), 'The rise of the "childfree"', March 31, http://news.bbc.co.uk/go/pr/fr/-/1/hi/world/Europe/4813590.stm, accessed July 2006.
Blumer, H. (1986), *Symbolic Interactionism: Perspective and Method*, Berkeley, CA: University of California Press.
Braithwaite, V. (1992), 'Caregiving burden: making the concept scientifically useful and relevant', *Research on Aging*, **14**, 3–27.

Breaugh, J.A. & Frye, N.K. (2007), 'An examination of the antecedents and consequences of the use of family-friendly benefits', *Journal of Managerial Issues*, **19**, 35–52.

Brief, A.P., Dietz, J., Cohen, R.R., Pugh, S.D. & Vaslow, J.B. (2000), 'Just doing business: modern racism and obedience to authority as explanations for employment discrimination', *Organizational Behavior and Human Decision Processes*, **81**, 72–97.

Bruzzese, A. (1999), 'Employers can overlook single workers' needs', *The Des Moines Register*, February 7.

Casper, L.M. & Bryson, K. (1998), *Current Population Reports: Population Characteristics*, Washington, DC: US Department of Commerce, Economic and Statistics Administration, March.

Casper, W.J., Eby, L.T., Bordeaux, C., Lockwood, A. & Lambert, D. (2007), 'A review of research methods in IO/OB work–family research', *Journal of Applied Psychology*, **92**, 28–43.

Cockerham, W.C. (1996), *Sociology of Mental Disorder*, Englewood Cliffs, NJ: Prentice-Hall.

Cohen, S. (1996), 'Psychological stress, immunity, and upper respiratory infections', *Current Directions in Psychological Science*, **5**, 86–90.

Conlin, M. (2003), 'Unmarried America: say good-bye to the traditional family. Here's how the new demographics will change business and society', *Business Week*, October 20.

Cooley, C.H. (1956), *Human Nature and the Social Order*, New York: Free Press.

Dalgin, R.S. & Gilbride, D. (2003), 'Perspectives of people with psychiatric disabilities on employment disclosure', *Psychiatric Rehabilitation Journal*, **26**, 306–11.

Dancey, C., Thagavi, M. & Fox, R. (1998), 'The relationship between daily stress and symptoms of irritable bowel syndrome', *Journal of Psychosomatic Research*, **44**, 537–45.

Dovidio, J.F. & Gaertner, S.L. (2000), 'Aversive racism and selection decisions: 1989 and 1999', *Psychological Science*, **11**, 315–19.

Eby, L.T., Casper, W.J., Lockwood, A., Bordeaux, C. & Brinley, A. (2005), 'A twenty-year retrospective on work and family research in IO/OB: a review of the literature', *Journal of Vocational Behavior*, **66**, 124–97.

Eisenberger, R., Huntington, R., Hutchison, S. & Sowa, D. (1986), 'Perceived organizational support', *Journal of Applied Psychology*, **71**, 500–507.

Eisenberger, R., Stinglhamber, F., Vandenberghe, C., Sucharski, I.L. & Rhoades, L. (2002), 'Perceived supervisor support: contributions to perceived organizational support and employee retention', *Journal of Applied Psychology*, **87**, 565–73.

Elmslie, B. & Sedo, S. (1996), 'Persistent consequences of initial discrimination: young black workers in the 1960s', *Review of Black Political Economy*, **24**, 97–113.

Epstein, H. (1998), 'Life and death on the social ladder', *New York Review of Books*, July.

Galinsky, E., Bond, J.T., Kim, S.S., Backon, L., Brownfield, E. & Sakai, K. (2005), *Over Work in America: When the Way We Work Becomes Too Much. Executive Summary*, New York: Families and Work Institute.

George, L.K. & Gwyther, L.P. (1986), 'Caregiver well-being: a multidimensional examination of family caregivers of demented adults', *Gerontologist*, **26**, 253–9.

Goodchild, S. (2004), 'Don't call us childless, call us child-free: the Bridget Jones', *The Independent on Sunday*, November 7.

Greenhaus, J.H. & Beutell, N.J. (1985), 'Sources and conflict between work and family roles', *Academy of Management Review*, **1**, 76–88.

Griffin, M.A., Patterson, M.G. & West, M.A. (2001), 'Job satisfaction and teamwork: the role of supervisor support', *Journal of Organizational Behavior*, **22**, 537–50.

Halpern, D.F. (2005), 'How time-flexible work policies can reduce stress, improve health, and save money', *Stress and Health*, **21**, 157–68.

Horvath, M. & Ryan, A.M. (2003), 'Antecedents and potential moderators of the relationship between attitudes and hiring discrimination on the basis of sexual orientation', *Sex Roles*, **48**, 115–30.

Karasek, R.A., Triantis, K.P. & Chaudhry, S.S. (1982), 'Coworker and supervisor support as moderators of associations between task characteristics and mental strain', *Journal of Occupational Behaviour*, **3**, 181–200.

Kossek, E.E., Colquitt, J.A. & Noe, R.A. (2001), 'Caregiving decisions, well-being, and performance: the effects of place and provider as a function of dependent type and work–family climates', *Academy of Management Journal*, **44**, 29–44.

Kossek, E.E. & Ozeki, C. (1998), 'Work–family conflict, policies, and the job–life satisfaction relationship: a review and directions for future organizational behavior human resources research', *Journal of Applied Psychology*, **83**, 139–49.

Lafayette, L. (1994), 'Fair play for the childless worker', *The New York Times*, October 16.

Landsbergis, P.A., Schnall, P.L., Belic, K.L., Baker, D., Schwarts, J.E. & Pickering, T.G. (2003), 'The workplace and cardiovascular disease: relevance and potential role for occupational health psychology', in Quick & Tetrick (eds), pp. 265–87.

LaRocco, J.M., House, J.S. & French, J.R.P. (1980), 'Social support, occupational stress, and health', *Journal of Health and Social Behavior*, **21**, 202–16.

LaRocco, J.M. & Jones, A.P. (1978), 'Coworker and leader support as moderators of stressor–strain relationships in work situations', *Journal of Applied Psychology*, **63**, 609–14.

Lee, J.A., Walker, M. & Shoup, R. (2001), 'Balancing elder care responsibilities and work: the impact on emotional health', *Journal of Business and Psychology*, **16**, 277–89.

Levinson, H. (1965), 'Reciprocation: the relationship between man and organization', *Administrative Science Quarterly*, **9**, 370–90.

McCafferty, D. (2001), 'Singles discrimination: are unmarried workers fighting an uphill battle?', http://content.careers.msn.com/WorkingLife/Workplace/gwp1070125.asp, accessed July 2003.

Mead, G.H. (1934), *Mind, Self, and Society*, Chicago, IL: University of Chicago Press.

Meyer, I.H. (2003), 'Prejudice, social stress, and mental health in lesbian, gay, and bisexual populations: conceptual issues and research evidence', *Psychological Bulletin*, **129**, 674–97.

Murray, K. (1996), 'The childless feel left out when parents get a lift', *The New York Times*, December 1.

Perrucci, R., MacDermid, S., King, E., Chiung-Ya, T., Brimeyer, T., Ramadoss, K., Kiser, S.J. & Swanberg, J. (2007), 'The significance of shift work: current status and future directions', *Journal of Family and Economic Issues*, **28**, 600–617.

Picard, M. (1997), 'No kids? Get back to work!', *Training*, **34**, 33–7.

Quick, J.C. & Tetrick, L.E. (2003), *Handbook of Occupational Health Psychology*, Washington, DC: American Psychological Association.

Rothausen, T. (1999), '"Family" in organizational research: a review and comparison of definitions and measures', *Journal of Organizational Behavior*, **20**, 817–36.

Rumbaut, R.G. (1994), 'The crucible within: ethnic identity, self-esteem, and segmented assimilation among children of immigrants', *International Migration Review*, **28**, 748–94.

Scott, M.P. (2001), 'Singling out singles: structuring employee services to accommodate the dating game', Employee Services Management Association: In The News, http://www.esmassn.org/news/indexsingles.htm, accessed July 2003.

Shirom, A. (2003), 'Job-related burnout: a review', in Quick & Tetrick (eds), pp. 245–64.

Sizemore, M.T. & Jones, A.B. (1990), 'Eldercare and the workplace: short-term training preferences of employees', *Educational Gerontology*, **16**, 97–104.

Strawbridge, W.J., Wallagen, M., Shema, S. & Kaplan, G. (1997), 'New burdens or more of the same? Comparing grandparent, spouse, and adult–child caregivers', *Gerontologist*, **37**, 505–10.

Swanberg, J. (2006), 'Making it work: informal caregiving, cancer and employment', *Journal of Psychosocial Oncology*, **24**, 1–18.

Swanberg, J., Kantazar, T., Mendiondo, M. & McCoskey, M. (2006), 'Caring for our elders: a contemporary conundrum for working people', *Families in Society*, **87**, 417–26.

Swim, J.K. & Stangor, C. (eds) (1998), *Prejudice: The Target's Perspective*, San Diego, CA: Academic Press.

Theil, S. (2006), 'Beyond babies; even in once conservative societies, more and more couples are choosing not to have kids. That means good things for restaurants and real estate. But a backlash has already begun', *Newsweek*, September 4.

Thompson, B.M., Kirk, A. & Brown, D.F. (2005), 'Work based support, emotional exhaustion, and spillover to the family environment: a study of policewomen', *Stress and Health*, **21**, 199–207.

Trentham, S. & Larwood, L. (1998), 'Gender discrimination and the workplace: an examination of rational bias theory', *Sex Roles*, **38**, 1–28.

US Census Bureau (1996), *United States Department of Commerce News*, http://www.census.gov/www/socdemo/hh-fam.html, accessed July 2003.

Wagner, D.L. & Hunt, G.G. (1994), 'The use of workplace eldercare programs by employed caregivers', *Research on Aging*, **16**, 69–84.

Westman, M. & Eden, D. (1997), 'Effects of a respite from work on burnout: vacation relief and fade-out', *Journal of Applied Psychology*, **82**, 516–27.

White, R.W. (1959), 'Motivation reconsidered: the concept of competence', *Psychological Review*, **36**, 953–62.

Williams, D.R. & House, J.S. (1991), 'Stress, social support, control and coping: a social epidemiologic view', in B. Badura & I. Kicksbusch (eds), *Health Promotion Research: Towards a New Social Psychology*, WHO regional publications, Europeans series, No. 37, Copenhagen: World Health Organization.

Young, M. (1996), 'Career issues for single adults without dependent children', in D.T. Hall (ed.), *The Career is Dead – Long Live the Career: A Relational Approach to Careers*, San Francisco, CA: Jossey-Bass, pp. 196–219.

Young, M. (1999), 'Work–family backlash: begging the question, what's fair?', *Annals of the American Academy of Political and Social Science*, **562**, 32–46.

Zedeck, S. & Mosier, K. (1990), 'Work in the family and employing organization', *American Psychologist*, **45**, 240–51.

Appendix 7A   Questions used in this research study

1. Do you feel your personal life is taken seriously by your employer? Probes: Why do you think this? Can you provide an example?
2. Do you think your employer recognizes your nonwork responsibilities as valid and important? Probes: Why do you think this? Can you provide an example?
3. Do you feel your nonwork responsibilities are perceived similarly to or differently from employees with families? If different, how?
4. Describe a situation at work in which you felt an organization you worked for was particularly supportive of your personal or nonwork needs.
5. Describe a situation at work in which you felt an organization you worked for was particularly unsupportive of your personal or nonwork needs.
6. Describe a situation at work in which you felt an organization you worked for was particularly supportive of a married co-worker's family needs.
7. Describe a situation at work in which you felt an organization you worked for was particularly unsupportive of a married co-worker's family needs.

8 Russian managers and doctors' indexes of latent motivation associated with social frustration
Vladimirn Kuznetsov

Introduction

Studies of motivation and frustration do not take language and cultural peculiarities into account. This is a comparative cross-sectional study aimed at researching the personal and motivational peculiarities of 102 managers and 99 doctors living in the Russian North, associated with frustration. The study found differences in the semantic field, which correlated with frustration indexes; for example, doctors and managers have different relationships between semantic field indexes and frustration level; doctors use feelings of discomfort to check many situations and are more focused on the inner world in comparison with managers. These findings require further research among other occupational groups.

Background

The development of the modern economic situation in Russia had both positive and negative consequences for human life. In spite of the fact that the number of poor people is decreasing by 5–6 million per year, the mortality level of those able to work is now increasing at a much faster rate than that of the whole population (Velichkovskii, 2005). The number of cases of disability is growing by 5% and the number of disability days by 1% per year. Mental health disorders morbidity has increased by 7.5% during the last two decades. Some 40% of the disability costs are related to a poor work environment (Trumel, 2002).

Typically, patients of 'standard' outpatient clinics are those aged 40–49 years (25.3%) and 20–29 years (24.1%), university graduates (57.8%) and those with chronic diseases (54.9%). The total percentage of people aged 60 and 20 is only 8.0% (Babenko et al., 2005).

Social stress is becoming an epidemic. The mortality rate of people able to work is higher than that in vulnerable groups of people (children and pensioners) in a situation of social stress. The main reason for social stress is specific – the loss of motivation to work (Velichkovskii, 2005).

The social and economic situation in Russia is changing dramatically, the level of emotional and informational pressure is increasing, and the competition is becoming very tough. People need more certainty about moral rules in society and more confidence in their abilities (Bandura, 1989), especially in their professional activities (Roginskaya, 2002). In Russia the situation is very specific because of a lack of definite rules in the labor market. Russian business is totally different from that in the West; what is seen as 'business' in Russia is sometimes a crime in the USA (Tretyakova et al., 2001).

The major burden rests with managers, because they have to organize other people's work. Managers' responsibilities differ from those in any other kind of occupation. They are constantly put under emotional and informational pressure.

These facts put managers' health increasingly at risk. Managers' duties are characterized by high intensity, diverse activities, numerous interpersonal contacts and oral communication with other people, which is why the study of frustration factors and managers' motivation is very important in terms of forecasting risks of diseases and health improvement (Gerchikova, 1995; Bobrovnikov, 2003; Bursak, 2005).

As an integral part of the country's economy, the Russian healthcare system is also in a state of flux. Charging for medicines is an emerging feature in the market. On the one hand, it is necessary to clarify the character of stress caused by diseases in order to apply new therapeutic strategies; on the other, changing the duties of medical staff is equally important.

'Burnout syndrome' is one of the manifestations of stress. This syndrome is more typically found in people from the communicative professions, including doctors and all types of managers (Bursak, 2005). Lack of motivation is one of the features of burnout. The substance and structure of human motivation are important signs of health and appropriate behavior (Mikhaylov, 2002; Krymov, 2004).

There is ample information about motivation and adaptation in Western scientific literature. But these models do not take into account national thinking patterns, based on semantic peculiarities, which are closely connected to values and motivation. The situation is very demanding in terms of studying mechanisms of stress development among the most vulnerable groups of people, including managers and doctors.

The objective of this study is to carry out a comparative study of managers' and doctors' personal and motivational peculiarities associated with frustration, and the following hypotheses were tested:

H1: (a) managers' social characteristics are different from those of doctors; (b) managers' estimations of job demands are higher than those of doctors.

H2: adaptation and social frustration levels correlate with values and behavior stereotypes in both groups.

H3: (a) managers' and doctors' behavior stereotypes are different in similar situations; (b) managers are more anxious.

H4: (a) the frequency of different life situations varies in these groups and the criteria for estimating these situations also vary; (b) managers use positive but doctors use negative criteria in estimating different situations.

H5: (a) future self-development is the main goal for both managers and doctors; (b) their basic values structures are different.

H6: (a) the main need for both groups is safety; (b) the need for rest is also very important.

H7: (a) semantic field characteristics are closely connected with adaptation and social frustration, taking profession into account.

Method

Participants
This cross-sectional survey of a sample of the population living in the Russian North was conducted in March–May 2006. In this typical northern industrial town there are three big factories and two big hospitals, including outpatient clinics. Within this framework, we randomly selected one factory and one hospital. In the factory, a department was randomly selected and interviewers sought a face-to-face interview with every *n*th eligible manager. In this department, the interviewer asked for a respondent matching an education grid. In the hospital, every doctor was asked to participate in the study. A total of 301 eligible respondents were identified: 163 managers, working in the big factory, and 138 doctors, working in the big city hospital. Of these, 67 were unable to answer because of poor health or other reasons, and 33 interviews were interrupted or rejected during a control session, yielding an overall response rate of 66.8%. This chapter is based on data obtained from questionnaires completed by the remaining 102 managers and 99 doctors. This sample comprised 87 males (43.3%) and 114 females (56.7%). Ages varied from 21 to 64 years.

Materials

Social characteristics   Vasserman's questionnaire (Vasserman et al., 2004) was used in this study. The questionnaire contains 20 points describing social characteristics (sex, age, education, marital status, number of children) and job conditions (intensity of physical, emotional and intellectual pressure at work, level of responsibility, contacts with people, monotony and work-related harmful aspects). Two points aimed at discovering compulsive thoughts and self-criticism were added to the questionnaire.

Social frustration   This was assessed using the 'scale of social frustration' (ibid.), devised at the Bekhterev psychoneurological institute for a rapid psychological diagnosis of satisfaction using different aspects of social life and evaluation of adjustment disorder emergency risk. This questionnaire is aimed at detecting areas where social frustration is most evident, with the help of subjective evaluation. These areas are most important for assessing personality in the micro- and macro-social milieus. Social frustration was tested in the 20 most important social fields for any adult person able to work and living in the defined society. Respondents used a five-point 'satisfaction–dissatisfaction' scale to indicate how they felt, ranging from 1 = very strongly to 5 = not at all. Extensive normative, reliability and validity data for this questionnaire are reported in the test manual (ibid.). There are five basic sets, each containing four questions, describing satisfaction with: relationships with close relatives (a spouse, parents and children); social environment (friends, colleagues, boss, opposite sex); social status (education, professionalism, field of professional activities and work as a whole); socioeconomic status (income, conditions of life, rest and social status); and health and working ability (physical health, emotional state, working ability and way of life). The sum of points in all five sets reflected the total level of social frustration.

Adjustment and personality   The multilevel personality questionnaire 'Adaptability' was used to measure a person's resilience. The questionnaire was based on an estimation of the psychophysiological and sociopsychological characteristics of personality, reflecting integral peculiarities of mental and social development. The theoretical basis of the test is that adjustment is the permanent process of active adaptation of the individual to the social environment, including all levels of human life and professional activities. The questionnaire consists of 165 questions and has four levels. Respondents are required to agree or disagree with each item with a 'yes' or a 'no'. Several scales of this questionnaire correspond to the basic Minnesota Multiphasic Personality Inventory (MMPI) scales. Another four scales show the level of adaptation of a person according to three groups: 5–10 points – high and normal level of adaptation; 3–4 points – satisfactory adaptation; and 1–2 points – low level of adaptation. Extensive normative, reliability and validity data for this questionnaire are reported in the test manual (Nikiforov et al., 2001).

Values structure and person's attitude to him/herself, other people and different types of activities This was tested using the 'Color Metaphors Test' (Solomin, 2001). This is the modified version of the 'Color Attitude Test', aimed at the diagnosis of a person's emotional attitude to concepts that are important for the person. The Color Attitude Test is based on the principle that assigning one color to different concepts is a sign of their subjective similarity. The Color Metaphors Test does not employ the total psychological meaning of colors and is based on two principles: first, a person assigns an attractive color to an attractive concept, and an unpleasant color to an unpleasant concept;[1] second, assignment of the same color to different concepts is a sign of their subjective similarity. So, if the person assigns the same color to two or more concepts, these concepts have something in common for this person and he/she treats them equally. The number of colors and their concept position are similar to the number of colors and their position in Lusher's (1993) standard test. In the test, respondents assigned one color of eight to each concept in the list. The list contaned 61 different concepts, defining different kinds of activities, different needs and life values, different emotional experiences of different people, including the respondent and at different periods (see Appendix 8A). After being shown the concepts, respondents indicated the position of colors according to the 'short eight-color Lusher test'.

Extensive normative, reliability and validity data for this questionnaire are reported in the test manual (Solomin, 2001).

Structure and content of a person's needs, of the motives for different kinds of activities, and of conscious and unconscious relationships These were studied using G. Kelly's 'Repertory Frames Method', modified by Solomin (2001). Respondents were shown scales developed by Solomin, their content was predetermined, and respondents' subjective bunching was later assessed using factor analysis and then evaluated. There were 23 different life situations, which served as the estimated objects (elements), and 26 different states, which were the subjective indicators of different needs. Situations included different spheres of human life (work, home, relaxation, relationships with different people, conflicts, illness etc.), and the states indicated such biological and social needs as food, sex, safety, impressions, activities, sleep and rest, emotional contacts, self-affirmation and so on (see Tables 8.3 and 8.4, below). Respondents estimated how often they experienced each state in each situation. The scale required respondents to agree or disagree with each item on a four-point scale of 1 (never) to 4 (always). Thus, respondents were given a form by the researcher, indicating elements and constructs. The situations were elements and the states were constructs. In contrast to conventional tests and inventories, this method is likely to yield a truthful response (Solomin, 2001).

Statistical analyses
Since we were interested in the determinants of vulnerable groups of people involved in communicative occupations with a high level of responsibility, only university graduates and executives participated in the survey. The objective was to compare managers and people who are not involved in managing. Senior doctors did not participate in the study. Qualitative data were represented as absolute frequencies and percentages. The mean (M) and standard deviation (SD) represented quantitative data. The normality of the distribution was assessed using the Kolmogorov–Smirnov criterion. Two groups were compared using qualitative criteria on the basis of Fisher's exact test (two-tailed). The comparison of two groups by normally distributed quantitative criteria was conducted using *t*-criteria for independent samples. When the data were not normally distributed, the Mann–Whitney U-criteria were applied to two groups using quantitative criteria. Bivariate correlation analysis was used for the detection of quantitative criteria relations using the Pearson correlation coefficient (for data with normal distribution) and the Spearman correlation coefficient (for data with abnormal distribution).

The data were analyzed using Microsoft Excel and the Statistical Package for Social Sciences SPSS 10.0) (Buhl & Zofel, 2000). Analysis of data received by the psychosemantic diagnosis of ulterior motivation method was realized using the original method of Solomin (2001) with the special program 'Psychosemantica', version 2.0 (ibid.), which included principal component analysis with varimax rotation with normalization.

Results

Managers' and doctors' social image
The managers' average age was 38.4 ± 10.4 and that of the doctors was 38.2 ± 9.0 years. Among the managers, the average period of living in the Russian North was 34.8 ± 11.5 and among the doctors it was 30.5 ± 12.1 years. All the respondents were university graduates.

The average time spent in the present position was 8.6 ± 0.8 years among managers and 9.5 ± 1.0 years among doctors. All the managers worked for a large machine building plant. Doctors worked for different departments in a town hospital; none of them was a senior doctor.

The marital status of the managers was as follows: 67.6% were married, 18.9% were single, 10.8% were divorced, and 2.7% were widows/widowers. The majority of the managers had children: 24.3% of them had no children, 27.0% had one child, 45.9% had two children, and 2.7% had more than two children. Among the doctors, 63.3% were married, 16.7% were single, 13.3% were divorced, and 6.7% were widows/widowers. The majority of the doctors also had children: 26.7% had no children, 30.0% had one child, 36.7% had two children, and 6.7% had more than two children.

The larger part of both groups did not associate their work with high physical strain: 97.3% of the managers and 93.3% of the doctors; however, the majority of respondents did associate their work with high emotional and intellectual pressure (Figure 8.1).

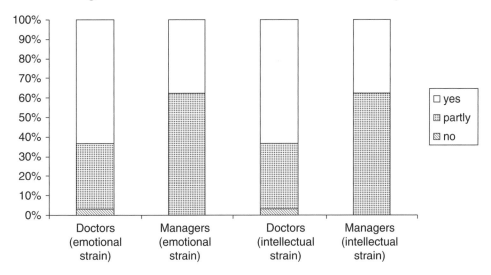

Figure 8.1   *Relationship between doctors' and managers' professional activity and high intellectual and emotional pressure*

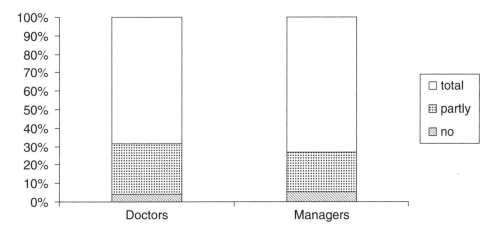

Figure 8.2   *Relationship between doctors' and managers' professional activity and decision making*

Both the managers' and the doctors' activities involve a high degree of decision making; only 5.4% of the managers and 4% of the doctors did not agree with this (Figure 8.2).

Both groups' responsibilities involve close relationships with people (Figure 8.3).

The majority of respondents did not consider their work to be monotonous; only some of them considered it to be somewhat monotonous (Figure 8.4).

The doctors associated their responsibilities with occupational hazards. Most of the managers faced no such hazards ($p < 0.001$) (Figure 8.5).

There were no differences in compulsive thoughts and self-criticism between the two groups (Figure 8.6).

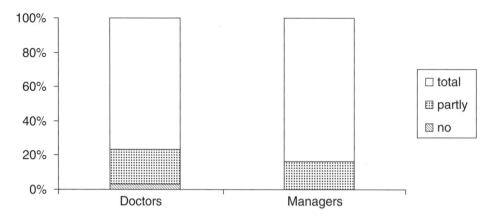

*Figure 8.3   Relationship between doctors' and managers' professional activity and
intensity of communication with people.*

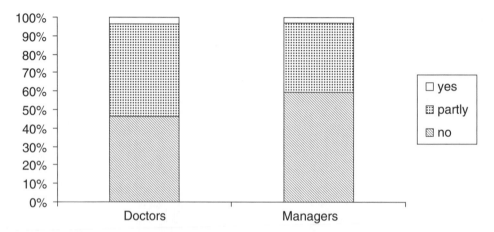

*Figure 8.4   Relationship between doctors' and managers' professional activity and
monotony*

On the whole, the social image of both groups was similar. They dealt with people, and were involved in decision making and subjected to high informational and emotional pressure. The doctors believed that their responsibilities involved occupational hazards, but the managers did not face such problems.

The social frustration level
The total social frustration level of both groups was estimated as medium, without significant differences. The level of satisfaction in each subscale was almost the same (Table 8.1).

The period of living in the Russian North and the respondents' age correlated negatively with satisfaction with the social environment ($r = -0.5; p = 0.002$), socioeconomic status ($r = -0.36; p = 0.03$), and total satisfaction ($r = -0.5; p = 0.003$). Satisfaction with their health correlated positively with high physical job strain ($r = 0.5; p = 0.006$).

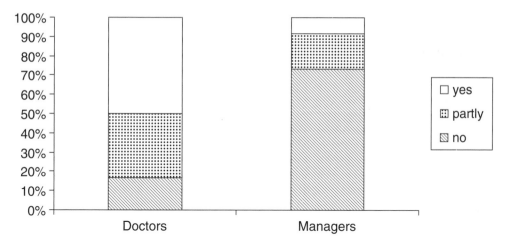

Figure 8.5   *Connection of doctors' and managers' professional activity with occupational hazards*

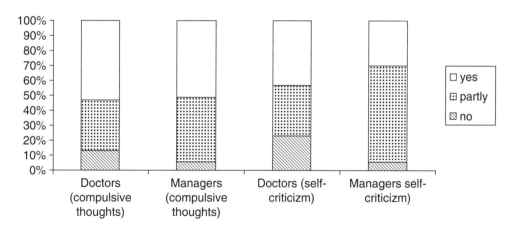

Figure 8.6   *Managers' and doctors' susceptibility to compulsive thoughts and self-criticism*

Table 8.1   *Level of social frustration of managers and doctors*

Index of frustration	Managers	Doctors
Close relations	7.9 ± 3.3	7.9 ±2.7
Relations with social environment	8.1 ± 3.6	7.6 ± 2.3
Social status	10.2 ± 3.5	8.6 ± 3.0
Socioeconomic status	10.3 ± 3.0	10.3 ± 3.2
Health and working ability	10.2 ± 2.77	10.1 ± 3.9
Total level of social frustration	46.7 ± 12.2	43.8 ± 9.9

Table 8.2   Doctors' and managers' indexes of adaptation

Index of adaptation	Managers	Doctors	p
Emotional stability	22.3 ± 8.2	29.9 ± 14.8	0.04
Communicative potential	13.3 ± 4.5	12.9 ± 3.7	0.98
Pursuit of moral standards	8.1 ± 3.1	8.5 ± 3.0	0.51
Personal adjustment potential	43.9 ± 12.3	51.9 ± 18.9	0.04

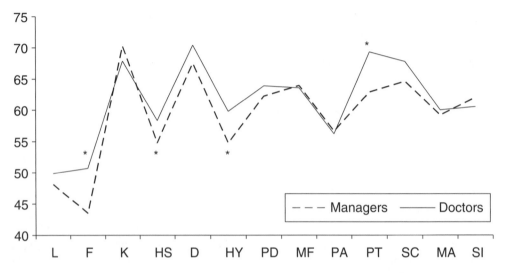

Notes:
L – Lie; F – Frequency; K – Correction; HS – Hypochondriasis; D – Depression; HY – Hysteria; PD –
Impulsivity; MF – Masculinity-Femininity; PA – Rigidity; PT – Psychasthenia (anxiety); SC – Individualism;
MA – Optimism; SI – Social introversion-extroversion.
*   Difference is significant at the 5% level.

Figure 8.7   Doctors' and managers' personality profiles

Among the doctors, the period of living in the region correlated positively with dissatisfaction with their social environment ($r = 0.42$; $p = 0.049$), and the increase in compulsive
thoughts frequency correlated positively with dissatisfaction with their socioeconomic
status ($r = 0.6$; $p = 0.022$), health ($r = 0.46$; $p = 0.001$), and total level of social frustration ($r
= 0.53$; $p = 0.002$). The indexes of adaptability of both doctors and managers were similar
(the indexes of emotional stability, communicative potential and pursuit of moral standards). Since they were of medium value (Table 8.2), the adaptability was satisfactory.

The doctors were more worried about their image than were the managers, as evidenced
by their higher indexes of hypochondria, hysteria and psychastenia ($p \leq 0.05$) (Figure 8.7).

Values of doctors and managers
The managers assigned an attractive color to the following concepts: 'Success', 'Contacts',
'Freedom', 'My father', 'Love', 'Power', 'My husband (wife)', 'My present reality', 'My

friend', 'Family', 'My child', 'Children', 'My future' and 'My company', and associated them with the first position. 'Interesting activity' and 'My hobby' were rated similarly. This confirmed that the basic values of the managers were self-actualization and self-affirmation in terms of friends, family, love and managing people. Concepts 'What I am in fact' and 'What I want to be in future' are on the same position as that above that that confirms assertiveness and future security. Thus the respondents were satisfied with themselves and had an adequate self-esteem, related to awareness of success at work and in their private relationships. The basic needs of the respondents were satisfied ('My present reality' was ranked accordingly) and managers subconsciously planned to satisfy them in the future ('My future'). Placing 'My future' far from the first position positively correlated with the dissatisfaction with their social environment ($r = 0.36; p = 0.03$), socioeconomic status ($r = 0.44; p = 0.007$) and total level of frustration ($r = 0.43; p = 0.01$). The majority of managers put 'My father' in this position. It may be assumed that there is some relationship between self-actualization and leadership abilities development and the manager comparing him/herself with the image of his/her father. Moreover, according to Lusher's test, these values are instrumental, which mean that managers use control of situations relations with their parents as instruments for self-actualization and planning for the future (Lusher, 1993).

The second position of the managers' values contained the following concepts: 'Joy', 'My work', 'My mother', 'Art', 'My home', 'Creativity', 'Wealth', 'My career', 'My profession', and 'Housekeeping'. This position was usually ranked as additional to the first one. It is closely connected with the basic personality values. Lusher's access theory allows us to assume that wealth and creation are basic aims for the majority of the managers. In fact, values determined by these concepts are complementary to the basic ones, but focused more on the process than on the result.

Managers associated 'My study', 'Knowledge', 'Education', 'Finances', 'Administration', 'Science', 'Information', 'Earnings', 'My clients', and 'Business' with the third and the fourth positions by assigning relatively indifferent colors. The majority of managers subconsciously consider their present reality to be a process of studying and administration, which was rewarding. Interestingly, the further from the first position that 'Business' and 'My clients' were situated, the higher was the level of their dissatisfaction with their socioeconomic status ($r = 0.53; p < 0.001$) and total level of dissatisfaction ($r = 0.38; p < 0.05$). The fifth and sixth positions contained the 'Machinery', 'People', 'Labor', 'Competition', 'Advertising', 'Changes', 'My boss', 'My duties', 'Psychology', and 'Service' concepts. Daily duties and relationships with the boss were estimated to be routine. Such concepts as 'Medicine', 'Sorrow', 'Failure', 'Illness', 'Conflicts', 'Worry', 'Threat', 'Fear', and 'Irritation' were put on the seventh and eighth positions by the majority of managers. This correlated with their profession and human values. Moreover, moving 'Threat' and 'Conflicts' away from the first positions correlated positively with an increased level of dissatisfaction with the social environment ($r = 0.4; p < 0.05$).

Thus, the managers were focused on the future and felt confident about it. They associated it with the satisfaction of the basic need of self-actualization, helped by mastery and private relationships building, considering them to be a creative process. The father image was often an indication of progress in those terms, but the mother image was an indication of progress in creativity. Moreover, the further 'My mother' was from the first positions, the higher the level of dissatisfaction with their socioeconomic status ($r = 0.48; p < 0.01$).

The doctors assigned the most attractive color to the same concepts as the managers. The differences involved only three concepts: 'Success' and 'Medicine' were placed at the second position and 'Administration' at the sixth ($p < 0.05$). For the doctors, there were more correlations between the level of social frustration and different positions of concepts compared to the managers. Thus, the further 'Failure' was from the first position, the higher the level of dissatisfaction with close relations ($r = 0.37; p = 0.048$), socioeconomic status ($r = 0.42; p = 0.02$), and total level of frustration ($r = 0.39; p = 0.03$). The further 'What I want to be in future' was from the first position, the higher the total level of dissatisfaction, as well as dissatisfaction with the social environment and socioeconomic status ($r = 0.4; p = 0.01$). There were similar correlations: 'Education' – social status ($r = 0.38; p = 0.008$) and 'Education' – socioeconomic status ($r = 0.48; p = 0.04$). The position of 'Earnings' correlated negatively with satisfaction with close relationships ($r = -0.48; p = 0.007$), social environment ($r = -0.4; p = 0.03$) and total level of satisfaction ($r = -0.42; p = 0.02$). Moving 'My profession' away from the first position correlated positively with the dissatisfaction with socioeconomic status ($r = 0.36; p = 0.049$) and the total level of dissatisfaction ($r = 0.47; p = 0.009$).

Thus, success, being the basic value for both groups, was associated unconsciously with real goals by doctors, and for managers success was of instrumental value. Managers associated administration with their daily routine, placing it at the third position, but the doctors did not recognize any such association. A similar situation could be observed with 'Medicine', which was a goal for doctors and a concern for managers.

The behavior strategy in different situations
Strong emotions emerged in situations connected with interpersonal relationships, rest and financial troubles in both groups. Professional activities did not provoke emotional reactions. Relationships with parents and intimate relations were significantly more important for the doctors than for the managers (Figure 8.8).

In spite of the fact that these situations were quite significant for both doctors and managers, they used different criteria in estimating them. Managers' criteria were the feelings of comfort, indicated by the following concepts: 'I feel cheerful and powerful', 'I'm calm and self-confident' and 'I feel sexual attraction'. Doctors more often estimated different situations by such feelings of physical and emotional discomfort as 'I worry', 'I would like to be alone', 'I need understanding and sympathy', 'I'm cold', 'I need peace and quiet', 'I'm depressed', 'I worry', 'I'm offended', 'I want to sleep', and 'I'm displeased' (Figure 8.9).

Factor analysis of the states of the managers revealed two factors, covering 65% of all states. The first (51.5%) was a factor of anxiety and emotional discomfort, and the second (14%) was the need of recognition. For the doctors, the first factor (47%) was that of depression and anxiety, associated with emotional discomfort and a need for relationships with people. The second (14%) expressed the need for recognition.

Thus, independently of respondents' awareness, the most important needs for them appeared to be safety, indicated by the first factor and rest, indicated by the second (Table 8.3).

Factor loadings of situations expressed the most important need for safety, revealed in the situations of conflicts and situations connected with physical discomfort in both groups. This need was least in situations connected with pleasant relationships with

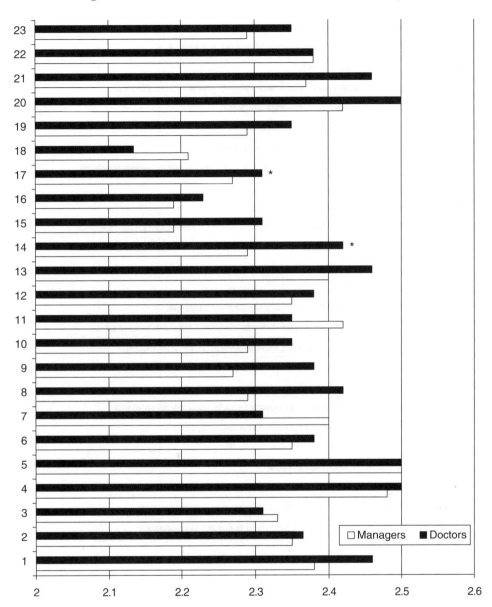

Notes:
1. In the evening after work; 2. With friends; 3. Being at odds; 4. During childhood; 5. At the weekend; 6. In unfamiliar company; 7. When I'm ill; 8. Today; 9. Alone; 10. With men; 11. With women; 12. At work; 13. Most of the time; 14. In an intimate situation; 15. In a difficult and important situation; 16. When I'm absorbed in an activity; 17. With my parents; 18. When I'm reading; 19. In bed; 20. With family; 21. In financial difficulties; 22. At a party; 23. When I'm being criticized.
* Difference is significant at the 5% level.

Figure 8.8 Ranking of frequency of different situation by doctors and managers

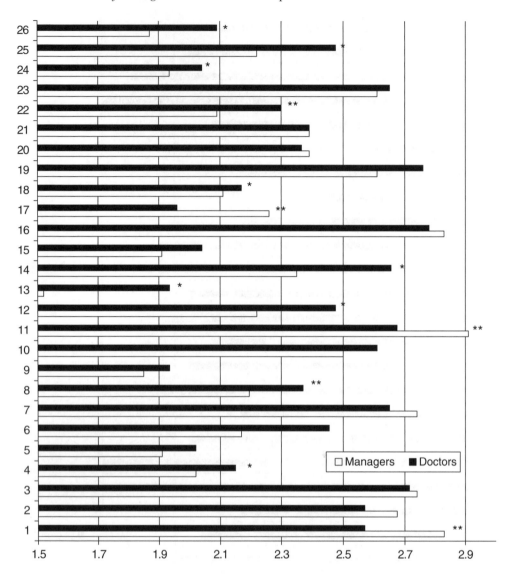

Notes:
1. I feel cheerful and powerful; 2. I want to eat tasty things; 3. I'm happy to communicate; 4. I worry; 5. I'm hot; 6. I'm tired and need a rest; 7. I'm enjoying myself; 8. I want to be alone; 9. I'm bored; 10. I want to breathe fresh air; 11. I'm calm and self-confident; 12. I need understanding and sympathy; 13. I'm cold; 14. I need peace and quiet; 15. I want to shout; 16. I try to keep independency; 17. I feel sexual attraction; 18. I'm depressed; 19. I want to drink tea or coffee; 20. I seek closer relationships; 21. I want some happiness; 22. I'm excited; 23. I want to be with you; 24. I'm offended; 25. I want to sleep; 26. I'm displeased.
* Difference is significant at the 5% level.

Figure 8.9   Ranking of frequency of experiences by managers and doctors

Table 8.3   Factor loadings of experiences of managers and doctors

Experiences		Managers		Doctors	
		Factor 1	Factor 2	Factor 1	Factor 2
1.	I feel cheerful and powerful	−0.90	0.02	−0.91	−0.01
2.	I want to eat tasty things	−0.69	0.54	−0.66	0.65
3.	I'm happy to communicate	−0.81	0.51	−0.81	0.42
4.	I worry	0.91	0.12	0.86	0.02
5.	I'm hot	0.28	−0.06	0.45	−0.59
6.	I'm tired and need a rest	0.70	0.25	0.79	0.30
7.	I'm enjoying myself	−0.95	−0.03	−0.95	−0.01
8.	I want to be alone	0.65	−0.54	0.76	0.05
9.	I'm bored	0.85	0.29	0.39	0.55
10.	I want to breathe fresh air	0.44	0.70	0.29	0.75
11.	I'm calm and self-confident	−0.87	−0.21	−0.85	0.06
12.	I need understanding and sympathy	0.55	0.69	0.46	0.47
13.	I'm cold	0.55	0.22	0.23	0.42
14.	I need peace and quiet	0.74	−0.44	0.67	0.13
15.	I want to shout	0.67	0.27	0.63	−0.03
16.	I try to keep independency	0.18	−0.02	0.25	−0.05
17.	I feel sexual attraction	−0.60	0.23	−0.63	−0.12
18.	I'm depressed	0.95	0.14	0.87	0.22
19.	I want to drink tea or coffee	−0.53	0.45	−0.26	0.76
20.	I seek closer relationships	−0.79	0.29	−0.86	0.08
21.	I want some happiness	−0.80	0.49	−0.86	0.15
22.	I'm excited	0.82	0.23	0.78	−0.05
23.	I want to be with you	−0.72	0.48	−0.70	0.28
24.	I'm offended	0.71	0.41	0.66	−0.05
25.	I want to sleep	0.34	0.43	0.37	0.64
26.	I'm displeased	0.92	0.26	0.88	−0.04
% of contribution		51.53	13.94	47.07	13.53

people. When the managers faced situations not related to definite duties and the work-load, the need for rest was indicated. For the doctors, the need for rest was expressed more in the situation associated with passivity, and less in situations related to active behavior (Table 8.4).

Thus, the needs for safety and rest were expressed by both the managers and the doctors in different situations. The major difference was that the need for rest was revealed differently by each group.

For the managers, three groups of situations are shown in a two-factor space scatter-gram (Figure 8.10). The first contained business relations and relations with friends in situations at and away from work. These situations did not provoke negative emotions; they were routine and frequent. The second group combined relations with friends of the same and opposite gender. The third involved situations arousing positive emotions and those related to rest.

Table 8.4   Factor loadings of situations of managers and doctors

Situations	Managers		Doctors	
	Factor 1	Factor 2	Factor 1	Factor 2
1. In the evening after work	0.07	5.89	−1.64	1.79
2. With friends	−17.8	−0.45	−18.1	2.39
3. Being at odds	29.83	−8.24	37.89	−1.74
4. During childhood	−8.71	3.32	−4.77	6.44
5. At the weekend	−3.80	4.68	−8.67	4.71
6. In unfamiliar company	−1.95	0.27	3.17	0.08
7. When I'm ill	23.98	3.94	29.89	2.23
8. Today	−1.89	2.87	−5.85	−0.42
9. Alone	5.61	1.48	2.75	−0.03
10. With men	−5.17	−1.11	−1.24	−1.12
11. With women	−1.31	−0.05	−8.01	2.51
12. At work	1.66	0.28	−0.19	0.34
13. Most of the time	0.44	1.18	−1.33	1.74
14. In an intimate situation	−12.1	−3.27	−13.3	−0.68
15. In a difficult and important situation	7.58	−2.76	5.39	−3.03
16. When I'm absorbed in an activity	−9.06	−6.13	−8.97	−7.69
17. With my parents	−8.50	2.97	−3.77	−0.58
18. When I'm reading	−5.22	−3.80	−4.86	−10.4
19. In bed	−10.8	−4.58	−8.18	−3.43
20. With family	−6.31	3.07	−6.67	3.63
21. In financial difficulties	18.70	2.80	13.84	1.61
22. At a party	−14.7	−0.46	−16.2	2.37
23. When I'm being criticized	19.69	−1.89	18.97	−0.70

For the doctors, four groups of situations are shown (Figure 8.11). The first and second groups were similar to those of the managers in similar situations. The third group contained situations related to family, including relationships with parents. Situations associated with intimate relationships, with high emotional reaction, formed the fourth group.

In both groups, the situations that provoked negative emotions were located at a distance, as were exciting activities and reading (Figures 8.10 and 8.11).

Correlation analysis showed a large number of links between the level of social frustration, the indexes of adaptation and the semantic field ($r > 0.5$).

For the managers, the level of dissatisfaction with their social environment correlated negatively with experiences of pleasant communication with people (Nos 3–7, Table 8.3) and positively with boredom (No. 9, Table 8.3), but the higher the level of dissatisfaction with their status, the closer to the first position was 'Business' (No. 44 in the Color Metaphors Test). Emotional stability and communicative potential correlated closely with the level of frustration.

For the doctors, the desire to be alone (No. 8, Table 8.3) and to be independent (No.

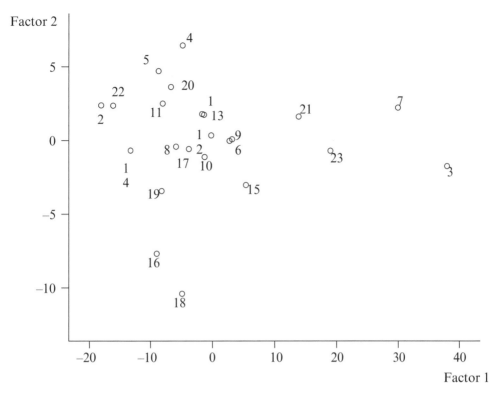

Notes:
1. In the evening after work; 2. With friends; 3. Being at odds; 4. During childhood; 5. At the weekend; 6. In unfamiliar company; 7. When I'm ill; 8. Today; 9. Alone; 10. With men; 11. With women; 12. At work; 13. Most of the time; 14. In an intimate situation; 15. In a difficult and important situation; 16. When I'm absorbed in an activity; 17. With my parents; 18. When I'm reading; 19. In bed; 20. With family; 21. In financial difficulties; 22. At a party 23. When I'm being criticized.

Figure 8.10   Scattergram of managers' situations

16, Table 8.3) correlated positively with dissatisfaction with their health; the desire to be independent (No. 16, Table 8.3) correlated positively with dissatisfaction with social status. Respondents felt depressed (No. 18, Table 8.3) in situations related to health and problems with relationships; health problems correlated closely with worries (No. 22, Table 8.3). Compulsive thoughts correlated positively with socioeconomic status problems and general dissatisfaction. The indexes of adjustment correlated negatively with the dissatisfaction with health.

Thus, in both groups there were strongly significant correlations between adjustment, frustration and the semantic field indexes. For the doctors, these correlations were evident in the field of health (Table 8.5).

In sum, the hypothesis that the managers in a large factory have personality traits and motivational peculiarities associated with the level of social frustration different from those of the doctors in a large clinic fits the current dataset well.

Hypothesis 1 is wrong: the social characteristics of the managers and doctors were

Factor 2

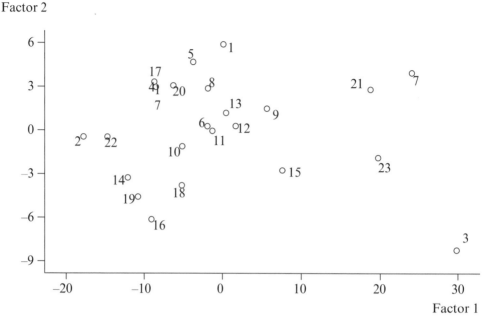

Notes:
1. In the evening after work; 2. With friends; 3. Being at odds; 4. During childhood; 5. At the weekend; 6. In unfamiliar company; 7. When I'm ill; 8. Today; 9. Alone; 10. With men; 11. With women; 12. At work; 13. Most of the time; 14. In an intimate situation; 15. In a difficult and important situation; 16. When I'm absorbed in an activity; 17. With my parents; 18. When I'm reading; 19. In bed; 20. With family; 21. In financial difficulties; 22. At a party; 23. When I'm being criticized.

Figure 8.11   Scattergram of doctors' situations

similar; the doctors' estimations of their job demands were higher than those of the managers.

Hypothesis 2 is true: the levels of adaptation and social frustration are satisfactory and correlated with values and behavior stereotypes.

Hypothesis 3 is partly true: the managers' and the doctors' behavior stereotypes are similar in similar situations, but the doctors have stronger emotional reactions, they tend to worry more and have an 'escape to illness' reaction.

Hypothesis 4 is not proved: life situations and criteria for estimating them are similar among both groups, but the suggestion that managers use positive but doctors negative criteria for estimating different situations is correct.

Hypothesis 5 is correct: the main goal for both groups is a future associated with self-development; however, their basic value structures are different.

Hypothesis 6 is also true: the main need for both groups is safety; then comes the need for rest.

Hypothesis 7 is correct: the semantic field indexes are closely connected with adaptation and social frustration, taking the profession into account; for the doctors, there are significant correlations in the field of health.

Table 8.5 *Correlation of social frustration level with indexes of values and experiences in managers and doctors*

	Level of social frustration					
	Close relations	Social environment relation	Social status	Socioeconomic status	Health and ability to work	Total
Managers						
I'm happy to communicate	–	r = 0.592 p = 0.0001	–	–	–	–
I'm enjoying myself	–	r = −0.599 p = 0.0001	–	–	–	–
I'm bored	–	r = 0.626 p < 0.0001	–	–	–	–
Business	–	–	r = 0.526 p = 0.001	–	–	–
Emotional stability	–	r = 0.558 p = 0.0001	–	–	–	r = 0.560 p = 0.0001
Communicative potential	r = 0.534 p = 0.0001	r = 0.653 p = 0.0001	–	–	–	r = 0.638 p = 0.0001
Doctors						
I want to be alone	–	–	–	–	r = 0.540 p = 0.002	–
I try to keep independency	–	–	r = 0.526 p = 0.003	–	–	–
I'm depressed	r = 0.579 p = 0.004	–	–	–	r = 0.514 p < 0.01	–
I'm excited	–	–	–	–	r = 0.552 p = 0.002	–
Compulsive thoughts	–	–	–	r = 0.581 p = 0.001	–	r = 0.534 p = 0.002
Emotional stability	–	–	–	–	r = 0.526 p = 0.003	–
Communicative potential	–	–	–	–	r = 0.509 p = 0.004	–
Personality adjustment potential	–	–	–	–	r = 0.512 p = −0.005	–

Discussion

This chapter provided a comparative study of managers' and doctors' personal and motivational peculiarities associated with frustration. Important and interactive peculiarities of personality and semantic field were discovered.

The social image of both groups was similar. The total level of social frustration was middling and homogeneous in both groups. The indexes of adaptability were similar to those of social frustration: those of emotional stability, communicative potential and pursuit of moral standards were satisfactory and homogeneous in both groups.

Note that frustration in these groups correlated with different aspects. The level of social frustration in the group of managers focused on the outer world correlated positively with the period of living in the region (quantitative index), while the level of social frustration in the group of doctors focused on the inner world correlated positively with the frequency of compulsive thoughts (qualitative index).

The managers' professional responsibilities involved little physical strain and the higher the level of physical job strain, the lower the level of dissatisfaction with their health ($r = -0.5; p = 0.006$). Their professional duties, requiring frequent social contacts and decision making, involved high informational and emotional pressure. Only the doctors considered their duties to be potentially harmful. This may be explained by the fact that doctors are more informed about health issues.

The doctors were more focused on their health, demonstrative and psychasthenic ($p < 0.05$) than the managers, which might also be related to their duties. Doctors have to work with symptoms, feelings and subtle differences in diseases – everything associated in Eastern philosophy with 'yin', that is, 'inner', 'passive' and so on. Managers have to work with external matters such as meetings, plans and production – everything associated in Eastern philosophy with 'yang', that is, 'outer', 'active' and so on. This was supported by value structures. Success was unconsciously associated with final goals by the doctors (the second position in the Colors Metaphors Test), and it was of instrumental value for the managers (the first position in the Colors Metaphors Test). Administration was routine for the managers, but it was of no value for the doctors. The father image (the first position in the Colors Metaphors Test) was often an indication of success for managers, but the mother image (the second position in the Colors Metaphors Test) was an indication of creativity. There were no significant differences in the choice of positions for 'My mother' and 'My father' made by either group, so we cannot conclude that such images affected these groups differently.

For the doctors, there was a greater correlation between the level of social frustration and different positions of concepts, than for the managers.

The most important unconscious needs for respondents of both groups were those for safety and for rest, revealed in different situations. For the managers, the need for rest manifested itself when they immersed themselves in situations not related to definite duties and the workload, and for the doctors when they immersed themselves in a situation associated with passivity. Both managers and doctors unconsciously grouped the situations similarly. Strong significant correlations between adjustment, frustration and semantic field indexes could be seen in both groups. For the doctors, these correlations appeared in the field of health.

Limitations of the study
The generalizability of the results is limited by the small size of the population sample as representatives of only two occupations were involved in the study and the findings may not be applicable to other occupations. The strength of the survey is that the sample was homogeneous and typical for the region. People of both genders were involved in the study and dispersion could be seen only in the age variable. Since the semantic field was culturally determined, it is important to study interrelations between social frustration and motivation, taking language aspects into consideration. Nevertheless, this fact also sets some limitation on the study, as the constructs cannot be translated into another language and culture without preliminary adaptation. Finally, it was a cross-sectional study and there is no information about stability and changes in motivation and frustration of

respondents. This limitation could partly be compensated by the similarity with results obtained by the Color Metaphors Test and the Repertory Frames Method.

Implications and Conclusions

This chapter has findings in relation to an under-researched aspect of motivation and behavior strategies of such stress vulnerable professions as managers and doctors, associated with social frustration. In spite of having similar social characteristics and social frustration levels, the doctors evaluated their activities as harmful, and revealed a tendency to 'escape into illness' but the managers did not react in the same way.

The semantic field indexes in both groups correlated closely with the different aspects of social frustration; these correlations were different for each group. The finding concerning personal and behavior strategy differences for each group is of particular interest. The doctors were more sensitive and used concepts of discomfort experiences. They were focused on feelings and thoughts more than on external manifestations, which has implications for the type of prevention strategies for these occupations. Several features of the current study suggest that behavior strategies correlate strongly with social frustration. Importantly, in contrast to including all professions in a 'burnout group', the current study finds different criteria for estimating the situations for managers and doctors.

In summary, the study found key differences in the semantic field, connected with frustration, for building prevention strategies in terms of stress. Specifically, (i) doctors use feelings of discomfort for checking many situations, (ii) doctors are focused on their inner world, managers on the outside one, and (iii) doctors and managers have different correlations of semantic field indexes with frustration. These findings require replication and extension in further research involving other occupations.

Acknowledgments

The author is deeply grateful to Pavel Sidorov, the rector of Northern State Medical University, who was the inspiration for the project, and two assistants, Elena Nazarova and Artem Tarakhtii, for collecting the data. The author acknowledges the help provided by the top management of the factory and the hospital where the data were collected, and would also like to thank Svetlana Pestovskaya, who helped him to express his ideas in English.

Note

1. An 'attractive color' is the color that respondents choose first and an 'unpleasant color' is the color that they choose last.

References

Babenko, A.I., Radchenko, L.P. & Tataurova, E.A. (2005), 'The opinion of the population about outpatient care organization (the results of a survey of a patients' polyclinic)' (in Russian), *Sibirskii consilium*, **2**: 54–7.

Bandura, A. (1989), 'Human agency in social cognitive theory', *American Psychologist*, **44**: 1175–84.

Bobrovnikov, P. (2003), 'Troubles, goals and problems in business' (in Russian), *Effektivnoye upravlenie*, **2**: 56–7.

Buhl, A. & Zofel, P. (2000), *SPSS: The Art of Information Processing. Analysis of Statistical Data and Reconstruction of Latent Rules* (in Russian), St Petersburg: DiaSoftUP.

Bursak, A. (2005), 'Emotional atmosphere in a team' (in Russian), *Secret firmy*, **11**: 26–8.

Gerchikova, I.N. (1995), *Management*, 2nd edn, oscow: Banki i Birghi, UNITI.

Kelly, G.A. (2000), *Theory of Personality. Psychology of Personal Constructs* (in Russian), St Petersburg: Rech.

Krymov, A.A. (2004), *You Are a Personnel Manager*, 2nd edn (in Russian), Moscow: Berator.

Lusher, M. (1993), *Signals of Personality* (in Russian), Voronezh: Voronezh.

Mikhaylov, G. (2002), 'Motivation as a management function' (in Russian), *Prikladnaya psychologia i psycho-analiz*, **1**: 15–30.

Nikiforov, G.S., Nikiforova, M.A. & Smetkov, V.M. (2001), *Handbook of the Psychology of Management and Professional Activities* (in Russian), St. Petersburg: Rech.

Roginskaya, T.I. (2002), 'Burnout syndrome in social professions' (in Russian), *Psychologicheskii Journal*, **3**: 85–95.

Solomin, I.L. (2001), *Psychosemantic Diagnostic of Latent Motivation. Manual* (in Russian), St Petersburg: Imaton.

Tretyakova, T.V., Ryshkov, V.I. & Palicyn, A.B. (2001), 'The management of entrepreneurial risk' (in Russian), *Problemy psychologii and ergonomiki*, **4**: 57–61.

Trumel, V.V. (2002), 'The health of the working population of the Russian Federation' (in Russian), *Medicina truda i promyshlennaya ekologiya*, **12**: 4–8.

Vasserman, L.I., Iovlev, B.V. & Beredin, M.A. (2004), *Method for the Psychological Diagnosis of Social Frustration and Its Practical Application. Manual* (in Russian), St Petersburg: NIPNI (V.M. Bekhterev).

Velichkovskii, B.T. (2005), 'Social stress, labor motivation and health' (in Russian), *Sibirskii consilium*, **2**: 47–53.

Appendix 8A   Concepts in the Color Metaphors Test

1. Success	21. Education	41. Worry
2. Failure	22. My spouse	42. Absorbing activities
3. Relationships	23. Medicine	43. School
4. Machinery	24. My present reality	44. Business
5. Illness	25. Competition	45. Children
6. Joy	26. Advertising	46. Fear
7. My study	27. Art	47. My duties
8. Freedom	28. My friend	48. My future
9. Knowledge	29. Family	49. Service
10. My father	30. My past	50. Creativity
11. People	31. Information	51. Wealth
12. What I want to be	32. What I am in fact	52. My personnel
13. Love	33. Earning	53. Irritation
14. My work	34. Changes	54. My career
15. Conflicts	35. Sorrow	55. Administration
16. Threat	36. My home	56. My profession
17. Nature	37. My boss	57. My company
18. My mother	38. My hobby	58. Housekeeping
19. Labor	39. Finances	59. Science
20. Power	40. My child	60. Psychology
		61. My clients

9 Enhancing occupational safety: non-technical skills
Rhona Flin

Introduction
For many workers the greatest occupational health risk is a workplace accident. An estimate of global occupational accidents for 1998 was 350,000 fatal accidents and 264 million non-fatal accidents (Hamalainen et al., 2006). Allowing for problems in estimation and deficiencies in reporting systems, these figures indicate that enormous numbers of people are injured or killed during the course of their work. There are significant differences between accident rates in developed and developing countries, but even in highly regulated, Western countries the accident rates remain a serious cause for concern. For example, in the UK, which has extensive safety legislation and required controls, there were 241 fatal injuries and 141,350 reported injuries to workers in 2006/07, with 6 million working days lost due to injury (HSE, 2007a).

In industrial safety research, a distinction is often drawn between major accidents, such as a refinery explosion or a plane crash which may kill and injure multiple workers (as well as members of the public), and individual accidents where a single worker is injured, typically by falling or being struck by machinery. While the patterns of causation are usually more complex for major accidents than for individual injuries, in both cases, a key contributing factor is frequently some form of human error (Reason, 1987). Analyses in a number of industrial sectors have indicated that up to 80% of accident causes can be attributed to human factors (Wagenaar & Groeneweg, 1987; Reason, 1990; Helmreich, 2000). We know that human error is common in all workplaces: for instance, observations on aircraft flightdecks have revealed that airline pilots make about two errors per flight segment, but most of these are discovered and corrected by the aircrew themselves (Helmreich et al., 2003). There are of course many other causes of workplace accidents, such as technical failures, unexpected environmental conditions and factors relating to the ways in which industries are regulated and organizations are managed. When industrial/organizational psychologists study safety, they are primarily interested in the behaviours of workers and managers that make a worksite safer or more dangerous (Glendon et al., 2006). This chapter presents one psychological approach to enhancing occupational safety, which involves identifying and training the non-technical skills that help to minimize the risks of accidents.

Recognizing the importance of non-technical skills
The term 'non-technical skills' was first applied to industrial safety by the European civil aviation regulator in relation to airline pilots' behaviour on the flightdeck. Non-technical skills can be defined as 'the cognitive, social and personal resource skills that complement technical skills, and contribute to safe and efficient task performance' (Flin et al., 2008, p. 1). In essence, they enhance workers' technical skills. The relationship between non-technical skills and human error is shown in Figure 9.1. This indicates that poor non-technical skills can increase the chance of error, which in turn can increase the chance of an

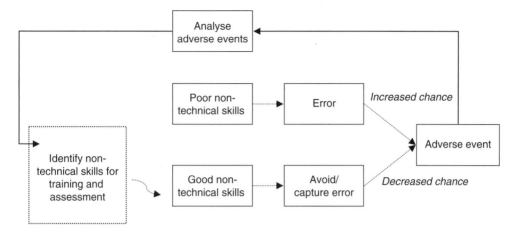

Source: From Flin et al. (2008), reprinted with permission from Ashgate.

Figure 9.1 Relationship between non-technical skills, errors and adverse events

adverse event. Good non-technical skills (e.g., high vigilance, clear communication, team coordination) can reduce the likelihood of error and consequently of accidents. Analysis of incidents, as well as studies of behaviour during routine tasks can reveal which workplace behaviours positively or negatively influence adverse outcomes. This knowledge can inform the design of non-technical skills training and competence assessment systems.

In the late 1970s, the aviation industry realized that failures in non-technical skills were linked to aircraft safety, when a series of major accidents occurred that did not have a primary technical cause. The most significant of these occurred in Tenerife in 1977, when two Boeing 747 aircraft (operated by KLM and Pan Am) crashed on a runway at Los Rodeos airport, killing 583 passengers and crew. Analysis of the accident revealed problems relating to communication with air traffic control, team coordination, leadership and decision making on the KLM flight deck, plus effects of fatigue (Weick, 1990). In other countries, similar accidents showing non-technical causes had been reported. In the USA, three United Airlines planes crashed in the late 1970s, and like the Tenerife accident, these were attributed to 'pilot error' rather than to technical faults. In response to this problem, an aviation industry conference was organized at NASA (US National Aeronautics and Space Administration) in 1979, when aviation psychologists and airline pilots were brought together to identify the human factors that were contributing to accidents (Wiener et al., 1993).

Once the aviation industry realized that maintaining high standards of safety was going to require paying more attention to non-technical skills, aviation researchers began to study safe and unsafe behaviours during flight operations. However, a flightdeck is a very remote and private workplace, so it was going to be difficult to discover what behaviours had contributed to these accidents. But the aviation industry had two important sources of information which helped to provide an answer. First, modern aircraft are fitted with cockpit voice recorders. The investigators and psychologists listened to what the pilots, flight engineers and air traffic controllers were saying in the minutes before an accident.

Analysis of their conversations suggested failures in leadership, poor team coordination, communication breakdowns, lack of assertiveness, inattention, inadequate decision making, and the influence of performance-limiting factors, relating to stress and fatigue. Second, aviation research centres, such as NASA, had high fidelity flightdeck simulators, so psychologists could make detailed observations of pilots' behaviour while they 'flew' the simulator in all kinds of operational conditions. In addition, experienced pilots were interviewed to discover which behaviours constituted what they called 'good airmanship'. The results from all these studies confirmed that good non-technical skills would help to reduce error, whereas inadequate non-technical skills contributed to increasing the risks for the flight (ibid.).

Once these skills had been identified, training courses ('crew resource management': CRM) were designed for pilots (and later for all the crew) to increase understanding of the importance of particular behaviours for safety and to provide opportunities to practise the skills in exercises and simulated flights (Walters, 2002). CRM is defined as 'a management system which makes optimum use of all available resources – equipment, procedures and people – to promote safety and enhance efficiency of flightdeck operations' (CAA, 2006, p. 1). Essentially, CRM courses train non-technical skills. Not only in aviation were cognitive and social skills found to contribute to workplace safety, but studies of accidents in other industries also revealed similar patterns of causation (Flin et al., 2008). CRM training is now widely used as a form of safety training and skills development. Courses are run in many different domains, such as nuclear power generation, the Merchant Navy, the military, prison services, emergency services and hospital medicine (Salas et al., 2001, 2006b; Flin et al., 2002; Musson & Helmreich, 2004; Okray & Lubnau, 2004). In the next section, the main categories of non-technical skill are briefly described.

Categories of non-technical skill
The principal categories of non-technical skills are shown in Table 9.1. These are broad skill categories relevant to most jobs but are particularly important in safety-critical operations, characterized by risk and time pressure, where errors can have significant costs in terms of damage to humans and equipment. Following the convention adopted in several taxonomies of non-technical skills, each category is subdivided into a number of component elements. The list in the table is intended to be generic. To identify the skill set for a particular occupation, a precise set of categories and elements should be established, using techniques such as task and accident analyses (see Flin et al., 2008).

These skills are not unfamiliar to most workers, but they may not have a common terminology. Moreover, they are not traditionally taught as part of technical training and they do not appear to be always used as effectively as required to maintain safe performance. Human error cannot be eliminated, but efforts can be made to minimize, recognize and mitigate errors by ensuring that people have appropriate non-technical skills to cope with the risks and demands of their work. Below, the main categories of non-technical skill are briefly described; more detailed accounts can be found elsewhere (Wiener et al., 1993; Salas et al., 2001; Flin et al., 2008).

Situation awareness
Situation awareness is related to perception and attention and is basically 'knowing what is going on around you' at the worksite. Endsley (1995a, p. 36) defines it as: 'the

Table 9.1 Main categories and elements of non-technical skills

Category	Elements
Situation awareness	Gathering information
	Interpreting information
	Anticipating future states
Decision making	Defining problem
	Considering options
	Selecting and implementing option
	Outcome review
Teamwork	Supporting others
	Exchanging information
	Coordinating activities
	Resolving conflicts
Leadership	Using authority
	Maintaining standards
	Planning and prioritizing
	Managing workload and resources
Managing stress	Identifying symptoms of stress
	Recognizing effects of stress
	Implementing coping strategies for stress
Coping with fatigue	Identifying symptoms of fatigue
	Recognizing effects of fatigue
	Managing fatigue

Source: Adapted from Flin et al. (2008).

perception of the elements in the environment within a volume of time and space, the comprehension of their meaning and the projection of their status in the near future'. The notion of situation awareness came from the military (i.e., knowing where the enemy was) and has been used extensively in aviation. The importance of situation awareness for occupational safety is clear (Stanton et al., 2001) and the concept has now been widely adopted for safety research and training in occupational fields such as anaesthesia (Gaba et al., 1995), nuclear plant process control (Patrick & Belton, 2004), and emergency response (Okray & Lubnau, 2004). Increasing interest in attention skills has been driven to some degree by the rapid development of computer-based monitoring systems, automated control processes, intelligent systems and other technological advances that serve to distance humans from the systems they are operating. Consequently the importance has been recognized of the human operator, for example, the control room supervisor, the fire officer, the anaesthetist, having a good 'mental model' representing the status of the current task and surrounding work environment.

Situation awareness is essentially a continuous monitoring of the task, noticing what is going on, and detecting any changes in the environment. It also functions as the first stage in the decision-making process. This cognitive skill is primarily about picking up and processing information from the work environment and using stored memories and mental models to make sense of it. The essential elements of this skill category are:

- gathering information;
- interpreting information; and
- anticipating future states.

Almost all aspects of safety-critical tasks rely heavily on situation awareness skills. Endsley (1995b) reviewed major air carrier accidents from 1989 to 1992 and found that situation awareness was a major causal factor in 88% of accidents associated with human error. These include 'controlled flights into terrain' accidents where a fully functioning plane has been flown into the ground (usually a mountain), as the pilots thought they were in a different location or at a safer altitude. In December 1995, a Boeing 757 crashed into a mountain near Cali, Colombia, killing 159 people. Analyses of the cockpit voice recording showed that while trying to resolve an error resulting from entering an incorrect navigation code, the pilots had not maintained awareness of the position of their aircraft in relation to the mountainous landscape. Although a cockpit alarm warned of ground proximity, they were unable to take the necessary action in time to avoid the mountain.

When 200 managers of offshore oil installations in the North Sea were asked what they thought were the main causes of offshore accidents, the leading causal factors they mentioned were attentional problems. While they did not use the term 'situation aware-ness', the most common answers were failures in situation awareness: 'not thinking the job through', 'carelessness', inadequate planning and inadequate risk assessment (O'Dea & Flin, 1998). A review of 332 offshore drilling accidents showed that 135 were attributed to problems associated with workers' attention (Sneddon et al., 2006).

Certainly errors relating to gathering and interpreting information and failures in anticipation are common contributing factors to adverse events at work. Situation aware-ness is a core component of non-technical skills training courses such as CRM, and there have been recent attempts to show that specific training can enhance task performance (Banbury et al., 2007). For further reading on situation awareness skills, see Endsley and Garland (2000) or Banbury and Tremblay (2004).

Decision making
Decision making during work tasks is a cognitive process for reaching a judgement, select-ing an option, or choosing which action to take to meet the needs of a given situation. In dynamic work environments, there is a continuous cycle of monitoring and re-evaluating the task environment, then taking appropriate action. Decision making is essentially a two-stage process: (i) carry out a situation assessment to establish the problem and (ii) use a decision method for choosing a course of action based on available options. The chosen method will be influenced by factors such as expertise, amount of time, level of risk or quantity of information. The main types of decision making are recognition-primed (a pattern recognition/intuitive process), rule based, analytical (i.e., comparing optional courses of action) and creative. Conditions for decision making can vary in relation to time pressure, task demands, feasibility of options and what level of constraint, support and resource exists for the decision maker. The basic elements of operational decision making in the workplace are:

- defining the problem;
- considering options;

- selecting and implementing option; and
- outcome review.

In the late 1980s, following a sequence of major incidents where poor decision making by military commanders, pilots, industrial managers and police officers was implicated, psychologists began to develop techniques to study expert decision makers in their work environments, such as flightdecks or military command posts (Klein et al., 1993; Flin et al., 1997; Zsambok & Klein, 1997; Montgomery et al., 2005). This approach to decision-making research is called 'naturalistic decision making' (NDM). The aim of NDM researchers is to describe how experts make decisions under conditions of high uncertainty, inadequate information, shifting goals, high time pressure and risk, usually working with a team and subject to organizational constraints. This naturalistic approach has now been applied in a range of safety-critical workplaces, such as acute medicine (e.g., surgery, anaesthesia, casualty, intensive care) where uncertain and risky judgements are common (Gaba, 1992; Flin et al., 2007). In hazardous industries, such as nuclear power generation, an NDM approach has been used to analyse decisions of control room supervisors (Carvalho et al., 2005) and emergency managers (Crichton et al., 2005).

The results of such studies are fed back into non-technical skills training on decision making which examines the different methods used for a given occupation, their strengths and weakness for particular workplace conditions, as well as factors affecting cognitive processing (e.g., stress and fatigue) and how to deal with them. Specific training techniques, such as tactical decision games (Crichton et al., 2000), can be used to provide directed practice.

Teamwork
In most modern work settings, the complexity of organizations and their supporting technologies means that the majority of people have jobs in some kind of team setting. Nowadays with electronic communication, teams may be co-located or distributed across several workplaces, sometimes even based in different countries. There is no shortage of evidence that good teamwork is important for safe and efficient task performance (Salas et al., 2001; Undre et al., 2006). Failures in team communication, coordination and conduct have been identified as accident precursors in a whole range of occupational settings (Turner & Parker, 2004). Key team skills for occupational safety relate to effective communication, task coordination, supporting other team members, negotiating and resolving conflicts, with generic elements from Table 9.1 listed as:

- supporting others;
- exchanging information;
- coordinating activities; and
- resolving conflicts.

There are many ways in which team members can support each other, for example, by sharing workloads, giving emotional support, or helping with work problems. Providing advice and sharing information can aid in task planning, as well as in task execution. Task coordination is enhanced where team members monitor each other and provide back-up behaviours when required. There are psychological, as well as safety and productivity benefits of working in a supportive team climate (West, 2004).

Open and efficient communication between team members minimizes the risk of adverse events, as errors are more likely to be avoided, or noticed and remedied (CAA, 2006). Effective information exchange involves not only clear and timely spoken and written communication but also active listening skills and attending to non-verbal channels and emotional signals (West, 2004). Also required for safe team practices are skills for negotiation and constructive conflict resolution. Conflicts can arise because of task or goal ambiguity, unclear roles and external influences. Airline pilots are trained in CRM courses that 'what is right' is much more important than 'who is right'. Lingard et al. (2002) have studied conflict situations in hospital operating theatre teams and shown that these events tend to have a more negative impact on junior staff, such as trainee surgeons with consequent risks to patient safety. A related skill, particularly useful for junior staff, which is taught on all CRM courses, is assertiveness. This is a communication method that focuses on protecting the individual's rights while respecting the rights of others. In another operating theatre study, team members who perceived themselves to be of lower status in the team were less likely to be fully involved in discussion or to speak up in order to challenge others or ask for help (Edmondson, 2003). Therefore assertiveness is an important element of non-technical skills training to ensure that team members have the skills and confidence to speak out when appropriate.

Leadership

A pivotal component of safe and effective teamwork is the skill of the team member who has the leadership position. Team leadership is about setting goals and targets, directing and coordinating the work tasks; encouraging cooperation; monitoring, assessing and reinforcing performance; developing group knowledge and abilities; motivating; planning and organizing; and establishing a positive team atmosphere (Hackman, 2002). There is an extensive literature on the psychology of leadership in the workplace; see Yukl (2005) and Northouse (2006) for recent reviews. In Table 9.1, the main elements of the leadership skill category are:

- using authority;
- maintaining standards;
- planning and prioritizing; and
- managing workload and resources.

Effective leadership has been shown across a number of industries to be crucial for maintaining safe performance in the workplace (Hofmann & Morgeson, 2004). For example, leaders influence key worksite safety behaviours such as compliance with rules and procedures, participation in safety activities, reporting of unsafe conditions and actions. The term 'safety leadership' is now used in the oil and gas industry and this refers to managers' and supervisors' leadership behaviours in relation to worksite safety. One underpinning aspect of safety leadership in this type of industry is being able to balance the competing demands of safety and production when these conflict.

The basic leadership skills described above such as careful planning, creating an open and supportive work climate, continuous monitoring and reinforcing appropriate behaviours are generally regarded as critical for maintaining safe operations. When team members must coordinate their actions in risky, uncertain, dynamic situations, effective leaders need to be able to communicate a motivating rationale for change and minimize concerns about status differences. This enables team members to speak up and engage in more proactive coordination. Edmondson (2003), studying teams in cardiac surgery, found that when the leading surgeon demonstrated these skills, the surgical team learned more quickly to utilize a new technique.

Managing stress

In safety-critical work environments, there can be two different kinds of work stress and both have implications for worker and system safety (Clarke & Cooper, 2004). Occupational or chronic stress relates to ongoing conditions and pressures from the job, co-workers, bosses and the organization. This type of stress has been extensively studied in a whole range of occupations and is fully discussed in other chapters in this volume. In almost all organizations, workers need to have knowledge to recognize the causes and effects of occupational stress and to have techniques for dealing with these, as well as knowing what sources of support are available from their employer (HSE, 2007b).

In non-technical (CRM) skills training courses, which tend to be used more often in the higher-risk industries, the focus tends to be more on the second type of stress, namely acute stress. This is due to a more immediate threat which can produce more severe reactions, and may be experienced by workers who have to deal with very high demand situations, such as life-threatening emergencies (see Flin, 1996). In this case, there is a focus on the physiological and psychological responses that constitute the reaction to perceived threat and how these will impact on critical survival skills such as decision making, teamwork and leadership. The training to improve stress coping shows how the stress effects can be managed and may include specific techniques such as breathing exercises or muscle relaxation to help to reduce physiological effects. In essence, the key skill components for managing both chronic and acute stress are:

- identifying symptoms of stress;
- recognizing effects of stress; and
- implementing coping strategies for stress.

Coping with fatigue

The higher-risk industries, healthcare and the military all have 24-hour operations that need to be staffed continuously, therefore employees need to be able to cope with working at night and working shifts, and if the sites are remote (such as the offshore oil industry), they may have to work for several weeks without a break before they can take their leave period. Some studies have indicated that longer working hours are increasingly hazardous due to the effects of fatigue (Dembe et al., 2005). Dawson and Reid (1997) studying problems related to fatigue and shiftwork, compared the performance impairment of fatigue and alcohol intoxication using a computer-based tracking task. They demonstrated that even moderate levels of sleep deprivation produce cognitive psychomotor performance impairment similar to that of moderate levels of alcohol intoxication. When workers, such as hospital doctors, have to be on-call for periods of time to deal with problems, they may suffer additional levels of fatigue (Howard et al., 2002). In addition, for airline pilots, and other employees in transportation industries, long-distance travel may mean that jet lag is an occupational hazard.

Not surprisingly, fatigue is common in many work settings and is regarded as a pervasive contributing factor to both major and minor occupational accidents (Coren, 1996; Horne, 2006). Therefore the final category of non-technical skills is coping with fatigue, the core elements of which are:

- identifying symptoms of fatigue;
- recognizing effects of fatigue; and
- managing fatigue.

A key aspect of fatigue management is recognizing when you are fatigued, understanding how this impacts on cognitive skills such as decision making, and adapting behaviour accordingly. A new study of long-haul pilots showed that when they were fatigued after a long flight, they adapted their team coordination behaviours such as using more read back and checking and taking decisions more systematically (Petrill et al., 2006). Other chapters in this volume (Chapters 5 and 15) deal with the effects of working hours and schedules on occupational health.

While the generic categories of non-technical skills described above appear to be relevant across many occupations, the component elements and behavioural examples for teaching and assessment need to be specified for a particular occupation and task set. The next section provides a brief example of a non-technical skills taxonomy developed for anaesthetists' work in the operating theatre.

Rating anaesthetists' non-technical skills (ANTS)

If non-technical skills are important for the maintenance of workplace safety, then workers need not only to be trained, but also to be assessed in the workplace or a simulator. In the UK, commercial pilots have an assessment of their non-technical as well as their technical skills on a regular basis (CAA, 2006). This competence assessment approach began to interest other professions which had already started to train non-technical skills in order to enhance workplace safety. Anaesthetists are one such group: they can suffer occupational accidents but their main concern is the safety of their patients.

Working with industrial psychologists, a team of consultant anaesthetists developed a taxonomy of non-technical skills and a method of rating them from behavioural observations of individual anaesthetists working in an operating theatre. The resulting ANTS system (Fletcher et al., 2003, see Figure 9.2), was developed using a similar design and evaluation process as was used for an earlier skills taxonomy and behaviour rating system for European airline pilots (Flin et al., 2003). The ANTS skill set was derived from the research literature on anaesthetists' behaviour, as well as observations, interviews, surveys and incident analysis (see www.abdn.ac.uk/iprc/ants for details).

The ANTS system is designed for experienced anaesthetists to rate observed behaviour of other anaesthetists. Two of the skill categories described above, managing stress and coping with fatigue, are not included as they can be difficult to detect unless extreme, and they influence the other performance skills. For anaesthetists, the category of leadership

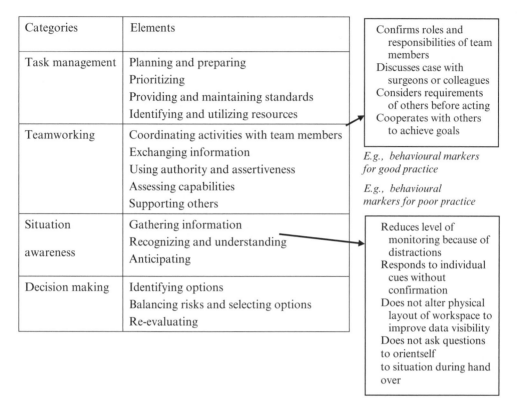

Categories	Elements
Task management	Planning and preparing
	Prioritizing
	Providing and maintaining standards
	Identifying and utilizing resources
Teamworking	Coordinating activities with team members
	Exchanging information
	Using authority and assertiveness
	Assessing capabilities
	Supporting others
Situation awareness	Gathering information
	Recognizing and understanding
	Anticipating
Decision making	Identifying options
	Balancing risks and selecting options
	Re-evaluating

Confirms roles and responsibilities of team members
Discusses case with surgeons or colleagues
Considers requirements of others before acting
Cooperates with others to achieve goals

E.g., behavioural markers for good practice

E.g., behavioural markers for poor practice

Reduces level of monitoring because of distractions
Responds to individual cues without confirmation
Does not alter physical layout of workspace to improve data visibility
Does not ask questions to orientself to situation during hand over

Figure 9.2   Anaesthetists' non-technical skills (ANTS) taxonomy

is incorporated into the teamwork category and they placed special emphasis on task management skills, which are shown as a separate category.

An evaluation of the ANTS behaviour rating method was carried out with 50 consultant anaesthetists who were given basic training on the system and were then asked to rate the non-technical skills of consultant anaesthetists shown in eight videotaped scenarios. The levels of rater accuracy were acceptable and inter-rater reliability was found to approach an acceptable level (Fletcher et al., 2003). Given that the raters had no previous experience of behaviour rating and minimal training (4 hours) in the ANTS system, it was concluded that these findings were sufficient to move on to usability trials. The first measures of usability and acceptability from consultants and trainees were promising (Patey et al., 2005). The ANTS system has now had preliminary trials in the UK through the Royal College of Anaesthetists and the Australia/New Zealand College has sponsored an evaluation study. ANTS has been translated into German and Hebrew and has been used to evaluate simulator training for anaesthetists in Canada and in Denmark. Anaesthetists Rall and Gaba (2005, p. 3088) discuss the ANTS system and conclude, 'On the whole, the ANTS system appears to be a useful tool to further enhance assessment of nontechnical skills in anaesthesia, and its careful derivation from a current system of nontechnical assessment in aviation (NOTECHS) may allow for some interdomain comparisons'.

Conclusion

In aviation, pilots are taught and examined in the psychological and physiological factors influencing safe task performance from the start of their training (human performance limitations courses). Consequently they are familiarized at an early stage of their career with the cognitive and social skills required for safe and efficient flight operations. They then undertake CRM training provided by their employing airline on a regular basis and also have checks of both their non-technical and technical skills.

This non-technical skills training is now widely used across the globe not only for pilots but increasingly for other workers in safety-critical occupations. The evidence that it enhances industrial safety is limited, partly because major accidents are infrequent in industries such as aviation and nuclear power generation. Anecdotal accounts from pilots and other professionals is that the training has helped them to manage difficult situations more effectively. The literature contains comparatively few studies in which the effects of the training have been evaluated, however reviews of these investigations have generally reported positive effects in relation to attitude and behaviour change, with some reports (e.g., military aviation) of reduced accident rates (Salas et al., 2001, 2006a; O'Connor et al., 2002).

References

Banbury, S., Dudfield, H., Hormann, J. & Soll, H. (2007), 'FASA: development and validation of a novel measure to assess the effectiveness of commercial airline pilot situation awareness training', *International Journal of Aviation Psychology*, **17**, 131–52.

Banbury, S. & Tremblay, S. (2004) (eds), *Situation Awareness: A Cognitive Approach*, Aldershot: Ashgate.

CAA (Civil Aviation Authority) (2006), *Crew Resource Management (CRM) Training. Guidance for Flight Crew, CRM Instructors (CRMIs) and CRM Instructor-Examiners (CRMIEs)*, CAP 737, Version 2, Gatwick: CAA, www.caa.co.uk, accessed 12 September 2008.

Carvalho, P., Santos, I. & Vidal, M. (2005), 'Nuclear power plant shift supervisor's decision making during microincidents', *Industrial Ergonomics*, **35**, 619–44.

Clarke, S. & Cooper, C.L. (2004), *Managing the Risks of Workplace Stress: Health and Safety Hazards*, London: Routledge.

Coren, S. (1996), *Sleep Thieves*, New York: Free Press.

Crichton, M., Flin, R. & McGeorge, P. (2005), 'Decision making by on-scene incident commanders in nuclear emergencies', *Cognition, Technology and Work*, **7**, 156–66.

Crichton, M., Flin, R. & Rattray, W. (2000), 'Training decision makers – tactical decision games', *Journal of Contingencies and Crisis Management*, **8**, 208–17.

Dawson, D. & Reid, K. (1997), 'Fatigue, alcohol and performance impairment', *Nature*, **388**, 23.

Dembe, A.E., Erickson, J.B., Delbos, R.G. & Banks, S.M. (2005), 'The impact of overtime and long work hours on occupational injuries and illnesses: new evidence from the United States', *Occupational and Environmental Medicine*, **62**, 588–97.

Edmondson, A. (2003), 'Speaking up in the operating room: how team leaders promote learning in interdisciplinary action teams', *Journal of Management Studies*, **40**, 1419–52.

Endsley, M. (1995a), 'Toward a theory of situation awareness in dynamic systems', *Human Factors*, **37**, 32–64.

Endsley, M. (1995b), 'A taxonomy of situation awareness errors', in R. Fuller, N. Johnson & N. McDonald (eds), *Human Factors in Aviation Operations*, Aldershot: Avebury, pp. 287–92.

Endsley, M. & Garland, D. (eds) (2000), *Situation Awareness: Analysis and Measurement*, Mahwah, NJ: LEA.

Fletcher, G., McGeorge, P., Flin, R., Glavin, R. & Maran, N. (2003), 'Anaesthetists' non-technical skills (ANTS). Evaluation of a behavioural marker system', *British Journal of Anaesthesia*, **90**, 580–88.

Flin, R. (1996), *Sitting in the Hot Seat: Leaders and Teams for Critical Incidents*, Chichester: Wiley.

Flin, R., Martin, L., Goeters, K., Hoermann, J., Amalberti, R., Valot, C. & Nijhuis, H. (2003), 'Development of the NOTECHS (non-technical skills) system for assessing pilots' CRM skills', *Human Factors and Aerospace Safety*, **3**, 95–117.

Flin, R., O'Connor, P. & Crichton, M. (2008), *Safety at the Sharp End: A Guide to Non-Technical Skills*, Aldershot: Ashgate.

Flin, R., O'Connor, P. & Mearns, K. (2002), 'Crew resource management: improving teamwork in high reliability industries', *Team Performance Management*, **8**, 68–78.

Flin, R., Salas, E., Strub, M. & Martin, L. (eds) (1997), *Decision Making under Stress*, Aldershot: Ashgate.

Flin, R., Youngson, G. & Yule, S. (2007), 'How do surgeons make intra-operative decisions?', *Quality and Safety in Health Care*, **16**, 235–9.

Gaba, D. (1992), 'Dynamic decision making in anaesthesia: cognitive models and training approaches', in D. Evans & V. Patel (eds), *Advanced Models of Cognition for Medical Training and Practice*, Berlin: Springer-Verlag, pp. 123–47.

Gaba, D., Howard, S. & Small, S. (1995), 'Situation awareness in anesthesiology', *Human Factors*, **37**, 20–31.

Glendon, I., Clarke, S. & McKenna, E. (2006), *Human Safety and Risk Management*, 2nd edn, Boca Raton, FL: CRC Press.

Hackman, J.R. (2002), *Leading Teams. Setting the Stage for Great Performances*, Harvard, MA: Harvard Business School Press.

Hamalainen, P., Takala, J. & Saarela, K. (2006), 'Global estimates of occupational accidents', *Safety Science*, **44**, 137–56.

Health and Safety Executive (HSE) (2007a), *Health and Safety Statistics 2006/2007*, London: HSE Publications, www.hse.gov.uk, accessed 22 December 2007.

Health and Safety Executive (HSE) (2007b), *Managing the Causes of Work Related Stress: A Step-by-step Approach Using the Management Standards HSG218*, 2nd edn, Sudbury: HSE Books.

Helmreich, R. (2000), 'On error management: lessons from aviation', *British Medical Journal*, **320**, 781–5.

Helmreich, R., Klinect, J. & Wilhelm, J. (2003), 'Managing threat and error: data from line operations', in G. Edkins & P. Pfister (eds), *Innovation and Consolidation in Aviation*, Aldershot: Ashgate, pp. 15–22.

Hofmann, D. & Morgeson, F. (2004), 'The role of leadership in safety', in J. Barling & M. Frone (eds), *The Psychology of Workplace Safety*, Washington, DC: APA Books.

Horne, J. (2006), *Sleepfaring. A Journey through the Science of Sleep*, Oxford: Oxford University Press.

Howard, S., Gaba, D., Rosekind, M. & Zarcone, V. (2002), 'The risks and implications of excessive daytime sleepiness in resident physicians', *Academic Medicine*, **77**, 1019–25.

Klein, G., Orasanu, J. Calderwood, R. & Zsambok, C. (eds) (1993), *Decision Making in Action*, New York: Ablex.

Lingard, L., Reznick, R., Espin, S., Regehr, G. & De Vito, I. (2002), 'Team communication in the operating room. Talk patterns, sites of tension and implications for novices', *Academic Medicine*, **77**, 232–7.

Montgomery, H., Lipshitz, R. & Brehmer, B. (eds) (2005), *How Professionals Make Decisions*, Mahwah, NJ: Lawrence Erlbaum.

Musson, D. & Helmreich, R. (2004), 'Team training and resource management in health care: current issues and future directions', *Harvard Health Policy Review*, **5**, 25–35.

Northouse, P. (2006), *Leadership: Theory and Practice*, 4th edn, London: Sage.

O'Connor, P., Flin, R. & Fletcher, G. (2002), 'Methods used to evaluate the effectiveness of CRM training: a literature review', *Human Factors and Aerospace Safety*, **2**, 217–34.

O'Dea, A. & Flin, R. (1998), 'Site management and safety leadership in the offshore oil and gas industry', *Safety Science*, **37**, 39–57.

Okray, R. & Lubnau, T. (2004), *Crew Resource Management for the Fire Service*, Tulsa, OK: PennWell.

Patey, R., Flin, R., Fletcher, G., Maran, N. & Glavin, R. (2005), 'Developing a taxonomy of anaesthetists' non-technical skills (ANTS)', in K. Hendriks (ed.), *Advances in Patient Safety: From Research to Implementation*, Rockville, MD: Agency for Healthcare Research and Quality, pp. 325–36.

Patrick, J. & Belton, S. (2003), 'What's going on?', *Nuclear Engineering International*, January, 36–40.

Petrill, R., Thomas, M., Dawson, D. & Roach, G. (2006), 'The decision making of airline crews following an international pattern', paper presented at the Australian Aviation Psychology conference, Manly, November, www.aavpa.org/seminars/ess2006 <http://www.aavpa.org/seminars/ess2006>, accessed 15 September 2008.

Rall, M. & Gaba, D. (2005), 'Human performance and patient safety', in R. Miller (ed.), *Anaesthesia*, Philadelphia, PA: Elsevier, pp. 3021–72.

Reason, J. (1987), 'The Chernobyl errors', *Bulletin of the British Psychological Society*, **40**, 201–6.

Reason, J. (1990), *Human Error*, Aldershot: Ashgate.

Salas, E., Edens, E. & Bowers, C. (eds) (2001), *Improving Teamwork in Organizations*, Mahwah, NJ: LEA.

Salas, E., Wilson, K.A, Burke, C.S. & Wightman, D.C. (2006a), 'Does CRM training work? An update, extension and some critical needs', *Human Factors*, **14**, 392–412.

Salas, E., Wilson, K., Burke, C., Wightman, D. & Howse, W. (2006b), 'Crew resource management training research and practice: a review, lessons learned and needs', in R. Williges (ed.), *Review of Human Factors and Ergonomics*, Vol. 2, Santa Monica, CA: Human Factors and Ergonomics Society, pp. 35–73.

Sneddon, A., Mearns, K. & Flin, R. (2006), 'Situation awareness in offshore drill crews', *Cognition, Technology and Work*, **8**, 255–67.

Stanton, N., Chambers, P. & Piggott, J. (2001), 'Situation awareness and safety', *Safety Science*, **39**, 189–204.

Turner, N. & Parker, S. (2004), 'The effect of teamwork on safety processes and outcomes', in J. Barling & M. Frone (eds), *The Psychology of Workplace Safety*, Washington: APA Books, pp. 35–62.

Undre, W., Sevdalis, N., Healey, A., Darzi, A. & Vincent, C. (2006), 'Teamwork in the operating theatre: cohesion or confusion?', *Journal of Evaluation in Clinical Practice*, **12**, 182–9.

Wagenaar, W. & Groeneweg, J. (1987), 'Accidents at sea: multiple causes and impossible consequences', *International Journal of Man–Machine Studies*, **27**, 587–98.

Walters, A. (2002), *Crew Resource Management is No Accident*, Wallingford, UK: Aries.

Weick, C. (1990), 'The vulnerable system: an analysis of the Tenerife air disaster', *Journal of Management*, **16** (3): 571–93.

West, M. (2004), *Effective Teamwork*: *Practical Lessons from Organizational Research*, 2nd edn, Leicester: BPS Blackwell.

Wiener, E., Kanki, B. & Helmreich, R. (eds) (1993), *Cockpit Resource Management*, San Diego, CA: Academic Press.

Yukl, G. (2005), *Leadership in Organisations*, 5th edn, Upper Saddle River, NJ: Prentice-Hall International.

Zsambok, C. & Klein, G. (eds) (1997), *Naturalistic Decision Making*, Mahwah, NJ: Lawrence Erlbaum.

10 The moderating role of interpersonal justice on the relationship between Eysenckian personality dimensions and employee voice and employee silence

*Alicia Omar**

Introduction

The effective functioning of an organization is highly dependent on spontaneous activities that are beyond prescribed role requirements. These behaviours were termed 'extra-role behaviours' by Katz and Kahn (1978) or 'organizational citizenship behaviours' by Smith et al. (1983). Organizational citizenship behaviour (OCB) has been described as 'individual behaviour that is discretionary, not directly or explicitly recognized by the formal reward system, and that in aggregate promotes the effective functioning of the organization' (Organ, 1988, p. 4). Examples of OCB include performing extra-job activities, helping colleagues, meeting workplace rules, and acting according to organizational policies and procedures regardless of personal inconvenience. A substantial body of organizational and industrial psychological research has shown that OCB benefits both the organization and its employees in numerous ways, which is evidenced by the increasing amount of research and theory on the topic (Podsakoff et al., 2000; LePine et al., 2002; Schnake & Dumler, 2003; Zellars & Tepper, 2003; Vey & Campbell, 2004).

Since the development of the concept, researchers have assumed that OCB is a multidimensional construct. In their seminal work, for example, Smith et al. (1983) identified two principal forms of OCB: altruism (helping behaviours directed at specific individuals), and general compliance (helping behaviours directed at the organizations as a whole). Subsequently, Organ (1988) proposed a model integrated by five dimensions: altruism, general compliance, civic virtue (participating in and being concerned about life of the organization), courtesy (informing others to prevent the occurrence of work-related problems), and sportsmanship (tolerating the inevitable inconveniences of work without complaining). Podsakoff et al. (1993) extended Organ's model by addressing the dimensions of interpersonal harmony (described as the avoidance of pursuing personal power and gain in the organization), and protecting company resources (defined as the avoidance of negative behaviours that abuse company policies and resources for personal use). Integrating frameworks from social history, philosophy and political science, Van Dyne et al. (1994) developed three new categories based on theories of civic citizenship. Their three categories (obedience, loyalty and civic participation) constitute what they called an 'active citizenship syndrome', wherein workers are engaged in responsible workplace participation. Afterwards, LePine and Van Dyne (1998) introduced the category of voice behaviour (intentionally expressing ideas, information and opinions with relevance to improvements in work and work organizations), whereas Morrison and Milliken (2000), developed the category of silence behaviour (intentionally withholding ideas, information and opinions about possible improvements).

Recently, Van Dyne et al. (2003) proposed a more refined conceptualization of employee voice and silence. Drawing on past research and theory in communication, social psychology and management, they described three different types of silence (acquiescent, defensive and prosocial), and three parallel types of voice (acquiescent, defensive and prosocial). Based upon prior management literature on silence (Morrison & Milliken 2000; Pinder & Harlos 2001), Van Dyne et al. (2003) described acquiescent silence (passive withholding of relevant ideas, based on resignation), and defensive silence (passive withholding of relevant ideas, based on fear, as a form of self-protection). Relying on the OCB literature (Organ, 1988), they proposed a third type of silence: prosocial silence (withholding work-related ideas, information, or opinions with the goal of benefiting other people or the organization itself). Similarly, they extended prior conceptualization of voice behaviour (constructive change-oriented communication, Van Dyne & LePine 1998), by describing prosocial voice (expressing work-related ideas, information, or opinions based on altruism or cooperative motives), and defined two additional types of voice: acquiescent voice (expressing work-related ideas based on resignation), and defensive voice (expressing relevant ideas based on fear). Van Dyne et al. (2003) argued that although employee voice and silence might appear to be polar opposites, they are separate and multidimensional constructs.

Much of the past research has concentrated on conventional OCB (Organ, 1988), such as altruism, generalized compliance and civic virtue. At the present time, the study of voice behaviour has begun to capture the scholar's attention (LePine & Van Dyne, 2001; Omar & Uribe, 2005; Platow et al., 2006), whereas silence behaviour has not yet been systematic and empirically studied. The current work will focus on prosocial voice and prosocial silence behaviours, the latest incorporations in the OCB nomological network, both of them considered as intentional, proactive, and other-oriented behaviours.

A sizeable literature documents the impact that organizational and dispositional variables have on OCB. Among the dispositional variables, personality traits have been specially considered. Some of this research involves the use of personality tests, generally placed within the five factor model framework. Conclusions based on meta-analyses have generally been that such tests predict OCB, with conscientiousness and agreeableness being the best predictors of altruism, general compliance and civic virtue (Organ & Ryan, 1995; Borman et al., 2001). Nevertheless, these results could be attributed to a certain degree of overlap among the items of these personality measures and the items used in OCB research (Borman et al., 2001). The other 'Big Five' factors (openness to experience, extroversion and emotional stability) have exhibited weak or controversial relationships with helping behaviour and civic virtue (Van Dyne et al., 2000; Sackett et al., 2006). Markedly less research has investigated whether voice (and silence) behaviour could be explained in terms of personality traits. Among the few studies that have explored such questions directly are those of LePine and Van Dyne (2001), and Omar and Uribe (2005). While the former, employing the Big Five dimensions, reported that agreeableness correlated positively with helping behaviour, but negatively with voice, the latter, employing the Eysenckian personality dimensions, found that voice correlated positively with extroversion, and negatively with neurotic tendencies. Extending this last perspective, the first aim of the present work is to verify whether employee prosocial voice and prosocial silence can be predicted by Eysenckian personality measures.

The four-scale Eysenck Personality Questionnaire (EPQ, Eysenck & Eysenck, 1975) has been used in several countries and cultures, and their psychometric properties are well documented. Extroversion (E) deals with traits such as sociability, activity, liveliness and optimism. Neuroticism (N) involves anxiousness, tenseness, guilt feelings and depression. Psychoticism (P) is related to aggressive, egocentric, impulsive and emotionally cold tendencies, and the L(ie) scale is intended to measure a propensity to 'fake good'. Several studies provide evidence that extroversion predisposes individuals towards positive affect, whereas neuroticism predisposes individuals towards negative affect (Costa & McCrae, 1980; Emmons & Diener, 1985). In this sense, following the logic of Organ (1994), if positive affective states generally elicit prosocial behaviours, then positive affectivity, as a dispositional variable, should predict the tendency to engage in prosocial behaviour. Conversely, if negative affect suppresses prosocial behaviour, then negative affectivity, as a trait, should be associated with less frequency of prosocial behaviours. In other words, high extroversion scorers (extroverts), due to their great tendencies to seek warm and positive social interactions, will possibly be more engaged in prosocial voice behaviours than introverts; whereas, the emotional stable ones (non-neurotic individuals), due to their marked disposition to be calm and relaxed, still under pressure, possibly will be more engaged in prosocial silence behaviours than neurotic ones. In addition, the Eysenckian psychoticism dimension (and L, the internal reliability scale of EPQ) could be indirectly associated with prosocial voice and/ or prosocial silence, via the patterns of behaviour to which they give rise. Psychotic individuals, due to their great predisposition to hostility, impulsivity, coldness and lack of empathy feelings, would hardly be engaged in prosocial voice. Whereas high L scale scorers, due to their great wish to give a more favourable picture of themselves, would hardly be engaged in prosocial silence. In this sense, for example, Finkelstein (2006) has indicated that individuals who wish to make a better impression are likely to choose activities visible to peers or supervisors. In line with these arguments, the following hypotheses are proposed:

Hypothesis 1: the positive pole (extroversion) of the Eysenckian 'introversion–extroversion' dimension and the negative pole (non-psychotic tendencies) of the Eysenckian psychoticism dimension will be associated with prosocial voice.

Hypothesis 2: the negative pole (emotional control) of the Eysenckian 'control–neuroticism' dimension and the negative pole (low lie tendencies) of the Eysenckian lie scale will be associated with prosocial silence.

Among the organizational variables, work satisfaction (Yoon & Suh, 2003; Van Dyne & Pierce, 2004), job involvement (Diefendorff et al., 2002), organizational commitment (Becker & Kernan, 2003), organizational values (Omar et al., 2007), perceived team support (Pearce & Herbik, 2004) and trust in supervisor (Aryee et al., 2002) have been specially considered as predictors of OCB. Nevertheless, organizational justice perception (Kickul et al., 2002; Ehrhart, 2004) is one of the workplace variables that has received more research attention in relation to OCB.

The impact of organizational justice perception on the personality–OCB relationship
Organizational justice is concerned with employee perception of fair or just treatment on the job (Cropanzano et al., 2001). Three main dimensions have been taken into

consideration in this area: distributive justice, which refers to the content of rewards and outcomes, that is, the justice of ends and results achieved; procedural justice, which relates to how the distribution is handled; and interactional justice, which is part of procedural justice and is related to the quality of interpersonal relationships between managers responsible for making those decisions and organizational members affected by them.

There is great controversy among authors whether the interactional justice is independent of procedural justice (Bies and Moag, 1986; Cropanzano & Greenberg, 1997). However, the latest trend in literature (Colquitt, 2001; Colquitt et al., 2001) has been to regard interactional justice as an autonomous dimension. It represents the social side of organizational justice and can be further divided into two different aspects: interpersonal and informational justice. Interpersonal justice refers to respect shown by managers when dealing with other members of an organization involved in distributive and procedural decisions. Informational justice, on the other hand, deals with the amount of information and explanations about decisions and procedures given by managers to other organizational members. Conclusively, there seems to be a consensus among organizational justice scholars in considering organizational justice as a multidimensional construct with four aspects: distributive justice, procedural justice, interpersonal justice and informational justice. The last two form the so-called 'interactional justice'.

Most studies have tried to verify the possible associations between distributive and procedural justice and OCB. Several of these investigations (Moorman et al., 1998; Masterson, 2001; Kickul et al., 2002) have collected evidence that procedural justice is a better predictor for OCB than distributive justice. In explaining such findings, the authors have made use of a two-factor model (Sweeney & McFarlin, 1993), according to which the justice of results and the justice of procedures, being different factors, lead to different kinds of reactions. Consequently, while the perceptions of distributive justice relate mainly to the satisfaction with specific results, namely salary payments, procedural justice relates to attitudes and behaviours which are more relevant to the organization, such as OCB. More recently, comparing the effects of procedural and interactional justice on OCB, Wayne et al. (2002) and Williams et al. (2002) have shown that interactional justice is more closely associated with OCB than is procedural justice. Nevertheless, up to the moment, relatively little research has analysed the relationships between the two facets of interactional justice (informational and interpersonal) and OCB, and none has tested the association among interpersonal and informational justice and prosocial voice, and prosocial silence. Taking into account that such dimensions are the social sides of organizational justice, it could be expected that both of them present associations with those OCBs. Based on these arguments the following hypothesis is proposed:

Hypothesis 3: the interpersonal and informational justice perceptions will be positively associated with prosocial voice and prosocial silence.

In line with the suggestions of Colquitt and Greenberg (2003), and Cropanzano et al (2001), the second aim of the present study is to analyse the moderating role of interpersonal justice perception on the relationship between personality and prosocial voice and silence. Colquitt and Cropanzano have called for research that expands beyond simply examining the direct effects of justice on employees' attitudes to exploring how justice perceptions work along with either contextual factor or individual differences to influence the attitudes of employees. Based on these suggestions, and as well as in some empirical evidence that indicates that interpersonal justice has the potential to enhance positive organizational outcomes (Laschinger, 2004), that fair interpersonal treatment leads to a smaller counterproductive behaviour (Aquino et al., 2004; Brennan & Skarlicki, 2004), that individual differences moderate the effects of interpersonal justice on job attitudes (Burnett et al., 2005), and that personality factors correlate with discretionary prosocial behaviours (Van Emmerik et al., 2004), it is possible to suppose, then, that interpersonal justice will act as a moderating variable in the relations between personality and prosocial voice and prosocial silence.

Hypothesis 4: the perceptions of interpersonal justice will moderate both the relationship between prosocial voice and extroversion/non-psychotic tendencies, and the relationship between prosocial silence and emotional control/non-lie tendencies.

Method

Participants
Participants were 316 employees from a variety of industries and companies (e.g., financial services, chemical industries, telecommunications, supermarkets, public services) in southern and central Rosario (Argentina). The majority of the participants were male (67%), almost half were married (48%), and 33% had a college education or were in the process of achieving it. The average age was 32.12 years (SD = 7.26) and the mean tenure was 6.28 years (SD = 3.10).

Procedure
Employees were asked to complete a survey on an individual or group basis, in their own companies, after obtaining authorization from the managers. Participation was voluntary, and individuals were assured that their responses would remain anonymous. All human subject procedures were followed in the conduct of this study. The survey included measures (described below) of personality dimensions, organizational justice perception, OCB behaviours and demographic information.

Measures
The personality dimensions were measured by an Argentinean version (Omar, 1988) of the EPQ (Eysenck & Eysenck, 1975). This is a 90-item questionnaire that contains four scales: (E) extroversion (21 items; $\alpha = 0.87$); (N) neuroticism (23 items; $\alpha = 0.82$); (P) psychoticism (25 items; $\alpha = 0.72$); and (L) lie (21 items; $\alpha = 0.79$) in a yes/no format. Higher values on the scales indicate greater tendencies to E, N, P and L.

   OCB was measured using the Argentinean validation (Omar et al., 2006) of the 10 items developed by Van Dyne et al. (2003) to assess employees' displayed prosocial voice (5 items: 'I express solutions to problems with the cooperative motive of benefiting the organization'; 'I develop and make recommendations concerning issues that affect the organization'; 'I communicate my opinions about work issues even if others disagree'; 'I speak up with ideas for new projects that might benefit the organization'; 'I suggest ideas for change, based on constructive concern for the organization'), and prosocial silence (5 items: 'I withhold confidential information, based on cooperation'; 'I protect proprietary information in order to benefit the organization'; 'I withstand pressure from others to tell organizational secrets'; 'I refuse to divulge information that might harm the organization'; 'I protect confidential organizational information appropriately, based on concern for the organization'). Both scales were modified in order that the focus of the questions was changed from the supervisor to the employee. Participants responded to each of these statements using a Likert-type scale ranging from 1 (never) to 5 (always). The coefficient alpha for the prosocial voice items was 0.80, and for the prosocial silence items was 0.76.

The organizational justice perceptions were measured by an Argentinean version (Omar et al., 2003) of Colquitt's (2001) justice scale. The participants indicated their responses to the 9-scale items using a 5-point Likert format with 'always' and 'never' as anchors. These items were distributed in two dimensions: interpersonal justice (4 items; $\alpha = 0.83$), and informational justice (5 items; $\alpha = 0.88$).

Data analysis
Moderated regression analysis was used as the recommended method for testing interaction effects (Cohen & Cohen, 1983). Two separate regression analyses were performed to detect main and interaction effects of personality dimension, and the moderator variable (interpersonal justice), on each of the OCB measures. In each of the regressions models, the standardized independent variables were introduced into the equation in five successive steps (Aiken & West, 1991). In the first step, age, sex and tenure were entered to control their possible influence, since past researchers have shown that sex (Wayne & Cordeiro, 2003; Sackett et al., 2006; Farrell & Finkelstein, 2007), age and tenure (Coyle-Shapiro & Kessler, 2003) contribute, at least, minimally to explain OCB. In the second and third steps, personality dimensions (E, N, P and L) and justice variables, respectively, were introduced as main effects. Finally, in the fourth and fifth steps, the interactions between personality variables and interpersonal justice were entered. In order to test interaction effects, multiplicative terms were created for the standardized independent variables (Cohen & Cohen, 1983). The outcome variables were prosocial voice and prosocial silence. The significant interaction effects would support hypothesis 4, whereas the significant main effects would support hypotheses 1–3, since the main effects of the independent variables generally constitute significant information (Jaccard et al., 1990).

Results
Means, standard deviations and intercorrelations of this study's variables are shown in Table 10.1. The correlation matrix shows that prosocial voice is correlated positively with extroversion ($r = 0.38, p < 0.01$), interpersonal justice ($r = 0.27, p < 0.01$) and informational justice ($r = 0.18, p < 0.01$), and weak, but negatively, with psychoticism ($r = -0.11$, $p < 0.05$). However, prosocial silence appears more strongly correlated, negatively, with neuroticism ($r = -0.22, p < 0.01$) than with lie ($r = -0.12, p < 0.05$), and positively with interpersonal justice ($r = 0.15, p < 0.01$).

To test for the interactions specified by the hypotheses, the data were analysed using moderated multiple regression. Separate analyses were conducted for each OCB variable (Table 10.2).

Hypothesis 1 predicted that the positive pole (extroversion) of the Eysenckian 'introversion–extroversion' dimension, and the negative pole (non-psychotic tendencies) of the Eysenckian psychoticism dimension would be associated with prosocial voice. As

Table 10.1   Means, standard deviations and correlations between the variables

		M	SD	1	2	3	4	5	6	7	8
1.	Extroversion	13.73	4.15	–	−0.12*	0.16**	0.07	0.23**	0.15**	0.38**	−0.09
2.	Neuroticism	12.75	4.40		–	0.32**	−0.19**	0.18**	0.10	0.07	−0.22**
3.	Psychoticism	5.45	2.71			–	−0.18**	−0.08	−0.07	−0.11*	0.02
4.	Lie scale	10.22	4.31				–	0.16**	0.09	0.05	−0.12*
5.	Interpersonal j.	4.25	0.70					–	0.12*	0.27**	0.15**
6.	Informational j.	3.82	0.81						–	0.18**	0.10
7.	Prosocial voice	3.95	0.73							–	−0.03
8.	Prosocial silence	3.38	0.98								–

Note: **$p < 0.01$; * $p < 0.05$.

Table 10.2   Summary of regression analysis for the moderating role of interpersonal justice between personality variables and prosocial voice, and prosocial silence

	Variables	Interpersonal justice perception as moderator	
		Prosocial voice	Prosocial silence
Step 1	Age	0.07	0.02
	Sex[a]	−0.05	0.09
	Tenure	0.01	0.01
		$R^2 = 0.01$	$R^2 = 0.01$
Step 2	Extroversion	0.32***	0.02
	Neuroticism	−0.07	−0.25**
	Psychoticism	−0.05	0.06
	Lie	0.10	−0.09
		$R^2 = 0.16$	$R^2 = 0.13$
		$\Delta R^2 = 0.15**$	$\Delta R^2 = 0.12**$
Step 3	Interpersonal justice	0.29**	0.12*
	Informational justice	0.07	0.09
		$R^2 = 0.21$	$R^2 = 0.16$
		$\Delta R^2 = 0.06*$	$\Delta R^2 = 0.04*$
Step 4	Extroversion × Interpersonal j.	0.28**	
		$R^2 = 0.25$	
		$\Delta R^2 = 0.04*$	
	Neuroticism × Interpersonal j.		−0.21*
			$R^2 = 0.23$
			$\Delta R^2 = 0.07*$
Step 5	Psychoticism × Interpersonal j.	0.02	
		$R^2 = 0.25$	
		$\Delta R^2 = 0.00$	
	Lie × Interpersonal j.		−0.01
			$R^2 = 0.23$
			$\Delta R^2 = 0.00$

Notes: *$p < 0.05$; ** $p < 0.01$; *** $p < 0.001$.
[a] Dummy coded: 1 'males'.

shown in Table 10.2, extroversion was positively related to prosocial voice ($\beta = 0.32$, $p < 0.001$), over and above that explained by the control variables. However, the hypothesized relationships between psychoticism and prosocial voice did not reach significance ($\beta = -0.05$, n.s.). Thus, hypothesis 1 was partially supported.

Hypothesis 2 predicted that the negative pole (emotional control) of the Eysenckian 'control–neuroticism' dimension and the negative pole (non-lie tendencies) of the Eysenckian lie scale will be associated with prosocial silence. The results showed that emotional control ($\beta = -0.25$, $p < 0.01$) had the greatest statistically significant effect on prosocial silence. Conversely, lie tendencies failed to make any contribution to the prediction of prosocial silence ($\beta = -0.09$, $p <$ n.s.), and hence, hypothesis 2 received only limited support.

Hypothesis 3 asserted that the interpersonal and informational justice perceptions would be positively associated with prosocial voice and prosocial silence. However, the results (Table 10.2) showed that only interpersonal justice had significant relationships with prosocial voice ($\beta = 0.29$, $p < 0.01$) and with prosocial silence ($\beta = 0.12$, $p < 0.05$), after accounting for the effects of the control variables. Consequently, hypothesis 3 was partially supported.

According to hypothesis 4, the perceptions of interpersonal justice would moderate, on the one hand, the relationships between prosocial voice and extroversion/non-psychotic tendencies, and, on the other, the relationship between prosocial silence and emotional control/non-lie tendencies. Entry, in step 4, of the two-way interactional term (extroversion × interpersonal justice) explained a significant amount of additional variance in prosocial voice, $\Delta R^2 = 0.04$; $F(1,406) = 6.05$, $p < 0.05$. However, the expected influence of the interaction of psychoticism and interpersonal justice on prosocial voice (step 5) did not receive support from the data. According to these findings, then, higher perceptions of interpersonal justice were only associated with higher levels of prosocial voice among employees with higher extroversion tendencies. With respect to prosocial silence, the interactional term (neuroticism × interpersonal justice), entered in step 4, explained a significant amount of additional variance of this dependent variable, $\Delta R^2 = 0.07$; $F(1,406) = 5.05$, $p < 0.05$; whereas the interactional term (lie × interpersonal justice) entered in step 5, did not reach significance. In the light of these results, higher perceptions of interpersonal justice were associated with higher levels of prosocial silence among employees with higher emotional control ($\beta = -0.21$, $p < 0.05$). In spite of these results, hypothesis 4 was partially supported since the hypothesized moderating effects of interpersonal justice on relation between prosocial voice/non-psychotic tendencies, and between prosocial silence/non-lie tendencies were not observed.

Discussion

The primary aim of this study was to investigate the relationship between Eysenckian personality dimensions and prosocial voice/prosocial silence. In this sense, the results gave partial support to the hypotheses suggested in the introduction. In line with the findings of Barrick et al. (2003), extroversion emerged as a better predictor of the occurrence of prosocial voice in the present study. The linkage observed would be an indicator that expressing work-related ideas, information or opinions based on altruism or cooperative motives (prosocial voice) is more closely associated with extrovert characteristics than with introvert ones. The association between extroversion and prosocial voice is also consistent with prior research (Graziano & Eisenberg, 1997) in showing that extroverted individuals may be more likely to engage in expressing opinions than introverted individuals when their cooperative motivation is high. In this sense, engaging in prosocial voice or silence can be viewed as an opposite activity, just as intro-extroversion are opposite poles of the Eysenckian temperamental dimension.

On the other hand, results indicated that withholding work-related ideas, information, or opinions with the goal of benefiting other people or the organization (prosocial silence) appear more closely associated with emotional control. The finding that non-neurotic individuals are more willing to engage in prosocial silence is similar to that reported by LePine and Van Dyne (2001), who found that neuroticism correlated negatively ($r = -0.12$) with voice. Baruch et al. (2004) and Sackett et al. (2006) also reported a similar effect and suggested that individuals with negative affective tones should engage in less prosocial activities. Although both emotional control and low lie tendencies were significantly correlated with prosocial silence in the univariate analysis (see Table 10.1), lie did not reach significance at the multivariate analysis. This lack of relationship between lie and prosocial behaviour is in line with the results of Finkelstein and Penner (2004) and Finkelstein (2006), who indicated that motives concerned with the desire to show better impressions did not prove to be good predictors of OCB.

Similarly, even though interpersonal and informational justice were significantly correlated with both OCB as well as with one another (see Table 10.1), only interpersonal justice perceptions emerged as a unique (and strong) predictor of voice, and a unique (although moderate) predictor of silence when shared variance was partialized by hierarchical regression analysis. According to this result it is possible to suppose that higher perception of interpersonal justice may result in a more general positive disposition to engage in prosocial behaviour. In this sense, it would be supposed that employees who personally believe that they are treated fairly by their supervisors are significantly more likely to exhibit prosocial citizenship behaviours than those who feel that their managers provide adequate explanations concerning decisions that affect their work (informational justice perception). In line with Moorman's earlier (1991) findings, the type of fairness perception was important in predicting the occurrence of OCB in the present study, and supports those of other researchers (Williams et al., 2002; Siegel et al., 2005), who suggested more recently that the treatment of employees may be one of the most important aspects in the manifestation of organizationally desirable actions. The current research also supported the explanation that the relations between some personality traits and some OCB can be better accounted for by investigating the moderating effect of justice perception. Indeed, interpersonal justice provides the impetus for prosocial voice among individuals who have an extroverted disposition, and for prosocial silence among individuals who have a disposition for great emotional control. In other words, the results showed that extrovert workers display more prosocial voice behaviour and non-neurotic workers display more prosocial silence behaviour when they perceive more interpersonal justice.

As with any empirical study, there are both strengths and limitations that warrant comment. One remarkable limitation of the present study is that it was based on OCB self-report data, and the results may be contaminated by the variance of the common method. Even though previous researchers (Konovsky & Organ, 1996) suggested that managerial-evaluated OCB can also produce bias, future research should include other sources of prosocial silence and prosocial voice (e.g., from supervisors, colleagues, sub-ordinates and customers), since observers should consider the nonverbal cues (such as facial expressions, gestures, posture and eye contact) provided in conjunction with the verbal cues (such as tone and inflection) in making judgements about employee voice or silence (Van Dyne et al., 2003). A further limitation is that any data collected by self-report measures may have been influenced by a social desirability response bias. Thus, although researchers have suggested that social desirability is generally not a source of bias in measuring organizational perceptions (Moorman & Podsakoff, 1992), it would be appropriate to complement the present measurements with others obtained through different methods. Finally, it would be useful to examine what role the 'spiral of silence' (Noelle-Neumann, 1991, cited by Bowen & Blackmon, 2003) plays in an employee's prosocial voice or silence. Noelle-Neumann's spiral of silence emphasizes the horizontal pressures that the threat of isolation and corresponding fear of isolation exert to keep people from being open and honest about their opinions. In this sense, Bowen and Blackmon (2003) suggested that individuals would be more likely to speak up when they believe that their position is supported by others, and remain silent when they believe that it is not.

However, the present study exhibited some strengths as well. Researchers emphasized that a sample involving a wider range of employees from a variety of organizations would likely result in improved external validity. Consequently, a wide variety of employees from a number of industries and companies were included in this work with the purpose of increasing the generalizability of the results. Results indicated, for example, that interpersonal fairness perceptions influenced OCB (prosocial voice and prosocial silence) across a number of companies and industries. Furthermore, the inclusion of demographic variables as control increased the validity of the design. After controlling for individual differences, findings showed that interpersonal justice perceptions still influenced OCB. These findings support those of other researchers (Williams et al., 2002), who suggested that interpersonal justice may be crucial in the manifestation of OCB, and showed that organizational members' perceptions of fair treatment is a key antecedent to perform prosocial behaviours.

The results also contribute to learning more about linkages between individual differences and relatively specific criterion constructs. In a broader context, these attempts to examine links between individual predictor constructs (e.g., personality traits) and criterion constructs (OCB) reflect Campbell's recommendations for building a science of personnel selection (Campbell et al., 1996).

Finally, despite the need of refinements, this research makes a contribution to the understanding of the impact of justice perceptions, having provided evidence that the effects of the personality of employees from Latin American countries on OCB are moderated by interpersonal justice perception. So, the findings could help human resource managers from these countries in implementing strategies designed to foster desirable actions of their employees in reaction to the fair treatment adopted by the organization. Therefore managers who desire to create an organizational atmosphere that elicits citizenship activity must strive to improve the perceived justice of their interactions with subordinates. Thus, it is an important goal of managers everywhere to make employees aware of the benefits of OCB (Bolino & Turnley, 2003) and, if possible, encourage it (Vigoda-Gadot, 2006).

Conclusion

The purpose of the present study was twofold: (i) to explore the relationships between Eysenckian personality dimensions and the new facets of OCB (prosocial voice and prosocial silence); and (ii) to examine the moderating role of interpersonal justice perceptions on such relationships. The findings provide evidence of the link between some global personality traits and some specific OCB since extroversion and neuroticism emerged as stronger predictors of prosocial voice and prosocial silence, respectively. Once again extroversion and neuroticism were demonstrated to be the Eysenckian 'Big Two' dimensions. The findings also provide preliminary support for understanding the role of justice perceptions in the relationship between dispositional and organizational variables. In particular, the results of this study suggest that interpersonal justice perception moderates the 'natural' tendencies of extrovert workers to engage in prosocial voice, and of non-neurotic workers to engage in prosocial silence. In sum, the promotion of high levels of interpersonal justice in work contexts can help workers to engage in more OCB, with positive effects on the organization as a whole. This is a real challenge for organizations, basically because previous studies (Podsakoff et al., 2000) have demonstrated that organizations with a strong emphasis on citizenship behaviour (and organizational justice) are healthier and more successful than other organizations that lack such a climate.

Acknowledgement

The research was funded by CONICET (National Council of Scientific and Technology Research): Award 5108.

Note

* Researcher, National Council of Scientific and Technological Research (CONICET), and Professor of National University of Rosario, Argentina.

References

Aiken, L.S. & West, S.G. (1991), *Multiple Regression: Testing and Interpreting interactions*, Sage, Newbury Park, CA.

Aquino, K., Galperin, B.L. & Bennett, R.J. (2004), 'Social status and aggressiveness as moderators of the relationship between interactional justice and workplace deviance?', *Journal of Applied Social Psychology*, **34** (5), 1001–29.

Aryee, S., Budhwar, P.S. & Chen, Z.X. (2002), 'Trust as a mediator of the relationship between organizational justice and work outcomes: test of a social exchange model', *Journal of Organizational Behavior*, **23**, 267–85.

Barrick, M.R., Mount, M.K. & Judge, T.A. (2003), 'Personality and performance at the beginning of the new millennium: what do we know and where do we go next?', *Journal of Applied Psychology*, **52**, 201–16.

Baruch, Y., O'Creevy, M., Hind, P. & Vigoda-Gadot, E. (2004), 'Pro social behavior and job performance: does the need for control and the need for achievement make a difference?', *Social Behavior and Personality*, **32**, 399–411.

Becker, T.E. & Kernan, M.C. (2003), 'Matching commitment to supervisors and organizations to in-role and extra-role performance', *Human Performance*, **16** (4), 327–48.

Bies, R.J. & Moag, J.F. (1986), 'Interactional justice: communication criteria of fairness', in R. Lewicki, B. Sheppard & M. Bazerman (eds), *Research on Negotiations in Organizations*, JAI Press, Greenwich, CT, pp. 43–55.

Bolino, M.C. & Turnley, W.H. (2003), 'Going the extra mile: cultivating and managing employee citizenship behavior', *Academy of Management Executive*, **17** (3), 60–71.

Borman, W.C., Penner, L.A., Allen, T.D. & Motowidlo, S.J. (2001), 'Personality predictors of citizenship performance', *International Journal of Selection and Assessment*, **9** (1–2), 52–69.

Bowen, F. & Blackmon, K. (2003), 'Spirals of silence: the dynamic effects of diversity on organizational voice', *Journal of Management Studies*, **40** (6), 1393–417.

Brennan, A. & Skarlicki, D.P. (2004), 'Personality and perceived justice as predictors of survivors' reactions following downsizing', *Journal of Applied Social Psychology*, **34** (6), 1306–28.

Burnett, M.F., Williamson, I.O. Bartol, K.M. (2005), 'Personality as a determinant of employees' reactions to justice and organizational reward perceptions: a cognitive affective perspective', *Academy of Management Best Conference Paper*, **1** (OB), E1–E6.

Campbell, J.P., Gasser, M.B. & Oswald, F.L. (1996), 'The substantive nature of job performance variability', in K.R. Murphy (ed.), *Individual Differences and Behavior in Organizations*, Jossey-Bass, San Francisco, CA, pp. 258–99.

Cohen, J. & Cohen, P. (1983), *Applied Multiple Regression/Correlation Analysis for the Behavioral Sciences*, Lawrence Erlbaum, Hillsdale, NJ.

Colquitt, J.A. (2001), 'On the dimensionality of organizational justice: a construct validation of a measure', *Journal of Applied Psychology*, **86**, 356–400.

Colquitt, J.A., Conlon, D.E., Wesson, M.J., Porter, C.O. & Ng, K.Y. (2001), 'Justice at the millennium: a meta-analytic review of 25 years of organizational justice research', *Journal of Applied Psychology*, **86**, 425–45.

Colquitt, J.A. & Greenberg, J. (2003), 'Organizational justice: a fair assessment of the state of the literature', in J. Greenberg (ed.), *Organizational Behavior: The State of the Science*, Lawrence Erlbaum, Mahwah, NJ, pp. 165–210.

Costa, P.T. & McCrae, R.R. (1980), 'Influence of extroversion and neuroticism on subjective well-being: happy and unhappy people', *Journal of Personality and Social Psychology*, **38**, 668–78.

Coyle-Shapiro, J.A.M. & Kessler, I. (2003), 'The employment relationship in the UK public sector: a psychological contract perspective', *Journal of Public Administration Research and Theory*, **13**, 213–30.

Cropanzano, R., Byrne, Z.S., Bobocel, D.R. & Rupp, D.E. (2001), 'Moral virtues, fairness heuristics, social entities, and other denizens of organizational justice', *Journal of Vocational Behavior*, **58**, 164–209.

Cropanzano, T. & Greenberg, J. (1997), 'Progress in organizational justice: tunelling through the maze', in C.L. Cooper & I.T. Robertson (eds), *International Review of Industrial and Organizational Psychology*, Wiley & Sons, New York, pp. 317–72.

Diefendorff, J.M., Brown, D.J., Kamin, A.M. & Lord, R.G. (2002), 'Examining the roles of job involvement and work centrality in predicting organizational citizenship behaviors and job performance', *Journal of Organizational Behavior*, **23**, 93–108.

Ehrhart, M.G. (2004), 'Leadership and procedural justice climate as antecedents of unit-level organizational citizenship behavior', *Personnel Psychology*, **57** (1), 61–94.

Emmons, R.A. & Diener, E. (1985), 'Personality correlates of subjective well-being', *Personality and Social Psychology Bulletin*, **11**, 89–97.

Eysenck, H.J. & Eysenck, S.B.G. (1975), *Manual of the Eysenck Personality Questionnaire*, Hodder & Stoughton, London.

Farrell, S.K. & Finkelstein, L.M. (2007), 'Organizational citizenship behavior and gender: expectations and attributions for performance', *North American Journal of Psychology*, **9** (1), 81–96.

Finkelstein, L.M. (2006), 'Dispositional predictors of organizational citizenship behavior: motives, motive fulfillment, and role identity', *Social Behavior and Personality*, **34** (6), 603–16.

Finkelstein, L.M. & Penner, L.A. (2004), 'Predicting organizational citizenship behavior: integrating the functional and role identity approaches', *Social Behavior and Personality*, **32** (4), 383–98.

Graziano, W.G. & Eisenberg, N. (1997), 'Agreeableness: a dimension of personality', in R. Hogan, J.A. Johnson & S.R. Briggs (eds), *Handbook of Personality Psychology*, Academic Press, San Diego, CA, pp. 795–824.

Jaccard, J., Turrisi, R. & Wan, C.K. (1990), *Interaction Effects in Multiple Regression*, Sage, Newbury Park, CA.

Katz, D. & Kahn, R.L. (1978), *The Social Psychology of Organizations*, Wiley, New York.

Kickul, J., Lester, S.W. & Finkl, J. (2002), 'Promise breaking during radical organizational change: do justice interventions make a difference?', *Journal of Organizational Behavior*, **23**, 469–88.

Konovsky, M.A. & Organ, D.W. (1996), 'Dispositional and contextual determinants or organizational citizenship behavior', *Journal of Organizational Behavior*, **17**, 253–66.

Laschinger, H.K.S. (2004), 'Hospital nurses' perceptions of respect and organizational justice', *Journal of Nursing Administration*, **34** (7–8), 354–64.

LePine, J.A., Erez, A. & Johnson, D.E. (2002), 'The nature and dimensionality of organizational citizenship behavior: a critical review and meta-analysis', *Journal of Applied Psychology*, **87** (1), 52–65.

LePine, J.A. & Van Dyne, L. (1998), 'Predicting voice behaviour in work groups', *Journal of Applied Psychology*, **83**, 853–68.

LePine, J.A. & Van Dyne, L. (2001), 'Voice and cooperative behavior as contrasting forms of contextual performance: evidence of differential relationships with Big Five personality characteristics and cognitive ability', *Journal of Applied Psychology*, **86** (2), 326–36.

Masterson, S.S. (2001), 'A trickle-down model of organizational justice: relating employees' and customers' perceptions of and reactions to fairness', *Journal of Applied Psychology*, **86**, 594–604.

Moorman, R.H. (1991), 'Relationship between organizational justice and organizational citizenship behaviors: do fairness perceptions influence employee citizenship?', *Journal of Applied Psychology*, **76**, 845–55.

Moorman, R.H., Blakely, G.L. & Niehoff, B.P. (1998), 'Does perceived organizational support mediate the relationship between procedural justice and organizational citizenship behavior?', *Academy of Management Journal*, **41**, 351–7.

Moorman, R.H. & Podsakoff, P.M. (1992), 'A meta-analytic review and empirical test of the potential confounding effects of social desirability response sets in organizational behavior research', *Journal of Occupational and Organizational Psychology*, **65**, 131–49.

Morrison, E.W. & Milliken, F.J. (2000), 'Organizational silence: a barrier to change and development in a pluralistic world', *Academy of Management Review*, **25**, 706–25.

Omar, A. (1988), 'Estandarización argentina de los cuestionarios de personalidad de Eysenck' ['Argentinean validation of Eysneck personality questionnaires'], *Revista Chilena de Neuro-Psiquiatría*, **42**, 83–95.

Omar, A., Maltaneres, V. & Paris, L. (2003), 'Análisis de la estructura factorial de una escala para explorar justicia organizacional' ['Factorial structure of an organizational justice scale'], *Proceedings of Marplatense Congress of Psychology*, National University of Mar del Plata, pp. 124–36.

Omar, A., Souto, S. & Uribe, H. (2006), 'Personality dimensions and citizenship organizational behaviour', *Revista Interamericana de Psicología Ocupacional*, **25** (1), 5–15.

Omar, A. & Uribe, H. (2005), 'Las dimensiones de personalidad como predictores de los comportamientos de ciudadanía organizacional' ['Personality dimensions as predictors of organizational citizenship behaviour'], *Estudos de Psicología (Natal)*, **10** (2), 35–47.

Omar, A., Uribe, H., Ferreira, M.C., Assmar, E.M., Souto, S., Terrones González, A. & Florez Galaz, M.M. (2007), 'Colectivismo, justicia y ciudadanía organizacional en empresas argentinas, mexicanas y brasileras' ['Collectivism, justice, and organizational citizenship in Argentinean, Mexican, and Brazilian organizations'], *Revista Mexicana de Psicología*, **24** (1), pp. 101–16.

Organ, D.W. (1988), *Organizational Citizenship Behavior: The Good Soldier Syndrome*, Lexington Books, Lexington, MA.

Organ, D.W. (1994), 'Personality and organizational behavior', *Journal of Management*, **20** (2), 465–78.

Organ, D.W. & Ryan, K. (1995), 'A meta-analytic review of attitudinal and dispositional predictors of organizational citizenship behavior', *Personnel Psychology*, **48**, 775–802.

Pearce, C.L. & Herbik, P.A. (2004), 'Citizenship behavior at the team level of analysis: the effects of team leadership, team commitment, perceived team support, and team size', *Journal of Social Psychology*, **144** (3), 293–310.

Pinder, C.C. & Harlos, K.P. (2001), 'Employee silence: quiescence and acquiescence as responses to perceived injustice', in K.M. Rowland & G.R. Ferris (eds), *Research in Personnel and Human Resources Management*, JAI Press, New York, pp. 331–69.

Platow, M.J., Filardo, F., Troselj, L., Grace, D.M. & Ryan, M.K. (2006), 'Non-instrumental voice and extra-role behaviour', *European Journal of Social Psychology*, **36**, 135–46.

Podsakoff, P.M., MacKenzie, S.B. & Hui, C. (1993), 'Organizational citizenship behaviour and managerial evolutions of employee performance: a review and suggestions for future resarch', *Research in Personnel and Human Resource Management*, **11**, 1–40.

Podsakoff, P.M., MacKenzie, S.B., Paine, J.B. & Bachrach, D.G. (2000), 'Organizational citizenship behaviours: a critical review of the theoretical and empirical literature and suggestions for future research', *Journal of Management*, **26**, 513–63.

Sackett, P.R., Berry, C.M., Wiemann, S.A. & Laczo, R.M. (2006), 'Citizenship and counterproductive behavior: clarifying relations between the two domains', *Human Performance*, **19** (4), 441–64.

Schnake, M.E. & Dumler, M.P. (2003), 'Levels of measurement and analysis issues in organizational citizenship behaviour research', *Journal of Occupational and Organizational Psychology*, **76** (part 3), 283–301.

Siegel, P.A., Post, C., Brockner, J., Fishman, A.Y. & Garden, C. (2005), 'The moderating influence of procedural fairness on the relationship between work–life conflict and organizational commitment', *Journal of Applied Psychology*, **90** (1), 13–24.

Smith, C.A., Organ, D.W. & Near, J.P. (1983), 'Organizational citizenship behaviour: its nature and antecedents', *Journal of Applied Psychology*, **68**, 653–63.

Sweeney, P.D. & McFarlin, D.B. (1993), 'Workers' evaluations of the "ends" and the "means": an examination of four methods of distributive and procedural justice', *Organizational Behavior and Human Decision Processes*, **55**, 23–40.

Van Dyne, L., Ang, S. & Botero, I.C. (2003), 'Conceptualizing employee silence and employee voice as multidimensional constructs', *Journal of Management Studies*, **40** (6), 1359–92.

Van Dyne, L., Graham, J.W. & Dienesch, R.M. (1994), 'Organizational citizenship behaviour: construct redefinition, operationalization, and validation', *Academy of Management Journal*, **37**, 765–802.

Van Dyne, L. & LePine, J.A. (1998), 'Helping and voice extra-role behaviour: evidence of construct and predictive validity', *Academy of Management Journal*, **41**, 108–19.

Van Dyne, L. & Pierce, J.L. (2004), 'Psychological ownership and feelings of possession: three field studies predicting employee attitudes and organizational citizenship behavior', *Journal of Organizational Behavior*, **25**, 439–59.

Van Dyne, L., Vandewalle, D., Kostova, T., Latham, M.E. & Cummings, L.L. (2000), 'Collectivism, propensity to trust and self-esteem as predictors of organizational citizenship in a non-work setting', *Journal of Organizational Behavior*, **21**, 3–23.

Van Emmerik, I.H., Jawahar, I.M. & Stone, T.H. (2004), 'The relationship between personality and discretionary helping behaviors', *Psychological Reports*, **95**, 355–65.

Vey, M.A. & Campbell, J.P. (2004), 'In-role or extra-role organizational citizenship behavior: which are we measuring?', *Human Performance*, **17** (1), 119–35.

Vigoda-Gadot, E. (2006), 'Compulsory citizenship behavior: theorizing some dark sides of the good soldier syndrome in organizations', *Journal for the Theory of Social Behaviour*, **36** (1), 77–93.

Wayne, J.H. & Cordeiro, B.L. (2003), 'Who is a good organizational citizen? Social perception of male and female employees who use family leave', *Sex Roles*, **49**, 233–46.

Wayne, S.J., Shore, L.M., Bommer, W.H. & Tetrick, L.E. (2002), 'The role of fair treatment and rewards in perceptions of organizational support and leader–member exchange', *Journal of Applied Psychology*, **87** (3), 590–98.

Williams, S., Pitre, R. & Zainuba, M. (2002), 'Justice and organizational citizenship behavior intentions: fair rewards versus fair treatment', *Journal of Social Psychology*, **142** (1), 33–44.

Yoon, M.H. & Suh, J. (2003), 'Organizational citizenship behaviors and service quality as external effectiveness of contact employees', *Journal of Business Research*, **56**, 597–611.

Zellars, K.L. & Tepper, B.J. (2003), 'Beyond social exchange: new directions for organizational citizenship behavior theory and research', in J.J. Martocchio & G.R. Ferris (eds), *Research in Personnel and Human Resources Management*, Elsevier Science, New York, pp. 267–79.

11 'Unhealthy' relationships at work and emerging ethical issues

Alexander-Stamatios G. Antoniou

Introduction

Work is considered to be an institution that permits each individual to create and develop relations with his or her economic, social and cultural environment. Work also has an important impact on a person's mental and emotional well-being. McGregor's (1960) 'Theory Y' and 'Theory X' offer two different ways of viewing this institution. According to Theory Y, work creates feelings of pleasure and self-fulfillment for the individual, and thus it becomes a source of satisfaction. Furthermore, Theory Y states that the objectives of the organization can be achieved not only through external control measures and the threat of punishment, but also by the satisfaction of the individual's ego and self-actualization.

According to Theory X, work's basic characteristic is to cause pain to the person. Thus work brings satisfaction not to the individual, but to the manager or the organization in general, which leads to the development in the individual of a feeling of inherent dislike and subsequently a need to avoid working. But since the individual is a member of a working group or an organization, and since that group or organization has specific objectives to be achieved, the next stage will involve coercive and control measures, imperative or compulsory directives and threats of punishment (Benton, 1972).

From these two theories the more general conclusion can be derived that in the context of an organization, there are certain relationships that are developed between individuals (that is, workers and managers). On the one hand, those relationships may be based on concordant cooperation that leads to the creation of feelings of satisfaction. On the other, they may be based on coercion and threats. The ethical and psychological analysis of healthy or unhealthy relationships between individuals (workers and managers) in an organization, is the aim of this chapter. But we shall begin by underling a few main points.

First, we must stress the significance of the psychological contract that is made between the individual and the organization. The psychological contract is defined as an implicit agreement that specifies what each is expected to give and to receive in that relationship. Individuals expect to receive a salary, status, advancement and opportunities. Organizations expect to receive loyalty, energy, talents and hard work in order to achieve their objectives. The contract is made with the entry of the worker into the firm and it is modified as the individual proceeds through his/her career (Gibson et al., 2000; Nelson & Quick, 2006).

According to Gibson et al., the psychological contract is violated when people believe that the firm has failed to fulfill its obligations towards them. Consequently, there are major emotional disturbances in their feelings of goodwill and trust towards the organization. In that case, the bond between the employer and the employee is weakened and the person feels disappointment. According to Jean Jacques Rousseau, the intensity of such feelings can result in moral outrage.

It is made explicit that through the psychological contract, there are certain human relationships which are created and developed between the individual and the organization and which are based on expectations between the two parties. Such relationships (and the consequent expectations), depend on the diversity of each individual's personality and on his/her psychological variables. That thought leads to the second main point of this introduction, which is the differences that exist between individuals concerning their character and psychology.

An individual's personality is a relatively stable set of characteristics, tendencies and temperaments that have been significantly formed by inheritance and by social, cultural and environmental factors. This set of variables determines the commonalities and differences in the behavior of the individual. In other words, it refers to a stable set of characteristics and tendencies that determine the common and different traits in people's behavior. Some basic factors determine the form that an individual's personality will take: (i) locus of control; (ii) self-efficacy; (iii) Machiavellianism; and (iv) creativity.

Apart from the special personality traits that create differences among individuals, there are also individual psychological variables that lead to the same point: the diversity between personalities, that is, 'perception', 'attribution', 'attitudes' and 'values'. In this chapter we shall emphasize 'perception', since this includes stereotypes which are defined as overgeneralized, oversimplified and self-perpetuating beliefs about people's personal characteristics. Stereotypes thus, are considered to be a cause of discrimination in the workplace that constitute problematic or unhealthy relations. 'Perception' is the process by which an individual gives meaning to the environment. It involves interpreting various stimuli and organizing them into a psychological experience. So, a stereotype is a form of perception that is related to how a person views others and how he/she categorizes them. The negative effect of stereotyping (on age, race, gender, ethnicity and lifestyle), can result in unfair programs of promotion, motivation, job design or performance evaluation. It can also lead to the rejection of the best person for a position (Gray & Starke, 1980; Rollinson, 1997; Gibson et al., 2000; Kreitner & Kinicki, 2001).

Our third main point refers to the rights of employees and specifically to the right of privacy which is related to cases of organizational invasion into a person's private life and the release of confidential information about a person, causing him/her emotional harm or suffering (Davis & Newstrom, 1989). This situation, apart from the psychological issues, also raises ethical ones that will be addressed later on in this chapter and which concern alcoholism, drug abuse and AIDS.

Unhealthy situations and ethical–psychological issues

Job satisfaction versus job dissatisfaction
According to Edwin Locke (1976), 'job satisfaction' is a pleasurable feeling that 'results from the perception that a person's job fulfills his important job values'. Three different conclusions emerge from that definition: (i) job satisfaction is a function of values, that is, satisfaction is strongly connected to 'what a person consciously or unconsciously desires to obtain'; (ii) different employees have different views concerning which values are important to them and which are not; and (iii) people's 'perception' of their present state is related to their values. The important issue in relation to stress in that case is that people's 'perception' of things does not depend on reality, which means that our perceptions

may not be an accurate reflection of reality. Consequently, people have different views of the same situation (Noe et al., 1997).

Job satisfaction can be attained if certain factors exist:

- *Mentally challenging work*   It is generally argued that people have a preference for jobs that give them the opportunity to use their skills and to fulfill diverse tasks. They also prefer jobs that offer them freedom of action and positive feedback. If those factors are present, then the job is defined as mentally challenging. On the contrary, if a job is described by the employee as being boring or causing feelings of failure and frustration, then either the job is not challenging enough or it is too challenging. If employees can obtain a moderate level of challenge, then they will experience feelings of pleasure and satisfaction.
- *Equitable rewards*   One way of creating satisfaction in the workforce of an organization is the implementation of a fair pay and promotion system that is in concordance with employees' expectations. Promotion, especially, provides opportunities for personal development, greater responsibilities and increased social status, leading to the creation of a feeling of satisfaction for the employee.
- *Supportive working conditions*   A working environment that provides employees with personal comfort and facilitating conditions can lead to job satisfaction. Studies have shown that employees have a preference for a safe and comfortable environment under normal conditions (temperature, light, noise).
- *Supportive colleagues*   In the field of work, apart from professional relationships, there are also social relationships, or social interactions. Employees will be more satisfied if they experience friendly and supportive relations with their co-workers and managers. According to some studies, the satisfaction that workers get from their job, is greatly increased if they are supervised by an understanding and amicable manager.
- *The job fits the personality of the worker*   According to Holland's (1997) 'personality–job fit theory', if there is strong agreement between employees' personality and occupation, then their behavior is characterized by satisfaction. Subsequently, they will reveal the whole range of their skills and talents and, thus, will be successful. This success results in the achievement of various feelings, such as happiness and satisfaction.
- *Genetic factor*   It has been argued that 30% of an individual's satisfaction is caused by hereditary elements, which leads to the conclusion that a significant portion of such satisfaction can be determined by genes. In other words, a person's general attitude is partly established by his/her genetic makeup (Robbins, 1998; Kreitner & Kinicki, 2001).

Note, however, that a person's attitude towards life is determined not only by genes, but also by his/her present lifestyle. Job satisfaction is only one part of life satisfaction. People's lifestyle outside of work has an important influence on their feelings about their job. Likewise, since work constitutes an important part of an individual's life, then the satisfaction that derives from work influences that person's satisfaction generally. This situation is defined as the 'spillover effect', which occurs in both directions between job and life satisfaction (Davis & Newstrom, 1989).

Another issue that is closely related to job satisfaction is its effects on employee performance. In other words, what we are interested in studying here is the impact of job satisfaction on an individual's performance in the workplace. According to Gibson et al. (2000), there are three views concerning the relationship between satisfaction and performance. The first argues that job satisfaction affects job performance, since a satisfied worker is more productive. According to the second view, job satisfaction is caused by job performance since the more productive worker is the one who experiences high levels of satisfaction. And finally, the third view asserts that there is no specific relationship between job satisfaction and job performance. According to Robbins (1998), job satisfaction has an important impact on employee productivity, absenteeism and turnover. Recent research has shown that there is a significant relation between satisfaction and productivity. If we examine the productivity factor not on the individual level, but on the whole organizational level, then we can draw the following conclusion: Organizations with more-satisfied employees tend to be more effective than organizations with less-satisfied employees.

Satisfaction is negatively related to absenteeism and turnover. In the case of absenteeism, it is argued that workers who are satisfied with their workplace conditions, performance and expectations do not feel the urge to avoid going to work. In the case of turnover, evidence indicates that an important moderator of this relationship is the employee's level of performance. Superior performers are generally satisfied by their job and they are less likely to leave. Organizations make considerable efforts to retain such high-level performers, for example, by offering pay rises, recognition and promotion.

Job dissatisfaction can be caused by many different factors:

- *The physical environment*   Extreme physical environments (temperature, lighting, lack of hygiene, noise), can affect both the individual's psychology and his/her job performance.
- *The social environment*   The social environment of the employee includes co-workers and supervisors. Three factors are involved in the feeling of satisfaction that derives from relationships with co-workers and supervisors: (i) sharing the same values and attitudes with co-workers and supervisors; (ii) the social support received from co-workers and supervisors, including sympathy and care; and (iii) the help that co-workers and supervisors can provide in helping the individual to clarify his/her goals and make the right choices. If these factors do not exist, then the immediate result will be dissatisfaction, disappointment and frustration, since the person is not supported by his/her social environment at work.
- *Behavioral settings*   Two important aspects of behavioral settings are: (i) social density (the number of people in an area divided by the number of square feet) and (ii) privacy (freedom from external observation). According to research, job satisfaction decreases as social density increases. Also, when the number of people at work increases, then the level of privacy decreases. Consequently, dissatisfaction and turnover increase.
- *Characteristics of the person*   Research shows that there are numerous differences in people's satisfaction. Those who have high levels of negative affectivity (that is, a basic characteristic of their personality and psychology), express more frequent feelings of dissatisfaction, anger, contempt, guilt, nervousness and fear,

both in and out of the workplace. They also focus more on the negative aspects of themselves and others than on the positive, both in and out of work. That general feeling, which is intrinsic in a person's psychology, is transferred from everyday life, to work life. So, people who have low levels of affectivity feel more satisfied in their job than those with high levels. Finally, dissatisfaction from other parts of a person's life can spill over into the workplace. General dissatisfaction can cause clinical depression that can become evident at work. Signs of such depression are: persistent sadness or anxiety, sleeping or eating disorders, lapses in concentration or in memory, irritability or excessive emotional displays, decreased performance, high absenteeism, apparent drug or alcohol abuse and apparent psychological disorders (Cartwright and Whatmore, 2005).

- *Organizational tasks* The three main aspects of tasks that affect job satisfaction are: (i) their complexity; (ii) the degree of physical effort and exertion; and (iii) the value that the employee puts on those tasks. First, with regard to task complexity, there is a strong positive relationship between complexity and satisfaction. Simple and repetitive jobs that do not challenge the worker and that cause boredom, lead to high levels of frustration and dissatisfaction. Second, physical effort is nowadays considered to be less, as a result of technological automation. Third, the value factor is very important and concerns the psychological state of mind that workers have about their job. For example, even if their job is low in complexity and high in physical effort, people with low-paying occupations tend to believe that the value of their job is of paramount importance to them.
- *Organizational roles* The person's role is defined as the set of expected behaviors that exists for that person in his/her job. Organizational roles can be influenced by: (i) role ambiguity, that is, the level of uncertainty about a person's organizational role. Employees need to know quite precisely what they are expected to do. When this is uncertain, then dissatisfaction arises; (ii) role conflict, which is characterized by the existence of contradictory demands on the person who occupies the role; and (iii) role overload, which is the state in which there are too many expectations placed on a person and this leads to job stress and dissatisfaction.

So far, we have examined in some detail the two 'rivals': job satisfaction and job dissatisfaction. Both conditions of human psychology form the source from where diverse and multiple feelings emerge. In the case of satisfaction, people continue to work as they did before or even harder, but in the case of dissatisfaction, apart from facing the risk of becoming depressed and frustrated, people also face the possibility of job withdrawal. According to Hulin (1991), job withdrawal is 'a set of behaviors that dissatisfied individuals enact in order to avoid the work situation'. Job withdrawal behavior takes four different forms. First, there may be a behavior change, that is, the effort made by individuals to change the conditions that cause their dissatisfaction. The immediate result, however, may be a supervisor–subordinate confrontation or conflict due to the fact that the employee is trying to make changes to organizational policies or in upper-level personnel. Second, there may be a physical withdrawal which largely involves either the employee's resignation or even frequent absenteeism if the person would prefer to resign, but does not have another employment opportunity. Another form of physical withdrawal is arriving late at work. Third, there may be psychological job withdrawal when the dissatisfied employee decides to remain at work physically, but psychologically and mentally, 'is disengaged'. This psychological disengagement can take different forms, for example, a low level of job involvement or organizational commitment. Fourth, if there is no psychological disengagement, the person may have health problems due to stress. According to research, there is a strong relation between stress and mental disorders. Stress-related mental disorders constitute a specific category of illnesses that are defined as occupational diseases. Stress is also connected to physical diseases such as coronary heart disease (CHD), hypertension and ulcers (Davis & Newstrom, 1989; Harris, 1997; Noe et al., 1997; Robbins, 1998; Spielberger & Reheiser, 2005; Zeidner, 2005).

According to Selye's theory (1956, 1974, 1982), stress is the 'non-specific response to the demands placed upon the body that leads to physical degeneration'. This is the General Adaptation Syndrome (GAS) theory, which asserts that stress is manifested in the whole body and it proceeds in three stages: the alarm reaction, the stage of resistance and the stage of exhaustion (Ivancevich & Matteson, 1996; Gordon, 2002; Miguel-Tobal & González-Ordi, 2005; Miller & Travers, 2005).

Workaholism is a basic factor of job stress since it is 'an irrational commitment to excessive work' (Cherrington quoted in Burke, 2005, p. 367). Workaholics devote more time and thoughts to their work than is demanded and gradually become emotionally crippled and addicted to control and power in order to gain approval and success (Burke, 2005). People trying to succeed make the mistake of relating job satisfaction and happiness to their work in an abnormal and excessive way.

Occupational stress can result in job burnout, which is defined as the prolonged response to chronic emotional and interpersonal stressors in the job, and is characterized by physical and emotional exhaustion, depersonalization and inefficacy (Davis & Newstrom, 1989; Bratton & Gold, 1999; Dessler, 2000; Kenny & McIntyre, 2005; Leiter & Maslach, 2005). Some of the consequences of burnout on the organizational level are turnover, absenteeism, low organizational commitment and use of violence. On a psychological level, there may be suicidal intentions, depression and anxiety (Shirom & Melamed, 2005).

Scapegoating
The phenomenon of scapegoating is based on an attitude of hostility towards one or more persons by the rest of a group or a company. The person who suffers the side-effects of such treatment is ceremonially and emotionally cast out of the group or the company with the charge of being unworthy of membership. As a phenomenon, scapegoating usually makes its appearance after an extremely difficult period or situation for the company when there is a harsh, but fair, assessment of responsibilities. What actually takes place is that only one person, or very few persons, take upon themselves all the blame for the problem. That person takes on all the guilt of the others who successfully avoid any unfair treatment and any charges. This occurs when all the workers are united against one single person who, as a scapegoat, becomes the target of hostility. The scapegoat is usually presented in stereotypic negative form in order to reassure the rest of the group or the company that he/she was basically a wicked person who was using deceitful or inappropriate methods to accomplish his or her own ends (Gabriel et al., 2000).

This phenomenon gives rise to two kinds of issues: ethical and psychological. With regard to the former, it is totally unethical to charge only one person with the wrongs and errors of a whole company (that is, a group of many people who work towards the same end). When only one worker is the scapegoat for a whole department, the ethical question is: 'Why only one person? Why only one subordinate and not the whole department including the manager?'.

When only the manager is charged with failure, the situation is different, since he/she is considered to be the 'head' of the department or the company and is in charge of making the right choices and taking the best decisions for the benefit of the firm. So, when the manager fails, it is widely felt that 'his/her head must fall'. But why? Supposing that the manager's action was not deliberate, and that the actions taken were considered to be in the company's best interests and according to the information that was available. No one can be perfect or have absolute knowledge, and thus, human nature is inherently imperfect. What we do throughout our life is to try to improve ourselves through the knowledge that we gain from our mistakes. So, in the case of the manager, it would be more ethical to conduct a detailed 'benefit–cost analysis' to assess why the failure occurred and what the manager should do to avoid such a situation in the future. Thus the manager, and also his/her subordinates, will gain important knowledge that will be useful to them at a later date.

With regard to the psychological issues, these can cause serious psychological disorders such as stress or depression. In this event, the person suffers from a psychological illness that may also have negative consequences for his/her physical health. As noted earlier, psychological stress can cause serious heart disease.

Fear: a way to motivate a worker or a psychologically stressful tactic?
The main target of a company is always profit, benefit, money. In order to succeed in its objectives, a firm has to raise its productivity and sales, and at the same time reduce its costs. To achieve this level of sure profit, many companies take unethical measures against their employees.

One of these measures, according to Dubrin (1981), is to create an atmosphere of fear, or else to threaten and terrorize the individual. This tactic is frequently applied against managers, that is, presidents of many firms threaten and terrorize their subordinate managers in order to make them do their best, usually through fear of losing their job. This strategy may be effective concerning the manager's performance, but only in a short time perspective. In the long run, the side-effects of such strategies become apparent.

Apart from the disadvantages that are evident in the workplace and which can cause serious economic harm to the company (since a manager who is threatened and fearful does not feel free to act, and does not dare to make decisions), there is also a more serious side-effect: the offense against human dignity and self-worth (ibid.). This situation is contrary to the Kantian perspective, which asserts that we should use others not only as means, but also as ends. People have the right to be respected as autonomous and responsible. Their value is more than mere economic profit. People live autonomously, they are responsible for their own actions and they can govern themselves. So they are capable of ethical judgments and, according to Kant, the immediate consequence is that simultaneously they have dignity and they must be treated with respect (Boylan, 1995; French, 1995; Bowie, 1999).

The psychological harm to a person's feelings and self-esteem can lead to an act of revenge, that is, sabotage. In such a case, the person may join another company and pass on to the new employer information regarding any secrets or innovation programs or the economic situation of the person's previous company (Dubrin, 1981). Indeed, such behavior is totally unethical and egoistic. We cannot of course characterize as unethical people who no longer wish to remain in a company where they are treated badly, but the ethical order is severely damaged if those people disclose all their company's secrets. The unethical issue is that there can be severe economic losses to the former company that will consequently lead to workers' dissatisfaction or even job loss. So, how ethical are people who cause harm to their former co-workers? Now, they are the ones who are not treating their co-workers with respect, but are using them merely as a means to their own end: to severely damage their former company without taking into consideration the fact that the company consists of a human workforce that may end without a job.

One reason why fear may be an effective motivator is that most people have an intrinsic psychological need for job security. However, according to Daniel Yankelovich's research (2007), fear is no longer considered to be a job motivator because people are less worried about unemployment (ibid.).

The 'clique': the company's guardian angel or the source of unethical planning?
The clique is defined as a group whose members are dispersed throughout a large part of the formal organization. The driving force of that specific group is the common purpose of its members. That is, people agree to take part because they feel that they all have something in common: their 'cause', which usually involves sharing the same belief about a certain policy (Benton, 1972).

The issue here is how ethical or unethical is this common shared 'cause'?. Does the group's policy coincide with company policy? Does the clique's objectives and actions constitute a harmonizing force or a highly disruptive one?

According to Benton, the manager has to observe very closely which way the wind blows – if the clique's influence and practices are harming the company's interests, then the manager will be compelled to break it up. On the contrary, if the group's actions aim at profiting the organization, then the manager should encourage it. Within the context of a firm, cliques use different methods to improve their position and promote their own plans. Their aims as well as their methods can be either detrimental to the company's interests or not. If it is decided by the firm that the group's efforts are compatible with company goals, then it is possible that the company's plans may require adjusting in order to be consistent with the group's aims, thereby gaining more profit (ibid.).

Discipline and punishment in the workplace
Discipline is an important factor of stability in the context of an organization which shows that each individual is not absolutely free to do whatever he/she wishes, but that there are certain rules that need to be followed in order to achieve a healthy working environment.

According to Davis and Newstrom (1989), there are two types of discipline: preventive and corrective. Preventive discipline is the action that a company takes in order to implement in the workforce certain standards and rules to be followed so that infractions do not occur. The main purpose of this kind of discipline is to encourage self-discipline in the employees. Corrective discipline is the action taken by the management after the infraction has occurred and aims at decreasing the possibility of other infractions so that future acts will be in compliance with standards. It is the disciplinary action taken in order to apply a penalty against an individual who has broken the rules and aims at: (i) reforming the offender, (ii) deterring others from similar actions and (iii) maintaining consistent and effective group standards.

Punishment is a form of corrective discipline that raises ethical and psychological issues. According to Gibson et al. (2000), punishment is an undesirable consequence of a particular behavior and serves as a message to a person not to do something. It is widely used as a method of changing behavior, despite its disadvantages.

According to Gray and Starke (1980), punishment is related to a number of disadvantages:

- *Punishment does not induce the desired response*   Punishment decreases or extinguishes the undesirable response but it does not stimulate or impose the desirable one.
- *Surveillance by the manager is necessary*   Punishment is considered to be an inefficient form of control because the physical presence of the manager is required.
- *Punishment leads to punishment*   Punishment leads only to temporary change and not to the acquisition of a more permanent character or behavior improvement.
- *Punishment has emotional consequences*   People who feel that they are punished unjustly may tend to express their feelings through non-productive actions such as direct sabotage. Another psychological problem is related to the dislike against the punisher (the manager) and future dysfunctional or problematic professional relations.
- *Punishment can cause behavior inflexibility*   The learning that arises from a particular punishment may be so permanent that it is overgeneralized and connected to every similar future situation. For example, an employee is punished by his/her manager because of an innovative process he/she had advanced. In the future, the same employee, due to overgeneralization, will not dare to make any effort towards any kind of innovation.
- *Punishment may have reinforcing consequences*   Punishment may itself be reinforcing and it can lead to more problems.

Since punishment has so many disadvantages, why is it meted out by managers? The answer to that question is that the act of punishing is reinforcing to the punisher him/herself, which means that the extinction of the problematic behavior is not the first and most important aim of the punisher.

Violence in the workplace

Violence is a workplace safety issue; it is the second most common cause of death among (usually female) employees (Fisher et al., 1999). Of all women who die at work, 39% are the victims of assault whereas only 18% of males who die at work were murdered. Fatal workplace violence against women is founded on three factors: (i) the assailant is unknown to the victim, (ii) the woman's employment involves serving the public and (iii) she works in order to survive (Dessler, 2000).

In order to reduce workplace violence, certain measures must be taken. One of these is more careful pre-employment screening, that is, the company should obtain a detailed employment application containing an applicant's employment history, educational background and references. This should also include a personal interview, personality testing and verification of all information provided by the applicant. Special attention should be paid when there is incomplete or false information in the application or reference, a criminal history, a history of depression or a history of drug and alcohol abuse (Fisher et al., 1999; Dessler, 2000).

A related method is the enhanced attention paid to retaining employees, which endorses avoidance of acts of violence, defensive, obsessive or paranoid tendencies, antisocial behavior, sexually aggressive behavior, overreactions to criticism, possession of weapons, violation of privacy rights of others and a retributory attitude (Dessler, 2000).

These two methods give rise to certain ethical issues that primarily concern two aspects. First, we are dealing with an invasion of a person's privacy since the main aim of the company is to know as much as possible about the employee. Of course, since this action has a preventive–defensive character, it cannot be defined as highly unethical in itself but is in its ultimate end, which is absolute knowledge of a person and the consequent prediction of his/her behavior. Further, if a company knows everything about its employees and if it can predict their movements, it can also prevent them from behaving in a certain way or even modify their actions through the application of preventive discipline. This would result in the total subjection of the person to the firm.

Second, it can be argued that the enhanced attention paid to the need to retain employees can lead to a kind of discrimination since those who are thought to have violent tendencies will not be hired. If that happens, the manager makes a double mistake: on the one hand, there is the assumption that such people fall into the category of existing stereotypes whereby those with attitude problems are rejected, which is unethical, and on the other, this leads to psychological irritation or feelings of frustration in the rejected person. It is quite possible that such feelings of frustration will become feelings of anger and revenge, leading to violent or even homicidal actions.

Conflict

Conflict is the process by which a party has the perception that a second party has negatively affected something that is important to the first (Robbins, 1998; Gordon, 2002). The issue of conflict has become the subject of intense interest and analysis and, consequently there are diverse views on its origins and basic character. According to the 'traditional' view, conflict is a dysfunctional consequence of: (i) poor communication, (ii) lack of openness and trust between people and (iii) the manager's failure to respond to the needs of his/her employees. Thus, conflict is considered to be a negative part of human relations: it is inherently bad and harmful and it should be avoided. According to the 'human relations' view, conflict is a natural and inevitable outcome that derives from the interaction, communication and cooperation among people who are members of a particular group. Finally, according to the 'interactionist' view, conflict can be a positive aspect of a group and sometimes its presence is necessary in order to motivate the members of the group to perform more effectively (Ivancevich & Matteson, 1996; Buchanan & Huczynski, 1997; Robbins, 1998).

Different kinds of conflict are based on the number of people involved. First, an 'intra-individual' conflict refers to the conflict within an individual about which activities to perform. This internal conflict may be caused when: (i) there is diversity between the person's morality and that of the instructions given to the person. In other words, the person believes that the action he/she is compelled to perform, is not morally 'right'; (ii) two different supervisors give contradictory instructions; and (iii) a certain activity will help the person, but at the expense of his/her co-workers. This inner type of conflict can cause serious psychological side-effects (apart from ethical dilemmas), such as stress. Second, an 'inter-individual' conflict refers to the conflict between two individuals. It is interesting from a psychological perspective to examine why an individual puts obstacles in the way of the goal achievement of his/her co-worker. One aspect of this issue is the basic character of a person, that is, if a worker has an absolute view about how things should be done and if he/she insists on imposing his/her own views about the goal-achievement process, then it is natural for the other individual (manager or co-worker who disagrees) to block the way and cause a conflict situation. Third, an 'individual–group conflict' which occurs when: (i) the individual is violating the group norms and (ii) the subordinates disagree with the manager's views and, consequently, try to change his/her attitude. Finally, a 'conflict between groups or intergroup conflict' is basically a conflict between different departments within the context of a firm (Gray & Starke, 1980; Nelson & Quick, 2006).

In this chapter, we emphasize 'intergroup' conflict, which can be 'functional' or 'dysfunctional'. Functional conflict has a positive meaning; it is defined as a healthy and constructive disagreement among individuals which results in a better relationship between the co-workers, and also in the achievement of self-knowledge. Since the major result of such conflict is the improvement in the relationships between co-workers, the next stage is the positive and innovative change within the organization. In contrast, dysfunctional conflict is an unhealthy and destructive disagreement between individuals. Its origin is usually emotional or behavioral, for example anger against a specific person. In other words, the main target of anger is not the problematic ideas or views or processes that a particular person recommends or even tries to impose, but rather that person's personality or character or psychology. This action also involves threats, deception and verbal abuse (Ivancevich & Matteson, 1996; Buchanan & Huczynski, 1997; Robbins, 1998; Gibson et al., 2000; Gordon, 2002; Nelson & Quick, 2006).

Intergroup conflict can be identified with the theory of ethical egoism. According to this teleological theory, what is right and wrong is determined according to the potential consequences for those who decide to act according to their own interest (Green, 1994). The 'ethical egoist', who is involved in a dysfunctional conflict, tries to harm another person not because of that person's ideas or choices but because of who he/she is and because of his/her character or spiritual beliefs. Thus the offender egoist is trying to harm the other person in order to reap the advantages of being the most successful or the best employee in the firm. According to this theory, the unethical behavior of the egoist is admissible.

Dysfunctional conflict is contrary to the beliefs of utilitarianism and deontology. Utilitarianism holds that one action is ethical if it results in the benefit for the greatest possible number of people (ibid.). But this kind of conflict does not benefit anyone, since it causes harm and drains the energy (of the people) that could be used in a more productive way. It also leads to psychological instability since a number of people are psychologically taxed.

Deontology holds that every person has to be respected by all the others and no one should be used as a means toward the achievement of a particular goal (ibid.). Dysfunctional conflict rejects the show of respect toward the other person since its basic characteristic is to harm that self-same person to whom respect must be shown.

The causes of conflict can be either structural or personal. Structural causes involve the following:

- *Specialization*   When jobs are highly specialized, the result is that some employees are experts on certain subjects. Conflict can arise because the others do not have the necessary knowledge to understand how those experts work.
- *Interdependence*   Different people and groups depend on each other in certain areas of work in order to achieve the goals of the firm, so if there are problems with or malfunctions of the processes, each party blames the other for behaving irresponsibly.
- *Common resources*   All the departments of the firm must share the available resources and if those sources are relatively scarce, then conflict may arise.
- *Goal differences*   This can arise when each department has no knowledge of the other departments' objectives. Each one sets different tasks, with the result that there is a lack of shared values and goals.
- *Authority relationships*   The manager issues the orders and the directives and this is not always tolerated by everyone.
- *Status inconsistencies*   Managers, due to their superior position, enjoy advantages such as flexible schedules or longer lunch breaks. These benefits are not available to the lower-level workers, and this can cause resentment and conflict.
- *Jurisdictional ambiguities*   The existence of unclear lines of responsibility can lead to misunderstandings and insufficient communication within the organization.

Personal factors consist of the following:

- *Skills and abilities*   There is a diversity of skills and abilities among the work-force. A highly skilled worker and an unskilled recruit may find it difficult to work together.
- *Personalities*   An organization employs groups of people who are very different, with diverse personality traits and characters. Those diversities may cause conflict, especially if they are based on abrasive critical feelings and behaviors.
- *Perceptions*   People hold different views about various issues and situations that arise in the context of an organization.
- *Values and ethics*   Each person has his/her own set of values and ethics which can be at odds with the different set of values and ethics held by another person.
- *Emotions*   The emotions of each person differ from those of another. Emotional problems that have their source in an out-of-work factor can spill over into the workplace, leading to conflict.
- *Communication barriers*   Physical separation and language, for example, can cause distortions in messages and consequently can lead to conflict.
- *Cultural differences*   These are strongly related to the lack of understanding of another culture (Gray & Starke, 1980; Dubrin, 1981; Ivancevich & Matteson, 1996; Gibson et al., 2000; Nelson & Quick, 2006).

According to Nelson & Quick, in the case of a conflict, the person involved usually feels frustrated, especially if he/she is criticized and is the target of negative feedback. In that case, the person develops defense mechanisms. There are three kinds of defense mechanisms: (i) aggressive (persistent and non-adjustive reaction, redirection of negative emotions toward the others, active or passive resistance); (ii) compromise (dedication to a particular pursuit, enhancement of self-esteem and rationalization of inconsistent or undesirable behavior); and (iii) withdrawal (abandonment, emotional conflicts expressed, bodily imaginative activity in order to escape from reality). According to Kenny and McIntyre (2005), interpersonal conflict in the context of work is a basic contributor to the onset of occupational stress and inability to do the job.

Conflicts of interest

According to Bowie (1983), a conflict of interest occurs when a person has two or more interests, such that if both are pursued, there might be an unjustifiable effect on another individual. According to Velasquez (1998), a conflict of interest arises when an employee is engaged in carrying out a task on behalf of the company and the employee has a private interest in the outcome of the task that is incompatible with the best interests of the company. In other words, a conflict of interest arises when the self-interest of employees in a position of trust, leads them to ignore the seriousness of their responsibilities and to act in a way that may not benefit the firm. A well-known situation is when employees of one company hold another job or consulting position in another (usually competitive) firm.

The ethical issue here is that such people not only give their energy and knowledge to two different parties, but they also pass on to one party the secrets and innovative or investment plans of the other. This action is considered to be highly unethical because these employees serve not their firm's interests firm (that is, a number of people or co-workers whose professional survival depends on them), but only their own. Accordingly, they are acting as 'ethical egoists' and not as 'utilitarians', since this particular action does not bring happiness to the larger possible number of people, but only to themselves. They cannot be characterized as 'ethical deontologists', since they show no respect for the other human beings who depend on them. In neither situation are they acting for the benefit of others, but rather they are harming the others. With regard to the ethical theory of egoism, Macklin's (1983) view is that 'ethical egoism' is not a moral basis of ethical behavior since it does not provide moral reasons for acting. Consequently, if a person's self-interest conflicts with both the interests of the organization and the society, then it cannot be defined as moral.

This view accords with McGuire's (1983, p. 50) concept of how a conflict of interest may be defined: 'a conflict of interest exists when a subsystem deliberately attempts to enhance its own interests or those of an alien system to the detriment of the larger system of which it is a part'. A subsystem is basically a person, and an alien system is another firm or person that is not an integral part of the larger system. This implies that both the system and the subsystem have different and totally opposed values which lead to harmful actions of one against another. And thus, if the subsystem wishes to profit, it will cause harm to the system.

Finally, there is a difference between the actual and potential conflicts of interest. An actual conflict occurs when people harm their firm out of self-interest. A potential conflict occurs when people are pressurized, tempted or motivated by self-interest to act against the firm's interest. Actual conflicts are unethical because they contravene and violate the professional contract that a worker establishes with one firm and according to which the employee has to advance the goal achievement and the profit of the firm (Velasquez, 1998).

Discrimination

This term is associated with a large number of wrongful acts that frequently occur in the occupational field of an individual and it is used to define the case where a person is deprived of some benefit or opportunity due to his/her membership of a particular group toward which there is substantial prejudice. Discrimination can take place under all the conditions of employment that directly affect the economic interests of employees, such as hiring (preferential hiring), promotion, payment or fringe benefits. The basic feature of such adverse treatment is that people are marked because of their race, gender, age or health (Velasquez, 1998; Treviño & Nelson, 1999; Boatright, 2000).

How can this treatment be explained psychologically? In order to answer that question, we need to describe the intentions of those who discriminate. The basic feature of discrimination is adverse treatment of a person due to his/her membership of a certain group, and the main intention in such cases is to treat all members of certain groups differently. Employers who refuse to hire, for example, black people or women, usually defend their choices by connecting race or gender to the job. They admit their intent to treat some people differently on the basis of a characteristic, but they refuse to admit that their behavior is racist or sexist. They claim that their behavior is based on business considerations (Boatright, 2000).

Thus, discrimination in employment must involve three elements: first, it concerns a decision that affects a person in a negative way which is not due to his/her ability to perform a certain task; second, such treatment derives from racial or sexual prejudice or from stereotypes; and third, the decision harms the individual's interests (e.g., loss of job or promotion) (Velasquez, 1998).

The ethical arguments against any form of discrimination are divided into three main categories. The first is the utilitarian view that is based on the idea that society's productivity will be optimized if every job is awarded according to a person's competency. In order to accomplish maximally productive jobs, every job should be assigned to those whose skills and personality traits fit the job. The second is the Kantian perspective, which holds that human beings should be treated not merely as means but as ends as well. It is a principle that refers to an individual's moral right to be treated as free and equal to other persons. Discrimination violates this principle in two ways. First, the main belief is that one group is inferior to others (black people, women). Racial or sexual discrimination is based on stereotypes that see minorities as 'lazy' or 'shiftless' and women as 'emotional' or 'weak'. Consequently, those persons' self-esteem is undermined and their right to be treated equally is violated. Second, the members of certain groups are placed in lower economic and social positions, that is, women and minorities have fewer job opportunities than men and they also have lower salaries, which leads to the conclusion that, again, their right to equal treatment is violated.

From the point of view of the offender, the Kantian perspective of the categorical imperative adds that those who actually discriminate would not want to see their action universalized because they would not want others to suffer. Consequently, it is morally wrong for offenders to discriminate.

The third ethical argument against discrimination, is from the point of view of justice. John Rawls refers to the 'principle of equal opportunity', and asserts that 'social and economic inequalities are to be arranged so that they are attached to offices and positions open to all under conditions of fair equality of opportunity' (Rawls, 1999, p. 28). Discrimination violates this principle by preventing minorities from having equal opportunities to acquire high-level positions (Velasquez, 1998; Boatright, 2000).

There are different kinds of discrimination in the workplace. In this chapter, we shall refer to only two cases: women, and people who suffer from addictions. The first and best-known form of discrimination against women is two-pronged: either it puts barriers in the way of their career advancement or it involves sexual harassment. Regarding the first issue, a well-known phenomenon is the 'glass ceiling', that is, an invisible barrier preventing women from advancing to higher levels within an organization (Harris, 1997; Drafke & Kossen, 1998; Gordon, 2002). Today the barriers are less harsh because certain social and economic factors are fueling the elevation of women into leadership or managerial positions. One of these is the 'women's movement', which promoted a more expanded role in society for women. Another is civil rights legislation, which forced companies to reverse their aggressiveness toward women. And finally, the unrelenting inflation has also led to the development of the need for a family to be supported economically by two salaries rather than only one. Nevertheless, the problem of discrimination still exists (Dubrin, 1981).

One explanation for this is that men do not take women seriously because women do not correspond to the 'instrumental innovative role' stereotype which is attributed to men. In other words, men cannot perceive and accept the concept of a woman who brings new ideas and special skills into company. Furthermore, even when a woman is recognized as having done a good job, her performance will not be attributed to her abilities but to other factors, and in addition there will not be any future expectation of a similar performance by her.

Conversely, an unsuccessful performance by a male will be attributed to bad luck and not to low qualifications or lack of ability. Finally, in the case of hiring a woman, a very frequent phenomenon is the devaluation or undervaluation of her qualifications. Often, women are more highly qualified than they appear to be or than others present them to be (Purdy, 1995).

The second form of discrimination against women is sexual harassment. This is considered to be an abuse of power, since it is a way of exerting power over a weaker person (Robbins, 1998; Gordon, 2002). The concept of power in the workplace should be taken seriously, since the idea of unequal power exists from the very beginning of the occupational relation between employer and employee. Supervisors decide, reward and coerce, and this gives them supervisory power which they may unethically abuse (Robbins, 1998; Bratton & Gold, 1999).

The psychological condition in a man who harasses is based on a feeling of victory, or on an inner need to be the center of attention or on the feeling that women are inferior and do not belong in the workplace (Gordon, 2002). On the other hand, serious psychological damage can be identified in the harassed person that leads to the development of stress (Bratton & Gold, 1999).

Sexual harassment is defined as

unwelcome sexual advances, requests for sexual favors and other verbal or physical conduct of a sexual nature that takes place under any of the following conditions:

1. Submission to such conduct is made either explicitly or implicitly a term or condition of an individual's employment.
2. Submission or rejection of such conduct by an individual is used as the basis for employment decisions affecting such an individual.
3. Such conduct has the purpose or effect of unreasonably interfering with an individual's work performance or creating an intimidating, hostile, or offensive work environment. (Velasquez, 1998; Boatright, 2000; Dessler, 2000)

Accordingly, there are two types of sexual harassment: the 'quid pro quo harassment' (which occurs when superiors use their power to grant or deny employment benefits to exact sexual favors from a subordinate) and the 'hostile working environment harassment' (which is the sexual nature of the conduct of co-workers that causes a woman to feel uncomfortable) (Harris, 1997; Bratton & Gold, 1999; Treviño & Nelson, 1999; Boatright, 2000; Dessler, 2000). Both cases concern the stereotypes that prevail outside the working environment where some men view women as sex objects. The conditions for stereotyping thus permit 'sex role spill over', in which women's roles outside of employment 'spill over' into the workplace where other roles related to job performance should prevail (Boatright, 2000).

The second kind of discrimination in the workplace is related to (i) addictions, such as smoking, alcohol and drugs, and (ii) HIV illness. These deficiencies in the workplace are closely related to the right to privacy and the right to maintain good health (in the case of non-smokers). In most working environments, strict discrimination against these people takes place which is characterized on the one hand as unethical, and on the other as psychologically harmful.

Smoking is a habit that harms health, so in most workplaces, either it is prohibited or the band of smokers are restricted to designated smoking areas within the company. In the case of hiring, an employer may reject a smoker (without of course admitting that the reason for the rejection is that specific habit) (Dessler, 2000). But how ethical is this discrimination? Smokers, unwillingly, are basically alienated by their co-workers, that is, they are not treated with the proper respect. But it would be highly unethical if smokers continued to work and smoke among the rest of the group who are non-smokers. Their habit could cause harm to the others' health, which means that the smokers are now the ones who are disrespectful of the others. On the other hand, this alienation of smokers could lead to serious psychological problems including frustration, depression and resentment.

The possibility of addiction to alcohol or drugs is addressed by the companies through a series of tests that employees are obliged to undergo (Davis & Newstrom, 1989; Harris, 1997; Fisher et al., 1999; Dessler, 2000). According to Kupfer (1995), employees are obliged to submit to drug testing. The ensuing debate concerns the privacy rights of individuals as opposed to the responsibility of the employers to have drug-free employees. Managers believe that drug-abusing workers cost the firm a lot of money in productivity, absenteeism and medical expenses (ibid.). This gives rise to the ethical question: 'Does a firm have the right to force people to do something against their will?'. We could answer, no, but since drug (or alcohol) abuse causes serious problems for the other workers in the firm and their general happiness, according to utilitarianism, drug testing could be ethical. But is the coerced person affected psychologically? Probably, to a certain extent, but many companies have special supportive programs to help such people.

The same problems arise in the case of those who are HIV positive. Some companies insist that their personnel undergo HIV testing. In Canada, this is considered to be an intrusion of individual rights, and employers are prohibited from subjecting their applicants to the procedure (Bratton & Gold, 1999). In the case of already hired employees who are infected, the employer should provide them with all the necessary support in order to help them deal with the problem (ibid.; Dessler, 2000; Nelson & Quick, 2006). There are also situations where those who are infected do not want to reveal their situation because they are afraid of being stigmatized (Nelson & Quick, 2006).

But what happens if the infected person is, say, a surgeon in a hospital? How ethical or right is it to remain in the job by keeping the condition a secret? And consequently, how ethical is it for the manager to intervene? People have the right to privacy, which means that, theoretically, they can conceal their condition. But from the point of view of ethics, a surgeon may become a danger to his (or her) patients: if during an operation he is cut, it is quite possible that he may infect the patient, which means that he is causing harm to another person without respecting that person's rights to health and well-being.

Conclusion

In this chapter we have analyzed situations that can negatively affect the healthy character of human and professional relations in the working environment of a company. Every situation is strongly related to ethical issues, as well as to psychological ones, since we are dealing with relationships between different kinds of people. Each individual has his/her own character, personality traits and psychological variables. An important aspect of the situations dealt with is the existence of stereotypes which impose a certain view and behavior. For example, the stereotype of 'female mental and physical weakness' causes problems in the communicative process between people in a company, and accordingly creates a permanent unhealthy working environment.

Generally speaking, problematic relations between co-workers or between superiors and subordinates are caused by the appearance, development and domination of certain 'models' that determine what is right and what is wrong. There is also a strong connection with the inequality of the relationship between workers and their managers that normally exists and that may lead to unhealthy relations at work.

The general conclusion is that in order to avoid the development of unhealthy relations, people should try to understand and accept the diversity between them. Such diversity can be at the level of race, gender, age or mental and physical condition, but it can also be at the level of culture, social status and economic background. As Gordon (2002) suggests, it is very important for a company's well-being that the management takes into account the uniqueness of each employee through developing effective relationships among people with different abilities, experiences and aspirations. Understanding the ways people differ, is a first step in dealing with diversity.

References

Antoniou, A.-S.G. & Cooper, C.L. (eds) (2005), *Research Companion to Organizational Health Psychology*, Cheltenham, UK and Northampton, MA, USA: Edward Elgar.

Beauchamp, T.L. & Bowie, N.E. (eds) (1983), *Ethical Theory and Business*, Englewood Cliffs, NJ: Prentice-Hall.

Benton, L.R. (1972), *Supervision and Management*, New York: McGraw-Hill.

Boatright, J.R. (2000), *Ethics and the Conduct of Business*, Englewood Cliffs, NJ: Prentice-Hall.

Bowie, N.E. (1983), 'Conflicts of interests and roles', in Beauchamp & Bowie (eds).

Bowie, N.E. (1999), *Business Ethics: A Kantian Perspective*, Oxford: Blackwell.

Boylan, M. (1995), *Ethical Issues in Business*, Fort Worth, TX: Harcourt and Brace College Publishers.

Bratton, J. & Gold, J. (1999), *Human Resource Theory and Practices*, Basingstoke: Macmillan Business.

Buchanan, D. & Huczynski, A. (1997), *Organizational Behavior: An Introductory Text*, Englewood Cliffs, NJ: Prentice-Hall.

Burke, R.J. (2005), 'Workaholism in organizations: work and well-being consequences', in Antoniou & Cooper (eds), pp. 336–81.

Cartwright, S. & Whatmore, L.C. (2005), 'Stress and individual differences: implications for stress management', in Antoniou & Cooper (eds), pp. 163–73.

Davis, K. & Newstrom, J.W. (1989), *Human Behavior at Work: Organizational Behavior*, New York: McGraw-Hill.

Dessler, G. (2000), *Human Resource Management*, Englewood Cliffs, NJ: Prentice-Hall.

Drafke, M.W. & Kossen, S. (1998), *The Human Side of Organizations*, New York: Addison-Wesley Longman.

Dubrin, A.J. (1981), *Human Relations: A Job Oriented Approach*, Englewood Cliffs, NJ: Prentice-Hall.

Fisher, C.D., Schoenfeldt, L.F. & Shaw, J.B. (1999), *Human Resource Management*, Boston, MA: Houghton Mifflin.

French, P.A. (1995), *Corporate Ethics*, Fort Worth, TX: Harcourt and Brace College Publishers.

Gabriel, Y., Fineman, S. & Sims, D. (2000), *Organizing and Organizations*, London: Sage.

Gibson, J.L., Ivancevich, J.M. & Donnelly, J.H. (2000), *Organizations: Behavior, Structure, Processes*, Boston, MA: McGraw-Hill.

Gordon, J.R. (2002), *Organizational Behavior: A Diagnostic Approach*, Englewood Cliffs, NJ: Prentice-Hall.

Gray, J.L. & Starke, F.A. (1980), *Organizational Behavior: Concepts and Applications*, Columbus, OH: Charles E. Merrill.

Green, R.M. (1994), *The Ethical Manager: A New Method for Business Ethics*, Englewood Cliffs, NJ: Prentice-Hall.

Harris, M. (1997), *Human Resource Management: A Practical Approach*, New York: Dryden Press, Harcourt & Brace College Publishers.

Holland, J.L. (1997), *Making Vocational Choices: A Theory of Vocational Personalities and Work Environments*, Odesa, FL: Psychological Assessment Resources.

Hulin, C.L. (1991), 'Adaptation, persistence, and commitment in organizations', in M.D. Dunnette and L.M. Hough (eds), *Handbook of Industrial and Organizational Psychology*, second edition, vol. 2, Palo Alto, CA: Consulting Psychologists Press, pp. 445–506.

Ivancevich, J.M. & Matteson, M.T. (1996), *Organizational Behavior and Management*, Chicago, IL: Irwin.

Kenny, D. & McIntyre, D. (2005), 'Constructions of occupational stress: nuisances, nuances or novelties?', in Antoniou & Cooper (eds), pp. 20–58.

Kreitner, R. & Kinicki, A. (2001), *Organizational Behavior*, Boston, MA: McGraw-Hill.

Kupfer, A. (1995), 'Drug testing good or bad?', in Boylan (ed.).

Leiter, M.P. & Maslach, C. (2005), 'A mediation model of job burnout', in Antoniou & Cooper (eds), pp. 544–64.

Locke, E.A. (1976), 'The nature and causes of job satisfaction', in M.D. Dunnette (ed.), *Handbook of Industrial and Organizational Psychology*, Chicago, IL: Rand McNally, pp. 1297–350.

Macklin, R. (1983), 'Conflicts of interest', in Beauchamp & Bowie (eds), pp. 240–46.

McGregor, D. (1960), *The Human Side of Enterprise*, New York: McGraw-Hill.

McGuire, J.M. (1983), 'Conflict of interest: whose interest? And what conflict?', in Beauchamp & Bowie (eds).

Miguel-Tobal, J.J. & González-Ordi, H. (2005), 'The role of emotions in cardiovascular disorders', in Antoniou & Cooper (eds), pp. 455–77.

Miller, G.V.F. & Travers, C.J. (2005), 'The relationship between ethnicity and work stress', in Antoniou & Cooper (eds), pp. 87–101.

Nelson, D.L. & Quick, J.C. (2006), *Organizational Behavior: Foundations, Realities and Challenges*, Cincinnati, OH: Thomson South-Western.

Noe, R.A., Hollenbeck, J.R., Gerhart, B. & Wright, P.M. (1997), *Human Resource Management: Gaining a Competitive Advantage*, Chicago, IL: McGraw-Hill.

Purdy, L.M. (1995), 'In defense of hiring apparently less qualified women', in Boylan (ed.).

Rawls, J. (1999), *A Theory of Justice*, Oxford: Oxford University Press.

Robbins, S.P. (1998), *Organizational Behavior: Concepts, Controversies, Applications*, Englewood Cliffs, NJ: Prentice-Hall.

Rollinson, D. (1997), *Understanding Employee Relations: A Behavioral Approach*, Reading, MA: Addison-Wesley.

Selye, H. (1956), *The Stress of Life*, New York: McGraw-Hill.

Selye, H. (1974), *Stress without Distress*, New York: Lippincott.

Selye, H. (1982), 'History and present status of the stress concept', in L. Goldberger & S. Breznitz (eds), *Handbook of Stress: Theoretical and Clinical Aspects*, New York: Free Press.

Shirom, A. & Melamed, S. (2005), 'Does burnout affect physical health? A review of the evidence', in Antoniou & Cooper (eds), pp. 599–622.

Spielberger, C.D. & Reheiser, E.C. (2005), 'Occupational stress and health', in Antoniou & Cooper (eds), pp. 441–54.

Treviño, L.K. & Nelson, K.A. (1999), *Managing Business Ethics: Straight Talk about How to Do It Right*, New York: John Wiley.

Velasquez, M.G. (1998), *Business Ethics: Concepts and Cases*, Englewood Cliffs, NJ: Prentice-Hall.

Yankelovich, D. (2007), *Profit with Honor*, New Haven, CT and London: Yale University Press.

Zeidner, M. (2005), 'Emotional intelligence and coping with occupational health', in Antoniou & Cooper (eds), pp. 218–39.

PART III

OCCUPATIONAL STRESS, WELL-BEING AND HEALTH

12 How altruism undermines mental health and happiness

Edwin A. Locke* and Ellen Kenner**

Introduction

It is taken as an axiom by most people that altruism is morally good and selfishness is morally evil. Our goal is to show that, not only is the opposite the case, but that altruism undermines mental health and happiness. Let's start with Amy, a mother of three, who has been in and out of therapy for years.

Amy has been diagnosed with depression and has tried medication after medication to no avail. She works part-time as a waitress while her children are in elementary school. She chauffeurs her father-in-law to his doctor visits, to the senior center and to his poker games. Her brother dumps his kids at her home on weekends so that all the kids can 'play together'. Amy's husband considers himself 'traditional' – she caters to him. Amy grits her teeth and assumes that this is the way life is – full of burdens.

Amy has had chronic back pain for years due to herniated discs. It's painful for her to wait on tables at work, to walk up stairs, to carry the laundry and to be active with the kids. Her medical doctors have urged her to get surgery, but she feels that she has no right to take time off from work or from household responsibilities. She feels guilty even considering this, a feeling she cannot bear to question. Amy's self-esteem is tied to feeling that she's a good wife, a good mother and a good daughter-in-law – yet that appraisal of 'good' comes at the expense of her own health and happiness. She finds herself becoming bitter and depressed – snapping at her kids, her husband and her father-in-law – the very people she wanted to love. And she feels chronic anxiety and self-doubt. Amy's medical doctor encourages her and her husband to see a psychologist. But her husband refuses to go, so she goes alone. Therapy goes nowhere. Her therapist encourages her to do what Amy 'feels is right'. Neither the therapist nor Amy question *by what standards* one judges something to be right or wrong, good or bad, healthy or unhealthy. 'Right' for Amy is putting others above herself – abiding by the moral code of altruism. And the therapist feels he cannot take any position; he has to be 'morally neutral'. Imagine going to a medical doctor who had no rational, scientific standards of physical health and felt it was 'ethical' to remain 'neutral' and let the patient's sense of a 'right cure' be the solution. No reasonable person would want a surgeon or cardiologist to behave in such a manner. Why should it be different in the realm of mental health?

Your mental health and happiness are not achievable by sacrificing your independent thinking or giving up pursuit of what you value most in life. Let's see why.

What is altruism?

Literally, altruism means other-ism – the doctrine that you should live for others, which means that you should sacrifice your time, your energy and your happiness for other people, as Amy is doing. Those others – the recipients of sacrifices – throughout history,

179

have taken numerous forms: the tribe, the ancient city-state, God, the master race, the proletariat, the state, society, the 'environment' or the family. What is the common element? To be moral, you must work to benefit someone or some collective or some entity other than yourself. Amy lives for others – she has not achieved self-esteem and happiness; rather, she feels empty, trapped, depressed and suffers chronic physical pain.

Of course, Amy, at times, does some things for herself – that is unavoidable (e.g., she buys clothes to keep warm in winter, takes prescribed medications, eats three meals a day including some foods she personally likes). Nobody could live consistently as an altruist – people who never did anything that benefits themselves would die. Even the act of breathing is self-valuing.

Short of total self-immolation, altruism must be practiced *inconsistently* – you sacrifice most of the time but guiltily smuggle in self-interest when you can. What is the consequence of cheating on this moral code? Insofar as you take morality seriously, it is *unrelenting guilt*. You feel like a hypocrite: you sacrifice to others often, but then act selfishly. You are not able to be a complete martyr, that is, you cannot fully live up to your own moral standards of the good.

What arguments are given to validate altruism?

Why should Amy live for others and not for herself? What proof is offered that altruism is the proper moral standard? No rational proof of this doctrine has ever been offered. Instead of proof, from her earliest days Amy was told that it was a matter of faith. She learned about religious martyrs (e.g., Jesus) and was told that these sacrificial heroes were the moral ideals to emulate. 'All good people have faith', she was told. She was given some stories, for example, of how God asked Abraham to sacrifice (i.e., murder) his favorite son. She remembers wincing but then concluding that faith required her to believe that this was good, or that it was God's way of 'testing us'. God, she was told, is the source of morality, and this is known through revelation.

But what is faith? Faith is acceptance of ideas based on feelings, in the absence of facts or counter to facts. No evidence is needed and no logic is applied. Faith and revelations are actually tactics to intimidate you into sacrificing, not your first-born son, but *your own mind and your own welfare*.

Amy was given a second 'reason' for embracing altruism: the assertion that the alternative, selfishness, is self-evidently evil. As a young child, Amy did not start life as a selfless person. Rather, she had dreams of being an actress, of earning enough to have a 'house with pretty gardens' and of traveling the world. When she shared these dreams with her mother she repeatedly heard that this was 'selfish'. She recalls her parents' lectures: 'If everyone did what they wanted to do, what kind of world would this be? People would do anything they want: rob, rape, kill, starve their children – just to please themselves'. Becoming an actress and owning a house with gardens did not quite seem the same as robbing, raping and starving children, but Amy's desires, acting and owning a home, did not involve living for others. And feeling insecure about her own ability to think about moral issues, Amy was left with no intellectual weapons with which to challenge altruism and validate her moral right to her personal values.

Amy also heard that selfish people have no capacity for love, kindness, consideration, compassion or generosity (see Smith, 2006, for a refutation). This is another common falsehood (which we shall deal with below) that makes the Amys of the world accept the code of altruism. She valued love and kindness, and thus, over time, studying to be an actress remained an unfulfilled dream – pushed to the depths of her subconscious as a *selfish* thought that must not be acknowledged.

The contradiction of altruism

There is an unacknowledged contradiction in the code of altruism. If it is right to sacrifice for others, is it not selfish of those others to accept the sacrifice? Should they not, in turn, sacrifice to others and so on, ad infinitum, thus resulting in no one getting anything they want? A frequent answer to this dilemma is that those who are rational, competent, productive and successful should sacrifice to those who are not. This means that the more successful you become, the more you become a slave to others – which means your life-supporting actions (e.g., being creative and productive, achieving a good education) work against your own life.

What is your 'self' and how does altruism destroy it?

One's first experience of the self occurs when one initially experiences awareness of something 'out there' in the world in contrast to 'in here', in one's mind – when one experiences that one's consciousness is separate from existence. One wordlessly, grasps that: 'It takes an act of consciousness to be aware of all this (e.g., this room) and it's I, my consciousness, that's performing the act' (Rand, 1990, p. 255). The experience of self is only implicit in an infant. Only later does one grasp conceptually that 'I am me, separate from the outside world'. Gradually one's concept of oneself expands. Most broadly, the self refers to every aspect of a given person: all his (or her) physical and personality characteristics, all his ideas, beliefs and values, all his habits and preferences, all his conscious and subconscious premises, all his experiences, memories and skills. (The person's actual self may or may not correspond to his *self-image*, which is the way he views himself.)

Most fundamentally, your self is your rational mind (Peikoff, 1991). At root it is your mind that makes the choices and actions that govern your life. But altruism says that your mind is not for you; what you think for yourself is of no moral import. Altruism declares war on you by claiming that your mind (and body) belong to others – that *your* independent judgment, *your* choices of what you want and what you value are not moral acts – and are, in fact, *immoral*. According to the code of self-sacrifice, the only proper use of your mind is to discover what others want and act accordingly. Your self is thus wiped out in principle. Altruism leads to self-immolation.

What is self-esteem and how does altruism destroy it?

Self-esteem is a judgment that one makes on oneself. It is one's estimate of one's fitness to live and one's worthiness of living (Locke, 2006–07). What is self-esteem based on? To quote Rand (1961, p. 128), 'Self-esteem is [man's] inviolate certainty that his mind is competent to think and his person is worth of happiness, which means: is worthy of living'.

Self-esteem is a profound psychological need. Man cannot tolerate the conviction that he is no good; the proof is that people who do not possess genuine self-esteem erect elaborate defenses against feelings of self-doubt or self-contempt (Locke, 2006–07). Feeling that you are worthless or 'wrong' as a person is intolerably painful. Without some sense of self-esteem, people are at risk for suicide or going insane. Feeling worthy of happiness is a selfish act; you are placing value on yourself.

Altruism destroys self-esteem at root. It says that as a separate individual you are worthless. The philosopher who most openly attacked self-esteem was Immanuel Kant. Kant regarded self-love as 'the very source of evil' (quoted in Peikoff, 1982, p. 78). Capitulation to self-love was, 'wickedness (the wickedness of the human heart) which secretly undermines the [moral] disposition with soul-destroying principles' (ibid.). Kant preached unrelenting self-sacrifice. The ideal man is 'a person who would be willing not merely to discharge all human duties himself . . . but even though tempted by the greatest allurements, to take upon himself every affliction, up to the most ignominious death' (Peikoff, 1982, p. 80). Kant himself did not preach literal altruism, not sacrifice to anyone, but *sacrifice for the sake of sacrifice*.

Kant argues:

> [I]t is a duty to preserve one's life, and moreover everyone has a direct inclination to do so. But for that reason the often anxious care which most men take of it has no intrinsic worth, and the maxim of doing so has no moral import. . . . But if adversities and hopeless sorrow completely take away the relish for life, if an unfortunate man, strong in soul, is indignant rather than despondent or dejected over his fate and wishes for death, and yet preserves his life without loving it from neither inclination nor fear but from duty – then his maxim has a moral import. (Quoted in Peikoff, 1982, pp. 73–4)

Kant's followers soon found recipients for the sacrifices: others or society. Altruism makes it clear: you are nothing – others are everything. As noted earlier, nobody could live consistently by Kant's moral code of pure self-sacrifice: sacrifice for the sake of sacrifice – or sacrifice for the sake of others.

Let us take the example of Mary, a 30-year-old woman, caring for her hypochondriac mother. Mary feels horribly guilty when planning a desperately needed romantic vacation to the Caribbean with her new boyfriend. She cannot say 'I *want* a vacation', but has to cloak her desire in the guise of a duty 'My doctor says I *have to* get away so that *I can take care of my mother better*'. When she is on vacation, her enjoyment is seriously undermined – what right does she have to enjoy herself when her mother needs her? Her boyfriend cannot understand why she cannot 'let go and enjoy'. She feels that there is something fundamentally wrong with her – she feels bitter when she sacrifices for her unappreciative mother (or others). She feels a growing hatred towards her mother whom she is 'supposed' to love. But her mother expects Mary to 'be there' for her. Mary wonders: 'Why should life have to be so hard?'. She is torn by inner conflict and guilt. She feels deep down that morality is a horrible burden.

With self-esteem destroyed and replaced by guilt and conflict, mental health is fundamentally undermined. Mental health requires that you place value on yourself and that you live *free of serious conscious or subconscious conflict*. Mary feels that she owes her life to her mother – and she also secretly feels, in her more rebellious moments, that she has some unspecified right to enjoy life and take a vacation. In this conflict, her altruist premises trump her rational, self-valuing ones, because she cannot morally defend self-interest. She feels guilt, not joy, on her 'vacation'.

Happiness requires the achievement of your values. How does altruism undermine values?
Values are things you want, things that you consider good and beneficial, things that you believe will make you happy. Altruism declares that the only legitimate values (morally) are the values of others. What they want counts; what you want for yourself does not. If

you have any personal values, they are to be sacrificed. The ideal state is one of complete personal value deprivation, a state of emptiness, except for one absolute: others. This is called 'selflessness' – a state which traditionally calls for the highest moral praise. Note the worship of saints and martyrs throughout history.

In reality, however, happiness requires that you pursue and attain *your own* values, but under altruism this is unethical. At best, as we noted, altruists will smuggle some personal values into their life, feel guilty about it and then work to please others to soothe the guilt. Since others will probably not reciprocate (e.g., Mary's mother), feelings of resentment, injustice and martyrdom will follow but may be suppressed or repressed.

What does altruistic duty do to one's motivation? To quote Rand (1970, p. 866):

> 'Duty' destroys values: it demands that one betray and sacrifice one's highest values for the sake of an inexplicable command – and it transforms values into a threat to one's moral worth, since the experience of pleasure or desire casts doubt on the moral purity of one's motives . . .

Altruism does not demand immediate death – that would prevent one from living for others. What it demands is a state of *living death*, action divorced from personal values and personal pleasure, action focused only on what others need or want. If altruism is self-destructive, what is the healthy alternative? Egoism. But what does egoism actually mean? It means rational selfishness.

What is rational selfishness?

Selfishness literally means concern with your own interests (Rand, 1964); the term itself does not specify what your interests are or how you discover them. But why should you be concerned at all with *your* own interests? The fundamental answer is: in order to live. As a human being you are mortal and failing to make the right choices is a threat to your survival and well-being. You need to make the right choices to physically keep yourself alive and thriving (e.g., food, shelter, clothing, medical care, earning a living) – and psychologically, to achieve self-esteem and happiness. 'Happiness', writes Ayn Rand, 'is the successful state of life' (Rand, 1992, p. 932):

> Happiness is that state of consciousness which proceeds from the achievement of one's values. A morality that dares to tell you to find happiness in the renunciation of your happiness – to value the failure of your values – is an insolent negation of morality. (Ibid.)

As humans, we do not possess any inborn moral code. We observe many people who choose actions that harm themselves because they do not know how to make rational choices. We observe this across many domains such as eating unhealthy foods, abusing alcohol and drugs, reckless gambling, putting up with abusive spouses, tolerating friends and relatives who cause misery, mismanaging money, failing to get an education, accepting jobs and careers that make us miserable, suffering financial exploitation, and so on.

As beings possessing free will (Peikoff, 1991) we constantly *face alternatives* and we have the *capacity to make choices* – furthermore, we need to make choices:

- Should Amy take the time to get back surgery – or not?
- Should she let her husband know that he needs to share household responsibilities – or just grin and bear it?

- Should she tactfully tell her father-in-law to make other arrangements to get to his poker games – or continue chauffeuring him?
- Should she set boundaries with her brother – or resentfully baby-sit for his kids every weekend?
- Should she pursue a career she loves – or stay at a boring job?

Observe that egoism and altruism give opposite answers to these questions and have opposite effects on her sense of self, self-esteem and happiness. If Amy accepts altruism, when she starts to think of her own well-being and desires, she feels immoral. She copes by burying (repressing) such selfish thoughts, telling herself: 'Don't think about it'. She must keep such thoughts out of conscious awareness. Amy is in a no-win situation: to be moral, she feels she must sacrifice herself – but that leaves her feeling bitter, depressed and unhappy. To be happy, she must think about what she wants – but that would violate her moral code and make her feel she is doing something wrong. This is the *psychological trap* set by altruism. It contradicts the very purpose of morality. Altruism, rather than furthering one's life, is anti-life. It flies in the face of reason.

Rand (1964; see also Peikoff, 1991) has shown that to identify and pursue one's own interests requires the exercise of reason, not mystical revelations, not whim, not blind obedience, but reality-based thinking. Unanalyzed feelings, emotions, are not a source of knowledge, and acting solely on feelings will simply lead to self-destruction. Your mind is your basic means of survival. Thus rationality, according to Rand (1964), is the highest virtue. Being rational requires you, not to unfocus your mind and take leaps of faith, or take the 'easy' way of going by gut feelings, but to take pride in having an active thinking mind. You need to understand and make sense of the world in order to live and enjoy life. In the Objectivist Ethics, Rand (1964, p. 26) elaborates on the virtue of rationality:

> It means a commitment to the principle that all of one's convictions, values, goals, desires and actions must be based on, derived from, chosen and validated by a process of thought – as precise and scrupulous a process of thought, directed by as ruthlessly strict an application of logic, as one's fullest capacity permits.

Using your mind rationally is effortful – and such effort brings you a sense of competency and self-esteem.

Other virtues implied by rationality are:

- *honesty* (the refusal to fake reality);
- *integrity* (acting in accordance with one's rational judgment);
- *independence* (thinking for oneself and working to support one's own life);
- *productivity* (working to produce, directly or indirectly, the goods one's life requires);
- *justice* (rationality applied to other men – judging them and acting toward them in accordance with their character and actions); and
- *pride* (striving to attain moral perfection).

(See Peikoff, 1991, and Smith, 2006, for a detailed discussion of these virtues.)

Acting in accordance with these virtues helps one prosper. (Note: we are concerned only with life on earth, not 'life' in another dimension – there are no other dimensions.) To give one example, dishonesty involves the negation of one's own rational judgment – seeing reality *as it isn't* rather than as it is. Amy's trying to 'put on a happy face' to her family and friends, when she is suffering terribly inside, will not make the suffering go away. Faking reality does not work – reality always wins in the end. A person will not benefit – and will ultimately be harmed by denying real problems, including psychological problems. By acknowledging such problems, however, the person is in a position to get better.

Rational egoism holds that the individual is the unit of value, an end in him/herself, not a means to the ends of others (Rand, 1992). By this code, Amy would have had a moral right to pursue a career of her choice – and to earn the money needed to eventually buy her 'house with pretty flower gardens'.

Politically, the concept of individual rights (freedom from government coercion) on which America was founded, is based on egoism (the right to the pursuit of happiness). Under the code of self-sacrifice, altruism, no such concept as rights would arise, because there would be no individual rights, only duties. (There can be no such thing as 'group' rights, since groups are not entities but only collections of individuals.)

Observe what the false 'package deal' of altruism offers: you can be 'moral', a good altruist, or you can be an immoral, selfish person. The term 'selfish', for the package-dealers, puts in the same category:

- amoral hedonists, criminals, and assorted rotten people (who are, in the end, *self-destructive*, not self-valuing); and
- moral, rational people who seek their own happiness without harming anyone (who are rationally selfish individuals).

The latter do not belong with the former. This life-defeating package deal must be totally rejected.

Can a rationally selfish person value or care about other people?

How would rational egoists view other people? First, they would *respect their rights*. No one could claim the protection of the principle of individual rights unless it applied equally to all. Second, they would deal with others through *voluntary trade*, giving value for value (see Smith, 2006, for details). This is obvious in the case of business, but it also applies in the realm of romantic love.

Let us look at romantic love more closely. To love another means that you selfishly value them, that this person's welfare and happiness is of critical importance to you. A 'selfless love' is a contradiction in terms. It would mean that you were indifferent to or disliked the person you love. But we hear that true love is altruistic. Imagine putting altruism into practice in your own life – marrying someone altruistically, that is, self-sacrificially, out of pity or duty. Such selfless love is anything but love.

Here is an imaginary 'love letter' written from a decent man under the sway of altruism, who married his wife, not for the joy she brought to his life, but out of pity and duty:

Dear Noreen,

I married you, not because I selfishly loved or admired or respected you, but because you needed me and said you couldn't be happy without me. I don't admire your character, because you're not always honest. I don't admire your independence,

because you depend on me for everything and cannot make even the smallest decision for yourself. You have no desire to grow and no ambition; you are content to
sit and watch mind-deadening soap operas. I notice that you never tell anyone what
you really feel, but what you think that person wants to hear. You do not seem to
have a real self. You always seem nervous and depressed and yet have no desire to
seek professional help. Although I get no selfish joy from being married to you, I
would feel too guilty to abandon you. I stay with you and serve your needs out of
pity and duty.

Sincerely,

David

You can see the obvious contradiction here. Altruistic love is not love at all. You
cannot love someone who means nothing to you. Romantic love is not selfless but selfish.
Although real love is not altruistic, nor is it narcissistic – a 'me-only', one-way street
relationship. Narcissists cannot really love; they use others to relieve their own sense of
inadequacy. True love is a mutually beneficial trade in which the currency is not money,
but the other person's self, body and soul.

You might ask: but couldn't you feel personal pleasure from helping others? Obviously
yes, if the person (such as your child or spouse) was someone you selfishly loved and
who was, say, recovering from an illness. You could help a friend in the same way. You
can want to do many things for your loved ones (e.g., bring flowers to your spouse, help
an adult child move to a new apartment, make meals for a friend who has lost a loved
one) and such 'giving' is rational and genuine when it comes from mutual respect and
valuing, not from duty and guilt. In such cases, you experience pleasure in helping, not
resentment. Even with strangers, it is sometimes proper and pleasurable to help, because
you love your life and value potentially good people. You have a generalized outlook
that, barring evidence to the contrary, a random stranger is a potentially good and possibly interesting person. Thus, as a rational person, you might kindly and generously help
an elderly couple put their luggage in the overhead lockers on a plane or let a couple,
stranded and freezing in a snowstorm, come into your home for warmth and to call for
help.

It is proper to help someone when it does not come at the expense of your higher
values, when the person you help is in difficulty through no fault of their own (e.g., not
a mooching, alcoholic relative), when it is temporary, when the person is appropriately
appreciative – and when it is not a risk to your life (which should be reserved for those
you love so much that you would not want to live without them).

A note about your children in relation to egoism: you should not choose to have
children unless you selfishly want them, that is, delight at the prospect of raising lovable
infants to become morally virtuous, independent, successful and happy adults. Because
children are born helpless, if you have chosen the responsibility to have them, then integrity demands that you fulfill your responsibility even if that might cause you fatigue and
stress at times. You also have to give up some other values (e.g., free time, money spent
elsewhere), but this should be because you value your children more than those other
values. (Tradeoffs between values is involved in all human action. Trade-offs are not
sacrifices unless you give up a higher value for a lower one, out of duty.) Similarly, you
marry your loved one because you value this person above all others; thus in your value

hierarchy of people, your spouse properly ranks at the top. It only becomes a sacrifice if you have children or get married out of duty or conformity.

But what about helping someone whom you do not value or actively dislike? Forcing yourself to spend your time helping those you do not value is a duty, a sacrifice. It is *anti-self*. What about charities? You can give to charities non-sacrificially, if you can afford the donation and if it is an organization whose work or cause you value and respect. But under altruism it would not work like this. Giving would not be based on your selfish values, but on duty – an unchosen sacrifice for the sake of others.

To see the extent of altruism's attack on self-esteem and happiness, we have included case vignettes from clinical practice. Specific details have been changed and cases are conglomerates to protect privacy:

- Case 1   Amy, our altruistic friend, who needs a back operation.
- Case 2   A 28-year old man who hates his career in a family business.
- Case 3   A couple whose sex life is destroyed due to altruistic ideas.
- Case 4   A successful cardiologist who feels too guilty to leave a loveless marriage to an unambitious woman.
- Case 5   A woman who has a lifetime career opportunity in Belgium but gives it up to stay with her alcoholic, mooching mother.

What do these cases have in common? Prior to therapy, the individuals involved have not yet discovered that the *philosophical cause* of their psychological pain, that is, their self-doubt, guilt and misery, is the code of altruism, self-sacrifice.

Case 1

Amy gave up on her first therapist since there was no progress. Amy's friend recommended a more rational therapist whom she started seeing weekly. Amy learned to uproot her selfless, altruistic standards, and to embrace rational moral standards (e.g., 'I *am* capable and worthy of achieving my personal values') and objective methods of thinking. She now feels, not guilt, but a sense of self-confidence and pride.

A year ago she had her back operation and wishes she had done this a decade earlier. Since then she has joined a gym and had found a more satisfying job. She felt a sense of growing strength – a sense of being in charge of her life. Amy now works part-time as a property manager for a resort condominium that has 'pretty gardens'. She became more assertive with her husband, insisting they make the relationship a *trade*, rather than a one-way street. When her husband realized she was serious, he found himself admiring her newfound courage and he agreed to couples therapy. Over the course of a year they learned how to make their relationship fair and mutually enjoyable. Amy's husband told his father that Amy would no longer be chaperoning him; he would need to make arrangements with the senior van service or rely on his poker friends for a lift. Amy told her brother that she no longer had an open-door babysitting policy – she agreed to take turns watching one another's children. This gave her a needed break. Amy's husband surprisingly encouraged her to join a community theater group. Amy felt closer than ever to him. She has not done this yet, but has considered getting involved with children's theater. Her children already enjoy putting on skits and this blends well with parenting and her reawakened passion for acting.

Case 2

Zachary, age 28, married, with a six-year-old son, sought therapy for anger management, 'shakiness' and depression. He hated his job: 'All day long I hear people's petty complaints or need to fill their stupid orders'. Zachary was chronically late for work; he took excessive coffee breaks and left early. He often called in sick.

Zachary worked in the furniture business, a business started by his father who had planned for this company to support his children throughout their adult lives. His father had carved out a position for each child: Zachary was the customer service coordinator, his younger sister was the visual merchandising manager, and his older brother was the purchasing manager. His mother was the receptionist.

When the therapist asked Zachary why he did not find a career that he would enjoy, he retorted, his hands trembling,

> You can't say no to my father. My father knows that I love being outdoors, and since childhood I've wanted to be a shipbuilder. But my father laughs at me when I mention this and then launches into mini-sermons:
>
> 1. The business supported us growing up – we have to give back to it.
> 2. Family members must stick together throughout life – we need each other.
> 3. We are lucky to have ready-made jobs and should feel grateful.
>
> I know my father is right – so I stay – but I hate my life.

Under his breath, he muttered, 'I hate my dad'.

Zachary was living a father-designed life, not his own. Many times he had fantasized about walking out and leaving the business forever. Yet he was torn. He knew that his father believed he was well meaning, and Zachary did not feel that he had a right to pursue his own interests. He could not betray the family or his father's generosity. He felt imprisoned with family members – walking into the office each day, as a 28-year-old, to be greeted by his mother.

Zachary did well in therapy. He had to grapple with and objectively answer each of his father's 'mini-sermons':

1. Yes, his father had supported him and the family through the business, but that did not mean that Zachary was his indentured servant for life. His father loved his career and why would he not want Zachary to choose his own career (shipbuilding) that offered Zachary similar excitement. Zachary realized that a 'good' dad is not one who forces his children to work for him (however well intentioned), but one who raises children to pursue their own rational careers.
2. Family members have a better chance of forming lasting friendships when they do not feel pressured to 'stick together'. Also, you cannot choose your family members and you may not like a particular family member's character – for good reason.
3. Discovering, through your own effort, that you can pursue your goals successfully, builds self-esteem. When life is planned for you, it robs you of your ability to discover and pursue your own interests, set challenging goals (e.g., shipbuilding), overcome obstacles, learn from mistakes, grow in confidence and earn self-esteem.

With clarity on these fundamental conflicts, Zachary made the decision to leave the family business. His mother was tearful for a full month following his departure. His father threatened to cut him out of his will. But Zachary, feeling a growing sense of inner dignity, left – he had learned he had a right to his own life.

Although Zachary initially experienced the conflict as a battle with his family, he discovered that his depression, 'shakiness' and anger stemmed from a battle within himself – between altruism and egoism. Once he discovered that it was proper and moral to pursue his dream career, he made the move. In the year following his departure, his wife noticed a marked improvement in his mood and his son found him more playful. Zachary made a promise to himself: that although he loved his new career at the shipyard, he would never manipulate with guilt or force his son to work in the shipbuilding trade. His son would have the pleasure of designing his own life.

Zachary's family gradually became more accepting of his move. His older brother secretly admired his leaving and is considering doing likewise. His sister truly loves the furniture business.

Case 3
Joe and Melanie, a childless couple celebrating their fifth anniversary, have decided to try therapy – their sex life is no longer pleasurable. Joe sees Melanie's low sexual desire as the problem. Joe wants sex daily; when he comes home from work he wants Melanie to enjoy pleasuring him. Melanie, who found Joe sexy when they first met, is bewildered. She went from being sexually adventurous to having no interest in sex with Joe – in five short years. As he increasingly told her what to do and how to do it, Melanie's feelings of inadequacy, guilt and resentment grew. His way was not her way, but she felt she could not speak up. She 'had' to put his needs first to feel like a good wife – not knowing that the moral code driving this was altruism. The result was worse than boring for her: sex turned into a distasteful, mechanical act that she dutifully performed to keep Joe satisfied. At first she even faked pleasure to make Joe feel pleased that he had turned her on.

Melanie was trapped: she did not feel worthy of expressing her own needs, and she could no longer force herself to fake pleasure. Joe became increasingly frustrated with her lack of emotional involvement and wondered if it might be 'hormonal'; Melanie had become depressed and withdrawn. In couples therapy, her male therapist gave her a diagnosis, not of altruism, but of hypoactive sexual desire disorder. This unexpectedly angered Melanie. Privately she knew she could arouse herself through self-pleasuring. But feeling guilty and embarrassed about this, she did not share this fact with Joe or her male therapist. She knew her 'hypoactivity' was not hormonal but due to years of resentment towards Joe's one-way lovemaking style.

Melanie quit couples therapy and tried individual therapy with a female therapist. When Melanie complained that Joe never tried to give her pleasure, the therapist asked, 'Melanie, how do you let Joe know what you want?'. Melanie confessed that she felt too guilty and embarrassed to talk about this with Joe. She noted that Joe initially begged her to share what makes her feel erotic and sensual. But feeling guilty about *receiving* personal pleasure from Joe, and eager to please him, Melanie pretended that she liked exactly what he liked. Then she faked pleasure. Melanie questioned aloud: 'I wonder if all these years, it wasn't that Joe didn't care, it's just that he gave up trying to help me value sexual pleasure'. With that, Melanie burst into tears. She saw that she was her own worst enemy – her altruistic approach to sex had ruined sex for both of them.

With her new insight and renewed hope, she invited Joe to join her with this new therapist for couples sessions. Armed with her new knowledge that selfish pleasure is both good and moral, Melanie gave herself permission to experiment sexually with Joe. Eventually she recaptured her sense of being sexually adventurous. Melanie and Joe had discovered that sexual intimacy requires honesty and mutual self-valuing.

Case 4

Alan, a successful cardiologist, wants to leave a marriage with a woman who has no ambition. She watches soap operas all day long while maids do everything at home. When they first married, he had encouraged her to have a career, but she had responded, 'What for?'. She is outraged when she learns he wants a divorce. She tells him that she would not have the same lifestyle if he leaves and that he has a responsibility to stay with her. He feels too guilty to 'abandon' her and both remain trapped in a loveless marriage. His wife wonders why he spends increasingly more time at work and has no time for her. She drags him into therapy to 'fix' *his* problem.

In therapy Alan remains quiet. He dare not hurt his wife by letting her know why he wants out of the marriage. Even thought he is a well-respected cardiologist, he feels like a failure at home. Couples therapy soon reaches a dead end.

In individual therapy, Alan levels with his therapist. He discovers that his policy of sacrificing himself, rather than dealing openly with the truth, has caused them both pain: this is not a romantic relationship – it's a fraud. Alan learns that it is proper to part ways when you are no longer soul mates, rather than faking a relationship that does not exist. Such a lie is not a value. He learns the difference between altruism and rational self-valuing. He learns how to let his wife know that he wants a divorce – this time with more tact and assertion, and to avoid accepting the torrent of unearned guilt that she will flood him with. Over the next year Alan is able to divorce with minimal inner moral conflict; three years later, he happily remarries.

Case 5

Connie, a young woman from Kansas, is offered a career opportunity in Belgium. Her mother tells her she could not survive if she were to move away. Her mother is an alcoholic and is always mooching off of her. Connie, an only child, feels that it is her job to support her mom and feels that she would be a bad person were she to pursue her dream career. She gives up the opportunity. She seeks therapy for depression and irritability, not knowing that it is her moral code of sacrificing which caused her to abandon her judgment about her future and to abandon her values (her career dreams). This puts her into a profound depression. Life no longer feels exciting, but heavy. She needs to discover a better moral code: rational egoism.

In therapy, Connie openly expresses how angry she is at her mother: 'I feel like I'm the parent and she's the child. I hate it'. Connie was brought up to 'be good to your parents', but realizes that her mom had *never* been good to her. She only used her over the years. In a tearful outburst, Connie said that the reason she catered to her mom (e.g., cleaning up her vomit after drinking binges, buying her a car, paying her bills) was out of duty: she thought it was her responsibility. Connie learned many thinking skills in therapy (e.g., how to understand her emotions, how to translate her emotions into thoughts, how to assess whether these thoughts were rational or not, how to focus on evidence as opposed to unanalyzed gut feelings, how to make decisions that will be more likely to result in enduring happiness). Connie learned assertiveness skills. In role plays, she and her therapist practiced how to stand up to her mother's manipulative, guilt-inducing methods with a sense of dignity and self-confidence. Connie became an expert in recognizing *un*earned guilt (a guilt she had not earned!) and refusing to accept such guilt. Connie cut off ties with her mother – without guilt.

Connie realized that the job opportunity in Belgium was not her only possibility. As she learned to value herself, she learned to actively job hunt. She interviewed with six international companies. One of these companies, delighted to find an energetic woman (no longer depressed or anxious), offered her a career opportunity in Italy. Connie had always loved Italy. Eight months later, the therapist received a lovely postcard from Venice, from an enthusiastic and happily employed Connie.

Such examples illustrate how most people feel that doing something that benefits themselves is, in some way, morally bad, and that sacrificing oneself, whether for one's parents, siblings, spouses, children, co-workers, employers, friends, the poor, the handicapped or the country, is somehow 'good'. Such sacrificing, as we have discussed, is referred to as 'altruistic', which is commonly taken to mean that the person is morally good for sacrificing.

But are these individuals, who have sacrificed, given up important values, put others above themselves, happier for doing so? Or are they privately suffering, feeling depressed, bitter or cynical? And if they are feeling these negative emotions, do they know to question their moral code? Once you allow yourself to think clearly about moral questions, and to see that the choices are not just being selfless or being mean, but that a third alternative exists – being rationally self-valuing – then mental health and happiness become well within reach.

Conclusion

Altruism requires that you give up what you value most in life – your dreams, your aspirations, your ambitions, your happiness; at root it means giving up your mind, which means: your self. What then would be a healthy, proper moral code, leading to both self-esteem and happiness? Rand (1961, pp. 120, 123) comments on this:

> For centuries, the battle of morality was fought between those who claimed that your life belongs to God and those who claimed that it belongs to your neighbors – between those who preached that the good is self-sacrifice for the sake of ghosts in heaven and those who preached that the good is self-sacrifice for the sake of incompetents on earth. And no one came to say that your life belongs to you and that the good is to live it . . . every man – is an end in himself, he exists for his own sake, and the achievement of his own happiness is his highest moral purpose.

Most psychologists have not fully discovered that true selfishness, self-valuing (not narcissism), is healthy, and that altruism is a cancer of the soul. Altruism is morally evil: it undermines mental health and happiness. Altruism has had an intellectual 'free ride' – going unchallenged – for too long. In this chapter we have shown that altruism is anti-life and that rational selfishness is moral, that is, good, and is the true basis for mental health and happiness.

Notes

   *   Dr Locke is Dean's Professor of Motivation and Leadership (Emeritus) at the University of Maryland, College Park. He has practiced psychotherapy part-time for 15 years.

**   Dr Kenner, a licensed clinical psychologist in private practice, has taught university courses in Introductory Psychology, Psychological Disorders and Theories of Personality. She hosts a syndicated call-in radio talk show, 'The Rational Basis of Happiness' (drkenner.com).

References

Binswanger, H. (1991), 'Volition as cognitive self-regulation', *Organizational Behavior and Human Decision Processes*, **50**: 154–78.

Locke, E.A. (2006–07), 'The educational, psychological and philosophical assault on self-esteem', *The Objective Standard*, **1** (4): 65–82.

Peikoff, L. (1982), *The Ominous Parallels*, New York: Stein & Day.

Peikoff, L. (1991), *Objectivism: The Philosophy of Ayn Rand*, New York: Dutton.

Rand, A. (1961), *For the New Intellectual*, New York: Signet.

Rand, A. (1964), *The Virtue of Selfishness*, New York: Signet.

Rand, A. (1970), 'Causality vs. duty', *The Objectivist*, July; reprinted in New York: *The Intellectual Activist*, 1986, 865–70.

Rand, A. (1990), *Introduction to Objectivist Epistemology*, 2nd edn, New York: NAL Books.

Rand. A. (1992), *Atlas Shrugged*, New York: Signet.

Smith, T. (2006), *Ayn Rand's Normative Ethics: The Virtuous Egoist*, Cambridge, UK: Cambridge University Press.

13 Work stress and health in the context of social inequality
Johannes Siegrist and Cristina Menni

Introduction

In this chapter we first argue that several highly prevalent chronic diseases are unequally distributed within and between modern societies. This distribution follows a social gradient: with each step one moves up on the social ladder or hierarchy, the better one's health. In a similar way, quality of work and employment is unequally distributed across the whole of a society, leaving those with lower occupational or educational standing in poorer quality of work and less secure employment. As will be demonstrated, poor quality of work is associated with increased risks of physical and mental disorders above and beyond the classical occupational diseases. This increased burden of disease at work is particularly relevant in the context of far-reaching changes in the nature of work and employment due to technological progress and economic globalization.

Based on these arguments we therefore address the following two questions:

1. Does quality of work, and more specifically work stress, mediate the association of socioeconomic position with health?
2. Alternatively, does socioeconomic position modify the effect of quality of work (work stress) on health, that is, are people with lower social standing more vulnerable to the adverse effects of work stress on health, compared to those in more privileged positions?

Following the discussion of these questions some policy implications of current knowledge in this field of scientific inquiry are addressed.

The social gradient of health and the social gradient of quality of work

Social inequalities in health between and within populations have been documented for decades, and there is convincing evidence that mean difference in life expectancy between those at the top and those at the bottom of modern societies' social structures (as defined by education, income, employment status) are anywhere from four to ten years (Mackenbach & Bakker, 2002; Marmot & Wilkinson, 2006). The same holds true for differences in life expectancy between countries, for instance between Western Europe and Central and Eastern Europe. Yet, the problem of inequalities in health is not confined to the poorest group of a society, but there is a social gradient of mortality and morbidity across the whole of a society (Townsend & Davidson, 1982). This was clearly demonstrated in the seminal Whitehall studies of British civil servants where position in the hierarchy shows a strong correlation with mortality risk (Marmot, 2004). Meanwhile, many more investigations confirmed and refined this evidence, testing explanations of this striking social gradient

(Siegrist & Marmot, 2006). A social gradient was seen not only for total mortality, but also for a majority of relevant causes of death, including coronary heart disease, stroke, lung cancer, type 2 diabetes, depression and accidents (Van Rossum et al., 2000). In addition to mortality data, a number of studies demonstrated the same social pattern for incidence of major diseases and disorders although some notable exceptions exist (e.g., breast cancer, asthma) (Kuh & Ben-Shlomo, 2004). Consequently, prolonged sickness absence and increased probability of disability pension add to the elevated burden of disease among those in lower socioeconomic positions (Krokstad & Westin, 2004; Dragano, 2007).

Traditional explanations of the social gradient of mortality and morbidity include (i) social selection, (ii) material resources, (iii) health-related lifestyles, and (iv) access to, and quality of healthcare (Townsend & Davidson, 1982). However, more recently it became clear that more refined explanatory approaches are needed that take into account a life course perspective where the interaction of genetic and early life circumstances is analysed and where a broad range of psychosocial phenomena with relevance to the social gradient are integrated into 'materialist' explanations (Siegrist & Marmot, 2006). This latter aspect is central to the content of this chapter, and we therefore ask what material and psychosocial aspects of the work environment are socially graded.

The most obvious aspect concerns physically strenuous work which is highly prevalent in unskilled and semi-skilled manual workers and much less frequent in professions. Yet, today fewer jobs are defined by physical demands and more by mental and emotional demands. Computer-based information processing is becoming a part of a growing number of job profiles, and employment in the service sector continues to rise. As a result, psychological and social stressors are becoming more prevalent, and their contribution to health and well-being at work is likely to parallel or even outweigh the contribution of 'traditional' occupational stressors. Some occupational groups with lower social standing are exposed to multiple stressors, such as physical demands and noise, or difficult posture and work pressure, or exposure to hazardous chemical substances and shiftwork. It should be noted that stressors such as noise are still rather frequent among the European workforce (between 25 and 30%), and the same holds true for exposure to chemical substances (about 15%; Parent-Thirion et al., 2007).

Concerning psychological and social stressors at work, these conditions cannot be identified by direct physical or chemical measurements. Rather, theoretical concepts are needed to identify those specific components within complex work environments that adversely affect health. These components are defined at a level of generalization that allows for their identification in a wide range of different occupations, and they are then translated into measures with the help of standardized questionnaires, interview schedules or observational devices.

A variety of theoretical concepts of psychosocial stress at work have been proposed and tested (for review, see Perrewé & Ganster, 2002; Schabracq et al., 2003; Antoniou & Cooper, 2005). Yet, few of these concepts were repeatedly analysed in the frame of prospective epidemiological investigations, a research design that is considered a gold standard in this field of inquiry because of the temporal sequence (exposure assessment precedes disease incidence), because of its large sample size that allows for statistical control of important confounders, and because of the quantification of disease probability as a function of exposure (relative risk).

Few of these concepts were additionally tested with respect to the psychobiological mechanisms that may mediate stressful experience at work with disease. Among the few models that fulfil these criteria, the demand–control model and the effort–reward imbalance model deserve special attention, given the amount of currently available empirical evidence. The demand–control model (Karasek & Theorell, 1990) posits that stressful experience at work results from a distinct job task profile defined by two dimensions, the psychological demands put on the working person and the degree of control available to the person to perform the required tasks. Jobs defined by high demands and low control are stressful because they limit the individual's autonomy and sense of control while generating continued pressure ('high job strain'). A third dimension, social support at work, was added to the original formulation where highest strain is expected to occur in jobs that are characterized by high demand, low control and low social support at work or social isolation ('iso-strain jobs'; Johnson & Hall, 1988). It is obvious that some of the traditional 'high strain' jobs are found in mass industry, especially under conditions of piecework and machine-paced assembly-line work. In particular, low control at work is highly frequent in jobs with a low level of qualification.

The effort–reward imbalance model is concerned with stressful features of the work contract (Siegrist, 1996). This model builds on the notion of social reciprocity, a fundamental principle rooted in an 'evolutionary old' grammar of interpersonal exchange. Social reciprocity lies at the core of the employment (or work) contract which defines distinct obligations or tasks to be performed in exchange for adequate rewards. These rewards include money, esteem and career opportunities, including job security. Contractual reciprocity operates through norms of return expectancy, where efforts spent by employees are reciprocated by equitable rewards from employers. The effort–reward imbalance model claims that lack of reciprocity occurs frequently under specific conditions (see below) and that failed reciprocity in terms of high cost and low gain elicits strong negative emotions with special propensity to sustained autonomic and neuroendocrine activation and their adverse long-term consequences for health. According to the theory, contractual non-reciprocity is expected if one or several of the following conditions are given: 'dependency', 'strategic choice' and 'overcommitment'. Dependency reflects the structural constraints observed in certain types of employment contracts, especially so in unskilled or semi-skilled workers, in elderly employees, in employees with restricted mobility or limited work ability, and in workers with short-term contracts. Strategic choice is a second condition of non-symmetrical exchange. Here, people accept high-cost/low-gain conditions of their employment for a certain time, often without being forced to do so, because they tend to improve their chances of career promotion and related rewards at a later stage. Third, there are psychological reasons for a recurrent mismatch between efforts and rewards at work. People characterized by a motivational pattern of excessive work-related overcommitment may strive towards continuously high achievement because of their underlying need for approval and esteem at work. Although these excessive efforts often are not met by adequate rewards, overcommitted people tend to maintain their level of involvement.

In summary, in addition to the burden of hazardous physical exposures at work, a health-adverse psychosocial work environment in terms of job strain (in particular low control), and in terms of failed reciprocity between effort and reward (in particular low reward) is more prevalent among employees with low occupational position or educational level. In the next section we ask what the current evidence is that links stressful work with reduced health.

Adverse health effects of stressful working conditions

The prospective epidemiological observational study is considered a gold standard approach in this field because of its temporal sequence (exposure assessment precedes disease onset), its usual sample size (based on statistical power calculation and allowing for adjustment for confounding variables in multivariate analysis) and the quantification of subsequent disease risk following exposure (odds ratio or relative risk of disease in exposed versus non-exposed people). Short reviews of main findings from prospective studies with respect to traditional occupational stressors, such as noise, heat, shiftwork and chemical hazards are available in Schnall et al. (2000) and in selected issues of specialized journals, for example, *Occupational and Environmental Medicine* or the *Scandinavian Journal of Work, Environment and Health*. Less well known are reviews of findings from prospective investigations on adverse health effects of psychosocial stress at work (for review, see Belkic et al., 2004; Kivimäki et al., 2006b; Marmot et al., 2006). A majority of these studies is devoted to cardiovascular diseases or affective disorders.

At least 15 prospective observational studies tested the demand–control and/or the effort–reward imbalance model with regard to cardiovascular disease. Ten studies are based on the former, and five on the latter model, with two studies testing both models simultaneously. In a majority of cases (10 out of 15 studies) significantly elevated relative risks were observed, based either on the full model or on one or several of its main components. Relative risks varied between 1.2 and 6.6. Findings are more consistent in men than in women and in middle-aged versus early-old populations. Incident fatal or non-fatal coronary heart disease and total cardiovascular morbidity or mortality are the main outcome measures. In addition to these primary endpoints, some studies documented an association of work stress with incident hypertension (Guimont et al., 2006), overweight (Kivimäki et al., 2006a) and the development of the metabolic syndrome (Chandola et al., 2006) as major cardiovascular risk factors. This epidemiological evidence is supported by a rich body of findings from experimental and naturalistic studies demonstrating direct effects of stressful experience on cardiovascular, hormonal and metabolic functioning (see below).

Depression is one of the more recently established risk factors of coronary heart disease (Van der Kooy et al., 2007), but in addition is considered an important stress-associated disorder. As such it has been included as an outcome measure in a number of prospective investigations of work stress in terms of the two models (five with the job strain, four with the effort–reward imbalance model, one of them testing both models simultaneously; for review, see Siegrist & Dragano, 2008). All studies reported elevated relative risks varying between 1.2 and 4.6. Additional health outcomes of prospective investigations testing these models include poor self-rated health (Cheng et al., 2000; Niedhammer et al., 2004), limited physical and mental functioning (Stansfeld et al., 1998; Kuper et al., 2002), alcohol dependence (Head et al., 2004) and risk of diabetes (Kumari et al., 2004; Chandola et al., 2006); among others.

It should be noted that results are drawn from a variety of different occupations in different modern societies, thus representing rich empirical support. These prospective findings are in line with a series of cross-sectional and case-control studies that are not reported here in detail (Tsutsumi & Kawakami, 2004; Marmot et al., 2006). Moreover, naturalistic and experimental studies supplement epidemiological evidence as they monitor the psychobiological responses to stressful exposure at work, such as cardiovascular reactivity, hormonal secretion, immune function or inflammatory response. In a recent review, Steptoe (2006) distinguished three different types of socioeconomic effects on psychobiological function that may be influenced, in part, by psychosocial stress at work. The first pattern concerns differences in the extent of physiological reactivity where employees with lower socioeconomic position exhibit greater increases in response to psychosocial challenge, compared to employees with higher status. A second pattern of socioeconomic difference in psychobiological function is found in the rate of post-stress recovery. In several studies, lower employment grade participants showed less effective recovery and delayed return to baseline levels. Third, some studies demonstrate an overall higher level of biological markers during stress among lower-status groups, both in experimental and naturalistic conditions. Yet, heightened responsiveness in the long run overtaxes an exhausted biological system which then responds to this load by blunted reactivity.

All three patterns are in line with the general hypothesis of chronic allostatic load that results from prolonged exposure to stressful conditions (McEwen, 1998). 'Allostatic load' refers to the wear and tear imposed on biological regulatory systems that is present more often in lower-status groups, possibly contributing to their increased burden of stress-related disorders. Importantly, two recent reports demonstrate that autonomic function is more often compromised among participants from lower employment grades (Hemingway et al., 2005) and that reduced functional capacity and delayed heart rate recovery after exercise testing are strongly related to socioeconomic status (Shishehbor et al., 2006). In this latter prospective study, some 30,000 patients with coronary symptoms underwent exercise testing where functional capacity and heart rate recovery were assessed. A strong social gradient of all-cause mortality was found. As both functional measures were associated with socioeconomic status, a multivariate model was calculated to test the degree of attenuation of the former relationship by adding these latter variables. In fact, reduced functional capacity and delayed recovery explained 47% of the association of social status with subsequent all-cause mortality (ibid.).

In addition to physiological vulnerability, psychosocial vulnerability needs to be assessed. In the next two sections this topic is further explored, referring to epidemiological research findings where the association of socioeconomic status with work stress and health is analysed in terms of mediation and effect modification.

Does work stress mediate the association of socioeconomic position with health?
If work stress is more prevalent in lower socioeconomic groups, and if both work stress and low socioeconomic position are associated with reduced health, it is tempting to conclude that work stress mediates the association of socioeconomic status with health. In fact, considerable support of the mediation hypothesis has been found. In the Whitehall II study, low control at work was independently associated with incident coronary disease and with low employment grade (Marmot et al., 1997). In multivariate analysis, low control in the workplace accounted for about half the social gradient of coronary heart disease as the odds ratio of coronary disease in the low employment group was reduced from about 1.4 to about 1.2 after respective adjustment. Importantly, the relation between low control and coronary disease was not removed by adjusting for socioeconomic position (ibid.; see also Bosma, 2006). Similar findings were obtained in a case-control study of coronary patients in the Czech Republic (Bobak et al., 1998) and in a prospective study of myocardial infarction in Denmark (Andersen et al., 2004). In this

latter study, a hazard ratio of 1.57 for unskilled workers compared to executive managers was observed. Yet, this hazard ratio was reduced to 1.07 after adjustment for low level of control (skill discretion) and other cardiovascular risk factors.

Additional studies were conducted to test the mediation hypothesis with respect to other health outcomes, sometimes using less explicit measures of an adverse psychosocial work environment, and their results were not always consistent (Schrijvers et al., 1998; Krokstadt et al., 2002; Melchior et al., 2005; Hagen et al., 2006; Rahkonen et al., 2006). Three such studies deserve particular attention.

Warren et al. (2004) examined the extent to which job characteristics mediate the relationship between socioeconomic position and musculo-skeletal disorders by study-ing 4,422 people from the Wisconsin Longitudinal Study, a random sample of men and women who graduated from Wisconsin (USA) high schools in 1975. After adjusting for health-adverse behaviours men and women with lower social standing exhibited a higher prevalence of musculo-skeletal disorders. Job characteristics played an important role in mediating this association where physical workload was a prominent mediator both in men and women, whereas psychosocial stress at work accounted for some of this associa-tion among women only.

Virtanen and Notkola (2002) estimated the degree to which unfavourable working conditions are responsible for socioeconomic inequalities in cardiovascular mortality, using data from the Finnish Longitudinal Census file. Poisson regression was performed to estimate the impact of independent variables on mortality. In a fully adjusted model with confounders, socioeconomic variables and two variables measuring high workload and low control at work parameters were used to calculate the number of expected car-diovascular deaths under the assumption of all occupations having the lowest exposure to stressful work. In this model, a reduction of about 10% in cardiovascular deaths was predicted. In conclusion, a moderate impact of an adverse psychosocial work environ-ment on socioeconomic differences in cardiovascular mortality was found.

Most recently, d'Errico et al. (2007) analysed hospital injury rates in relation to socio-economic status and working conditions in different occupational groups of two private hospitals in Massachusetts. While a strong social gradient of injury rates was found, this gradient was greatly attenuated when controlling for psychosocial and ergonomic work-place exposures. These exposures were decision latitude, reward (psychosocial), bending, kneeling and forceful exertion (ergonomic).

In summary, adverse physical and psychosocial working conditions attenuate the asso-ciation of socioeconomic position with health to some extent, but in general this effect is moderate and it depends on disease outcome and occupational characteristics included. Therefore, it is worth exploring an alternative hypothesis, effect modification.

Does socioeconomic position modify the effect of work stress on health?
In the previous sections it was shown that many prevailing diseases in modern societies are socially graded. The same holds true for quality of work and employment, which is consid-erably poorer among those in lower socioeconomic positions. Having argued that stress-ful work adversely affects the health of employees, we concluded that there is reason to assume that poor quality of work mediates the association of socioeconomic position with health. The findings of several investigations demonstrate that, to some extent, this is in fact the case. However, some components of the two work stress models, 'demand', 'social

support', 'effort' and 'overcommitment' are not consistently related to occupational position. On the contrary, in some studies a higher prevalence in better-qualified occupational groups was observed (Karasek & Theorell, 1990; Siegrist et al., 2004). Therefore, alternative ways of disentangling the association of social position, work stress and health are needed. The effect modification hypothesis represents one such strategy. It posits that susceptibility to an exposure (such as work stress) is higher among lower-status compared to higher-status people and that among people with lower socioeconomic position, the effect size produced by the exposure is more pronounced. Several explanations can account for this fact. First, it is likely that stressful experience resulting from different conditions of social disadvantage is accumulated in people with lower socioeconomic standing, thus overtaxing their coping resources and increasing their vulnerability. It is more difficult to meet the challenges of stressful work if financial hardship or chronic interpersonal strain outside work are experienced simultaneously (Ross & Mirowski, 1989).

A second explanation points to socially graded coping abilities and coping strategies (Kristenson, 2006). For instance, Lachman and Weaver (1998) and Bosma (2006) argued that low sense of control or low control beliefs are part of a distinct socialization pattern that reflects a sense of powerlessness in the face of deprived social circumstances. Low control beliefs are not only socially graded, but are independent predictors of poor health (ibid.). Faced with the same stressors, people with lower social standing may be less effective in meeting stressful demands and threats compared to more privileged people, because they lack adequate mastery, self-efficacy and positive outcome expectancy.

The effect modification hypothesis was tested in several studies that document a stronger effect of high demand and low control at work, or of high effort and low reward at work, on health among lower compared to higher employment grades. One of the earlier studies was conducted by Johnson and Hall (1988), who analysed the association of job strain with cardiovascular disease in a random sample of the Swedish working population in a cross-sectional design. A significantly elevated odds ratio of job strain (including low social support at work) was observed among blue-collar, but not among white-collar workers. In a later Swedish study comparing patients with acute myocardial infarction with healthy controls, Hallqvist et al. (1998) replicated this finding, testing the interaction of occupational group with job strain by the synergy index. A significant synergy effect of job strain with manual workers was observed. In the frame of the Whitehall II study, Kuper et al. (2002) analysed the association of effort–reward imbalance to coronary disease incidence (quartiles of the effort–reward ratio) in an 11-year follow-up period in the Whitehall II study. While they found an increased disease risk in the upper quartile of scores in the effort–reward ratio within the total study population, this effect was relatively strongest in the lowest employment group, especially so for fatal and non-fatal acute myocardial infarction.

In a recent analysis of baseline data from a population-based prospective study of employed middle-aged men and women in Germany the effect modification hypothesis was tested using both work stress models (Wege et al., 2008). Socioeconomic position was defined by two indicators, level of education and occupational grade. Poor self-rated health, angina pectoris and depressive symptoms were assessed based on standardized interviews and self-completed questionnaires. Figures 13.1 and 13.2 show the results of logistic regression analyses testing an interaction of socioeconomic position (occupational grade) with work stress on depressive symptoms, as measured by the CES-D

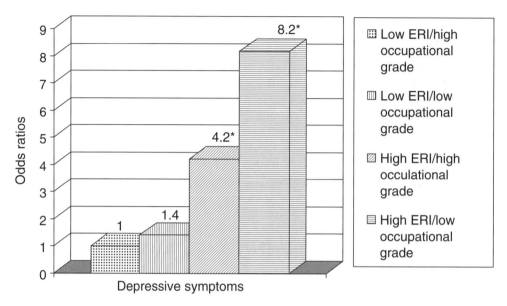

Note: *p<0.05.

Source: Adapted from Wege et al. (2008).

Figure 13.1   Relationship of work stress (effort–reward imbalance (ERI)) and social position (occupational grade) with depressive symptoms (synergy index = 1.99 (CI 1.02–2.23))

scale (Radloff, 1977). Models are adjusted for age, gender, body mass index, smoking and physical inactivity. A significant synergy effect of occupational grade with effort–reward imbalance is observed, leaving the high-stress/low-grade group at an eight times higher risk of experiencing depressive symptoms compared to the low-stress/high-grade reference group. The probability of depressive symptoms is also clearly increased in the job-strain/low-grade group although no synergy effect is present. This latter pattern of results was obvious for the two remaining health indicators as well. In all instances, the high-stress/low-grade group exhibited relatively highest risks of poor health.

Concluding remarks and policy implications
The evidence presented on work stress and health in the context of social inequality is limited in different ways. First, we referred to a body of recent research that is largely restricted to information obtained from employed populations in modern Western societies. In general, welfare policies and technological progress in these countries contribute to a relatively high level of health protection at work and social security measures in the case of unemployment and precarious life events. Although the Nordic welfare states in Europe whose respective achievements are most pronounced still face strong social inequalities in health (Dahl et al., 2006), the extent of physical and psychosocial stress at work and the burden of disease evolving from them may have been underestimated by this restriction. Employment and

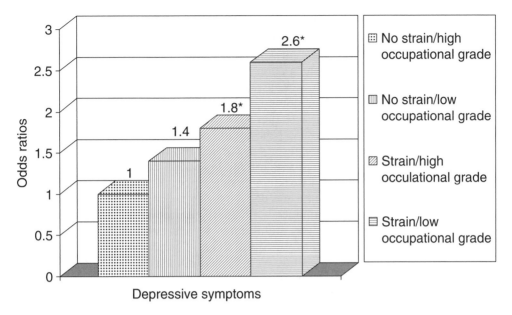

Note: *p<0.05.

Source: Adapted from Wege et al. (2008).

Figure 13.2   *Relationship of work stress (job strain) and social position (occupational grade) with depressive symptoms (synergy index = 1.28 (CI 0.42–3.91))*

working conditions in rapidly developing countries, such as China and India, or in countries that underwent political and economic upheaval, such as Russia and former communist countries in Central and Eastern Europe, are likely to be more dangerous and more stressful and, thus, may aggravate the impact of work on social inequalities in health.

Second, we limited this review to two established theoretical concepts of stressful work, demand–control and effort–reward imbalance, because up to now relatively largest amounts of empirical data are available from them. This does not preclude further theoretical developments as additional important dimensions of stressful experience at work may be bypassed by these models. For instance, the notion of organizational injustice developed in organizational psychology (Greenberg & Cropanzano, 2001) was applied to health where procedural and relational injustice were shown to predict adverse health (Elovainio et al., 2002; Kivimäki et al., 2007). As the effort–reward imbalance model is rooted in the notion of social reciprocity or exchange justice, one might assume that these constructs overlap to some extent. Yet, as recent comparative analyses demonstrate, they must be considered complementary rather than redundant models (Kivimäki et al., 2007).

In addition, prevailing concepts of work stress should take into account far-reaching recent changes of the nature and economic context of paid work. With the advent of economic globalization, pressures towards an increase of return on investment have been growing, increasing work pressure and competition (Ostry & Spiegel, 2004). Another consequence of economic globalization concerns the expansion and mobility of labour markets, the rapid dislocation of production sites, mergers, downsizing and increased redundancy. With recent progress in information technology and automatization, the traditional separation of the spheres of work and home is vanishing. These and related challenges deserve attention in contemporary research on work stress and health.

A third limitation concerns the lack of scientific evidence derived from intervention studies. The number of theory-based intervention studies following a rigorous research design is still scarce. Some of these studies were successful in changing coping behaviour (Kompier et al., 2002), leadership behaviour (Theorell et al., 2001) or in improving the development of health-promoting organizational features (Bond & Bunce, 2001; Bourbonnais et al., 2006). Among these last developments, increasing control at work by changing tasks and division of work, improving support at work and strengthening education and qualification are measures derived from the demand–control model. The effort–reward model offers opportunities of gain sharing, introducing compensatory wage systems, strengthening non-monetary gratifications such as esteem reward, or reducing workload while providing job security at critical stages of occupational trajectories. Yet, to our knowledge, no intervention study yet has demonstrated that social inequalities in health are attenuated as a result of improved quality of work.

Despite these limitations, some policy implications of current scientific evidence on the link between work stress and health are obvious. First, worksite health protection measures are to be improved in countries and economic branches with less developed standards. Specific occupational high-risk groups deserve particular attention, such as migrant workers, workers in precarious or temporary employment, transport workers or employees with high mobility, occupations with high risks of accidents and injuries and those exposed to chemical hazards. Improving standards of health protection at work by legislation, control systems and economic incentives is considered a powerful way of reducing work-related social inequalities in health. In this context, the rights of trade unions and their demands of fair wages, reduced workload and improved employment security need to be emphasized.

A second policy implication concerns improved monitoring of the newly identified psychosocial stressors at work in order to develop measures of worksite health promotion. To this aim, standardized questionnaires measuring the demand–control (Karasek et al., 1998) or the effort–reward imbalance models (Siegrist et al., 2004) or additional concepts (e.g., Kristensen et al., 2005) are available in several languages, offering programs of data analysis and reference data (www.jcqcenter.org; www.uni-duesseldorf.de/medicalsociology). In addition, companies can use their administrative data to identify targets of worksite health promotion, by establishing task forces or committees devoted to the development and implementation of respective initiatives. Studies are needed to demonstrate the medium-term cost savings of investments into healthy work, as there is still strong resistance among managers and stakeholders against such investments, in particular in medium-sized or smaller enterprises.

Reducing psychosocial stress at work by implementing theory-based interpersonal and structural measures is a most important target. It is hoped that improved health results from such interventions. However, it is not clear whether such interventions are sufficient to reduce that part of social inequalities in health that is attributed to stressful work. In the previous section, we argued that lower socioeconomic groups are more vulnerable to the adverse effects of stressful work than more privileged employees. What are the policy implications of results supporting the effect modification hypothesis? In our view at least one implication is obvious: improving coping skills of exposed people by strengthening capabilities and abilities of less privileged groups of working populations (Sen, 1999; Marmot, 2004). Strengthening capabilities and abilities refers to two types of measures. First to psychosocial resources, such as mastery, perceived control, self-efficacy, and options of receiving support, esteem and reward. Second, the biomedical dimension of coping needs to be strengthened. Biological signs of dysfunction and exhaustion due to prolonged exposure to stressful work, as mentioned above, need to be monitored, reduced and prevented. By this approach, a relevant part of sub-clinical burden of stress-related diseases can be detected and eventually controlled. In conclusion, recent progress in research on work stress and health resulted in the discovery of new risk factors of an adverse psychosocial work environment. It is hoped that this new evidence, in combination with established knowledge of traditional occupational risks, is translated into activities of worksite stress prevention and health promotion. Most importantly, such measures may contribute to the reduction of social inequalities in health that still prevail in working populations of modern societies.

References

Andersen, I., Burr, H., Kristensen, T.S., Gamborg, M., Osler, M., Prescott, E. & Diderichsen, F. (2004), 'Do factors in the psychosocial work environment mediate the effect of socioeconomic position on the risk of myocardial infarction? Study from the Copenhagen Centre for prospective population studies', *Occupational and Environmental Medicine*, **61**, 886–92.

Antoniou, A.-S.G. & Cooper, C.L. (eds) (2005), *Research Companion to Organizational Health Psychology*, Edward Elgar, Cheltenham, UK and Northampton, MA, USA.

Belkic, K.L., Landsbergis, P.A., Schnall, P.L. & Baker, D. (2004), 'Is job strain a major source of cardiovascular disease risk?', *Scandinavian Journal of Work Environment and Health*, **30**, 85–128.

Bobak, M., Hertzman, C., Skodova, Z. & Marmot, M. (1998), 'Association between psychosocial factors at work and non-fatal myocardial infarction in a population-based case-control study in Czech men', *Epidemiology*, **9**, 43–7.

Bond, F.W. & Bunce, D. (2001), 'Job control mediates change in work organization intervention for stress reduction', *Journal of Occupational Health Psychology*, **6**, 290–302.

Bosma, H. (2006), 'Socio-economic differences in health: are control beliefs fundamental mediators?', in Siegrist & Marmot (eds), pp. 153–66.

Bourbonnais, R., Brisson, C., Vinet, A., Vezina, M. & Lower, A. (2006), 'Development and implementation of a participative intervention to improve the psychosocial work environment and mental health in an acute care hospital', *Occupational and Environmental Medicine*, **63**, 326–34.

Chandola, T., Brunner, E. & Marmot, M. (2006), 'Chronic stress at work and the metabolic syndrome: prospective study', *British Medical Journal*, **332**, 521–5.

Cheng, Y., Kawachi, I., Coakley, E.H., Schwartz, J. & Colditz, G. (2000), 'Associations between psychosocial job characteristics and health functioning in American women: prospective study', *British Medical Journal*, **320**, 1432–6.

d'Errico, A., Punnett, L., Cifuentes, M., Boyer, J., Tessler, J., Gore, R., Scollin, P., Slatin, C. & Promoting Healthy and Safe Employment in Healthcare Research Team (2007), 'Hospital injury rates in relation to socio-economic status and working conditions', *Occupational and Environmental Medicine*, **64**, 325–33.

Dahl, E., Fritzell, J., Lahelma, E., Martikainen, P., Kunst, A. & Mackenbach, J.P. (2006), 'Welfare state regimes and health inequalities', in Siegrist & Marmot (eds), Oxford University Press, Oxford, pp. 193–222.

Dragano, N. (2007), *Arbeit, Stress und krankheitsbedingte Frührenten* (Work, stress and disability-related pensions), VS Verlag, Wiesbaden.

Elovainio, M., Kivimäki, M. & Vahtera, J. (2002), 'Organizational justice: evidence of a new psychosocial predictor of health', *American Journal of Public Health*, **92**, 105–8.

Greenberg, J. & Cropanzano, R. (eds) (2001), *Advances in Organization Justice*, Stanford University Press, Stanford, CA.

Guimont, C., Brisson, C., Dagenais, G.R., Milot, A., Vézina, M., Mâsse, B., Moisan, J., Laflamme, N. & Blanchette, C. (2006), 'Effects of job strain on blood pressure: a prospective study of male and female white-collar workers', *American Journal of Public Health*, **96**, 1436–43.

Hagen, K.B., Tambs, K. & Bjerkedal, T. (2006), 'What mediates the inverse association between education and occupational disability from back pain? A prospective cohort study from the Nord-Trondelag health study in Norway', *Social Science and Medicine*, **63**, 1267–75.

Hallqvist, J., Diderichsen, F. & Theorell, T. (1998), 'Is the effect of job strain on myocardial infarction due to interaction between high psychological demands and low decision latitude? Results from the Stockholm Heart Epidemiology Program (SHEEP)', *Social Science and Medicine*, **46**, 1405–15.

Head, J., Stansfeld, S.A. & Siegrist, J. (2004), 'The psychosocial work environment and alcohol dependence: a prospective study', *Occupational and Environmental Medicine*, **61**, 219–24.

Hemingway, H., Shipley, M., Brunner, E., Britton, A., Malik, M. & Marmot, M. (2005), 'Does autonomic function link social position to coronary risk? The Whitehall II study', *Circulation*, **111**, 3071–7.

Johnson, J.V. & Hall, E.M. (1988), 'Job strain, workplace social support and cardiovascular disease: a cross-sectional study of a random sample of the Swedish working population', *American Journal of Public Health*, **78**, 1336–42.

Karasek, R., Brisson, C., Kawakami, N., Houtman, I., Bongers, P. & Amick, B. (1998), 'The job content questionnaire (JCQ): an instrument for internationally comparative assessment of psychosocial job characteristics', *Journal of Occupational Health Psychology*, **3**, 322–55.

Karasek, R.A. & Theorell, T. (1990), *Healthy Work*, Basic Books, New York.

Kivimäki, M., Head, J., Ferrie, J.E., Shipley, M.J., Brunner, E., Vahtera, J. & Marmot, M.G. (2006a), 'Work stress, weight gain and weight loss: evidence for bidirectional effects of job strain on body mass index in the Whitehall II study', *International Journal of Obesity*, **30** (6), 982–7.

Kivimäki, M., Vahtera, J., Elovainio, M., Virtanen, M. & Siegrist, J. (2007), 'Effort–reward imbalance, procedural injustice and relational injustice as psychosocial predictors of health: complementary or redundant models?', *Occupational and Environmental Medicine*, Online, doi:10.1136/oem.2006.031310.

Kivimäki, M., Virtanen, M., Elovainio, M., Kouvonen, A., Väänänen, A. & Vahtera, J. (2006b), 'Work stress in the etiology of coronary heart disease – a meta-analysis', *Scandinavian Journal of Work, Environment and Health*, **32**, 431–42.

Kompier, M.A., Aust, B., van den Berg, A.M. & Siegrist, J. (2002), 'Stress prevention in bus drivers: evaluation of 13 natural experiments', *Journal of Occupational Health Psychology*, **5**, 11–31.

Kristenson, M. (2006), 'Socio-economic position and health: the role of coping', in Siegrist & Marmot (eds), pp. 127–52.

Kristensen, T.S., Hannerz, H., Hogh, A. & Borg, V. (2005), 'The Copenhagen psychosocial questionnaire – a tool for the assessment and improvement of the psychosocial work environment', *Scandinavian Journal of Work, Environment and Health*, **31**, 438–49.

Krokstad, S., Johnsen, R. & Westin, S. (2002), 'Social determinants of disability pension: a 10-year follow-up of 62,000 people in a Norwegian county population', *International Journal of Epidemiology*, **31**, 1183–91.

Krokstad, S. & Westin, S. (2004), 'Disability in society – medical and non-medical determinants for disability pension in a Norwegian total county population study', *Social Science and Medicine*, **58**, 1837–48.

Kuh, D. & Ben-Shlomo, Y. (2004), *A Life Course Approach to Chronic Disease Epidemiology: Tracing the Origins of Ill-health from Early to Adult Life*, Oxford University Press, Oxford.

Kumari, M., Head, J. & Marmot, M. (2004), 'Prospective study of social and other risk factors for incidence of type II diabetes in Whitehall 2 study', *Annals of Internal Medicine*, **164**, 1873–80.

Kuper, H., Singh-Manoux, A., Siegrist, J. & Marmot, M. (2002), 'When reciprocity fails: effort–reward imbalance in relation to coronary heart disease and health functioning within the Whitehall II Study', *Journal of Occupational and Environmental Medicine*, **59**, 777–84.

Lachman, M.E. & Weaver, S.L. (1998), 'The sense of control as a moderator of social class differences in health and well-being', *Journal of Personality and Social Psychology*, **74**, 763–73.

Mackenbach, J.P. & Bakker, M. (eds) (2002), *Reducing Inequalities in Health: A European Perspective*, Routledge, London.

Marmot, M. (2004), *Status Syndrome. How Your Social Standing Directly Affects Your Health and Life Expectancy*, Bloomsbury, London.

Marmot, M., Bosma, H., Hemingway, H., Brunner, E. & Stansfeld, S. (1997), 'Contribution of job control and other risk factors to social variations in coronary heart disease', *Lancet*, **350**, 235–40.

Marmot, M., Siegrist, J. & Theorell, T. (2006), 'Health and the psychosocial environment at work', in Marmot & Wilkinson (eds), pp. 97–130.

Marmot, M. & Wilkinson, R. (eds) (2006), *Social Determinants of Health*, 2nd edn, Oxford University Press, Oxford.

McEwen, B. (1998), 'Protective and damaging effects of stress mediators', *New England Journal of Medicine*, **338**, 171–9.

Melchior, M., Krieger, N., Kawachi, I., Berkman, L.F., Niedhammer, I. & Goldberg, M. (2005), 'Work factors and occupational class disparities in sickness absence: findings from the GAZEL cohort study', *American Journal of Public Health*, **95**, 1206–12.

Niedhammer, I., Tek, M.L., Starke, D. & Siegrist, J. (2004), 'Effort–reward imbalance model and self-reported health: cross-sectional and prospective findings from the GAZEL cohort', *Social Science and Medicine*, **58**, 1531–41.

Ostry, A.S. & Spiegel, J.M. (2004), 'Labor markets and employment insecurity: impacts of globalization on the healthcare workforce', *International Journal of Occupational and Environmental Health*, **10**, 368–74.

Parent-Thirion, A., Macias, E.F., Hurley, J. & Vermeylen, G. (2007), *Fourth European Working Conditions Survey*, Office for Official Publications of the European Communities, Luxembourg.

Perrewé, P.L. & Ganster, D.C. (eds) (2002), *Historical and Current Perspectives on Stress and Health*, JAI Elsevier, Amsterdam.

Radloff, L.S. (1977), 'The CES-D scale: a self-report depression scale for research in the general population', *Applied Psychological Measurement*, **1**, 385–401.

Rahkonen, O., Laaksonen, M., Martikainen, P., Roos, E. & Lahelma, E. (2006), 'Job control, job demands, or social class? The impact of working conditions on the relation between social class and health', *Journal of Epidemiology and Community Health*, **60**, 50–54.

Ross, C.E. & Mirowsky, J. (1989), 'Explaining the social patterns of depression: control and problem solving – or support and talking?', *Journal of Health and Social Behavior*, **30**, 206–19.

Schabracq, M.J., Winnubst, J.A.M. & Cooper. C.L. (eds) (2003), *The Handbook of Work and Health Psychology*, Wiley, London.

Schnall, P.L., Belkic, K., Landsbergis, P. & Baker, D. (eds) (2000), 'The workplace and cardiovascular disease', *Occupational Medicine: State of the Art Reviews*, **15**, 1–334.

Schrijvers, C.T.M., van de Mheen, H.D., Stronks, K. & Mackenbach, J.P. (1998), 'Socioeconomic inequalities in health in the working population: the contribution of working conditions', *International Journal of Epidemiology*, **27**, 1011–18.

Sen, A. (1999), *Development and Freedom*, Alfred A. Knopf, New York.

Shishehbor, M.H., Litaker, D., Pothier, C.E. & Lauer, M.S. (2006), 'Association of socio-economic status with functional capacity, heart rate recovery, and all-cause mortality', *Journal of the American Medical Association*, **295**, 784–92.

Siegrist, J. (1996), 'Adverse health effects of high-effort/low-reward conditions', *Journal of Occupational Health Psychology*, **1**, 27–41.

Siegrist, J. & Dragano, N. (2008), 'Psychosocial stress and disease risks in occupational life', *Bundesgesundheitsblatt*, Gesundheitsforschung Gesundheitsschutz, **51** (3), 305–12.

Siegrist, J. & Marmot, M. (eds) (2006), *Social Inequalities in Health*, Oxford University Press, Oxford.

Siegrist, J., Starke, D., Chandola, T., Godin, I., Marmot, M., Niedhammer, I. & Peter, R. (2004), 'The measurement of effort–reward imbalance at work: European comparisons', *Social Science and Medicine*, **58** (8), 1483–99.

Stansfeld, S.A., Bosma, H., Hemingway, H. & Marmot, M. (1998), 'Psychosocial work characteristics and social support as predictors of SF-36 functioning: the Whitehall II Study', *Psychosomatic Medicine*, **60**, 247–55.

Steptoe, A. (2006), 'Psychobiological processes linking socio-economic position with health', in Siegrist & Marmot (eds), pp. 101–26.

Theorell, T., Emdad, R., Arnetz, B. & Weingarten, A.M. (2001), 'Employee effects of an educational program for managers at an insurance company', *Psychosomatic Medicine*, **63**, 724–33.

Townsend, P. & Davidson, N. (eds) (1982), *Inequalities in Health: The Black Report and the Health Divide*, Penguin Books, Harmondsworth.

Tsutsumi, A. & Kawakami, N. (2004), 'A review of empirical studies on the model of effort–reward imbalance at work: reducing occupational stress by implementing a new theory', *Social Science and Medicine*, **59**, 2335–59.

Van der Kooy, K., van Hout H., Marwijk, H., Marten, H., Stehouwer, C. & Beekman, A. (2007), 'Depression and the risk for cardiovascular diseases: systematic review and meta analysis', *International Journal of Geriatric Psychiatry*, **22**, 613–26.

Van Rossum, C.T.M., Shipley, M., Van de Mheen, H., Grobbee, D.E. & Marmot, M. (2000), 'Employment grade differences in cause-specific mortality. A 25-year follow-up of civil servants from the first Whitehall study', *Journal of Epidemiology and Community Health*, **54**, 178–84.

Virtanen, S.V. & Notkola, V. (2002), 'Socioeconomic inequalities in cardiovascular mortality and the role of work: a register study of Finnish men', *International Journal of Epidemiology*, **31**, 614–21.

Warren, J.R., Hoonakker, P., Carayon, P. & Brand, J. (2004), 'Job characteristics as mediators in SES–health relationships', *Social Science and Medicine*, **59**, 1367–78.

Wege, N., Dragano, N., Stang, A., Erberl, R., Jöckel, K.H. & Siegrist, J. (2008), 'When does work stress hurt? Testing the interaction with social economic position in the Heinz Nixdorf RECALL Study', *Journal of Epidemiol Community Health*, **62**, 338–41.

14 The challenges facing the temporary workforce: an examination of stressors, well-being outcomes and gender differences

Sarah E. Crozier and Marilyn J. Davidson

Introduction

This chapter aims to discuss the psychological literature concerning the temporary workforce, with a particular focus on some of the challenges that temporary workers face in this type of employment, and their links with well-being and stress outcomes. It should be noted that until recently, only a few studies have addressed this type of alternative working. Furthermore, gender diversity is examined as a preliminary examination of how certain diversity demographics are shown to impact on the types of challenges experienced and their associated outcomes. First, this chapter will give a brief overview of the definitions and circumstances relating to temporary working. Second, empirical research examining a number of workplace characteristics relevant to this workforce is reviewed. This is followed by an examination of the possible stress outcomes experienced by temporary workers and how outcomes can differ dependent upon gender. Finally, recommendations are suggested for how any negative outcomes could be mitigated, and avenues for further research are discussed.

Who are the temporary workforce?

Temporary workers are defined in many ways and many synonyms exist for such work (contingency workers, contract workers, casual workers, agency workers and so on: Isaksson & Bellagh, 2002). This chapter focuses on workers employed by a recruitment agency who work *within* an organization but not *for* the organization, on a contract that is not permanent or secure. Temporary workers employed by a recruitment agency work on contracts of various length in order to fulfil organizations' fluctuations in demand (Garsten, 1999). Such workers provide organizations with a flexible solution to their 'man-power' needs: workers are hired when workload increases, and then disposed of when workload decreases (Weins-Tuers & Hill, 2002). In economic terms, temporary work seems to make sense, and its benefits are described in a number of social economy publications (Reilly, 1998). While from a 'business' perspective, temporary work is believed to *solve* problems, from an occupational health psychology perspective it is also important to focus on the individuals involved in this way of working, and examine whether any problems are *caused* at an individual and organizational level.

The number of temporary agency workers in the UK constitutes almost 6% of the UK workforce (Biggs & Swailes, 2006), is a multi-million pound industry and represents a 'non-standard' way of working (Benevides et al., 2000). Statistics gathered by the TUC (2005) suggest that temporary agency workers are disproportionately female, of younger age groups and of ethnic minorities. This seems to be the case in other countries also, particularly the USA (Boyce et al., 2007). These facts suggest that the issue of diversity and possible discrimination should be addressed carefully.

Job characteristics for temporary workers
The general trend in the research reviewed concerning temporary workers, is to measure participants' perceptions of their job characteristics in order to benchmark such workers' positive or negative experiences. Warr (1987, 2002) explains that job characteristics can give a good indication of psychological well-being. Job characteristics defined by the reviewed research concentrated on factors derived from theories on dissatisfaction, stress and health (Rogers, 1995; Siegrist, 1996; Isaksson & Bellagh, 2002). Simply, factors present in the workplace that could influence individual outcomes either positively or negatively are measured as a way of determining a general picture of what temporary work is like and what it consists of.

Each of the job characteristics reviewed in the literature is outlined here. The emphasis for the purpose of this chapter is to examine possible challenges to the temporary workforce, thus the research reviewed generally focuses on the problematic aspects of temporary working. For each characteristic, an explanation of how this can be construed as a stressor is presented, along with any stress and well-being outcomes identified by research findings.

Training and skill acquisition
Employees who have the appropriate training to understand and perform well in their job are of benefit to an organization and its productivity. Individuals who receive training are likely to be more motivated in their work, and thus may be more satisfied (Wheeler & Buckley, 2001). Weins-Tuers and Hill (2002) investigated the training provisions for temporary workers. They predicted that temporary workers would receive less training than permanent workers due to the theory of human capital, whereby employers will only invest in an employee if the input made by the employee is greater than the costs of such training. Because temporary workers are by definition with the organization for a short length of time, it follows that employers are not prepared to use resources to further the training of such individuals. It is important for temporary workers to receive some form of training in order to understand the job and to fulfil their role, but this is seen to take place in an informal manner from co-workers, which may not be as effective (Gordon, 1996).

In their study, Weins-Tuers and Hill (2002) looked at two types of temporary workers: those employed by an organization on a temporary contract, and intermediate temporary workers employed by a recruitment agency. Interestingly, they found that the latter type received significantly less and inefficient training than workers employed by the organization. This is of relevance for two reasons. First, it consolidates the idea that temporary workers are invested in less so than employees who hold a contract with the organization, lending support to the idea that organizations treat temporary employees with less regard. Second, this suggests that temporary employees are in some way denied the opportunity for learning and development, which may impact upon chances of promotion and career progression (Lynch, 1992). These findings are supported by other research, for example, Virtanen et al. (2003) found that contingent workers received substantially less occupational training and career planning than permanent workers, concluding that inequality in the workforce is potentially increased because of this.

Underemployment

The issue of underemployment can be linked to training opportunities and skill acquisition. Maynard et al. (2006, p. 509) describe underemployment as 'holding a job that is in some way inferior or of lower quality, relative to some standard' (see also Feldman, 1996) adding that underemployment is shown to have many negative consequences for the individual, such as depression, a poor job attitude, and poor psychological health (Johnson & Johnson, 1996, 2000). In their study, Maynard et al. found that temporary workers often experienced underemployment, where perceived overqualification was an important factor. This refers to individuals believing that they hold qualifications, skills or abilities above the level required for the role. This can result in feeling undervalued and worthless.

Social isolation

A number of researchers have found that temporary workers can experience social isolation within their job, in that they are not accepted by others working within the organization and do not receive appropriate support from co-workers and management. Rogers (1995) describes temporary workers as experiencing feelings of exclusion and alienation that are unavoidable due to the very nature of temporary work. He explains that temporary workers often have very little control or autonomy over their work, and are often expected to do a lot in a short space of time. This can be explained by a number of factors. Crozier (2005) found that the expectations placed on temporary workers can reflect the organization's expectations of the individual who would normally carry out that job role. For example, if a temporary worker is employed to cover an individual who is absent due to sickness, the former is often not welcomed if he/she displays different attributes from the latter, or if he/she conducts work tasks in a different way. This can also be compounded by a backlog of work that builds up during the time it takes to hire a temporary replacement and can result in the temporary worker being treated unfairly by other employees (ibid.).

Job security

Working on temporary contracts carries with it the risk of low job security. Temporary workers' contracts often specify that only a minimum notice period is required before employment can be terminated by the hiring organization. This presents a number of difficulties to temporary employees, particularly with regard to financial security. Crozier and Davidson (2006) found that this issue was prominent within their sample and was a great cause of dissatisfaction and anxiety. Some temporary contracts are much more secure than others in that the employee is told at the beginning of the employment that the assignment will last for a number of months. For others, employees are told at the end of the day or week whether they are still required, and this can understandably create feelings of uncertainty, anxiety and stress.

Stigmatization, discrimination and harassment

Boyce et al. (2007) investigated the stigmatization of temporary workers in the USA. They argue that temporary workers, while used as a flexible solution for organizational demand, are in fact devalued in their daily working lives. In addition, the authors present a model of stigmatization, where individual and organizational influences are integrated together to show outcomes in terms of extent of stigmatization. In examining the concept of discrimination for temporary workers, it is important to consider stigmatization as a component of this. In their model, Boyce et al. first focus on the concept of stereotyping and question what the stereotype of a temporary worker can be. They conclude that the work status of temporary workers is the key facet of how stereotypes are formed. This is based around the premise that because a temporary worker's status is unstable, he or she is believed by others to have low skill levels, a lack of intelligence and be inferior to permanent workers. Crozier and Davidson (2007) have gathered evidence via qualitative interviews that explore the concepts of discrimination and harassment as experienced by the temporary workforce. Evidence from the interviews suggest that temporary workers can be bullied because of their job status, and believe that they are more likely to be the focus of sexual harassment, compared to their permanent counterparts. Workers in this sample commented that they believed they were an easy target because they were temporary, and were often blamed for others' mistakes and wrongdoings. Further research is currently being conducted to understand the intricacies involved in these issues.

The importance of individual differences
Individual differences can have an impact upon how temporary working affects an individual. Ellingson (1998) defined the reasons for partaking in temporary work as either voluntary or involuntary. Voluntary temporary workers are those that have willingly entered into a temporary contract despite the option of permanent work being available. In contrast, involuntary temporary workers are those who would prefer a permanent job but cannot acquire one for reasons such as lack of qualifications, job loss and difficulty in locating a permanent job. Ellingson suggested that voluntary temporary workers are more likely to have more positive attitudes and experiences than involuntary workers. Tan and Tan (2002) conducted an empirical analysis of job attitudes and behaviour of temporary workers in Singapore, finding that the reasons given for undertaking a temporary contract had a significant impact on their attitudes towards their work. They discovered that individuals who undertook temporary work for reasons such as self-improvement (i.e., gaining new experiences and skills in a variety of environments, as a means to gaining a permanent job, and as a flexible way of earning *extra* income when needed), were generally happier than those who felt that temporary work was their only option. This suggests that an individual's motives for carrying out such work can significantly affect his/her experiences.

Stress and well-being outcomes
Being subject to a number of negative workplace characteristics is shown to impact upon stress outcomes in a number of workforces (Sutherland & Cooper, 2000; Arnold et al., 2005). The challenges facing temporary workers in their direct work environment, as described above, are shown to have consequences for individuals' health, well-being and stress status as implied in a number of research publications.

Research has addressed whether temporary workers are more likely than permanent workers to suffer from adverse health and well-being outcomes, as a result of their work. Isaksson and Bellagh (2002) suggested that the perception individuals hold about their type of employment may affect the amount of somatic complaints they experience. With regard to health and well-being outcomes, Isaksson and Bellagh found that whether or not the employee had chosen to carry out temporary work had significant impact on well-being outcomes. In other words, if temporary work was their contract of choice, they had fewer health complaints in terms of anxiety and distress, than if they did not want to be employed on a temporary contract. Further, the concept of job perception was taken into consideration. This included factors such as perceived workload, and perceived organizational support which were shown to influence health and well-being outcomes, where if individuals believed that less support was given from others in the workplace, and workload was high, they were shown to have more health complaints. This was also related to intentions to quit but not to actual quitting. In other words, individuals who had these negative perceptions of their work wanted to quit, but did not (ibid.). This is of interest in terms of well-being, particularly with regard to issues such as satisfaction and stress, where temporary workers may stay within a post because they see no other option.

Crozier and Davidson (2005) explored the job characteristics that temporary workers were exposed to and measured psychological well-being by utilising the GHQ-12 (General Health Questionnaire, Goldberg, 1979). They found that temporary workers showed evidence of psychological morbidity. A regression analysis showed that the workplace characteristics most likely to impact on the GHQ score were contract preference (i.e., whether or not an individual wanted to work as a temporary worker, Ellingson, 1998; Isaksson & Bellagh, 2002), satisfaction with job security, and the opportunity for acquisition for new skills. These findings support the evidence from Isaksson and Bellagh's work.

Moreover, it is of use to explore what the specific stressors present in temporary workers' employment may be and investigate how these may differ from those of permanent workers. Research on occupational stress has identified a number of stressors that can potentially be present in any workforce, namely factors intrinsic to the job, role, relationships and support, barriers to career progression, and home–work interface (Sutherland & Cooper, 2000; Arnold et al., 2005; Sulsky & Smith, 2007). These are discussed in turn below, with specific reference to the temporary workforce.

First, factors intrinsic to the job can be a source of stress. In terms of temporary working this can encompass a number of issues, specifically workload. The research discussed explains that temporary workers are often over- or underloaded. Temporary workers are often employed to conduct another person's work for a given amount of time and research has highlighted the importance of temporary workers being appropriately matched to their job via a thorough selection process (Crozier, 2005). In reality however, some temporary workers witnessed few or no formal selection methods being used by recruitment agencies which has resulted in them undertaking a job that they believe they are not suited to (Crozier & Davidson, 2005). The impact of inadequate selection processes can be exacerbated by poor integration into the role, characterized by the aforementioned poor training opportunities and lack of support from the organization. The extent to which these job characteristics and conditions are managed by the organization can therefore impact substantially on the type of stress outcome experienced as a result of a workload which is not matched to the temporary workers' expectations or capabilities.

In terms of their role within the organization, temporary workers are often exposed to role ambiguity, where they are unsure what is expected of them. Cooper and Cartwright (1997) found that if individuals experienced a lack of clarity with regard to their role and how to fulfil it, they were likely to withdraw from the role and endure negative consequences with regard to satisfaction and stress. It is likely that in some temporary roles, individuals may be unsure of their place within the organization (Garsten, 1999), and as a result be irresolute about the characteristics of their job role. This may be weighted by length of contract and how much detail is communicated to the temporary worker about the role, before the assignment commences or during the initial stages of the assignment.

Role ambiguity can be caused by many things including a lack of training or the provision of inadequate information about the role an employee is supposed to undertake. This phenomenon is related to tension and fatigue, intention to quit and actual quitting, and high levels of anxiety, physical and psychological strain, and absenteeism (Sutherland & Cooper, 2000). Interestingly, Ivancevich and Matteson (1980) suggest that starting a new job is when role ambiguity is likely to be at its most prevalent. Temporary workers (especially those employed on a variety of short-term assignments) are constantly in the phase of beginning new jobs. Role ambiguity is therefore an important consideration in assessing the impact of health and stress on temporary workers. This is related to the concept of adjustment into a new role, where in any new job, individuals are more likely to feel stressed or anxious during their initiation period. While with permanent work this feeling should reduce as time goes on, individuals who undertake temporary employment for long periods are constantly within an adjustment phase, and are more likely to display stress outcomes.

Some temporary assignments are defined as 'temporary to permanent' where individuals are hired as a temporary worker, and if they satisfy the organization in their ability to do the job, there is the option for a permanent role. Bauer and Truxillo (2000) investigated stress in this type of temporary employment and found that employees faced more stress due to constantly having to prove themselves in order to advance into a more permanent position. This suggests that temporary workers who strive to gain a more permanent post or solely undertake temporary employment with the aim of becoming a permanent member of staff, would experience more stress than those who were satisfied with maintaining a temporary post. Crozier and Davidson (2006) found that many employees' motivations for undertaking temporary work were focused around attaining a permanent job within a specific organization or a specific industry, even if the present temporary assignment did not overtly offer such opportunities. Taken together these findings suggest that this is an important aspect of stress for the temporary workforce.

Barriers to career progression can also be a potential stressor for employees (Arnold et al., 2005). The research reviewed in this chapter has highlighted problems with career progression for the temporary workforce, particularly with regard to training and learning outcomes. The concept of underemployment is also a pertinent factor to career progression outcomes, in that being undervalued in this sense can cause great dissatisfaction (Maynard et al., 2006). This in turn has been linked with stress outcomes, at an individual level in terms of anxiety and at an organizational level in terms of desire to quit. Another important aspect of career development according to some researchers (Sulsky & Smith, 2007) is the facet of job security, where lack of job security is believed to cause a number of stress outcomes. Depending upon the type and length of temporary role undertaken, it is likely that this is a relevant stressor for the temporary workforce. Support for this comes from Crozier's (2005) work where self-ratings of job security were shown to be an important predictor of psychological health score.

Relationships at work are a potential source of stress (Arnold et al., 2005; Colligan &

Higgins, 2005). Within the temporary workforce, the provision of supportive relationships within the work environment is shown in research to be sparse (Rogers, 1995). This can be exacerbated by the very nature of the role as 'temporary' – any relationships formed are only temporary themselves, and new relationships must be formed once a new temporary assignment begins. Moreover, the quality of relationships within the work environment is believed to be substandard, according to many research findings, where little support is given from co-workers and temporary workers are excluded from partaking in social situations at work (Crozier & Davidson, 2006). Bernin and Theorell (2001) found that sufficient social support at work is crucial to health and well-being. The quality of the relationships temporary workers enter in to could therefore play an important outcome in terms of health and well-being outcomes.

Finally, the home–work interface is an important concept for organizational stress and is very relevant to the temporary workforce. The benefits of temporary working are its flexibility and status as temporary, in that people with other commitments outside of the workplace can, in theory, use temporary work as a way of gaining employment when it suits them and for a duration that is appropriate, without having to commit to an organization, and being free to give a short notice period. Some research has suggested that because of its flexibility, temporary working can actually aid health and well-being outcomes (Benevides et al., 2000). What is of vital importance here are the individual characteristics and circumstances the temporary workers face in both their home and work life. For people who have a spouse with a secure income, the factor of job security should be less of a stressor than those who live alone and have a child to support, for example. This illustration begins to highlight the importance of individual characteristics, or diversity and its relationship with particular outcomes for temporary workers (Crozier & Davidson, 2007). The next section of this chapter examines gender diversity as an important facet of diversity and attempts to exemplify why it is important to take individual differences into account when surveying the occupational health status of a workforce such as this.

Gender differences

It is of relevance to consider that the 'temping' phenomenon is stereotypically a female-dominated work environment, particularly with regard to clerical or administration jobs which make up a large percentage of the temporary workforce (TUC, 2001). Further, statistics show that the number of males in temporary work is increasing. In explaining the relevance of this, a brief overview of the literature on gender diversity followed by the authors' research findings into this arena will be discussed.

Gender diversity forms a major part of the literature on diversity, and is an issue that has been prevalent in society for centuries. The differences in perceptions about male and female roles are of particular interest in the workplace. Fincham and Rhodes (1999) argue: 'it can be readily shown that all societies distinguish between the work that men do and the work that women do' (p. 478). Women are believed to be more suited to certain roles, reflective of other responsibilities they are perceived to have, such as child rearing (Sly et al., 1997). This leads to a division of labour, where women are encouraged to pursue occupations that are reflective of their 'domestic roles' as wives and mothers (Fincham & Rhodes, 1999). Further, women are more likely than men to undertake part-time and temporary work, in order to fit in other responsibilities, traditionally the raising of children (Neathey et al., 2005). Temporary work may be more suited to females for this very reason.

Because such roles are deemed to be stereotypically female dominated, particularly with regard to clerical and administration roles (Cockburn, 1985), it is of interest to consider how males' and females' experiences may differ from one another. Cockburn suggests that men often feel alienated and indignant if they are required to do work they believe to be stereotypically female. Crozier and Davidson (2006) found that male and female temporary workers faced different challenges from one another and were exposed to different workplace characteristics. Both male and female temporary workers showed dissatisfaction with their jobs as temporary workers; however, the factors causing such dissatisfaction were different. Male temporary workers rated their opportunities for training and learning as higher than females, whereas female temporary workers believed that they were treated better and had higher levels of organizational support (ibid.). Taken together, these findings suggest that gender can play an important role in the experiences that temporary workers face.

To elaborate, Crozier and Davidson (ibid.) exposed some statistically significant differences between males and females with regard to self-perceptions of the job characteristics in their work environment. First, females scored higher than males on the satisfaction and treatment from others scale, which encompassed how satisfied participants were with how other people within the work environment interacted with, and responded to them. This suggests that females are happier in temporary work than males, and are welcomed more and treated in a more favourable manner by other people within the workplace, and by the recruitment agency. With reference to gender diversity theory, this finding would suggest that females fare better than males in this type of occupation. Because temporary work, particularly within a clerical domain is 'gendered' as a feminized occupation (Fincham & Rhodes, 1999; Henson & Rogers, 2001), males are more likely to be treated less well than females due to their 'mismatch' with the role.

There is evidence from previous research findings (Henson & Rogers, 2001) that males are perceived by others to be incompetent if undertaking temporary work, as the very nature of the work is far removed from their traditional gender role of full-time breadwinner (Kimmel, 1996). Crozier and Davidson's research (2006) supports this framework. Further, Rogers (1995) explains that all temporary workers irrespective of gender, experience exclusion and alienation due to the very nature of their definition as a disposable workforce. It would appear that these negative experiences are somewhat exacerbated for males, in reflection of the stereotypes associated with the roles suited to the male workforce. Henson and Rogers (2001) also found that male temporary workers suffered threats to their masculinity as a result of their status as a temp. This is further supported by Crozier and Davidson's (2007) work, where male temporary workers reported more bullying and harassment than their female counterparts, particularly with respect to sexual issues.

Paradoxically, although males are seen as being treated in a poorer sense than females in terms of the relationships they undergo at work, in other areas, males are shown to have the advantage. Crozier and Davidson (2006) found that male temporary workers rated their training and learning opportunities as significantly higher than their female counterparts. This measure was related to the acquisition of skills that would help the employee in further career development (Isaksson & Bellagh, 2002). This gives support to the research on gender diversity that suggests males find it easier to attain routes to improving their careers (O'Neil, 1985; Davidson & Fielden, 2003). Based on gender stereotyping, where males are assumed to be the individual responsible for financial security within a family unit, some researchers have found that males are excluded from temporary roles completely (Cohany, 1998). It seems in this instance that the employers of temporary workers do not exclude males from temporary roles, but instead provide them with more learning experiences as a way of progressing out of such roles, and into better (possibly more permanent) roles. This could suggest that employers believe that males should be given the chance to progress into permanent positions more so than their female counterparts, in alignment with their traditional status as breadwinners (Kimmel, 1996).

Moreover, Hicks-Clarke and Iles (2003) put forward the idea that males find it easier to progress more careerwise than females due to a belief in their natural abilities, resulting in utilizing a mechanism of overshadowing and deferring attention from females' achievements. While this concept is difficult to define in a practical sense, the findings concerning learning may be, in part, attributable to this hypothesis. Further, in a work environment where males (as the minority) are 'competing' more with other females as opposed to males, male temporary workers may find it easier to progress based on gender stereotypes. To clarify, if males are presumed to be more competent in undertaking high-level, high-status roles in alignment with the traditional gender stereotype of males as more assertive and more likely to progress (Schein et al., 1975; Cockburn, 1985), *and* in addition do not face competition from similar males, then they may experience greater opportunity to reach a higher position or attain permanent status. These theories can possibly account for why males learn more skills for future career progression, than females in temporary roles.

To summarize, the findings presented here concerning gender differences in temporary working highlight the following important conclusions. First, temporary working does not manifest itself in the same way for all temporary employees. Second, the extent to which temporary employees are subjected to negative job characteristics is dependent, at least in part, upon gender and personal circumstances. Finally, the examination of gender as a preliminary investigation of gender diversity illustrates how complex the relationship between these different variables and their associated health and stress outcomes appear to be.

Implications for organizations

The research findings discussed in this chapter have important implications for organizations hiring temporary workers, and for recruitment agencies. There are certain practical recommendations for managers and employers of temporary staff that can be put forward following a consideration of the empirical research in this domain. First, recruitment consultants should aim to gather an understanding of why each temporary worker wants or needs to undertake temporary work. They should focus their search for an appropriate assignment for the individual based upon the individual's career aspirations, where possible. With regard to temporary workers seeking permanent work, recruitment consultants should aim to find organizations where this is a possibility. By having an increased understanding of employee motivations for such work, recruitment consultants should be educated on the benefits that this will bring the recruitment agency; that is, less absenteeism/staff turnover and so on, and happier and healthier temporary workers. Second, given the research findings concerning the importance of training and learning for temporary workers, recruitment agencies should develop training and learning strategies for the temporary workers if they should want it. This might involve the opportunity to learn certain skills relating specifically to job tasks, and could involve the option of vocational qualifications. Organizations hiring temporary workers should be made aware of the possible increases in performance and efficiency that could arise if temporary workers are entitled to some of the benefits that permanent workers receive. By explaining to employers that providing investment to temporary workers in the form of training or organizational support may save later costs in replacing such workers who have quit or who are absent due to stress or ill health, should act as a motivation for recruitment agencies to take note of.

Limitations of the research reviewed and avenues for further research

This chapter reviews literature on an emerging area of occupational health psychology. While the theories relating to occupational stress in general are more than well established, they are seldom applied to the temporary workforce. In this chapter the authors present some of their preliminary work in this area. It is recognized that much more research is needed into the types of stressors and well-being outcomes relevant to this workforce, and more research studies are underway at present.

In terms of methodology, this chapter highlights the importance of specifying and distinguishing between different types of temporary workers. Some of the work reviewed in this chapter does not specify for how long participants have been undertaking temporary working. It is important to consider that some temporary contracts can be less than a week in length, and some can be as long as six months. It may be that as temporary workers' contracts increase, their negative experiences may increase or decrease dependent on circumstances within their work. One cannot use the term 'temporary worker' in a collective sense and must ensure that the length of contract is taken into account as this is likely to prove an interesting area for further investigation. Longitudinal studies following temporary workers from the beginning of their assignments are currently being carried out by the present authors in order to assess how potential stressors and well-being outcomes vary at different stages of the employment.

The literature specifies that temporary workers face fewer benefits than permanent workers as a result of their temporary status and organizations' reluctance to invest in them (Rogers, 1995; Garsten, 1999). A large proportion of temporary workers are employed within a clerical capacity. Research on clerical workers (of a permanent status) also suggests that negative experiences arise from the fact the job is of a low status, and individuals have little control over the way they conduct their work (Turner & Roszell, 1994). What the present research fails to do is ascertain to what extent the findings are attributable to the fact that the workers are temporary, and to what extent the findings are due to the workers being employed in a clerical domain. In order to rectify this, future studies could compare temporary and permanent clerical workers in order to assess how much the two features of work interact. At present, it is difficult to generalize the findings because it is not certain as to whether the results are reflective purely of the participants' status as temporary workers. What is interesting, however, is the way that the two types of job impact upon one another. It would be worthwhile perhaps examining temporary workers in different domains in order to better understand how the specific job role (in this case clerical work) interacts with the definition of the work as 'temporary'.

Conclusions

Temporary working is a precarious form of employment, and can in some circumstances bring with it a number of challenges to individuals, such as lack of benefits, poor treatment from co-workers, little job security, a lack of organizational support, few opportunities for training and career progression, and social isolation. The issues impacting on these workers are a complex interaction among individual characteristics, the conditions of employment and the management of this type of workforce. The research reviewed in this chapter reveals a number of important findings in understanding the challenges for temporary workers and how these can impact on well-being and stress outcomes. It is evident that a lot of the job characteristics present within the environment of temporary working fit well with the organizational theories on workplace stressors, thus suggesting that this workforce might be vulnerable to such stress-related outcomes. Furthermore, the research highlights how individual preferences (such as whether employees actively choose to be a temporary worker, and their aspirations for future employment), as well as gender diversity, can vary the outcomes for the individual. As this chapter has shown, further research is needed in order to further explore the intricacies and interrelated factors that impact on occupational health of individuals, and the organizational outcomes for this industry.

References

Arnold, J., Silvester, J., Patterson, F., Robertson, I., Cooper, C.L. & Burnes, B. (2005), *Work Psychology. Understanding Human Behaviour in the Workplace*, 4th edn, Harlow, UK: Pearson Education.

Bauer, T.N. & Truxillo, D.M. (2000), 'Temp–permanent employees: a longitudinal study of stress and selection success', *Journal of Occupational Health Psychology*, **5** (3), 337–46.

Benevides, F.G., Benach, J., Diez-Roux, A. & Roman, C. (2000), 'How do types of employment relate to health indicators? Findings from the second European survey of working conditions', *Journal of Epideminological Community Health*, **54**, 494–501.

Bernin, P. & Theorell, T. (2001), 'Demand–control support among female and male managers in 8 Swedish companies', *Stress and Health*, **17** (4), 231–43.

Biggs, D. & Swailes, S. (2006), 'Relations, commitment and satisfaction in agency workers and permanent workers', *Employee Relations*, **28** (2), 130–43.

Boyce, A.S., Ryan, A.M. & Imus, F.P.M (2007), '"Temporary worker, permanent loser?" A model of the stigmatization of temporary workers', *Journal of Management*, **33**, 5–29.

Cockburn, C. (1985), *Machinery of Dominance: Women, Men and Technical Knowhow*, London: Pluto Press.

Cohany, S.R. (1998), 'Workers in alternative employment arrangements, a second look', *Monthly Labor Review*, **121**, 3–21.

Colligan, T.W. & Higgins, E.M. (2005), 'Workplace stress: etiology and consequences', *Journal of Workplace Behavioral Health*, **21** (2), 89–97.

Cooper, C.L. & Cartwright, S. (1997), 'Healthy mind: health organisation – a proactive approach to occupational stress', *Human Relations*, **47**, 455–71.

Crozier, S.E. (2005), 'Examining the health and well-being of the UK clerical "temp" workforce: a preliminary investigation of gender diversity and cross-cultural comparison', dissertation submitted to the University of Manchester for the degree of MSc in Organisational Psychology, unpublished.

Crozier, S.E. & Davidson, M.J. (2005), 'Temporary workers, well-being and gender diversity: a preliminary study', MSc dissertation submitted to the University of Manchester, unpublished.

Crozier, S.E. & Davidson, M.J. (2006), 'An examination of gender as a possible barrier to career progression for UK temporary clerical workers: implications for management and selection practices', paper presented at EURAM (European Academy of Management) Conference, Oslo, May.

Crozier, S.E. & Davidson, M.J. (2007), 'Challenges faced by male clerical temporary workers: examining implications for the individual and for management practices', paper presented at EURAM (European Academy of Management) Conference, Paris, May.

Davidson, M.J. & Fielden, S. (eds) (2003), *Individual Diversity and Psychology in Organisations. A Handbook in the Psychology of Management in Organisations*, Chichester, UK: Wiley.

Ellingson, J.E. (1998), 'Factors relating to the satisfaction and performance of temporary workers', *Journal of Applied Psychology*, **83**, 913–21.

Feldman, D.C. (1996), 'The nature, antecedents and consequences of underemployment', *Journal of Management*, **22**, 385–407.

Fincham, R. & Rhodes, P. (1999), *Principles of Organisational Behaviour*, 3rd edn, Oxford and New York: Oxford University Press.

Garsten, C. (1999), 'Betwixt and between: temporary employees as liminal subjects in flexible organisations', *Organisation Studies*, **20** (4), 601–17.

Goldberg D. (1979), 'A scaled version of the General Health Questionnaire', *Psychological Medicine*, **9**, 139–45.

Gordon, J. (1996), cited in Weins-Tuers & Hill (2002), p. 544.

Henson, K.D. & Rogers, J.K. (2001), 'Why Marcia you've changed! Male clerical temporary workers doing masculinity in a feminised occupation', *Gender and Society*, **15** (2), 218–38.

Hicks-Clarke, D. & Iles, P. (2003), 'Gender diversity', in Davidson & Fielden (eds), pp. 173–92.

Isaksson, K.S. & Bellagh, K. (2002), 'Health problems and quitting among female "temps"', *European Journal of Work and Organisational Psychology*, **11** (1), 27–45.

Ivancevich, J.M. & Matteson, M.T. (1980), *Stress and Work*, Glenview, IL: Scott Foresman.

Johnson, G.J. & Johnson, W.R. (1996, 2000), cited in Maynard et al. (2006), p. 510.

Kimmel, M.S. (1993, 1996), cited in Burke, R.J. & Nelson, D.L. (2001), 'Organisational men: masculinity and its discontents', in C.L. Cooper & I. Robertson (eds), *Wellbeing in Organisations: A Reader for Students and Practitioners*, Chichester: John Wiley, pp. 209–38.

Lynch, L.M. (1992), 'Private sector training and the earnings of young workers', *American Economic Review*, **82** (1), 299–312.

Maynard, D.C., Joseph, T.A. & Maynard, A.M. (2006), 'Underemployment, job attitudes and turnover intentions', *Journal of Organizational Behaviour*, **27**, 509–36.

Neathey, F., Willison, R., Akroyd, K., Regan, J. & Hill, D. (2005), 'Equal pay reviews in practice', Equal Opportunities Commission (EOC) Working Paper series No. 33, http://www.employment-studies.co.uk/pubs/report.php?id=eoc33.

O'Neil, J. (1985), 'Role differentiation and the gender gap in wage rates', in L. Larwood, A. Stromnerg & B. Gutek (eds), *Women and Work, An Annual Review*, London: Sage, pp. 169–88.

Reilly, P. (1998), 'Balancing flexibility – meeting the interests of employer and employee', *European Journal of Work and Organizational Psychology*, **7**, 7–22.

Rogers, J.K. (1995), 'Just a temp – experience and structure of alienation in temporary clerical employment', *Work and Occupations*, **22** (2), 137–66.

Schein, V.E., Mueller, R. and Jacobson, C. (1975), 'The relationship between sex role stereotypes and requisite management characteristics among female managers', *Journal of Applied Psychology*, **60**, 340–44.

Siegrist, J. (1996), 'Adverse health effects of high effort/low reward conditions', *Journal of Occupational Health Psychology*, **1** (1), 27–41.

Sly, F., Price, A. & Risdon, A. (1997), 'Women in the labour force: results from the spring 1996 labour survey', *Labour Market Trends*, London: HMSO.

Sulsky, L. & Smith, C. (2007), 'Work stress: macro-level work stressors', in A. Monat, R.S. Lazarus & G. Reevy (eds), *The Praeger Handbook on Stress and Coping*, vol. 1, Westport, CT: Praeger/Greenwood, pp. 53–86.

Sutherland, V. & Cooper, C.L. (2000), *Strategic Stress Management*, London: Macmillan.

Tan, H.H. & Tan, C.P. (2002), 'Temporary employees in Singapore: what drives them?', *Journal of Psychology*, **136** (1), 83–102.

Trades Union Congress (TUC) (2001, 2002), 'Report: Agency Work in Britain Today: Working on the Edge', unpublished.

Turner, R.J. & Roszell, P. (1994), 'Psychosocial resources and the stress process', in W.R. Avison & I.H. Gotlib (eds), *Stress and Mental Health: Contemporary Issues and Prospects for the Future*, New York: Plenum Press, pp. 179–210.

Virtanen, M., Kivimaki, M., Virtanen, P., Elovainio, M. & Vahtera, J. (2003), 'Disparity in occupational training and career planning between contingent and permanent employees', *European Journal of Work and Organisational Psychology*, **12** (1), 19–36.

Warr, P.B. (1987), *Work, Unemployment and Mental Health*, Oxford: Clarendon Press.

Warr, P.B. (ed.) (2002), *Psychology at Work*, 5th edn, Harmondsworth: Penguin Books.

Weins-Tuers, B.A. & Hill, E.T. (2002), 'Do they bother? Employer training of temporary workers', *Review of Social Economy*, **60** (4), 543–66.

Wheeler, A.R. & Buckley, M.R. (2001), 'Examining the motivation process of temporary employees: a holistic model and research framework', *Journal of Managerial Psychology*, **16** (5), 339–54.

15 Affect regulation and well-being in the workplace: an interpersonal perspective

Karen Niven, Peter Totterdell and David Holman

Introduction

During and outside of work, the ways in which people manage their own and others' emotions and moods can impact on their own and others' well-being. For example, in relation to managing one's own affect, constantly having to present a happy face towards customers can result in emotional exhaustion, particularly if this expression of emotion is not consistent with one's internal affective state. Likewise, with respect to managing others' affect, if a team member were to joke with a colleague who was feeling anxious about an upcoming deadline, this could reduce the tension experienced by the colleague, and also make the team member feel better.

Over the last 25 years, there has been a great deal of research regarding the management of one's own affect. However, research concerning the management of other people's affect is still in its infancy. It is important to recognize the interpersonal aspects of affect regulation, for both theoretical and practical reasons. Theoretically, researchers interested in emotions are increasingly suggesting that emotions are social in nature, with interpersonal functions such as communication (e.g., Manstead, 1991; Mowday & Sutton, 1993; Leach & Tiedens, 2004; Parkinson et al., 2005). Practically, it is evermore important to understand relationships in the workplace, owing to the changing nature of work (e.g., the rise in service jobs) and the changing structure of organizations (e.g., increases in team working). As Barsade et al. (2003) put it, 'the workplace [comprises] many people working together, and it is very helpful to understand how the social aspects of affect influence work life' (p. 19).

In this chapter we seek to integrate the available literature on the effects of both intra- and interpersonal affect regulation processes on well-being at work. We discuss evidence for links between both types of affect regulation and well-being in organizational contexts, and suggest possible mechanisms for these effects.

Well-being at work

Individuals' well-being at work can have important implications for both organizations and individuals themselves. For example, individuals' work-related strain can result in changes in health-related behaviours (e.g., smoking, alcohol intake), psychological problems (e.g., sleep disturbance), and medical problems (e.g., immune deficiencies) (Quick et al., 1986; Danna & Griffin, 1999). Work-related well-being can also enhance or compromise work performance (e.g., Price & Hooijberg, 1992) and affect rates of absenteeism (e.g., Elkin & Rosch, 1990; Johnson & Indvik, 1997). Accordingly, well-being at work has long been recognized as a major concern among occupational health psychologists. It is therefore considered important to understand the factors that contribute towards well-being in the workplace.

Traditionally, research to this end has focused on the role of job characteristics as antecedents of job satisfaction and strain. For example, Hackman and Oldham's classic job characteristics model contends that characteristics including skill variety, autonomy and task significance are important contributors to outcomes such as job satisfaction (Hackman & Oldham, 1976). Likewise, Karasek's job demands–control model predicts that job demands and decision latitude have an interactive effect on individuals' job-related strain (Karasek, 1979). However, more recently there has been a change in emphasis away from looking at job characteristics and individuals' responses to these, and towards looking at the active role that individuals play in terms of their work experiences.

Intrapersonal affect regulation

In particular, there has been increasing attention paid to the active role that individuals play in the regulation of affect at work. Affect regulation has been defined as 'the process of initiating, maintaining, modulating, or changing the occurrence, intensity, or duration of . . . feeling states' (Eisenberg et al., 2000, p. 137). Researchers have usually conceptualized affect regulation as an intrapersonal process. As such, researchers have been largely concerned with the deliberate[1] regulation of individuals' own affective states (i.e., their emotions and moods). Intrapersonal affect regulation is most frequently performed with the aim of improving or maintaining one's own positive affect (Parrott, 1993; Wegener & Petty, 1994; Westen, 1994). For example, an individual might choose to think about happy memories in order to improve a negative mood state. But it should be noted that intrapersonal affect regulation is conceptually distinct from coping, since affect regulation can refer to upward and downward regulation of affect and affect maintenance, and it specifically concerns the influence of one's own affect, as opposed to general life events (Parkinson & Totterdell, 1999).

Intrapersonal affect regulation in the workplace

Within organizational contexts, intrapersonal affect regulation has predominantly been studied under the theoretical framework of emotional labour. Hochschild's (1983) book *The Managed Heart* regarding flight attendants first brought to light the notion of emotional labour, which she defined as 'the management of feeling to create a publicly observable facial and bodily display' (p. 7). As such, emotional labour can be seen as a form of deliberate intrapersonal affect regulation (Grandey, 2000). Emotional labour is distinct from other forms of affect regulation that occur within or outside of organizations in that it is exchanged for a wage, and is performed in accordance with 'display rules' that require employees to express particular emotions as part of the job role. According to Hochschild, there are two major types of emotional labour: 'deep acting' refers to the manipulation of one's experienced emotion; and 'surface acting' refers to the manipulation of one's emotional expression only. Grandey further clarified the distinction between these two types of regulation, contending that deep acting is achieved using antecedent-focused regulation strategies (e.g., reframing a situation), whereas surface acting is achieved using response-focused strategies (e.g., suppressing an unwanted emotion).

Most occupations that involve some sort of contact with other people require some degree of emotional labour (Briner & Totterdell, 2002). For example, Mann's (1999) investigation of emotional labour among office workers suggested that these employees attempted to manage their emotions in almost two-thirds of their work-based communications with colleagues. But emotional labour is most prevalent in jobs that involve a high degree of contact with customers or clients, in particular in service roles. Indeed, emotional labour has been studied in a variety of service occupations, for example, among fast-food workers (Leidner, 1991), supermarket cashiers (Rafaeli & Sutton, 1990), debt collectors (Sutton, 1991), hairdressers (Parkinson, 1991), and call-centre workers (Holman et al., 2002; Totterdell & Holman, 2003).

Intrapersonal affect regulation and well-being
Outside of the work domain, a number of researchers have reported links between intrapersonal affect regulation and well-being. In particular, research has found effects of regulating one's own affect on indicators of well-being such as depression and life satisfaction (e.g., Nolen-Hoeksema & Morrow, 1993; Gross & John, 1997, 2003; Davis et al., 1998; Gross, 1998, 2002).

However, the majority of research that links intrapersonal affect regulation and well-being has come from research in organizational settings, and has concerned emotional labour. In fact, over the 24 years since Hochschild's seminal work, the topic of emotional labour has transformed from a sociological into a key occupational health concern. A recent review by Holman et al. (2007) presents the mounting body of evidence suggesting important relationships between the performance of emotional labour and individuals' work-related well-being.

But *how* does affect regulation affect individuals' well-being? Based on literature concerning emotional labour performed to meet organizational requirements, and affect regulation performed in the pursuit of other goals (e.g., to improve one's affective state), a change in resource levels has been proposed to be the main mechanism of the effects of intrapersonal affect regulation on well-being (ibid.). Conservation of resources theory contends that people strive to obtain, protect and enhance valued resources such as energy, self-esteem and social support (Hobfoll, 1989, 2001). People do this because a reduction in one's resources is typically associated with a reduction in well-being, whereas a bolstering of one's resources improves well-being (e.g., Schaufeli et al., 1996; Ito & Brotheridge, 2003). Intrapersonal affect regulation causes changes in individuals' resource levels for three main reasons: effort, dissonance, and others' responses (Holman et al., 2007).

With regard to effort, many researchers have identified the process of regulating affect as effortful, claiming that the act of regulating consumes valuable resources such as energy (Muraven & Baumeister, 2000; Brotheridge & Lee, 2002; Demerouti et al., 2004). Using response-focused regulation (e.g., surface acting) has been found to heighten physiological responding (Gross & Levenson, 1993, 1997; Gross, 1998), and to involve more effort (Richards & Gross, 1999, 2000) compared to antecedent-focused regulation (e.g., deep acting). Dissonance refers to the mismatch between expressed and felt emotion that can occur during intrapersonal affect regulation, especially when individuals regulate only their emotional response (i.e., surface act). A state of dissonance can threaten an individual's sense of self and self-authenticity, both of which are valuable resources (Zapf et al., 1999; Brotheridge & Lee, 2002; Gross & John, 2003; Lewig & Dollard, 2003; Zapf & Holz, 2006). Others' responses to intrapersonal affect regulation are also important determinants of the effects of this process, as suggested in interactive feedback models of affect and affect regulation (e.g., Côté, 2005; Hareli & Rafaeli, 2007). Taking the example of emotional labour, when a customer responds positively to the emotional labour display, this can provide the employee with valued resources, for instance a sense of personal accomplishment. In contrast, a negative response from a customer can diminish such a resource. Past research has demonstrated that antecedent-focused regulation produces a more authentic displayed emotion compared to response-focused regulation, and thus produces more favourable customer or client responses (Brotheridge & Grandey, 2002; Gross & John, 2003).

This evidence therefore suggests that using response-focused affect regulation is likely to result in a worsening of an individual's well-being, whereas using response-focused regulation may not. This is supported by numerous studies regarding emotional labour (e.g., Brotheridge & Grandey, 2002; Totterdell & Holman, 2003; Bono & Vey, 2005; Martínez-Iñigo et al., 2007), which have reported surface acting to result in worsened well-being, but deep acting to result in no change or an improvement in well-being. As such, regulating one's own affect can act as a source of work-related strain, or as a means of dealing with strain, depending on the strategies adopted.

Interpersonal affect regulation
While extant research has shown robust links between intrapersonal aspects of affect regulation and well-being, to date there has been little attention paid to the interpersonal aspects of affect regulation. As such, the full picture of how affect regulation impacts on well-being is not clear.

Interpersonal affect regulation is defined as the deliberate and socially induced initiation, maintenance or modification of the occurrence, intensity, or duration of feeling states. So, for example, if a work colleague feels anxious about a deadline, an employee might try to make the colleague feel calmer by talking the work through with him or her, or by praising his or her efforts. Given these examples, it is important to note that just as intrapersonal affect regulation was highlighted as being conceptually distinct from coping, interpersonal affect regulation can also be viewed as separate from social support. While individuals may regulate others' affect with the intention of support, the concept of interpersonal affect regulation is specifically focused on the management of affect. Moreover, interpersonal affect regulation may also be performed to worsen others' affect. For example, if an employee was irritated by a colleague, he or she might try to upset that colleague by shouting at or ignoring the person.

It can be argued that emotional labour is also an interpersonal form of affect regulation, in that it is done with respect to someone else – the customer (e.g., Côté, 2005). However, emotional labour involves the regulation of an individual's own affective state. Here, it is argued that individuals can and do deliberately try to regulate *other people's* affect. Indeed, the idea of regulating others' affect has been recognized by researchers within the emotional labour tradition (e.g., Rafaeli & Sutton, 1990; Sutton, 1991; Pugliesi, 1999), but has yet to be examined in depth.

Interpersonal affect regulation in the workplace
While the topic of interpersonal affect regulation *per se* is relatively new, there is a great deal of evidence that interpersonal affect regulation occurs within organizations, especially between colleagues. For example, research concerning team member relationships has indicated the importance of interpersonal affect regulation with regard to resolving

team conflicts (Gobeli et al., 1998; Von Glinow et al., 2004). Interpersonal affect regulation is also used as 'caregiving' or 'toxin handling' between colleagues (Kahn, 1993, 1998; Frost & Robinson, 1999; Frost, 2003; Martens et al., 2003). Humour in particular is used in medical organizations to help colleagues cope with distress (e.g., Francis, 1994; Francis et al., 1999). In fact, studies in settings as diverse as law firms (Lively, 2000) and debt collection agencies (Sutton, 1991) have reported the occurrence of interpersonal affect regulation among colleagues.

Interpersonal affect regulation is also used by leaders towards their followers. Literature suggests that transformational leaders deliberately try to influence the affect of their followers, for example energizing them, in order to gain support and allegiance (e.g., Conger & Kanungo, 1998; Lewis, 2000; Cross & Parker, 2004; Brown & Moshavi, 2005). Conversely, interpersonal affect regulation may also be used by employees towards their superiors. For example, Pierce's (1999) research into the roles of paralegals suggests that they are frequently expected to improve their lawyers' moods and emotions.

There is also a great deal of evidence that interpersonal affect regulation is used by employees towards individuals external to their organization. More and more frequently, interpersonal affect regulation is becoming a key part of service roles, with employees regulating the affect of their customers or clients. In some cases, interpersonal affect regulation by employees towards customers or clients is a means of giving care. For example, medical professionals use tactics such as humour (Francis, 1994; Locke, 1996; Francis et al., 1999) to encourage more positive emotions among their patients. In other cases, interpersonal affect regulation is performed more instrumentally. Sutton's (1991) study regarding the interpersonal emotional behaviours of debt collectors highlighted the fact that these types of employees use interpersonal affect regulation towards debtors in order to influence debtors to pay the money they owe. For example, collectors were found to display irritation or anger towards friendly debtors in order to make the debtors feel more anxious and therefore to create a sense of urgency towards making a payment. Rafaeli and Sutton (1990) and Lee and Dubinsky (2003) also discuss the instrumental use of interpersonal affect regulation towards customers in retail settings.

Our own recent research has identified a full range of behaviours, or strategies, that individuals use to regulate others' affect (Niven et al., 2007a). The research generated 378 distinct strategies used to elicit, intensify, suppress and eliminate particular affective states such as happiness, calmness, enthusiasm, pride, anger, misery, guilt and jealousy. Some of the most commonly mentioned strategies for improving others' affect included listening, joking and complimenting. Some of the most commonly mentioned strategies for worsening others' affect were ignoring, mocking and criticizing.

Interpersonal affect regulation and well-being
Although it is clear that interpersonal affect regulation does occur in a variety of workplaces, research has only recently begun to draw links between this process and well-being. We contend that the emerging research area of interpersonal affect regulation could provide a fresh perspective on understanding well-being in the workplace. More specifically, the process of interpersonal affect regulation (in addition to the process of *intra*personal affect regulation) can have important implications for the well-being of both the person whose affect is being regulated (the target) and also the person who is performing the regulation (the agent).

Effects on targets' well-being   Interpersonal affect regulation strategies are used with the express intention of influencing the way that the strategy target feels. As such, a successful interpersonal affect regulation attempt should result in a change in the targets' affective state. Indeed, there is some evidence for this assertion. Our own study examining the effects of interpersonal affect regulation in a prison setting found shorter-term effects of interpersonal affect regulation on strategy targets' moods (Niven et al., 2007c). Further research in this setting also highlighted effects of interpersonal affect regulation on strategy targets' well-being, particularly in terms of enthusiasm and tension (Niven et al., 2007b). In addition, other researchers have reported effects of interpersonal affect regulation-type behaviours such as listening and aggression on aspects of well-being including strain and burnout (e.g., Henderson & Argyle; 1985; Kahn, 1993, 1998; Thoits, 1995; LeBlanc & Kelloway, 2002).

We propose that interpersonal affect regulation influences targets' well-being through various pathways. One mechanism is a change in the target's resource levels. This pathway assumes that particular resources will be bolstered or threatened when a person's affect is regulated. As discussed above, a change in an individual's resource levels has implications for that person's well-being (e.g., Ito & Brotheridge, 2003). Accordingly, interpersonal affect regulation would exert an impact on targets' well-being, through its effects on valued resources. Targets' resources are likely to be bolstered following the use of strategies to improve affect. For example, being listened to would enhance a person's levels of social support. In contrast, targets' resources are likely to be threatened following the use of strategies to worsen affect. For instance, being criticized or insulted might diminish a person's self-esteem.

Another mechanism is *intra*personal affect regulation. This pathway assumes that some strategies take effect through provoking a response from the target that involves intrapersonal affect regulation, and through this response impact on the target's well-being. For example, the strategy of pointing out the upsides of someone's situation might induce the target to reappraise and reframe this situation. Alternatively, being mocked might result in the target faking a smile, in order to give the agent the impression that his or her words had little impact on the target. Intrapersonal affect regulation has been consistently reported to relate to individuals' well-being, as discussed previously. Therefore, the use of intrapersonal affect regulation, as induced by interpersonal affect regulation, would cause a change in the target's well-being.

From the above proposed pathways, it is clear that using positive interpersonal affect regulation strategies is likely to result in an improvement in the target's well-being, while using negative strategies is likely to result in the worsening of targets' well-being, although individuals may be able to resist these effects to differing extents. This is consistent with the evidence for effects of interpersonal affect regulation on well-being cited above. As such, some strategies used to influence others' feelings may help others to cope with work-related stressors, while others may be maladaptive, acting as a source of strain or impeding coping efforts.

Effects on agents' well-being   Rind and Kipnis (1999) ask, 'can we change other people without changing ourselves as well?' (p. 141). In other words, does the use of interpersonal affect regulation impact on the strategy agent, as well as on the target? Our own research has provided some support for the proposed effect of interpersonal affect regulation on strategy agents' well-being. Our first prison study found effects of interpersonal affect reg-ulation on strategy agents' moods (Niven et al., in press), and the second found effects on aspects of well-being, particularly enthusiasm and tension (Niven et al., 2007b). However, to date, there has been little other research investigating this proposition.

Again, we contend that interpersonal affect regulation can influence agents' well-being through a number of pathways. Here, a change in the agent's resource levels may be an important mechanism. It is likely that the act of using interpersonal affect regula-tion behaviours is effortful. For example, speaking aggressively towards someone could be both physically and emotionally draining. The effort expended through the use of interpersonal affect regulation towards others would therefore cause a change (more specifically, a worsening) in strategy agents' well-being. However, the effortful nature of some types of interpersonal affect regulation might be offset by a resource-enhancing effect. For instance, effectively improving someone else's affect might bolster valuable resources including self-esteem and personal accomplishment. As such, the overall effect of some interpersonal affect regulation strategies could be an improvement in agents' well-being.

A second mechanism is the reciprocation of interpersonal affect regulation by the target. This pathway assumes that the use of interpersonal affect regulation might provoke targets to use similar strategies towards the initial agent. According to theo-ries of interpersonal behaviour, every individual's interpersonal behaviours constrain or elicit subsequent behaviours from those they are directed towards, with a pattern of complementarity usually followed, such that positive interpersonal behaviours most often produce a positive behavioural response, and so on (e.g., Tracey, 1994; Losada & Heaphy, 2004). This seems likely in the case of interpersonal affect regulation. For example, if a target were to be spoken to aggressively, he or she might choose to ignore the initial strategy agent. The initial agent would then effectively become the target of the new regulation attempt, with effects on his or her well-being therefore expected through the pathways discussed above. This iterative proposition resembles the feedback loops of Côté's (2005) social interaction model and the emotion cycle model discussed by Hareli and Rafaeli (2007).

From these pathways, it appears that the use of positive interpersonal affect regula-tion strategies will result in an improvement in strategy agents' well-being, while negative strategies will result in the worsening of agents' well-being. This is again consistent with the evidence for effects of interpersonal affect regulation on well-being cited above. The act of trying to influence someone else's feelings can therefore have positive or negative effects on the agent's well-being, depending on the strategy chosen. Accordingly, regulat-ing others' affect may be seen as both a stressor and a means of coping with strain.

Other factors influencing the effects of interpersonal affect regulation   The effects of interpersonal affect regulation on well-being are likely to vary according to a number of factors. For instance, the characteristics of either of the two individuals involved in the interpersonal affect regulation process (i.e., the agent or target) might moderate the effects of interpersonal affect regulation on either of these individuals' well-being. Characteristics such as emotional skills (e.g., emotional expressivity, emotional intel-ligence) and interpersonal skills (e.g., empathy, interpersonal control) are especially relevant here. The context within which interpersonal affect regulation is used might also moderate the effects of interpersonal affect regulation on strategy agents' and targets' well-being. For instance, interpersonal affect regulation strategies are interpreted in different ways in different contexts. Finally, characteristics of the relationship within which interpersonal affect regulation occurs could also vary the effects of regulation on well-being. In particular, the relative status of the agent and target, and perceptions of shared (ingroup) versus non-shared (outgroup) membership are important factors.

Summary

In this chapter, we have presented evidence that two forms of affect regulation – intrapersonal and interpersonal – influence well-being at work. We have also described a number of possible mechanisms by which these effects may occur, and suggested a number of additional factors that might moderate the effects of interpersonal affect regulation on well-being. However, some of the propositions regarding interpersonal effects are as yet untested. Elucidating the underlying processes and boundary conditions will help to understand how, when and why well-being at work is likely to be affected by the regulation of affect. This in turn will aid both researchers and practitioners in identifying fruitful points of intervention to alleviate occupational health problems.

Note

1. While it has been argued that individuals can and do automatically regulate their own affect (e.g., Forgas et al., 1998; Forgas & Ciarrochi, 2002), this chapter is concerned with more deliberate regulation processes.

Bibliography

Barsade, S.G., Brief, A.P. & Spataro, S.E. (2003), 'The affective revolution in organizational behavior: the emergence of a paradigm', in J. Greenberg (ed.), *Organizational Behavior: The State of the Science*, Mahwah, NJ: Erlbaum.

Bono, J.E. & Vey, M.A. (2005), 'Toward understanding emotional management at work: a quantitative review of emotional labor research', in C.E. Hartel & W.J. Zerbe (eds), *Emotions in Organizational Behavior*, Mahwah, NJ: Lawrence Erlbaum.

Briner, R.B. & Totterdell, P. (2002), 'The experience, expression and management of emotion at work', in P. Warr (ed.), *Psychology at Work*, 5th edn, London: Penguin Books.

Brotheridge, C.M. & Grandey, A.A. (2002), 'Emotional labour and burnout: comparing two perspectives of "people work"', *Journal of Vocational Behavior*, **60**: 17–39.

Brotheridge, C.M. & Lee, R.T. (2002), 'Testing a conservation of resources model of the dynamics of emotional labour', *Journal of Occupational Health Psychology*, **7**: 57–67.

Brown, F.W. & Moshavi, D. (2005), 'Transformational leadership and emotional intelligence: a potential pathway for an increased understanding of interpersonal influence', *Journal of Organizational Behavior*, **26**: 867–71.

Conger, J.A. & Kanungo, R.N. (1998), *Charismatic Leadership in Organisations*, Thousand Oaks, CA: Sage.

Côté, S. (2005), 'A social interaction model of the effects of emotion regulation on work strain', *Academy of Management Review*, **30**: 509–30.

Cross, R. & Parker, A. (2004), 'Charged up: creating energy in organisations', *Journal of Organizational Excellence*, **23**: 3–14.

Danna, K. & Griffin, R.W. (1999), 'Health and well-being in the workplace: a review and synthesis of the literature', *Journal of Management*, **25**: 357–84.

Davis, C.G., Nolen-Hoeksema, S. & Larson, J. (1998), 'Making sense of loss and benefitting from the experience: two construals of meaning', *Journal of Personality and Social Psychology*, **75**: 561–74.

Davis, M.H. (1983), 'Measuring individual differences in empathy: evidence for a multidimensional approach', *Journal of Personality and Social Psychology*, **44**: 113–26.

de Rivera, J. (1984), 'The structure of emotional relationships', in P. Shaver (ed.), *Review of Personality and Social Psychology: Emotions, Relationships, and Health*, Beverly Hills, CA: Sage.

de Rivera, J. & Grinkis, C. (1986), 'Emotions as social relationships', *Motivation and Emotion*, **10**: 351–69.

Demerouti, E., Bakker, A.B. & Bulters, A.J. (2004), 'The loss spiral of work pressure, work–home interference and exhaustion: reciprocal relations in a three-wave study', *Journal of Vocational Behaviour*, **64**: 131–49.

Eisenberg, N., Fabes, R.A., Guthrie, I.K. & Reiser, M. (2000), 'Dispositional emotionality and regulation: their role in predicting quality of social functioning', *Journal of Personality and Social Psychology*, **78**: 136–57.

Elkin, A.J. & Rosch, P.J. (1990), 'Promoting mental health at the workplace: the prevention side of stress management', *Occupational Medicine: State of the Art Review*, **5**: 739–54.

Forgas, J.P. & Ciarrochi, J.V. (2002), 'On managing moods: evidence for the role of homeostatic cognitive strategies in affect regulation', *Personality and Social Psychology Bulletin*, **28**: 336–45.

Forgas, J.P., Johnson, R. & Ciarrochi, J. (1998), 'Mood management: the role of processing strategies in affect control and affect infusion', in M. Kofta, G. Weary & G. Sedek (eds), *Personal Control in Action: Cognitive and Motivational Mechanisms*, New York: Plenum.

Francis, L.E. (1994), 'Laughter, the best mediation: humour as emotion management in interaction', *Symbolic Interaction*, **17**: 147–63.

Francis, L.E., Monahan, K. & Berger, C. (1999), 'A laughing matter? The uses of humor in medical interactions', *Motivation and Emotion*, **23**: 154–77.

Frost, P.J. (2003), 'Emotions in the workplace and the important role of toxin handlers', *Ivey Business Journal Online*, www.iveybusinessjournal.com.

Frost, P. & Robinson, S. (1999), 'The toxin handler: organisational hero and casualty', *Harvard Business Review*, **77**: 96–106.

Gobeli, D.H., Koenig, H.F. & Bechinger, I. (1998), 'Managing conflict in software development teams: a multilevel analysis', *Journal of Product Innovation Management*, **15**: 423–35.

Grandey, A. (2000), 'Emotion regulation in the workplace: a new way to conceptualize emotional labour', *Journal of Occupational Health Psychology*, **5**: 95–110.

Gross, J.J. (1998), 'Antecedent- and response-focused emotion regulation: divergent consequences for experience, expression, and physiology', *Journal of Personality and Social Psychology*, **74**: 224–37.

Gross, J.J. (2002), 'Emotion regulation: affective, cognitive, and social consequences', *Psychophysiology*, **39**: 281–91.

Gross, J.J. & John, O.P. (1997), 'Revealing feelings: facets of emotional expressivity in self-reports, peer ratings, and behaviour', *Journal of Personality and Social Psychology*, **72**: 435–48.

Gross, J.J. & John, O.P. (2003), 'Individual differences in two emotion regulation processes: implications for affect, relationships, and well-being', *Journal of Personality and Social Psychology*, **85**: 348–62.

Gross, J.J. & Levenson, R.W. (1993), 'Emotional suppression: physiology, self-report, and expressive behavior', *Journal of Personality and Social Psychology*, **64**: 970–86.

Gross, J.J. & Levenson, R.W. (1997), 'Hiding feelings: the acute effects of inhibiting positive and negative emotions', *Journal of Abnormal Psychology*, **106**: 95–103.

Hackman, J.R. & Oldham, G.R. (1976), 'Motivation through the design of work: test of a theory', *Organizational Behavior and Human Performance*, **1**: 250–79.

Hareli, S. & Rafaeli, A. (2007), 'Emotion cycles: on the social influence of emotion in organizations', *Research in Organizational Behavior*, **28**: 35–59.

Henderson, M. & Argyle, M. (1985), 'Social support by four categories of work colleagues: relationships between activities, stress and satisfaction', *Journal of Occupational Behaviour*, **6**: 229–39.

Hobfoll, S.E. (1989), 'Conservation of resources: a new attempt at conceptualising stress', *American Psychologist*, **44**: 513–24.

Hobfoll, S.E. (2001), 'The influence of culture, community, and the nested-self in the stress process: advancing Conservation of Resources theory', *Applied Psychology: An International Review*, **50**: 337–70.

Hochschild, A.R. (1983), *The Managed Heart*, Berkeley, CA: University of California Press.

Holman, D., Chissick, C. & Totterdell, P. (2002), 'The effects of performance monitoring on emotional labour and well-being in call centres', *Motivation and Emotion*, **26**: 57–81.

Holman, D., Martínez-Iñigo, D. & Totterdell, P. (2007), 'Emotional labour and employee well-being', in N. Ashkanasy & C.L. Cooper (eds), *Research Companion to Emotion in Organizations*, Cheltenham, UK and Northampton, MA, USA: Edward Elgar, pp. 301–15.

Ito, J.K. & Brotheridge, C.M. (2003), 'Resources, coping strategies, and emotional exhaustion: a conservation of resources perspective', *Journal of Vocational Behaviour*, **63**: 490–509.

Johnson, P.R. & Indvik, J. (1997), 'The boomer blues: depression in the workplace', *Public Personnel Management*, **26**: 359–65.

Kahn, W.A. (1993), 'Caring for the caregivers: patterns of organisational caregiving', *Administrative Science Quarterly*, **38**: 539–63.

Kahn, W.A. (1998), 'Relational systems at work', *Research in Organizational Behavior*, **20**: 39–76.

Karasek, R.A. (1979), 'Job demands, job decision latitude and mental strain: the implications for job redesign', *Administrative Science Quarterly*, **24**: 285–308.

Leach, C.W. & Tiedens, L.Z. (2004), *The Social Life of Emotions*, Cambridge: Cambridge University Press.

LeBlanc, M.M. & Kelloway, E.K. (2002), 'Predictors and outcomes of workplace violence and aggression', *Journal of Applied Psychology*, **87**: 444–53.

Lee, S. & Dubinsky, A.J. (2003), 'Influence of salesperson characteristics and customer emotion on retail dyadic relationships', *International Review of Retail, Distribution and Consumer Research*, **13**: 21–36.

Leidner, R. (1991), 'Serving hamburgers and selling insurance: gender, work, and identity in interactive service jobs', *Gender and Society*, **5**: 154–77.

Lewig, K.A. & Dollard, M.F. (2003), 'Emotional dissonance, emotional exhaustion and job satisfaction in call centre workers', *European Journal of Work and Organizational Psychology*, **12**: 366–92.

Lewis, K.M. (2000), 'When leaders display emotion: how followers respond to negative emotional expression of male and female leaders', *Journal of Organizational Behavior*, **21**: 221–34.

Lively, K.J. (2000), 'Reciprocal emotion management: working together to maintain stratification in private law firms', *Work and Occupations*, **27**: 32–63.

Locke, K. (1996), 'A funny thing happened: the management of consumer emotions in service encounters', *Organisation Science*, **7**: 40–59.

Losada, M. and Heaphy, E. (2004), 'The role of positivity and connectivity in the performance of business teams: a nonlinear dynamic model', *American Behavioural Scientist*, **47**: 740–65.

Mann, S. (1999), 'Emotion at work: to what extent are we expressing, suppressing, or faking it?', *European Journal of Work and Organizational Psychology*, **8**: 347–69.

Manstead, A.S.R. (1991), 'Emotion in social life', *Cognition and Emotion*, **5**: 353–62.

Martens, M.L., Gagné, M. & Brown, G.R. (2003), 'Toxin handler behaviour: an initial assessment of a new measure', *Proceedings of the 2003 ASAC Conference*, available at SSRN: http://ssrn.com/abstract=602841.

Martínez-Iñigo, D., Totterdell, P., Alcover, C.M. & Holman, D. (2007), 'Emotional labour and emotional exhaustion: interpersonal and intrapersonal mechanisms', *Work and Stress*, **21**: 30–47.

Mowday, R.T. & Sutton, R.I. (1993), 'Organisational behaviour: linking individuals and groups to organisational contexts', *Annual Review of Psychology*, **44**: 195–229.

Muraven, M. & Baumeister, R.F. (2000), 'Self-regulation and depletion of limited resources: does self-control resemble a muscle?', *Psychological Bulletin*, **126**: 247–59.

Niven, K., Totterdell, P. & Holman, D. (2007a), 'A conceptual classification of strategies used to deliberately influence others' affect', Working Paper, Institute of Work Psychology, University of Sheffield.

Niven, K., Totterdell, P. & Holman, D. (2007b), 'The effects of interpersonal emotion management on staff and inmates in a high-security prison', paper presented at the European Congress of Work and Organisational Psychology, Stockholm, May.

Niven, K., Totterdell, P. & Holman, D. (2007c), 'Changing moods and influencing people: the use and effects of emotional influence behaviours at HMP Grendon', *The Prison Service Journal*, **172**: 39–45.

Nolen-Hoeksema, S. & Morrow, J. (1993), 'Effects of rumination and distraction on naturally occurring depressed mood', *Cognition and Emotion*, **7**: 561–70.

Parkinson, B. (1991), 'Emotional stylists: strategies of expressive management among trainee hairdressers', *Cognition and Emotion*, **5**: 419–34.

Parkinson, B. (1995), *Ideas and Realities of Emotion*, London: Routledge.

Parkinson, B. (1996), 'Emotions are social', *British Journal of Psychology*, **87**: 663–83.

Parkinson, B., Fischer, A.H. & Manstead, A.S.R. (2005), *Emotion in Social Relations: Cultural, Group, and Interpersonal Processes*, New York: Psychology Press.

Parkinson, B. & Totterdell, P. (1999), 'Classifying affect regulation strategies', *Cognition and Emotion*, **13**: 277–303.

Parrott, W.G. (1993), 'Beyond hedonism: motives for inhibiting good moods and for maintaining bad moods', in W.A. Pennebaker (ed.), *Handbook of Mental Control*, Englewood Cliffs, NJ: Prentice-Hall.

Pierce, J.L. (1999), 'Emotional labour among paralegals', *Annals of the American Academy of Political and Social Science*, **561**: 127–42.

Price, R.H. & Hooijberg, R. (1992), 'Organizational exit pressures and role stress: impact on mental health', *Journal of Organizational Behavior*, **13**: 641–51.

Pugliesi, K. (1999), 'The consequences of emotional labour: effects on work stress, job satisfaction, and well-being', *Motivation and Emotion*, **23**: 125–54.

Quick, J.D., Horn, R.S. & Quick, J.C. (1986), 'Health consequences of stress', *Journal of Organizational Behavior Management*, **8**: 19–36.

Rafaeli, A. & Sutton, R.I. (1990), 'Busy stores and demanding customers: how do they affect the display of positive emotion?', *Academy of Management Journal*, **33**: 623–37.

Richards, J. & Gross, J.J. (1999), 'Composure at any cost? The cognitive consequences of emotion suppression', *Personality and Social Psychology Bulletin*, **25**: 1033–44.

Richards, J.M. & Gross, J.J. (2000), 'Emotion regulation and memory: the cognitive costs of keeping one's cool', *Journal of Personality and Social Psychology*, **79**: 410–24.

Rind, B. & Kipnis, D. (1999), 'Changes in self-perceptions as a result of successfully persuading others', *Journal of Social Issues*, **55**: 141–56.

Schaufeli, W.B., Van Dierendonck, D. & Van Gorp, K. (1996), 'Burnout and reciprocity: towards a dual-level social exchange model', *Work and Stress*, **10**: 225–37.

Sutton, R.I. (1991), 'Maintaining norms about expressed emotions: the case of bill collectors', *Administrative Science Quarterly*, **36**: 245–68.

Thoits, P.A. (1995), 'Stress, coping, and social support processes: where are we? What next?', *Journal of Health and Social Behaviour*, **35**: 53–79.

Totterdell, P. & Holman, D. (2003), 'Emotional regulation in customer service roles: testing a model of emotional labour', *Journal of Occupational Health Psychology*, **8**: 55–73.

Tracey, T.J. (1994), 'An examination of the complementarity of interpersonal behaviour', *Journal of Personality and Social Psychology*, **67**: 864–78.

Von Glinow, M.A., Shapiro, D.L. & Brett, J.M. (2004), 'Can we talk, and should we? Managing emotional conflict in multicultural teams', *Academy of Management Review*, **29**: 578–92.

Wegener, D.T. & Petty, R.E. (1994), 'Mood management across affective states: the hedonic contingency hypothesis', *Journal of Personality and Social Psychology*, **66**: 1034–48.

Westen, D. (1994), 'Towards an integrative model of affect regulation: applications to social–psychological research', *Journal of Personality*, **62**: 641–67.

Zapf, D. & Holz, M. (2006), 'On the positive and negative effects of emotion work in organizations', *European Journal of Work and Organizational Psychology*, **15**: 1–28.

Zapf, D., Vogt, C., Seifert, C., Mertini, H. & Isic, A. (1999), 'Emotion work as a source of stress: the concept and development of an instrument', *European Journal of Work and Organizational Psychology*, **8**: 371–400.

16 Well-being and stress in small and medium-sized enterprises
Chris Brotherton, Carolyn Deighan and Terry Lansdown

Introduction

No matter how we define small firms they constitute the bulk of enterprises in all economies in the world, yet our approach to studying stress and well-being in organizations seems to take no direct account of the size of the organizations involved in our studies. Our books on the management of stress are generally silent on the issue of small and medium-sized enterprises (SMEs) and searches through our journals find very few papers indeed on such companies. One systematic review of over 15,000 workplace interventions on mental health showed that there was not one that reported any such interventions in SMEs (Seymour, 2005).

In this chapter we shall discuss the issues that SMEs face and put forward some proposals on stress and well-being that may address the challenges. This is not to be critical of research colleagues. Organizational researchers face several problems when they consider SMEs, not least in deciding what is included or excluded by such categorization. Many of these issues will also arise when occupational physicians have patients, employed in SMEs, who are exhibiting signs of stress and looking for positive ways forward.

In his book *Understanding the Small Business Sector* (1994), David Storey says:

> There is no single, uniformly acceptable, definition of a small firm. This is because a 'small' firm in, say, the petrochemical industry is likely to have much higher levels of capitalisation, sales and possibly employment, than a 'small' firm in the car repair trades. Definitions, therefore, which relate to 'objective' measures of size such as number of employees, sales turnover, profitability, net worth etc. when examined at a sectoral level, mean that in some sectors all firms may be regarded as small, while in other sectors there are possibly no firms which are small. (Deakin and Freel, 2003, p. 28)

Storey then goes on to illustrate how the Bolton Committee (Bolton, 1971) attempted to overcome the problem of definition by formulating what they called an 'economic' definition and a 'statistical' definition. The economic definition regarded firms as being small if they satisfied three criteria: (i) they had a relatively small share of their marketplace; (ii) they were managed by owners or part-owners in a personalized way, and not through the medium of a formalized management structure; and (iii) they were independent, in the sense of not forming part of a large enterprise.

Given this economic definition, Bolton then devised a 'statistical' definition which was designed to address three main issues. The first was to quantify the current size of the small firm sector and its contribution to economic aggregates such as gross domestic product, employment, exports, innovation and so on. The definitions were devised so as to enable measurement of change of the size of the contribution as well as to allow international comparisons to be made. Small firms are probably subject to considerable change, in terms of both structure and product innovation (Pavitt et al., 1987).

Taking the economic definition first, Bolton's criteria was that a small business is 'managed by its owners or part owners in a personalised way, and not through the medium of a formal management structure' (Deakins and Freel, 2003). Storey points out that this was incompatible with the statistical definition of small manufacturing firms, which could have up to 200 employees. While Bolton recognized that some smaller firms which may have one or more intermediate layers, for example, supervisors or foremen to interpret their owner–manager decisions and transmit them to employees, it still regarded small-firm owners as taking all the principal decisions and exercising the principal management functions.

Size increases the scale of management functions. Atkinson and Meager (1994) demonstrate that managerial appointments – not simply supervisors or foremen – are made when firms reach a size of between 10 and 20 workers. At that size, owners are no longer the exclusive source of managerial decisions. By the time a business has in excess of 100 employees, the owners of businesses are starting to assemble significant teams of managers and have to devolve responsibilities to those teams.

In terms of structure and decision making, small firms, particularly new small firms, vary considerably not only between each other but between themselves and larger firms. Small firms also seem exposed to conditions that are likely to induce considerable stress. Small firms face a great amount of uncertainty since they have a limited customer and product base. Small firms may simply act as subcontractors to larger firms (McHugh & Brotherton, 2000) and so be unduly dependent and vulnerable. On the other hand, small firms can internalize control and locate it in the hands of a small number of people, thereby reducing the internal conflict that can exist in many larger firms.

We can only estimate the number of small companies because, in most countries of the world, official statistics do not adequately record the numbers. The estimates indicate that almost two-thirds of UK firms throughout the 1980s had two employees or less. In 1979 it is estimated that 1.1 million firms had two employees or less, out of a total of 1.79 million firms – constituting 61% of all businesses in the UK (McCann, 1993). Across Europe small companies vary in size, as judged by the number of employees. Germany has 17% of its enterprises employing between 0 and 9% while Greece has 59%. The majority of countries fall around the 30–35% mark. There is a much higher proportion of employment in larger companies in the United States: 49% of all employment is in enterprises that have more than 500 workers – which is two-thirds higher that the average for Europe. If we take the number of small firms as a proportion of all firms, no matter how they are defined, then small enterprises in Europe constitute at least 95%. These figures seem to be broadly upheld in more recent figures that are provided by Deakins and Freel (2006). Nevertheless there is variation across countries as well as change – for example, by the time Deakins and Freel's figures were available, the percentage of small firms in Germany had grown to over 48%, with medium companies contributing over 11% of employment (or in total terms over 3.5 million enterprises).

Storey (1994, p. 49) states:

> The birth and death of firms occurs on a huge scale. In the United Kingdom each year 14 per cent of all businesses have registered for VAT (Value Added Tax) during the previous 12 months; they contributed a gross stock addition to the stock of UK businesses of approximately 235,000 in 1990. Each year there are almost as many firms deregistering for VAT (185,000) in 1990. Hence, in 1990 the net contribution to stock i.e. births minus deaths, was only 50,000.

Storey also reports: 'The fundamental characteristic, other than size *per se*, which distinguishes small firms from large, is their higher probability of ceasing to trade'. Ganguly (1985) shows that, in the United Kingdom in the 1980s, firms with an annual sales turnover of less than £13,000 in 1980 were six times more likely to deregister for VAT than firms with a turnover in excess of £2 million. In the United States, Dunne et al. (1989) show that, for manufacturing plants, those with between five and 19 employees had an exit rate which was 104.7% higher than for plants with more than 250 employees. It is hard for anyone with an interest in small firms to fail to see that the death rate of firms carries with it considerable stress, anguish and often hardship at both a financial and a psychological level.

Many individuals starting up a new company will have raised finance through the re-mortgaging of their own homes, or by sizeable borrowings secured on their family's surety. In our own research we have found that many founders of new small companies have been through periods of redundancy prior to embarking on new ventures. The families of owner–managers are frequently involved in supporting the business activities of small companies (Keogh, 2006). There are other potential sources of stress in the relationship between families in the management of businesses. Family positions may affect the role in the business or the stance that members may take over various business decisions. Politics within family factions can arise, such as giving too much credence to the heir in a family, the decision-making process within the company can prove difficult because of the dominance of certain family members and this can give rise to interpersonal conflict, and so on (ibid.). These are all questions that an occupational physician or an occupational psychologist may raise in a counselling session with an owner–manager of an SME or with an employee in respect to the stresses faced by the owner–manager if the social climate of the company looks to be a source of possible stress.

The restricted time and resources experienced by owner–managers in small companies are frequently highlighted as barriers to attending seminars on health and well-being, along with many similar activities. The relevance of advice on health matters provided to small companies will be questioned by them because the advice is often based on the experience that advisers have of larger-scale operations. Policies and procedures to protect healthy working have also been found to be of low priority for many new small companies because their business operation demands so much of their time and activity (Brotherton et al., 1987; Lansdown et al. 2007). SMEs often fail to create adequate records of information on health and safety issues so that research tasks are not easily accomplished. There are, then, a significant number of possible sources of stress and ill-health for small business owner–managers as well as very probably their employees. There are also considerable problems for researchers in this area.

There is a large and growing literature on work and well-being which, like the stress literature, is not taking account of the presence of SMEs and of those who run them. One exception is the text *Stress, Self-esteem, Health and Work* by Simon Dolan (2007), which has several sections on entrepreneurship, stress and well-being, most of which seem designed to offer self-help considerations, and presents some observations of leadership and confidence. Dolan comments (p. 201):

> The higher the leader moves up through the hierarchical levels of the company, the less time he has to read, to understand what he is reading, to care for his partner and his children, to have relaxation with his friends, to think, to reflect or simply to enjoy life or take time out to do

nothing in particular. This stress or adaptive failure has important negative emotional, commercial and social consequences. The many conventional leaders (clichéd) work very hard, almost always too much, administering hierarchies, resources and numbers. They also treat 'human resources' as just another resource. By contrast, the few new breed of leaders have the special value of being able to think differently, to decide to develop themselves as people, to release the creative energies of their colleagues, to contribute to the creation of a more solidarity-oriented society and to create conversational spaces for the true construction of shared values. The management of their own fears and the fears of others is their main value. . . . in essence what is expected of the new leaders is the capacity for building confidence and overcoming fear. Fear is feeling vulnerable when confronted by lack of control or stress. Stress is uncontrollability, fear, mistrust, hostility, inhibition, avoidance, displeasure, submission and illness.

Dolan's is a readable text based on an organizational behaviour approach derived from scholarly writing – perhaps in contrast to the more rigorous methods that psychologists and medical scientists utilize. What Dolan offers is a set of considerations that may be of some initial help in exploring a patient's or a client's approach to their work when they present with symptoms of stress.

The Handbook of Positive Psychology, edited by C.R. Snyder and Shane J. Lopez (2005) is the benchmark text for well-being research. In Chapter 52, entitled 'Positive psychology at work', Nick Turner and his colleagues argue that it is time to extend the research focus from the detrimental effects of organizational decisions on workers and to explore more fully the positive sides of work so as to gain a full understanding of the meaning and the effects of working: 'We firmly believe that a healthy and positive work focus is achievable. Indeed, we will argue that, in its truest sense, healthy work means the promotion of both psychological and physical well-being' (p. 715).

Turner et al. concentrate on job-related well-being because it is well established in research, and it provides a positive foundation for examining the determinants of healthy work. They cite Warr (1987, 1990), who characterizes general well-being as an 'active state', consisting of positive affect and high arousal. In the work context more specifically, they tell us that Warr considers job satisfaction, job involvement and organizational commitment (reflections of how employees feel about their jobs) as but a few of many measures of job-related well-being. Second, they remind us that work experiences translate directly into other mental health outcomes and indirectly affect life satisfaction.

Turner et al. argue that one of the most important ways to improve the experience of work is to design jobs so as to encourage workers to engage actively with their tasks and their work environment. By providing workers with autonomy in performing their jobs, challenging work, and the opportunity for social interaction, they are encouraged to exert choice and to feel competent. It is this form of work redesign that maximizes employee effectiveness and well-being.

The owner–managers of new small enterprises ought to be in a very good position to design their work so as to bring to the fore the positive and healthy aspects. So too should, or could be, the employees in SMEs, providing that the management adopt appropriately supportive strategies. Elsewhere in this *Handbook* (see Chapter 13) there is a discussion of Karasek's (1979) demand/control model which has been quite widely used to design jobs that enhance psychological and physical well-being. According to this model, healthy work environments are those in which appropriate demands, such as production goals, are made for workers which allow the ability to control the pace or the method of work. Turner et al. draw their readers' attention to the more recent dynamic version of the

Karasek model devised by Theorell (1990, cited in Turner et al., 2005), which proposes 'spirals of behaviour' to explain the effects of work design on well-being through a learning and development mechanism. Jobs with high demands and high control can inhibit strain by promoting both confidence and active learning. Workers with active jobs are more likely to apply coping strategies and seek challenging situations that promote mastery, thereby encouraging skill and knowledge acquisition. On the other hand, a relaxed job, with low demands and high control, does not provide employees with such extrinsic motivation. Similarly high-strain jobs, with high demands and low control, are likely to overwhelm employees and encourage a form of helplessness that can undermine employees' sense of mastery and dissuade them from developing and using skills. Finally, a passive job, which has low demands and low control, does not encourage skill development and can result in employee helplessness similar to that found in a high-strain job.

Miller (1979) saw Karasek's demands and control model to be in accord with his own minimax hypothesis, which proposes that a belief in situational control reduces negative responses to stressful situations because it provides individuals with the knowledge that they can minimize the maximum aversiveness of a stressful event. In other words, the potential for situational control can be used to avoid the experiences of unbearable adversity. In the context of understanding work stress, Karasek's job demands–control model is potentially important because it directs attention towards the organizational-level factors that may need to be addressed in order to mitigate the effects of work stress. There are, as this handbook undoubtedly demonstrates, many individual-level interventions whereas what is needed in many situations is to reduce job demands in the workplace.

In our own work on owner–managers of new small firms we found that business was often judged by 'busyness'. It often took the owner–manager several years to determine a more strategic approach to the business, in which profitability was calculated by measuring costs and determining financial returns rather than simply adding a percentage and waiting to see whether a profit emerged historically (Brotherton et al., 1987). Our sample reported long hours and a rushed approach to meeting customers' requirements rather than a balanced approach to production or to service that enabled a positive approach to the jobs and tasks to be designed into the business.

Role clarity and role load are seen as important features of well-being by researchers in job design. The way in which workers, co-workers and supervisors 'enact' their work roles is related to their experience. The balance between challenge and latitude is important and it is also important that an appropriate load is most beneficial to the worker and to the organization. Here the owner–manager might require to see how to obtain balance and clarity. In our own research, many owner–managers seemed to wish to take on every task and challenge that came before them with strong possibilities for stress and burnout being raised.

Parker (1998) explored how work characteristics, such as autonomy, affected employees' confidence, or self-efficacy, that they actually could carry out a broader set of role responsibilities. Using a longitudinal design, Parker found that employees who had high amounts of task control in an environment with high-quality communication exhibit greater confidence in their ability to undertake a more proactive set of work tasks than employees with fewer of these job characteristics.

Reviewing one's own role and its performance is probably a difficult set of tasks for anyone, let alone for people with responsibility for their own business success as well as for the livelihoods of people working with them. There is a broad base of research that has explored how having sufficient information and predictability in one's own work restricts the demands and expectations and makes work more challenging yet more manageable. Job satisfaction and organizational commitment are consistently and positively related to role clarity as a lack of anxiety and employee well-being.

The extent to which SMEs can be developed so as to maximize their opportunities for working as teams might well be important for positive health and well-being. Turner et al. (2005) take Guzzo and Dickson's (1996) review of team effectiveness and similarly define a workgroup as an entity comprising individuals who perform tasks in an interdependent fashion to meet the goals of an organization, and who can distinguish themselves from other groups. New SMEs should be well placed to capitalize in this respect since their goals should be set well within the purview of each company member and the identity of the company clearly distinct from any other. Turner et al. tell us that studies conducted in a range of contexts have associated team working with better individual well-being, and they cite Greller et al. (1992) and Sonnentag (1996) in support of this position. Turner says that there are a number of reasons for such benefits. First, working with a group of people provides a social network. Further, group membership can provide companionship, as well as the emotional and practical assistance that can help themselves and others cope successfully with tasks and interpersonal demands.

SMEs ought to be well placed to take advantage of the group level of interaction within their organizations. Given their organizational size, groups in SMEs are likely to be sufficiently close in proximity and in sociability for high-quality social interaction to take place. Accomplishing important goals in groups, organizations and societies has always depended on the ability of individuals to identify the capabilities of others and to harness these abilities to accomplish common goals. In the positive psychology literature, Bandura's (1997) theory of self-efficacy has had considerable influence. By self-efficacy, Bandura means that it is important that we believe in our own ability and that any effort we make will lead to outcomes that we seek. At a collective level, a group's shared belief in its conjoint capabilities to organize and execute the courses of action required to produce levels of attainment is seen as the expression of self-efficacy. Put simply, collective self-efficacy is the extent to which we believe that we can work together effectively to accomplish our shared goals. There is a considerable amount of research to suggest that collective self-efficacy is important in collective situations such as athletics, academic achievement, self-managed work teams, group brain storming and collective political action. However, there is no research that we know of on collective efficacy in SMEs.

Positive psychology emphasizes the development of positive human qualities and the facilitation of positive human health over the mere remediation or prevention of illness. It embraces the notion that individuals can be self-initiating agents for change in their own lives and in the lives of others. Self-efficacy theory also places emphasis on the development of enablement – providing people with the skills for selecting and attaining the life goals that they desire – over prevention and risk reduction. Self-efficacy concerned with enhancing our understanding of self-regulation will enhance our understanding of how to provide people with these enablement skills. Positive psychology emphasizes the social embeddedness of the individual and acknowledges that individual success and happiness depends to a large extent on the individual's ability to cooperate, collaborate, negotiate and otherwise live in harmony with other people. Collective efficacy in organizations such as SMEs provides many questions for future research.

Although it would be hard for anyone to argue that the notion of effective leadership contributes to the positive health of the organization of SMEs there has been precious little research. The concept of transformational leadership offers particular promise in the small business context. Transformational leadership occurs when leaders increase followers' awareness of the mission or vision towards which they are working, thereby creating a situation where followers feel excited and interested in common goals. Bass (1985) related transformational leadership to Abraham Maslow's (1971) hierarchy of needs and demonstrated that, in such a situation, followers are rewarded internally with achievement and self-actualization rather than externally with safety and security. In particular, the elements of transformational leadership (idealized influence, inspirational motivation, intellectual stimulation and individualized consideration) have potential for enhancing well-being (Avoloio, 1999). Put simply, asking what the CEO is like in a large organization or what the owner–manager is like in a small company can be fruitful in terms of understanding how well-being may be promoted. It seems that even a small change in a leader's behaviour can have profound effects on followers' perception of their own well-being. SMEs ought to be particularly well placed to promote well-being through the communication of leaders and the groups represented within the company.

Leaders show individualized consideration when they care for the work-related development of their employees. For example, when leaders listen and demonstrate empathy for given employers, they are extending a special personalized form of social support. Transformational leadership affects performance by mediating different forms of employee morale. Transformational leadership is associated in research studies with higher levels of trust in management and in group cohesion, both of which promote commitment to the organization. Transformational leadership elevates employee morale in general and effective commitment to the organization in particular. Transformational leadership, then, has the potential to result in positive employee well-being.

When people are engaged in challenging but controllable tasks that are intrinsically motivating, they experience a psychological state that Csikszentmihalyi (1992, 1997) has termed 'flow'. Motivation can be extrinsic – we do things because the outcomes of these activities bring about situations that we like or which allow us to avoid unpleasant events. So, we work to earn money to pay for food and entertainment and to avoid the horrors that come with poverty. When we are intrinsically motivated we do things because we like the activities themselves, as we might enjoy art or sport. For flow experiences to occur we must have a good chance of completing the tasks that we are engaged in. These tasks require total concentration and we become deeply and effortlessly involved in them, so that we no longer think about the frustrations and worries of everyday life (Carr, 2004). Our sense of self disappears when we are involved in these tasks and the sense of self emerges as strengthened after the task is completed. Time perception is altered during flow experiences. Hours can pass in what seems to be minutes and minutes can seem like hours.

Researching with new owner–managers has shown us that there are many aspects of flow involved in their work, particularly when manufacture or production of goods was at the core of the new company. 'Busyness' leads them to spend very long hours at work (Brotherton et al., 1987). The processes of flow in the production itself though may lead to the finance and accounting side of the business taking second place until there was a crisis in the business. In our research we saw this as being a possible cause of company failure. There was an obvious training and support issue here that might be taken forward by occupational psychologists. From the perspective of occupational medicine, the long hours and total engagement of new owner–managers in their work might at first be seen as a threat to good health and to work–life balance, but on deeper analysis to indicate a separation between the levels of cognitive processing required to keep business activity and business financial monitoring together. Both are vital to the success of the small firm and this unity is generally overlooked by texts on SMEs.

The notions of 'flow' and of 'busyness' may provide a mechanism for appraisal and intervention in the promotion of well-being and the reduction of unreasonable stress. Researchers need to explore whether there are common features of flow and busyness, and whether, if they are exploited together, they facilitate more effective working practices and provide prior warning of detrimental stress agents. It seems that features of working life that are conducive to the development of a flow state provide a real opportunity for enhanced productivity and enriched well-being. The ever-present danger, however, as indicated by Brotherton et al., exists in the form of flow without regard to profitability, both financial and emotional. That is, working smart, rather than working hard. The literature provides evidence of the practical benefits of, for example, understanding the real cost of one's time to the business (Reijers & Liman Mansar, 2005), the scope of broader economic strategy, and the right time to say no (Steffens et al., 2007). If such notions were taken up systematically within the flow state, triggering productivity–appraisal iterations, then overall efficiency may be preserved. Reijers and Liman Mansar (2005) have developed an evaluation framework which they call 'the devil's quadrangle' consisting of four dimensions – cost, versus time and quality versus flexibility – which may be traded against each other in business activity appraisal. Further, it is anticipated that such processes may mediate unreasonable 'busyness' and more broadly enhance autonomous control and well-being, while protecting the individual from undue stress. Fascinating research potential exists for the identification of, development of supporting tools for, and evaluation of such cycles of productivity and appraisal.

From a psychological perspective on SMEs, it is perhaps worth considering the context in which the motivational possibilities of the new owner-manager are faced. Intrinsic motivation is weakened by punishment, threats of punishment, pressurized evaluation and by imposing goals, deadlines and directives. Carr (2004) cites Deci et al. (1999) who found, surprisingly and controversially, that intrinsic motivation is also weakened by giving people rewards for completing interesting tasks, particularly if these rewards are perceived as controlling. Both punitive and positive incentives reduce intrinsic motivation because they reduce people's perception of autonomy and increase their perception that their performance was caused or controlled by external rather than internal factors. That is, they perceive their performance as being a response to the promise of external rewards or the threat of external punishment rather than arising from internal interest. The sources of threat to which a business might be exposed are deadlines imposed by customers as well as by the need to meet the requirements of legislation and taxation. Sources of reward to small businesses might come from the considerable benefits to be had by the nature of the delivery of goods and services to customers who are frequently known to the staff of the company rather than being at the end of a long supply chain. There may be taxation changes that encourage or pose threats to SMEs – even though they may not be designed as such by our legislators. The effects on motivation and satisfaction of policy-level decisions have hardly been looked at in the social and behavioural sciences involved in the study of business activity. There is an important set of issues here for researchers.

Positive psychology, which is at the heart of the discussion on well-being, is seen by many researchers as being largely anecdotal or qualitative. In our view, the vignettes that form the illustrative basis of the study of flow have enormous power. Of course, much of the discourse on positive psychology at work comes to us in the form of reported studies conducted by a range of people, not necessarily directly from the researchers themselves. This is the case in the chapter written by Turner et al. (2005), cited in the opening of this discussion. However, Turner is reporting a sizeable body of empirical research in which robust statistical comparisons have been conducted.

Nevertheless, positive psychology is well placed to make a further move forward scientifically in that there are now quite a wide range of measures and techniques available to those who wish to analyse psychological well-being and health.

The Oxford Handbook of Methods in Positive Psychology, edited by Anthony D. Ong and Manfred H.M. van Dulmen (2007) and published by Oxford University Press contains over 40 contributions to the measurement of positive psychology, many of which apply to health issues in general but some of which might be applicable in research in SMEs. Many of the methods demand the application of multilevel modelling but these enable motivation to be seen as a dynamic phenomenon that is sensitive to both person and situational changes. Seeing motivation as dynamic seems crucial to the proper understanding of SME activity. Discovering the strength of the interaction between person and situation, particularly in small businesses, is vital to researchers and to clinicians in occupational settings. Emotional competence is an issue that is discussed in this *Handbook* (Chapters 26 and 27). Since many business partnerships break down at the level of personal relationship malfunction, emotional competence might well provide some useful insights into the situation. One intervention strategy that suggests itself is to get both parties to complete an emotional competence inventory for themselves and to comment upon how they expect the other party to complete it. Exploring differences in the patterns of competence between the parties might also be a fruitful way of exploring relationships and how they are perceived. This *Handbook* has considerable promise for researchers and practitioners in positive psychology and for SMEs.

SMEs provide new challenges and significant demands of researchers, particularly in terms of stress and well-being. For the practitioner faced with patients who are stressed or who are low in well-being, the need for greater research effort in this area is pressing. The approaches to stress reduction that are available in larger organizations are not likely to be possible in SMEs. Because of their prevalence in the world economies, SMEs will generate a sizeable proportion of workers who experience stress. The rewards to researchers and to practitioners for increasing well-being in these companies are huge and the potential on the working population is at least commensurate.

References

Atkinson, J. & Meager, N. (1994), 'Running to a standstill: the small business in the labour market', in J. Atkinson & D. Storey (eds), *Employment, the Small Firm and the Labour Market*, London; Routledge.
Avoloio, B.J. (1999), *Full Leadership Development: Building the Vital Forces in Organizations*, London: Sage.
Bandura, A. (1997), *Self-efficacy*, New York: Freeman.

Bass, B. (1985), *Leadership and Performance Beyond Expectations*, New York: Free Press.

Bolton, J. (The Bolton Committee) (1971), *Report of the Committee on Small Firms*, CMND 4811, London: HMSO.

Brotherton, C., Leather, P. & Simpson, S. (1987), 'Job creation – new work for women?', *Work and Stress*, 1, 249–59.

Carr, A. (2004), *Positive Psychology: The Science of Happiness and Human Strengths*, Hove and New York: Brunner-Routledge.

Czikszentmikhalyi, M. (1992), *Flow*, London: Rider.

Czikszentmikhalyi, M. (1997), *Finding Flow: The Psychology of Engagement with Everyday Life*, New York: Basic Books.

Deakins, D. & Freel, M. (eds) (2003; 2006), *Entrepreneurship and Small Firms*, 3rd edn; 4th edn, London and Maidenhead: McGraw-Hill.

Deci, E.L., Keostner, R. & Ryan, R.M. (1999), 'A meta-analytic review of experiments examining the effects of extrinsic rewards or intrinsic motivation', *Psychological Bulletin*, 125, 627–68.

Dolan, S.I. (2007), *Stress, Self-Esteem, Health and Work*, Basingstoke: Palgrave-Macmillan.

Dunne, P., Roberts, M.J. & Samuelson, L. (1989), 'The growth and failure of US manufacturing plants', *Quarterly Journal of Economics*, 104 (4), 671–91.

Ganguly, P. (1985), *UK Small Business Statistics and International Comparisons*, London: Harper & Row.

Greller, M.M., Parsons, C.K. & Mitchell, D.R.D. (1992), 'Additive effects and beyond: occupational stressors and social buffers in a police organization', in J.C. Quick, L.R. Murphy & J.J. Hurrell, Jr (eds), *Stress and Well-being at Work: Assessments and Interventions for Occupational Mental Health*, Washington, DC: American Psychological Association, cited in Turner et al. (2005).

Guzzo, R.A. & Dickson, M.W. (1996), 'Teams in organizations: recent research on performance and effectiveness', *Annual Review of Psychology*, 47, 307–38.

Karasek, R.A. (1979), 'Job demands, job decision latitude, and mental strain: implications for job re-design', *Administrative Science Quarterly*, 24, 285–308.

Keogh, W. (2006), 'Family businesses', Chapter 10 in Deakins and Freel (eds).

Lansdown, T., Deighan, C. & Brotherton, C. (2007), *Health and Safety in the Small to Medium-sized Enterprise: Psychosocial Opportunities for Intervention*, London: Health and Safety Executive.

Maslow, A. (1971), *The Furthest Reach of Human Nature*, New York: Viking.

McCann, A. (1993), 'The UK enterprise population – 1979–91', *The Nat-West Review of Small Business Trends*, 3 (1), 5–13.

McHugh, M. & Brotherton, C. (2000), 'Strategic warning: powerful buyers can seriously damage organizational health', *International Journal of Management and Decision Making*, 1, 28–43.

Miller, S.M. (1979), 'Controllability and human stress: method, evidence and theory', *Behaviour Research and Therapy*, 17, 287–304.

Ong, A.D. & van Dulmen, M.H.M. (2007), *The Oxford Handbook of Methods in Positive Psychology*, Oxford: Oxford University Press.

Parker, S.K. (1998), 'Enhancing role breadth self-efficacy: the role of job enrichment and other organizational interventions', *Journal of Applied Psychology*, 83, 835–52.

Pavitt, K., Robson, M. & Townsend, J. (1987), 'The size and distribution of innovating firms in the UK: 1945–1983', *Journal of Industrial Economics*, 45, 297–306.

Reijers, H.A. & Liman Mansar, S. (2005), 'Best practices in business process redesign: an overview and qualitative evaluation of successful redesign heuristics', *Omega*, 33, 283–306.

Seymour, L. (2005), *Workplace Interventions for People with Common Mental Health Problems*, London: British Occupational Health Research Foundation.

Snyder, C.R. & Lopez, S.J. (eds) (2005), *The Handbook of Positive Psychology*, Oxford: Oxford University Press.

Sonnentag, S. (1996), 'Work group factors and individual well-being', in M.A. West (ed.), *The Handbook of Work Group Psychology*, Chichester: Wiley, pp. 346–67.

Steffens, W., Martinsuo, M. & Artto, M. (2007), 'Changing decisions in product development projects', *International Journal of Project Management*, 25, 702–13.

Storey, D. (1994), *Understanding the Small Business Sector*, London: Thomson.

Turner, N., Barling, J. & Zacharatos, A. (2005), 'Positive psychology at work', Chapter 52 in Snyder & Lopez (eds).

Warr, P. (1987), *Work, Unemployment and Mental Health*, Oxford: Oxford University Press.

Warr, P. (1990), 'The measurement of well-being and other aspects of mental health', *Journal of Occupational Psychology*, 63, 193–210.

PART IV

PROFESSIONAL BURNOUT, COPING AND PREVENTION

17 Value congruence, burnout, and culture: similarities and contrasts for Canadian and Spanish nurses

Michael P. Leiter,* Santiago Gascón** and Begoña Martínez-Jarreta***

Introduction

People work in organizational environments that have enduring structures, policies, and procedures that influence their experience of their work and themselves. To some extent, people contribute their time and effort to meet the demands of their jobs. Through the effective application of their talent and abilities, they respond to work demands. But this process is not the full story of worklife, especially for people who are bringing highly developed skills to work of personal importance. In these situations, the organization's priorities as well as its task demands become important aspects of the work experience. When things are going well on both dimensions, employees experience work engagement, characterized by energy, involvement, and efficacy. When these processes are operating poorly, employees are vulnerable to burnout. To examine these processes and their generalizability across distinct settings, this study explores a two-process model of burnout with hospital-based nurses from Spain and from Canada.

The research model

The Maslach Burnout Inventory (MBI) (Maslach et al., 1996) reflects a three-factor model of burnout in terms of energy, involvement, and efficacy. Although some researchers have used the term, 'burnout', to refer to exhaustion (see Shirom, 1989), the syndrome is more complex than chronic fatigue. The second aspect of burnout, involvement, includes a specific inability to care about service recipients (depersonalization) or to be absorbed in work activities (cynicism). This dimension expands the focus from individuals' concern with physical or emotional well-being to consider their capacity to connect with the external world. The third dimension, efficacy, describes employees' self-evaluations. Contrary to the process of building efficacy through mastery experiences (Bandura, 1982), the experience of chronic exhaustion and cynicism erodes employees' belief in their capacity to exert influence on their work world. These three interdependent experiences form the full burnout syndrome.

Limiting the definition to the exhaustion aspect of burnout encourages an exclusive focus on the adverse impact of work overload and exhaustion. This relationship is central to job stress and burnout research. Employees have a limited capacity to apply energy to work demands. Eventually, they will experience fatigue if they encounter excessive demands and have insufficient time for recovery. This dynamic is an important part of the burnout process, but it is not the only process occurring. Although this dynamic is important and factual, it does not have the complexity needed to support a worldwide research program for three decades, as has occurred with burnout.

The second, and more complex, dynamic at work in burnout is value congruence. The burnout syndrome is especially relevant to occupations that require dedication. The original focus of burnout was on human service professions (Freudenberger, 1974; Maslach & Jackson, 1981). Its importance was not solely that people felt exhausted from too much work, but that they lost the capacity for involvement in their work. They no longer cared about their service recipients. Further, they lost their sense of accomplishment, concluding that they no longer made a meaningful contribution through their work. When broadening the burnout syndrome beyond human services in the MBI–General Scale (also General Survey) (Leiter & Schaufeli, 1996), the three-component framework continued. Although exhaustion continued to be an important part of the framework, burnout encompassed both employees' capacity for involvement in their work and the sense of profession efficacy that they derived from their contribution.

From this perspective, workload leading to exhaustion is only one process to consider with burnout. Considering the balance of demands to resources, as in the job demand/resources (JD/R) model of burnout (Bakker et al., 2002) includes more relevant information, but remains incomplete. A complete perspective on the organizational context of burnout considers value congruence as well (Maslach & Leiter, 1997; Leiter & Maslach, 2004).

At issue is the correspondence of two distinct sets of values. One set includes individual values of employees. Individuals through various processes, including personal experience, cultural background, or professional training, develop a set of values pertaining to their work. Some people can clearly articulate their work values as a structured framework, assigning relative importance to activities, settling ethical conflicts, and guiding plans. Others have only a general idea of values. They may not be aware of their values until they encounter an event that offends their expectations. The second set includes the corporate values of the organization. Corporate values are expressed through organizational mission, vision, and values statements. These may be prominently displayed, guiding major organizational policy decisions and influencing the organization's day-to-day operational decisions. In other situations, corporate values are poorly articulated in a generic fashion, including nothing unique to the specific organization. The values-in-action that guide the organization's important decisions may differ considerably from the documented values.

A central proposition presented here is that employees monitor the congruence of their personal values with those of the organization. Their judgments of congruence are a defining factor in their psychological relationship with work. Congruence of personal and organizational values confirms individuals of their relevance to the organization. It also assures them that they are properly positioned to pursue what is truly important in their careers. Organizations provide the resources, networks, and opportunities through which people can have a significant impact in their careers. The lone individual has only a modest impact in a post-industrialized work world. People working in an organization with congruent values are motivated to pursue shared objectives and are reassured that they possess the efficacy to achieve those objectives.

In contrast, the experience of value conflicts with an employer can be the occasion for a career crisis. When in conflict, pursuing personal values at work incurs risk. Employees may encounter conflict with supervisors or other organizational personnel for neglecting organizational priorities for other activities. When complying with organizational values, employees may judge that they are wasting their talents and time on trivial matters. In extreme situations, they may conclude that pursuing organizational values requires them to behave unethically.

The model considers value congruence within three timeframes. On the broadest scale, values define individuals' understanding of their career. Positioning for a career in contemporary information/services economies requires a series of long-term commitments. Training and credentialing require years of study, practice, guidance, and mentoring. Gaining access to these experiences requires the commitment of serious monetary resources, often entailing long-term debt. It requires the active collaboration of other people, including family, friends, teachers, and colleagues. A clear value structure is a great asset for individuals who are positioning themselves for a career, becoming established in an occupation, and gaining access to its opportunities. Clear values support unconflicted motivation and confidence in critical decisions.

In the medium term, clear values guide individuals in setting annual or quarterly goals within their training and their work (Austin & Klein, 1996). Employees are more likely to identify and strive for challenging goals when they further that which they truly value. By focusing on employees' values, goals become meaningful.

In the short term, clear values provide a guide for day-to-day decisions. They reduce the processing time required for decisions by pointing decisions in the direction of employees' intrinsic preferences. They permit employees to avoid becoming bogged down in indecision, moving on to other issues in their worklife.

People lack value clarity for various reasons. Superficial reflection on life plans or occupational issues leaves individuals with little insight into their personal perspectives. They may simply not know their preferences in a specific situation. They may lack a capacity to articulate a rationale for choosing one option over another. External sources of value conflict arise for individuals with clear values in interaction with others with different values. This conflict is especially intense when the other party includes individuals or social systems with authority. When employees find that their personal values conflict with those of the organization, they experience distress from the conflict itself. They are also vulnerable to additional distress by losing a strong basis for guiding their decisions – long term, medium term, and short term – in their work.

Value incongruity has implications for all three aspects of burnout. First, the strain of ongoing conflict with the organization or central people within that organization depletes employees' energy. Both the strain of conflict and the futility of wasted talent are exhausting. Second, value conflicts decrease employees' involvement in their work. Employees experience a de-motivating situation in which they are discouraged from pursuing what they truly value. Third, they lose their sense of efficacy and accomplishment as they devote their time and talents to activities of little personal importance. The total impact of value congruence constitutes a major process in the development of burnout. By going beyond an exclusive focus on the exhausting impact of excessive work demands, the model provides a deeper consideration of employees' application of personal values to understand their worklife.

Method

Participants: Spanish sample

Participants in the study included 834 nurses working in three public hospitals in northern and eastern Spain. The hospitals had varying numbers of employees: 4,500,

2,500, and 550. They included inpatient services as well as outpatient primary health services.

The participants included 187 males (21.4%) and 687 females (78.6%). Most (463, 53.0%) were in permanent positions, with the remainder in temporary positions of varying contract length. Most were married (694, 79.4%) and most had dependent children (542, 62.0%). Specialty areas included laboratory (13, 1.5%), internal medicine (101, 11.6%), surgery (127, 14.5%), emergency medicine (98, 11.2%), cardio (88, 10.1%), neurology (30, 3.4%), oncology (33, 3.8%), ophthalmology (16, 1.8%), otology (5, 0.8%), psychiatry (49, 5.6%), and gynecology (71, 8.1%), with the remainder in other specialties. Participants had worked in their profession for varying times: less than two years (225, 25.7%), 2 to 5 years (186, 21.3%), 5 to 10 years (172, 19.7%), 10 to 15 years (149, 17.0%), 15 to 20 years (94, 10.8%) and more than 20 years (48, 5.5%).

Participants: Canadian sample

Most of the sample (*n* = 725) were female (687) (25 respondents did not specify their gender). Respondents included registered nurses (*n* = 589), licensed practical nurses (*n* = 85), clinical nurse specialists (*n* = 5), clinical nurse educators (*n* = 5), nurse practitioners (*n* = 3), and 'other' (*n* = 15; 23 respondents did not specify their job title). Participants worked in tertiary hospitals (*n* = 226), regional hospitals (*n* = 362), community hospitals (*n* = 89), or other settings (24; 24 respondents did not specify their work environment). The majority of participants worked full-time (*n* = 437), with 135 respondents working part-time, and 46 respondents working on a casual basis (107 did not specify their work status). The majority of respondents were staff nurses (*n* = 601), and there were 29 managers and 68 classified as 'other' (27 respondents did not indicate their position). Respondents included members of the District Nurse Advisory Council (*n* = 19) and members of the Practice Council (*n* = 37), but most respondents were not members of either type of council (*n* = 669). Of the participants, 54 of them had worked at their present organization for less than a year; 240 for 2–10 years, 210 for 11–20 years, and 199 for over 20 years (22 participants did not specify their time with their organization). The sample represents a 29% response rate for the 2,500 surveys distributed to acute care settings in Atlantic Canada. The large proportion of full-time, female, point-of-care registered nurses is representative of the population in this region (Canadian Institute for Health Information, 2005a, 2005b).

Procedure: Spanish sample

The research team conducted a series of meetings at the participating hospitals. They described the rationale, objectives, and procedures for the survey and invited attendees to complete the survey package. The researchers distributed brochures and posters describing the study to informed potential participants who could not attend the meetings. Participants completed the questionnaires over the following two weeks, depositing the completed questionnaire in a locked box at the work setting. Participation was anonymous. The researchers conducted sessions at the hospitals describing the research results.

Procedure: Canadian sample

Participation in the study involved completion of the questionnaire package. The researchers distributed paper questionnaire packages to nurse managers at selected hospitals in all four Atlantic Provinces in Canada. Nurse managers were responsible for distributing the packages to point-of-care nurses working on their units either during unit meetings, by placing the packages in mailboxes, or by leaving a stack of packages with ward clerks to help distribute. All of the packages included the survey, an information letter detailing the procedures and reason for the study, a flyer to advertise the online version of the survey, and a ballot and ballot envelope. As an incentive to participate, all nurses who completed the survey were given the opportunity to enter their name into a prize draw.

Instruments: both samples

Burnout Burnout was measured using the MBI–GS (Schaufeli et al., 1996), which measures the three dimensions of burnout: exhaustion, cynicism, and inefficacy. The items are framed as statements of job-related feelings (e.g., 'I feel burned out from my work'; 'I feel confident that I am effective at getting things done'), and are rated on a 6-point frequency scale (ranging from $0 =$ never to $6 =$ daily). Burnout is reflected in higher scores on exhaustion and cynicism, and lower scores on efficacy, whereas the opposite pattern is consistent with greater work engagement. Developed from the original MBI (Maslach et al., 1996), which was designed for human service occupations, the MBI–GS is a 16-item measure that evaluates burnout among people in all occupations.

Areas of worklife The Areas of Worklife Scale (AWS) (Leiter & Maslach, 2000, 2004) comprises 29 items that produce distinct scores for six areas of worklife – manageable workload (6), control (3), reward (4), community (5), fairness (6), and values (5). The items are worded as statements of perceived congruence or incongruence between oneself and the job. Each subscale includes positively worded items of congruence, e.g., 'I have enough time to do what's important in my job' (manageable workload) and negatively worded items of incongruence, e.g., 'Working here forces me to compromise my values' (values). Respondents indicate their degree of agreement with these statements on a 5-point Likert-type scale ranging from 1 (strongly disagree), through 3 (hard to decide), to 5 (strongly agree). The scoring for the negatively worded items is reversed. For each of the six subscales, the AWS measure defines congruence as a high score (greater then 3.00), indicating a higher degree of perceived alignment between the workplace and the respondent's preferences. Conversely, it defines incongruence as a low score (less than 3.00), indicating more perceived misalignment or misfit between the worker and the workplace. The AWS items were developed from a series of staff surveys conducted by the Centre for Organizational Research and Development (Maslach & Leiter, 1997; Leiter & Harvie, 1998) as a means of assessing the constructs underlying our analysis of the six areas of worklife. The scale has yielded a consistent factor structure across samples (Leiter & Maslach, 2004).

For the Spanish sample, the research team translated the questionnaires from English into Spanish. Back translations were evaluated in consultation with native English speakers and revised. This study is the first large-scale application of the translation.

Results
A series of *t*-tests contrasted the Spanish and Canadian samples on the nine variables in the study, using a criterion of $p < 0.0056$ as a Bonferoni correction for multiple comparisons. As indicated in Table 17.1, the two groups differed on all measures, but the direction of the difference varied across the measures.

Table 17.1   Comparisons of Spanish and Canadian nurses

Measure	Spain		Canada				99.44%	confidence
	Mean	SD	Mean	SD	t	Sig.	Lower	Upper
Exhaustion	2.40	0.91	2.65	1.46	−4.18	0.0001	−0.42	−0.08
Cynicism	1.63	1.27	1.83	1.42	−2.93	0.0034	−0.39	−0.01
Efficacy	3.86	1.09	4.45	0.98	−11.13	0.0001	−0.74	−0.44
Manageable workload	2.97	0.75	2.75	0.73	5.62	0.0001	0.11	0.32
Control	2.96	0.77	3.08	0.79	−3.09	0.0021	−0.23	−0.01
Reward	2.90	0.83	3.10	0.79	−4.71	0.0001	−0.31	−0.08
Community	3.07	0.74	3.46	0.69	−10.85	0.0001	−0.49	−0.29
Fairness	2.50	0.65	2.75	0.65	−7.54	0.0001	−0.34	−0.16
Values	2.95	0.67	3.23	0.61	−8.41	0.0001	−0.36	−0.18

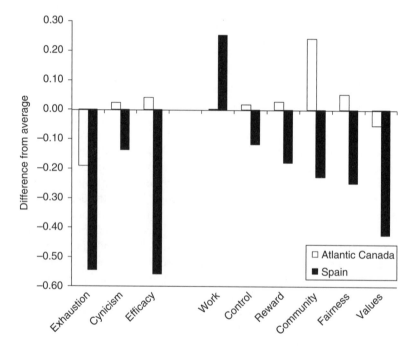

Figure 17.1   Comparisons between Spanish and Canadian nurses relative to norms

The Canadian nurses reported higher scores on exhaustion and cynicism, indicating more negative experiences regarding energy and involvement. They also reported higher scores on efficacy, indicating a more positive experience on the third component of burnout. For all six areas of worklife, a larger score indicates a more positive evaluation, or greater congruence, on that dimension. As indicated in Table 17.1 and displayed in Figure 17.1, the Spanish nurses reported more positive evaluations of workload than

Table 17.2   Contrasts of Spanish and Canadian nurses with norms

Measure	Norms		Spain		Canada	
	Mean	SD	t	Sig.	t	Sig.
Exhaustion	2.95	1.56	26.36	0.001	9.21	0.001
Cynicism	1.80	1.30	5.84	0.001	−0.99	n.s.
Efficacy	4.41	1.02	21.29	0.001	−1.55	n.s.
Manageable workload	2.75	0.72	9.36	0.001	0.09	n.s.
Control	3.08	0.78	−4.45	0.001	0.68	n.s.
Reward	3.10	0.94	−6.68	0.001	1.02	n.s.
Community	3.46	0.83	−8.07	0.001	8.63	0.001
Fairness	2.75	0.77	−8.93	0.001	1.88	n.s.
Values	3.23	0.66	−14.52	0.001	−1.84	n.s.

Table 17.3   Correlations and alphas for the Spanish sample

Variable	α	2	3	4	5	6	7	8	9
1. Exhaustion	0.91	0.51	−0.18	−0.47	−0.21	−0.33	−0.19	−0.25	−0.23
2. Cynicism	0.81		−0.41	−0.35	−0.24	−0.41	−0.32	−0.31	−0.32
3. Efficacy	0.78			0.16	0.28	0.26	0.20	0.15	0.20
4. Manageable workload	0.74				0.31	0.28	0.23	0.25	0.17
5. Control	0.62					0.46	0.33	0.37	0.35
6. Reward	0.78						0.34	0.35	0.28
7. Community	0.77							0.31	0.32
8. Fairness	0.74								0.46
9. Values	0.65								

Note: $N = 834$; all correlations significant $p < 0.01$.

did the Canadian nurses, but reported more negative evaluations of the other five areas of worklife.

The midline of the graph in Figure 17.1 represents normative scores on the measure. The bars, representing the scores for Canadian and Spanish nurses, are the differences divided by the standard deviation of the normative sample. The reference scores for the MBI–GS subscales are the nursing norms from the MBI Manual (Maslach et al., 1996). The norms for the AWS are from its Manual based upon 17,079 responses to the questionnaire, encompassing 35 surveys of diverse occupations in seven languages from around the world (Leiter & Maslach, 2007). The Canadian nurses scored more positively than the normative group on exhaustion and community (see Table 17.2). The Spanish nurses differed significantly from the norms on every measure. They scored more positively on exhaustion, cynicism and workload and more negatively on all the other measures.

Table 17.3 displays correlations among the measures for the Spanish sample; Table 17.4 displays this information for the Canadian sample. The correlations follow similar

Table 17.4 Correlations and alphas for the Canadian sample

Variable	α	2	3	4	5	6	7	8	9
1. Exhaustion	0.92	0.59	−0.26	−0.61	−0.35	−0.45	−0.25	−0.36	−0.29
2. Cynicism	0.76		−0.38	−0.39	−0.40	−0.53	−0.30	−0.41	−0.39
3. Efficacy	0.86			0.24	0.39	0.32	0.20	0.27	0.34
4. Manageable workload	0.80				0.40	0.35	0.28	0.31	0.27
5. Control	0.71					0.45	0.28	0.51	0.47
6. Reward	0.81						0.38	0.52	0.39
7. Community	0.82							0.39	0.27
8. Fairness	0.76								0.53
9. Values	0.74								

Note: $N = 667$; all correlations significant $p < 0.01$.

Table 17.5 Multiple regression of workload and values on burnout

	Spain			Canada		
	Exhaustion	Cynicism	Efficacy	Exhaustion	Cynicism	Efficacy
Exhaustion	−	0.46	−	−	0.51	−
Cynicism	−	−	−0.33	−	−	−0.29
Workload	−0.44	−	−	−0.56	−	−
Values	−0.15	−0.22	0.12	−0.12	−0.21	0.20
$F(2,871)$	138.64	188.80	90.08	268.51	257.00	54.66
R^2	0.24	0.30	0.17	0.39	0.41	0.18
Sig.	0.001	0.001	0.001	0.001	0.001	0.001

Note: All coefficients in the table: $p < 0.01$; nonsignificant coefficients for workload are not displayed.

patterns across the two samples. For both samples, the strongest correlation of an area of worklife with an aspect of burnout is that of manageable workload with exhaustion (Spanish, $r = -0.47$; Canadian, $r = -0.61$). In contrast, all of the other areas of worklife have their largest correlation with either cynicism or efficacy.

A series of multiple regression analyses examined this pattern further. The outcome variables were the three aspects of burnout: exhaustion, cynicism, and efficacy. For cynicism, exhaustion was entered as a predictor on the first step; for efficacy, cynicism was entered as a predictor on the first step, following a process model of burnout (Leiter, 1993; Leiter & Maslach, 2004). In the second step of these analyses, both values and workload were allowed to enter in a stepwise fashion: either or both of the predictors could enter the equation if their coefficient was significant at the 0.05 level. For exhaustion, values and workload were entered in this fashion in Step 1. As indicated in Table 17.5, workload was a significant predictor in the regression only on exhaustion. In contrast, values was a predictor of all three aspects of burnout in the context of the other predictors.

Discussion

The study found major differences between burnout and worklife evaluations by Canadian and Spanish nurses. These findings supported the concept of burnout as encompassing two processes. One process is evident in the relationship of workload with exhaustion. The other arises in the relationship of values with all three aspects of burnout. Replicating these patterns across two distinct samples of hospital-based nurses from Spain and Canada confirmed that these processes are relevant to both settings. The results are discussed in reference to their relevance to burnout research and the importance of cross-cultural projects.

The two-process model of burnout is reflected in the distinct pattern of scores across the measures in the study. One process is the link of workload with exhaustion. This connection is a mainstay of burnout research (Maslach et al., 2001; Halbesleben & Buckley, 2004). Through its connections with the other two aspects of burnout, exhaustion mediates the relationship of workload. The regression analyses confirmed this relationship in both samples. The second process is the impact of value congruence on the full burnout syndrome. The distinct relationships of values with all three aspects reflect its broad relevance. This dynamic defines burnout as something more than an exhaustion syndrome. That quality of burnout is captured adequately in the workload process. The issue of value congruence confirms employees as active participants in their worklife. They are not merely functionaries performing tasks until they are too tired to continue. They enter their work world with a set of values and perspectives that they use to make sense of the experiences, structures, and procedures they encounter. When they conclude that personal and organizational values are in conflict, they are vulnerable not only to fatigue, but also to losing their capacity to work in a dedicated and fulfilling manner.

The two samples differed regarding the relevance of these two processes to their experience of worklife. The profile of scores for the Canadian nurses indicated a strong workload process. They were less content with their workload and expressed more negative scores on exhaustion and cynicism than did the Spanish nurses. In contrast, the Spanish nurses provided more negative evaluations of the other areas of worklife, especially value congruence, and reported more negative levels of professional efficacy. While these results cannot be generalized to characterize the two nations' public health systems, they do indicate the extent to which two groups of hospitals can differ on the processes pertaining to job burnout.

The pattern of responses on areas of worklife differs strongly across the two samples. The Canadian sample has only one complaint about their worklife: there are too many work demands. This single complaint is not sufficient to prompt a major crisis in burnout: although they are significantly more exhausted than nurses in the Spanish sample, they remain less exhausted than the normative group. On the other areas of worklife, they score at the normative level or more positively. In general, they experience a reasonable level of congruence of their personal values with those of their employing hospital. In contrast, the nurses in the Spanish sample have a broad range of concerns about their worklife. These doubts are most strongly indicated by a negative score on values: they perceive conflict between their personal values and those of their employers. The survey did not identify the specific issues within this conflict. This general assessment of work values suggests that a value clarification process within these hospitals may be beneficial.

The overall value congruence for healthcare professionals reflects elements of national culture to some degree. It may be that the stronger value congruence for the Canadian nurses reflects the central role of the healthcare system in that country. For example, in the most recent national election, healthcare was identified in polls as the most important issue to the electorate (Canadian Medical Association, 2006). The high priority for excellent healthcare among the general public and the political sector may influence the healthcare administrators to develop organizational environments more congruent with the values of healthcare providers.

The study is limited by a reliance on cross-sectional, self-report data. The two samples are convenience samples regarding this analysis because the hospitals were not systematically selected to establish the contrasts explored in this study. Although using the same measures, the original research studies occurred without reference to one another. As such, the research cannot be taken as a definitive contrast of Canadian and Spanish nurses. The differences between the samples may reflect differences in the hospital missions, funding, or local issues rather than national culture. However, a strength of the comparison is that both the Canadian and the Spanish samples included nurses from multiple public sector hospitals. Although they do not constitute representative national samples, they do provide a diverse perspective on their national regions.

The research questions raised in this study would benefit from longitudinal research projects that track the development of the workload and values processes over time. Also, the work would be enhanced by integrating the survey responses with other sources of data regarding nurses' experience of their worklife. Through a more extensive research network spanning both countries, researchers could develop the capacity to conduct definitive research addressing cross-cultural issues.

In summary, the research reported here found support for a two-process model of burnout. The research also found striking differences between a Spanish and a Canadian sample of nurses. The Canadian nurses appeared to encounter greater challenges with the workload process while the Spanish nurses encountered greater challenges with the values process. A more extensive examination of these processes has the potential to make a significant contribution to understanding and addressing burnout.

Notes

*   Professor, Centre for Organizational Research and Development, Acadia University, Wolfville, NS, Canada.
**   Associate Professor of Occupational Medicine, Faculty of Medicine, University of Zaragoza, Zaragoza, Spain.
***   Full Professor of Occupational Medicine, Director of the School of Occupational Medicine, Faculty of Medicine, University of Zaragoza, Zaragoza, Spain.

References

Austin, J.T. & Klein, H.J. (1996), 'Work motivation and goal striving', in K.R. Murphy (ed.), *Individual Differences and Behavior in Organizations*, San Francisco, CA: Jossey-Bass, pp. 209–56.

Bakker, A.B., Demerouti, E. & Schaufeli, W.B. (2002), 'Validation of the Maslach Burnout Inventory–General Survey: an internet study', *Anxiety, Stress and Coping: An International Journal*, **15**, 245–60.

Bandura, A. (1982), 'Self-efficacy mechanism in human agency', *American Psychologist*, **37**, 122–47.

Canadian Institute for Health Information (2005a), *Workforce Trends of Registered Nurses in Canada, 2004*, Ottawa: Canadian Institute for Health Information.

Canadian Institute for Health Information (2005b), *Workforce Trends of Licensed Practical Nurses in Canada, 2004*, Ottawa: Canadian Institute for Health Information.

Canadian Medical Association (2006), 'Health care, not Gomery, is *the* election issue', *CMA Bulletin*, **174**, 277.

Freudenberger, H.J. (1974), 'Staff burnout', *Journal of Social Issues*, **30**, 159–65.

Halbesleben, J.R.B. & Buckley, M.R. (2004), 'Burnout in organizational life', *Journal of Management*, **30**, 859–79.

Leiter, M.P. (1993), 'Burnout as a developmental process: consideration of models', in W. Schaufeli, C. Maslach & T. Marek (eds), *Professional Burnout: Recent Developments in Theory and Research*, Washington, DC: Taylor & Francis, pp. 237–50.

Leiter, M.P. & Harvie, P. (1998), 'Conditions for staff acceptance of organizational change: burnout as a mediating construct', *Anxiety, Stress, and Coping*, **11**, 1–25.

Leiter, M.P. & Maslach, C. (2000), *Preventing Burnout and Building Engagement: A Training Package*, San Francisco, CA: Jossey-Bass.

Leiter, M.P. & Maslach, C. (2004), 'Areas of worklife: a structured approach to organizational predictors of job burnout', in P. Perrewé & D.C. Ganster (eds), *Research in Occupational Stress and Well Being: Volume 3. Emotional and Physiological Processes and Positive Intervention Strategies*, Oxford: JAI Press/Elsevier, pp. 91–134.

Leiter, M.P. & Maslach, C. (2007), *The Areas of Worklife Scale Manual*, Wolfville, NS, Canada: Centre for Organizational Research and Development.

Leiter, M.P. & Schaufeli, W.B. (1996), 'Consistency of the burnout construct across occupations', *Anxiety, Stress, and Coping*, **9**, 229–43.

Maslach, C. & Jackson, S.E. (1981), 'The measurement of experienced burnout', *Journal of Occupational Behaviour*, **2**, 99–113.

Maslach, C. & Leiter, M.P. (1997), *The Truth about Burnout*, San Francisco, CA: Jossey-Bass.

Maslach, C., Jackson, S.E. & Leiter, M.P. (eds) (1996), *Maslach Burnout Inventory Manual*, 3rd edn, Palo Alto, CA: Consulting Psychologists Press.

Maslach, C., Schaufeli, W.B. & Leiter, M.P. (2001), 'Job burnout', *Annual Review of Psychology*, **52**, 397–422.

Schaufeli, W.B., Leiter, M.P., Maslach, C. & Jackson, S.E. (1996), 'The Maslach Burnout Inventory–General Survey', in Maslach et al. (eds), p. 14.

Shirom, A. (1989), 'Burnout in work organizations', in C.L. Cooper & I. Robertson (eds), *International Review of Industrial and Organizational Psychology*, New York: Wiley, pp. 25–48.

18 Coping with burnout: a theoretical perspective and a corresponding measure

*Ayala Malach Pines**

Introduction

'Coping is among the most widely studied topics in contemporary psychology' declare Mark R. Somerfield and Robert R. McCrae in their review of stress and coping research (Somerfield & McCrae, 2000, p. 620). Close to 14,000 research articles that were published in the last decade alone (according to the Psych Info database) support this claim. Few of these articles (a mere 200, according to the same source) address coping with burnout. This is surprising because coping with burnout has been the focus of interest for both practitioners and researchers since burnout was introduced to the scientific literature in the mid-1970s (Freudenberger, 1974; Maslach, 1982; Pines & Aronson, 1988; Schaufeli et al., 1993; Maslach & Leiter, 1997; Schaufeli & Enzmann, 1998; Maslach et al., 2001).

Most studies on coping with burnout used conceptual frameworks that were developed in stress research. These include the distinction between problem-focused versus emotion-focused coping proposed by Lazarus and Folkman (1984) in their seminal work on coping with stress (e.g., Chan & Hui, 1995; Hurst & Hurst, 1997), conservation of resources stress theory proposed by Hobfoll (1989) (e.g., Hobfoll, & Freedy, 1993; Freedy & Hobfoll, 1994), as well as a variety of other conceptual formulations such as: positive as compared to negative coping (Ogus, 1995), adaptive versus maladaptive coping (Seidman & Zager, 1991), control-oriented versus avoidance-oriented coping (Koeske et al., 1993) and low versus high internal control (Greenglass et al., 1998).

Studies of coping with burnout used a variety of measures that were also developed in stress research, including the Ways of Coping Questionnaire (Chan & Hui, 1995; Hurst & Hurst, 1997; Gueritault et al., 2000), the Coping Resources Inventory (Turnipseed & Turnipseed, 1991), the coping skills subscale from the Occupational Stress Indicator (Butterworth et al., 1999; McElfatrick et al., 2000), and Latack's Coping Questionnaire (Jarvis et al., 1996).

However, burnout is a special and unique response to stress and more related to a disappointment in the existential quest for meaning (Pines & Keinan, 2005). According to its pioneer researchers, burnout is the end result of a process that erodes the spirit of highly motivated and committed individuals, until they reach a point at which they feel they cannot take things any longer (Freudenberger, 1980; Maslach, 1982; Pines & Aronson, 1988).

Coping with burnout: the current research

What coping strategies do individuals employ when they experience signs of burnout? This is the question that will be addressed in this chapter. The question is addressed from two perspectives: one theoretically derived, and the other based on people's actual reports of the way they cope with burnout.

While different definitions of burnout exist (see Maslach et al., 2001 for a review), one of the most cited definitions (Schaufeli & Enzmann, 1998) describes it as a state of physical, emotional and mental exhaustion (Pines & Aronson, 1988). Research has also shown that exhaustion is the central, dominant, and most significant component of burnout (Koeske & Koeske, 1989; Wallace & Brinkeroff, 1991; Burke & Richardsen, 1993; Schaufeli & Van Dierendonck, 1993) and its most intrinsic dimension (Garden, 1987; Evans & Fischer, 1993).

Based on the definition of burnout as a state of exhaustion, an important dimension in coping with it is the level of energy or exhaustion involved in the coping. This dimension is inherent in the distinction between active and inactive coping or the version that received considerable attention in the coping literaure: approach versus avoidance (e.g., Roth & Cohen, 1986; Moos, 1997; Rutherford & Endler, 1999; Dempsey et al., 2000; Anshel, 2001; Finset et al., 2002). In the case of burnout, active coping or approach involves active attempts to change the cause of burnout or oneself, whereas inactive coping or avoidance represents giving up and giving in and involves attempts to avoid, deny, withdraw or escape from the burnout-causing situation.

The second dimension, implied in the definition of coping suggested by Lazarus (1993) as 'efforts to manage demands that tax or exceed our resources' (p. 34) involves the direction of the coping efforts: outwardly towards the cause of burnout, or inwardly towards one's responses to it. The distinction between outward and inward directed coping is somewhat similar to the problem- versus emotion-focused coping suggested by Lazarus and Folkman (1984). In problem-focused coping, the person tries to master a stressful transaction with the environment; in emotion-focused coping the person attempts to reduce his or her own emotional distress. However, outwardly directed coping with burnout does not necessarily involve problem-solving efforts and inwardly directed coping with burnout does not necessarily involve a focus on emotions.

The same two dimensions of coping: active versus inactive and outward versus inward, emerged from the discussion of coping during burnout workshops with a wide range of human service professions (Pines, 2000). The goal of burnout workshops (which in most cases are voluntary and done at the workers' request) is to introduce the concept of burnout, describe the symptoms associated with it, identify its probable causes and help participants cope with it more effectively.

The experiential part of the workshop includes a series of structured exercises that help participants identify the causes of their burnout and their characteristic strategies for coping with it. In the first of these exercises, participants are asked to write down the aspects of their work that are most responsible for their burnout. They are then put into groups of four and asked to identify the causes of burnout they share. The shared causes of burnout are then presented to the full forum. It turns out that these shared causes tend to be very similar for most foursomes in a certain occupation.

In the next stage of the exercise, participants are asked how they cope with these causes of burnout. The coping strategies are discussed in the foursomes and afterwards, once again, presented to the full forum. It turned out that the coping strategies mentioned, despite differences due to burnout causes associated with particular occupations and organizational settings, could almost always be placed along two dimensions: active versus inactive and outward directed versus inward directed.

Here is an example. In a burnout workshop with 147 human service workers, 20% used outward-directed active coping (confronted the source of their burnout), 20% indicated that they used outward-directed inactive coping (avoided it), 49% used various inward-directed active coping techniques such as talking about it (20%), thinking about it (12%) and getting involved in other activities (17%), and 11% reported inward-directed inactive techniques such as accepting the situation, crying, drinking, eating and smoking (Pines & Aronson, 1988).

The consistency with which these strategies emerged in burnout workshops suggested again a rudimentary taxonomy of coping with burnout that includes, like the taxonomy that was theoretically derived, two dimensions: active versus inactive coping and outward- versus inward-directed coping.

On the basis of both these perspectives, the theoretical and the practical, a measure was developed. It is both a 'grassroot' measure that was developed based on people's actual descriptions of the way they cope with burnout, and it is theory based because these descriptions match a theoretically derived rudimentary taxonomy of coping with burnout.

The two dimensions generate four categories of coping: outward-directed active, outward-directed inactive, inward-directed active and inward-directed inactive. Each of these generic categories includes a variety of related strategies. While there were differences in specific coping strategies mentioned by different professionals in different contexts, the most often mentioned 'generic' strategies associated with the four coping categories were as follows (note that there were two dimensions of coping with burnout: active–inactive and outward–inward directed):

- *Outward-directed active*:
  confronting the person or situation that is the cause of burnout;
  changing the source of burnout, solving the issue; and
  finding the positive aspects in the situation.
- *Outward-directed inactive*:
  ignoring the person or situation that is the cause of burnout;
  avoiding the person or situation that causes burnout; and
  leaving the burnout-causing person, situation or job.
- *Inward-directed active*:
  talking about the cause of burnout;
  changing self to cope better; and
  getting involved in distracting activities (sport, hobbies, etc.).
- *Inward-directed inactive*:
  drinking alcohol, using drugs, taking medication;
  doing nothing, obsessing, sleep; and
  collapsing, getting sick.

Despite some item differences (for example, in some samples, talking had a positive connotation of talking constructively about the problem with a supportive friend, and in others it had a negative connotation of obsessing about the problem), these 12 generic strategies provided the basis for the Coping with Burnout Measure. The measure was presented to five different samples in which various psychometric properties of the measure were tested.

Hypotheses

The main hypothesis was that the active–inactive dimension, which addresses the level of exhaustion which is the central, dominant, and most significant component of burnout will emerge as the primary dimension in coping with burnout.

It was further hypothesized that the direction of the coping effort (inward or outward) will also emerge as an important dimension, but less so than the active–inactive dimension.

As for correlations with burnout, it was hypothesized that outward-directed active coping, which is likely to change the burnout-causing situation, will be negatively correlated with burnout whereas the other coping strategies will be positively correlated to different degrees.

Method

Participants

Five different samples took part in testing different aspects of these hypotheses. One was a sample of MBA students whose data were collected twice, three months apart; the other four samples were samples of professionals all working with people whose data were collected during burnout workshops

The students' sample included 66 Israeli MBA students, all of them working (34% men and 66% women, average age 26.4, SD = 5.06). The second sample included 1,942 police officers (85% men and 15% women): 495 were regular police, 492 were border police, and 476 were prison police. The third sample included 216 dialysis nurses (20% men and 80% women). The fourth sample included 503 human service professionals (43% men and 57% women) including social workers, teachers, managers and counselors. The fifth included 220 human service professionals (21% men and 79% women) including social workers, counselors, therapists, nurses, teachers, administrators and managers.

Measures

The Coping with Burnout Measure is a self-report questionnaire in which each of the four categories of coping with burnout is represented by three coping strategies. The 12 strategies are presented in random order. Respondents are asked how frequently they use each strategy to cope with burnout causes they encounter in their work. They are asked to respond using 7-point scales ranging from 1 = never, to 7 = always (see Appendix 18A).

The Burnout Measure (BM) (Pines & Aronson, 1988) is a self-report measure of burnout that includes 21 items evaluated on 7-point frequency scales (from 1 = never to 7 = always). The items assess the level physical (e.g., feeling tired), emotional (e.g., feeling depressed), and mental (feeling worthless), exhaustion. The BM is the second most frequently used measure of burnout (Enzmann et al., 1998) and is considered a reliable and valid instrument (Schaufeli & Enzmann, 1998) with internal consistency coefficients exceeding 0.85.

Procedure

In all five samples the two measures were group administered. Respondents were assured anonymity. The 220 human service professionals were also asked about the perceived effectiveness of various strategies (on a 7-point scale ranging from 1 = not at all to 7 =

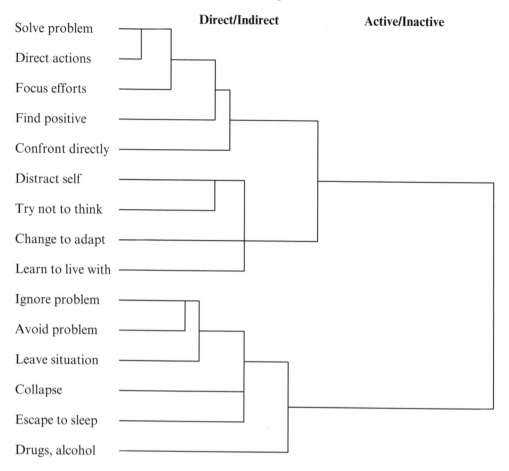

Figure 18.1   Hierarchical cluster analysis (66 MBA students)

very effective). The 66 MBA students responded to the coping measure twice, at the start and the end of the semester three months later. The police officers were given items that were specific to their work (e.g., outward-directed active: talk to direct commander).

Results
Hierarchical cluster analysis using the responses of the 66 MBA students (see Figure 18.1) revealed two main clusters – active versus inactive – each separated into two additional clusters: outward directed versus inward directed. The active outward-directed subcluster included: solve problem/change, direct action, focus my efforts, find the positive and confront directly. The active inward-directed subcluster included: distract self with activities, try not to think about the problem, change self to adapt and learn to live with the problem. The inactive outward-directed subcluster included: ignore the problem, avoid the problem or person and leave the situation. The inactive outward-directed subcluster included: collapse/get sick, escape to sleep and take drugs/use alcohol.

   Test–retest reliability of the Coping with Burnout Measure was assessed by correlating

Table 18.1   Alpha Cronbach values for the different police samples

Coping category	Blue police N = 495	Border police N = 492	Prison police N = 476
	Alpha	Alpha	Alpha
Outward-directed active	0.60	0.63	0.70
Inward-directed active	0.70	0.73	0.77
Outward-directed inactive	0.57	0.57	0.51
Inward-directed inactive	0.64	0.74	0.73

the responses of 66 MBA students at the beginning and the end of the semester. The correlation between time 1 and time 2 for the inward-directed inactive items was highest (0.81, $p < 0.0001$), for the outward-directed active items it was also very high (0.79, $p < 0.01$). It was lower for the outward-directed inactive items (0.63, $p < 0.01$) and lowest for the inward-directed active items (0.49, $p < 0.01$). As for correlations with burnout, the only negative correlation was for the outward-directed active strategy (-0.37, $p < 0.0001$), whereas both inactive strategies were positively correlated with burnout (outward-directed inactive: 0.32, $p < 0.001$; inward-directed inactive: 0.56, $p < 0.001$). Internal consistency coefficients (alpha Cronbach) of the measure as a whole were low, suggesting that the items do not represent a single construct. Alpha coefficients were higher when the four categories of coping were analyzed separately. Alpha value for outward-directed active coping was the highest (0.78), followed by outward-directed inactive coping (0.71). The inward-directed coping strategies had lower alphas: inward-directed inactive coping somewhat higher (0.49) and inward-directed active coping ranking lowest (0.41).

Similar internal consistency coefficients were found in the samples of the professionals, but they varied between samples. For example, Table 18.1 presents alpha values for the three police samples.

As can be seen in Table 18.1, alpha values for inward-directed active coping are highest, ranging around 0.73. Values for outward-directed inactive coping come next, ranging around 0.70, followed by outward-directed active coping with alpha values ranging around 0.64. The lowest alpha values are for outward-directed inactive coping, ranging around 0.55.

Table 18.2 presents Pearson correlations between the use of the 12 coping strategies and burnout among the samples of police officers, dialysis nurses, and human service workers.

As can be seen in Table 18.2, correlations between the different coping strategies and burnout showed a consistent pattern: outward-directed active coping (especially confronting and finding the positive) was negatively correlated with burnout; outward-directed inactive coping (especially avoiding and leaving) was positively correlated with burnout as was inward-directed active coping (especially talking about problems or trying to change oneself). However, the highest positive correlations were between burnout and inward-directed inactive coping such as getting sick and collapsing.

For the second sample of 220 human service workers, correlations were also calculated between the perceived effectiveness of the various coping strategies and burnout. These

Table 18.2   Pearson correlations between burnout and the use (and in one case effectiveness) of 12 coping strategies

Coping strategy	1942 officers' use r/burnout	216 nurses' use r/burnout	503 human service workers' use r/burnout	220 human service workers' use r/burnout	220 human service workers' effectiveness r/burnout
Confront	−0.28**	−0.02	−0.29**	−0.32**	−0.26*
Solve/change	−0.49**	−0.28**	−0.02	−0.09	−0.40*
Find positive	−0.08*	−0.14*	−0.24**	−0.19*	−0.33*
Ignore	0.45**	0.23**	0.04	0.05	−0.26*
Avoid	0.48**	0.17*	0.23**	0.21**	−0.03
Leave	0.49**	0.20**	0.25**	0.15*	−0.08
Talk/obsess	0.08*	0.18**	0.18**	0.09	−0.25*
Change self	0.07*	0.18**	0.12**	0.03	−0.17*
Activities	0.09*	0.12	0.17**	0.09	−0.13
Drugs	0.41**	0.17*	0.35**	0.21**	−0.09
Collapse/get sick	0.41**	0.40**	0.41**	0.35*	0.19*
Sleep	0.59**	0.40**	0.38**	0.33*	0.13

Note: $* < 0.05$; $** < 0.01$.

are presented in the last column in Table 18.2. It can be seen in the table that the correlations between the perceived effectiveness of the various coping strategies and burnout suggest that the perceived effectiveness of outward-directed active coping (especially confronting the source of burnout and finding the positive in the situation) had the highest negative correlations with burnout. The perceived effectiveness of outward-directed inactive coping (ignoring the person or situation causing the burnout) and of inward-directed active coping (talking to a close friend and changing oneself) were also negatively correlated with burnout. But the perceived effectiveness of inward-directed inactive (such as collapsing or getting sick) was positively correlated with burnout.

Discussion

Unlike other studies on coping with burnout that used conceptual frameworks that were developed in stress research (e.g., Hobfoll & Freedy, 1993; Freedy & Hobfoll, 1994; Chan & Hui, 1995; Hurst & Hurst, 1997) and used measures that were developed in stress research (e.g., Turnipseed & Turnipseed, 1991; Chan & Hui, 1995; Hurst & Hurst, 1997; Butterworth et al., 1999; Gueritault et al., 2000; McElfatrick et al., 2000) the conceptual framework proposed in this chapter was theoretically derived from the notion that, unlike the more general concept of stress, for burnout exhaustion is central, intrinsic, dominant, and most significant (Garden, 1987; Koeske & Koeske, 1989; Wallace & Brinkeroff, 1991; Burke & Richardsen, 1993; Evans & Fischer, 1993; Schaufeli & Van Dierendonck, 1993). The measure that derives from this conceptual framework also emerged in people's actual reports of the way they cope with burnout.

Based on this notion, a crucial dimension in coping with burnout was assumed to be the level of activity versus inactivity (or exhaustion) involved. Thus, the rudimentary taxonomy of coping that served as the foundation for both the conceptual framework and measure includes as a primary dimension active/inactive (confronting and trying to change versus avoiding and giving up). This dimension is further divided in terms of direction into outward versus inward directed (directed at the cause of burnout versus directed at one's reactions to it). The hierarchical cluster analysis supported this basic taxnonomy. It revealed two main clusters – active versus inactive – each separated into two additional clusters: outward versus inward directed, thus supporting the main hypothesis of the study.

Data collected from five different samples (including MBA students and of four samples of people working with people whose data were collected during burnout workshops: police officers, nurses and human service professionals) tested various psychometric properties of the Coping with Burnout Measure. Analysis of data obtained from MBA students at the beginning and end of the semester, and which showed correlations varying in size but all statistically significant, suggests two things: (i) the measure seems reliable; and (ii) it probably assesses both trait and state coping, since even after three months the correlations between items were significant, but not high enough to suggest that a trait is being assessed. The state interpretation assumes that the low test–retest reliability is a result of measuring something different between time 1 (the start of the semester) and time 2 (the end of the semester, before exam period and a time of high stress for students).

As hypothesized, the data obtained from four samples of human service professionals show that the use of outward-directed active coping is negatively correlated with burnout, whereas the use of the other coping strategies, especially inward-directed inactive coping, is positively correlated with burnout. Similarly, the perceived effectiveness of outward-directed active coping had the highest negative correlations with burnout whereas the perceived effectiveness of inward-directed inactive coping is positively correlated with burnout. In both cases, the presentation of individual items helped clarify where the main effect of the particular category derives from.

It should be noted that the Coping with Burnout Measure has high face validity. Use of the measure with hundreds of professionals from different occupations in burnout workshops around the globe suggests that people relate to it very comfortably and can easily suggest the specifics in their own work that correspond to the generic items. This may be the place to note that while 'collapsing' and 'getting sick' are usually not viewed as 'coping', some people (mostly women) still report using them when all else fails.

The chapter did not address personality, gender and culture. However, other studies that used the Coping with Burnout Measure showed cross-cultural and gender differences in the use of different coping strategies. In a study of cross-cultural differences in coping with burnout, for example, Israelis were found to be more likely to use the active- and outward-directed strategy of confrontation, while Americans were more likely to use such inactive inward-directed strategies as drink alcohol, use drugs, get sick, collapse, get involved in other activities and leave (Pines & Kafry, 1981; Etzion & Pines, 1986).

In the same study, women were found to be more likely to use such inward-directed strategies as talk, get sick and collapse, while men were found to be more likely to use such outward-directed strategies as confront the cause of burnout or ignore it. These latter findings replicated other studies that demonstrated gender differences in coping, showing men to be more outward directed and women to be more inward directed. Thus, for example, Vingerhoets and Van Heck (1990) found that men preferred problem-focused coping strategies whereas women preferred emotion-focused coping.

As for personality, different attachment styles (secure, anxious–ambivalent and avoidant) were found to be correlated with different coping strategies: a positive correlation was found between secure attachment and attempts to find the positive aspects in the situation and a negative correlation was found with a tendency to ignore the cause of burnout.

However, both insecure attachment styles showed a negative correlation with making active attempts to solve the problem and positive correlations with attempts to avoid the problem or a tendency to collapse in the face of one (Pines, 2004).

All in all, the findings presented provide tentative support for the proposed theoretical perspective on coping with burnout that focuses on the unique aspect of burnout – the centrality of exhaustion – and a two-dimensional taxonomy of coping with it, as well as the validity and reliability of the 12-item generic measure that was developed on the basis of this taxonomy. The taxonomy has the advantage of being both theoretically derived as well as 'grassroot', based on people's actual reports of the way they cope with burnout.

Neither the two-dimensional taxonomy nor the 12 generic strategies that derive from it is intended as a final statement about coping with burnout, but merely the first step toward developing a theoretical perspective as well as a psychometrically sound instrument specific to coping with burnout.

Future studies will need to increase the number of items in each of the four categories of coping represented in the current measure to four or even five items. This will no doubt increase the size of the alpha coefficients, establish a more adequate reliability and make it possible to analyze the dimensionality of the scales representing the four categories. Test–retest reliabilities may also be higher with more items per dimension. In order to assure the measure's universality, however, it seems important for the items to be stated generically rather than elaborated with detailed specific to a particular profession.

Future studies will also need to use the measure with large samples, of different occupational groups, in different contexts and different cultures. And they will need to address other limitations of the study, including the reliance on self-report data with all the problems inherent in this type of methodology, the fact that it is not possible to assume causation since the variables all correlate with each other, and the additional problem of shared variance between the variables. Such studies may determine the causal relationship between the frequency and effectiveness of using different coping strategies and the likelihood of burnout. They will also, no doubt, fine-tune the proposed theoretical perspective, the taxonomy of coping with burnout as well as the measure based on it.

The findings reported in this chapter have both theoretical and practical implications for occupational health psychology. On the theoretical sphere, the view of burnout as a special response to stress that is related to a disappointment in the existential quest for meaning (Pines & Keinan, 2005) can be seen as part of the general framework of occupational health psychology, which developed in part in response to the limitations in occupational stress literature, and the growing body of empirical evidence for positive outcomes such as growth and thriving through coping following exposure to stress (e.g., Park, 1998; Hart & Cooper, 2001). The notion that coping with burnout can result in both adverse as well as positive outcomes, provides organizations with the potential to make choices regarding these outcomes. Increasing the likelihood of growth and thriving outcomes as a result of coping with burnout requires identifying the mechanisms that are responsible for such outcomes. Identifying resources that can be influenced by organizational practices (e.g., selection, training, organizational change), can help organizations develop a prevention strategy for coping with burnout.

Acknowledgements

The study of police officers was supported by a grant from the Israeli Ministry of Public Security. The author wishes to thank the Chief Scientist of the Israeli Ministry of Public Security, the Head of its Social Sciences Division and the members of the study's Steering Committee for their invaluable help and support during all stages of the study. The views and opinions presented in this chapter represent the views of the author who bears sole responsibility for the chapter's content.

The dialysis nurses' data was collected by Mahamed Haskia BSN RN, a dialysis nursing supervisor at the Rabin Medical Center. The author wishes to thank Mahamed Haskia for this valuable contribution.

Note

*   Professor Ayala Malach Pines is Chair of the Department of Business Administration at the School of Management, Ben-Gurion University, Beer-Sheva, Israel.

References

Anshel, M.H. (2001), 'Qualitative validation of a model for coping with acute stress in sport', *Journal of Sport Behavior*, **24**, 223–44.

Burke, R.J. & Richardsen, A.M. (1993), 'Psychological burnout in organizations', in R.T. Golembiewski (ed.), *Handbook of Organizational Behavior*, New York: Marcel Dekker, pp. 263–99.

Butterworth, T., Carson, J., Jeacock, J., White, E. & Clements, A. (1999), 'Stress, coping, burnout and job satisfaction in British nurses: findings from the Clinical Supervision Evaluation Project', *Stress Medicine*, **15**, 27–33.

Chan, D. & Hui, E.K.P. (1995), 'Burnout and coping among Chinese secondary school teachers in Hong Kong', *British Journal of Educational Psychology*, **65**, 15–25.

Dempsey, M., Overstreet, S. & Moely, B. (2000), '"Approach" and "avoidance" coping and PTSD symptoms in inner-city youth', *Current Psychology: Developmental, Learning, Personality, Social*, **19**, 28–45.

Enzmann, D., Schaufeli, W.B., Janssen, P. & Rozeman, A. (1998), 'Dimensionality and validity of the Burnout Measure', *Journal of Occupational and Organizational Psychology*, **71**, 331–51.

Etzion, D. & Pines, A.M. (1986), 'Sex and culture in burnout and coping among human service professionals', *Journal of Cross Cultural Psychology*, **17**, 191–209.

Evans, B.K. & Fischer, D.G. (1993), 'The nature of burnout: a study of the three factor model of burnout in human service and non human service samples', *Journal of Occupationl and Organizational Psychology*, **66**, 29–38.

Finset, A., Stein, S., Haugli, L., Steen, E. & Laerum, E. (2002), 'The brief approach/avoidance coping questionnaire: development and validation', *Psychology, Health and Medicine*, **7**, 75–85.

Freedy, J. & Hobfoll, S.E. (1994), 'Stress inoculation for reduction of burnout: a conservation of resources approach', *Anxiety Stress and Coping: An International Journal*, **6**, 311–25.

Freudenberger, H.J. (1974), 'Staff burnout', *Journal of Social Issues*, **30**, 159–65.

Freudenberger, H.J. (1980), *Burn-out: The High Cost of High Achievement*, Garden City, NY: Doubleday.

Garden, A.M. (1987), 'Depersonalization: a valid dimension of burnout?', *Human Relations*, **40**, 545–60.

Greenglass, E.R., Burke, R.J. & Konarski, R. (1998), 'Components of burnout, resources, and gender related differences', *Journal of Applied Social Psychology*, **28**, 1088–106.

Gueritault, C.V., Kalichmnan, S.C., Demi, A. & Peterson, J.L. (2000), 'Work-related stress and occupational burnout in AIDS caregivers: test of a coping model with nurses providing AIDS care', *AIDS Care*, **12**, 149–61.

Hart, P.M. & Cooper, C.L. (2001), 'Occupational stress: toward a more integrated framework', in N. Anderson, D.S. Ones, H.K. Sinangil & C. Viswesvaren (eds), *International Handbook of Work and Organizational Psychology, Volume 2: Organizational Psychology*, London: Sage, pp. 93–114.

Hobfoll, S.E. (1989), 'Conservation of resources. A new attempt at conceptualizing stress', *American Psychologist*, **52**, 18–26.

Hobfoll, S.E. & Freedy, J. (1993), 'Conservation of resources: a general stress theory applied to burnout', in

W. Schaufeli, C. Maslach & T. Marek (eds), *Professional Burnout: Developments in Theory and Research*, Washington, DC: Taylor & Francis, pp. 115–29.

Hurst, T.E. & Hurst, M.M. (1997), 'Gender differences in mediation of severe occupational stress among correctional offices', *American Journal of Criminal Justice*, **22**, 121–37.

Jarvis, H., Burge, F.I. & Scott, C. (1996), 'Evaluating a palliative care program: methodology and limitations', *Journal of Palliative Care*, **12**, 23–33.

Koeske, G.F., Kirk, S.A. & Koeske, R.D. (1993), 'Coping with job stress: which strategies work best?', *Journal of Occupational and Organizational Psychology*, **66**, 319–35.

Koeske, G.F. & Koeske, R.D. (1989), 'Construct validity of the Maslach Burnout Inventory: a critical review and conceptualization', *Journal of Applied Behavioral Science*, **25**, 131–44.

Lazarus, R. (1993), 'Why we should think of stress as a subset of emotion?', in L. Goldberger & S. Breznitz (eds), *Handbook of Stress*, New York: Free Press, pp. 21–39.

Lazarus, R.S. & Folkman, S. (1984), *Stress, Appraisal and Coping*, New York: Springer.

Maslach, C. (1982), *Burnout: The Cost of Caring*, Englewood Cliffs, NJ: Prentice-Hall.

Maslach, C. & Leiter, M.P. (1997), *The Truth about Burnout: How Organizations Cause Personal Stress and What to Do About It*, San Francisco, CA: Jossey-Bass.

Maslach, C., Schaufeli, W.B. & Leiter, P.M. (2001), 'Job burnout', *Annual Review of Psychology*, **53**, 397–422.

McElfatrick, S., Carson, J., Annett, J., Cooper, C.L., Holloway, F. & Kuipers, E. (2000), 'Assessing coping skills in mental health nurses: is an occupation specific measure better than a generic coping skills scale?', *Personality and Individual Differences*, **28**, 965–76.

Moos, R.H. (1997), 'Assessing approach and avoidance coping skills and their determinants and outcomes', *Indian Journal of Clinical Psychology*, **24**, 58–64.

Ogus, E.D. (1995), 'Burnout and coping strategies: a comparative study of ward nurses', in R. Crandall and P.L. Perrewé (eds), *Occupational Stress: A Handbook. Series in Health Psychology and Behavioral Medicine*, Philadelphia, PA: Taylor & Francis, pp. 249–61.

Park, C.L. (1998), 'Stress-related growth and thriving through coping: the roles of personality and cognitive processes', *Journal of Social Issues*, **54**, 267–77.

Pines, A.M. (2000), 'A burnout workshop: design and rationale', in R. Golembiewski (ed.), *Handbook of Organizational Consultation*, 2nd edn, New York: Marcel Dekker, pp. 110, 841–50.

Pines, A.M. (2004), 'Adult attachment styles and burnout', *Work and Stress*, **18**, 66–80.

Pines, A.M. & Aronson, E. (1988), *Career Burnout: Causes and Cures*, New York: Free Press, ch. 7.

Pines, A.M. & Kafry, D. (1981), 'Coping with burnout', in J.W. Jones (ed.), *The Burnout Syndrome*, Berkeley, CA: University of California Press, pp. 139–50.

Pines, A.M. & Keinan, G. (2005), 'Stress and burnout: the significant difference', *Personality and Individual Differences*, **39**, 625–35.

Roth, S. & Cohen, L.J. (1986), 'Approach, avoidance and coping with stress', *American Psychologist*, **41**, 813–19.

Rutherford, A. & Endler, N. (1999), 'Predicting approach–avoidance: the roles of coping styles, state anxiety, and situational appraisal', *Anxiety, Stress and Coping*, **12**, 63–84.

Schaufeli, W.B. & Enzmann, D. (1998), *The Burnout Companion to Study and Practice: A Critical Analysis*, London: Taylor & Francis.

Schaufeli, W.B., Maslach, C. & Marek, T. (eds) (1993), *Professional Burnout: Developments in Theory and Research*, Washington, DC: Taylor & Francis, pp. 1–16.

Schaufeli, W.B. & Van Dierendonck, D. (1993), 'The construct validity of two burnout measures', *Journal of Organizational Behavior*, **14**, 631–47.

Seidman, S.A. & Zager, J. (1991), 'A study of coping behavior and teacher burnout', *Work and Stress*, **5**, 205–16.

Somerfield, M.R. & McCrae, R.R. (2000), 'Stress and coping research', *American Psychologist*, **55**, 620–25.

Turnipseed, D.L. & Turnipseed, O.H. (1991), 'Personal coping resources and the burnout syndrome', *Journal of Social Behavior and Personality*, **6**, 473–88.

Vingerhoets, A.J. & Van Heck, G.L. (1990), 'Gender, coping and psychosomatic symptoms', *Psychological Medicine*, **20**, 125–35.

Wallace, J. & Brinkeroff, M.B. (1991), 'The measurement of burnout revisited', *Journal of Social Service Research*, **14**, 85–111.

Appendix 18A   Coping with burnout
Following are 12 strategies for coping with burnout. Please indicate how frequently you use each one of these techniques to cope with burnout causing stresses in your work using the following scale:

1	2	3	4	5	6	7
never	almost never	rarely	sometimes	often	very often	always

1.   I change the source of burnout, I solve the issue____
2.   I ignore the person or situation that is the source of burnout ____
3.   I talk about it ____
4.   I drink alcohol, use drugs, take medication ____
5.   I confront the person or situation that is the cause of burnout ____
6.   I avoid the person or situation that causes burnout ____
7.   I try to find the positive aspects in the situation ____
8.   I tend to get sick, I collapse ____
9.   I change myself, so I can cope better ____
10.   I leave the burnout causing person, situation or job ____
11.   I get involved in distracting activities (sport, hobbies, etc.) ____
12.   I do nothing, I sleep____
13.   Other, please explain _____

19 Implications of burnout for health professionals

Timothy P. Munyon, Denise M. Breaux and Pamela L. Perrewé

Introduction

Health professionals function in practice environments marked by a variety of vocational, regulatory, and relational strictures. These environments place substantial job demands on professionals who sometimes exercise little control over outcomes. Indeed, the acts of psychological and physical caregiving require the dedication of personal resources which may be reciprocated in minimal patient improvement or loss. Research suggests that these practice environments are replete with stress and the potential for burnout. Individual factors also play an important role in the perception and management of personal stress and burnout.

Burnout is an especially salient condition with significant ramifications for individual and organizational functioning. Additionally, research suggests that burnout is not an isolated phenomenon. Burnout has been cited by doctors, nurses, social workers, therapists, and a variety of other specializations. Accordingly, the purpose of this chapter is to examine the phenomenon of burnout and its implications for health professionals.

Our discussion is structured as follows. First, this chapter provides a conceptualization of burnout and its major antecedents. Considerable research has helped clarify the psychological symptoms and causes of burnout (see Maslach et al., 2001; Halbesleben & Buckley, 2004 for reviews). Second, the primary consideration of this chapter is directed toward consequences and implications of burnout. We consider stakeholders inside and out of the organization in our analysis. Finally, the chapter evaluates new areas of research to guide future inquiry. Despite the prevalence of burnout among health professionals, there is hope that an improved understanding of the condition will illuminate its mitigation.

Defining burnout

Burnout is a psychological response to chronic stressors characterized by emotional exhaustion, depersonalization, and reduced personal accomplishment (Maslach & Jackson, 1986; Maslach et al., 2001). The syndrome is typically associated with individuals working in service occupations marked by heavy interpersonal client contact. An important distinguishing feature of burnout is a general feeling of hopelessness experienced by the subject (Zellars et al., 1999).

When experiencing burnout, individuals report a variety of major symptoms. One symptom, emotional exhaustion, is typified by a general lack of energy and emotional resources experienced by the individual. A second symptom of burnout, depersonalization, is the loss of humanity that an individual ascribes to patients or clients during interactions. Through the lens of burnout, an individual may begin to view patients as objects rather than people. This is largely characteristic of withdrawal. The third major symptom, diminished personal accomplishment, reflects a decreased sense of achievement on the job and during personal interactions (Cordes & Dougherty, 1993). Diminished personal accomplishment generally signals a loss of efficacy by the individual that may extend to the collective (Zellars et al., 1999).

Burnout researchers have recently expanded inquiry into job engagement, which is viewed as the theoretical converse of burnout (Maslach et al., 2001). Job engagement describes a positive affective state of fulfillment characterized by vigor, dedication, and absorption (Schaufeli & Bakker, 2004). Vigor is viewed as the theoretical converse of exhaustion and describes a state of energy, persistence, and a willingness to invest in work. Dedication is the theoretical converse of depersonalization (or cynicism) and describes feelings of meaning, pride, and inspiration in work. Finally, absorption is the converse to diminished personal accomplishment and describes a contented engrossment and efficacy with work.

While job engagement and burnout are theoretically and empirically related, they have different predictors (ibid.). For example, burnout is strongly linked to both excessive work demands and a lack of resources. However, job engagement is generally fostered through the availability of resources. Accordingly, managerial interventions designed to reduce burnout may fail in fostering job engagement. Likewise, interventions intended to encourage job engagement may reduce but not prevent the occurrence of burnout in organizations. Consequently, a discussion of burnout is important because of its distinct implications for organizations.

Modeling burnout

While a complete discussion of burnout antecedents is beyond the scope of this chapter, it is useful to briefly describe factors that influence the incidence and severity of burnout among health professionals. In general, burnout is not caused by a single factor. Rather, research suggests that a 'cocktail' of environmental and individual factors is responsible. Models of burnout generally evaluate the influence of job demands and available resources that are stressors or moderate the stressor–strain relationship. One heavily researched area evaluates environmental stressors related to role analysis and social support.

Role analysis and stressors

Role analysis refers to specific stressors and resources in an employee's practice environment that may contribute to or alleviate burnout. Role stressors are generally associated with perceived uncertainty of managerial expectations (i.e., role ambiguity), excessive workload or feelings of inadequacy (i.e., role overload), and differing expectations concerning performance (i.e., role conflict) (Cordes & Dougherty, 1993). Role stressors may be especially prevalent in poorly organized practice environments, even when staffed with well-trained professionals (Aiken et al., 2002a).

Characteristics of a practice environment also present stressors that contribute to burnout. For example, many health professionals experience secondary trauma stressors from their exposure to patients suffering physical and mental duress (Canfield, 2005). Countertransference is the mechanism that affects the response of a health professional to secondary trauma stressors, potentially resulting in vicarious traumatization (Dunkley & Whelan, 2006). Vicarious traumatization refers to a 'pervasive effect on the identity, world-view, psychological needs, beliefs, and memory systems of therapists who treat trauma survivors' (Canfield, 2005, p. 87). Vicarious traumatization has been tied to burnout.

The nature of many health occupations also presents stressors. Health professionals may frequently be called on to hide or fake emotions, especially during interactions with patients. Faking emotions is known as surface acting and can result in emotional exhaustion, one symptom of burnout (Brotheridge & Grandey, 2002). To reduce emotional labor and the stress of surface acting, health professionals may begin to limit overall emotive expressions and withdraw from stressful circumstances.

Staff work levels also influence the incidence of burnout. Essentially, an increase in the level of work increases the demands on an employee while reducing time available for resource building (i.e., recuperation). An example of work demands is illustrated in a study by Aiken et al. (2002b), who found that each additional patient assignment to a nurse resulted in a 23% increase in the likelihood of burnout and a 15% increase in the likelihood of job dissatisfaction. Interestingly, increased caregiver workload is also positively related to patient mortality in hospitals (ibid.).

Role analysis and resources

In addition to the analysis of job demands, role analysis evaluates personal resources available in a practice environment. These factors may include autonomy, advancement and growth opportunities, and skill utilization (Lee & Ashforth, 1996). The prevalence of vocational and regulatory strictures among health professionals is a likely contributory factor toward burnout as it decreases autonomy and skill utilization. For example, health practitioners may be substantially limited in their ability to respond to patient needs because the necessary intervention lies outside their vocational or regulatory sanctioned area of expertise. Professional liability concerns would likely preclude or limit autonomy and reduce skill utilization in these instances.

The highly specialized nature of health occupations presents a paradox for professionals with ramifications for burnout. In one instance, high levels of specialization may act as entry barriers that contribute to above-average wages and job security. In another, these same barriers can preclude mobility into and out of roles, potentially contributing to burnout. Occupational entry barriers may also limit the number of professionals entering a field, leading to increased workload and potential for role overload. Entry barriers may also decrease the quality of entrants into a field, exacerbating stress inherent in a given practice environment.

The costs of specialization for health professionals may also limit advancement and growth opportunities. For example, prior investments made to gain licensure in a profession may limit future opportunities, especially if education expenses were offset by loan financing. These prior investments can act as a sunk cost that may limit advancement and growth opportunities into other potentially more desirable occupations. Since many health professionals lack mobility and opportunities for advancement out of a practice environment, the focus of burnout research logically moves to quality *within* the practice environment. The quality of a practice environment can be highly influenced by the presence and type of social support perceived by the individual.

Social support refers to expressions of sympathy or empathy for a distressed individual that can be a powerful buffer against burnout (Zellars & Perrewé, 2001). The presence of social support from managers, in particular, has a strong impact in mitigating burnout. Likewise, the absence of social support is a contributory factor toward burnout.

Individual differences

Individual differences also play an important and emergent role in the incidence and severity of burnout. Individual differences describe the personal characteristics of employees on the job and include factors such as personality, political or social skill, and demography.

Locus of control is a personality characteristic referring to the perceived level of control that individuals exert over their own fate. People with a high internal locus of control believe that their fate is largely self-determined, while a high external locus of control denotes a level of determinism over one's fate. In a recent study, Ng et al. (2006) found that internal locus of control was significantly related to lower levels of stress and burnout among respondents. In contrast, external locus of control was significantly related to stress and burnout. These results suggest that individuals who feel out of control are more susceptible to burnout.

Specific personality traits also influence the incidence of burnout. One popular taxonomy of personality is the five-factor model (see Digman, 1990). When researching personality and burnout, Zellars et al. (2000) extended work by Piedmont (1993) and found that neuroticism was positively related to the burnout symptom of emotional exhaustion. Neuroticism describes the relative emotional stability of an individual. Individuals high in neuroticism are generally less emotionally stable.

Zellars et al. also found that extroversion, agreeableness, and openness to experience were all significant negative predictors of depersonalization, another symptom of burnout. Finally, extroversion and agreeableness were significant negative predictors of diminished personal accomplishment. These results suggest that introverts who prefer highly structured and routine environments are more likely to experience burnout. The unpredictable nature of client care in many practice environments could represent an especially salient stressor for these individuals. In addition, extroversion is positively associated with successful coping and social support (Amirkhan et al., 1995). This implies that introverts may be more susceptible to stressors and burnout in the absence of social support.

Political skill has also been cited as a neutralizer to stress and burnout. Political skill is an interpersonal style construct that combines social astuteness with the ability to relate well, and otherwise demonstrate situationally appropriate behavior in a disarmingly charming and engaging manner that inspires confidence, trust, sincerity, and genuineness (Ferris et al., 2000). Individuals with high levels of political skill generally view interpersonal interactions as opportunities and seem better able to navigate potential stressors within organizations (Perrewé et al., 2004). Logically, these same individuals would be less likely to experience burnout, holding other factors constant.

Demographic characteristics also influence burnout. Burnout has been found to be negatively correlated with age and to be more prevalent among females than males. Burnout has also been found to be more prevalent among single than among married respondents (Cordes & Dougherty, 1993). This implies that the nature of a marital relationship can provide social support and resources for a distressed individual. Finally, job tenure and burnout have been positively related, implying that the risk for burnout increases as tenure increases. Logically, repeated exposure to stressors could decrease personal resources and increase the chances of burnout. Nonetheless, it remains uncertain how job tenure influences burnout longitudinally and causally.

Burnout is generally conceptualized as a long-term response. Accordingly, factors linked to burnout logically function cyclically to influence continuation and severity of the syndrome and related consequences. This cyclical nature of burnout (Zellars et al., 1999) necessitates a review of consequences which may exacerbate or alleviate the severity and duration of the syndrome.

Consequences of burnout

The consequences of burnout are pervasive and affect a variety of stakeholders in and out of health organizations. Research suggests that burnout syndrome influences the quality of work and home for health professionals. We consider implications for both environments here.

Consequences in the workplace

Perhaps the most salient consequences of burnout are those experienced by the subject. Ironically, burnout may serve to reduce the health of professionals charged with maintaining the well-being of others. Specifically, the experience of burnout may lead to physical consequences for individuals through maladaptive coping and somatic disorders. For example, one study of physicians (Gundersen, 2001) found that burnout was significantly related to substance abuse and emotional distancing. The ease of accessibility to controlled substances for some health professionals may increase the risk of this maladaptive coping behavior. Unfortunately, research into maladaptive behaviors can be difficult due to social desirability bias and the extreme potential liability for respondents. Nonetheless, available evidence suggests that some health professionals engage in maladaptive behaviors to cope with stress and burnout (Felton, 1998).

Another study by Schaufeli and Bakker (2004) found that burnout partially mediated the relationship between job demands and health problems. This implies that the job demands occurring in a practice environment may lead to health problems for professionals experiencing burnout. Although we are not aware of any study demonstrating the relationship, this partial mediation may be caused by a decrease in immunity partially resulting from burnout. This concern is especially important for professionals exposed to high levels of disease-causing pathogens in their practice environments.

Individual performance may also suffer as a result of work stressors and burnout. A recent meta-analysis by Gilboa et al. (2006) found a significant negative correlation between work stressors and performance. This suggests that stressors generally reduce performance in organizations. Gilboa et al. noted that role ambiguity and situational constraints were especially salient stressors in organizations. Burnout is also significantly related to turnover intentions, absenteeism, reduced organizational commitment, and actual turnover (e.g., Leiter & Maslach, 1988; Bakker et al., 2003; Schaufeli & Bakker, 2004).

Evidence suggests that burnout negatively influences the quality of clinical care (Felton, 1998). The emotional disengagement of health professionals from their patients can result in lower levels of perceived care and empathy for suffering patients. Lower perceived levels of care can be exacerbated by the depersonalization that occurs in burned-out health professionals.

Research has shown a link between burnout and reduced self-esteem and efficacy (e.g., Rosse et al., 1991). Conventional wisdom dictates that losses in individual self-efficacy add an additional element of uncertainty to treatment recommendations and referrals that could have a substantial impact on client care and well-being. Finally, increased rates of turnover caused by burnout may lead to an overall decrease in the cumulative tenure and training available from practitioners. Inadequately trained practitioners may offer lower levels of care and suffer from role overload, perpetuating the cycle of organizational burnout.

Next, Zellars et al. (1999) postulated that a loss of individual efficacy from burnout may extend to the collective. A study by Jung and Sosik (2003) found that collective efficacy was linked to group effectiveness, suggesting that collective losses in efficacy negatively influence group performance. However, this study also notes the potential for collective efficacy to positively influence individual efficacy over time. Given available evidence, it is apparent that burnout can influence collective efficacy and its related outcomes.

As we have shown, the consequences of burnout are not limited to the subjects or their patients. There is additional evidence that burnout negatively affects the quality of work for co-workers. For example, higher levels of absenteeism from burnout subjects may lead to a greater workload for the remaining staff. An increased frequency of turnover also increases the administrative burden of staffing and training new employees. As previously discussed, new employees may be susceptible to the same or worse burnout conditions as their predecessors, especially when considering the context of burnout contagion.

A recent study by Bakker et al. (2005) found evidence for burnout contagion in organizations. Exposure to subjects experiencing burnout may consciously or subconsciously influence its occurrence among health professionals not suffering from burnout syndrome. Essentially, the exposure to burnout may drain critical resources from health professionals already placed in stressful practice environments that make them susceptible to burnout.

Many health professionals function in communities of practice or work teams. Evidence for burnout contagion has also been found at these levels. The results of a multilevel study (Bakker et al., 2006) indicate that team-level burnout exists and negatively influences individual positive work engagement within the team. This means that burned-out health professionals can undermine others' feelings of engagement in their work. However, it also implies that team-level engagement may ease individual burnout among members through social support mechanisms.

We postulate at least three reasons why engaged individuals may be susceptible to burnout contagion. First, the same occupational strictures that limit mobility in a practice environment can impede individual withdrawal from psychologically stressful environments and co-workers. Thus, individuals may be embedded in their work and unable to withdraw from draining co-workers. Second, many health professionals are naturally 'helping' individuals drawn to assist others (Felton, 1998). These individuals may engage with burnout subjects and become susceptible to the same syndrome they seek to alleviate. Third, emotions are contagious within workgroups (Barsade, 2002), implying that the respective emotional outcomes of burnout and engagement spread within a group. We purport that these factors, potentially working in concert, influence the prevalence of burnout within a team structure.

The relational impacts of burnout likely influence the formation and quality of social capital at multiple levels within health organizations. Social capital refers to 'resources embedded in a social structure which are accessed and/or mobilized in purposive actions'

(Lin, 2001, p. 12). While there is generally little overlap between psychological and socio-logical explanations of behavioral outcomes, we suggest that social capital, a sociological theory, offers a useful complement to psychological explanations of burnout syndrome and its contagion within social systems.

Based on extant theory (e.g., Burt, 2001), individuals most likely to experience burnout are those with few ties and not in structural holes within an organization. These same individuals would likely lack personal resources and social support important in coun-tering workplace stressors and burnout. The tendency of burned-out individuals to withdraw may also negatively influence organization efforts to form social capital with external stakeholders.

Consequences at home

The same burnout mechanisms that degrade work relationships likely have an impact on relationships at home. First, longitudinal research has shown that general work distress decreases marital satisfaction (Neff & Karney, 2007). When one partner is feeling dis-tressed, he or she may lack available resources needed to maintain a healthy relationship. Consequently, the quality of the relationship may suffer. Additional research has shown that burnout negatively influences one's satisfaction with life in general (e.g., Demerouti et al., 2000). Consequently, burnout rooted in work may negatively influence the quality of life for health professionals.

One way in which quality of life suffers is the crossover of stress and burnout between partners (e.g., Westman & Etzion, 1995). Stress and burnout crossover occurs when the psychological distress of one partner affects the occurrence of stress and burnout in the other. While research has shown that stress and burnout cross over from one partner to another (e.g., Westman et al., 2001), a decrease in marital satisfaction was significant for husbands and wives when they are experiencing above-average levels of stress (Neff & Karney, 2007). Thus, burnout is likely to spread within a practice environment and also to the home.

In summary, there is substantial evidence that experienced burnout has an impact on health professionals, their fellow employees, patients, and their relationships at home. The syndrome of burnout can lead to increased absenteeism, turnover, decreases in client care, decreases in social capital, relational erosion, and the degradation of physical and mental health for practitioners. These substantial consequences have far-reaching impli-cations for the healthcare industry and its stakeholders. In the next section, we consider these specific implications.

Implications of burnout

One major assumption of health professionals and researchers is that burnout mitigation and intervention is necessary. Unfortunately, this perspective fails to adequately address the status quo conditions for health professionals. Specifically, what is likely to occur to health professionals in practice environments if nothing is done about burnout syn-drome? We suggest that there are changes already manifesting in the healthcare industry that present fundamental challenges for professionals and burnout researchers.

First, many health professionals, especially in North America and Europe, are coping with increasing demand for services as national populations grow older. In the United States, over 78 million baby-boomers will reach their senior years by the year 2020

(*Health Care News*, 2007). This development parallels the anticipated experiences of many Western European nations and Japan. High birthrates in some developing countries are also straining existing healthcare systems (Mills & Shillcutt, 2004). In general, the evidence supports increasing demand for healthcare services.

At the same time, the available supply of healthcare is expected to be at critically low levels. For example, a shortage of 200,000 physicians is expected by the year 2020 in the United States (*Health Care News*, 2007). Parallel shortages in other health occupations are not difficult to envisage, with several potential net effects.

First, it is possible that health services may become inaccessible to individuals as demand exceeds supply. Economic factors would likely influence accessibility to healthcare as costs become prohibitively expensive for some individuals. A second potential scenario is that existing practitioners will work under more demanding circumstances. These factors may manifest in concert with one another, placing greater strain on health professionals and the system in general. Following logically, it is easy to envisage a scenario where systematic increases in job demands dramatically increase the incidence of burnout among health professionals. In such a scenario, one could expect a dramatic increase in the consequences of burnout to professionals, their patients, co-workers, and families. Accordingly, maintenance of the status quo could have serious negative ramifications for healthcare professionals, their patients, and families. Consequently, intervention and mitigation of burnout is a more practicable alternative. In fact, we suggest that the intervention and mitigation of burnout may represent a source of competitive advantage for organizations. Accordingly, it is useful to consider the implications of burnout from a mitigation perspective. Two general management tools are available to mitigate burnout. First, human resource management (HRM) may offer organizations with a tool useful in preventing burnout. Second, job redesign may offer an opportunity to mitigate burnout. Finally, intervention may ease the causes and consequences of burnout.

Mitigation through human resource management
There are several effective ways in which HRM can be used to reduce the incidence and severity of burnout within organizations. First, organizations can recruit and select individuals with characteristics resistant to burnout syndrome. This chapter has cited several individual characteristics that enhance resistance to burnout. Second, organizations can engage in training and development for existing employees designed to reduce the causes and effects of burnout. HRM professionals may be especially well-equipped to facilitate this training.

Recruiting and selecting burnout-resistant employees
The evidence on individual differences suggests that certain individuals are more prone to burnout than others. Thus, human resource staffing mechanisms may have a strong mitigating influence by purposefully recruiting and selecting individuals resistant to burnout. Certain traits, in particular, have buffering effects against burnout. For example, individuals high in extraversion, agreeableness, openness to experience, and political skill are less likely to experience burnout (Perrewé et al., 2000; Zellars et al., 2000). In addition, individuals with a high internal locus of control experience burnout less than individuals with high external locus of control. Thus, selection of these individuals into organizations should have a net effect of decreasing burnout, *ceteris paribus*.

Unfortunately, there are practical and theoretical complications that should be considered with this approach. First, the healthcare industry is currently suffering from shortages of available skilled personnel. Shortages of skilled personnel place downward pressure on the selection criteria used to hire employees (Lievens et al., 2002). Essentially, organizations may begin to reduce the extent of selection criteria with which they hire. Thus, the quality of new employee hires can suffer as employers settle for potentially less desirable employees. To circumvent this, organizations may engage in recruitment strategies designed to increase the number and quality of applicants (Rynes & Barber, 1990). These may include pursuit of non-traditional applicants, the enhancement of applicant inducements, and modification in the timing of recruitment endeavors. Organizations may also pool their individual recruitment efforts into collective action through alliances. Alliances may be a particularly salient answer for industrywide shortages of skilled personnel. Specifically, alliances can provide individual organizations with resources needed to compete effectively (Ireland et al., 2002). In the healthcare industry, organizations may use alliances with competitors to reduce manpower and staffing needs. Organizations may also use alliances with education institutions to supplement traditional recruitment efforts. Since education institutions are the primary medium through which professionals enter the market, the formation of alliances with these essential labor suppliers may represent a viable alternative that increases total industry entrance.

A second complication derives from the attraction–selection–attrition (ASA) framework (Schneider, 1987). The ASA framework suggests that organizations tend toward personnel homogeneity over time. Accordingly, organizations may have a difficult time attracting desirable burnout-resistant employees if those employees are substantially different from the existing personnel composition within the hiring organization. In this case, organizations may face pressures toward personnel homogeneity that actually increase the number of burnout-prone individuals within the practice environment. It would seem that misery *attracts* company. Despite the presence of this pressure, managerial intervention in the selection process may be an effective counter. Specifically, organization managers can formalize recruitment and selection mechanisms designed to encourage hiring of burnout-resistant employees.

A third potential complication in staffing burnout-resistant employees derives from competitive pressure. Specifically, one study by Gardner (2005) demonstrated that organizations compete against each other for desirable labor and may challenge competitor attempts to gain desirable labor. The implication here is that organizations are largely competing against one another for scarce skilled labor, leading to upward compensation and benefits pressure. Organizations may also recruit from one another to gain desirable labor, contributing to potential competitive responses and disrupting operations (ibid.). While traditional incentive and compensation mechanisms may counter competitive actions, the enhancement of organizational reputation and image can also be a powerful draw for employees. For example, Turban and Greening (1996) found that the social reputation of a firm influences its attractiveness to prospective employees.

Finally, empirical work has shown that the use of evaluation instruments in the selection process may be viewed unfavorably, even by those successfully hired into the organization (see Ryan & Ployhart, 2000 for a review). While there are risks inherent in the use of evaluation instruments, the potentially contagious impacts of burnout would suggest a strong argument for policies designed to encourage the selection of burnout-resistant individuals.

Training and development to mitigate burnout
While efforts to recruit and select burnout-resistant individuals may result in partial mitigation of burnout, these efforts do little to help existing employees. For these health professionals, burnout prevention programs may be useful. Such programs can be used to teach individuals how to identify burnout and modify individual coping strategies (Maslach & Goldberg, 1998). Specific training strategies include targets to provide more realistic expectations of work, better time management strategies, facilitation of social support, and improvements in self-analysis (ibid.). This approach focuses on modification of personal coping with the stressors inherent in a given practice environment.

There are factors that should be considered when implementing a training and development program designed to mitigate burnout. One of the most important and perhaps neglected concepts in training is actual implementation of the training and development program. Training and development initiatives require a commitment of resources from both the organization *and* its employees. Ironically, stressed and potentially overworked employees may perceive training and development initiatives as an additional stressor detracting from their normal duties. Consequently, implementation of training and development must be exercised with appropriate forethought to scheduling impacts lest these initiatives fail or backfire.

It may also be beneficial to train employees between communities of practice. Given the complexity and rigidity of modern healthcare, exposure to different occupational specialties may foster shared understanding. Each occupational specialty is likely to have its own regulatory strictures. Thus, an increased understanding of these strictures may foster trust and social support among health professionals while decreasing the potential for burnout.

Organizations seeking to implement burnout prevention training would also be wise to include partners. The inclusion of spouses or partners in training may provide a vantage with which to understand how stress and burnout cross over to the home. It can also affirm an organization's commitment to family and social support.

Mitigation through job design
Job design efforts focus on modifying inherently stressful elements of work to reduce burnout. Job design efforts generally include efforts to reduce occupational demands and increase the availability of resources. One study by Bakker et al. (2003) suggested that job demands can be lowered by decreasing the workload. The same study suggested that increasing individual autonomy and control over jobs is effective in promoting job resources. Finally, Bakker et al. suggest that participation in decision making can be effective in reducing burnout. These remediation tactics imply a level of change in the position to realize a reduction in the negative ramifications of stressors.

Despite the intuitive appeal of these tactics in reducing burnout, there are practical implications that should be considered by management. For example, decreasing workload will likely reduce burnout; however, the net effect of such actions is an increase in staffing levels potentially not feasible under existing labor-shortage conditions. Of course, this assumes workload reductions for all employees. Selective use of this technique for employees may actually increase the likelihood of burnout in others who now face a greater workload.

Increases in autonomy and control over jobs may, in some instances, be effective in reducing burnout. However, regulatory and liability concerns are typically restrictive in the healthcare industry, reducing the viability of this strategy. One alternative is to provide employee cross-training into different occupational specialties to promote autonomy and a greater sense of control over jobs through the mechanism of trust and cooperation (e.g., McAllister, 1995).

Mitigation through intervention
Thus far, this chapter has analyzed general mechanisms for burnout mitigation. First, we have suggested ways to decrease burnout by hiring individuals less prone to the syndrome. This has perhaps the most serious implications for long-term mitigation of burnout. A second method of mitigation deals with changing the nature of the job by design. The provision of autonomy, discretion, and reduced workload will all likely contribute to mitigation of burnout. A third method of burnout mitigation suggests intervention for those individuals either with a propensity toward burnout or currently experiencing burnout.

One way in which intervention can occur is through mentoring relationships. Mentoring can positively influence a protégé's efficacy, occupational competence, image, and well-being within an organization (Noe, 1988). Organizational mentoring initiatives may be formal or informal. Formal mentoring occurs when a mentor and protégé are placed together by a third party. Informal mentoring occurs when two individuals develop a relationship on the basis of shared understanding and mutual identity (Ragins & Cotton, 1999). Research suggests that the most effective mentoring relationships are those between a supervisor and a subordinate. Further, informal mentoring relationships are generally more effective than formal arrangements, although formal mentoring relationships still provide benefits to the protégé (ibid.). Accordingly, organizations that encourage informal and formal mentoring relationships may be successful in mitigating burnout through this very unique form of social support.

Short-term interventions may also be effective in reducing the incidence of burnout. For example, Cooley and Yovanoff (1996) tested the impacts of two short-term interventions designed to reduce burnout. One intervention was a series of weekly stress management workshops designed to teach coping skills to practitioners. The second provided practitioners with a structured time designed to provide social support. A longitudinal analysis of the results showed significant improvements in the symptoms of burnout and organizational commitment. Consequently, well-designed interventions may be effective in reducing burnout.

There is a caveat to the use of these interventions. Zellars and Perrewé (2001) found that social support can decrease but also *increase* burnout in certain contexts. Specifically, employees who engaged in negative-content conversations ('gripe sessions') increased the symptoms of burnout while employees engaged in positive-content conversations decreased the symptoms of burnout. Consequently, efforts to encourage social support may be most effective when accompanied by clarified and intentional managerial intervention.

Strategic implications of burnout

The prevalence of burnout in the healthcare industry may afford organizations with an opportunity to improve strategic performance relative to competitors. The primary assumption of this statement is that burnout is a widespread problem among healthcare organizations. We suggest that organizations can develop competencies in burnout mitigation that positively impact on their performance at multiple levels.

First, organizations successful in mitigating burnout should experience a reduction in the negative consequences of burnout. This implies that organizations will have more productive employees, less turnover, greater organizational commitment, and lower home impacts. These same organizations should devote fewer resources to turnover staffing and managerial intervention.

Next, organizations successful in mitigating burnout may augment their reputation. Improvements in reputation can enhance the attractiveness of the organization to current and prospective employees (Turban et al., 1998). Resultant increases in the applicant pool should enable these organizations to select better employees, further enhancing organizational reputation in a cyclical manner. Residual benefits may include increases in the quality of client care and available managerial resources.

Finally, the development of burnout-mitigation competencies may decrease the need for future investments in burnout mitigation. For example, organizations successful in creating burnout-resistant cultures may require less intervention as the incidence of burnout decreases. Thus, we would anticipate a tangible benefit for organizations that invest in burnout mitigation.

Remaining questions

While considerable work has helped clarify our understanding of burnout syndrome, there is much left undone for health professionals and researchers alike. In this section, we address some remaining questions important in accentuating our understanding of burnout syndrome and its specific implications for health professionals.

First and perhaps ironically, limited work has evaluated the role of patients throughout the burnout process. Empirically and conceptually, patients represent a substantial stressor to health professionals. Yet, not all patient interactions are stressful. Indeed, some patient interactions may be highly fulfilling and rewarding to health professionals. Accordingly, more analysis is needed to examine the conditions under which patient interactions become stressful. Specifically, it is possible that early patient interactions influence the subsequent quality of relationship between patients and the professionals treating them.

Next, evidence has shown that burnout syndrome can be contagious (e.g., Bakker et al., 2005). However, little is known about the specific mechanisms that trigger burnout contagion in organizations. Laboratory research may be especially fruitful in identifying the specific cognitive and affective mechanisms that spread burnout from person to person.

Third, longitudinal evaluations of burnout mitigation are absolutely critical. We need to know how proposed mitigation techniques work and the net impact of burnout reductions in organizations. It would also be fruitful to explore the role of alliances in increasing applicant pools for health organizations.

References

Aiken, L.H., Clarke, S.P. & Sloane, D.M. (2002a), 'Hospital staffing, organization, and quality of care: cross-national findings', *Nursing Outlook*, September/October, 187–94.

Aiken, L.H., Clarke, S.P., Sloane, D.M., Sochalski, J. & Silber, J.H. (2002b), 'Hospital nurse staffing and patient mortality, nurse burnout, and job dissatisfaction', *Journal of the American Medical Association*, **288**(16), 1987–91.

Amirkhan, J.H., Risinger, R.T. & Swickert, R.J. (1995), 'Extraversion: a "hidden" personality factor in coping?', *Journal of Personality*, **63**(2), 189–212.

Bakker, A.B., Demerouti, E., de Boer, E. & Schaufeli, W.B. (2003), 'Job demands and job resources as predictors of absence duration and frequency', *Journal of Vocational Behavior*, **62**, 341–56.

Bakker, A.B., Le Blanc, P.M. & Schaufeli, W.B. (2005), 'Burnout contagion among intensive care nurses', *Journal of Advanced Nursing*, **51**(3), 276–87.

Bakker, A.B., van Emmerik, H. & Euwema, M.C. (2006), 'Crossover of burnout and engagement in work teams', *Work and Occupations*, **33**(4), 464–89.

Barsade, S.G. (2002), 'The ripple effect: emotional contagion and its influence on group behavior', *Administrative Science Quarterly*, **47**, 644–75.

Brotheridge, C.M. & Grandey, A.A. (2002), 'Emotional labor and burnout: comparing two perspectives of "people work"', *Journal of Vocational Behavior*, **60**, 17–39.

Burt, R.S. (2001), 'Structural holes versus network closure as social capital', in N. Lin, K. Cook & R.S. Burt (eds), *Social Capital: Theory and Research*, New York: Aldine De Gruyter, pp. 31–56.

Canfield, J. (2005), 'Secondary traumatization, burnout, and vicarious traumatization: a review of the literature as it relates to therapists who treat trauma', *Smith College Studies in Social Work*, **75**(2), 81–101.

Cooley, E. & Yovanoff, P. (1996), 'Supporting professionals-at-risk: evaluating interventions to reduce burnout and improve retention of special educators', *Exceptional Children*, **62**(4), 336–55.

Cordes, C.L. & Dougherty, T.W. (1993), 'A review and integration of research on job burnout', *Academy of Management Review*, **18**, 621–56.

Demerouti, E., Bakker, A.B., Nachreiner, F. & Schaufeli, W.B. (2000), 'A model of burnout and life satisfaction amongst nurses', *Journal of Advanced Nursing*, **32**(2), 454–64.

Digman, J.M. (1990), 'Personality structure: emergence of the five-factor model', *Annual Review of Psychology*, **41**, 417–40.

Dunkley, J. & Whelan, T.A. (2006), 'Vicarious traumatisation: current status and future directions', *British Journal of Guidance and Counselling*, **34**(1), 107–16.

Felton, J.S. (1998), 'Burnout as a clinical entity: its importance in health care workers', *Occupational Medicine*, **48**, 237–50.

Ferris, G.R., Perrewé, P.L., Anthony, W.P. & Gilmore, D.C. (2000), 'Political skill at work', *Organizational Dynamics*, **28**, 25–37.

Gardner, T.M. (2005), 'Interfirm competition for human resources: evidence from the software industry', *Academy of Management Journal*, **48**(2), 237–56.

Gilboa, S., Shirom, A., Fried, Y. & Cooper, C.L. (2006), 'A meta-analysis of work demand stressors and job performance: examining main and moderating effects', *Personnel Psychology*, **61**, 227–71.

Gundersen, L. (2001), 'Physician burnout', *Annals of Internal Medicine*, **135**(2), 145–8.

Halbesleben, J.R.B. & Buckley, M.R. (2004), 'Burnout in organizational life', *Journal of Management*, **30**, 859–79.

Health Care News (2007), 'Health care demand rising, population aging. The imperative to increase physician supply', *Healthcare News In-Depth*, July 23.

Ireland, R.D., Hitt, M.A. & Vaidyanath, D. (2002), 'Alliance management as a source of competitive advantage', *Journal of Management*, **28**(3), 413–46.

Jung, D.I. & Sosik, J.J. (2003), 'Group potency and collective efficacy: examining their predictive validity, level of analysis, and effects of performance feedback on future group performance', *Group and Organizational Management*, **28**(3), 366–90.

Lee, R.T. & Ashforth, B.E. (1996), 'A meta-analytic examination of the correlates of the three dimensions of job burnout', *Journal of Applied Psychology*, **81**(2), 123–33.

Leiter, M.P. & Maslach, C. (1988), 'The impact of interpersonal environment on burnout and organizational commitment', *Journal of Organizational Behavior*, **9**, 297–308.

Lievens, F., van Dam, K. & Anderson, N. (2002), 'Recent trends and challenges in personnel selection', *Personnel Review*, **31**(5), 580–601.

Lin, N. (2001), 'Building a network theory of Social Capital', in N. Lin, K. Cook & R.S. Burt (eds), *Social Capital: Theory and Research*, New York: Aldine De Gruyter, pp. 3–30.

Maslach, C. & Goldberg, J. (1998), 'Prevention of burnout: new perspectives', *Applied and Preventive Psychology*, **7**, 3–74.

Maslach, C. & Jackson, S.E. (1986), *MBI: The Maslach Burnout Inventory Manual, Research Edition*, Palo Alto, CA: Consulting Psychologists Press.

Maslach, C., Schaufeli, W.B. & Leiter, M.P. (2001), 'Job burnout', *Annual Review of Psychology*, **52**, 397–422.

McAllister, D.J. (1995), 'Affect- and cognition-based trust as foundations for interpersonal cooperation in organizations', *Academy of Management Journal*, **38**(1), 24–59.

Mills, A. & Shillcutt, S. (2004), 'Communicable diseases', in B. Lomborg (ed.), *Global Crises, Global Solutions*, Cambridge: Cambridge University Press, pp. 62–114.

Neff, L.A. & Karney, B.R. (2007), 'Stress crossover in newlywed marriage: a longitudinal and dyadic perspective', *Journal of Marriage and Family*, **69**, 594–607.

Ng, T.W.H., Sorensen, K.L. & Eby, L.T. (2006), 'Locus of control at work: a meta-analysis', *Journal of Organizational Behavior*, **27**, 1057–87.

Noe, R.A. (1988), 'An investigation of the determinants of successful assigned mentoring relationships', *Personnel Psychology*, **41**(3), 457–79.

Perrewé, P.L., Ferris, G.R., Frink, D.D. & Anthony, W.P. (2000), 'Political skill: an antidote for workplace stressors', *Academy of Management Executive*, **14**, 115–23.

Perrewé, P.L., Zellars, K.L., Ferris, G.R., Rossi, A.M., Kacmar, C.J. & Ralston, D.A. (2004), 'Neutralizing job stressors: political skill as an antidote to the dysfunctional consequences of role conflict', *Academy of Management Journal*, **47**(1), 141–52.

Piedmont, R.L. (1993), 'A longitudinal analysis of burnout in the health care setting: the role of personal dispositions', *Journal of Personality Assessment*, **67**, 457–73.

Ragins, B.R. & Cotton, J.L. (1999), 'Mentor functions and outcomes: a comparison of men and women in formal and informal mentoring relationships', *Journal of Applied Psychology*, **84**(4), 529–50.

Rosse, J.G., Boss, R.W., Johnson, A.E. & Crown, D.F. (1991), 'Conceptualizing the role of self-esteem in the burnout process', *Group and Organizational Management*, **16**(4), 428–50.

Ryan, A.M. & Ployhart, R.E. (2000), 'Applicants' perceptions of selection procedures and decisions: a critical review and agenda for the future', *Journal of Management*, **26**(3), 565–606.

Rynes, S.L. & Barber, A.E. (1990), 'Applicant attraction strategies: an organizational perspective', *Academy of Management Review*, **15**(2), 286–310.

Schaufeli, W.B. & Bakker, A.B. (2004), 'Job demands, job resources, and their relationship with burnout and engagement', *Journal of Organizational Behavior*, **25**(3), 293–315.

Schneider, B. (1987), 'The people make the place', *Personnel Psychology*, **40**, 437–53.

Turban, D.B., Forret, M.L. & Hendrickson, C.L. (1998), 'Applicant attraction to firms: influences of organization reputation, job and organizational attributes, and recruiter behaviors', *Journal of Vocational Behavior*, **52**, 24–44.

Turban, D.B. & Greening, D.W. (1996), 'Corporate social performance and organizational attractiveness to prospective employees', *Academy of Management Journal*, **40**(3), 658–72.

Westman, M. & Etzion, D. (1995), 'Crossover of stress, strain, and resources from one spouse to another', *Journal of Organizational Behavior*, **16**(2), 169–81.

Westman, M., Etzion, D. & Danon, E. (2001), 'Job insecurity and crossover of burnout in married couples', *Journal of Organizational Behavior*, **22**(5), 467–81.

Zellars, K.L. & Perrewé, P.L. (2001), 'Affective personality and the content of emotional social support: coping in organizations', *Journal of Applied Psychology*, **86**, 459–67.

Zellars, K., Perrewé, P.L. & Hochwarter, W. (1999), 'Mitigating burnout among high NA employees in health care: what can organizations do?', *Journal of Applied Social Psychology*, **29**, 2250–71.

Zellars, K.L., Perrewé, P.L. & Hochwarter, W.A. (2000), 'Burnout in health care: the role of the five factors of personality', *Journal of Applied Social Psychology*, **30**(8), 1570–98.

20 Self-efficacy training programs to cope with highly demanding work situations and prevent burnout

Carmen Tabernero, Alicia Arenas and Elena Briones

Introduction

The work environment is constantly changing and increasingly competitive, which necessitates the development of new skills, facing risky situations and making difficult decisions. The perception of personal capacity to carry out the demands of a job influences stress levels and, consequently, professional health. Employees with low self-efficacy levels will suffer from more emotional and physical stress when faced with a workload which they feel exceeds their capabilities, whereas those whose perceived self-efficacy is higher, do not seem to be negatively affected by high-demand work situations. In this chapter we explore the role that judgements of self-efficacy play in moderating the effect of certain variables associated with burnout, and show the steps needed to train oneself in self-efficacy in order to avoid occupational stress. First, we define the concept of self-efficacy as a self-regulatory mechanism inside a dynamic social cognitive model. Second, we show the relationship between self-efficacy and burnout. In order to do this, we carried out a study in which, after constructing a self-efficacy scale for facing complex organizational situations, we evaluated the levels of self-efficacy in a sample group of workers, who were also questioned on their levels of burnout and organizational satisfaction. Finally, we present a self-efficacy training programme, based on existing models, for preventing burnout.

Self-efficacy and the dynamic social cognitive model

Social cognitive theory includes a framework to analyse how people face up to and react to the changes and demands imposed by companies. This theoretical model helps us to understand the role that personal and situational factors play with regard to motivation, self-regulatory processes, performance, commitment and absenteeism in the workplace (Mischel & Shoda, 1995; Bandura, 1997). Social cognitive theory explains human behaviour, focusing on the cognitive and emotional processes which influence how people react to different situations, such as new or complex tasks, which require them to react in a way that is directly linked to the perceived level of occupational stress. Different ways of facing up to situations can unleash either upward or downward spirals, depending on where those people perceive themselves to be in the company hierarchy, on their perceived efficacy to competently carry out the tasks and on their relationship with their colleagues (Bandura, 2006).

Social cognitive theory has shown self-efficacy to be a construct which directly affects other self-regulatory mechanisms, moderates the relationship between other variables and greatly influences behaviour (Bandura & Locke, 2003; Schunk & Meece, 2006). When people feel capable of successfully carrying out an action, they develop the

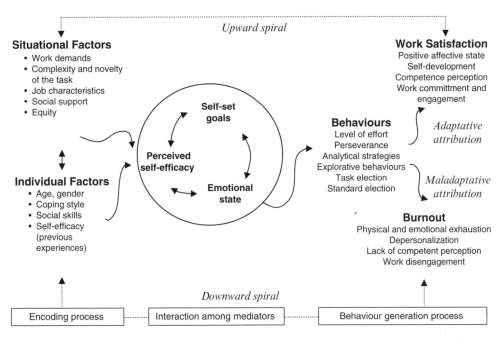

Note: * Proposed to explain the development of burnout versus job satisfaction from personal–situational interaction and the mediating role of self-regulatory mechanisms.

Figure 20.1   Social–cognitive dynamic model*

necessary analytical strategies and, because of this, are more likely to succeed in the task. Various studies have analysed the influence of self-efficacy on performance when we are faced with different issues or in laboratory situations (Holden, 1991; Multon et al., 1991; Stajkovic & Luthans, 1997), although others believe that other conditional variables can play an equally important part (Colquitt et al., 2000; Chen et al., 2001; Judge et al., 2007). But, as previously mentioned, perceived self-efficacy not only plays a central role in explaining behaviour, it also directly influences other self-regulatory mechanisms such as goals, the expectation of results, how difficult we perceive a task to be, our state of mind or the analytical strategies developed to carry out the necessary course of action. That is to say, the perception of self-efficacy influences the social constructs that we develop when we are faced with a certain situation, as well as the goals and expectations that we give ourselves and, finally, the achieved result.

Bandura (1986, 1997) presents self-efficacy as the best cognitive–emotional variable to understand and explain how personal and situational factors influence behaviour. Bandura (1986) defines self-efficacy as the belief (or confidence) in our own capacity to organize and manage the necessary courses of action in order to face certain situations in the immediate future and achieve the desired results (p. 361). In this way, perceptions of self-efficacy influence the goals people set themselves and their emotional reactions to how far they have achieved them. In Figure 20.1, adapted from the models of Mischel and Shoda (1995), we present a theoretical model to understand how the personal and situational factors which lead to job satisfaction and burnout influence behaviour.

In this model, the impact of the situation on behaviour is explained by how individuals perceive and socially construct the situation. The interaction between personal and situational characteristics, such as the novelty or complexity of the task, perceived social support, the relationship with colleagues or the way of facing the situation, influence this encoding process and that is why people differ so much in their perception of a situation. In a study carried out by Saks (1994), we see an example of the moderating effect of self-efficacy in the relationship between the methods used in training and the anxiety caused by learning. Those trainees with low self-efficacy levels experience more anxiety when receiving tutorial training, making a difficult new task, such as learning new technology, seem threatening to a person who does not feel able to carry it out effectively. The way in which people encode situations can affect the emotional reactions they use to overcome them. The perceived properties of the situation activate the self-regulatory mechanisms. Because of this, the goals people set themselves, their perceived self-efficacy and their emotional reactions to the task are all influenced by how the situation is interpreted (Bandura, 1997; Mischel & Shoda, 1995).

Self-efficacy not only guarantees a level of effort and involvement necessary to face threatening and uncertain professional situations, it also provides the necessary motivation to persist in the presence of failure and to face risks and possible mistakes. Those who have a high level of self-efficacy and keep adapting their attributional style (e.g., ascribing success to effort) will develop upward spirals more easily in this process (Lindsey et al., 1995). These spirals are built from our own perception of our capability and self-efficacy determines the level of effort put in and the desire to achieve a high success rate in those goals set when we are faced by the threatening situation. As people experience different situations and receive feedback, they will evaluate their skills, which will allow them to adapt their strategies, their level of effort and their goals, with the aim of anticipating future situations. However, when people feel unable to face threatening situations, downward spirals develop as a result of interpreting the feedback that their own experience has brought. If they are not adaptable when evaluating their attributes, such people will blame themselves for the results, will stop making any effort and will eventually become so depressed that they will abandon the task. Because of this, as we shall see later (see Table 20.1), it is useful to show various strategies which help individuals face the situations they have coded as threatening when making a training programme to prevent burnout.

It has been shown that people's perception of their capability to fulfil the demands of a job influences stress levels and therefore occupational health. Employees with low self-efficacy levels will experience more emotional and physiological stress when they feel that their workload exceeds their capabilities, whereas those with high levels of self-efficacy will not be affected by increased demands on them in the workplace (Jex & Bliese, 1999).

We are aware that people differ in areas of life where feelings of efficacy are developed. Our personal belief in our efficacy to face and manage our social life, our family life, our professional life and our health vary significantly according to these different areas. So, the system of beliefs of efficacy is not a global trait, but a group of beliefs in oneself linked to different functional areas (Bandura, 1986, 1997). Because of this, both the evaluation and the participation programmes to generate self-efficacy evaluations must be linked to a specific area. In this chapter we have chosen to include data collected in the Spanish organizational context which supports the proposed relationship between self-efficacy and burnout.

Self-efficacy and burnout

In recent years, more and more investigators of burnout have looked into the moderate yet systematic role that self-efficacy plays on burnout (Leiter, 1992; Cherniss, 1993; Friedman, 1999, 2003; Brouwers & Tomic, 2000; Evers et al., 2002). In the Spanish context, Grau et al. (2001) found that self-efficacy modulates the relationship between stress and the stressful situation. However, this modulating effect seems to depend on how self-efficacy is used (generally or specifically), on the nature of the cause of the stress (related to the task or social), on the characteristics of the job (resources and demands) and on the types of consequences of stress (burnout, job satisfaction or organizational commitment). Specifically, these authors found that employees with a low level of generalized self-efficacy showed more emotional turmoil when left to work alone; whereas those who had low levels of professional self-efficacy showed higher levels of impersonalization when routine and job incompatibility were high, and lower levels of organizational commitment when they had high levels of job incompatibility. Furthermore, they showed that both general and specific self-efficacy are strong modulators in the relationship between the cause of the stress and the burnout experience. Therefore, if we take these results and put them into the model shown in Figure 20.1, self-efficacy influences how we encode a threatening situation, what self-regulatory strategies are used and what behaviour ensues.

In an educational context, Brouwers and Tomic (2000) examined leadership and the type of relationship between the self-efficacy perceived in the management of a class and the three dimensions of burnout for teachers. These authors found that the self-efficacy used for teaching had a longitudinal effect on impersonalization and a simultaneous effect on personal fulfilment. Management showed the opposite in the case of perceived self-efficacy and emotional exhaustion. On the other hand, Evers et al. (2002) found that self-efficacy beliefs were significantly and negatively related to impersonalization and emotional exhaustion, but significantly and positively related to personal fulfilment. More recently, Skaalvik and Skaalvik (2007) have found similar results by working with a multidimensional educational self-efficacy scale, comprising six interrelated scales, each dealing with a different educational field: instruction, adaptation to students' needs, student motivation, maintaining discipline, colleague cooperation and dealing with change. These authors point out a strong relationship between each of the six dimensions and the three components of burnout (the values of Cronbach's alpha correlation fall between -0.22 and -0.39).

In the studies carried out using a multifaceted approach to the study of the relationship between self-efficacy and burnout in teachers, Friedman (2003) observed differences between the levels of efficacy experienced in the classroom and those experienced during preparation time. Friedman maintains that teachers reported a higher level of efficacy in the classroom than in relation to organization. He explains this by pointing out that during the process of teacher training in his native country (Israel), more emphasis is put on performance in the classroom than performance in the school as an organization. Furthermore, as in previous studies, Friedman found a negative relationship between self-efficacy and burnout. However, given the cyclical nature of self-efficacy, we cannot

---

BOX 20.1   SCALE OF SELF-EFFICACY WHEN FACING
COMPLEX SITUATIONS IN AN ORGANIZATIONAL
CONTEXT

Keeping in mind your daily job, think of the most challenging situation you have
had to deal with in the past week (e.g., making a complicated decision). Now, if
a similar situation were to arise in the future, you can:

1. Find a way to solve the problem, even if someone (e.g., the director) objects.
2. Solve the problems that arise if you put enough effort in (e.g., time pressure)
3. Continue with what you had planned to do despite the setbacks (e.g., being
   the only person who believes in the solution).
4. Cope capably with unexpected events (e.g., team members' abandonment).
5. Find the necessary resources to overcome unexpected problems (e.g., lack
   of a budget).
6. Keep calm and confident when encountering difficulties (e.g., when a
   mistake has been made).
7. Cope with situations which could be risky for you or your colleagues (e.g.,
   reacting to an accident).
8. Find an acceptable alternative when faced with a difficult situation (e.g.,
   sending economic or material resources to just one beneficiary).

---

determine whether this relationship is unidirectional, that is, whether the level of self-efficacy causes burnout or whether burnout affects the level of self-efficacy. Basing our theory on reciprocal natural law, self-efficacy can act both as a dependent and as an independent variable. In this way, Friedman (2000) suggested that burnout is a symptom of a feeling of professional failure, but in the presence of repeated professional failures and high levels of burnout, it can also diminish perceived professional efficacy (Bandura, 1997). The relationship between the variables is reciprocal (Bandura, 2006), so personal self-efficacy determines how a person perceives professional difficulties, but also the presence of high levels of professional burnout can cause a lack of confidence in our own capability to face complex situations.

Self-efficacy to face difficult situations
Various studies (Bandura, 1997; Jex & Bliese, 1999) have shown that the moderating effect of self-efficacy on behaviour is determined by the generality–specificity of the measurement used. Note that Bandura (2006) recommends the creation of self-efficacy scales specific to the task they are to explain. In this section we have included data collected in the Spanish organizational context which supports the proposed relationship between self-efficacy and burnout. We have created a self-efficacy scale to face complex organizational contexts using eight items reflecting day-to-day situations which require the development of complex strategies in order to solve them (see Box 20.1). We applied the scale

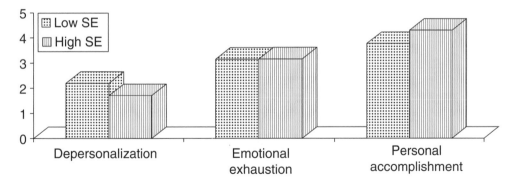

Note: Test group of service-industry employees.

Figure 20.2   Relationship between self-efficacy and the dimensions of burnout

to a group of 326 service-industry employees, 60% male and 40% female, of the following age categories: 35.3% between 18 and 29, 36.8% between 30 and 39, 19.6% between 40 and 49, and the rest aged 50 and above. More than 53% of the test group have held a medium responsibility role for over two years. None of the aforementioned variables was deemed to be significant in the levels of self-efficacy perceived by the workers.

The proposed scale has a suitable psychometric quality. To prove this, we carried out a factor analysis with a Varimax rotation, and we saw that the eight items show a 59% variation. Furthermore, the eight items come together in one factor presenting values which oscillate between 0.812 and 0.647. The reliability of the scale was high ($\alpha = 0.90$).

Using an abbreviated version of the Maslach Burnout Inventory Scale (see Figure 20.2) (Maslach et al., 1996), we find that the level of perceived self-efficacy is significantly and negatively related to the level of impersonalization experienced ($F_{(1,181)} = 13.20$, $p < 0.001$, $\eta^2 = 0.07$) and positively related to the level of personal fulfilment experienced by the workers ($F_{(1,182)} = 25.14$, $p < 0.001$, $\eta^2 = 0.12$). Our data do not show any relationship between self-efficacy and emotional weakening ($F_{(1,397)} = 0.001$, n.s., $\eta^2 = 0.00$).

On the other hand (see Figure 20.3), those employees who have greater self-efficacy to face complex situations show more satisfaction in both support received ($F_{(1,182)} = 6.14$, $p < 0.001$, $\eta^2 = 0.03$) and development opportunities ($F_{(1,182)} = 4.12$, $p < 0.05$, $\eta^2 = 0.02$). This relationship is also reflected in the overall level of job satisfaction ($F_{(1,182)} = 15.38$, $p < 0.001$, $\eta^2 = 0.08$).

There are still some aspects that need clarifying with regard to the relationship between self-efficacy beliefs and burnout. The meta-analysis carried out by Guertin and Courcy (1999) to analyse the relationship between self-efficacy and the concept of occupational adaptation and stress, found only a moderate relationship between self-efficacy and stress, and the results indicated that most of the differences between the two studies were due to the presence of moderators, for example, the perception of support, strategies of facing problems, or the perception of equity. Halbesleben (2006) carried out a meta-analysis in which there is no difference in the role that social support plays in the three dimensions of burnout. Differences do appear, however, when we specify whether the social support comes from the working environment or not. When we consider social

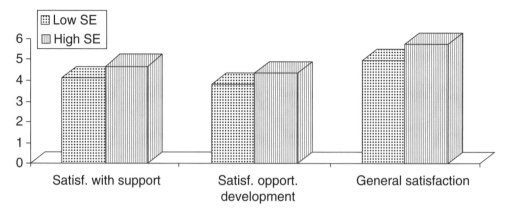

Note: Test group of service-industry employees.

Figure 20.3 Relationship between self-efficacy and different dimensions of organizational satisfaction

support from work, its influence is greater on emotional exhaustion that on the other dimensions.

The perception of lack of support from colleagues and managers has a significant effect on self-efficacy beliefs in asking for support and predicting the level of burnout. Furthermore, social support reduces the perception of overwork and 'mobbing' which can cause stress and burnout. Social support and self-efficacy act as moderators in the relationship between these variables (Van Dick & Wagner, 2001), a fact also corroborated by our studies. Those employees who have a higher self-efficacy, experience lower levels of mobbing compared to their colleagues ($F_{(1,171)} = 4.10$, $p < 0.05$, $\eta^2 = 0.02$). The level of burnout and mobbing experienced influence the way in which workers perceive the lack of support from their colleagues (Brouwers et al., 2001) and self-efficacy acts as a moderator in this relationship. Continuing this discussion, Halbesleben and Bowler (2007) present motivation as a moderator in the relationship between emotional exhaustion and performance.

Participation programmes to generate perceptions of efficacy
When introducing the concept of self-efficacy, Bandura (1986) shows the four sources from which we can generate perceptions about capability in training programmes. Specifically, Bandura shows that it is necessary to combine three elements in these programmes: first, we must promote the basic skills that are essential to the job by establishing a series of rules and operational strategies via an *instructive model* training programme; second, in order that all of the trainees learn to judge their own capabilities, they should use *simulation practice* related to their actual job, but where they can develop more confidence in their capabilities; finally, they should present day-to-day work situations in which they can practise and *transfer the skills learned* which helps increase their perception of achievement and control over their capabilities.

One of the most popular training programmes for generating self-efficacy in the workplace was developed by Latham and Saari in 1979. This training programme has three stages, based first on the use of a model to show supervisors or section managers the interpersonal skills necessary to carry out their job efficiently. It is a leadership exercise used to influence the morale and efficacy of the team in order to increase company productivity. To develop the programme, Latham and Saari highlight the influencing skills associated with the job which supervisors can use when dealing with their staff in order to generate better motivation. They then show a video of a model facing and resolving the day-to-day situations of a supervisor's job. Specifically, the model uses different strategies to motivate the staff, and the supervisors are shown how to use feedback, the repercussions that can be caused, which goals to establish and how to cope with problematic absenteeism or resistance to change. Subsequently, they present scenes of real-life behaviour so that the supervisors can discuss which working methods are the most useful; they carry out role playing so that the supervisors can confer and prove that they are capable of dealing with day-to-day situations, receiving specific feedback which helps them to improve their skills. Finally, to aid the transfer of learned skills to their working environment, the supervisors are instructed to use the skills they have learned on the course for one working week in their normal job. After the week, they meet up to discuss the difficulties they encountered when putting the skills into practice and also the results they had achieved. In order to solve any possible problems, the supervisors are re-trained using an instructive model on how to deal with complex situations. To monitor the effect of the training programme, Latham and Saari compared the effectiveness of those supervisors who had received training and those who had not. They carried out the evaluation in two phases: immediately after the training and one year after undergoing the programme. The results showed that the training programme had a positive effect both on the morale of the teams and on the productivity achieved. The training programme has also been applied to other aspects of work, and its effects have been noticed both in the improvement of decision-making and problem-solving skills and in the levels of absenteeism and rotation.

Returning to the effect of self-efficacy on the reduction of burnout, Bandura (2000) points out that this type of training programme can be used for various applications, not only to improve performance. For example, it could be used to help reduce the anxiety associated with stressful situations or phobias which develop when we are facing threatening situations, since people tend to avoid such situations and this can lead to them being out of touch with the reality of their job. On the other hand, the use of model-based and guided-learning training has a positive and rapid effect on the way people face those situations that are perceived as threatening. People are trained in developing confrontational strategies which allow them to use their own experience to convince themselves that they are capable of controlling potential threats. For this training to be useful, all of the situations in which people doubt their ability to cope must be covered.

Another training programme for developing organizational self-efficacy was introduced by Gist et al. (1990). This is a guided-model training programme for negotiation skills. This programme includes a module on the development of capabilities for facing difficulties. Following a similar three-phase strategy as the previous programme, Gist et al. suggest that the final phase should encourage workers to anticipate all of the situations which could potentially cause them stress, to think of ways to overcome them, to evaluate the efficacy of the strategies used to face the situations, and to call on their internal resources to persevere and not give up. This cognitive training strategy seeks to teach people how to react to negative results and to anticipate the strategies that will allow them to maintain their level of effort.

Bandura (2000) comments that there are an increasing number of programmes that use guided-model strategies, but most of them fail because they do not develop the third phase of generating self-efficacy and the anticipation of strategies that will help people face up to bad results or failures in a real-life context.

Taking into account the training programmes mentioned, we have adapted the three-phase training programme developed by Latham and Saari (1979) and applied it to a stressful work situation:

1. *Instructive model*   First, the programme should show a model efficiently facing those threatening activities so as to help trainees overcome them. In order to do this, we must first make a list of the tasks that intimidate people and divide them into sub-tasks so that they can be tackled in smaller steps. The model should show how to face these situations step by step until the trainees manage to complete them success-fully. People develop their sense of self-efficacy by watching and identifying with the model, which deals with what the trainee sees as threatening. In this case it is essential that the trainee identifies with the model in order to generate self-efficacy, since this process is based on social comparison. As we saw in Figure 20.1, the social construc-tion that is caused by the situation being encoded as threatening can be rebuilt when the person sees that certain strategies are successful.

2. *Development of past experiences in a simulation and/or through role-playing*   Bandura (2000) shows that another good way to overcome anxiety is to carry out threaten-ing tasks for only a short period. This method could be used as the second step of the programme, as in Latham and Saari (1979). As people begin to feel more sure of themselves and confident in the task, the amount of time spent on the task can be increased. The success of this method stems from the fact that people experience for themselves that they are capable of dealing with and overcoming the situations that they once considered as threatening, and this helps them develop a strong sense of self-efficacy.

3. *Transferring skills into a real-life context*   In the final phase of the programme it is important to select those activities or tasks that give trainees the opportunity to put into practice the newly-learned strategies and therefore realize that they are capable of dealing with stressful situations, that is, to generalize their perception of their day-to-day self-efficacy. This last phase is where the perceived self-efficacy is rein-forced and the meaning of the increase in excitement or adrenaline that certain situ-ations provoke is understood and reconstructed.

As we have seen, a three-phase training programme such as that in Table 20.1 is an efficient way to reduce or prevent the development of chronic occupational stress in the workplace. In this programme we use four sources to generate self-efficacy in each of the phases. The programme is based on confrontational skills training, protection against stress and the support of the trainers and the team. In this training programme, the sources of self-efficacy which feature in the process are clearly identified so as to reduce perceived capabilities and to strengthen perceived self-efficacy: own experience, vicarious experience, persuasion and physiological states.

Table 20.1   Template for a proposed training programme to prevent burnout

Strategies	Examples	Sources of self-efficacy
Phase 1 Instructive Model		
A. Make a list of: • the specific skills needed for your job	*Motivate colleagues or influence management decisions*	Interpreting the physiological symptoms experienced when faced with stressful situations
• the situations you see as threatening	*Disagreement/conflict with colleagues or lack of equity in the sharing out of jobs*	The use of knowledge gained from past stressful experiences (recoding)
B. Divide those skills into subtasks	*A subtask to motivate colleagues would be to organize tasks according to the interests and strengths of the individual*	The use of your own and others' experiences in order to succeed in your profession
C. Presentation of a model way in which to face these situations (subtasks), using different strategies, successfully resolving the situations	*Record some of your colleagues' presentations, watch them back and analyse the strategies they have used to motivate their subordinates*	Observing and modelling yourself on others (identification and generation of an evaluation of the capabilities you possess which are similar to those of the model): 'If he can do it, so can I' Learning how the model persuades using messages or the verbalization of his/her strategies
Phase 2 Development of Past Experiences in a Simulation and/or through Role Playing		
A. Present scenes showing real-life situations in order to discuss the most useful working methods with which to resolve them	*Present a real case of an underperforming employee before the group and discuss how you would deal with it* *Swap/exchange the roles of boss and subordinate among the course participants in order to practise the different strategies covered/learned*	Learning how to resolve problems and develop skills by experiencing and overcoming situations similar to those which you face at work
B. Use role-playing techniques		

Table 20.1   (continued)

Strategies	Examples	Sources of self-efficacy
Phase 3 Transferring Skills into a Real-Life Context		
A. Give instructions to use the skills learned during their normal working week	*Keep a diary of all situations faced, along with the strategies to be used and note down any achievements or difficulties encountered*	Generalization of real-life self-efficacy evaluation using the four sources: your own experience, observation, persuasion, and the interpretation of physiological symptoms
B. Evaluation of the difficulties encountered and achievements made in practice	*Personal evaluation of the results achieved by following the strategies and analysis of possible alternatives*	
C. Anticipation of strategies to be used to face future problems	*Note down any different stressful situations experienced by your colleagues along with the strategies used to overcome them*	

Conclusions

Personal experience and the structure, content and patterns of behaviour followed in past successes and failures are one of the most important sources when generating individual, group or collective judgements of capability (Pajares, 1997; Bong & Skaalvik, 2003). According to Jonge and Dormann (2006), internal resources are more powerful at combating stress factors than the corresponding external resources. For these internal resources, burnout could be an emotional response to an emotionally stressful task. Because of this, we strongly believe in the need to generate perceptions of self-efficacy in the individual in order to deal with stressful situations.

The learning process we go through when we face difficult and demanding tasks partly depends on the meaning feedback brings to us. In this way, when facing a positive result, people with a high perceived self-efficacy will tend to attribute this good result to their capability (stable internal attribution), whereas those with low self-efficacy would put it down to luck (unstable external attribution), that is, an attribution over which they have no control, leaving their future in the hands of fate. On the other hand, when facing an unsatisfactory or negative result, for example when looking for work, people with high self-efficacy will tend to make attributions based on effort (unstable internal attribution), which will not reduce their perception and will give them the opportunity to make more of an effort in the future, and therefore achieve their desired goals. Those who have a low perception of their self-efficacy, however, will attribute this result to their lack of capability (stable internal attribution), which will further lower their perception of self-efficacy. Once again we find ourselves with an illustration of the spirals which are formed in the relationship between self-efficacy and performance and proof of the implications that these self-fulfilled prophecies have. Because of this, when carrying out training courses for the prevention of burnout, we must focus on the processes of attribution/giving credit made when we receive feedback on our performance.

Following on from this, it is useful to emphasize that some authors have mentioned the negative effects that self-efficacy can have on behaviour (Vancouver et al., 2001; Vancouver & Kendall, 2006), meaning that when perceived self-efficacy is too high for their capabilities, they will set themselves goals that are too ambitious and will not get satisfactory results. Contrary to this, Bandura and Locke (2003) claim that these unreal expectations of capability do not have any negative effect on self-efficacy, and in fact are signs that such people do not correctly interpret the information that the results of their performance brings, and they therefore generate incorrect self-efficacy perceptions. Another problem could be that people misinterpret the task they must face. This is why we have previously stressed how important it is that people correctly interpret the information given in their performance feedback so as to choose those tasks that correspond to their level of capability, as well as the level of effort required in order to carry out the tasks successfully.

Learning by using a model is one of the most effective training methods. On a practical level, when using participation to face threatening situations and prevent burnout, it is necessary for people who have similar characteristics to those we are trying to emulate to give us their view on the strategies they use, and what led them to recode those situations they once thought of as threatening. In the training programme successfully used by Eden and Aviram (1993), they use role-playing games as well as videos showing people successfully carrying out the tasks, so that trainees will learn to perceive self-efficacy in practice, not just in theory.

Some training programmes focus on using social support to motivate and show trust in the person's ability to deal successfully with the situation. It is important that the person acting as persuader should be seen to be an expert if he/she is to be effective. There must also be a level of consensus between the two parties in order to help those who are doubtful of their capabilities to overcome the threatening situation. Finally, they must both have a similar level of experience in the task. Often, the person who is trying to persuade the trainees of the strategies they should use is much more familiar with the task, and therefore it is difficult for the less-experienced trainee to emulate such behaviour.

The state of mind experienced when faced with a certain situation, stemming from physiological or psychological states such as excitement, inhibition, apathy, anxiety and so on can significantly affect the perceived self-efficacy. Although it is normal to suffer certain physiological symptoms such as palpitations, sweating or stammering when faced with a stressful situation, such as an assessment meeting with one's boss, we also know that how we interpret our anxiety can lead us to face the situation either feeling confident in our abilities, or leaving the assessment feeling weak, impotent and insecure. In the first case, the anxiety generated activates our levels of arousal/adrenaline which makes us more open/ready to receive information in this context, whereas in the second case the level of anxiety is interpreted as an indicator of our insecurity to be able to face this situation successfully.

In conclusion, the social cognitive model is the theoretical framework from which we can explain how perceived efficacy can significantly affect performance when dealing with threatening situations, both directly and indirectly via the increase in persistence and effort. In this way, self-efficacy perceptions play an important role in explaining persistence in the face of failure and in transferring or generating similar perceptions to other tasks. When faced with the continuous changes brought about in the workplace, companies require the development of training programmes to prevent the development of burnout.

References

Bandura, A. (1986), *Social Foundations of Thought and Action: A Social Cognitive Theory*, Englewood Cliffs, NJ: Prentice-Hall.
Bandura, A. (1997), *Self-efficacy: The Exercise of Control*, New York: Freeman.
Bandura, A. (2000), 'Cultivate self-efficacy for personal and organizational effectiveness', in E.A. Locke (ed.), *Handbook of Principles of Organizational Behavior*, Oxford: Blackwell, pp. 120–36.
Bandura, A. (2006), 'Guide for constructing self-efficacy scales', in F. Pajares & T. Urdan (eds), *Adolescence and Education, Volume 4: Self-efficacy Beliefs of Adolescents*, Greenwich, CT: Information Age Publishing, pp. 307–37.
Bandura, A. & Locke, E.A. (2003), 'Negative self-efficacy and goal effects revisited', *Journal of Applied Psychology*, **88**, 87–99.
Bong, M. & Skaalvik, E.M. (2003), 'Academic self-concept and self-efficacy: how different are they really?', *Educational Psychology Review*, **15**, 1–40.
Brouwers, A. & Tomic, W. (2000), 'A longitudinal study of teacher burnout and perceived self-efficacy in classroom management', *Teaching and Teacher Education*, **16**, 239–53.
Brouwers, A., Evers, W. & Tomic, W. (2001), 'Self-efficacy in eliciting social support and burnout among secondary-school teachers', *Journal of Applied Social Psychology*, **31**, 1474–91.
Chen, G., Casper, W.J. & Cortina, J.M. (2001), 'The roles of self-efficacy and task complexity in the relationships among cognitive ability, conscientiousness, and task performance: a meta-analytic examination', *Human Performance*, **14**, 209–30.
Cherniss, C. (1993), 'Role of professional self-efficacy in the etiology and amelioration of burnout', in W.B. Shaufeli, C. Maslach & T. Marek (eds), *Professional Burnout: Recent Developments in Theory and Research*, Washington, DC: Taylor & Francis, pp. 135–49.
Colquitt, J.A., Lepine, J.A. & Noe, R.A. (2000), 'Toward an integrative theory of training motivation: a meta-analytic path analysis of 20 years of research', *Journal of Applied Psychology*, **58**, 678–707.
Eden, D. & Aviram, A. (1993), 'Self-efficacy training to speed reemployment: helping people to help themselves', *Journal of Applied Psychology*, **78**, 352–60.
Evers, W.J., Brouwers, A. & Tomic, W. (2002), 'Burnout and self-efficacy: a study of teachers' beliefs when implementing an innovative educational system in the Netherlands', *British Journal of Educational Psychology*, **72**, 227–44.
Friedman, I.A. (1999), 'Turning our schools into a healthier workplace: bridging between professional self-efficacy and professional demands', in R. Vandenberghe & A.M. Huberman (eds), *Understanding and Preventing Teacher Burnout*, Cambridge: Cambridge University Press, pp. 166–75.
Friedman, I.A. (2000), 'Burnout in teachers: shattered dreams of impeccable professional performance', *Journal of Clinical Psychology*, **56**, 595–606.
Friedman, I.A. (2003), 'Self-efficacy and burnout in teaching: the importance of interpersonal relations efficacy', *Social Psychology of Education*, **6**, 191–215.
Gist, M.E., Bavetta, A.G. & Stevens, C.K. (1990), 'Transfer training method: its influence on skill generalization, skill repetition, and performance level', *Personnel Psychology*, **43**, 501–23.
Grau, R., Salanova, M. & Peiró, J.M. (2001), 'Moderator effects of self-efficacy on occupational stress', *Psychology in Spain*, **5**, 63–74.
Guertin, C. & Courcy, F. (1999), 'Self-efficacy, work adaptation and occupational stress: two meta analyses', *Science et Comportement*, **28**, 19–38.
Halbesleben, J.R.B. (2006), 'Sources of social support and burnout: a meta-analytic test of the conservation of resources model', *Journal of Applied Behavioral Science*, **42**, 244–66.
Halbesleben, J.R.B. & Bowler, W.M. (2007), 'Emotional exhaustion and job performance: the mediating role of motivation', *Journal of Applied Psychology*, **92**, 93–106.
Holden, G. (1991), 'The relationship of self-efficacy appraisals to subsequent health related outcomes: a meta-analysis', *Social Work in Health Care*, **16**, 53–93.
Jex, S.M. & Bliese, P.D. (1999), 'Efficacy beliefs as a moderator of the impact of work-related stressors: a multilevel study', *Journal of Applied Psychology*, **84**, 349–61.
Jonge, J. de & Dormann, C. (2006), 'Stressors, resources, and strain at work: a longitudinal test of the triple-match principle', *Journal of Applied Psychology*, **91**, 1359–74.

Judge, T.A., Jackson, C.L., Shaw, J.C., Scott, B.A. & Rich, B.L. (2007), 'Is the effect of self-efficacy on job/task performance an epiphenomenon?', *Journal of Applied Psychology*, **92**, 107–27.

Latham, G.P. & Saari, L.M. (1979), 'Application of social learning theory to training supervisors through behavioral modeling', *Journal of Applied Psychology*, **64**, 239–46.

Leiter, M.P. (1992), 'Burnout as a crisis in self-efficacy: conceptual and practical implications', *Work and Stress*, **6**, 107–15.

Lindsey, D.H., Brass, D.J. & Thomas, J.B. (1995), 'Efficacy–performance spirals: a multilevel perspective', *Academy of Management Review*, **20**, 645–78.

Maslach, C., Jackson, S.E. & Leiter, M. (1996), *Maslach Burnout Inventory: Manual*, 3rd edn, Palo Alto, CA: Consulting Psychologists Press.

Mischel, W. & Shoda, Y. (1995), 'A cognitive-affective system theory of personality: reconceptualizing situations, dispositions, dynamics, and invariance in personality structure', *Psychological Review*, **102**, 246–68.

Multon, K.D., Brown, S.D. & Lent, R.W. (1991), 'Relation of self-efficacy beliefs to academic outcomes: a meta-analytic investigation', *Journal of Counseling Psychology*, **38**, 30–38.

Pajares, F. (1997), 'Currents directions in self-efficacy research', in M. Maehr & P. Pintrich (eds), *Advances in Motivation and Achievement*, Greenwich, CT: JAI Press, pp. 1–49.

Saks, A.M. (1994), 'Moderating effects of self-efficacy for the relationship between training method and anxiety and stress reactions of newcomers', *Journal of Organizational Behavior*, **15**, 639–54.

Schunk D.H. & Meece, J. (2006), *Student Perceptions in the Classroom: Causes and Consequences*, Hillsdale, NJ: Lawrence Erlbaum.

Skaalvik, E.M. & Skaalvik, S. (2007), 'Dimensions of teacher self-efficacy and relations with strain factors, perceived collective teacher efficacy, and teacher burnout', *Journal of Educational Psychology*, **99**, 611–25.

Stajkovic, A.D. & Luthans, F. (1997), 'A meta-analysis of the effects of organizational behavior modification on task performance, 1975–95', *Academy of Management Journal*, **40**, 1122–49.

Van Dick, R. & Wagner, U. (2001), 'Stress and strain in teaching: a structural equation approach', *British Psychological Society*, **71**, 243–59.

Vancouver, J.B. & Kendall, L.N. (2006), 'When self-efficacy negatively relates to motivation and performance in a learning context', *Journal of Applied Psychology*, **91**, 1146–53.

Vancouver, J.B., Thompson, C.M. & Williams, A.A. (2001), 'The changing signs in the relationships between self-efficacy, personal goals and performance', *Journal of Applied Psychology*, **86**, 605–20.

21 The relationship between unfairness, bullying, stress and health problems in organizations

Herman Steensma

Introduction

In this chapter attention will be paid to the relationship between injustice, bullying, stress and burnout. It will be shown that theories of organizational stress and injustice share many similarities. The injustice stress theory is worked out and empirical evidence will be presented. The chapter then focuses on aggression, and particularly on bullying. The role of weak and dysfunctional leadership in the development of bullying and burnout will be explained. Finally, the chapter will conclude with suggestions for how justice theories may be used to reduce stress.

Stress

Stress is a rather fuzzy concept that is defined in different ways by different authors. However, although authors differ in several respects, they also share a lot of common ground. Most authors share the idea of stress as a stimulus–organism–response model, and almost all authors emphasize the existence of a stress cycle (see, e.g., French et al., 1982; Lazarus & Folkman, 1984; Edwards, 1992). This stress cycle has the following form. People sense their environment. The perceived environment is compared with a criterion (or, actually, several environmental characteristics are compared with several reference criteria). If there is a discrepancy or 'gap' between the perceived characteristic and the criterion value, the sensing person feels stress. If the discrepancy is seen as important, the stress will be rather large, and the larger the gap and the stress, the more the sensing person will try to reduce the discrepancy. Attempts to change the gap between perceived environment and criterion value will have consequences for the person. These consequences may be desired – that is, the discrepancy is successfully reduced – but sometimes there are consequences that were not intended. The new situation is then sensed again, and a new chain of events follows.

This is the general basic framework of the stress cycle, on which many authors elaborate. Most social scientists adhere to a stress model in which a distinction is made between stressors, stress and strains. Stressors are defined as the objective and/or the perceived environmental characteristics or 'stimuli'. In organizations, for example, stressors may be a high workload, ambiguous roles, monotonous jobs; dirt and noise; unpleasant social relationships; low pay, lack of promotion opportunities; and so on. If these stressors and (job) demands exceed the adaptive resources of the individual, an unpleasant state will be experienced, that is, 'stress'. The stress leads to *strains*, and there are several possibilities, that is, strains are behavioral, physiological, or psychological responses. Examples of such responses are alcohol consumption and smoking; higher blood pressure and more heart activity; dissatisfaction and low motivation. In the long run, strains can cause sickness, and the accumulation of stress may cause burnout (in particular, emotional exhaustion and depersonalization) and sickness absenteeism of workers. However, the relationship between stressors and strains, and between strains and long-term effects, may be moderated by moderator variables such as personality differences (for example, type A or type B personality; see Friedman & Rosenman, 1974), and social support by significant others, for example, in organizations by colleagues and/or supervisors. It should be noted here that sometimes lack of social support is seen as a direct stressor, too. The stress model described here and applied to the situation in organizations is the 'Michigan model', and it integrates earlier models developed by Kahn (1970) and French and Caplan (1972). In a refined version of this model, known as the person–environment (P–E) fit model, work stress is defined as a 'misfit' between environmental factors and resources, and individual needs and abilities (French et al., 1981).

Theories of stress in organizations can be clustered in two categories, based on different assumptions about human nature. In the *reactive* models, people are seen as rather passive, and stress 'happens to people'. In the *coping* models, persons are seen as willing, and often very able, to cope with stressful situations. Coping can take several forms, for example problem-focused coping, in which active attempts are made to solve problems by altering the relationship between the person and the environment. Coping efforts may also take the form of avoidance, or of emotion-focused coping. Coping ceases when the problems have been solved, or the emotions have been regulated satisfactorily. In cases of successful coping, general well-being may result; but if coping fails, negative consequences are to be expected. Lazarus and Folkman (1984) present a dual appraisal model of stress and coping. In a primary appraisal process, the threat value of an event is assessed. If the event is threatening, a secondary appraisal process will evaluate the options for coping with the threat, and a coping method will be selected. This model is frequently used to describe the coping efforts of workers, trying to improve their 'fit' into the environment.

Justice

There are two general classes of justice theories in social and organizational psychology. In *distributive* justice, the emphasis is on the fairness of outcomes and of allocation judgments. *Procedural* justice theories emphasize the fairness of the decision-making procedures and some other aspects of social process.

Distributive justice theories differ in terms of what is seen as the most important principle of justice. Equity theory (Adams, 1965) is probably the best-known theory of distributive justice. The focus in equity theory is on the proportionality of inputs and outcomes. Inequity exists for people whenever they perceive that the ratio of their outcomes to inputs and the ratio of a comparison other's outcomes to a comparison other's inputs are unequal. Inequity results for people not only when they are relatively underpaid, but also when they are relatively overpaid. However, underpayment is generally seen as more unpleasant than overpayment. The presence of inequity in a person creates an unpleasant tension, proportional to the magnitude of inequity present. This tension motivates the person to eliminate or reduce it. Therefore, the presence of inequity will motivate people to restore equity or reduce inequity. The proportionality principle may be applied to compare own outcome–input ratios with the outcome–input ratio of a comparison other ('own equity'). It is also possible to compare the present ratio with an internal standard, based on outcomes received in the past for inputs, invested in the past. Later distributive

---

BOX 21.1 ASPECTS OF PROCEDURAL AND INTERACTIONAL JUSTICE

- Decision control (influence on outcomes)
- Process control; voice (opportunity to give opinion and to present evidence)
- Neutrality (lack of bias; honesty)
- Trust (authority can be trusted)
- Standing (respect for position of person in group; status recognition)
- Consistency rule (procedures are the same for different persons, and consistent over time)
- Bias suppression (including suppression of personal self-interest)
- Accuracy (decisions should be based on accurate information)
- Correctability (existence of methods for modifying decisions)
- Representativeness rule (take into account the concerns and viewpoints of persons and groups affected by the decision)
- Ethicality rule (use ethical principles)
- High quality of interaction (treat all persons well)
- Information (supply adequate and correct information to all persons involved)

---

justice researchers added other distributive justice principles. The equality principle states that equality of outcomes should exist across the group. A third principle suggests that a fair distribution is reached by allocating outcomes according to 'need'. For a more thorough discussion, see Deutsch (1975).

Procedural justice focuses on the methods, the procedures by which outcomes (tasks, money, social outcomes and rewards in general) are distributed. Perceptions of fair procedures may be influenced by several aspects. Interactional justice is the quality of the interpersonal treatment people receive during the enactment of organizational procedures (Bies & Moag, 1986). Frequently, interactional justice is seen as a subset of norms and rules of procedural justice. The main criteria of procedural and interactional justice are summarized in Box 21.1, which is based on the studies by Thibaut and Walker (1975), Leventhal et al. (1980), Bies and Moag (1986), Greenberg (1986), and Tyler and Lind (1992).

All justice theories share the assumption that injustice is unpleasant and that it creates distress. Therefore, people strive for fairness. Fairness is supposed to have positive effects on the attitudes and behaviors of the persons involved. Most authors on justice in organizations mention one or more of the following positive effects of fairness: job satisfaction; motivation; perceived legitimacy of authority; and loyalty and commitment to the authority and to the group or organization.

Moderator variables: personality factors
Moderator variables may affect the strength of the link between objective characteristics and perceived (in)justice, and the link between perceived (in)justice and people's attitudes and behaviors. For instance, Greenberg (1979) studied the relation between

the Protestant work ethic, reward allocation and fairness of equity inputs. Koper et al. (1993) studied the role that self-esteem plays in situations where procedural fairness is important. Self-esteem as a trait moderated the relation between injustice and reactions to injustice. Tornow (1971) introduced the concept of input–outcome orientation, that is, the inclination to perceive job elements as inputs or outcomes. The more input oriented a worker is, the more (s)he perceives that (s)he is underrewarded. The personality factor that received by far the most attention of justice researchers is the 'just world belief' (JWB), the belief that the fate of people corresponds to what they 'deserve' (Lerner & Simmons, 1966; Lerner, 1980). Since those with a strong JWB are inclined to see the world as just, they will 'see' more justice in organizations than will be seen by those with a weak JWB.

Moderators: cross-cultural influences
Culture influences powerfully the norms, expectations, intentions and behaviors of people. Therefore, it seems only logical that culture also affects the perceptions of what is (un)fair, and the reactions to unfairness. But what are the relevant aspects of culture in the context of injustice perceptions? Most researchers examining cultural differences use the categorization of cultural value dimensions developed by Hofstede (1980). Briefly, these dimensions are characterized as individualism–collectivism, uncertainty avoidance (tolerance for ambiguity), power distance (inequality of power and influence), and masculinity–femininity (striving for rationality versus an emphasis on social relationships). Often, a fifth dimension is added: time perspective (long-term or future-oriented versus short-term orientation).

Some research has studied the effects of cultural differences on perceptions of, and reactions to, injustice. Most studies focused on distributive justice, and particularly on reward allocation. These studies indicate the existence of some differences in preference for distributive justice norms: in individualistic countries equity tends to be preferred, whereas in collectivistic countries equality and need are emphasized. However, contextual factors *within* a country are often more important determinants of rule preferences (see McFarlin & Sweeney, 2001). As for procedural justice, Lind et al. (1997) suggest that in countries where power distance is large, people are particularly concerned about relational aspects of fairness. 'Voice' seems to be more important in cultures characterized by individualism and low power distance, and cultural dimensions are important determinants of the role of procedural justice rules in personnel selection (see the review by McFarlin & Sweeney, 2001).

Apparently, different cultural dimensions affect the salience of justice rules. Therefore, managers should pay special attention to the applications of justice rules that are seen as important in their national culture.

A general justice model
It is not possible to give a complete overview of all justice theories and all justice research. But all the important elements have been discussed, and by combining these elements a general model of justice can be built (see Figure 21.1). In the box of moderator variables, goals and (prior) outcomes have been added to the list. In the box of effects, a section is added with effects that play a prominent role in the recently developed injustice stress theory.

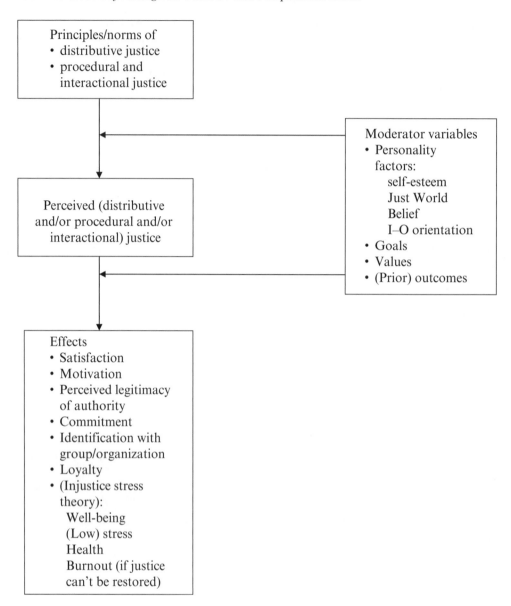

Figure 21.1   A general model of justice

Injustice stress theory

Deviations from justice norms create distress, and people try to remove the distress by reducing the injustice. Note the similarity with the stress cycle that has been described and with the coping models of stress. The discrepancy between perceptions and criteria, the importance of these discrepancies, and the 'coping efforts' to reduce the stress and the discrepancies are core elements in both the general justice and the stress models. Stress and injustice have structural as well as substantive properties in common. Vermunt and

Steensma combined notions from stress theory and the general justice model in their injustice stress theory (Steensma, 1999; Vermunt & Steensma, 2001, 2003, 2005). This theory is useful to explain the relation between injustice, dissatisfaction, stress, health problems and burnout in organizations. Vermunt and Steensma apply the Lazarus and Folkman model of psychological stress. They argue that a distributive or procedural injustice will be evaluated as a threat only if additional information gives reasons to perceive it this way. Otherwise, it may be evaluated as a challenge or as irrelevant. If, however, the combined injustice is evaluated as a threat, the second appraisal process will be triggered in which the available resources and options are evaluated to cope with the threat. The second appraisal process leads to the selection of coping strategies. Failure to cope effectively may, in the long run, lead to negative consequences for health, to burnout, and to sickness absenteeism. Whether injustice will be felt depends, in this model as in the general justice model, not only on the objective and subjective, perceived characteristics of environmental stimuli, but also on the effects of moderator variables.

In the injustice stress theory special attention is paid to the role of the superior, in particular to the 'authority' who is supervising the workers. These managers allocate outcomes (rewards, but also tasks) to the workers, apply procedures, and have social interactions with the workers which may or may not meet the criteria of interactional justice. The special attention to the role of managers, the inclusion of all three forms of (in)justice (procedural, interactional, distributive) and the relatively sharp focus on the effects of possible moderator variables differentiate the injustice stress theory from two other models in which notions of justice theories are used to explain stress: the effort–reward imbalance model (Siegrist, 2001) and the work of Tepper (2001). In the following sections, empirical evidence will be presented to demonstrate the explanatory value of the injustice stress model. Part of the evidence rests on the interpretation of studies done by other researchers.

Empirical evidence
Vermunt et al. (1998, study 2) conducted a 2 × 2 scenario study to find out how respondents would evaluate combinations of procedural (interactional) and distributive justice. The scenarios described the allocation of workload (high versus medium), and the treatment by a supervisor (fair versus unfair). Participants were asked how stressed they would be in the described situation. The results showed that highest stress was reported in the high workload–unfair procedure condition. Lowest stress was reported in the medium workload–fair procedure condition. This suggests additive effects of workload and interactional unfairness on stress. In another study, stress and fairness were induced experimentally (Vermunt & Steensma, 2003). Subjects performed an arithmetic task. Half of the subjects got ample time to perform the task, the other half of the subjects got hardly any time at all. After the task performance, subjects were treated fairly (voice: they could explain why their performance was as it was) or unfairly (no voice). Before, during and after the task and the manipulations, heart action and blood pressure were measured. The results supported the expected effect of fair treatment, in that lower cardiovascular activity was measured after fair treatment but not after unfair treatment. Moreover, three-way interactions showed that participants with type-A behavior in the low mental pressure condition had lower cardiovascular activity after fair treatment but not after unfair treatment, while participants with type-B behavior showed lower cardiovascular activity after fair treatment in the high mental pressure condition. Physiological changes,

that is, increases in skin conductance after induction of inequity, were also found in a study by Markovsky (1988). Tomaka and Blascovich (1994) asked high and low believers in a just world to perform a mentally stressful task. The high believers in a just world had, as predicted, psychophysiological responses that indicated low stress levels, and their self-reports confirmed their low stress. A survey study in Finnish hospitals found that procedural and interactional injustice were related to absenteeism (Elovainio et al., 2002). In another Finnish study, procedural and interactional injustice in organizations correlated with stress (Elovainio et al., 2001). Based on the evidence presented up to now, it is clear that injustice may explain stress and strains. But what can be said about the long-term effects of injustice on burnout? This will be the topic of the next (sub)section.

Injustice, stress, and burnout
Burnout is a multidimensional concept, including the dimensions of emotional exhaustion, depersonalization (detached cynicism) and lack of accomplishment (decline of competence). Several studies have shown that perceived inequity is a strong predictor of burnout. However, most studies did not make clear how the underlying psychological process actually operates. In what is perhaps the most impressive article on the relation between inequity, job stress, and burnout, this problem was examined by Taris et al. (2001). They studied burnout among two samples of Dutch teachers as a function of inequity and experienced job stress in three different exchange relationships (i.e., relationships with students, colleagues, and the school organizations). The main hypothesis was that inequity would be linked to burnout through the job stress, resulting from the several forms of inequity. Analysis of a cross-sectional survey sample ($N = 271$) revealed that this was indeed the case. Perceived inequity could be explained by high investments and, particularly, by low rewards. Effects of inequity on burnout dimensions were not only mediated via the three kinds of stress (student stressors; colleague stressors; organizational stressors), but there were also some direct effects of (some forms of) inequity on (some) burnout dimensions. The main findings of the first cross-sectional study were replicated in a second, two-wave longitudinal survey study using a nationally representative sample of 940 teachers (Taris et al., 2001; study 2). Again, more investments in, and particularly, lower rewards from a relationship were associated with perceived inequity of the relationship. And the (student; colleague; organizational) stressors or variables were influenced by the perceived inequity. Stress had, in general, the predicted effects on the burnout dimensions. And, again, there were some direct paths between perceived inequity and burnout variables. Thus, not all effects of inequity are mediated via stress. An interesting finding of the longitudinal study was that the lagged effects of the time 1 stressors on the time 2 burnout indicators were either not significantly different from zero or even in the reverse direction. This supports the reasoning that (some) participants who experience much stress are to some degree successful in mitigating the negative effects of the stressors.

The study by Taris et al. shows convincingly that distributive unfairness may cause stress and (partly directly, partly through this stress) burnout. However, effects of procedural and interactional injustice were not studied in their research program. These effects were studied, though, by Steensma and Willemstein (2006). In their survey study, employees ($N = 56$) working in 10 profit organizations filled out a questionnaire on P–E fit. As was predicted, procedural injustice seemed to be a cause of burnout. In particular, informational injustice and interactional injustice by managers were strong predictors of burnout. Aspects of distributive justice, in particular fair distribution of social and 'intrinsic' job rewards, correlated negatively with burnout. Moreover, it was found that people who perceive that their personal values conflict with the values adhered to in the organization run the risk of becoming a victim of burnout.

In conclusion, we can say that both experimental and survey studies largely support the predictions derived from justice theories, and in particular the injustice stress theory. In the following sections, attention will be paid to a special stressor in organizations: aggression.

Aggression in the workplace
Aggression in the workplace is one of the most troubling issues facing many organizations today. It is estimated that each year about 4% of all European workers are subjected to physical violence; 8% are subjected to intimidation and bullying; and about 2% are subjected to sexual harassment (Paoli, 1997). Exposure rates differ between organizations and between employees. A large-scale European survey found that aggression at work clearly seems to lead to an increase in health complaints. In addition, health-related absenteeism increased with aggression at work (ibid.). American society has the same problems of aggression in the workplace. Millions of workers in the USA are physically attacked, while many more receive threats or are the target of one of the forms of harassment (O'Leary-Kelly et al., 1996).

Aggression is a special stressor. Beyond health complaints and absenteeism, many additional negative effects of organizational violence can be mentioned, including high financial costs of healthcare, decreased productivity, damage to property, dissatisfaction, weaker employee morale, and increased turnover. To develop a successful anti-aggression policy, it is necessary to gain insight into the intricate network of real and perceived causes and consequences of the several forms of aggression in the workplace. A distinction should be made between two different forms: 'external' aggression and 'internal' aggression. External aggression is the violent or threatening behavior of organizational 'outsiders', such as robbers, dissatisfied customers, and the general public. Internal aggression, on the other hand, is committed by colleagues, supervisors, or (sometimes) subordinates. In continental Europe, researchers often use the term 'mobbing' to refer to internal aggression. This form of workplace aggression includes behaviors such as socially isolating a person, verbal threats, physical attacks, spreading rumors, attacking the victim with organizational measures, and so on (Leymann, 1993; Zapf et al., 1996). Bullying (mobbing) is the continual and deliberate repeated malicious treatment of a target person (or a small group of individuals). It is treatment that persistently provokes, pressures, frightens, intimidates or otherwise causes discomfort (Einarsen, 1996).

Causes of aggression in the workplace
External aggression can be explained as a function of the characteristics of both the perpetrator and the 'environment', and the interaction between these characteristics (Steensma et al., 1997). There are four levels of environmental characteristics:

1. macro-level characteristics (for example, societal norms; legislation);
2. characteristics and procedures of the organization (for example, organizations may use procedures that are perceived as unfair, and the unfairness could cause aggressive reactions);

3. workplace characteristics (e.g., unpleasant physical characteristics, but also factors such as 'crowding'); and
4. characteristics of the work itself (e.g., work that includes many difficult social contacts implies a higher risk that conflicts arise).

Relevant person characteristics of the aggressor are sex, age, and personality factors such as emotional reactivity and low frustration tolerance. Characteristics of workers also affect the risks of becoming a victim of external aggression.

Environmental and 'person' factors are important in the explanation of internal aggression, too. It should be stressed here that, although characteristics of the work, the workplace, the organization and the society covary with violence in the workplace, these characteristics are not 'aggressive' in and of themselves. Aggression is an act of people, not of things. Researchers should study why some environmental and personality characteristics affect aggressive behaviors of some people, and not others. In this chapter, the focus is on the causes and consequences of internal aggression and the relations with interactional (in)justice and leadership behaviors.

Internal aggression: the boss as a bully?
In his pioneering study on the effects of job demands and job decision latitude, Karasek (1979) demonstrated convincingly that high job demands do not necessarily lead to high levels of stress and strain. It is the combination of job demands and decision latitude (job control) that matters, that is, high job control enables workers to handle high job demands effectively and efficiently, without negative health consequences. But in particular the combination of high job demands and *low* job control will result in high stress levels (and, therefore, lead to negative health consequences). It should be noted that job demands and job control of workers are based on decisions by higher management and often also on decisions by direct supervisors of employees. Therefore, aspects of fair allocation (of workload) and fair procedures play an important role here. Actually, high job control meets the fair procedure criterion of giving a certain amount of 'voice' to workers, and demonstrates that workers are seen as competent members of the organization. Lack of job control may be frustrating to workers, in particular in combination with high job demands. Since frustration often leads to aggression (Dollard et al., 1939), this may result in higher levels of internal aggression. Of course, there are more variables that may be related to bullying in the workplace, but job demands and job control certainly belong to the ones that are interesting, both for theoretical reasons (the core variables of a stress model), and for practical reasons (implications for change are clear). Therefore, job demands and job control were included by Hubert et al. (2001) in a theoretical model, and a third central variable was added: leadership style. The supervisor is responsible for leading and coaching his/her subordinates, and for the quality of the group 'climate' in the team or department. This model postulates that negative work characteristics and low quality of leadership contribute to high bullying risks. Health complaints may be caused both by bulling and by low quality of working life (QWL) and poor leadership. Health complaints will, in the end, result in higher sickness absenteeism. The model was tested in two studies. Briefly, the model stood its test well. Bullying, low QWL and poor leadership correlated as predicted with health problems, and bullying could be explained by lack of job control, high workload, and poor socioemotional leadership (ibid.; study 1, a

survey study with $N = 3011$ participants). In a second survey study, with 427 employees, poor leadership and lack of decision latitude again correlated strongly with bullying and bullying correlated strongly with sickness absenteeism (ibid.; study 2). A rather alarming finding of the study by Hubert et al. was that bullying not only had negative effects on the somatic and mental health of victims. Victims had, as was predicted, more health complaints, less job satisfaction, more need for recovery, stronger emotional reactions and more worries than had the members of a control group (employees working in departments where no bullying was reported). But there were ripple effects: bystanders who had been witnesses of bullying demonstrated the same significant pattern of symptoms, although the effects were somewhat less extreme. The existence of ripple effects implies that the group of people who may obtain relief from effective anti-bullying policies is far larger than only the group of victims.

Poor leadership may cause bullying in two ways. First, leaders may neglect group dynamics. Frustrating conditions may lead to mounting tensions in the group of subordinates, and finally this may result in the bullying of one or more employees by (some of) their colleagues. The bullying goes on, unnoticed by the supervisor, and/or the leader does not intervene successfully. Second, and very alarming, there is the direct causal path: the leader/supervisor is the initiator of the bullying behavior, and/or (s)he is participating actively in bullying one or more victims. Unfortunately, this seems to happen rather frequently. Many researchers reported high rates of bullying by formal leaders/ supervisors and managers (see, e.g., Ashforth, 1994; Rayner, 1995; Vartia, 1996; Hubert et al., 2001). Hubert et al. found that more than one-third of the victims participating in their survey studies indicated that their supervisor was the perpetrator of bullying. To gain more insight into this problem, a series of in-depth interviews with victims of bullying was planned. Some 55 in-depth interviews with victims were held, and in about 35 of these, special attention was paid to the behavior of leaders and supervisors.

Interviews with victims
Many interviewees had been bullied, both by their colleagues and by their supervisors; many were bullied only by their colleagues, and about one-third of all interviewees had been bullied mainly or even only by their supervisors. Bullying behavior by supervisors shares many characteristics with bullying behaviors by colleagues or 'peers'. For example, social isolation of victims is one of the most preferred ways of hurting people, and both supervisors and colleagues of the victim often use this isolation option. But there are also differences, and these differences have to do with the hierarchically higher positions of supervisors. Supervisors have more structural 'bully resources' at their disposal than have the colleagues of the victims, and often they use these resources. For example, supervisors may use performance appraisals to frustrate ambitions of victims, and to damage the public image of victims. Another way in which bullying supervisors use their legitimate power to reward and punish subordinates, is the 'systematic' allocation of unpleasant tasks to the same person – the victim – time and again. This is, of course, a clear example of distributive injustice. A majority of the interviewed victims mentioned many examples of stress-causing behaviors by their supervisors. Often, the examples amount to transgressions of norms of distributive, procedural and/or interactional justice. Refusal to delegate responsibility to some subordinates and publicly demonstrating a lack of trust is rather frequently reported. Emphasizing existing status differences and neglecting the ideas and

suggestions offered by some unpopular subordinates is a procedurally unfair method to lower the status of victims in their group. Sometimes, the quality of the workplace, the office furniture and the equipment of victims is lower than the quality of the workplace, furniture and equipment of their colleagues, and no attempts are made to undo this state of distributive unfairness. Moreover, a rather rigid application of formal rules without concern for the needs of subordinates and without consideration of their views is not unusual behavior for many managers. The conclusion is clear: supervisors are in a good position to take organizational measures against subordinates they do not like, and many bosses use these opportunities. The consequences are very negative. Almost all victims reported stress symptoms. About half of the victims were interviewed by a clinical psychologist, and in this group of victims about one-third of the interviewees were diagnosed as suffering from post-traumatic stress symptoms according to the criteria of DSM-IV (American Psychiatric Association, 1994).

Dysfunctional leadership, bullying, and burnout
Effects of leadership behavior on stress and burnout, and the relationships between leadership styles, bullying, stress, burnout, and aspects of injustice were also studied by means of a survey study with visitors of a burnout website as participants (participants differed strongly in the extent to which they suffered from burnout, so even though there is some reduction in the range of burnout variance, correlation and regression analyses could be used). In this study by Steensma and Van de Veerdonk (2002), special attention was paid to two types of dysfunctional leadership: obstructive leadership and failure behaviors of leaders. Obstructive leadership is demonstrated by leaders who, for example, constantly intervene and disturb the workflow of activities. Often, obstructive leaders speak disparagingly about their subordinates in public. So, obstructive leaders show negative attitudes and negative behaviors towards their subordinates. Leaders who are characterized by the performance of failure behaviors (i.e., ineffective or 'failed' leaders) want perhaps to do things right and to treat their subordinates well, but unfortunately, their leadership skills and competencies (e.g., knowledge, problem-solving skills and social judgment skills) are of low quality. Many of these failed leaders have a *laissez-faire* leadership style. The survey study demonstrated strong relationships between, on the one hand, obstructive and failed leadership with, on the other hand, the three main forms of unfairness, that is, procedural, interactional and distributive injustice. All unfairness aspects were related to bullying, while bullying correlated with obstructive leadership, stress, and with the burnout dimension emotional exhaustion. Failed leadership was related not only to exhaustion, but also to the depersonalization dimension of burnout. As was expected, there was a clear link between unfairness and stress. In spite of the already mentioned risk of some restriction of range, the survey study demonstrated that leadership, bullying, injustice, stress and burnout are all connected with each other. So, efforts to reduce stress and burnout of workers should pay attention to the role played by leaders, allocations and procedures in organizations.

Using justice to reduce stress
Apparently, unfair allocations and unfair behaviors of managers and supervisors may explain (partly) stress, health problems, and burnout of workers in organizations. But this implies that it should be possible to use justice criteria to improve the mental

and somatic health of employees. The supervisor should have a very active role in this method of managing stress. Let there be no misunderstanding. The methods proposed here are not identical with the social support factor of the 'Michigan' stress model. Social support, as well as coping, are generally initiated by the worker (e.g., by seeking support from other persons). But another way to reduce (and to prevent) stress is one in which the direct superior takes the initiative. The superior or manager at the supervisory level of an organization is an 'authority' who allocates resources (tasks, time, rewards) to subordinates by applying rules and procedures, and often (s)he is doing this while having direct social interaction with the subordinate. Both resources and the procedures and interactions may fail to meet the criteria of fairness. This is highly unpleasant and threatening for the subordinates. Unfair distributions of resources widen the gap between environmental demands and capacities of the worker. Moreover, unfair procedures and interactions indicate the possible existence of a negative relationship with an important authority. However, by compensating for possible injustices, superiors may reduce the stress of their subordinates. Folger introduced the term 'fair process effect', to refer to the beneficial effects of a fair procedure on an unfair outcome (e.g., Folger et al., 1979). Expressing one's view (voice) leads to higher satisfaction with outcomes, and this may be true even in the case of negative outcomes. However, this is not the only way to overcome the unfairness of previous decisions. Actually, there are at least four tactics for overcoming initial injustices. These four ways to reduce injustice are the results of a combination of the (un)fairness of prior distributions/allocations and procedures, with 'new' procedures and allocation processes. A distribution as well as a procedure may be judged as fair or unfair. An unfair distribution may be followed by a fair distribution as well as by a fair procedure. An unfair prior procedure may be followed by a fair distribution or by a fair procedure. The combinations result in four modes of acting fairly after an unfairness (see Table 21.1). The four methods to manage stress are described by Vermunt and Steensma (2001).

Here, only a short description will be given of the four methods. An unfair distribution may be judged as more fair, if it is followed by another, fair outcome allocation. This method to restore justice is called 'compensation'. For example, an employee who perceives his/her demotion as unfair may be compensated for the unfairness by a raise in salary. By using 'justifications' in allocating a resource, the negative effects of an unfair distribution may be overcome. Often, there are good reasons for some unfairness in allocations and by communicating adequately these reasons to the persons involved, the participants feel less unfairness. Justification is a form of fair process effect. A fair end state may have beneficial effects and reduce the stress caused by prior unfair procedures.

Table 21.1   Four modes of using justice to manage stress

		Acting fairly via	
		Distribution	Procedure
Prior unfairness	Distribution	Compensation	Justification
	Procedure	Appreciation	Mitigation

Source: Adapted from Vermunt & Steensma (2001).

This fair end state of outcomes demonstrates 'appreciation', and is a form of fair outcome effect. Finally, in 'mitigation', the negative effects of an unfair prior procedure may be softened by another but fair procedure. These four methods may be seen as rather 'pure', but it is, of course, possible to combine methods. For example, to reduce the negative effects of a prior unfair distribution, compensation may be combined with the justification method. Moreover, there are several ways to implement a certain method to manage injustice stress. For instance, compensation can be given in the form of a permanent salary increase, but also in the form of a financial bonus, or a special sabbatical leave, and so on. Therefore, managers have many alternative ways to reduce or prevent stress. However, not all combinations of methods will have the same positive effects. Knowing beforehand that one has voice in an inaccurate procedure, may even lower the trust in the authority (Vermunt & Shulman, 1996). Therefore, one should be careful in combining different methods of stress management.

Managers may effectively reduce injustice stress in organizations. And certain styles of leadership should be used to prevent and/or reduce bullying. To do this effectively, managers and supervisors should have certain skills and abilities. It is sometimes believed that good leaders are born, not made. However, leadership research has made it clear that most knowledge, skills and abilities which are needed for effective leadership can be learned and developed. Effective leadership depends on several competencies, that is, problem-solving skills, social judgment skills, and the technical knowledge to perform certain tasks as well. These competencies are influenced by individual attributes (i.e., motivation, personality factors) and by career experiences and environmental influences. But they can be developed and learned over time through education and experience (Mumford et al., 2000). Knowledge of the causes and consequences of distributive, procedural, and interactional fairness should become a central module in management training programs.

Stress and aggression management: the integral approach
Developing the competencies of managers and giving them information about the influences of leadership style and (in)justice on stress, burnout and bullying is highly desirable. It is even better, though, to make this a part of a more integral approach. The integral approach is a general model for improving the QWL. This approach, useful for all efforts to reduce stress, burnout and sickness absenteeism and to improve satisfaction, motivation, performance and well-being of workers might be called the 'IDPIE model', after its five core elements (phases):

- *Intention*   All parties involved, and particularly the managers, commit themselves to the intention to improve QWL or a special aspect of QWL (e.g., reduction of bullying). Workers have 'voice' in expressing the desire and intention to improve QWL.
- *Diagnosis* (data gathering and trying to develop a body of knowledge of the causes and consequences of the aspect of QWL (e.g., the bullying). Aspects of procedural justice are important here: accuracy, correctability, voice.
- *Prioritize* (often it is not possible to do all things, so choices should be made: what to do first? Again, voice and representativeness are important).
- *Implementation* of actions (preferably in close cooperation with workers and their representatives).

- *Evaluation* (both of results and of the processes used to reach results; this may lead to the continuous improvement seen in total quality management).

Management should strive for a close cooperation with workers and their representatives in all phases of the IDPIE approach. For example, the Works' Council should express its support for QWL programs, and job consultation may be used to reach better diagnoses of QWL – a lot of 'local knowledge' will become available – and to facilitate the implementation of planned changes. Actually, the IDPIE approach is built on principles of procedural and interactional justice, and its results demonstrate the value of this model. For example, stress absenteeism had been halved in a project using this approach (Steensma & Van der Vlist, 1998).

Conclusions

Bullying, stress and burnout of workers are influenced heavily by distributive, procedural and interactional injustice and by poor leadership. Effective programs to reduce bullying, stress and burnout should pay attention to all forms of fairness.

References

Adams, J.S. (1965), 'Inequity in social exchange', in L. Berkowitz (ed.), *Advances in Experimental Social Psychology*, Vol. 2, New York: Academic Press, pp. 267–99.

American Psychiatric Association (1994), *Diagnostic and Statistical Manual of Mental Disorders*, 4th edition, Washington, DC: American Psychiatric Association.

Ashforth, B. (1994), 'Petty tyranny in organizations', *Human Relations*, **47**(7), 755–78.

Bies, R.J. & Moag, J.S. (1986), 'Interactional justice: communication criteria of fairness', in R.J. Lewicki, B.H. Shepard & M.H. Bazerman (eds), *Research on Negotiation in Organizations*, Vol. 1, Greenwich, CT: JAI Press, pp. 43–55.

Deutsch, M. (1975), 'Equity, equality and need: what determines which value will be used as the basis of distributive justice?', *Journal of Social Issues*, **31**, 137–49.

Dollard, J., Miller, N.E., Doob, L.W., Mowrer, O.H. & Sears, R.R. (1939), *Frustration and Aggression*, New Haven, CT: Yale University Press.

Edwards, J.R. (1992), 'A cybernetic theory of stress, coping, and well-being in organizations', *Academy of Management Review*, **17**, 238–74.

Einarsen, S. (1996), 'Bullying amd harassment at work: epidemiological and psychological aspects' (dissertation), University of Bergen, Norway.

Elovainio, M., Kivimaki, M. & Helkama, K. (2001), 'Organizational justice evaluations, job control, and occupational strain', *Journal of Applied Psychology*, **86**, 418–24.

Elovainio, M., Kivimaki, M. & Vahtera, J. (2002), 'Organizational justice: evidence of a new psychosocial predictor of health', *American Journal of Public Health*, **92**(1), 105–8.

Folger, R., Rosenfield, D., Grove, J. & Corkran, L. (1979), 'Effects of "voice" and peer opinions on responses to inequity', *Journal of Personality and Social Psychology*, **37**, 2253–61.

French, J.R.P. & Caplan, R.D. (1972), 'Organizational stress and individual strain', in A.J. Marrow (ed.), *The Failure of Success*, New York: Amacom, pp. 30–67.

French, J.R., Caplan, R.D. & Harrison, R.V. (1982), *The Mechanisms of Job Stress and Strain*, New York: Wiley.

French, J.R.P., Rogers, W. & Cobb, S. (1981), 'A model of person–environment fit', in L. Levi (ed.), *Society, Stress and Disease*, Vol. 4, Oxford and New York: Oxford University Press, pp. 39–44.

Friedman, M. & Rosenman, R. (1974), *Type A Behavior and Your Heart*, New York: Alfred Knopf.

Greenberg, J. (1979), 'Protestant ethic endorsement and the fairness of equity inputs', *Journal of Research in Personality*, **13**, 81–90.

Greenberg, J. (1986), 'Determinants of perceived fairness of performance evaluations', *Journal of Applied Psychology*, **71**, 340–42.

Hofstede, G. (1980), *Culture's Consequences: International Differences in Work-related Values*, Beverly Hills, CA: Sage.

Hubert, A., Furda, J. & Steensma, H. (2001), 'Mobbing, systematisch pestgedrag in organisaties. Twee studies naar antecedenten en gevolgen voor de gezondheid' ['Mobbing, systematic bullying behavior in organizations: two studies of antecedents and effects on health'], *Gedrag & Organisatie*, **14**(6), 378–96.

Kahn, L. (1970), 'Some propositions towards a researchable conceptualization of stress', in J.W. McGrath (ed.), *Social and Psychological Factors of Stress*, New York: Holt, Rinehart, Winston, pp. 97–104.

Karasek, R.A. (1979), 'Job demands, job decision latitude, and mental strain: implications for job design', *Administrative Science Quarterly*, **24**, 285–308.

Koper, G., Van Knippenberg, D., Bouhuys, F., Vermunt, R. & Wilke, H. (1993), 'Procedural fairness and self-esteem', *European Journal of Social Psychology*, **26**, 313–25.

Lazarus, R.S. & Folkman, S. (1984), *Stress, Appraisal and Coping*, New York: Springer.

Lerner, M.J. (1980), *Belief in a Just World: A Fundamental Delusion*, New York: Plenum Press.

Lerner, M.J. & Simmons, C.H. (1966), 'Observers' reaction to the "innocent victim": Compassion or rejection?', *Journal of Personality and Social Psychology*, **4**, 203–10.

Leventhal, G., Karuza, J. & Fry, W.R. (1980), 'Beyond fairness: a theory of allocation preferences', in G. Mikula (ed.), *Justice and Social Interaction*, Bern: Huber, pp. 167–218.

Leymann, H. (1993), '*Mobbing: Psychoterror am Arbeitsplatz und wie man sich dagegen wehren kann [Mobbing; Psychoterror in the Workplace and how to Defend Oneself Against it]*, Reinbeck: Rohwolt.

Lind, E.A., Tyler, T.R. & Huo, Y.J. (1997), 'Procedural context and culture: variation in the antecedents of procedural justice judgments', *Journal of Personality and Social Psychology*, **47**, 793–804.

Markovsky, B. (1988), 'Injustice and arousal', *Social Justice Research*, **2**, 223–33.

McFarlin, D.B. & Sweeney, P.D. (2001), 'Cross-cultural applications of organizational justice', in R. Cropanzano (ed.), *Justice in the Workplace*, Vol. 2, Mahwah, NJ: Erlbaum, pp. 67–95.

Mumford, M.D., Zaccaro, S.J., Harding, F.D., Jacobs, T.O. & Fleishman, E.A. (2000), 'Leadership skills for a changing world: solving complex social problems', *Leadership Quarterly*, **11**(1), 11–35.

O'Leary-Kelly, A.M., Griffin, R.W. & Glew, D.J. (1996), 'Organization-motivated aggression: a research framework', *Academy of Management Review*, **21**(1), 225–53.

Paoli, P. (1997), *Second European Survey on the Work Environment 1995–1996*, Dublin: European Foundation for the Improvement of Working and Living Conditions.

Rayner, C. (1995), *The Incidence of Workplace Bullying*, paper presented at the Bruce Burns Memorial Trust Conference, Birmingham, 10 October.

Siegrist, J. (2001), 'A theory of occupational stress', in J. Dunham (ed.), *Stress in the Workplace: Past, Present and Future*, London: Whurr, pp. 52–66.

Steensma, H. (1999), 'Injustice stress and the bullying leader: a new research model', paper presented at the 9th European Congress on Work and Organizational Psychology, Espoo-Helsinki, 12–15 May.

Steensma, H., Hubert, A., Van Duijn, S. & Evers, G. (1997), 'Geweld op het werk. Omgevings- en persoonskenmerken, verklarende modellen' ['Violence in the workplace. Context and personality factors, explanatory models'], *Tijdschrift voor Toegepaste Arbowetenschap*, **10**(2), 24–9.

Steensma, H. & Van de Veerdonk, R. (2002), 'Dysfunctional leadership, bullying in the workplace, and burnout of workers', paper presented at the 25th International Congress of Applied Psychology, Singapore, 7–12 July.

Steensma, H. & Van der Vlist, R. (1998), 'Action research to reduce sickness absenteeism: a case study', *Concepts and Transformation*, **3**(3), 179–206.

Steensma, H. & Willemstein, A. (2006), 'Value conflicts, injustice, and burnout', paper presented at the 11th International Social Justice Conference, Berlin, 2–5 August.

Taris, T.W., Peeters, M.C.W., Le Blanc, P., Schreurs, P.J.G. & Schaufeli, W.B. (2001), 'From inequity to burnout: the role of job stress', *Journal of Occupational Health Psychology*, **6**(4), 303–23.

Tepper, B.J. (2001), 'Health consequences of organizational injustice: tests of main and interactive effects', *Organizational Behavior and Human Decision Processes*, **86**(2), 197–215.

Thibaut, J. & Walker, L. (1975), *Procedural Justice: A Psychological Analysis*, Hillsdale, NJ: Erlbaum.

Tomaka, J. & Blascovich, J. (1994), 'Effects of justice beliefs on cognitive appraisal and subjective, physiological, and behavioral responses to potential stress', *Journal of Personality and Social Psychology*, **67**(4), 732–40.

Tornow, W.W. (1971), 'The development and application of an input–outcome moderator test on the perception and reduction of inequity', *Organizational Behavior and Human Performance*, **6**, 614–38.

Tyler, T. & Lind, E.A. (1992), 'A relational model of authority in groups', in M.P. Zanna (ed.), *Advances in Experimental Social Psychology*, Vol. 25, San Diego, CA: Academic Press, pp. 115–91.

Vartia, M. (1996), 'The sources of bullying. Psychological work environment and organizational climate', *European Journal of Work and Organizational Psychology*, **5**, 203–14.

Vermunt, R., Oskam, M. & Steensma, H. (1998), 'Van baas tot bazig. Stress als gevolg van onheuse bejegening door de baas' ['The bossy boss. Stress caused by unjust behavior of supervisors'], *Gedrag & Organisatie*, **11**(6), 354–71.

Vermunt, R. & Shulman, S. (1996), 'Responding to an unfair procedure', *Nederlands Tijdschrift voor de Psychologie*, **51**, 35–46.

Vermunt, R. & Steensma, H. (2001), 'Stress and justice in organizations: an exploration into justice processes with the aim to find mechanisms to reduce stress', in R. Cropanzano (ed.), *Justice in the Workplace*, Vol. 2, Mahwah, NJ: Erlbaum. pp. 27–48.

Vermunt, R. & Steensma, H. (2003), 'Physiological relaxation: stress reduction through fair treatment', *Social Justice Research*, **16**(2), 135–49.

Vermunt, R. & Steensma, H. (2005), 'How can justice be used to manage stress in organizations?', in J. Greenberg & J.A. Colquitt (eds), *Handbook of Organizational Justice*, Mahwah, NJ: Erlbaum, pp. 383–410.

Zapf, D., Knorz, C. & Kulla, M. (1996), 'On the relationship between mobbing factors, and job content, social work environment, and health outcomes', *European Journal of Work and Organizational Psychology*, **5**(2), 215–37.

PART V

IMMIGRATION, ACCULTURATION AND HEALTH

22 Immigration, unemployment and career counseling: a multicultural perspective

Alexander-Stamatios G. Antoniou and Marina Dalla

Introduction

Migration in Europe: the social, demographic and political context

Migration is considered as a movement responding to the societal pressures to move from one country to another because of social, economic and political problems and opportunities (Bierbrauer & Pedersen, 1996). More than 191 million persons, documented or undocumented immigrants, currently reside in a country other than where they were born, about 3% of the world's population (IOM, 2003). In Europe, mass migration is not new. During the twentieth century Europe has experienced three major periods of movements: during the First and Second World Wars and the last decades. Modern mass immigration differs from past migration in part because it is characterized by new movements, especially from Eastern and Central European countries. Moreover, some countries in Europe, such as Spain, Italy or Portugal, which have traditionally been exporters of immigrants, have shifted to becoming importers. With regard to the characteristics of the migrants, it is no longer the poorest who emigrate, as the migration process involves a material cost. Migration of elites and skilled personnel is increasing, as is the participation of women as independent actors in the migration process (Castles & Miller, 1998). Another new feature of the migration is that immigrants are not simply looking for an immediate job, but for situations which give them a higher quality of life, together with better future possibilities for themselves and their children.

In the literature, migration has been divided into involuntary and voluntary migration (Berry, 2006). Voluntary migrants are immigrants and sojourners. They are distinguished by the fact that the stay of immigrants is longer and more permanent compared to that of sojourners (who include students, diplomatic personnel and international executives), whose stay in the country of destination is quite temporary and whose return is already planned ahead of the migration. Refugees and asylum seekers, often called 'forced migrants', are involuntary migrants, and their life has often been stressful before the migration. Another distinction is made between first- and second-generation immigrants (Berry et al., 2006). First-generation immigrants are persons who have moved from one society to another and settled in the new society while second-generation immigrants are persons born in the new society. The presence of undocumented immigrants is a well-established fact in most European countries, although the European Union (EU) members have been practicing a policy of closing borders with the development of processes of regularization of immigrants.

Migration in Greece: the main immigrant groups

In many ways, immigration to Greece has much in common with the other southern EU member states such as Portugal, Spain and Italy. First, the East–West dimension dominates. Second, most of the immigrants are clandestine, at least initially. Third, the new forms of mobility are also evident: transit, temporary, seasonal and cross-border migration. Finally, geographic proximity and cultural or historical links with countries of origin and migrant populations (in terms of religion, ethnicity, etc.) can also be identified (King et al., 2000). According to the 2001 census, immigrants constitute 7% of the total Greek populations, though other sources estimate that this percentage reaches 10% (Zavos, 2006). Major population inflows towards Greece include Albanian immigrants, who constitute 57% of the total foreigners in the country, immigrants from other former socialist countries of Eastern Europe (Bulgaria, Romania, Georgia), ethnic Greeks from the Black Sea region (Pontics) who were entitled to Greek passports, ethnic Greek Albanian citizens (Vorioepirotes) and a smaller number of returning Greek migrants from Northern Europe, the US, Canada and Australia (Cavounidis, 2004; Gropas & Triandafyllidou, 2005). Greece has always had a relatively small inflow of asylum seekers, compared to other EU states, such as the UK and Germany.

The role of migration in Greece has been discussed during recent years from the point of the policy of regulation of undocumented migrants (Sitaropoulos, 2003; Cavounidis, 2002), the consequences of migration on different sectors of society and economy (Labrianidis & Lyberaki, 2001; Rovolis & Tragaki, 2005) or the study of acculturation of immigrants with a specific emphasis on the transformation of social and ethnic identity (Georgas & Papastylianou, 1996). Little attention has been given to integration of immigrants into the labor market and the career behavior of individuals with culturally different backgrounds. There are several reasons why studies of career development of immigrant groups are still in the early stages. First and foremost, the vast majority of immigrants in Greece perform manual work, whatever their educational and technical qualifications. The overwhelming majority of employed Albanians, Bulgarians and Romanians are classified in craft and related work, as plant and machine operators and in elementary occupations which include unskilled occupations in agriculture, industry and services (Cavounidis, 2004). Second, current models of career development and counseling do not take into consideration the effect of the transitional experience of immigrants who are settling in a new country (Sue et al., 1996). Third, theories of career development are usually based on Eurocentric worldviews that may differ from those of the immigrant groups. For instance, they usually assume an individualistic perspective regarding behavior and choices, whereas members of immigrant groups may prefer a collectivist orientation to choices and decisions (Aycan, 2000; Triandis & Trafimov, 2003). Fourth, many assessment instruments used in career counseling may not cover the salient aspects of behavior of immigrants due to lack of similarity of the meaning of test scores across culture groups (Gainor, 2000; Van de Vijver, 2000).

An examination of the career behavior and development of immigrant groups in Greece reveals both areas of immigration as a transition experience and areas of divergence between groups. The purpose of this chapter is to present a range of issues relevant to career development of immigrants. It begins with concepts and issues within the field of acculturation together with a presentation of basic needs and health problems of immigrants. This is followed by the unemployment of immigrants as a risk factor for adaptation to the new situation. The subsequent section includes theories about career development and counseling of diverse cultural groups, followed by a section that reviews research findings on career development of immigrant groups in Greece and presents a comparative study about some psychological aspects of work-related behavior and the experiences of unemployed Pontic remigrants and native Greeks in comparison with employed coethnics. The final section is concerned with a model of career development (career behavior and counseling), drawing upon both theory and empirical findings to address issues that may arise in plural societies as a result of immigration.

Immigration, needs and health problems of immigrants

Immigration has been regarded by social scientists and mental health professionals as one of the most stressful processes of loss and change. The first phase starts when a person leaves the familiar environment, family and friends, community ties and job, customs and language in the hope of finding new opportunities. The second phase is the initial period after arriving in a new country. The difficulties related to culture contact are characterized as culture shock (Ward et al., 2001), which includes emotional reactions such as confusion, anxiety, disorientation, and bewilderment in response to difficulties and restrictions connected to being an immigrant. After this, there is acculturation that involves the ongoing process of changes over time in beliefs, emotions, attitudes, values, and behavior and identification patterns of one person in first-hand contact with another from another culture (Liebkind, 2001). Acculturation may proceed along diverging options: assimilation and integration, separation and marginalization (Berry, 2003). The integration option is chosen where the individual seeks to participate as an integral part of a larger society. The second option, assimilation, is chosen if the individual does not wish to maintain his or her identity. Separation is the preferred strategy where the individual wants to hold on to his or her original culture, but avoids interaction with the larger society. Marginalization results from little possibility or interest in cultural maintenance or intergroup relations (Liebkind, 2001; Berry, 2003).

Adaptation refers to long-term ways in which people rearrange their lives and settle down to a more or less satisfactory existence (Berry, 2006). Successful psychological adaptation involves one's psychological and physical well-being (Schmitz, 1992) and is predicted by personality variables, life-change events and social support (Berry, 2006), while sociocultural adaptation is the ability of an individual to manage daily life in the new cultural context and is associated with cultural knowledge, degree of contact and positive intergroup attitudes (Ward et al., 2001). Economic adaptation is conceptualized as the sense of accomplishment and full participation in the economic life in a new country (Aycan & Berry, 1996). The extent to which one's original professional identity can be resumed upon immigration affects the adaptation process. Immigrants who maintain their professional identity, especially when other aspects of themselves are challenged, ensure an inner continuity in change and feel vocationally efficacious (Akhtar, 1999). But it is widely recognized that migratory experience is associated with a number of difficulties within the host country. Ability to find work, questions of pay, seasonal availability, safety, and the unpleasantness of the job play an important role in adaptation. Whether or not the immigrant is documented or undocumented affects the opportunity to participate in a new culture as well as the general quality of life (Suárez-Orozco, 2000).

Because of status loss, immigrants may not initially enjoy the same economic success as natives for the following reasons (Aycan & Berry, 1996; Hayfron, 2006). First, migrating individuals are less likely to find employment at the level for which their education and training has prepared them because different countries have different educational systems and labor-market operation, and employers in the host country may have less information about the educational qualifications and work experience most immigrants bring with them to the host country. Non-recognition of the individual observable characteristics such as educational qualifications and years of work have as a consequence devaluation of different unobservable characteristics such as innate ability, motivation, values, beliefs and interests, since employers believe that there is a positive correlation between observed and unobserved characteristics. Second, language difficulties, depending on the linguistic distance between immigrants' native language and the host country's language, may lead to acculturation difficulties and an exclusion of immigrants from higher-paying jobs in the labor market (Berman et al., 2003). Third, the quantity and quality of occupational opportunities available to immigrant groups are limited due to barriers that are the result of discrimination and oppression against members of immigrant groups.

Discrimination as inappropriate treatment to individuals due to their membership is inextricably linked to notions of justice and equality (Mummendey & Otten, 2003). According to sociological perspectives, immigrants experience occupational discrimination that is perpetuated by the structure of the economic system. There are two main reasons for the discrimination process of immigrant people. The delays in the regulation process of immigrants, which has been criticized either for operating too slowly to respond to the expansion of immigrant population or for the restrictiveness it has placed on employers who sought to legally recruit migrants from abroad (Cavounidis, 2002; Gropas & Triandafyllidou, 2005). Second, entrance into the core economic system that consists of large firms that have control over a large amount of resources, especially for high salary and prestigious positions, is restrictive for members of immigrant groups. Institutions often set up formal and informal rules in terms of educational background, values, beliefs and cultural characteristics that lead to creating a reality of certain typically occupations of immigrants. Structural discrimination is at least partly responsible for the under-representation of immigrant groups in professional and managerial occupations, which are usually positions that carry higher prestige and wages. A comparison of 25 OECD member countries indicated that Greece exhibits the most extreme concentration of migrants in manual occupations. Specifically, the percentages of immigrants working in non-manual jobs in Greece are 10% compared to 40% of the total labor force (Cavounidis, 2002; Rovolis, & Tragaki, 2005). Most of the jobs are non-skilled, manual, and well below the immigrants' level of education and qualifications. According to Kasimis and Kassimi (2004) nearly half of all migrants have secondary education (including technical-skill schools), one-third have either completed or had some primary school education and approximately one-tenth have higher education.

The social experiences of discrimination can cause some immigrants to restrict the range of occupations they consider. Actual or perceived discrimination may discourage them from choosing some occupations or can create a sense of hopelessness about their occupational future. Furthermore, discrimination has been associated with social skill deficits and less willingness to adopt host culture identity (Ward et al., 2001) that have negative consequences in the formation of vocational self-concept, a construct that has a significant influence on the psychological and social functioning of immigrants (Swanson

& Fouad, 1999). When people – and groups – are consistently denied employment opportunities, and when they are also provided with inferior training opportunities, perceive law enforcement as providing little protection, and face discrimination in other aspects of community life, the combination adds up to a powerful recipe for exclusion – the antithesis of inclusion, which is the fundamental notion of integration to the host country.

Adversity experienced in employment results in 'acculturative stress', a term coined to describe a stress reaction in response to life events that are rooted in the experience of acculturation (Berry, 2006). Acculturative stress is usually manifested in the form of depression because of the multiple cultural losses and anxiety due to uncertainties. Work-related problems and low economic status were found to be associated with depressive symptoms and stress in various immigrant groups (Aycan & Berry, 1996). Several studies have evidenced association between discrimination against immigrants and poor health status (Karlsen & Nazroo, 2002; Wiking et al., 2004). Increasingly, the contextual discrimination, particularly in relation to residential segregation, is detrimental to health status (Williams & Collins, 2001) and increases the risk of morbidity (Acevedo-Garcia, 2001) and mortality (Fang et al., 1998). Mental health professionals in Europe refer to 'chronic and multiple stress syndrome' in immigrants who experience difficult conditions (Achotegui, 2002; Bhui et al., 2003). Immigrants affected by this syndrome present depressive symptomatology with atypical characteristics, where depressive symptoms are mixed with anxiety, somatoform and dissociative symptoms. The symptoms develop progressively as the immigrants encounter the obstacles that take place during the migration process, such a distance from their home environment: difficulties in finding a job and obtaining documents, and discrimination in the receiving context.

Unemployment as a risk factor for the mental health of immigrants
Despite their aspirations for financial security, immigrants encounter more barriers to economic success than natives. They are often unemployed or underemployed, especially if they migrate from non-traditional or cultural distant locations (Ward et al., 2001). Across Western Europe, immigrants have far higher rates of unemployment and economic inactivity than the native-born populations (Phalet & Kosic, 2006). In Britain, Asian and Muslim communities have been vulnerable to unemployment or low-paid work (Modood et al., 1997; Wilson, 2003).

Although economists view unemployment or inadequate employment as an economic problem and attribute psychological effects to financial disadvantage, a comprehensive view of the literature underlies the correlation between employment status and mental health (Winefield, 2002). Mental health refers to the embodiment of social, emotional and spiritual well-being that provides individuals with the vitality necessary for active living, to achieve goals, and to interact with others in ways that are respectful and just (VicHealth, 1999). It is well documented that unemployment, or job loss results in significant deterioration in psychological and physical well-being for the majority, including increased rates of depressive symptomatology, and re-entry leads to significant improvement in mental health (Murphy & Athanasou, 1999; Catalano et al., 2000; Dooley et al., 2000). Furthermore, researchers also argue that satisfaction with employment is the key ingredient differentiating employment and unemployment experiences. Being satisfactorily employed enhances psychological growth and self-esteem, but being unsatisfactorily employed is psychologically as bad as being unemployed (Winefield, 2002).

Although employment problems are considered to generate similar mental health outcomes for any individual in society, Aycan and Berry (1996) suggest that unemployment of immigrants results not only in the typical incidence of psychological problems but also in adaptation difficulties. They reported that adapted immigrants were those who experienced satisfaction with their employment condition. The authors state that having work provided not only an income, but also status and identity, which enabled the individual to establish relationships with others in society. The importance of employment issues among other stress factors in the settlement process has been highlighted by Sharareh et al. (2004), who suggest that immigrants in Sweden may also occupy an inferior position in the labor market, which leads to poor health. The influence on health is more marked for immigrant women than for immigrant men. Similar results were reported by Lev-Wiesel and Kaufman (2004) who found that duration of unemployment among immigrants was also positively correlated with anxiety. Australian immigrants are found to have poorer mental health six months after arrival in Australia compared with assessments at 18 and 42 months. Furthermore, unemployment, and especially a long duration of unemployment, is found to be associated with poor mental health (Kennedy & Mcdonald, 2006). Collected data on Canada indicated that living in areas of high unemployment is associated with poor physical and mental health of immigrants in comparison to non-immigrants. Among first-generation immigrants, community unemployment was associated with psychological distress. Among second-generation immigrants, the probability of obesity and poor self-rated health increased significantly for those living in areas with high unemployment, but these associations were statistically significant only for men. Findings among first-generation immigrants are interpreted with respect to the effects of possible discrimination in areas with low job availability. Among second-generation men, poor physical health and obesity may be the result of poor health habits stemming from perceived lack of life opportunities (Zunzunegui et al., 2006). Studies from Australia and New Zealand indicated that immigrant mental illness is related to social aspects such as difficulties at home and at work and loss of status (Sang & Ward, 2006).

The role of career development and counseling from a multicultural perspective
Career development is a term that came into general use in the 1960s and was broadened in definition through the 1970s. During the 1980s, theorists expanded and extended career development from an occupational to a life perspective in which occupation (and work) has place and meaning. They defined 'life career development' as self-development over the life span through the integration of the roles, settings, and events of a person's life (Gysbers & Moore, 1975). The concept of *life* career *development* includes recognition of life-span aspects (career tasks in each of a series of life stages: growth, exploration, establishment, maintenance, decline) and life-space aspects (multiple contexts of individuals' lives) of career development, and the view of work as embedded within other life roles (Swanson et al., 2000). As such, career development involves one's whole life, not just occupation. It concerns the whole person, needs and wants, capacities and potentials, excitements and anxieties. More than that, it concerns him/her in the ever-changing contexts of his/her life.

The contemporary use of the term 'career development' describes both the total constellation of factors that combine to shape individual career behavior over the life span and the interventions or practices that are used to enhance a person's career development or to enable that person to make more effective career decisions. Thus, inherent in the current usage of the term are two sets of theories, or conceptual categories, one which explains the development of career behavior across the life span and the other which describes how career behavior is changed by particular interventions (Erwin, 2001).

Although there is growing consensus in vocational psychology for career counseling to be culture centered, relatively little is known empirically about how, exactly, culture influences vocational processes (Fouad, 2001). Early work regarding issues of career behavior of minority groups focused on between-group differences (e.g., career behavior of African American and Caucasian students). The next stage of research focused on within-group differences and investigated variables such as identity attitudes or perceptions of opportunities among immigrant groups (Swanson et al., 2000). The review of the literature (Walsh, 2001) shows that identity attitudes significantly predict career choices, career-related self-efficacy, and the ability to use bicultural strategies for managing two cultural contexts. Although biculturalism can be a positive coping mechanism, it may also contribute to stress, for example, when an individual is the only member of his/her cultural group in a non-traditional occupation (Carter & Constantine, 2000; Walsh, 2001). Other researchers have integrated the issues of diversity and the career behavior of minority groups into the mainstream vocational and counseling psychology (Gysbers et al., 1999; Swanson et al., 2000). Models of career counseling have also been criticized for not including the critical variables of migration, poverty and discrimination (Leung, 1995). Such external issues have a disproportional effect on the process of career development and on the content of career choices, because they limit the options that individuals may consider and restrict their opportunities for success. On the other hand, the strong relationship between socioeconomic status and educational and occupational levels lead to a continuous cycle of poorly educated minority individuals.

No one theoretical framework has been developed to explain the career behavior of immigrant groups. Rather, various models have developed to help counselors conceptualize ways for appropriate career counseling among such groups. The integrative–sequential conceptual framework for career counseling (Leong & Hartung, 2000) involves identifying culturally relevant ways to assist individuals to make career decisions, adjust to those decisions, and manage work relative to other life roles. Augmenting the longstanding emphasis on person variables (e.g., interests, aptitudes, personality traits), with a focus on cultural context variables, such as social roles and values, should give incremental validity to career development theory and counseling practice. Hartung et al. (2002) studied the relationship between the individualist–collectivist (I–C) values and the occupational choices, career planning behaviors, work values, and family background of 269 college students of African, Asian, Hispanic, and European American descent. They found some significant though moderate relationships between I–C values and the values students sought in work, the career choices they made, and the ways they planned to achieve career goals. Community college students from four cultural groups (white, black, Hispanic, Asian) displayed significant differences on a number of career values (Teng et al., 2001). For example, having a good starting income was more important to black people, while job security, performance, and use of prior experience were more important to black and Hispanic people in comparison to whites and Asians.

Leung's context model (1995) focuses on career intervention by exploring the effect of two variables on the career behavior of minority groups: racial discrimination and social class. Working with multicultural middle school students, Jackson and Nutini (2001) identified contextual barriers and resources affecting career-related learning of minority students: (i) external barriers (unsafe environment, low income, negative social support, discrimination); (ii) internal barriers (negative self-efficacy, negative academic performance, perception of equal opportunity); (iii) external resources (role models, social and cultural support); and (iv) internal resources (bicultural competence, coping efficacy).

Fouad and Bingham (1995) and Fouad and Byars-Winston (2005) used the culturally appropriate career counseling model (CACCM), by incorporating culture as a critical factor in every aspect of the counseling process. The CACCM includes the following steps: counselor's establishment of a culturally appropriate relationship with the person, identification of career issues, assessment of the impact of cultural factors on identified career issues, appropriate process and goal setting, and developing specific career counseling strategies to address the client's career concerns.

Examination of career development of immigrant groups in Greece: a comparative study

Albanian immigrants
Following the political changes in 1990, it is estimated that one million Albanians left the country, with Greece and other countries as their destination. According to the National Statistics Service of Greece, more than half of all foreigners registered in the 2001 Greek census are Albanian citizens (Kasimis & Kassimi, 2004). The majority of these stated that they came to Greece to find employment, while the others came for family reunion.

Albanian immigrants experience anxiety, frustration and emotional states of anger due to acculturation issues, although the majority of them choose integration as the prime acculturation strategy (Dalla et al., 2004; Dalla & Georgiadhou, 2005). The integration as a modification of one's construal of ethnic identity by adding to it aspects of a new culture allow many Albanian immigrants to see migration as a positive experience because it allows them to think that the host country may offer more opportunities than their home country. The past is associated with economic, social and educational difficulties such as poverty, and insecurity in everyday life. The study 'Personality and mental health among Albanian immigrants in Greece in comparison to their coethnics in Albania and native Greeks' (Dragoti et al., 2006) indicated that Albanian immigrants, although living in a new country, demonstrated fewer psychological problems in comparison with their coethnics. At the same time, the lack of psychological problems is associated with high levels of openness to the new challenges and low negative affect (low neuroticism) (Dragoti et al., 2006).

The findings in relation to the educational and career development of Albanian immigrants can be linked to a variety of structural factors, including the prolonged undocumented status of many migrants, racism, and other acculturative factors such as lack of knowledge of the Greek language, ignorance of the labor market networks, the risk of employing immigrants due to the ignorance of employers regarding the personal and other characteristics of immigrants and the restrictions imposed on the labor market by the regulation of many professions (Lianos, 2004). About a third of Albanians work in the construction sector and a fifth in agriculture. The fact that so many Albanian immigrants are employed in heavy manual labor reduces their chances of improving their professional qualifications and familiarizing themselves with modern skills and technologies, and leads to occupational segmentation due to the lack of opportunities for incremental upward mobility through well-paid, blue-collar positions. Employment in poorly paid sectors is a way of survival – it is not a means of integration in the new country.

Research data also show that Albanian immigrant children tend to fare worse in academic performance than their native counterparts (Motti-Stefandi et al., 2008), although they and their parents bring with them high aspirations with regard to school success (Dalla, 2002). They tend to have lower educational and occupational expectations due to perceptions of lack of opportunity, although youth of immigrants do not differ from the majority in their career development interests or aspirations (Suárez-Orozco, 2000). According to Nikolaou (2000) increasingly high percentages of immigrant students are entering schools at the secondary level, and yet the majority of programs designed to help Greek-language learners tend to be concentrated at the elementary school level. Some children are particularly at risk of dropping out. Some of these students arrive with interrupted schooling that has not prepared them well for the new setting. Others may have received an adequate or even superior education, but often find that they encounter resistance to finding a job that reflects their educational level (Ruiz-de-Velasco & Fix, 2001).

Regarding the structure of attitudes of the host country toward Albanian immigrants, there are four factors that give rise to prejudice: negative stereotypes, intergroup anxiety, realistic threats and symbolic threats (Stephan & Renfro, 2003). The literature indicates that a set of negative attributes is ascribed to Albanian immigrants: a low status and inferior group; 'casual workers'; 'marginalized, unemployed, homeless'; often 'illiterate with no skills'; of low potential and ability; and 'doomed to work in heavy and badly paid jobs'. Realistic threats are related to group conflict and competition for scarce resources or threats to physical well-being of an ingroup member. As a result, Albanians may be regarded as illegitimate competitors who are depriving native people of material resources, jobs, wages, social benefits and services (Constantinidou, 2001). Some interesting findings indicated that Albanian immigrants cope actively with prejudice. They display a relatively positive view toward their own group and pursue hetero stereotyping and prejudice to a lesser extent than the Greeks toward Albanians (Dalla & Georgiadhou, 2005). Albanians attribute to themselves virtues such as friendly, helpful, social, peaceful, honest, enthusiastic and negative emotional traits to a lesser extent such as inactive, undisciplined and lazy. Immigrants reject any personal responsibility for their status and attribute responsibility to the political system and complex bureaucratic procedures (Lyberaki & Maroukis, 2004).

Pontic Greeks

Pontic Greeks are descendants of the ancient Hellenic communities of the southern shores of the Black Sea, who were scattered by Stalin to different areas of the Soviet Union. These ethnic Greeks have retained the Greek culture, language, religion, and customs, but have never lived in Greece (Georgas & Papastylianou, 1996). More than half of them (about 80,000) came from Georgia, 31,000 from Kazakhstan, 23,000 from Russia and about 9,000 from Armenia (Gropas & Triandafyllidou, 2005). People coming to Greece from these countries are considered ethnic migrants, they are given special status and are treated as non-immigrants, even though in most cases, they face the same difficulties integrating in Greek society as other migrants. The main factors contributing to the migration of Pontic Greeks were a personal desire for return to their ancestral homeland, the presence of relatives already residing in Greece, the expectation of a better life and working conditions, the desire to raise their children where the existing language and religion would reinforce their ethnic identity, the civil war and persecution of minorities in the former Soviet Union and the neglect by the post-Soviet state with its lack of support for Pontic Greeks.

Regarding acculturation issues, Pontic Greeks can be described in terms of inclination toward integration (Georgas & Papastylianou, 1996). Most of them prefer to downplay the difference between them and the host society. Pontic Greeks maintain national and international connections. More than 300 different associations of Pontic Greeks exist in Greece. The local associations are organized in a larger body, 'Nostos', which since 1995 has brought together the Southern Greece Federation of Pontic Associations and the Pontic Associations of a number of major Greek cities and of neighborhoods across Athens. Nostos has participated in EU-funded programmes and has developed education, training, leisure and other activities aimed at Pontic Greeks' and their children's integration into Greek society and the labor market (Gropas & Triandafillidou, 2005).

Pontic Greeks have a higher educational level than the native-born population. Specifically, over 27% of Pontic Greeks have a higher educational degree compared with only 7% of the native populations. Two-thirds of Pontic Greeks have completed secondary education, compared with only one-third of the native population (Kassimati, 1992). Yet, most of them work as construction workers, cleaners, marker vendors, farm workers or craftspeople, jobs that bear little relevance to their previous experience and education. Part-time employment, unemployment and underemployment are the defining characteristics of the Pontic immigrant's work and occupation in Greece (Kassimati, 2001). The difficulty of integrating into Greek society and economy, which partly reproduces experiences of exclusion and 'Otherness', places Pontic Greeks somewhere between the ethnic Greeks and the ethnic minorities.

A comparative study of work behavior and experience of unemployed Pontic and native Greeks compared to employed coethnics
We conducted a study whose purpose was to examine some psychological aspects of work-related behavior and experience of unemployed Pontic remigrants and native Greeks in comparison with employed coethnics. The work-related behavior and experience was examined in relation to personality attributes such as personality traits and personal values, and occupational variables such as vocational interests and work values. Participants included people aged from 18 to 64 years, 121 Pontic remigrants and 294 Greeks who provided comparative data. The total sample included 104 males and 311 females. More than two-thirds of the sample (84.3%) were unemployed, 88 Pontic Greeks (73.3%) and 259 (88.4%) native Greeks. The employed sample comprised 66 people, 32 remigrants and 34 natives.

Personality traits   Personality factors could function as psychological resources for psychosocial and economic adaptation of immigrants (Ward & Leong, 2004). This study examined whether personality traits function as moderator variables between immigration and employment. A short version of the Adjective Check List – Five Factors (ACL–ff; Williams et al., 1998) was used to measure personality traits. The instrument measures neuroticism (N), extraversion (E), openness (O), agreeableness (A), and conscientiousness (C). Each scale has six items, and responses are scored on a 7-point rating scale, ranging from 'not at all' to 'very much'.

It was found that some personality factors correlate with both immigration and employments status. Both employed and unemployed immigrants presented a significantly high level of conscientiousness. Neuroticism, which encompasses facets of anxiety, hostility, and impulsiveness, is associated with a high level of unemployment for both natives and immigrants. It is a negative predictor of extrinsic success – for example, income and occupational status – and has been broadly linked to skills deficits (Judge et al., 1999). Furthermore, immigrant status makes economic adaptation for Pontic Greeks more anxiety raising because they experience many changes that take place as a result of culture contact and participation in a new society.

Personal values   Values specify an individual's personal beliefs about how he or she 'should' or 'ought' to behave in their social environments (Schwartz, 1994). Change and societal insecurity would result in emphasis on conservation and self-enhancement values, whereas societal security would result in emphasis on openness-to-change and self-transcendence values (Schwartz & Sagie, 2000). The Schwartz Values Survey was used to determine value differences between immigrants and natives and their relation to employment status. The Schwartz survey identifies 10 universal values that are organized into a system of four types of higher-order values: openness to change (self-direction, stimulation), conservation (conformity, security, tradition), self-enhancement (achievement, hedonism, power), and self-transcendence (benevolence, universalism). Openness-to-change values relate to the importance of personal autonomy and independence, variety, excitement and challenge. Conservation values relate to the importance of self-control, safety and stability in societal and personal relationships, and respecting cultural traditions. Self-enhancement values relate to achieving personal success through demonstrated competence, attaining social status and prestige, and control over others. Self-transcendence values relate to protecting and enhancing the well-being of those with whom one has close contact, as well as the welfare of all people and the environment.

According to the results, Pontic remigrants attribute less importance to openness to change (stimulation and self-direction), to self-enhancement (hedonism) and to self-transcendence, including benevolence. The dissimilar values and orientations of immigrants and native Greeks could be attributed to different socioeconomic and cultural environments and to immigration changes that do not engender modernist survival values, such as the pursuit of personal power and success. Furthermore, employed native Greeks were found to be significantly more open to change and self-enhancement but less conservative than unemployed natives and immigrants. One implication of this study is a need for flexible managerial and human resource practices using work team formation, and career development to accommodate values differences and to facilitate workplace coordination and long-term organizational success (Kupperschmidt, 2000).

Vocational interests   Vocational interests refer specifically to those activities, objects or processes associated with work activities. People obtain satisfaction by performing the particular kind of work activity that closely fits their personality preferences. Holland (1997) articulated a model of vocational interests which included six dimensions, or interest types. Realistic individuals enjoy working with mechanical devices and working outdoors using machines, tools and objects. Investigative individuals enjoy scientific pursuits, working with abstract ideas, researching and analyzing. Artistic individuals value aesthetics and enjoy using their imagination and creativity. Social individuals value service to others and enjoy teaching, helping, and working with people. Enterprising people value status and enjoy directing, organizing, and leading. Conventional individuals prefer structured tasks, and enjoy practical pursuits and working with things, numbers or machines to meet precise standards.

The Vocational Interests Inventory for Adults was also used (Holland et al., 2001). Vocational interests were measured using 48 items rated on a 5-point Likert scale (1 = strongly disinterested, 5 = strongly interested).

Compared to natives, remigrants from the former Soviet Union seem to avoid high occupational goals and ambitions, and are focused much less on activities that relate to social, investigate, artistic, enterprising and conventional occupations. Immigrants have to deal with different kinds of adaptation problems because of their different cultural background, the different labor market and the language barrier. Consequently, factors such as job satisfaction and even finding a job that suits the person's preferences are of peripheral importance. Immigrants who have assigned less importance to job satisfaction and their vocational preferences are more likely to find employment. Fulfilling this need therefore becomes far more important than job satisfaction.

Work values   A person's expectations from a job are determined by the personal goals (material enjoyment, prestige, social harmony) and the cultural values in which the person is socialized. Many of these values are related to work (Hui, 1990). Within the literature, several classifications of work values exist (Super, 1992). Based upon the categorization of values proposed by Super, we focused on six basic types of work values: (i) intellectual stimulation, which is associated with work that provides opportunity for independent thinking and learning how and why things work; (ii) creativity, which is associated with work that permits individuals to invent new things, design new products or develop new ideas; (iii) independence, which permits individuals to work their own way, doing what they want according to their level of achievement and direction; (iv) group orientation, which is associated with work that brings people into contact with fellow workers whom they like; (v) prestige, which is associated with work that gives people standing in the eyes of others and evokes respect; and (vi) security, which is associated with work that provides people with the certainty of having a job, even in hard times. Intellectual stimulation, creativity and independence reflect intrinsic rewards derived from pleasurable activities and goal accomplishment, while social orientation concerns extrinsic social concomitants of work and prestige and security extrinsic values in the form of rewards. The Work Value Inventory consisted of 38 items rated on a 5-point Likert scale ranging from 'not well at all' to 'very well'.

It was found that in most scales, immigrants did not differ in their work values from native Greeks. However, statistical significant differences were found in the social orientation scale, where immigrants look for social values within their work situation less than natives and are more material rather than affective at work. Concerning employment, it was found that despite their ethnicity, unemployed people look for social values and intellectual stimulation within their work situation more than employed people. This finding is consistent with other studies that suggest that nearly all people seem to value intrinsic work-related rewards such as achievement and independence, whereas others seek socialization and stimulation (Seligman, 1994). The multiple sources of job satisfaction help to address problems presented by unstimulating jobs and unemployment.

Model of career development for culturally different individuals

Career theory and practice have long emphasized 'person' variables such as an individual's skills, abilities, and interests; understanding personality, values, and beliefs; and matching these variables with appropriate potential careers (Flores et al., 2003). But in the context of immigration, people experience changes and transition. These changes place the understanding of career development in a broader sociocultural context, and other factors such as acculturation, intergroup relations and the broader immigration policy of the settlement country (Figure 22.1). Immigration and acculturation are also important variables to assess in the career development of immigrants. Information about the way in which immigrants acculturate (integration, assimilation, separation, and marginalization) should inform about their self-identification, the language proficiency and the acculturative stress as these factors influence the ability of immigrants to integrate into the workforce (Stewart, 2003). Furthermore, they should determine the kind of information that immigrants have about the structure of the labor market in the new country and about the experiences they may encounter upon entering the workforce. Immigrants may also encounter systematic racism in career and employment practices, especially if natives feel insecure about the stability of their own job during economic slumps (Arthur, 2005).

In addition to the individual level, career development processes of immigrants take place at the institutional level. The general public institutions of the receiving society, such as the educational system and institutional arrangement in the labor market, might promote or hinder integration processes of immigrants (Penninx & Roosblad, 2000). A critical step in improving immigrant outcomes is to help adult immigrants improve their

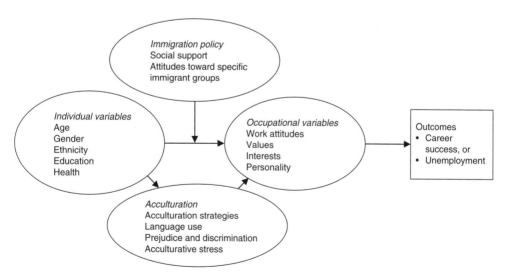

Figure 22.1   Model of career development for culturally different individuals

language skills, so that they can integrate more quickly and effectively into the labor market. Obtaining citizenship is a significant step in the integration process for newcomers because it signifies full participation in a new society. Perhaps the most frustrating barrier that immigrants may have to face is that their previous educational achievements and credentials may not be recognized (Arthur, 2005). Therefore, if immigrants want to re-enter their previous professions, they will have to re-take their training or upgrade their degrees. People working in the public services that deal with immigrants and within organizations for the support of immigrants should be trained on the direct issues concerning immigrants in order for them to have a better understanding of how they should approach this social group, how they can help them become integrated into the new society and how they can provide counseling for the labor market and other relevant areas.

According to the model of career development presented in Figure 22.1, career counseling of immigrants includes different modes and areas of intervention. The modes of intervention at the institutional level involve activities that seek to change and modify the environments of immigrants so that obstacles to their career and educational development can be reduced. In the context of the individual, career issues of immigrants can be understood in terms of the cultural background and acculturation issues. Descriptive information about variables such as vocational interests, work values, personality and aspirations is a starting-point for researchers and practitioners. But they also need to understand the range of variables that affect the career development of immigrant groups, such as acculturation, ethnic identity development and acculturative stress.

References

Acevedo-Garcia, D. (2001), 'Zip code-level risk factors for tuberculosis: neighborhood environment and residential segregation in New Jersey, 1985–1992', *American Journal of Public Health*, **91** (5), 734–41.

Achotegui, J. (2002), *La depresion en los immigrantes: una perspectiva transcultural* [Depression and Loss Among Immigrants: a Multicultural Perspective], Barcelona: Editorial Mayo.

Akhtar, S. (1999), *Immigration and Identity. Turmoil, Treatment and Transformation*, Jason Aronson.

Arthur, N. (2006), 'Infusing culture into constructivist approaches to career counseling', in M. McMahon & W. Patton (eds), *Career Counseling: Constructivist Approaches*, New York: Routledge, pp. 57–68.

Aycan, Z. (2000), 'Cross-cultural industrial and organizational psychology: contributions, past development and future directions', *Journal of Cross-Cultural Psychology*, **31**, 110–28.

Aycan, Z. & Berry, J.W. (1996), 'Impact of employment-related experiences on immigrants' psychological well-being and adaptation to Canada', *Canadian Journal of Behavioural Science*, **28** (3), 240–51.

Berman, E., Lang, K. & Siniver, E. (2003), 'Language skill complementarity: returns to immigrant language acquisition', *Labor Economics*, **10** (3), 265–90.

Berry, J.W. (2003), 'Conceptual approaches to acculturation', in K. Chun, P. Balls-Organista & G. Martin (eds), *Acculturation: Advances in Theory, Measurement and Applied Research*, Washington, DC: American Psychological Association, pp. 17–37.

Berry, J.W. (2006), 'Contexts of acculturation', in D.L. Sam & J.W. Berry (eds), *The Cambridge Handbook of Acculturation Psychology*, Cambridge: Cambridge University Press, pp. 27–43.

Berry, J.W., Phinney, J.S., Kwak, K. & Sam, D.L. (2006), 'Introduction: goals and research framework for studying immigrant youth', in J.W. Berry, J.S. Phinney, D.L. Sam & P. Vedder (eds), *Immigrant Youth in Cultural Transition. Acculturation, Identity and Adaptation across National Contexts*, Mahwah, NJ: Lawrence Erlbaum, pp. 1–15.

Bhui, K. Abdi, A., Abdi, M., Pereira, S., Dualeh, M., Robertson, D., Sathyamoorthy, G. & Ismail, H. (2003), 'Traumatic events, migration, characteristics and psychiatric symptoms among Somali refugees – preliminary communication', *Social Psychology and Psychiatric Epidemiology*, **38**, 35–43.

Bierbrauer, G. & Pedersen, P. (1996), 'Culture and migration', in G.R. Semin & K. Fiedler (eds), *Applied Social Psychology*, London: Sage, pp. 399–423.

Carter, R.T. & Constantine, M.G. (2000), 'Maturity, life role salience, and racial/ethnic identity in Black and Asian American college students', *Journal of Career Assessment*, **8** (2) 173–87.

Castles, S. & Miller, M. (1998), *The Age of Migration*, 2nd edn, London: Macmillan.

Catalano, R., Aldrete, E., Vega, W., Kolody, B. & Aguilar-Gaxiola, S. (2000), 'Job loss and major depression among Mexican Americans', *Social Science Quarterly*, **81** (1), 477–87.

Cavounidis, J. (2002), 'Migration in Southern Europe and the cases of Greece', *International Migration*, **40** (1), 45–69.

Cavounidis, J. (2004), 'Migration to Greece from the Balkans', *South-Eastern Europe Journal of Economics*, **2**, 35–59.

Constantinidou, C. (2001), *Social Representations of Crime: Images of Albanian Immigrants' Criminality in the Athenian Press*, Athens: Sakkoulas (in Greek).

Dalla, M. & Georgiadou, E. (2005), 'The effect of intergroup emotions on intergroup stereotypes', paper presented at the 27th International School Psychology Colloquium, Athens, Greece.

Dalla, M., Karademas, V. & Prapas, Ch. (2004), 'Immigration and mental health. Immigrant from Albania and repatriated from former Soviet Union' (in Greek), *Tetradhia Psixiatrikis*, **87**, 103–13.

Dooley, D., Prause, J. & Ham-Rowbottom, K. (2000), 'Underemployment and depression: longitudinal relationships', *Journal of Health and Social Behavior*, **41**, 421–36.

Dragoti, E., Dalla, M. & Pavlopoulos, V. (2006), 'Personality and mental health among Albanian immigrants in Greece in comparison to their coethnics in Albania and native Greeks', presentation at 13th European Conference of Personality, Athens, Greece, 22–26 July.

Fang, J., Madhavan, S., Bosworth, W. & Alderman, M.H. (1998), 'Residential segregation and mortality in New York City', *Social Science and Medicine*, **47** (4), 469–76.

Flores, L.Y., Spanierman, L.B. & Obasi, E.M. (2003), 'Ethical and professional issues in career assessment with diverse racial and ethnic groups', *Journal of Career Assessment*, **11** (1), 76–95.

Fouad, N. (2001), 'The future of vocational psychology: aiming high', *Journal of Vocational Behavior*, **59**, 183–91.

Fouad, N. & Bingham, R. (1995), 'Career counseling with racial/ethnic minorities', in W.B. Walsh & S.H. Osipow (eds), *Handbook of Vocational Psychology*, Hilsdale, NJ: Lawrence Erlbaum, pp. 331–66.

Fouad, N. & Byars-Winston, A. (2005), 'Cultural context of career choice: meta-analysis of race/ethnicity differences', *Career Quarterly*, **53** (3), 223–33.

Gainor, K.A. (2000), 'Vocational assessment with culturally diverse populations', in L.A. Suzuki, J.G. Panterotto & P.J. Meller (eds), *Handbook of Multicultural Assessment*, San Francisco, CA: Jossey-Bass, pp. 169–91.

Georgas, J. & Papastylianou, D. (1996), 'Acculturation and ethnic identity: the remigration of ethnic Greeks to Greece', in H. Grad, A. Blanco & J. Georgas (eds), *Key Issues in Cross-Cultural Psychology: Selected Papers from the Twelfth International Congress of the International Association for Cross-Cultural Psychology*, Lisse: Swets & Zeitlinger, pp. 114–28.

Gropas, R. & Triandafyllidou, A. (2005), 'Active civic participation of immigrants in Greece', Country Report prepared for the European research project POLITIS, Oldenburg, www.uni-oldenburg.de/politis-Europe. pdf.

Gysbers, N.C. & Moore, E.J. (1975), 'Beyond career development – life career development', *Personnel and Guidance Journal*, **53**, 647–52.

Gyspers, N.C., Heppner, M.J. & Johnston, J.A. (1999), *Career Counseling: Process, Issues and Techniques*, Boston, MA: Allyn & Bacon.

Hartung, P.J., Fouad, N.A., Leong, F.T.L. & Hardin, E. (2002), 'Cultural value orientation, family expectations, and career development', paper presented at the Annual Meeting of the American Psychological Association, Chicago, IL, August 22–25.

Hayfron, J.E. (2006), 'Immigrants in the labor markets', in D.L. Sam & J.W. Berry (eds), *The Cambridge Handbook of Acculturation Psychology*, Cambridge: Cambridge University Press, pp. 439–51.

Holland, J.L. (1992), *Making Vocational Choices*, 2nd edn, Odessa, FL: Psychological Assessment Resources, Inc.

Holland, J.L. (1997), *Making Vocational Choices*, Odessa, FL: Psychological Assessment Resources, Inc.

Holland, J.L., Reardon, R.C., Latshaw, R.J., Rarick, S.R., Schneider, S., Shortridge, M.A. & James, S.A. (2001), Self-Directed Search Form R Internet Version 2.0 (online), available at http://www.self-directed-search.com.

Hui, C.H. (1990), 'Work attitudes, leadership styles, and managerial behaviors in different countries', in R.W. Brislin (ed.), *Applied Cross Cultural Psychology*, London: Sage, pp. 186–209.

International Organization for Migration (IOM) (2003), *Managing Migration – Challenges and Responses for People on the Move*, Vol. 2 of the IOM World Migration Report Series.

Jackson, M.A. & Nutini, C.D. (2002), 'Hidden resources and barriers in career learning assessment with adolescents vulnerable to discrimination', *Career Development Quarterly*, **51** (1), 56–77.

Judge, T.A., Higgins, C.A., Thoresen, C.J., Barrick, C.J. & Murray, R. (1999), 'The Big Five personality traits, general mental ability and career success across the life span', *Personnel Psychology*, **52**, 621–52.

Karlsen, S. & Nazroo, J.Y. (2002), 'Relation between racial discrimination, social class, and health among ethnic minority groups', *American Journal of Public Health*, **92** (4), 624–31.

Kasimati, K. (1992), *Pontiac Immigrants from Former Soviet Union. Social and Economic Adaptation* (in Greek), Athens: General Secretariat of Greek Diaspora.

Kasimati, K. (ed.) (2001), *Social Exclusion. The Greek Experience*, Athens: Gutenberg.

Kasimis, C. & Kassimi, C. (2004), 'Greece: a history of migration', Migration Information Source, www.migrationinformation.org/pdf.

Kennedy, S. & Mcdonald, J.T. (2006), 'Immigrant mental health and unemployment', *Economic Record*, **82** (259), 445–59.

King, R., Lazaridis, G. & Tsardanidis, C. (2000), *Eldorado or Fortress? Migration in Southern Europe*, London: Macmillan.

Kupperschmidt, B.R. (2000), 'Multigeneration employees: strategies for effective management', *Health Care Manager*, **19**, 65–76.

Labrianidis, L. & Lyberaki, A. (2001), *Albanian Immigrants in Thessaloniki: Integration Paths and Public Projections*, Thessaloniki: Paratiritis.

Leong, F.T.L. & Hartung, P.J. (2000), 'Adapting to the changing multicultural context of career', in Collin & R. Young (eds), *The Future of Career*, Cambridge: Cambridge University Press, pp. 212–27.

Leung, S.A. (1995), 'Career development and counseling: a multicultural perspective', in J.G. Ponterotto, J.M. Casas, L.A. Suzuki & C.M. Alexander (eds), *Handbook of Multicultural Counseling*, Newbury Park, CA: Sage, pp. 549–67.

Lev-Wiesel, R. & Kaufman, R. (2004), 'Personal characteristics, unemployment, and anxiety among highly educated immigrants', *International Migration*, **42** (3), 57–75.

Lianos, Th. P. (2004), *Report on Immigration*, European Migration Network, Greek National Contact Point, Center for Planning and Economic Research, Greece.

Liebkind, K. (2001), 'Acculturation', in R. Brown & S.L. Gaertner (eds), *Blackwell Handbook of Social Psychology*, Oxford: Blackwell, pp. 386–409.

Lyberaki, A. & Maroukis, T. (2004), *Albanian Immigrants in Athens: Some Recent Findings*, Athens: Hellenic Foundation for European & Foreign Policy.

Modood, T., Berthoud, R., Lakey, J., Nazroo, J., Smith, P., Virdee, S. & Beishon, S. (1997), *Fourth National Survey of Ethnic Minorities in Britain: Diversity and Disadvantage*, London: Policy Studies Institute.

Motti-Stefanidi, F., Pavlopoulous, V. Obradović, J., Dalla, M., Takis, N., Papathanasiou, A. & Masten, A. (2008), 'Immigration as a risk factor for adolescent adaptation in Greek urban schools', *European Journal of Developmental Psychology*, **5** (2), 235–61.

Mummendey, A. & Otten, S. (2003), 'Aversive discrimination', in R. Brown & S. Gaertner (eds), *Blackwell Handbook of Social Psychology*, Oxford: Blackwell, pp. 112–33.

Murphy, G.C. & Athanasou, J.A. (1999), 'The effect of unemployment on mental health', *Journal of Occupational and Organizational Psychology*, **72** (1), 83–99.

Nickolaou, J. (2000), *Integration and Education of Immigrant Children at Primary School. From Homogeneity to Multiculturalism* (in Greek), Athens: Ellinika Grammata.

Penninx, R. & Roosblad, J. (2000), *Trade Unions, Immigration and Immigrants in Europe, 1960–1993: A Comparative Study of the Attitudes and Actions of Trade Unions in Seven West European Countries*, New York: Berghahn Books.

Phalet, K. & Kosic, A. (2006), 'Acculturation in European societies', in D.L. Sam & J.W. Berry (eds), *The Cambridge Handbook of Acculturation Psychology*, Cambridge: Cambridge University Press, pp. 331–49.

Rovolis, A. & Tragaki, A. (2005), 'The regional dimension of migration in Greece: spatial patterns and causal factors', paper presented to the 45th Congress of the European Regional Science Association on Land Use and Water Management in a Sustainable Network Society, Vrije Universiteit, Amsterdam, 23–27 August.

Ruiz-de-Velasco, J. & Fix, M. (2001), *Overlooked and Underserved: Immigrant Students in U.S. Secondary Schools*, Washington, DC: Urban Institute.

Sang, D.L. & Ward, C. (2006), 'Acculturation in Australia and New Zealand', in D.L. Sam & J.W. Berry (eds), *The Cambridge Handbook of Acculturation Psychology*, Cambridge: Cambridge University Press, pp. 253–73.

Schmitz, P. (1992), 'Immigrant mental and physical health', *Psychology and Developing Societies*, **4**, 117–31.

Schwartz, S.H. (1994), 'Are there universal aspects in the structure and content of human values?', *Journal of Social Issues*, **50** (4) 19–45.

Schwartz, S.H. & Sagie, G. (2000), 'Value consensus and importance: a cross-national study', *Journal of Cross-Cultural Psychology*, **31**, 465–97.

Seligman, L. (1994), *Developmental Career Counseling and Assessment*, London: Sage.

Sharareh, A., Bilat, C.O., Franzén, E.C. & Wamala, S. (2004), 'Health in relation to unemployment and sick leave among immigrants in Sweden from a gender perspective', *Journal of Immigrant Health*, **6** (3), 103–18.

Sitaropoulos, N. (2003), *Immigration Law and Management in Greece. Towards an Exodus from Underdevelopment and a Comprehensive Immigration Policy*, Athens: Sakkoulas.

Stephan, W.G. & Renfro, C.L. (2003), 'The role of threat in intergroup relations', in D.M. Mackie & E.R. Smith (eds), *From Prejudice to Intergroup Emotions: Differentiated Reactions to Social Groups*, New York: Psychology Press, pp. 191–209.

Stewart, J.B. (2003), 'Career counselling multicultural immigrant groups', NATCON Papers 2003, http://www.contactpoint.ca/natcon-conat/2003/pdf/pdf-03-14.pdf, 28 October 2004.

Suárez-Orozco, C. (2000), 'Identities under siege: immigration stress and social mirroring among children of immigrants', in C.G.M. Tobben & C. Suárez-Orozco (eds), *Cultures Under Siege. Collective Violence and Trauma*, Cambridge University Press, pp. 195–226.

Sue, D.W., Ivey, A.E. & Pedersen, P.B. (1996), *Multicultural Counseling Theory*, Belmont, CA: Brooks/Cole.

Super, D.E. (1992), 'Towards a comprehensive theory of career development', in D. Montross & C. Shinkman (eds), *Career Development: Theory and Practice*, Springfield, IL: Thomas.

Swanson, J.L. & Fouad, N.A. (1999), *Career Theory and Practice: Learning through Case Studies*, Thousand Oaks, CA: Sage.

Swanson, J.L., Paul, A. & Gore, P. Jr. (2000), 'Advances in vocational psychology. Theory and research', in S.D. Brown & R.W. Lent (eds), *Handbook of Counseling Psychology*, Chichester, UK and New York: John Wiley, pp. 233–70.

Teng, L.Y., Morgan, G.A. & Anderson, S.K. (2001), 'Career development among ethnic and age groups of Community College Students', *Journal of Career Development*, **28** (2), 115–27.

Triandafyllidou, A. & Mariangela, V. (2002), 'The hierarchy of Greekness – ethnic and national identity consideration in Greek immigration policy', *Ethnicities*, **2** (2), 189–208.

Triandis, H.C. & Trafimov, D. (2003), 'Culture and its implications for intergroup behavior', in R. Brown & S. Gaertner (eds), *Blackwell Handbook of Social Psychology*, Oxford: Blackwell, pp. 367–86.

Van de Vijver, F. (2000), 'The nature of bias', in R.H. Dana (ed.), *Handbook of Cross-Cultural and Multicultural Personality Assessment*, Mahwah, NJ: Lawrence Erlbaum, pp. 87–107.

VicHealth (1999), *Mental Health Promotion Plan Foundation Document: 1999–2002*, Melbourne: Victorian Health Promotion Foundation.

Walsh, W.B. (2001), *Career Counseling for African Americans*, Mahwah, NJ: Lawrence Erlbaum.

Ward, C., Bochner, S. & Furnham, A. (2001), *The Psychology of Culture Shock*, 2nd edn, New York: Routledge.

Ward, C. & Leong, C. (2004), 'Personality and sojourner adjustment. An exploration of the Big Five and the cultural fit proposition', *Journal of Cross-Cultural Psychology*, **35** (2), 137–51.

Wiking, E., Johansson, S.E. & Sundquist, J. (2004), 'Ethnicity, acculturation, and self-reported health. A population-based study among immigrants from Poland, Turkey, and Iran in Sweden', *Journal of Epidemiology and Community Health*, **58** (7), 574–82.

Williams, D.R. & Collins, C. (2001), 'Racial residential segregation: a fundamental cause of racial disparities in health', *Public Health Report*, **116** (5), 404–16.

Williams, J.E., Satterwhite, R.C. & Saiz, J.L. (1998), *The Importance of Psychology Traits: A Cross-Cultural Study*, Plenum Press.

Wilson, M. (2003), 'The mental health of black and minority ethnic people', *Mental Health Review*, **8**, 7–15.

Winefield, A.H. (2002), 'Unemployment, under-employment, occupational stress and psychological well-being', *Australian Journal of Management*, **27**, 137–48.

Zavos, A. (2006), 'Migration management as a political necessity. Objectives and characteristics of a modern Greek migration policy', in D.G. Papademetriou & J. Cavounidhis (eds), *Managing Migration: The Greek, EU, and International Context*, Hellenie Migration Policy Institute (IMEPO), pp. 10–20.

Zunzunegui, M.V., Forster, M., Gauvin, L., Raynault, M.F. & Douglas, W. (2006), 'Community unemployment and immigrants' health in Montreal', *Social Science of Medicine*, **63** (2), 485–500.

23 Migration and health: psychosocial determinants
Bruce Kirkcaldy, Adrian Furnham and Georg Siefen

Introduction

This chapter reviews contemporary literature on the social and psychological factors which are associated with migration. The potential stressful impact of migration is examined with respect to psychological and physical health, incidence of psychopathology, family and their offspring, and drug and chemical abuse. In addition, the implications of linguistic factors, familiarity of culture, cross-cultural differences in temperament (cultural disparity), and accessibility to healthcare are examined. Economic and psychological adaptation are explored as well as differences in coping with stress and the moderating effects of social networks on the link between stress and health outcomes. Finally, concluding remarks are offered, together with a short discussion of the implication of these findings for social and health policy makers.

Magnitude of the problem

The number of migrants in the world has more than doubled since 1975, so that by 1990, migrants represented over 15% of the population in 52 countries. Whereas in the past Europe has been a continent of emigrants, it is now one of immigrants (Carta et al., 2005). The last decade has been labelled the 'decade of ethnicity', with theoretical interest revolving around the manner in which 'culture and psyche' interact (Shweder & Sullivan, 1993). Economic factors have played a major role in the migration process, which is particularly evident from the immigration patterns towards more industrialized, economic stable countries. There are push and pull factors in migration. Migrants are pushed by poverty, famine, illness and political oppression while being pulled by opportunities for a better life for themselves and their families.

For example, Germany is one of the nations with a high immigration intake. Just over half a century ago, foreigners made up only 1% of the German population. By the end of 2003, this had risen to almost 9% of the population (7.3 million, including 2.3 million citizens from EU countries). On the other hand, 20% of foreigners living in Germany were born here and are therefore second- or third-generation immigrants. In 1992, 1.5 million immigrated to Germany, although this number was halved (800,000) by 2003. This increase was due primarily to ethnic Germans from Eastern Europe and the former Soviet Union (until the mid-1990s), asylum seekers and refugees from war/civil unrest (who for the most part have returned to their native countries).[1]

Migration and stress

Migration is unanimously described as a critical life event which may overwhelm previously existing adaptive capabilities, coping and problem-solving strategies (Lantermann & Hänze, 1999). Berry (1997) argued that stress is a direct effect of the acculturation process, and subsequently leads to inferior physical and psychological well-being, with migrants typically complaining of fatigue, headaches and sleep irregularities (Sundquist, 1993).

Haasen and Yagdiran (2000) specified various stressful factors associated with migration, including unresolved separation anxiety related to one's immediate and extended family, alienation and isolation due to prolonged separation and changing relational ties, marital and intergenerational norm and role conflicts, persistent ambivalence and discord, conflicting lifestyles and goals of individual family members, difficulties in orientation due to unpredictable and unstable work prospects, disappointment in educational attainments of the children, uncertainties relating to living conditions/housing and legal rights of residency, chronic occupational stress, (the threat of) unemployment, stigmatization, social rejection and hostility towards foreigners.

Carta et al. (2005) also referred to the chronic and multiple stress syndrome associated with the risky and strenuous journey that some immigrants take, for example, in reaching the coasts of Spain and Italy. The term 'Ulysses syndrome', used by psychiatrists in Barcelona in the Psychosocial Assistance Service team trying to help these immigrants, refers to an independent category between adjustment and post-traumatic disorders. It is manifested by a variety of symptoms including anxiety, somatoform and dissociative experiences coupled with depressive symptomatology.

The length of settlement seems to influence the physical and mental well-being of immigrants. Bagley (1993) observed that recent Chinese migrants to Canada exhibited more anxiety and depression than the long-term established ones. Furthermore, those migrants who had settled in Canada some 20 years previously revealed physical and psychological health profiles similar to those of Euro-Canadians. It may be argued that this is related to familiarity with the new language and increasing proficiency of linguistic fluency.

There is, in brief, no shortage of data to suggest that there is a certain amount of stress associated with migration. However, whether that stress is chronic or acute depends largely on the psychological make-up of the individual, his/her social network, and the particular circumstance of the travel experience.

Psychological aspects of migration

There has been widespread research on migration and psychological ill health. Migration can be a highly traumatizing experience. The process involves uprooting, being detached from family and traditional values, and being in novel social and cultural situations where job and legal security may be negligible. Many experience direct and indirect prejudice (Carbello & Nerukar, 2001). Social integration will seldom be unproblematic:

> Among all the changes a human being must face throughout his life, few are so wide and complex as those which take place during migration. Practically everything that surrounds the person who emigrates changes. Aspects ranging from diet, family and social relations to climate, language, culture, and status are subject to change . . . Every person who emigrates experiences affective loss, but is buoyed up in the hope of finding the first world paradise they often so little about. (Carta et al., 2005)

A vast array of empirical studies would seem to support the notion of migration being particularly stressful (Furnham & Bochner, 1986; Ward et al., 2001). For example, Jews from the former Soviet Union displayed more symptoms of demoralization (low self-esteem, sadness, anxiety, hopeless and psychosomatic ailments) than Israeli-born settlers of European descent (Zilber & Lerner, 1996).

Studies on different migrant groups in different countries have tended to yield similar findings, namely that there are often social, medical and behavioural consequences of the process of migration.

Psychological health, psychopathology and migration

How does the physical and mental health of migrants differ from that of the natives? If it does, is this evidence of cultural differences, selective migration, the stress of migration or some combination of the above?

In the United Kingdom, Irish immigrants have a higher rate of suicide, and Afro-Caribbeans are more often diagnosed as schizophrenic than native Britons (Balarayan, 1995). Janca and Helzer (1992) reported that a group of foreign students in Yugoslavia who were hospitalized in psychiatric clinics displayed higher rates of depressive and paranoid responses, which may have resulted from maladaptation to the novel living conditions, causing feelings of isolation and alienation coupled with depression. Rosmond et al. (2000) observed that female immigrants from Nordic, other European and non-European countries and natives of Sweden showed a high level of psychiatric ill health. In a German study (Storch and Poutska, 2000) involving psychiatric inpatients, there were more frequent suicidal attempts among females from Mediterranean countries than among their German female counterparts.

The relatively high prevalence of depressive disorders among immigrants and their offspring in many European countries has also been connected with high rates of suicidal behaviour, which may be related to unemployment. In the Netherlands, where the unemployment rate among immigrants in the mid-1990s was 2.5 times that of Dutch nationals (31% and 13%, respectively), the incidence of suicide among immigrant children was also substantially higher than in the general population (see Carbello & Nerukar, 2001).

Ponizovsky et al. (1999) found that Jewish children who had emigrated to Israel from Russia displayed a 6-month rate for suicidal ideation of 10.9%, which was higher than that of the Jewish adolescents living in Russia (3.5%). The incidence rate was higher, albeit non-significant, compared to that of children of similar ages in Israel (8.7%). It has been argued that this corresponds to a greater gravitation among adolescents towards the suicidal attitudes of the host nation. Others (Bengi-Arslan et al., 1997) have observed that among Turkish parents, their children who had immigrated to the Netherlands were perceived as more anxious, depressive and aggressive compared to their counterparts in Turkey. On the other hand, they felt they displayed less physical ailments.

However, several studies do not reveal differences in terms of physical or psychological distress between migrant and non-migrant groups (Noh & Kaspar, 2003). One explanation is that for migrants as opposed to refugees, it is the better off, hardier and more robust that choose to and are allowed to migrate and that these were therefore more psychologically and physically resilient.

Others have argued for *less* psychopathology among immigrants. Migrants who move to obtain a better lifestyle and environment may display improvement in health. For instance, Southeast Asian migrants in the United Kingdom exhibited lower levels of depression compared to the white majority (Berthoud & Nazroo, 1997). Sam (1998) found that adolescent migrants in Norway who originated from Third-World countries had fewer behavioural problems than their native-born peers. Much depends on the education, work skills and social–emotional support in migrant groups.

Drug and alcohol usage

One of the problems inherent in using figures for the incidence rates of drug and alcohol use among immigrants is that many societies such as Canada and the USA are reluctant to implement measures of ethnic/racial origin when exploring antisocial behaviour, because they believe that inherent racial prejudices are thereby reinforced. Nevertheless, some studies have focused on the relationship between drug and alcohol use and migrants. Furthermore, abuse of alcohol and drugs is strongly culturally determined. Thus, there is very low alcohol abuse among Muslims and in Muslim countries even where alcohol is permitted (e.g., Malaysia). There are traditionally low rates of alcoholism among Jews and high levels among Northern European peoples. Drug consumption is likewise culturally determined, so that some drugs are rarely used outside a particular region, though this pattern may be changing.

When differences have been observed, they have been cited as support for competing theories such as culture conflict (culture shock); marginalization (alternatively sociocultural isolation); absence of protective factors (social supportive networks); personality factors (traits such as sensation and novelty seeking); goal-striving success (aspirations of individuals); and parental attitudinal dissonance. The problem is that these theories are *not* mutually exclusive and are generally operating simultaneously. More specifically, if we confine a review to sociological variables and neglect psychobiological variables, then we are unlikely to observe the relative magnitude of effect of these two variable sets.

One explanation of differences between migrants and native populations focuses on the economic–geographical factors. For example, a study (Bankston & Zhou, 1997) on the bifurcation of Vietnamese American youth hypothesizes that the tendency of Vietnamese young people to become achievers or delinquents is attributable to their relationship to their own community in the context of settlement in economically underprivileged neighbourhoods. The authors concluded that the delinquent group consisted of those who have relatively numerous ties to *non-Vietnamese* American youth in the low-income neighbourhoods and who adopt interests and activities associated with this part of American youth culture. Conversely, non-delinquents were more inclined to display social ties linking them to other Vietnamese, expressing interests and activities associated with Vietnamese ethnic society.

Various studies have shown that abuse of alcohol and other drugs by young people is primarily a function of parental values and parenting style, their social group (peers and friends) and educational level.

There is some indication that migrants may be overrepresented among drug users in some cultures. In the Netherlands, an estimated 25,000–28,000 hard drug addicts (cocaine and heroin) are assumed, and of these, from one-quarter to just over one-third are assumed to be migrants (6,400–9,900), mainly from the former colonies (Surinamese, Antillian, and Moluccan) as well as Moroccan and Turkish (Trautman, 1998). Such figures give some indication of the magnitude of the problem, but little detail of the underlying mechanism that may be operating to determine drug abuse. Clearly, incidence rates in themselves do not permit inferences about causal mechanisms.

For many new immigrants in a host nation, there will certainly be initial 'practical' problems with respect to inferior wages, long working hours (including night shifts), over-crowding and bad housing, which in turn will increase the risk of health problems and impact on their children's psychological development. Added to these difficulties, racism can lead to direct or indirect racial discrimination, abuse, inequality and disadvantage with regard to employment, housing, educational and training opportunities, access to healthcare, welfare, local amenities, and environmental quality, as well as to the under-mining of their culture, identity and self-image (Dwivedi, 1999). Such racism degrades and dehumanizes communities, and leads to lowering of their self-esteem, increases their sense of worthlessness and exacerbates depression.

In a large-scale epidemiological study, Johnston et al. (1999) found that for 8th graders, no differences were observed in the annual rate of use of marijuana of white and black pupils (approximately 16.3%), but Hispanics had higher rates (22.7%). Furthermore, Hispanics displayed higher usage of crack (3.6%), heroin (1.7%), cocaine (5.2%), LSD (4.2%) and hallucinogens (4.6%) for this age group. Blacks had the lowest rates of all three ethnic groups. For the 12th graders, the pattern had changed, with whites showing the highest prevalence of marijuana usage (39.9%, compared to 30% and 37.2% for blacks and Hispanics, respectively), inhalants, hallucinogens, LSD, MDMA, heroin and amphetamines. Blacks displayed the *lowest* levels throughout. Hispanics revealed the highest prevalence among the 12th graders for the categories of drugs, cocaine, crack, and other cocaine derivatives. Furthermore, not all studies have been consistent in their find-ings of 'cultural differences'. Swaim et al. (1997) compared tobacco use between migrant and non-migrant Mexican and Mexican–American youth. Using a self-report survey of cigarette use among 10th- and 12th-grade Mexican and Mexican-American pupils, they found no differences in rates of use by migrant status.

Occasionally, further studies have shown that not only are ethnic differences in drug usage observed, but they are moderated by gender differences (Kandel et al., 1997) based on three aggregated waves between 1991 and 1993 of nationally representative samples of the general population. Among adolescents, rates of dependence on alcohol, marijuana and cocaine were higher among females than males (in contrast to adults, whose rates of dependence were higher among males than among females for alcohol and marijuana, but lower for nicotine). Moreover, ethnic group seems to influence drug usage, with whites being more likely than any other ethnic group to be dependent on nicotine and blacks to be dependent on cocaine.

Drug and alcohol abuse has many causal factors, but one is the problems associated with migrant status. Cultural factors related to country of origin and country of destina-tion are primary causal factors in when, why and what form abuse takes place.

Immigrant families and their offspring

Migration is likely to have a different impact on the adults who decided to migrate to their host country compared to their children and those who may have more opportuni-ties to familiarize themselves with the new society, or indeed may have been born in that adopted society.

Other researchers (Siefen et al., 1996) have argued that parental relationships may centre on issues of conformity, minimizing conflict and maintenance of national tradi-tions, which is a key area for research into cultural adaptation and human relations involving parental attitudes. This is because the integration of adolescent immigrant groups into a host culture is mirrored by parental attitudes and relationships. Some attitudes are relatively flexible and amenable to change, while others form a stable part of the culture and social personality of a national group, often due to strong religious norms.

There is some evidence that adolescents take on the values and attitudes of the host culture more rapidly than do their parents, and the differences that emerge regarding attitudes between parents and their offspring may represent a source of conflict among immigrant families (Heras & Revilla, 1994; Ward et al., 2001).

Sethi (1990) also argued that adolescence is likely to be more turbulent for Indian youth in the United States than in their country of origin. The society with which they are most familiar and in which they were educated, which underlines critical thinking and questioning, will make them more reluctant to accept the traditional and cultural values of their parents. On the other hand, Patel et al. (1996) have observed that parental values are not static and are susceptible to change, so that Indian families (particularly those from the Hindu culture) are often selective in the retention of traditional as opposed to acceptance of modern values. Fathers were shown to retain their traditional values regarding interpersonal relations at home, especially with their daughters, while espousing American directives concerning interactions at other levels, such as in the workplace. Conversely, Sam (1998) was able to demonstrate that these value conflicts between generations were not confined to immigrants, and could be observed equally between Norwegian immigrant and non-immigrant families – manifested in intergenerational discrepancies in value systems.

Overall, there is evidence that parents exert a powerful influence upon their children's acculturation experiences and behaviours. Furthermore, their attitudes and behaviours have consequences for their children's sociocultural and psychological adaptation. Adolescents who had maintained a strong sense of ethnic identity had parents who exhibited a conscious effort to prepare their offspring for life in a diverse society (Phinney & Nakayama, 1991). Assimilated parents are more likely to have children who display high social competence (Lasry & Sayegh, 1992), and parental acceptance of the host culture is generally associated with superior health among their children (Barankin et al., 1989).

Barriers to healthcare: linguistic factors and 'health availability'
One issue of great importance is individual access to healthcare and whether this is affected by being a migrant.

Clinical and epidemiological studies may prove to be useful, but the inferences will be tenuous because there are several methodological and conceptual difficulties. They include problems associated with the cross-cultural equivalence of the psychometric and medical instruments for assessment, potential cultural biases in diagnoses, and disparities in access to the use of medical, psychological and therapeutic facilities (Tanaka-Matsumi & Draguns, 1997).

It can be expected that inadequacy in language proficiency in the host country may serve as a barrier to effective communication. The ability to communicate is likely to influence health-seeking behaviour, inferior explanations of health problems and symptoms, misdiagnoses and an underreporting of symptoms, both physical and more especially psychological (see Carbello & Nerukar, 2001).

Kirkcaldy et al. (2004) have explored the relationship between healthcare variables and health outcome factors for physical and psychological health, and analysed this across nations. Whenever psychological healthcare is analysed among immigrants in a

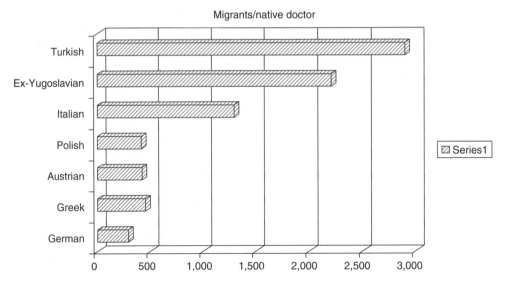

Figure 23.1   Number of 'native' migrants living in Germany per doctor originating from that original country

host country, it is essential to have information concerning the level and effectiveness of health treatment in that country. Added to this, it has been suggested that mistrust and unfamiliarity with the 'new' health system frequently leads to a lack of confidence in the effectiveness of healthcare (Wittig et al., 2004).

One explanation of the differences in an individual's inclination to seek medical treatment may be the lack of availability of medical professionals familiar with the immigrant's own culture and language. This seems to be one reason why minority groups will fear or feel ill at ease with the host nations' mental health systems. Moreover, medical doctors may be insensitive and/or misinterpret the problems that the immigrants confront them with. Kirkcaldy and Siefen (2002) analysed the figures for the German population and the largest immigrant subpopulations (Turks, Poles, Greeks, Italian, ex-Yugoslavians and Austrians). The data are given in Figure 23.1.

The value of having medical care provided in one's native language was demonstrated by a study by Grube (2001). A bilingual setting was introduced by employing a Turkish psychologist as counsellor for the diagnostic and therapeutic teams. Health outcome comparisons between Turkish patients and non-Turkish migrants as controls revealed significantly shorter duration of hospitalized treatment for Turkish non-schizophrenic in-patients, and Turkish schizophrenic patients demonstrated superior levels of rehabilitation.

Crijnen et al. (2000) observed that Turkish staff teaching Turkish immigrant children reported higher levels of anxiety and depression among immigrant children which apparently go unnoticed by native Dutch teachers. A German study (Hansen et al., 2001) found that increased incidence of hostility and depression was diagnosed among Turkish as opposed to German schizophrenics: increased rates which may be attributable to misdiagnoses.

The likelihood that a migrant will seek professional help concerning emotional problems will depend to some extent on the availability of mental health professionals and the cultural attitudes towards mental health problems. Family doctors may differ in their willingness to refer patients to a mental health specialist. There are also national differences in treatment-seeking behaviour for mental health problems. Using the Eurobarometer and the World Health Organization (WHO-FHA) databases (European Commission, 2004), the probability of consulting a general practitioner for help with such a problem was the highest in Belgium, France, Germany and Austria, and the lowest in the Netherlands, Portugal, Sweden and Spain. On the other hand, the likelihood of consulting another 'provider' (presumably non-medical professional counsellor or therapist) is the highest for the Netherlands, followed by Belgium, Sweden, France and Austria, and the lowest in Italy, Spain and Portugal. It was concluded that in some countries the non-medical professions were an important source of care. When the types of providers were examined, Germans (both new and old federal states) were much more likely to consult a general practitioner, followed by the Portuguese, Austrians, Belgians and French, compared with the Italians, Luxemburgers, and Dutch, who were least likely to see a GP concerning mental health problems. Psychotherapists and therapists were least sought among the Germans and Portuguese, and most often among the Spanish, Dutch, Italians and French. Thus, how a distressed, ill person sees a professional helper, how that helper diagnoses the problem and what treatment is received may well be a function of the culture of the patient, the helper and of the wider society.

Cultural disparity
The fact that migrants may report more (or less) distress of particular kinds than natives could, of course, be due to cultural norms in manifesting distress. Thus while some cultures may emphasize *stoicism* under stress, others may value emotional venting of distress. Furthermore, the extent to which psychosomaticization and its opposite occur for particular problems (such as depression) may well be powerfully influenced by culture.

Kirkcaldy and Siefen (2002) have underlined the value of comparing the psychological distress of migrants and non-migrants for those nations being compared with their 'host' country. In Figure 23.2, we have compared European nations' scores on two variables assessing psychological health, well-being and happiness scores. It could also be argued that it is essential to compare the rates of psychological ill health with the population scores for their country of origin rather than the country of immigration. For example, Russia, Hungary and Greece and to some extent Poland are all countries which consistently display comparatively low (psychological) well-being and happiness scores, while nations such as Holland, Iceland, Ireland, Sweden and Norway display high happiness scores. Immigrants arriving from Russia to a country such as Holland, Ireland or Sweden are probably more likely to show exaggerated negative affect which may not be related to the impact of migration *per se*, but which is due to inherent cross-cultural differences in personality and/or emotionality.

Assuming that these figures reflect to some extent the overall trend towards the psychological health of a nation, it is quite possible that differences observed among migrant groups may well reflect innate differences in personality traits, such as emotionality, which were present prior to migration. Clearly, it may be an 'illegitimate' comparison when psychological profiles of immigrants are compared to the population of the host nation. The complexity of the causal pattern is explained by Furnham and colleagues

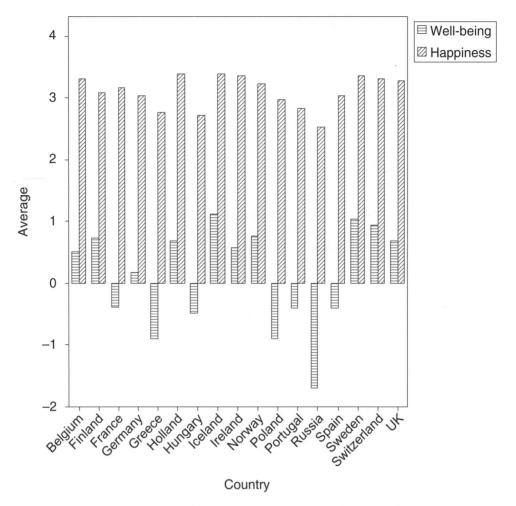

Sources: Well-being adapted from Diener et al.'s (1995) data for specified countries, and happiness scores from Veenhoven (2001b).

Figure 23.2   Well-being and happiness scores for European nations

(Furnham & Bochner, 1986; Ward et al., 2001) who explored the early studies in this field dating back to the 1930s.

Mirsky (1997) had also suggested that differences in psychological distress between migrants and non-migrants might originate from differences between the normative levels of discomfort in the original culture and the society of destination, exploring 'psychological phenomena among immigrants in the perspectives of cultural relativity and in the light of the society from which they arrived' (p. 226). Psychological well-being has been shown to be lower among Russians (Veenhoven, 2001a) compared to other nations, and this appears to be associated with the stagnation of the country's crippled economy. An alternative explanation for the negative cognitive bias may be a reflection of a 'folklore of misanthropy and lamentation' in which embellishment of unhappiness is a facet of Russian temperament.

Psychological adaptation

Do some groups – that is, young people, the better educated – or individuals (extroverts, stable individuals) adapt better than others? Kirkcaldy et al. (2008) looked at this issue in a sample of almost 1,000 adolescents, over half of whose families had migrated to Germany. Adolescents whose parents had migrated from their native countries to Germany did not display any significant differences in terms of physical health, but they did report inferior psychological health, as assessed through anxiety and depression measures.

In a more recent cross-cultural study involving some 50 countries, Kirkcaldy[2] found a significant negative correlation between the trait neuroticism and the percentage of migrants, indicating that those nations with a higher proportion of migrants are more inclined to show greater emotional stability (in terms of lower neuroticism scores). It could be argued that this relationship was due to differences in economic factors, that is, wealthy nations tending to display superior psychological well-being (lower neuroticism) and migration to such countries will reflect the economic wealth to a greater degree.

In Germany, it has been estimated that approximately 13% of immigrants seen for depressive disorders developed their problems during the first year of being away from home. A further 25% manifested their problems within the following 2–5 years. It has frequently been observed that immigrants report exaggerated memories of their style of living, familial events and the events they had experienced as children. Such 'migrant's opium' can be psychologically incapacitating, for instance in families whose migration was effected by forced dispersion (e.g., refugees in areas plagued by civil war) (Carbello & Nerukar, 2001).

The famous U-curve hypothesis suggests that adaptation occurs over time. Psychological distress seems to be associated with the first few years after arrival (ibid.), beginning with an initial phase of euphoria followed by disillusionment and demoralization with elevated negative affect during the second year and eventual return to well-being. Migrants have been shown to develop more psychosomatic ailments than nationals during the early stages of integration, for example, headaches, peptic ulcers, anxiety attacks, sleeping disorders, alcohol and chemical substance abuse and somatization of problems (European Commission, 2004).

Berry (1992) proposed a multiphase model of the integration process, beginning with contract/observation and transition into a conflict phase with an increase in stress, which will eventually decrease in a stage of adaptation or stabilization. This theory is supported by others (e.g., Ritsner & Ponizovsky, 1999).

In the recent study by Kirkcaldy et al. (2005), attempts were made to monitor physical complaints of Russian immigrants in Germany within the first 18 months after migration. There was an increase in complaints during the first six months after arrival, which was consistent with the migration hypothesis. They were cautious in assuming that physical complaints were necessarily related to actual physical health. The pain symptoms and signs of headaches and fatigue indicate excessive strain that may result from the enormous demands of communication in an unfamiliar language and reorientation in the host country. After 18 months, the degree of complaints was below that of the level on arrival, supporting the concept of adaptation over time. They further found that migrants exhibiting a high degree of personal satisfaction with their lives in Germany were more likely to experience superior health.

There does appear to be some evidence that certain groups have adapted better than others. However, it is difficult to isolate a number of separate factors, as these tend to be complex and often confounded.

Economic adaptation

A significant number of immigrants select countries that offer them economic advantages with a better quality of life for themselves and their immediate families. These aspirations for financial security and economic success are frequently thwarted. This occurs because their qualifications may not be recognized and they gravitate towards dirty, demeaning, difficult and badly paid jobs. In this sense, they may feel worse off than in their country of origin. Swan et al. (1991) have shown that immigrants are more often unemployed and encounter more problems in obtaining recognition of their educational (and professional) qualifications and occupational experience, particularly if transition was from a non-traditional or culturally distant location.

Inferior economic resources are related to increased health risks and impediments to medical care. Potter[3] compared the use of immigrant resources – classified as human capital, cultural capital, financial capital, personality and social capital – in achieving integration outcomes. Most of those outcomes were financial/economic in nature, although a 'health and well-being' outcome was also analysed. In terms of health and well-being, social networks were shown to dominate. Human capital resources did not figure in the end – other factors did (such as having experienced hardship in Canada, even if someone was doing well). Hence the context in which these children are living – extended families, isolated, within ethnic enclaves, and so on – was deemed a critical parameter in the process of cultural 'accommodation'.

There is evidence that even in instances when employment is secure, migrants are frequently disadvantaged compared to the native-born. Winter-Ebmer (1994) found that economic migrants to Austria, including those from Yugoslavia, Eastern Europe and Turkey, display lower growth in wages than natives, and this economic inequality persists over time. Similarly, in Canada it has been observed that Third-World immigrants will be unlikely to match the average income levels for natives in the same age groups with equal occupational experience and educational qualifications (Borjas, 1988). Disadvantaged groups in European populations would appear to exhibit more anxiety and depression than more-privileged groups. The suffering that results is witnessed in serious loss of production and social functioning, with implications for family life and work which follow from poor social integration and social withdrawal (European Commission, 2004).

Aycan and Berry (1996) examined the economic status of Turkish migrants in Canada before and after migration. Socioeconomic (and to some extent occupational) status showed a decrease six months after immigration, but steadily increased over the years, albeit without regaining its original level. On the other hand, income, in terms of purchasing power, did eventually surpass that of the country of origin. 'These figures are striking in light of the widespread economic motivation of migration and the impact of economic success in migrant adaptation more generally' (Ward et al., 2001, p. 20).

During the last decade, national statistics have shown that in the United Kingdom, the unemployment rates for the minority ethnic working population have doubled in comparison to the majority working population, possibly due to differences in educational achievement, family size and discrimination.

In a Canadian study (Aycan & Berry, 1996) of migrants who relocated for financial reasons and who suffered less status loss and fewer/shorter periods of unemployment and made significant gains in relative status displayed positive evaluations of accomplishment in the economic domain. Adaptation was further associated with social and psychological factors such as superior self-image, less acculturation stress, improved family relationships, reduced feelings of alienation and less perceived discrimination.

Work stress as well as under- or unemployment are clearly related to mental and physical health and well-being. There are psychological benefits of good work: it gives one a source of activity and money and creativity, it helps to structure time, it provides important social contacts with natives of the host nation and it provides a source of self-esteem and identity. We know that employment status is clearly linked to well-being. It is not surprising, then, that migrants in poor jobs are clearly unhealthy.

The healthy migrant effect

There is evidence (Kirkcaldy et al., 2005) that on several health outcome measures, first-generation immigrants often emerge as healthier than native-born residents who share ethnic and racial backgrounds. On the other hand, the advantage in health rapidly diminishes, so that the longer the period of time spent in the host country, the greater the risk of adolescent risk behaviours, anxiety and depression. Noh and Kaspar (2003) suggest that this deterioration in health may be due to migrants adopting poor health behaviours and inferior lifestyles found in Western industrialized nations, gravitating away from previous resources such as social networks and cultural practices. As a consequence, resilience and robustness are steadily eroded through adaptation.

There is even some evidence that immigrants may enjoy better mental health than the natives of the countries on arrival. Lechner and Mielck (1998) compared data from cross-sections of the German Socioeconomic Panel taken at four-yearly intervals from 1984 to 1992. Migrants who had arrived in Germany prior to 1973 manifest better health than the German population. The healthy-migrant phenomena was found consistently across all three morbidity measures, including chronic illness, disablement and limitations of daily activities due to poor health. Once age had been controlled for, restriction of daily activities showed higher morbidity rates for migrants than for German subjects (in 1984). As age increased, morbidity also increased (for the 1984–92 period), and this effect was most pronounced for the migrants.

Wu and Schimmele (2005) explored the epidemiological paradox that immigrants initially display superior health compared to non-immigrants, including low levels of depression, although this 'advantage' is short-lived. They observed a large, heterogeneous Canadian sample, studying three trajectories of depression among the immigrant community. They were able to confirm the healthy migrant effect to the extent that initially these groups were especially healthy, but depression began increasing shortly after arrival in Canada and continued for several decades.

Personal coping and social networks

The stress of migration is always moderated by personal coping techniques and mechanisms. The coping and problem-solving strategies differ across ethnocultural backgrounds. Strohschneider (1999) found that German students were more active and problem oriented compared with Indian students, who expressed more interest in immediate feedback and details of contextual information. It has been proposed that such cultural differences in coping methods among children and adolescents are attributable to parental child-rearing differences with respect to styles of coping with stress (Siefen et al., 1996). Another moderator variable between acculturation stress and health outcome was the intrinsic motivation to migrate to Germany. Those migrant youths who expressed a more favourable attitude towards the move to Germany were more likely to integrate by rapidly forming new social networks, in contrast to those children who had been forced to come by their parents (Silbereisen & Schmitt-Rodermund, 1999). Expectations concerning self-efficacy have also been shown to exert a favourable influence on the relationship between migration stress and health (Schwarzer, 2002).

Migration inevitably involves adaptation and resettlement and is frequently associated with loneliness and social isolation. Relief provided by transitory friendship and supportive social networks may counter the potentially negative impact of seclusion.

Neto (1995) has shown that loneliness is a major difficulty for migrants entering a new community, and it has been associated with life dissatisfaction. A major resource in times of coping with stress is social support. It represents a significant factor (and family members, friends and acquaintances) in determining both physical health and psychological adjustment during the process of transition between two cultures (Kirkcaldy et al., 2005). There is much evidence suggesting that social support is associated with enhanced psychological well-being (e.g., Kirkcaldy & Furnham, 1995).

Overall, there is evidence that the emergence of psychiatric symptomatology is less likely in instances where an adequate social support system is available (ibid.). One primary source of support is the spouse, and Naidoo (1985) found that having a supportive husband was generally associated with less stress being experienced by Asian women who had immigrated to Canada.

In a Dutch study, Elich and Blauw (1981) examined returnees, and observed that although economic incentives had motivated many to emigrate, their reasons for returning to their native society were connected more often with relationship problems. Berry (1997) has confirmed the value of relationships that promote intercultural adaptation, underlining the fact that there need not be a large number of relationships. Rather, these should be diverse, including host nationals and coethnics who can fulfil emotional and informational requirements.

Social support represents one of the most important forms of coping with stress. The stress and coping model of adaptation has been implemented to explain and predict adaptation processes. In a study of Korean immigrants (average residence of 12 years) in Canada (Noh & Avison, 1996) with a one-year follow-up, a longitudinal path analysis revealed that psychological resources reinforce levels of both psychological and social resources. Self-esteem facilitated mastery and coethnic social support. In turn, mastery enhanced self-esteem and coethnic support. The extent of coethnic social support had a stress suppression impact, suggesting an indirect effect on depression through life events.

Kirkcaldy et al.'s (2005) study investigates the influence of satisfaction with life in the host country and the individual acculturation strategy of the physical health of Russian migrants to Germany. Migrants who actively attempt to establish and maintain favourable relationships with members of the host country are healthier than those who avoid or have a low interest in social contact. The findings support the positive impact of social networks in mitigating the adverse effects of acculturative stress.

On the other hand, Aroian et al. (1996) showed that family support may not only be a source of instrumental and emotional support for Soviet immigrants, but due to being beleaguered through stresses imposed by immigration, offering support to others may represent an additional source of stress (see doubled-edged sword hypothesis of social support, Kirkcaldy & Furnham, 1995).

Noh and Kaspar (2003) found that although potential risk factors such as age, length of residency and occupational status may not be significantly related to depression, social support from ethnic networks on arrival in the host country appeared to benefit immigrants and had a powerful impact on their enduring mental health.

Erim-Frodermann (1997) described the problems inherent in many Turkish migrant families which strongly adhere to a rigid concept of role and relational structures. On the other hand, she underlines the value of strong family relationships as a resource in instances where self-development is possible. There is also evidence that there is seldom overt aggression within Turkish families. Frei et al. (1999) have found support that depressive disorders and suicidal behaviour is dealt with more favourably among family units.

Native Germans emerged as less likely to believe in the influence of personal factors, the medical profession or fate in the development of their health than the ethnic German migrants (Kirkcaldy et al., 2005). One explanation of these findings was that Russia has a medical care service requiring that the individual patient contributes a significant share of their medical fees, and health prevention and maintenance are generally not included (Ensor & Savelyeva, 1998). Thus individuals will be expected to display a higher degree of personal responsibility for their personal health. Furnham and Bochner (1986) make a distinction between voluntary and involuntary (refugees) migration: migrants who choose to leave their native country of Russia ('selective migration') for Germany are presumably prepared to take greater personal risks and assume considerable personal responsibility and control over their own affairs, whether social, familial or financial, and subsequently display a marked internal locus of control.

Conclusion

Many, but not all, migrants experience stress and difficulty soon after migration. Most refugees do. Many, but not all, learn to adapt. The sort of factors that have been implicated in trying to understand why some groups are obviously better off than others include: motives for migration, the selective policies of host countries, the education, skills and work attitudes of migrant groups, the social support networks open to individuals, economic and welfare policies in the country of destination, as well as disparities between the cultures of origin and destination.

The sheer number of migrants moving from one country and continent to another make it imperative that we understand these issues so that we are in a position to assist migrants and refugees to become healthy, happy and integrated members of the society to which they have elected to come.

Notes

1. Federal Ministry of the Interior.
2. Unpublished study, Kirkcaldy (2006).
3. Personal communication, Stephanie Potter.

References

Aroian, K., Spitzer, A. & Bell, M. (1996), 'Family stress and support among former Soviet immigrants', *Western Journal of Nursing Research*, **18**, 655–74.
Aycan, Z. & Berry, J.W. (1996), 'Impact of employment-related experiences on immigrants' psychological well-being and adaptation to Canada', *Canadian Journal of Behavioural Science*, **28**, 240–51.
Bagley, C.R. (1993), 'Mental health and social adjustment of elderly Chinese immigrants in Canada', *Canada's Mental Health*, **41**, 6–10.
Balarayan, R. (1995), 'Ethnicity and variations in the nation's health', *Health Trends*, **27**, 114–19.
Bankston, C.L., III & Zhou, M. (1997), 'Valedictorians and delinquents: the bifurcation of Vietnamese American youth', *Deviant Behavior*, **18** (4), 343–64.
Barankin, T., Konstantareas, M.M. & de Bossett, F. (1989), 'Adaptation of recent Soviet Jewish immigrants and their children to Toronto', *Canadian Journal of Psychiatry*, **34**, 512–18.
Bengi-Arslan, L., Verhulst, F.C., van der Ende, J. & Erol, N. (1997), 'Understanding childhood (problem) behaviors from a cultural perspective: comparison of problem behaviors and competencies in Turkish immigrant, Turkish and Dutch children', *Social Psychiatry Psychiatric Epidemiology*, **32**, 477–84.
Berry, J.W. (1992), 'Acculturation and adaptation in a new society', *International Migration*, **30**, 69–85.
Berry, J.W. (1997), 'Immigration, acculturation and adaptation', *Applied Psychology: An International Review*, **46**, 5–34.
Berthoud, R. & Nazroo, J. (1997), 'The mental health of ethnic minorities', *New Community*, **23**, 309–24.
Borjas, G.J. (1988), 'Economic theory and international migration', *International Migration Review*, **23**, 457–85.
Carbello, M. & Nerukar, A. (2001), 'Migration, refugees, and health risks', *Emerging Infectious Diseases*, **7** (3), 556–60.
Carta, M.G., Bernal, M., Hardoy, M.C. & Haro-Abad, J.M. (2005), 'Migration and mental health in Europe (The State of the Mental Health in Europe Working Group: Appendix 1)', *Clinical Practice and Epidemiology in Mental Health*, **1**, 13, www.cpementalhealth.com/content/T/1/13.
Crijnen, A.A., Bengi, Arslan, L. & Verhulst, F. (2000), 'Teacher reported problem behaviour in Turkish immigrant and Dutch children: a cross-cultural comparison', *Acta Psychiatrica Scandinavica*, **102**, 439–44.
Diener, E., Diener, M. & Diener, C. (1995), 'Factors predicting the subjective well-being of nations', *Journal of Personality and Social Psychology*, **69**, 851–64.
Dwivedi, K.N. (1999), *Meeting the Needs of Ethnic Minority Children*, Priority Lodge Education, http://priory.com/psych/chneeds.htm.
Elich, J.H. & Blauw, P.W. (1981), *En toch terug* (Yet returned), Rotterdam: Department of Sociology, Erasmus University.
Ensor, T. & Savelyeva, L. (1998), 'Informal payments for health care in the former Soviet Union: some evidence from Kazakhstan', *Health Policy Plan*, **13** (1), 41–9.
Erim-Frodermann, Y. (1997), 'Kulturspezifische Aspekte der sozialmedizinischen Begutachtung von ausländischen Rentenbewerbern mit psychiatrischen und psychosomatischen Krankheitsbildern. Erfahrungen einer muttersprachlichen Gutachterin' ['Culture-specific aspects of social medical assessment of foreigners – with psychiatric and psychosomatic disorders – applying for pensions. Experiences with a case-file native speaker'], in J. Collatz, E. Koch, R. Salman & W. Machleidt (eds), *Transkulturelle Begutachtung*, Berlin: Verlag für Wissenschaft und Bildung, 141–7.
European Commission (2004), *The State of Mental Health in the European Union*, Health & Consumer Protection, Directorate-General, Luxembourg: Office for Official Publications of the European Communities.
Frei, A., Finzen, A. & Hoffmann-Richter, U. (1999), 'Alternativen zum Suizid? Doppelkasuistik zweier kurdisch-alevitischer Frauen' ['Alternatives to suicide? Double, casuistry of two Kurden-alevic women'], *Psycho*, **25**, 131–6.
Furnham, A.F. & Bochner, S. (1986), *Culture Shock: Psychological Reactions to Unfamiliar Environments*, London and New York: Routledge.
Grube, M. (2001), 'Evaluation of a special project for treatment of psychiatrically ill Turkish migrants', *Psychiatrische Praxis*, **28**, 81–3.
Haasen, C. & Yagdiran, O. (2000), *Beurteilung psychischer Störungen in einer multikulturellen Gesellschaft* [*Assessment of Psychological Disorders in a Multicultural Society*], Freiburg Lambertus.
Hansen, C., Yagdiran, O., Mass, R. & Krausz, M. (2001), 'Schizophrenia disorders among Turkish migrants in Germany. A controlled study', *Psychopathology*, **34**, 203–8.

Heras, P. & Revilla, L.A. (1994), 'Acculturation, generational status, and family environment of Filipino Americans: a study in cultural adaptation', *Family Therapy*, **21**, 129–38.

Janca, A. & Helzer, J.E. (1992), 'Psychiatric morbidity of foreign students in Yugoslavia: a 25 year retrospective analysis', *International Journal of Social Psychiatry*, **38** (4), 287–92.

Johnston, L.D., O'Malley P.M. & Bachman, J.D. (1999), *National Survey Results on Drug Use from the Monitoring of the Future Study 1975–1998*, US Department of Health and Human Services, National Institute of Health, University of Michigan Institute of Social Research.

Kandel, D.B., Chen, K., Warner, L., Kessler, R. & Grant, B. (1997), 'Prevalence and demographic correlates of symptoms of dependence on cigarettes, alcohol, marijuana and cocaine in the U.S. population', *Drug and Alcohol Dependence*, **44**, 11–29.

Kirkcaldy, B.D. (2006), 'Cross-cultural differences in personality correlates of migration', Düsseldorf: International Centre for the Study of Occupational and Mental Health, unpublished manuscript.

Kirkcaldy, B.D. & Furnham, A. (1995), 'Coping, seeking social support and stress among German police management', *European Review of Applied Psychology*, **45** (32), 121–6.

Kirkcaldy, B.D. & Siefen, R. (2002), 'Darstellung englischsprachiger wissenschaftlicher Literatur zu Migration und Sucht' ['Summary of the English research literature on migration and chemical dependency'], in U. Boos-Nünning, G.R. Siefen, B.D. Kirkcaldy, B.O. Otyakmaz & D. Surall (eds), *Migration und Sucht. Expertise im Auftrag des Bundesministerium für Gesundheit*, [*Migration and Chemical Dependency. Expert Report for the German Ministry of Health*], Vol. 141/II, Schriftenreihe des Bundesministeriums für Gesundheit, Baden-Baden: Nomos Verlagsgesellschaft.

Kirkcaldy, B.D., Richardson, R., Furnham, A. & Siefen, R. (2008), 'The effects of gender and migrant status on physical and psychological well-being', Düsseldorf: International Centre for the Study of Occupational and Mental Health, submitted manuscript.

Kirkcaldy, B.D., Siefen, G. & Furnham, A. (2004), 'The relationship between health efficacy, educational attainment and well-being among 30 nations', *European Psychologist*, **2**, 107–19.

Kirkcaldy, B.D., Siefen, R.G., Wittig, U., Schüller, A., Brähler, E. & Merbach, M. (2005), 'Health and emigration: subjective evaluation of health status and physical symptoms in Russian-speaking migrants', *Stress Health*, **21** (5), 295–309.

Lantermann, E.D. & Hänze, M. (1999), 'Werthaltungen, materieller Erfolg und soziale Integration von Aussiedlern' ['Value Attitudes, Material Success and Social Integration of Emigrants'], in R.K. Silbereisen, E.D., Lantermann & E. Schmitt-Rodermund (eds), *Aussiedler in Deutschland. Akkulturation von Persönlichkeit und Verhalten* [*Migrants in Germany. Acculturation of Personality and Behaviour*], Opladen: Leske & Budrich, 165–84.

Lasry, J.C. & Sayegh, L. (1992), 'Developing an acculturation scale: a bi-dimensional model', in N. Grizenko, L. Sayegh & P. Migneault (eds), *Transcultural Issues in Child Psychiatry*, Montreal: Editions Douglas, pp. 67–86.

Lechner, I. & Mielck, A. (1998), 'Decrease in the health migrant effect: trends in the morbidity of foreign and German participants in the 1984–1992 Socioeconomic Panel', *Gesundheitswesen*, **60** (12), 715–20.

Mirsky, J. (1997), 'Psychological distress among immigrant adolescents: culture specific factors in the case of immigrants from the Former Soviet Union', *International Journal of Psychology*, **32** (4), 221–30.

Naidoo, J. (1985), 'A cultural perspective on the adjustment of South Asian women in Canada', in I.R. Lagunes & Y.H. Poortinga (eds), *From a Different Perspective: Studies of Behaviour across Cultures*, Lisse: Swets & Zeitlinger, pp. 76–92.

Neto, F. (1995), 'Predictors of satisfaction with life among second generation migrants', *Social Indicators Research*, **35**, 93–116.

Noh, S. & Avison, W.R. (1996), 'Asian immigrants and the stress process: a study of Koreans in Canada', *Journal of Health and Social Behaviour*, **37**, 192–206.

Noh, S. & Kaspar, V. (2003), *Diversity and Immigrant Health*, Toronto: University of Toronto Press.

Patel, N., Power, T.G. & Bhavnagri, N.P. (1996), 'Socialisation values and practice of Indian immigrant parents: correlates of modernity and acculturation', *Child Development*, **67**, 302–13.

Phinney, J.S. & Nakayama, S. (1991), 'Parental influences on ethnic identity formation in adolescents', paper presented at the Meeting of the Society for Research and Child Development, Seattle, WA, 18–20 April.

Ponizovsky, A.M., Ritsner, M.S. & Modai, I. (1999), 'Suicidal ideation and suicide attempts among immigrant adolescents from the former Soviet Union to Israel', *Journal of the American Academy of Child and Adolescent Psychiatry*, **38**, 1433–41.

Ritsner, M. & Ponizovsky, A. (1999), 'Psychological distress through immigration. The two-phase temporal pattern', *International Journal of Social Psychiatry*, **45**, 125–39.

Rosmond, R., Nilsson, A. & Bjorntorp, P. (2000), 'Psychiatric ill-health and distribution of body fat mass among female immigrants in Sweden', *Public Health*, **114**, 45–51.

Sam, D.L. (1998), 'Predicting life satisfaction among adolescents from immigrants families in Norway', *Ethnicity and Health*, **3**, 5–18.

Schwarzer, R. (2002), 'Selbstwirksamkeitserwartung' ['Self-efficacy expectations'], in R. Schwarzer, M. Jerusalem & H. Weber (eds), *Gesundheitspsychologie von A bis Z. Ein Handwörterbuch [Health Psychology from A to Z]*, Hogrefe: Göttingen, Bern, Toronto, Seattle, pp. 521–4.

Sethi, R. (1990), 'Intercultural communication and adaptation among first generation Asian–Indian immigrants', paper presented at the Korean Psychological Association International Conference on Individualism–Collectivism: Psychocultural Perspectives from East and West, Seoul, Korea, 9–13 July.

Shweder, R.A. & Sullivan, M.A. (1993), 'Cultural psychology: who needs it?', *Annual Review of Psychology*, **44**, 497–523.

Siefen, G., Kirkcaldy, B.D. & Athanasou, J. (1996), 'Parental attitudes: a study of German, Greek and second generation Greek migrant adolescents', *Human Relations*, **49** (6), 837–51.

Silbereisen, R. & Schmitt-Rodermund, E. (1999), 'Wohlbefinden der jugendlichen Aussiedler' ['Well-being among adolescent migrants'], in R.K. Silbereisen, E.D. Lantermann & E. Schmitt-Rodermund (eds), *Aussiedler in Deutschland. Akkulturation von Persönlichkeit und Verhalten [Migration in Germany: Acculturation of Personality and Behavior]*, Opladen: Leske & Budrich, pp. 257–75.

Storch, G. & Poutska, F. (2000), 'Mental disorders in hospitalised children of migrant families from the Mediterranean', *Praxis der Kinderpsychologie und Kinderpsychiatrie*, **49**, 199–208.

Strohschneider, S. (1999), 'On the cultural relativity of problem-solving styles: exploration in India and Germany', in W.J. Lonner, D.L. Dinnel, D.K. Forgays & S.A. Hayes (eds), *Merging Past, Present and Future in Cross-Cultural Psychology*, 14th International Congress of the International Association for Cross-Cultural Psychology, Bristol, PA, Lisse: Swets & Zeitlinger, pp. 188–204.

Sundquist, J. (1993), 'Ethnicity as a risk factor for mental illness: a population-based study of 338 Latin American refugees and 996 age-, sex-, and education-matched Swedish controls', *Acta Psychiatrica Scandinavia*, **87**, 208–12.

Swaim, R.C., Beauvais, F., Chavez, E.L. & Oetting, E.R. (1997), 'The effect of school dropout rates on estimates of adolescent substance use among three racial/ethnic groups', *American Journal of Public Health*, **87**, 51–5.

Swan, N., Auer, L., Chenard, D., dePlaa, A., deSilva, A., Palmer, D. & Serjak, J. (1991), *Economic and Social Impacts of Immigration*, Ottawa: Economic Council of Canada.

Tanaka-Matsumi, J. & Draguns, J.G. (1997), 'Culture and psychopathology', in J.W. Berry, M.H. Segall & C. Kagitcibasi (eds), *Handbook of Cross-cultural Psychology: Volume 3. Social Behaviour and Applications*, 2nd edn, Boston, MA: Allyn & Bacon, pp. 449–91.

Trautman, F. (1998), 'Drogenarbeit mit Migranten in der Niederlanden' ['Drug work with migrants in Netherlands'], in Deutsche Gesellschaft gegen die Suchtgefahren [German Society against Risks of (Chemical) Dependency] (eds), *Sucht in unserer multikulturellen Gesellschaft*, Freiburg: Lambertus.

Veenhoven, R. (2001a), 'Are the Russians as unhappy as they say they are? Comparability of self-reports across nations', *Journal of Happiness Studies*, **2**, 111–36.

Veenhoven, R. (2001b), 'State of Nations: world database of happiness', Erasmus University of Rotterdam, Faculty of Social Sciences.

Ward, C., Bochner, S. & Furnham, A. (2001), *The Psychology of Culture Shock*, 2nd edn, New York & London: Routledge, Taylor & Francis.

Winter-Ebmer, R. (1994), 'Motivation for migration and economic success', *Journal of Economic Psychology*, **12**, 269–84.

Wittig, U., Merbach, M., Siefen, R.G. & Brähler, E. (2004), 'Beschwerden und Inspruchnahme des Gesundheitswesens von Spätaussiedlern bei Einreise nach Deutschland' ['Ailments and demands on the health services of late immigrants on arrival in Germany'], *Gesundheitswesen*, **66**, 85–92.

Wu, Z. & Schimmele, C.M. (2005), 'The healthy migrant effect on depression: variation over time?', Population Association of America Annual Meeting Program, Philadelphia, PA, March 31–April 2.

Zilber, A. & Lerner, Y. (1996), 'Psychological distress among recent immigrants from the former Soviet Union to Israel, I: Correlates of level of distress', *Psychological Medicine*, **26**, 493–501.

24 Acculturative stress in professional immigrants: towards a cultural theory of stress

Rabi S. Bhagat, Charlotte A. Davis and Manuel L. London

Introduction

Since the 1960s, the liberalization of US immigration laws as well as the immigration laws of other countries and the continuous interconnectedness of various countries in the global economy have created a significant growth of immigrants in the G8 countries. While a majority of them are legal immigrants who move from their country of origin to the host country in search of better occupational opportunities, professional growth, and better quality of living, there has also been a corresponding growth of illegal immigrants. Illegal immigrants are those individuals who move across the national boundaries without having obtained legal permission to either live or work in the host country. Census data and data collected by the US Department of Homeland Security reveals that over 13 million immigrants currently living in the US are illegal, that is, they have no legal permission to either work or live in the US. Similar situations exist in the UK, France, Canada, and other Western European countries. Research on illegal immigrants, especially dealing with their work experiences, has been rare – there have been some economic analyses pertaining to their contribution to the regions of the US where they tend to settle. These regions include the western and southwestern states of California, Arizona, New Mexico, Texas, and Florida in the South in the US. In the Asian context, the flow of illegal workers to rapidly globalizing countries, such as India, has also created social upheavals. While economic analyses pertaining to the impact of illegal immigration provide interesting data and implications for public policy, we know relatively little regarding the psychological adaptation of this group of immigrants to the cultural context of the host country.

Professional immigrants are those who have attained professional status in their home country, through either experience or education, and intend and are able to continue their profession in the host country, for example, doctors, nurses, professors, managers, and engineers. Professional immigrants have considerable training, high expectations, are self-regulated and self-directed, have internal control (were not forced to make the move), and believe that they can bring about positive outcomes. They also have resources to stay in touch with relatives, friends, and colleagues in their home country, and have resources to help with their adjustment and thus quickly achieve a higher standard of living.

Figure 24.1 depicts the flow of legal professional residents in the US since 1900. It shows that there has been a dramatic increase in the growth of legal immigrants between 1990 and 2000. The issue of immigration has also been a topic of considerable economic and cultural attention in Western Europe. As reported in *Time Europe* (London, 2000), in 1999 the number of legal immigrants into Western Europe was 16 million, and many of these immigrants are entrepreneurs and professionals, who add to the economic growth and development of their countries of settlement.

Millions

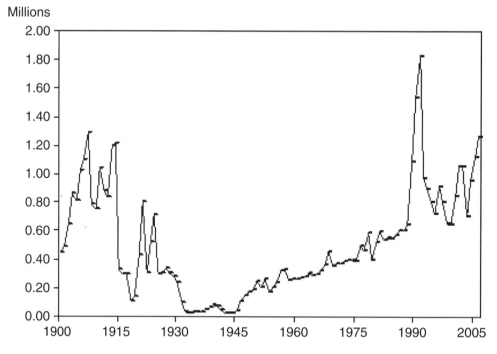

Source: Office of Immigration Statistics (2006).

Figure 24.1   Legal permanent resident flow to the US, 1900–2008

The focus of this chapter is on professional immigrants and their work experiences in the culturally dissimilar context of the host country. Our goal in this chapter is:

1.   to present a detailed analysis of how professional immigrants appraise various stressful reactions in their work and non-work lives;
2.   to discuss the significance of different styles of coping (i.e., problem focused, emotion focused, etc.) in dealing with stresses that accompany the process of acculturation in the work organizations of the host country;
3.   to present patterns of acculturation stresses in four grids of societal cultural variations; and
4.   to draw implications for developing a cultural theory of stress.

Acculturation, acculturative stress, and valued work outcomes: a conceptual model
Immigrants undergo some distinctive changes that occur as a result of personal contact with individuals from dissimilar cultural origins. Collectively these changes are termed 'acculturation' (Redfield et al., 1936; Graves, 1967; Berry & Kim, 1988; Ward, 1996; Berry & Sam, 1997). Graves differentiated among collective- or group-level acculturation and acculturation experienced by individuals known more distinctively as 'psychological acculturation'. In the former type, changes are observed in the cultural patterns of the acculturating group, whereas in the latter, acculturation

is seen as a change in the beliefs, attitudes, values, and behavioral intentions of the individual.

In this chapter, we are concerned with the antecedents and consequences of psychological acculturation in professional immigrants. In recent years, research has begun to focus more on the dynamics of immigration to countries outside of the US. For example, studies have examined stressors surrounding the resettlement of Central Americans in Canada (Pottie et al., 2005) and workplace stress of women in the People's Republic of China and Hong Kong as well as the US (Shaffer et al., 2000). The phenomenon of flow of professional immigrants and the accompanying acculturative stresses is not limited to the US. In fact, there have been parallel incidents of acculturative stresses in countries such as France, the UK, Germany, Israel, and Russia. What we notice in each of these cases is that acculturation and acculturative stresses are primarily confined to the professional immigrant groups who migrate from collectivistic countries of Southeast and South Asia (e.g., China, the Philippines, South Korea, India, and Vietnam) to G8 countries (e.g., the US, Canada, the UK, France, Germany, Italy, Japan, and Russia). Pottie et al. (2005) examined acculturation and acculturative stress of Central American male immigrants into Canada. There have also been several studies focusing on Russian immigrants to Israel in the 1980s (Kozulin & Venger, 1995; Ponizovsky et al., 1998); however, our research shows that there have been considerably more studies of acculturation and acculturative stresses of immigrants from developing nations into the US and Canada.

The distinction between group- or community-level acculturation and individual or psychological acculturation is important for two reasons. First, these two phenomena are different and are concerned with different types of outcomes. At the group level, changes in (i) outcomes such as patterns of interconnectedness between various ethnic groups in a plural or multicultural society; (ii) economic improvements of the acculturating group; and (iii) political participation in the larger society, are often the foci of interest. However, at the individual level, the research is directed to observe changes in such social psychological phenomena as cultural identity, cultural-specific values, and attitudinal orientations. A second reason for distinguishing between the two types of acculturation is that not all professional immigrants in the acculturating group participate in the collective changes that are underway in their cultural group. To correctly assess the relationship between culture contact of the ethnic immigrant group and the host society, one has to develop separate measures for detecting changes at the group or community level and the extent of participation in these ethnic group-specific changes by members of these groups, and then relate these changes to the psychological and related work outcomes for the individual.

Acculturative stress (Berry, 1970) is a major experience that occurs during individual-level acculturation and is largely responsible for generating adverse psychological, psychosomatic, and behavioral reactions. It is a response by individuals to both positive and negative stressful experiences, including life events that are present during intercultural contact. Acculturative stress occurs when professional immigrants face the challenges of new types of opportunities and at the same time come to appreciate the types of demands and constraints that are present in the new cultural environment of the society to which they have migrated. For example, a civil engineer from Pakistan who travels to Canada with the hope of finding a job in his or her field may be surprised to find that there is limited acceptance of the professional qualifications obtained in his or her country of origin. Acculturative stress in this case comes from reduced level of status that he or she might have to accept, but also from the lack of knowledge in dealing with various issues pertaining to the demands of the culturally dissimilar organization. In a related vein, a professional accountant from India who accepts the job of a clerk while pursuing a CPA degree in the US also experiences acculturative stress. Until the person is able to upgrade his or her professional training obtained in India to US standards, such acculturative stresses persist. Many professional immigrants may develop a sense of resentment toward the immigration system of the globalized countries because, while there is encouragement to migrate, there might not be enough realistic preview of what they might have to undergo in the process of finding adequate employment and moving up in their career.

Bhagat and London (1999) provide a detailed typology of the kinds of stresses that are present in the development of acculturative stress. Like other facets of work stress, acculturative stresses are generated when the demands associated with cultural-specific changes that accompany acculturation (in the context of both work and non-work) exceed the capacity of the individual to deal with them (Berry & Ataca, 2000). Some of these reactions include heightened levels of dissatisfaction with the work role, depression associated with the experience of possible changes to cultural identity, and of anxieties linked to uncertainties regarding how one should interpret the various unfamiliar experiences and events occurring during the process of acculturation and how one should live in the dissimilar context of the host society. These reactions largely depend on the differences in the work environment in the country of settlement from the work environment of the country of origin, as well as the quality of social support that the professional immigrant is able to access in the new context.

The notion of acculturative stress is similar to the notion of culture shock (Oberg, 1960), but the concept of acculturative stress is preferred by occupational health psychologists for two reasons. First, the term 'shock' has pathological overtones. The term 'stress' has a theoretical foundation in psychological studies of how individuals deal with negative experiences. For instance, they engage in various types of coping strategies and seek emotional and social support from members of their ethnic group and understanding others in the host country. Second, as John Berry (2001) has argued, by using the term 'acculturative', one clearly signals that the root of such stressful experiences lies in the intercultural interactions of two or more groups. In Figure 24.2, we present a conceptual model of acculturation and acculturative stress, and their effects on valued work outcomes.

To comprehend the nature of acculturative stress that is likely to evolve for a professional immigrant in a given context, one needs to understand the nature of the two societal contexts: those of origin and settlement. The cultural characteristics that accompany the individuals into the acculturation process need clear description to understand literally where the person is coming from and in part to establish comparative analyses of the nature of the underlying cultural dimensions that are relevant. The combination of economic, political and demographic conditions of the country of origin in comparison with those of the country of settlement are also important. For example, Russian doctors migrating to Israel encounter a significant amount of acculturative stress because of striking differences among all of these important features of Russia versus Israel. It is often reported that they experience stresses from significant losses in status. In Israel, there is more attention to migrating doctors from the West and they are generally compensated better compared to those coming from Russia and Eastern Europe.

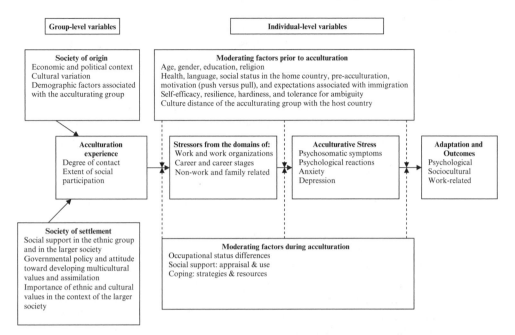

*Figure 24.2   A conceptual model depicting the factors affecting acculturation,
acculturative stress and outcomes as moderated by group- and individual-
level variables*

The nature of social support available in the ethnic group of the society in which the professional immigrant is to settle and also in the larger context of the host society is quite important. The importance of multicultural values that is placed in the host society along with the history of conflict, if any, between the country of origin and the country of settlement should also be taken into account. Triandis (1994) noted that cultural distance, perceived similarity with the members of the host country, knowledge of the language of the host country, and equal status contact, coupled with existence of superordinate goals, are important in facilitating the acculturation process which in turn will reduce acculturative stress. Smith et al. (2006) note that successful acculturation depends to a large extent on the degree and quality of contact between immigrants and the members of the host society. Professional immigrants who are able to initiate and sustain meaningful relationships with members of the host society (both in the context of work and non-work) are more likely to acculturate faster and in the process experience reduced levels of stress.

Individual-level moderating factors which either facilitate or hinder acculturation include age, gender, education, and religious preference. Health status, occupational experience in the society of origin, and the motivation for migration are also clearly important. We suggest that young males with strong motivation to migrate to the country of settlement and who have had some prior work experience in their home country are likely to experience less acculturative stress compared to older females, who, with inadequate occupational preparation are less inclined to migrate because of strong family connections in the country of origin. Refugees and others who accept immigration as an accident in their lives because they are *pushed* into this condition are likely to have difficulty in acculturating and therefore will experience considerable acculturative stress. For example, refugees – especially those who have had a professional career in Central European countries such as Bosnia and Herzogovina and the former republics of Yugoslavia who had to settle in the northwestern part of the US (i.e., Idaho and Washington) experience considerable acculturative stress. Not only do these immigrants experience sudden loss of status due to involuntary migration, but they also do not find comparable professional work due to their lack of knowledge of the language. In addition, if some of these immigrants practice the Islamic faith, they are less likely to find places of worship in the northwestern part of the US, which is predominantly populated by Anglo-Saxon Christian communities.

However, professional immigrants who have the opportunity to migrate because they experience considerable *pull* from the various occupational opportunities in the country of settlement (i.e., Indian high-tech professionals working for global software companies such as IBM or Microsoft) are likely to experience little or no acculturative stress in the process of settling in the US or UK. In a recent trip from India, the first author encountered a significant number of young (both male and female) computer science graduates from leading engineering schools who were coming to the US to work for a varied length of time. They spoke fluent English and some of them had already worked with their US-based superiors and colleagues in the subsidiaries of these companies in India. They were excited at the opportunity to learn advanced computer science-related techniques and were not the least bit worried about settling in cities such as Seattle, Dallas, Los Angeles and so on. They noted that they would be settling with other Indian professionals who had come before. The point is: we speculate that those immigrants who perceive a strong opportunity for growth and advancement (Bhagat & London, 1999) in the context of their work in the country of settlement (whether it is short or long term) are not likely to experience as much acculturative stress.

Immigration can often be physically demanding and those with higher degrees of self-efficacy, resilience, and hardiness are likely to experience significantly lower levels of acculturative stress. The role of religious orientation has not been sufficiently understood, but we can speculate that individuals with strongly dissimilar religious backgrounds are likely to find the host country less receptive for practicing their beliefs and religious ideologies. Professional immigrants' career motivation may indicate their propensity to adapt successfully. London (see London & Noe, 1997; Bhagat & London, 1999) identified three elements of career motivation, each one of which is a set of individual difference characteristics. Career resilience is the ability to overcome career barriers. It encompasses such characteristics as self-esteem, self-efficacy, and self-regulation. People develop these traits by the time they reach young adulthood. Career insight consists of understanding one's own strengths and weaknesses and the opportunities and challenges in the environment. Career identity consists of the goals and expectations people have for themselves relative to the goals and expectations of others in the same occupation. Insight is the motivational spark. Identity is the direction of motivation. Resilience maintains motivation. Professional immigrants are likely to be high in resilience to begin with; otherwise they would not have taken the initiative to immigrate. However, this is a hypothesis that should be tested. Employers and other sources of support can increase immigrants' career identity and insight by providing performance feedback, coaching, and information about career opportunities.

Moderating factors during acculturation which affect the nature of stressors from the domains of work and non-work, career and career stages are depicted in Figure 24.2. Immigrants who are migrating either voluntarily or involuntarily from the country of origin to the country of settlement are likely to undergo considerable acculturative stress, especially if they have to settle for professions and careers which are less prestigious than what they had before. This phenomenon is more pronounced for Eastern European immigrants who have migrated or are migrating to the UK and other countries of Western Europe. *The International Herald Tribune* (19 October, 2007) reports that while Polish immigrants are doing better economically, they often find themselves accepting positions which are characterized by lower occupational status compared to the jobs that they had in Poland. Because the pay is better, they accept this incongruent situation, but they nevertheless still experience acculturative stress. They are much less satisfied compared to those who were fortunate to find jobs in the same occupation that they had before, in part because of the difference in their status as a result of the career change. Such experiences are rarely reported or seriously analyzed by occupational stress researchers.

The role of social support, especially how it is appraised by the professional immigrants during the time of acculturation, is very important. In fact, our research reveals that a significant amount of empirical work has been conducted in this area. The more social support a professional immigrant is able to receive from either his or her ethnic group or from the host society at large, the less stressful would be his or her experiences with the process of acculturation (Furnham & Alibhai, 1985; Vega & Rumbaut, 1991; Jayasuriya et al., 1992; Furnham & Sheikh, 1993). Immigrants who tend to settle in communities where there are large concentrations of other ethnic groups (especially ethnic groups from their country of origin) generally have little difficulty in learning the various 'ropes to know and ropes to skip' pertaining to the dynamics of their work role as well as various culture-specific cues and signals that are likely to expedite their adjustment. The various types of social support (e.g., informational, affective, and structural) that they receive from their ethnic community enables them to understand the intricacies of both economic and cultural scenarios that are likely to affect them in the present and also in the future.

Berry and his colleagues (Berry et al., 1987, 1989; Berry & Sam, 1997) note that in evaluating the series of dissimilar cultural experiences, an immigrant is likely to appraise some events as benign, some as demanding, and some as opportunities. The outcome of this appraisal is multifaceted. Some of the outcomes are positive and satisfying, whereas others can lead to psychosomatic symptoms and adverse psychological reactions resulting in anxiety and depression. Immigrants who migrate with a strong motivation to adjust to and succeed in the occupational context of the host society are likely to engage in coping – they will also be more effective in accessing various societal resources that can aid the process of coping with and adapting to stresses during the process of acculturation.

Research reported in Noh and Kaspar (2003) found that the use of problem-focused coping (i.e., action strategies directed at lowering the problematic levels of various situations or events embedded in the work or non-work context) reduced adverse emotional reactions of perceived discrimination, while emotion-focused coping strategies (i.e., attempts to reduce or manage distress associated with the experience of stress) increased the impact of such perceived discrimination on the mental health outcomes. Chang (2001) found behavioral (i.e., action oriented) and emotional coping to be positively related to life satisfaction and negatively related to depression in a sample of Asian Americans.

Recent theoretical approaches focusing on the cultural maintenance hypothesis (Roesch et al., 2006) suggest that individuals from collectivistic cultures (i.e., Korean or other Southeast Asian groups) who treat family as the basic unit of the society to which one must show unwavering loyalty (i.e., strong adherence to Confucianism) and who fear 'loss of face' (avoidance of disclosure of deep-seated personal emotions) are predisposed to use avoidance- rather than problem-focused coping (Noh et al., 1999).

The cultural maintenance hypothesis has been found useful in delineating the role of different types of coping strategies in dealing with the dilemma of acculturation and acculturative stresses. However, more research needs to be conducted into the nature of interactions between cultural values of the immigrants and the demands of the acculturating situation. Coping resources that one may be able to access may be a function of the multicultural policies of the host government, coupled with the resources that are brought to bear to enable the newcomers to adjust to the demands of work and non-work roles. From the research we have reviewed in writing this chapter, it seems that Canada provides a significant number of community-based mechanisms for coping with various types of disorientations and related disorders that might accompany the process of acculturation. More research needs to be conducted on the effects of those policies on the actual experiences of professional immigrants. Governmental policies favoring multiculturalism and maintenance of the cultural mosaic of various immigrant groups are most helpful in identifying the nature of various coping resources that professional immigrants might be able to utilize during the acculturation process. This cultural mosaic is indicative of an integrative mode of acculturation (Bhagat & London, 1999), in which immigrants attempt to participate in the culture of the country of settlement while at the same time retaining their ethnicity of the country of origin. Berry (1997) delineated four acculturation strategies which immigrants may adopt in attempting to cope with the stresses of acculturation: integration, assimilation, separation/segregation, and marginalization. According to him, the integration strategy is most likely to lead to successful acculturation and adjustment in the country of settlement. Professional immigrants who adopt this integrative mode of acculturation are less likely to experience acculturative stress than those who adopt an assimilation mode, in which they denounce their ethnic backgrounds and attempt to become full members of the culture of the country of settlement. Those immigrants who adopt the strategies of separation/segregation or marginalization are likely to experience high levels of acculturative stress and will also find it more difficult to adapt to the host society.

Immigrants adapt when they are able to rearrange the various disorienting aspects of their lives by selectively accessing the various coping resources as well as social support mechanisms that are present in the work organization and the social context in which they live. Adaptation and the outcomes of the process of acculturation and experience of acculturative stress are multifaceted (Altrocchi & Altrocchi, 1995). The distinction between psychological and sociocultural adaptation is proposed and validated by Ward and her colleagues (Searle & Ward, 1990; Ward, 1996; Ward & Rana-Deuba, 1999). Psychological adaptation is concerned with the immigrant individual's psychological and physical well-being, while sociocultural adaptation refers to how an acculturating individual is able to manage daily life in the new cultural context. These two interact and predict work-related adaptation.

Immigrant groups which are composed of individuals with a high tolerance for ambiguity, resilience, self-efficacy and hardiness, and who are high in sociocultural adaptation, are able not only to manage the transition into the new culture flawlessly and maintain a desired level of performance and work adjustment in the new context, but often excel. 'Resilience' reflects the capacity to maintain a stable equilibrium during stressful and unsettling experiences. 'Hardiness' is concerned with being committed to finding meaningful purpose in life, having strong beliefs that one can influence one's external surroundings and the outcome of life events and that one can indeed learn and grow from both positive and negative life experiences (Bonanno, 2004). Resilient immigrants are much more likely to accept the circumstances that are often present in their lives from the time of arrival and develop strategies to cope with them. Hardy individuals are likely to appraise stressful life events as less threatening, and are able to employ appropriate coping mechanisms in reducing the experience of acculturative stresses, both in the short and long terms. Whereas the research reviewed in this chapter is largely concerned with coping with stressful consequences of acculturation and acculturative stress, it is important to remember that some immigrant groups experience this process in a positive manner. It would be interesting to develop a taxonomy of various kinds of adaptational outcomes as a result of interactions among the various constructs depicted in Figure 24.2.

Prevalence of acculturative stress in four grids of societal cultural variations

In Figure 24.3, we depict a culture-based matrix of the prevalence and recognition of acculturative stress, use of social support, and differential emphasis on various types of coping. The point of this culture-based matrix is to emphasize the fact that the recognition of acculturative stress and methods to deal with it largely depend on the cultural context of the organization and the society of settlement. Organizations which are located in countries characterized by strong relationship orientation (i.e., found in collectivistic cultures of the world) and are also employee oriented (Hofstede, 2001) are likely to be quick in recognizing the importance of stresses that immigrants experience during the process of acculturation (Cell 1). Immigrants working in these types of organizations are also likely to engage in different emotion-focused coping, that is, avoidance coping, selective ignoring, hoping for a better scenario in the future and tolerating the present state of stress (Menaghan & Merves, 1984). Other forms of emotion-focused coping are distancing, self-controlling, and unrealistic positive appraisal (Yeh et al., 2006). These organizations may be found in countries such as Mexico, Brazil, and countries of the Middle East and Africa. Organizations located in countries characterized by cultural variations of strong rule and employee orientation (Cell 2) are likely to have moderate recognition of the importance of acculturative stress and also will provide moderate emphasis on various social supports systems. Immigrants in these organizations will find that the importance of emotion- and problem-focused coping will also be moderate in nature. Examples of organizations in Cell 2 may be found in newly globalizing countries such as India, China, and South Korea.

Organizations in countries characterized by strong rule and job orientation (Cell 3) are quick to recognize the growing importance of acculturative stresses experienced by professional immigrants. There is more of a tendency for professional immigrants in these organizations to emphasize problem-focused coping and employee assistance programs and have less emphasis on emotion-focused coping and social support-related

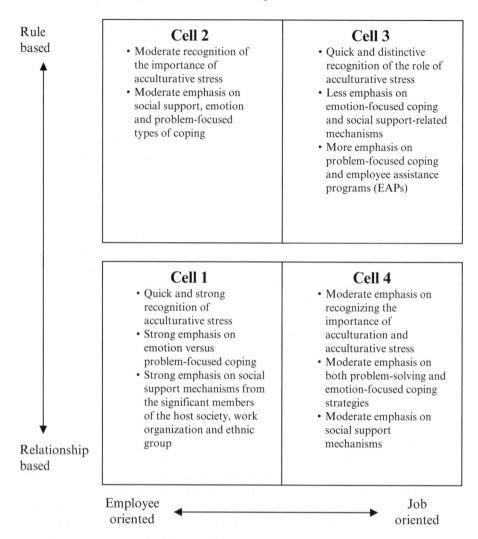

Figure 24.3   A culture-based matrix of the prevalence and recognition of acculturative stress, use of social support, and differential emphasis on various types of coping: impact of organizational and societal focus on immigrant acculturation

mechanisms (see Bhagat et al., 2008, for further discussion on the role of these types of cultural variations in fostering the role of social support and coping). These organizations are likely to be found in more individualistic countries such as those in Western Europe, and the US, Canada, and Australia. Organizations in Cell 4 are relationship based and job oriented, and show moderate emphasis on the importance of acculturation and acculturative stress. Professional immigrants in these organizations will place moderate emphasis on both problem-solving and emotion-focused coping and social support mechanisms. These organizations may be found in countries such as South Korea, Thailand,

Taiwan, Singapore, and globalized urban areas of India and China. The point of this culture-based matrix is to emphasize the fact that the recognition of acculturative stress and methods to deal with it largely depend on the cultural context of the organization and the society of settlement.

It is typically recognized that stresses of acculturation are much less in work organizations in Canada, which falls in Cell 3 of Figure 24.3. In countries where emphasis on developing relationships is important, for example, Brazil, China and South Korea, which are demonstrated by Cell 2, immigrants are likely to experience more stress in the initial phases of their adjustment compared to later phases. Development of relationships, particularly in the collectivistic context of these East Asian countries such as Japan, South Korea, China, and Singapore takes time. The nature of relationships in these cultures is highly differentiated (Triandis, 1994) and one must learn to appreciate the various types of relationships that exist in the work organization as well as in the societal context, before one can effectively utilize the resources that are inherent in these relationships for enhancing adjustments and dealing with acculturative stresses.

In countries that are more rule based, chances are high that immigrants can quickly learn to access various resources that are likely to be helpful in ameliorating the effects of stresses during the process of acculturation. However, it does not necessarily mean that one will be able to deal with the various stresses by utilizing the resources. Our research indicates that relationship-based cultures are more effective in providing appropriate social support mechanisms for helping immigrants to adjust to the demands of the work role and other roles in the broader societal context. However, adjusting to the demands of work roles in such cultures takes more time because the expectations associated with how one ought to behave and perform are much more implicit and context bound compared to countries which are more rule oriented and focused on immediate performance in the work role.

Toward a cultural theory of acculturative stress and adaptation
In Figure 24.4 we provide a model that has elements toward developing a culture-based theory of acculturative stress and adaptation. It shows that acculturative stress is a function of the differences between the salient cultural dimensions of the country of origin and the country of settlement. The differences between the levels of globalization of the country of settlement and the country of origin are also important. Immigrants coming from countries such as the developing economies of South America, Africa and Asia are likely to have more difficultly in deciphering the demands of work role that are present in the globalized economies of Western Europe, the US, Canada, and Australia. Immigrants to Japan also complain of significant amounts of role overload and the use of employment assistance programs in dealing with dysfunctional aspects of acculturative stress are common (Bhagat et al., 2008). International and cultural variations operate in the generation of acculturative stresses in ways not easily discerned from a casual glance at the literature. In fact, there have been hardly any systematic investigations into the interplay of culture-specific factors in the organizational context with the cultural characteristics that are rooted in the country of origin of the immigrants. For a robust theory of acculturative stress and adaptation to develop we need more systematic investigations into the joint effects of societal as well as organizational culture-based differences. For immigrants who have not had much work experience in their country of origin, it is

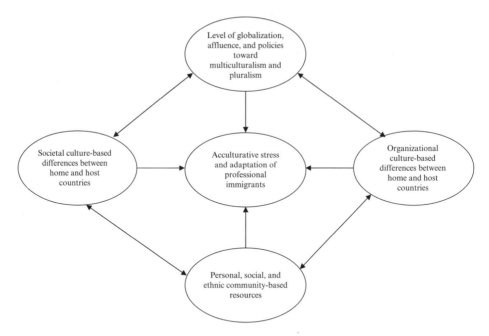

Figure 24.4   Distinctive facets of acculturative stress

important to focus on the nature of various experiences they have had in the institutions where they were educated.

Sessa and London (2006) propose that people are generative and transformative learners when they are ready to learn and are prompted by the needs of their environment. Readiness to learn is a function of individual differences such as self-efficacy, openness to new ideas, high learning orientation (wanting to learn for its own sake as well as for material rewards), ability to permeate social boundaries, developmental maturity, insight into how systems work, and conscientiousness. People who are low on these characteristics are likely to have a more difficult time adjusting and creating an experience of renewal for themselves and their families compared to those who are high on these characteristics. Pressure for moving beyond adaptation depends on social support from one's work organization (i.e., helpful co-workers and colleagues from whom one can learn valuable skills) and from one's ethnic group and community. Rewards that one might obtain at the end of successful personal change and adaptation will facilitate the motivation for changing. Sessa and London distinguish between adaptive, generative, and transformative learning. Adaptive learning is essentially a form of reactive coping. It consists of making incremental improvements, often through trial and error, and serves to reduce external pressures. Generative learning is proactive. The individual learns to seek new knowledge, experiments with new behaviors, obtains feedback, and improves. It is an explorative process and results in incorporating new skills, behaviors, and knowledge into one's job, career, and life. Transformative learning is concerned with developing a radical new lifestyle. It consists of giving up older forms of behaviors and interaction patterns in order to create new goals, roles, relationships, and work methods.

We propose that professional immigrants are more likely to be successful when they discover how to learn generatively and transformatively as opposed to learning in a reactive mode. Research into these learning styles and how they are implemented by professional immigrants will provide valuable insights for human resource managers in global and multinational organizations which employ them.

The nature of resources, both social and institutional, that are available to the immigrants in the country of settlement as well as the interplay of the significance of these resources with personal and ethnic group characteristics is also important to consider in developing the theory.

Implications for future research
Since about 100 years ago when the US society dealt with notions of American identity and the turn against immigration, the situation at the beginning of the twenty-first century reflects remarkable change. There has been a significant amount of research dealing with the psychosocial adjustments of immigrants in countries such as Canada, the US, Australia, the UK, and France, and one gets a clear impression that the issues of identity and the national credo (Huntington, 2004) are not only limited to the US society but are emerging as significant issues that need to be addressed comprehensively by social scientists from disciplines such as economics, sociology, psychology, and law. Psychological issues concerning acculturation, acculturative stress, and work-related adjustments and performance of culturally dissimilar professional immigrants in the work organizations of G8 countries are becoming quite important. A variety of issues are reflected in books such as the *Handbook of Multicultural Perspectives on Stress and Coping* (Wong & Wong, 2006), and *The Psychology of Culture Shock* (Ward et al., 2001).

The purpose of our chapter has been to further highlight the importance of this phenomenon in the context of increasing mobility of professional immigrants in the twenty-first-century global economy. While illegal immigration (about 13 million foreign-born persons in the US) is an issue that arises from time to time in the political arena in the US, the issue of global migration of legal and professional immigrants is always debated positively. At the time of writing this chapter, the percentage of professional immigrants in multinational and global corporations is on the rise: about 20% of professional software engineers at the higher ranks of Microsoft Corporation and a similar percentage in IBM, Oracle, Apple, Cisco Systems, FedEx, Texas Instruments, and others are foreign born. They are not only valued highly for their sustained professional contribution for enhancing the global competitiveness of these corporations, but are often sought after because they can be recruited at competitive wages in the global economy.

There is no doubt that a primary factor motivating the movement of professional immigrants from their countries of origin (often collectivistic in orientation and not fully globalized) to the country of settlement (often individualistic in orientation and fully globalized) lies in the differential nature of compensation. However, increasingly these professional immigrants are seeking jobs which allow them to experience not only job-related opportunities for growth and advancement, but also opportunities for maintaining strong ethnic ties with their native cultures and ethnic groups. Difficult experiences with the process of acculturation and acculturative stress make the contribution of these professional immigrants problematic, especially in the initial stages of their career.

We have attempted to portray the full range variables that come into play in understanding the process of acculturation, acculturative stress, and work-related adaptation (Figure 24.2), and in Figure 24.4 we delineate the four distinctive facets that are responsible for the development of acculturative stress in professional immigrants. In terms of future research, we propose the following:

1. Since cultural differences between the country of origin and the country of settlement are crucial aspects of the acculturation process, more robust methods should be employed in measuring the culture distance between the countries. These measures should be obtained at the individual level – using measures such as the one proposed by Triandis (1998) and his associates (Singelis et al., 1995) – and at the level of the nation, as shown in the works of Schwartz and Sagiv (1995). It is quite likely, as we have discussed earlier, that certain members of the professional immigrant group might acculturate a lot faster compared to the group as a whole. Positive occupational experiences coupled with high self-esteem, self-efficacy, and hardiness facilitate the process of acculturation for some individuals. It will be of interest to have a better understanding into the nature of these variables and their interaction with pre-acculturation-based individual-level variables. The gap in acculturation experiences between some individuals and the members of their ethnic group should be the focus of future studies involving professional immigrants. It is often noted that challenging professional experiences and assignments expedite the process of acculturation and lower acculturative stresses remarkably. While qualitative data collected by the first author and other anecdotal evidence points in this direction, we need more empirical insights into the validity of this phenomenon. This also has significant practical implications for facilitating adaptation of professional immigrants into multinational and global organizations in the twenty-first century.

2. A second issue of importance is the unfolding of the process of acculturation, adaptation, and assimilation over the career path of the professional immigrant. While cross-sectional surveys provide us with interesting information regarding the pattern of correlations of various adaptational outcomes with the variables listed in Figure 24.2, we need a better grasp of the causal pathways among these variables in order to discern their relative influences and importance over time. Findings in this area will provide valuable insights into the nature of variables that are likely to be more important in the initial stages of career development processes of professional immigrants versus later stages. This will also aid human resource management departments in designing effective training modules to facilitate development of multicultural and pluralistic attitudes and values in the professional immigrants as well as their co-workers and supervisors.

3. It is important to develop a taxonomy of adaptational outcomes as a result of interactions among the various constructs depicted in Figure 24.2. More research into the pattern of intercorrelations between the moderating factors both prior to and during acculturation would help in developing a better understanding of the type of outcomes that occur.

4. Future research should also be directed at assessing the intensity of career motivation (i.e., resilience, insight, and identity) of professional immigrants from the time they arrive in order to better predict later acculturation and acculturative stress-related outcomes. This calls for longitudinal designs that measure pre-immigration, personal

characteristics and situational conditions (i.e., challenges, barriers, and pressure) at initial as well as later stages of acculturation. There is also a distinct need to examine changes in learning styles, progress toward adaptive, generative, and transformative outcomes. One would expect that immigrants who are open to new ideas, proactive in seeking and applying new knowledge and skills, experimenting with new interpersonal and social relationships and new kinds of behavior are more likely to overcome career barriers (London, 1998). In the process, they also create expanded career opportunities for themselves and improved quality of life for their families.

Concluding thoughts

Immigration is a transformative (i.e., 'frame-breaking') experience. This chapter focuses on adaptation, and indicates that immigrants need to be adaptive learners. They also create new experiences for themselves, and as such, they engage in generative and transformative learning and behavior.

As globalization intensifies and the flow of educated and professional immigrants increases from the developing countries to more developed ones, the issues surrounding their economic impact and psychological adaptation will also become important. In this chapter we have examined the nature of acculturation that must occur over time in order for the professional immigrants to make their move professionally and personally satisfying. A larger part of our focus has been on examining the movement of collectivistic individuals from developing regions of the world to the more developed ones which are more individualistic in orientation. However as various economies of East, Southeast and South Asia as well as BRIC (Brazil, Russia, India and China) economies continue to expand at higher rates compared to the First-World countries of Western Europe, the US, Canada, and Japan, there is a reverse trend of people migrating from individualistic nations to the more collectivistic nations. Such migrations essentially have the same motivation which is present in the motivation of collectivistic individuals to the individualistic nations, which has been the focus of our analysis in this chapter. While the processes of adaptation and acculturative stress of this reverse type of immigration are concerned with similar kinds of processes, it might be necessary to modify our theoretical framework to accommodate interesting developments, the nature of which we have not yet fully comprehended. *The Economist* (2008) provides an interesting appraisal of the current status of global migration to include both professional and non-professional immigrants. We urge future researchers to incorporate some of the issues raised by this chapter and take a more comprehensive approach in understanding the nature of acculturation and acculturative stress. It is our hope that the ideas offered in this chapter will stimulate further research into this phenomenon.

References

Altrocchi, J. & Altrocchi, L. (1995), 'Polyfaceted psychological acculturation in Cook Islanders', *Journal of Cross-Cultural Psychology*, **26**, 426–40.

Berry, J.W. (1970), 'Marginality, stress and identification in an acculturating Aboriginal community', *Journal of Cross-Cultural Psychology*, **1**, 239–52.

Berry, J.W. (1997), 'Immigration, acculturation and adaptation', *Applied Psychology: An International Review*, **46**, 5–34.

Berry, J.W. (2001), 'A psychology of immigration', *Journal of Social Issues*, **57**, 615–31.

Berry, J.W. & Ataca, B. (2000), 'Cultural factors in stress', in G. Fink (ed.), *Encyclopedia of Stress*, vol. I, San Diego, CA: Academic Press, pp. 604–11.

Berry, J.W. & Kim, U. (1988), 'Acculturation and mental health', in P. Dasen, J.W. Berry & N. Sartorius (eds), *Health and Cross-Cultural Psychology*, Newbury Park, CA: Sage, pp. 207–36.

Berry, J.W., Kim, U., Minde, T. & Mok, D. (1987), 'Comparative studies of acculturative stress', *International Migration Review*, **21**, 491–511.

Berry, J.W., Kim, U., Power, S., Young, M. & Bujaki, M. (1989), 'Acculturation attitudes in plural societies', *Applied Psychology*, **38**, 185–206.

Berry, J.W. & Sam, D.L. (1997), 'Acculturation and adaptation', in J. Berry, M.H. Segall, & C. Kagitcibasi (eds), *Handbook of Cross-Cultural Psychology, Volume 3: Social Behavior and Application*, Needham Heights, MA: Allyn & Bacon, pp. 291–326.

Bhagat, R.S. & London, M. (1999), 'Getting started and getting ahead: career dynamics of immigrants', *Human Resource Management Review*, **9**, 349–65.

Bhagat, R.S., Steverson, P.K. & Segovis, J.C. (2008), 'Cultural variations in employee assistance programs in an era of globalization', in D.L. Stone & E.F. Stone-Romero (eds), *The Influence of Culture on Human Resource Management Processes and Practices*, New York: Lawrence Erlbaum, pp. 207–33.

Bonnano, G.A. (2004), 'Loss, trauma, and human resilience: have we underestimated the human capacity to thrive after extremely aversive events?', *American Psychologist*, **59**(1), 20–28.

Chang, E.C. (2001), 'A look at the coping strategies and styles of Asian Americans: similar and different', in C.R. Snyder (ed.), *Coping with Stress*, Oxford and New York: Oxford University Press, pp. 222–39.

Economist, The (2008), 'Global migration: keep the borders open', January 3.

Furnham, A. & Alibhai, N. (1985), 'The friendship networks of foreign students: a replication and extension of the functional model', *International Journal of Social Psychology*, **20**, 709–22.

Furnham, A. & Sheikh, S. (1993), 'Gender, generational and social support correlates of mental health in Asian immigrants', *International Journal of Social Psychiatry*, **39**, 22–33.

Graves, T.D. (1967), 'Psychological acculturation in a tri-ethnic community', *Southwestern Journal of Anthropology*, **23**, 337–50.

Hofstede, G. (2001), *Culture's Consequences*, 2nd edn, Thousand Oaks, CA: Sage.

Huntington, S.P. (2004), *Who Are We: The Challenges to America's National Identity*, New York: Simon & Schuster.

Jayasuriya, L., Sang, D. & Fiending, A. (1992), *Ethnicity, Immigration and Mental Illness: A Critical Review of Australian Research*, Canberra: Bureau of Immigration Research.

Kozulin, A. & Vengar, A. (1995), 'Immigration without adaptation: the psychological world of Russian immigrants in Israel', *Journal of Russian and East European Psychology*, **33**(2), 26–38.

London, M.L. (1998), *Career Barriers: How People Experience, Overcome and Avoid Failure*, Mahwah, NJ: Lawrence Erlbaum.

London, M.L. & Noe, R.A. (1997), 'London's career motivation theory: an update on measurement and research', *Journal of Career Assessment*, **5**(1), 61–80.

London, R.R. (2000), 'Knocking on Europe's door', *Time Europe*, July 3, **155**(5).

Menaghan, E. & Merves, E.S. (1984), 'Coping with occupational problems: the limits of individual efforts', *Journal of Health and Social Behavior*, **25**, 406–23.

Noh, S., Beiser, M., Kaspar, V., Hou, F. & Rummens, A. (1999), 'Perceived racial discrimination, coping, and depression among Asian refugees in Canada', *Journal of Health and Social Behavior*, **40**, 193–207.

Noh, S. & Kaspar, V. (2003), 'Perceived discrimination and depression: moderating effects of coping, acculturation, and ethnic support', *American Journal of Public Health*, **93**, 232–8.

Oberg, K. (1960), 'Cultural shock: adjustment to new cultural environments', *Practical Anthropology*, **7**, 177–82.

Office of Immigration Statistics (2006), 'US Permanent Legal Residents', Department of Homeland Security, Washington, DC.

Ponizovsky, A., Ginath, Y., Durst, R., Wondimeneh, B., Safro, S., Minuchin-Itzigson, S. & Ritsner, M. (1998), 'Psychological distress among Ethiopian and Russian Jewish immigrants to Israel: a cross-cultural study', *International Journal of Social Psychiatry*, **44**(1), 35–45.

Pottie, K., Brown, J.B. & Dunn, S. (2005), 'The resettlement of Central American men in Canada: from emotional distress to successful integration', *Refuge*, **22**(2), 101–12.

Redfield, R., Linton, R. & Herskovits, M.J. (1936), 'Memorandum for the study of acculturation', *American Anthropologist*, **38**, 149–52.

Roesch, S.C., Wee, C. & Vaughn, A.A. (2006), 'Relations between the Big Five personality traits and dispositional coping in Korean Americans: acculturation as a moderating factor', *International Journal of Psychology*, **41**, 85–96.

Schwartz, S.H. & Sagiv, L. (1995), 'Identifying culture specifics in the content and structure of values', *Journal of Cross-Cultural Psychology*, **26**, 92–116.

Searle, W. & Ward, C. (1990), 'The prediction of psychological and sociocultural adjustment during cross-cultural transitions', *International Journal of Intercultural Relations*, **14**, 449–64.

Sessa, V.I. & London, M. (2006), *Continuous Learning*, Mahwah, NJ: Erlbaum.

Shaffer, M.A., Joplin, J.R.W., Bell, M.P., Lau, T. & Oguz, C. (2000), 'Disruptions to women's social identity: a comparative study of workplace stress experienced by women in three geographic regions', *Journal of Occupational Health Psychology*, **5**(4), 441–56.

Singelis, T.M., Triandis, H.C., Bhawuk, D.S. & Gelfand, M. (1995), 'Horizontal and vertical dimensions of individualism and collectivism: a theoretical and measurement refinement', *Cross-Cultural Research*, **29**, 240–75.

Smith, P.B., Bond, M.H. & Kagitcibasi, C. (2006), *Understanding Social Psychology across Cultures*, London: Sage.

Triandis, H.C. (1994), *Culture and Social Behavior*, New York: McGraw-Hill.

Triandis, H.C. (1998), 'Vertical and horizontal individualism and collectivism: theory and research implications for international comparative management', *Advances in International Comparative Management*, **12**: 7–35.

Vega, W. & Rumbaut, R. (1991), 'Social networks, social support, and their relationship to depression among immigrant Mexican women', *Human Organization*, **50**, 154–62.

Ward, C. (1996), 'Acculturation', in D. Landis & R.S. Bhagat (eds), *Handbook of Intercultural Training*, 2nd edn, Thousand Oaks, CA: Sage, pp. 124–47.

Ward, C., Bochner, S. & Furnham, A. (2001), *The Psychology of Culture Shock*, Hove, UK: Routledge.

Ward, C. & Rana-Deuba, A. (1999), 'Acculturation and adaptation revisited', *Journal of Cross-Cultural Psychology*, **30**, 422–42.

Wong, P.T.P. & Wong, L.C.J. (eds) (2006), *Handbook of Multicultural Perspectives on Stress and Coping*, New York: Springer.

Yeh, C.J., Arora, A.K. & Wu, K.A. (2006), 'Culture: a fundamental context for the stress and coping paradigm', in P.T.P.Wong & L.C.J. Wong (eds), *Handbook of Multicultural Perspectives on Stress and Coping*, New York: Springer, pp. 29–53.

25 Immigration, acculturation and drug abuse: multicultural aspects of treatment

Marina Dalla, Alexander-Stamatios G. Antoniou and Katerina Matsa

Introduction

Migration in Europe

Immigrants and refugees are an increasingly substantial subset of the European societies. During the year 2000, more than 22 million foreign nationals resided in Western Europe, comprising over 5.5% of the total population (Salt, 2003). This number includes legal immigrants, asylum seekers, and undocumented immigrants arriving each year. Projections suggest that the numbers of first- and second-generation residents will continue to expand rapidly. The future of Europe is ultimately related to the adaptation of immigrants and their children, even with possible future efforts to reduce immigration.

Immigrants arrived in two waves to Greece. The first was during the early 1990s, in which Albanians dominated. The second arrived after 1995, and involved much greater participation of immigrants from other Balkan states, the former Soviet Union, Pakistan, India, Iraq and Iran. According to the 2001 Census, the largest group of immigrants draws its origins from the Balkan countries of Albania, Bulgaria, and Romania. People from these countries make up almost two-thirds of the total 'foreign population'. Migrants from the former Soviet Union (Georgia, Russia, Ukraine, Moldavia, etc.) comprise 10% of the total and are mainly of Greek origin; the EU countries approximately 6%. A heterogeneous group of people from places such as the United States, Canada, and Australia (mostly first- or second-generation Greek emigrants returning home), also account for around 6%. Finally, a residual group from a wide variety of countries makes up 13% (Labrianidis & Lyberaki, 2001).

Drug abuse is a significant health problem for all European societies. There are an estimated 2 million drug abusers in Europe alone and the numbers are growing steadily, particularly among young people (Diamanduros, 2005). In Greece the number of problem drug users appeared to increase in 2004, compared to 2003. Among the users, non-Greek nationals accounted for 2.5%. In addition, from 1993 up to 2001 a sharp increase in drug-related deaths was observed. Non-Greek nationals accounted for 5.8% (Terzidou, 2005). A 1996 World Health Organization (WHO) report noted that the consumption of tranquillizers and antidepressants by young immigrants across Europe is growing. Most of the research and literature that examines drug abuse problems identify risk factors for the general population, but, more specifically find immigrant youth to be particularly at risk of beginning the use of drugs because of their minority status (Robbins & Mikow, 2000). In order to design effective intervention programs and services for minority people, it is important to understand the process of immigration as a transition, and also the differences in culture that may affect the decision of an immigrant to use different substances.

This chapter provides an overview of the relationship between immigration, acculturation and drug abuse in immigrants. In this section, immigration and acculturation factors which play a role in immigrants' adaptation are presented. The focus then moves to the relationship between acculturation and drug abuse with greater emphasis on risk factors that are related to immigrants' drug addiction. The subsequent section deals with the accessibility of substance abuse and mental health services by immigrants, followed by a section that is more focused on comparative research regarding differences and similarities in drug abuse among native Greeks and immigrants. The penultimate section pays attention to the integration of culture concepts into intervention programmes for the rehabilitation of addicted immigrants, and the final section concludes.

Immigration and acculturation
The process of migration can be understood as a profound non-normative life transition (Suárez-Orozco, 2000) consisting of the pre-migration and departure phase, and the transition and adaptation to a new country. Even under the best of conditions, migration involves a series of events that can be highly traumatizing and that can place migrants at risk. The decision to migrate as a perceived lack of prospects that people have in their own country due to economic or political conditions (Ward et al., 2001) removes them from predictable contexts (family, friends, customs, language) and leads to a keen sense of loss (Suárez-Orozco & Suárez-Orozco, 2001). During the initial period following arrival, many immigrants experience a sense of confusion, including anxiety, disorientation, suspicion and bewilderment (Oberg, 1960), but as the realities of the new situation are confronted, they begin to experience a variety of psychological problems due to acculturation.

Acculturation implies changes over time in beliefs, emotions, attitudes, values, behaviors and identification pattern of persons in first-hand contact with persons representing another culture (Sam, 2006). Pressures on the individual to contend with the host society can lead to increased stress, or acculturative stress (Berry, 2003) as a generalized physiological and psychological state brought about by the experience of stressors in the environment, and which requires some reduction through a process of coping until some satisfactory adaptation to the new situation is achieved. When behavioral shifts have taken place without difficulty, stress is likely to be minimal and personal consequences are generally positive. When acculturative problems do arise, but have been successfully coped with, stress will be low and the immediate effects positive. But when an individual's adaptive resources are insufficient to support adjustment to a new cultural environment, stress will be higher and the effects more negative (ibid.). Acculturative stress is a common experience of first-generation immigrants (Ward et al., 2001). Second- and later-generation immigrants experience acculturative stress owing to the conflicts that arise out of their bicultural socialization (Roysircar-Sodowsky & Maestas, 2000). Accumulative evidence suggests that acculturative stress may have important implications for the mental health of immigrants, including psychosocial, somatic and social aspects (Organista et al., 2003).

Substance abuse among immigrants
Important considerations in studying the relationship between immigration and drug abuse are differences in substance use patterns between the general population and immigrants. A body of research that we have found useful assesses whether foreign-born

individuals demonstrate higher or lower rates of substance use than their native-born counterparts, and the variety of variables (the nature of migration, culture differences, lack of support) that mediate the relationship between acculturation and mental health and make people vulnerable to substance abuse (Gfroerer & Tan, 2003). Comparison across groups often includes the role of psychosocial characteristics across two or more culture groups, or in the medical context the treatment in which the specialist and the patient belong to different cultures (Westermeyer, 2004).

Research findings on substance use patterns among immigrant populations are mixed, with some studies indicating that substance use increases with increased time in the new country (Gfroerer & Tan, 2003). Other studies showed decreased substance use and mental health problems over time and with increased levels of acculturation (NIDA, 2001; Caetano & Clark, 2003). Even within subgroups of immigrants, there is wide variability in substance use patterns. According to Isralowitz et al. (2002), immigrants from the former Soviet Union (FSU) faced with the highly complex challenge of acculturation often develop emotional and behavioral problems that include mental illness, delinquency, and alcohol and drug abuse. Their experiences in their new countries, where drugs and alcohol are readily available at low prices, lead immigrants who are experiencing difficulty to turn to substance abuse as a way of coping. Early research shows that FSU substance abusers, especially those using drugs, are mainly bilingual males in their early twenties. Unlike other young people in the New York City area, this population does not start with 'gateway' drugs, such as marijuana or ecstasy, but goes straight to injecting heroin.

The mixed findings from research with immigrant and minority populations have pointed to the need for considering coexistence of stressors that increase vulnerability to personal problems of immigrants such as drug use. Most studies have relied on acculturation and acculturative stress effects on licit and illicit drug use by immigrant adolescents (EMCDDA, 2002). Additional research addresses the culture itself, including the norms for the abuse of alcohol, tobacco and other drugs within the specific culture and their meaning and effect on the initial or continued abuse of drugs by minority youth (Robbins & Mikow, 2000).

Risk factors that are related to drug abuse among immigrants: a review of the literature
Acculturative stress, or the challenge of assimilating into the dominant culture, has been implicated as a mechanism for increased substance use among immigrants (NIDA, 2001). The process of acculturation implies role strains, cognitive manipulations, and affective states that are potentially stressful and responsible for the non-adaptive attitudes and behaviors of immigrants (Berry, 1997). An important premise of the acculturative stress process is that stressors are harmful only when coping resources are inadequate for solving problems; demands must exceed resources to produce a negative outcome. Drug use is one possible negative outcome (Alaniz, 2002; Castillo & Henderson, 2002). Mental health professionals have described the common symptoms that most immigrants present and have called it 'chronic and multiple stress syndrome' in immigrants (Carta et al., 2005). Immigrants affected by this syndrome present depressive symptomatology with atypical characteristics, where depressive symptoms are anxiety, somatoform and dissociative symptoms. The development of this condition occurs progressively as the immigrants encounter difficulties that take place during the migration and acculturation process, difficulties in finding a job and housing, in obtaining documents, or with

the racism encountered in a new country. According to specialists, chronic and multiple stress syndrome should constitute a category situated in between adjustment disorders and post-traumatic stress disorder.

Another hypothesis is that exposure to a new culture brings with it increasing familiarity with the social contexts of drug use, as well as opportunities for drug use in peer group situations, in which youth often construct spaces of competence in the underground (Suárez-Orozco, 2000). These peer groups function on the periphery of multiple sociocultural worlds and include individuals who may feel confused, frustrated, and inferior. Therefore, the use of substances is adapted as a method of socialization into the new society. Thus, the addicts have friends or peers and are in this way grown up, independent, and 'successful'.

Despite the plausibility of both explanations, they are neither satisfactory nor comprehensive. Becoming a drug user is a complex, multipath process that has no unitary explanation. While it is evident that immigrant youth who have greater exposure to a new culture may be more delinquent or use more illicit drugs, this fact alone cannot explain which youth are susceptible among all youth so exposed. Similarly, the argument that acculturative stress increases drug use among immigrants fails to identify the factors or conditions that differentiate users from non-users. Added stressors from the process of immigration itself can lead to increased risk for emotional disturbance and drug abuse in newer immigrants. These include previous traumatic exposure in their homelands (war, torture), many of which prompt the decision to emigrate in the first place. These are often compounded by the loss of extended family and kinship networks (and even separation from nuclear family members, such as children from their parents) as well as the lack of social support and assimilation or marginalization (Caetano et al., 1998; Makimoto, 1998; Elder et al., 2000). Such experiences create vulnerability in children and adolescents due to their incomplete biopsychosocial development, dependency, inability to understand certain life events and underdevelopment of coping skills. These risk factors for drug use operate through increasing the probability of incorporation of deviant norms generally, by increasing the chances of involvement with deviant peers (Beauvais & Oetting, 1999).

Accumulating data indicate that unaccompanied children and adolescents and those separated from family members are consistently at greater risk of having psychiatric and mental health problems than their accompanied peers (Sourander, 1998). By definition, an unaccompanied immigrant child is an individual under 18 years of age who has been separated from both parents and is not being cared for by a responsible adult (Servan-Schreiber et al., 1998; Sourander, 1998). Unaccompanied adolescents and youths are particularly vulnerable as their increasing autonomy causes them to relive past separations, creating difficulties in adjustment. Separation of children from their parents (for whatever reason) can directly affect the parent–child relationship and may result in increased vulnerability and risk for children. On reunification, parents and children have to adjust to living together again. The parental viewpoint of separation–reunion is often very different from that of their children. Parents have expectations that their children will be happy, affectionate and obedient. In the absence of such behaviors, parents may perceive the child as ungrateful and experience hurt and anger when faced with a hostile or unappreciative child (Suárez-Orozco, 2000). The symptom of addiction in these cases provides a form of 'pseudo-individuation' at several levels, containing elements of the fear of being separated or abandoned and presenting an attempt to punish the parents by engaging in acting-out behavior.

Moreover, a variety of problems exist when one parent, especially the father, migrates first and, if married, leaves behind a wife and children, and the reunion occurs after he had become established in the new country (Suárez-Orozco & Suárez-Orozco, 2001). The temporary loss of relationships and contact with the family, and the disruption of family support, are related to the sense of loneliness and the lack of an attachment figure (Peplau & Perlman, 1982). Drug addiction in this case, especially to heroin, does indeed appear to have many adaptive, functional qualities that fuel negative emotional states of isolation and loneliness in addition to the 'pleasurable' features that serve to fulfill the unconscious need to entertain and to enact various kinds of homosexual and perverse fantasies, and at the same time to avoid taking responsibility for this.

Contact with the new culture and conflicts that are rooted in different rates of acculturation in the family (e.g., highly assimilated children, adherence of parents to the traditional values) lead to the disruption of the core family processes (perceived roles, hierarchy, exercise of power, models of interaction), even in cases where the entire family immigrate. The weakness of the parents in supporting their children, either because their economic needs force them to leave their children alone without supervision for long periods, or because of mental disturbance or divorce (Hjern et al., 1998; Suárez-Orozco & Suárez-Orozco, 2001), and the faster acculturation of the children due to their young age together with their integration into the educational system, together result in parent–child conflicts that concern issues such as dress code, dating, and school performance, and also rights and obligations within the family (Booth et al., 1997). When the intensity of conflicts becomes unbearable and the youngster is unable to trust other people outside of the familial environment, then drug abuse is a way of making the negative emotions more tolerable. Using drugs is considered to be a way of expressing frustration and anger, especially when the young people are unable to deal with their parents directly. Young drug abusers are bound in a simultaneous need to defy their parents and to punish themselves for their own rebellion.

Acculturation strategies, regarding the way in which immigrants regulate the proximity and the distance in the transformation of identity and in their relationships with the country of origin and the country of reception (Akhtar, 1999) are considered to have different effects on mental health (Sam, 2006). The issue of substance abuse. If young people feel isolated because they are unable to integrate, or feel rejected by the mainstream culture, or if their ethnic group is viewed by the majority culture as devalued and denigrated, they may identify and internalize these negative perceptions, which may lead to negative self-emotions, which in turn may lead to substance abuse. At the other end of the continuum, they may develop an adversarial identity, standing in defiance of the majority culture, which is seen as depriving them of social and financial aspirations and marginalizing them. In these situations, some young people who are not able to embrace their own culture and who develop an adversarial identity against the mainstream culture, construct spaces of competence in the underground and may join gangs. For them, gangs offer a sense of belonging, solidarity, protection, discipline, and warmth. These groups structure the anger many feel towards the society that violently rejected their parents and themselves (Suárez-Orozco, 2000).

Additional factors that are connected with the pathology of usage are the low economic and social level of the parents (Howard & Hodes, 2000), economic poverty, low social status connected with the national group, failure at school as the basic institution of children's socialization (Hyman et al, 2000), and also the lack of future opportunities (Caetano et al., 1998; Elder et al., 2000).

Healthcare services and drug dependence in immigrants: the experience in Greece

Studies in drug abuse document that immigrant groups have less access to, and availability of, mental health services and they are less likely to receive needed mental health care. They often receive a poorer quality of mental health care in terms of treatment and are underrepresented in mental health research (EMCDDA, 2002). A constellation of barriers deters minorities from obtaining treatment. Many of these barriers operate for all people: cost, fragmentation of services, lack of availability of services, and societal stigma toward dependence from illicit substances. But additional barriers deter racial and ethnic minorities: personal beliefs, mistrust and fear of treatment, racism and discrimination, and differences in language and communication (Israelowitz, 2004).

Personal cultural beliefs have a great impact on the perception of substance use. Culture determines how people understand and deal with substance use and abuse. For example, people from traditional cultures may avoid substance abuse services due to the fear of stigmatization. For them, substance abuse is a moral problem and a source of family shame (Sue, 2002). Cultural factors influence the type of symptoms displayed and conceptions of mental health and disturbance. People from collectivistic cultures tend to have more organic or somatic involvement in emotional disturbance. They also believe that the exercise of willpower, and the avoidance of morbid thoughts, are means of enhancing psychological well-being. As a consequence they may avoid Western forms of mental health treatment and seek medical treatment for emotional problems (Tanaka-Matsumi & Draguns, 1997)

Experiences of discrimination and stereotyping, alienation, healthcare providers' biases, as well as communication problems can prevent immigrants from utilizing health services. Discrimination and stereotyping play a role in mistrust and subsequent service utilization in immigrants and in greater use of informal services and help seeking from friends or relatives, but not in the use of formal services (Spencer & Chen, 2004). The ability to communicate with one another is essential for all aspects of healthcare, yet it carries special significance in the area of mental health because drug abuse and substance abuse treatment is based on encompassing thoughts, moods, and the highest integrative aspects of behavior. People often respond to the language barrier by remaining silent, appearing withdrawn, moody, and fearful. Thus, the treatment of substance abuse dependence greatly depends on verbal communication and trust between patient and specialist. The lack of culturally and linguistically appropriate services and mistrust of mental health providers constitute significant elements of social exclusion.

Although in Greece the officially recognized drug treatment programs operating in the country add up to 51 in total and deliver different types of treatment services (Terzidou, 2005), little attention has been paid to the examination of utilization of drug abuse treatment services by immigrants. There are different sources of information, but up to the present there has not been any attempt to design comprehensive surveys regarding the handling of immigrant populations and mental health. The interest in different treatment services has focused on the characteristics of immigrant groups, recording changes in patterns of use and trying to better understand their needs.

In terms of the treatment services available, integrated culture-specific treatment is provided by two programs for immigrant drug users. More specifically, the Drug Dependence Unit 18 (ANO) (Psychiatric Hospital of Attica), which comes under the Ministry of Health, has been working in recent years to respond to the needs of addict immigrants and refugees by developing and integrating a culturally sensitive plan of substance abuse intervention. According to this plan, the multistage therapeutic process consisting of sensitization, psychological recovery (main treatment) and social reintegration is sensitive to cultural values and experiences of immigrant groups, while addressing the common etiological factors of substance abuse. The main treatment services offered integrate different needs of immigrants. The therapeutic team provides bridges to social resources in the community to provide information about supportive networks that facilitate the reintegration of immigrants and refugees (document and housing aid, language learning).

The Therapy Center for Dependent Individuals (KETHEA) has established the MOSAIC Transitional Centre in Athens in order to provide psychosocial support to dependent individuals from vulnerable social groups, such as repatriated Greeks, refugees and immigrants. The program delivers healthcare services, motivation, empowerment, dependence treatment and social activation, adapting a cross-cultural approach (Terzidou, 2005).

Drug abuse among native and immigrant adults: a comparative study in Greece
This study presents information on the prevalence of illicit drug use among immigrants aged 18 or older in Greece, in comparison to native Greeks. Estimates for immigrants and native drug abusers are based on data collected during 2005–06 from adults in the Drug Dependence Unit at the State Psychiatry Hospital of Attica. Sample sizes were: $N = 53$ (51%) immigrants and $N = 51$ (49%) native Greeks. Some 60% (31) of immigrants were from the FSU, 17% (8) from Arabic countries (Iraq, Iran), 15% (7) from countries of Eastern Europe (Albania, Poland, Bulgaria) and 8% (5) were repatriated Greek immigrants from the FSU, Australia and Germany. In the above sample, 18 people (17.5%) were married, 72 (69.9%) were single and 12 (11.9%) were divorced. Although the immigrants were married, their children and wives lived in their country of origin.

Materials
The data collection method used in this study involved in-person structured interviews with the sample population, incorporating procedures that would be likely to increase respondents' cooperation and willingness to report honestly about their illicit drug use behavior. The interview included personal and demographic information (age, education in years, and country of birth), marital status, living conditions and housing, health status (HIV/AIDS), criminal and deviant behaviors, and information regarding lifetime use of illicit substances. The interview was conducted after the person had decided to participate in the drug rehabilitation program.

Results

Education level   Immigrant abusers displayed a considerably higher education level compared with Greek abusers. Some 49% of immigrants compared to approximately 24% of native Greeks held a university degree: $\chi^2(1, n = 104) = 3.16, p = 0.05$.

Employment status   In terms of the kind of jobs that people did there were no differences between immigrants and natives. The main occupations for all drug abusers were paid employment in construction (54.5%), in manufacturing sectors (27.7%) and in the scientific sector (5.9%), with a small percentage in self-employment (2%). With regard to employment participation, immigrants also displayed a considerably higher unemployment rate compared with Greek natives (63% compared to approximately 47.1%, respectively: χ^2(1, $n = 104$) = 6.36, $p = 0.01$. Moreover the rate of immigrants without social security (50%) is considerably higher than that of natives: χ^2(1, $n = 104$) = 5.06, $p < 0.05$.

Health status   The rate of immigrants that were users of the healthcare system (53.8%) was considerably lower than the rate of native Greeks (29.4%): χ^2(1, $n = 104$) = 9.0, $p < 0.01$. In terms of acquired immuno-deficiency syndrome (AIDS) more immigrants (26.4%) than natives (13.7%) have no information about AIDS infection: χ^2(1, $n = 104$) = 6.8, $p < 0.01$.

Substance abuse   With respect to the main illicit substance there were no differences among groups. Specifically, heroin is the main illicit substance that the majority of the group 86.5% (90) use, 6.7% reported that they use cocaine as a main substance, and the remaining 6.7% reported using other drugs such as amphetamines, benzodiazepines, marijuana and hashish. However, differences were found with regard to methods of substance use: χ^2(1, $n = 104$) = 3.5, $p = 0.05$. Compared with natives (36.7%), substance use among most immigrants occurs intramuscularly, through multiperson use of needles and syringes (51%). More natives than immigrants use illicit substances orally, or inhaled. With respect to the multiperson use of a common syringe there were no differences between the groups. Some 32% of people reported multiperson use of syringes.

The path to drug addiction begins with the act of taking hashish or marijuana for 72.6%, 9.9% use narcotics such as heroin and opium, and the remainder (7.7%) begin with using depressants, cocaine and amphetamines. With regard to concurrent use of different types of substances, differences between groups were observed: heroin was associated with marijuana use in immigrants, whereas among natives multiple substance use was observed: χ^2(1, $n = 104$) = 23.9, $p = 0.001$.

Age of first involvement with illicit substance use   The age of first involvement with elicit substances is older for immigrants ($M = 18$) than for natives ($M = 15.6$): $F(1, 96) = 8.5$, $p < 0.01$. The mean age of first illicit substance use for immigrants is 18 years, with the youngest aged 10 and the oldest aged 40. Natives appeared to have a mean initiation age of 15.6 years, with the youngest aged 12 and the oldest aged 30.

Although immigrants appeared to have been initiated into illicit substance use at an older age, their developmental sequence of substance use involvement increases faster compared to natives. Immigrants advance to intramuscular substance use more rapidly than Greeks. The average time of dependency does not differ among groups. The mean length of use reported by natives was 7 years and by immigrants 5.2 years. The longest time of use for natives is 25 years and for natives 36.6 years.

Legal status   According to statistics, there are differences in drug-related offences between groups: χ^2(1, $n = 103$) = 23.9, $p < 0.05$. Immigrants reported fewer offences than natives. However, more immigrants than natives do not give information about their legal status. Differences were found with regard to trial or court decisions: $\chi^2(1, n = 100) = 6.7, p < 0.01$ and to awaiting such trial or court decision: $\chi^2(1, n = 100) = 3.0, p < 0.05$. More specifically, a lower proportion of drug users among immigrants than among natives reported that they are awaiting a hearing and a decision concerning a past offense. But a higher proportion of immigrants than Greeks provide no information about their previous history of trial or court decisions. Regarding prior punishment and imprisonment there were no differences between the groups. A total of 45.6% reported the outcome of their case: prior arrest and prison was reported by 23.8%; self-report data indicated that 29.7% had committed a serious violent offense; suspension of judgment was reported by 18%; and trial by jury by 33.3%.

Counseling and substance abuse treatment   The length of involvement of immigrants and natives in a treatment program was the same. However, immigrants are twice as poor as natives at keeping their appointments: $F(1, 95) = 5.5, p < 0.05$. In addition, immigrant drug abusers tend to seek a medical solution for their addiction. It appears that many of them use treatment to reduce their level of drug abuse, not to eliminate the problem: $\chi^2(1, n = 96) = 4.3, p < 0.05$.

Conclusions   Immigrant status (i.e., being an immigrant) does appear to influence the attitudes and behavior of drug abusers. Drug abusers, natives and immigrants, are more inclined to use heroin as a main illicit substance and their behavior is mostly related to a combination of heroin with other substances. But numerous factors tend to differentiate immigrants and native drug abusers, including patterns of injected heroin use: intramuscular in combination with multiperson use of needles and syringes was present among most immigrants. Multiperson sharing of syringes is associated with rapid transition of HIV among illicit drug users, with HIV incidence rates as high as 20–50 per 100 person years at risk. Moreover, most illicit drug users who continue to inject may be unable to obtain a sufficient number of syringes to effectively reduce their risk of acquiring and transmitting blood-born viral infections (Batki & Nathan, 2004).

The second important result refers to the speed at which immigrant substance users progress from mild to more severe involvement. Faster progression of immigrants compared to natives is in contrast to the later initiators of substance use among immigrants. The results also suggest that it is important to investigate whether immigration and acculturation may play a role in addictive liability, above and beyond what is accounted for by other factors.

Descriptive findings confirm that immigrants have less access to mental health services than natives; and they are less likely to receive needed care because immigrants are unlikely to use formal mental health and primary healthcare services. To understand ethnic disparities in specialty care, the effects of ethnicity should be analyzed in combination with other factors including the financial costs involved. According to the results, a higher rate of immigrant drug users face a social and economic environment of inequality that includes greater poverty, unemployment and lack of social security. Other barriers that affect utilization of mental health options may be categorized as follows: differences in language and culture, stigmatization and the failure of services to target immigrant groups (Makimoto, 1998; Elder et al., 2000; EMCDDA, 2002).

Similarly, immigrants are seen to differentiate their behavior in relation to drug abuse treatment. Immigrants are seen as having an increased probability of missing appointments and also of seeking a medical solution for their addiction. Culturally based factors such as shame and stigma, conceptions of mental health, and alternative options are important factors that affect utilization and appropriateness of mainstream services (Sue, 2002). The tendency to have more organic or somatic involvement in drug abuse disturbance has to do with the cultural meaning of somatic complaints (Tanaka-Matsumi & Draguns, 1997). Somatic complaints are less stigmatized among some cultures and somatization justifies an acceptable medical intervention. On the other hand, specialists must be cognizant of the immigration experience itself because of stress and the lack of social and economic resources for coping, which may deter immigrants from using services and receiving appropriate care.

Importance of adapting an integrated multicultural approach to drug dependence problems of immigrants

Recently, there has been a demand for cultural sensitivity and competence in treating refugees and immigrants. It is a common task of mental health professionals to understand the role of culture in order to help people from different contexts to optimize their functioning and well-being. Culture is usually defined as a way of life or the totality of the individual artifacts, behaviors, and mental concepts transmitted from one generation to the next in a society. It is visible and invisible, cognitive and affective, conscious and unconscious, internal and external, rational and irrational at the same time (Draguns, 2002). Comparisons across cultures in a treatment context are often termed 'etic', whereas noncomparable, culture-specific elements or patterns are termed 'emic' (Westermeyer, 2004).

The influence of culture in the treatment process can be understood in terms of two dimensions: (i) the specific sets of environments that influence the individual's experience such as family, school and community, and (ii) the specific meanings of social phenomena including patterns of social behavior, self-concept, interpersonal interaction, beliefs about social gender roles and sexuality (Draguns, 2002). Many studies have shown that people differ in their experience of pain, in what they label as a symptom, how they communicate their pain or symptoms, in their beliefs about its cause, the attitudes toward therapists and the treatment they desire or expect (McGoldrick & Giordano, 1996). Furthermore, a careful, well-documented treatment plan necessitates an addicted individual detailing the nature of stressful events and acculturative stress, information about the cultural context that influences the behavior of the individual, and the therapists' awareness and self reflection about their own possible prejudice and cultural biases (Azima, 2002). It is important to be aware of the challenges that face addicted immigrants and refugees: acculturation and acculturative stress, parental acculturation and related stress, disruption in the family structure and 'parentification' of the child, a new identity based on certain features of the culture of origin and the host culture.

Diversity within cultural groupings

It is also important that mental health professionals are sensitive to variations within a culture. For example, Middle Eastern ethnic groups share many similarities in culture and traditions which include the importance of family, spirituality, and a collectivistic set of societal expectations. But they also have many differences including language (e.g., Arabic, Farsi, Armenian, and Lebanese) as well as differences in religion. The family attitudes and traditions in smaller cultural groups are also likely to be different and need to be understood in order for an addicted individual to become more trusting of the therapist (ibid.).

Legal status

Immigrants' legal status is a key factor for their well-being. Undocumented immigrants constantly appear to do worse in many health and social indicators than their legal counterparts. Legal status directly affects immigrants' wages and work conditions. Many health problems of this group often remain undiagnosed and without treatment due to undocumented underutilization of health services. More than half of undocumented immigrants are uninsured compared to legal immigrants (Passel, 2005). The lack of access to drug services contributes to the hidden nature of drug abuse among immigrants and to the employment of alternative strategies to keep the drug abuse within the family or community.

Acculturation modes

Knowing how addicted individuals feel about their culture allows for an understanding of their adaptation process. Some individuals will be ashamed of their culture and will feel rejected in a new environment. The conflicting values put an extra burden upon the individual's ego, rendering identity consolidation difficult. Such individuals have to create a 'third reality', not of their homeland or of the adopted land, but something uniquely different (Akhtar, 1999). Other individuals remain comfortable in their homoethnic group, but find it difficult to mingle with the culture at large (Suárez-Orozco, 2000). Youths clustering around the assimilation, leave their ethnic group behind, and feel embarrassed by their parents' attachment to traditional culture. The frequent difficulties facing young immigrants arise from the struggles to balance the demands of the new culture with those of traditionally minded parents.

Acculturative stress

There are also significant sources of acculturative stress that immigrants must respond to (Chope & Fang, 1999), for example:

- physical stress in adjusting to a new, unfamiliar physical environment with different housing standards and climate;
- psychological stress when values, beliefs, attitudes, and sense of belonging change;
- family stress when generational differences are magnified by disparate contact with the host culture;
- social stress effected by vast changes in employment opportunities, educational instruction, and ethnic and social status, history of discrimination; and
- cultural stress in the encounter with a new language, religion, and purchasing power.

Migration history

Adaptation is affected by whether one family member migrated alone or whether many members of the family came together. Family migration can take different forms, for example: (i) parents will migrate with their family (family migration); (ii) parents will migrate either singly or together with the intention of sending for the rest of their family at a later date (serial migration); (iii) parents will migrate either singly or together for a defined period or indefinitely but have no intention of having their children live in the overseas country (parental migration) (Crawford-Brown & Rattray, 2002); (iv) parents (or a single parent) who migrate for up to six months at a time to work in the host/receiving country (seasonal migration); and (v) unaccompanied children and adolescents when placed with adults of similar or dissimilar cultural backgrounds (Sourander, 1998). When working with immigrant families, the theme of migration, which in turn includes issues of acculturation, acculturation stress, changes in socioeconomic status, minority status, and ethnic identity, is very powerful. Therapists are advised to explore the circumstances surrounding the family's migration including the decision making around the migration, and immigration-related attachment disruptions.

Acculturation processes in the family
There may be conflicts in the family over just assimilating in the new culture. The intergenerational conflict due to differing rates of acculturation between parents and children makes family interactions stressful and leads to a weakened quality of parent–child communication and creates overreaction by parents to perceived loss of control over adolescent children (Szapocznik & Williams, 2000). The end point of this process is adolescent resistance to parental expectations, personal distress and possibly acting out through delinquency and drug use.

Migration often creates changes within the structure of the family. Former family leaders may be demoted and the nature of the gender relationships may shift (Suárez-Orozco, 2000). For example, when employment conditions are such that a woman from a traditional couple can obtain a job more easily than a man, her new role as the breadwinner may create tensions and stress in the family structure. Furthermore, in maladaptive relationships, the reconfiguration of the power structure and the redefinition of family roles result in rules and consequences that are unclear and unpredictable. The children become part of a triangle in the parental system conflict. They may become entangled in destructive coalitions with a parent, act out in response to ineffective control, or disengage from the family to avoid distressing interactions (Chun & Akutsu, 2003).

Acculturation plays a role in the disruptions of parent–children relationships. Immigrant parents often have to make considerable sacrifices for a better future for their children. Within the new country, they set limits that are significantly more stringent than if they had stayed in their country of origin. At the same time they are often dependent upon their children. The children often learn the new language more quickly than their parents and consequently they often take on new roles as translators and advocates for their families. Alternating between 'parentifying' the children and at the same time severely constricting their activities may create significant tensions within the family, adolescent defiance and loss of family cohesiveness (Brook et al., 2001).

Emotional and physical closeness is another dimension in which it is important to be sensitive to culture-specific differences (Santisteban & Mitrani, 2003). Immigrant families place a relatively higher value on collectivism and give precedence to the needs of the family rather than to the needs of the individual. If those who are assimilated are rebelling because they are not allowed to be individuals, then the tendency for greater emotional and psychological closeness in the family is related to the emergence of symptomatic behavior. A strategy of working with such families is to recognize the strengths of self-autonomy while trying to make some small changes in the willingness of family members to band together in a time of need or crisis.

Multicultural competence

To meet the needs of addicted persons from culturally diverse groups, healthcare providers must engage in the process of becoming culturally competent. 'Multicultural competence' refers to the process by which the therapist continuously strives to achieve the ability and availability to effectively work within the cultural context of an individual, family or community. This process includes addressing the importance of awareness, knowledge and skills. Cultural awareness may be equated with the ability of therapists to judge the situation from both their own viewpoint and from the viewpoint of members of other cultures. If multicultural competence helps the therapist to ask the right questions, cultural knowledge is the process of understanding the worldview of members of other cultures to explain how they interpret their illness and how it guides their thinking, doing, and being. Multicultural skill is the ability to collect relevant cultural data regarding the presenting problem as well as accurately performing a culturally based assessment that helps to determine explicit needs and intervention practices within the context of the people being served (Draguns, 2002; Pedersen, 2002).

In general, intervention in drug rehabilitation of immigrants needs to be more culturally sensitive by combining specific culture patterns, experience of immigration and acculturation with universal aspects of treatment approaches. Therapists should also assess the socioeconomic and educational levels of the addicted immigrant and his/her family, as well as their level of acculturation into the new culture, because these variables are responsible for variations in belief systems and value orientations and contribute, to an important extent, to the way in which the intervention and intervention goals are structured. Failure to take these variables into account may lead to erroneous cultural oversimplifications and stereotyping that will damage the intervention process.

Conclusion

This chapter has focused on drug abuse issues among immigrants: acculturation and acculturative stress as risk factors contributing to drug abuse in these groups, as well as treatment and services approaches for addressing their unique needs. There is general agreement in the published literature that a myriad of stresses that often accompany immigration (breaking with family, friends, and established social networks, departing from traditional routines, value systems, and accepted ways of behaving and having to adapt to new social and psychosocial environments) are related to mental health problems among immigrants. Although substance abuse has increased in recent years among general populations, insufficient attention has been paid to illicit substance use among immigrant populations.

It is important to understand that the presentation of substance abuse among immigrants may be different from that of non-immigrants. Furthermore, there is a need to understand what symptoms of substance abuse mean to the individual and the immigrant family (adaptation to the host environment, different rates of acculturation in the family, 'parentification' of the child, disruption in the family structure, marginalization) and what their expectations are of the treatment they seek. The principles of culturally competent mental health services are most applicable to the development and delivery of mental health services for immigrants and refugees. This includes addressing differences in symptom expression and factors that affect the accessibility and acceptability of services such as stigmatization, linguistic barriers, documentation and legal status, and cultural competence of professionals.

Much more research is needed for a better understanding of the prevalence of drug addiction in immigrants, and for developing protective programs and interventions that may be required to help these groups. Research needs to be more sensitive by combining an integrative approach that recognizes how people from all populations are both similar and different at the same time. The dual emphasis on the universal and particular becomes a central professional issue in counseling and treatment of different cultural groups.

References
Akhtar, S. (1999), *Immigration and Identity. Turmoil, Treatment and Transformation*, New York: Jason Aronson.

Alaniz, M.L. (2002), 'Migration, acculturation, displacement: migratory workers and "substance abuse"', *Substance Use and Misuse*, **37**, 1253–57.

Azima, F.J.C. (2002), 'Transcultural training models for therapists treating refugee and immigrant children and families', in F.J.C. Azima & N. Grizenko (eds), *Immigrant and Refugee Children and Their Families: Clinical, Research, and Training Issues*, Madison, CT: International Universities Press, pp. 189–212.

Batki, S.L. & Nathan, K.I. (2004), 'HIV/AIDS and substance use disorders', in M. Galanter & H.D. Kleber (eds), *Textbook of Substance Abuse Treatment*, Washington, DC: American Psychological Association, pp. 555–63.

Beauvais, F. & Oetting, E.O. (1999), 'Drug use, resilience and the myth of the golden child', in M.D. Glantz & J.L. Johnson (eds), *Resilience and Development. Positive Life Adaptations*, Dordrecht: Kluwer Academic/Plenum, pp. 101–6.

Berry, J.W. (1997), 'Immigration, acculturation and adaptation', *Applied Psychology: An International Review*, **46**, 5–68.

Berry, J.W. (2003), 'Conceptual approaches to acculturation', in Chun et al. (eds), pp. 17–37.

Booth, A., Crouter, A.C. & Landale, N.S. (1997), *Immigration and the Family: Research and Policy on U.S. Immigrants*, Hillsdale, NJ: Lawrence Erlbaum.

Brook, J.S., Brook, D.W., de la Rosa, M., Whiteman, M., Johnson, E. & Montoya, I. (2001), 'Adolescent illegal drug use: the impact of personality, family, and environmental factors', *Journal of Behavioral Medicine*, **24**, 183–203.

Caetano, R. & Clark, L.C. (2003), 'Acculturation, alcohol consumption, smoking, and drug use among Hispanics', in Chun et al. (eds), pp. 207–23.

Caetano, R., Clark, C.L. & Tam, T. (1998), 'Alcohol consumption among racial/ethnic minorities: theory and research', *Alcohol Health and Research World*, **22**, 233–8.

Carta, M.G., Bernal, M., Hardoy, M.C. & Haro-Abad, J.M. (2005), 'Migration and mental health in Europe (The State of the Mental Health in Europe Working Group: Appendix I)', *Clinical Practice and Epidemiology in Mental Health*, 1–13.

Castillo, M. & Henderson, G. (2002), 'Hispanic substance abusers in the United States', in G.X. Ma & G. Henderson (eds), *Ethnicity and Substance Abuse: Prevention and Intervention*, Springfield, IL: Charles C Thomas, pp. 191–206.

Chope, R. & Fang, F. (1999), 'Career counseling for new Chinese immigrants: clinical issues and practical recommendations', *College of Education Review*, **10**, 54–9.

Chun, K.M. & Akutsu, P.D. (2003), 'Acculturation among ethnic minority families', in Chun et al. (eds), pp. 95–119.

Chun, K.M., P.B. Organista & G. Marín (eds) (2003), *Acculturation: Advances in Theory, Measurement and Applied Research*, Washington, DC: American Psychological Association.

Crawford-Brown, C. & Rattray, J.M. (2002), 'Parent–child relationships in Caribbean families', in N. Boyd Webb & D. Lum (eds), *Culturally Diverse Parent–Child and Family Relationships*, New York: Columbia University Press, pp. 107–30.

Diamanduros, N. (2005), 'The European Ombudsman and EU Drugs Policy', in *10th European Conference on Rehabilitation and Drug Policy – Drug Addiction Treatment and Prevention in a United Europe: Diversity and Equality*, KETHEA & EFTC, pp. 13–23, http://www.ombudsman.europa.eu/report/el/default.htm/pdf.

Draguns, P.J. (2002), Universal and cultural aspects of counseling and psychotherapy', in P.B. Pedersen, J.G. Draguns, W.J. Lonner & J.E. Trimble (eds), *Counseling across Cultures*, 5th edn, Newbury Park, CA: Sage, pp. 25–50.

Elder, J.P., Campbell, N.R., Litrownik, A.J., Ayala, G.X., Slymen, D.J., Parra-Medina, D. & Lovato, C.Y. (2000), 'Predictors of cigarette and alcohol susceptibility and use among Hispanic migrant adolescents', *Preventive Medicine*, **31**(2 Pt 1), 115–23.

European Monitoring Centre for Drugs and Drug Addiction (EMCDDA) (2002), *Workgroup Review of Qualitative Research on New Drug Trends*, Lisbon.

Gfroerer, J.C. & Tan, L.L. (2003), 'Substance use among foreign-born youths in the United States: does the length of residence matter?', *American Journal of Public Health*, **93**, 1892–5.

Hjern, A., Angel, B. & Jeppson, O. (1998), 'Political violence, family stress and mental health of refugee children in exile', *Scandinavian Journal of Social Medicine*, **26**(1), 18–25.

Howard, M. & Hodes, M. (2000), 'Psychopathology, adversity and service utilization of young refugees', *Journal of the American Academy of Child and Adolescent Psychiatry*, **39**(3), 368–77.

Hyman, I., Vu, N. & Beiser, M. (2000), 'Post-migration stresses among Southeast Asian refugees youth in Canada: a research note', *Journal of Comparative Family Studies*, **31**(2), 281–93.

Isralowitz, R. (2004), *Drug Use: A Resources Handbook*, Denver, CO: ABC-CLIO.

Isralowitz, R., Straussner, L., Vogt, I. & Chtenguelov, V. (2002), 'Toward an understanding of Russian speaking drug addicts in Israel, Germany and the United States', *Journal of Social Work Practice in the Addictions*, **2**(3/4), 119–36.

Labrianidis, L. & Lyberaki, A. (2001), *Albanian Immigrants in Thessalonika. Integration Paths and Public Projection* (in Greek), Thessalonika: Paratiritis.

Makimoto, K. (1998), 'Drinking patterns and drinking problems among Asian-Americans and Pacific Islanders', *Alcohol Health and Research World*, **22**, 270–75.

McGoldrick, M. & Giordano, J. (1996), 'Overview: ethnicity and family therapy', in M. McGoldrick, J. Giordano & J.K. Pearce (eds), *Ethnicity and Family Therapy*, New York: Guilford Press, pp. 1–31.

National Institute on Drug Abuse (NIDA) (2001), Monitoring the Future: National Survey Results on Drug Use, 1975–2000. Volume II: College Students and Adults, Ages 19–40, NIH Publication No. 01-4925, Bethesda, MD: US Department of Health and Human Services.

Oberg, K. (1960), 'Cultural shock: adjustment to new cultural environments', *Practical Anthropology*, **7**, 177–82.

Organista, P.B., Organista, K.S. & Kurasaki, K. (2003), 'The relationship between acculturation and ethnic minority mental health', in Chun et al. (eds), pp. 95–119.

Passel, J.F. (2005), 'Unauthorized migrants: numbers and characteristics', Washington, DC: Pew Hispanic Center, http://pewhispanic.org/reports/report.php?ReportID=44./pdf.

Pedersen, P. (2002), 'Ethics, competence and other professional issues in culture-centered counseling', in P.B. Pedersen, J.G. Draguns, W.J. Lonner & J.E. Trimble (eds), *Counseling across Cultures*, 5th edn, Newbury Park, CA: Sage, pp. 3–24.

Peplau, L.A. & Perlman, D. (1982), *Loneliness: A Sourcebook of Current Theory, Research and Therapy*, New York: Wiley.

Robbins, S.P. & Mikow, J. (2000), *Tobacco, Alcohol and Other Drug Use Among Minority Youth: Implications for the Design and Implementation of Prevention Programmes*, Philadelphia, PA: University of Pennsylvania Center for the Study of Youth Policy.

Roysircar-Sodowsky, G. & Maestas, M.V. (2000), 'Acculturation, ethnic identity and acculturative stress: evidence and measurement', in R.H. Dana (ed.), *Handbook of Cross-Cultural and Multicultural Personality Assessment*, Hillsdale, NJ: Lawrence Erlbaum, pp. 113–31.

Salt, J. (2003), *Current Trends in International Migration in Europe*, Strasbourg: Council of Europe.

Sam, D.L. (2006), 'Acculturation and health', in D.L. Sam & J.W. Berry (eds), *The Cambridge Handbook of Acculturation Psychology*, Cambridge: Cambridge University Press, pp. 452–68.

Santisteban, D. & Mitrani, V.B. (2003), 'The influence of acculturation processes on the family', in Chun et al. (eds), pp. 121–36.

Servan-Schreiber, D., Le Lin, B. & Birmaher, B. (1998), 'Prevalence of posttraumatic stress disorder and major depressive disorder in Tibetan refugee children', *Journal of the American Academy of Child and Adolescent Psychiatry*, **37**(8), 874–9.

Sourander, A. (1998), 'Behavior problems and traumatic events of unaccompanied refugee minors', *Child Abuse and Neglect*, **22**(7), 719–27.

Spencer, M.S. & Chen, J. (2004), 'Effect of discrimination on mental health service utilization among Chinese Americans', *American Journal of Public Health*, **94**(5), 809–14.

Suárez-Orozco, C. (2000), 'Identities under siege: immigration stress and social mirroring among the children of immigrants', in C.G.M. Tobben & Suárez-Orozco (eds), *Cultures under Siege: Collective Violence and Trauma*, Cambridge: Cambridge University Press, pp. 195–226.

Suárez-Orozco, C. & Suárez-Orozco, M. (2001), *Children of Immigration*, Cambridge, MA: Harvard University Press.
Sue, S. (2002), 'Asian American mental health: what we know and what we don't know', in W.J. Lonner, D.L. Dinnel, S.A. Hayes & D.N. Sattler (eds), *Online Readings in Psychology and Culture* (Unit 3, Chapter 4), http://www.wwu.edu/~culture, Center for Cross-Cultural Research, Western Washington University, Bellingham, WA.
Szapocznik, J. & Williams, R.A. (2000), 'Brief strategic family therapy: twenty five years of interplay among theory, research, and practice in adolescent behavior problems and drug abuse', *Clinical Child and Family Psychology Review*, **3**(2), 117–35.
Tanaka-Matsumi, J. & Draguns, J.G. (1997), 'Culture and psychopathology', in J.W. Berry, M.H. Segall & C. Kagiteibasi (eds), *Handbook of Cross-Cultural Psychology: Volume 3. Social Behaviour and Application*, Boston, MD: Allyn & Bacon, pp. 449–91.
Terzidou, M. (2005), *National Report to the EMCDDA by the Reitox National Focal Point GREECE: New Development, Trends and In-Depth Information on Selected Issues*, Athens: University Mental Health Research Institute.
Ward, C., Bochner, S. & Furnham, A. (2001), *The Psychology of Culture Shock*, 2nd edn, New York: Routledge.
Westermeyer, J. (2004), 'Cross-cultural aspects of substance abuse', in M. Galanter & H.D. Kleber (eds), *Textbook of Substance Abuse Treatment*, Arlington, VA: American Psychiatric Publishing, pp. 89–101.
World Health Organization (1996), *Mental Health of Refugees*, Geneva, Switzerland.

PART VI

EMOTION AT WORK

26 Emotional intelligence and coping with occupational stress: what have we learned so far?
Moshe Zeidner

Overview

Emotional intelligence (EI) has figured prominently in both the academic literature and mass media as a pivotal factor contributing to organizational processes and outcomes (see Zeidner et al., 2006; Zeidner et al., 2009). EI is frequently claimed to be part and parcel of what it takes to be an effective organizational citizen and as a prerequisite for performing effectively on the job. It is readily apparent that EI has become an integral part of the discussion surrounding effective organizational recruiting and placement, functioning, leadership, and occupational training.

In the rapidly changing world of business and commerce, characterized by dynamic growth and development, constant change and economic competition, both cognitive and technical skills are of the essence. In order to succeed at work, employees need a broad arsenal of emotional and social skills. Among the socio-emotional competencies essential for success in the modern workforce are: motivation to work hard towards effectively achieving group goals; adaptability in the face of obstacles and setbacks; communication and negotiation skills; emotion regulation to maintain a positive and energetic mood and to contain negative emotions; and effective transformational leadership skills to lead work teams.

Much of the interest surrounding EI in organizational settings is based on the working assumption that EI can play a major role in making the workplace a more productive, profitable, as well as enjoyable place. Proponents of EI claim that the integration of both explicit cognitive knowledge and tacit emotional knowledge on the part of the individual may help us see what pure logic overlooks and thereby help us steer the best, safest course to business success. Thus, sweeping claims have been made about the value of EI, which has been hyped as the ultimate solution for the majority of management problems and integrated into every human resource product or service offered (Schmit, 2006). With respect to the concerns of this chapter, proponents of EI have claimed that emotional competencies are systematically related to individual differences in coping with stress at the workplace, which, in turn, should confer generally more or less successful occupational outcomes on the individual (see Salovey et al., 2002). Despite the popular interest in the role of EI in occupational stress and coping, there is a paucity of studies on how EI is related to coping with organizational stress, and knowledge of the mechanisms is quite limited.

In this chapter we review what we have learned so far about the role of EI in coping with organizational stress (for a recent review of the role of EI in contributing to organizational outcomes, see Zeidner et al., 2009). We begin by briefly describing the importance of EI and emotional competencies at the workplace. We move on to discuss key sources and outcomes of organizational stress and how people typically cope with such stress. We survey the empirical literature on the role of EI in coping with organizational stress and present a number of concerns regarding attempts to explicate the EI–occupational stress relationship. We conclude by surveying efforts made in coping skills training at the worksite.

Emotions and emotional competencies at work

Emotions at the workplace
Emotions are on-line indicators of how well we are coping with environmental demands, pressures, and opportunities. It is now readily apparent that emotions may be useful sources of information that can help us interpret and navigate our social environment. Accordingly, our emotions and feelings on the job reflect spontaneous emotional responses to the appraisals and interpretations we make of ongoing events involving challenges, threats, and losses, in the workplace. When we believe we are successfully coping with environmental demands, challenges, and affordances, we tend to feel good about ourselves; when we feel we are not successfully coping with ongoing demands and challenges we tend to feel bad. Thus, if we work backwards from the emotions we experience, emotions experienced on the job are capable of providing us with rich information about the appraisals of events and relational meanings that we share inside our organizational environment. This may often alter our thinking and actions at work in such a way as to allow us to negotiate organizational challenges and threats in a more adaptive manner. Furthermore, emotion issues may be critical for organizational success, to the extent that a better understanding of emotions will help workers reach organizational goals, and thus give organizations a competitive edge (Ashkanasy et al., 2002).

Affective processes saturate daily life at the workplace. An employee's mood may swing from moments of contentment, interest, satisfaction, confidence, pride, gratitude and joy, to moments of boredom, anger, fear, sadness, shame, guilt, envy, hate and disgust (Pekrun & Frese, 1992; Ashforth & Humphrey, 1995). However, until recently, the importance of emotions at the workplace has, as a rule, been ignored by researchers, with emotions given short shrift in organizational thinking, research and applications. It appears that cognitive, motivational, and performance factors have traditionally been viewed as being more urgent for occupational life than emotions. Because emotions were viewed as antithetical to rationality, they were glossed over, discouraged, or relegated to a relatively minor role in occupational research (Ashforth & Humphrey, 1995; Ashkanasy et al., 2002).

Fortunately for emotion research, the current *zeitgeist* at the turn of the millennium has offered an alternative view on the interface of reason and emotions. Current research in the cognitive and affective sciences suggests that emotions are inextricably intertwined with cognition and necessary for sound judgement and decision making (Damasio, 1994). Furthermore, as processing increases in complexity, affect may play an especially crucial role – with specific moods affecting cognition in different ways. More and more organizational psychologists and researchers over the past few years have come to realize that emotions are really a central part of organizational life and crucial for organizational functioning and success. It is of note that the spiralling research on EI over the past 15 years or so has inadvertently served as a 'soupstone' (Matthews et al., 2002) and major catalyst for the resurgent interest in emotions in organizations and its emergence as a flourishing area of research (Ashkanasy & Tse, 2000).

Emotions and occupational life are most plausibly construed as being mutually determined. On one hand, emotions are among the primary determinants of day-to-day interactions and achievement at the worksite, impacting upon, life satisfaction, well-being, social climate, as well as individual productivity (i.e., emotions → work). Emotions may influence work-related cognitive and motivational processes, which, in turn, affect task and social behaviours. On the other hand, given that work is a sphere of life that is of key importance to most people in modern society (i.e., workplace → emotions), an individual's professional life is among the primary determinants of emotional life and well-being. Given the importance of work for a person's income, self-esteem, and social status, occupational life is a major source of both positive and negative emotions. A person's affective development and health may influence success or failure at work, through the mediation of emotions.

Overall, the diverse emotions experienced at work are slippery and difficult to classify (Rafaeli & Sutton, 1989). Depending on the perspective adopted, the same emotion can be viewed as positive or negative. For example, the forced smile of a customer service representative may be construed as friendly by customers, but artificial, negative and patronising by the same (or another) customer service representative. One tentative typology of emotions at the workplace (Pekrun & Frese, 1992) attempts to specify the universe of work-relevant emotions based on two major dimensions, that is, valence (positive versus negative) and focus (task versus social). These two dimensions reasonably cross-partition the domain of emotions in the workplace into four discrete categories:

- positive task-related emotions (e.g., happiness, joy, relief, pride);
- negative task-related emotions (e.g., anger, anxiety, guilt, boredom);
- positive social-related emotions (e.g., empathy, gratitude, admiration, compassion); and
- negative social-related emotions (e.g., envy, jealousy, contempt, embarrassment).

Emotional competencies at work
Ever since the popularization of EI, efforts to apply emotional competencies to work settings have been emerging at an accelerated rate, with four out of five companies trying to promote EI in their employees according to a recent benchmarking survey. It appears that much of the popularity accorded to EI in the scientific and popular press derives from its potential applications in practical settings, particularly in predicting and shaping on-the-job performance. Recent reviews of the literature show that EI modestly predicts a wide array of organizational outcomes, ranging from job performance to job satisfaction, organizational citizenship and leadership (Zeidner et al., 2009).

Emotional abilities are likely to contribute to the quality of relationships that people establish at work because emotions serve valuable communicative and social functions (Lopes et al., 2005). Furthermore, high EI employees should be more adept at regulating both their own and others' emotions to foster positive interactions, which results in positive organizational citizenship and higher performance (see Sy et al., 2006). High EI individuals might be more capable of using both positively toned and negatively toned emotions to their advantage to improve performance. Thus, positive emotions, such as enthusiasm and pride, could stimulate employees to provide better customer service, complete their work assignments with alacrity, or contribute more of their time to the organization. Conversely, negative emotions such as fear, envy and sadness, could adversely impact on employees' ability and motivation to focus on their work tasks. Accordingly, if company leaders and employees are are emotionally intelligent, the company will then have a competitive advantage over other companies.

Whereas EI designates the *potential* to learn certain emotional responses and skills, emotional *competencies* are learned capabilities, based on EI, that result in successful performance at work (Goleman, 2001). That is, whereas EI may determine a person's potential for learning practical job-related emotional and social skills, the level of emotional competencies manifested by that person shows how much of that potential she or he has actually realized. Thus, it is emotional competence that directly translates EI into on-the-job capabilities. For example, in order to be able to actually empathize with a co-worker's plight, one needs to have used EI to learn the specific empathic skills that translate into caring and compassionate behaviours at the worksite (Cherniss & Goleman, 2001).

Within this general framework, myriad skills and social and emotional competencies have been claimed to be critical for success in occupational settings (see, e.g., Cooper & Sawaf, 1997; Weisinger, 1998; Boyatzis et al., 2000). Goleman (1998), for example, lists 25 different competencies necessary for effective performance in various occupational contexts. It is of note that with respect to the 180 competence models identified by Goleman, over two-thirds of the abilities deemed essential for effective performance were identified as *emotional* competencies. EI is purportedly related to coping with tasks where there is a clear emotional skill required for successful performance (e.g., sales, customer relations, helping professions, schoolteaching). Thus, trust and empathy appear vital for psychotherapists, social workers, and marriage counsellors, whereas confidentiality is crucial for loan officers and priests. EI may also be useful in facilitating coping with organizational stress, a theme we address next.

EI and organizational stress

Psychological stress is frequently described as the 'Black Plague' of the modern era, taxing the resources of individuals and organizations, and threatening individual and societal health and well-being. From a transactional perspective (see, e.g., Lazarus & Folkman, 1984), organizational stress may be conceptualized as a dynamic interaction between the individual and various facets of the organizational environment, which has demands, constraints and pressures that are perceived to tax, threaten or exceed a person's resources and coping capabilities (McGrath, 1976; Beehr & Newman, 1978). In order to understand the experience of occupational stress, one must consider both the subjective and the objective environments impinging on the person, along with stable individual differences that influence both the nature and strength of occupational stresses that are perceived. The complex and dynamic interaction between occupational conditions and the worker's personal resources (coping skills, dispositions, values, commitments and beliefs) constitutes a call for action, resulting in a meaningful change (disruption or enhancement) of the worker's personal condition, such that the person is forced to deviate from normal functioning.

Organizational stress is a major problem across different national sites (Mack et al., 1998). In fact, cross-national research has demonstrated striking similarities across countries with respect to specific sources of work stress, levels of occupational stress, and personal characteristics that cause workers to be susceptible to stress in various occupational settings across the globe (ibid.). The stress process may contribute to a wide range of physical and mental disorders, including: depression, cardiovascular disease, chronic respiratory ailments, infectious disease and cancer (House, 1981). Schuler (1980) identified a number of diseases related to stress in organizations (i.e., high blood pressure, peptic ulcers, coronary heart disease) which are major contributing factors to disability and hospital care in the United States. Moreover, a large proportion of premature deaths in Western countries are attributed to stress-related illness. Although US industry loses approximately 550 million working days due to absenteeism, 54% of these absences have been estimated to be stress related in some way (Elkin & Rosch, 1990). Furthermore, it has been estimated that the total cost of stress to American organizations, as assessed by absenteeism, reduced productivity, direct medical expenses, health insurance and compensation claims, adds up to more than $150 billion a year (Karasek & Theorell, 1990).

Sources of occupational stress
Over three decades of systematic study in the area of occupational stress have generated a substantial body of evidence on numerous factors, often in complex interactions, that contribute to stress at the workplace (O'Driscoll & Cooper, 1994). Thus, work stress can be caused by factors such as time pressures and deadlines; too much or too little work; overload in number of decisions to make; fatigue from the physical strains of work (assembly line); excessive travel; mobbing and supervisor/co-worker bullying; excessive emotional labour; having to cope with frequent changes at the workplace; and errors in making financial decisions (Cooper & Marshall, 1978). Curiously, job requirements to regulate negative emotions and express positive emotions (i.e., emotional labour) are by themselves a frequent source of stress and physical symptoms (Schaubroeck & Jones, 2000). For almost every job description these will include factors that for some individuals and point of time will be a source of pressure.

We now briefly survey a number of broad categories of work stress, based in part on a useful taxonomy suggested by Cartwright and Cooper (1996). Poor emotional intelligence would be expected to be a major factor at play in aggravating a number of the following sources of stress.

Factors intrinsic to the job, task, or workplace   This category includes task-related sources of stress as well as physical conditions (Schuler, 1980). Task-related sources of stress include: work overload/underload, disruption of work patterns (e.g., shift in workload), long and unconventional hours, shiftwork, extensive travel, high risk, uncertainty, lack of autonomy, and new technology. French and Caplan (1973) differentiated between 'qualitative' overload, where a task is too difficult for the worker, and 'quantitative' overload, where a worker has too much to do. Research by Cooper and Marshall (1978) suggests that work overload is indeed a major source of stress, with chronic and serious consequences including absenteeism, escapist drinking and coronary heart disease. Furthermore, a number of physical working conditions that may be stress evoking are excessive levels of noise, inadequate lighting, crowded workspace, lack of privacy, pathogenic agents and physical danger.

Role in the organization   Ambiguity, conflict, and powerlessness are key dimensions of role-related stress at the workplace. Role ambiguity arises when a person has incomplete information about the scope and responsibilities of the job or where there is a lack of clarity about work objectives associated with this role or about work colleagues' expectations of the work role (ibid.). Role conflict evolves when inconsistent expectations about behaviours in the organization are held by the individual and others in the organization (managers, supervisors, co-workers; Hamner & Tosi, 1974). For example, a novice college instructor may perceive incompatible work demands from college administrators (to publish and secure grants), fellow instructors (assume committee responsibilities, attend faculty seminars, cooperate with others on research projects, etc.) and students (to teach well, prepare valid exams, return grades on time, hold liberal office hours, etc.). Employees in a particular work role may be torn by conflicting job demands or engaged in things they really do not want to do (Cooper & Marshall, 1978). Powerlessness, another major source of job stress, refers to the perception that an individual simply cannot control outcomes at the workplace. Thus, lack of control over outcomes has been linked to high anxiety, job dissatisfaction, low self-esteem and poor job performance (Kottkamp & Travlos, 1986). Feelings of personal control and ability to tolerate ambiguity were linked with stress in a sample of 180 AT&T employees who coped with divestiture and transition to an unregulated entity (Ashford, 1988).

Poor interperonsal relationships   Some data suggest that negative interactions with co-workers, supervisors and clients are one of the most frequently reported sources of work-related stress (Cooper & Marshall, 1978). Aggression and workplace violence is a particularly stressful and disturbing aspect of organizational life. This topic has been dealt with under various headings, including 'mobbing', 'bullying', 'harassment', 'interpersonal abuse' and 'victimization'. All these terms refer to potentially harmful and unpleasant interpersonal relationships and interactions at the workplace (Baron & Neuman, 1996). Workplace aggression and violence ranges from minor acts of incivility (low-intensity behaviours, such as ridicule and gossip) to extreme antisocial behaviour (e.g., physical manhandling or sexual harassment), which harms both workers and organizations. When interpersonal relations are disrupted at work, this negatively affects the person's need for acceptance and recognition, often resulting in anxiety and dissatisfaction at work (Schuler, 1980). This is often manifested by a low sense of trust in co-workers, low supportiveness, and minimal interest handling problems that confront organizational members.

Organizational structure, climate and culture   This category subsumes stressors related to the organizational culture and milieu. This may include lack of a person–role fit, inadequate training and skills for the job on hand, inappropriate management style, poor communication and lack of feedback from co-workers and superiors, a culture tolerant of harassing subordinates, and ugly office politics. Threat to an individual's freedom, autonomy and identity (e.g., minimal participation in the decision-making process, minimal sense of belonging, poor communication, and office politics) is a source of stress for many. Human service jobs, in particular, may pose demands that are different from those of other professions because workers must use themselves as the technology for meeting the needs of clients, who, in turn, do not always express gratitude or appreciation. Organizational culture may play an important role in determining various forms of harassment at the workplace. Thus, in some organizational cultures, sexual harassment, mobbing, and other forms of aggression and violence seem to be more or less permitted as the way things are done to most expediently achieve organizational goals (Salin, 2003). The perpetrator may perceive the costs and expected sanctions by management as minimal, thus increasing risky and deviant behaviour at the worksite, such as bullying and harassing workers. Individuals who operate in a work environment where others are rewarded for aggressive behaviours are more likely to engage in similar acts themselves to attain various incentives (promotion, salary increases and social status).

Career development This category includes reaching a career plateau, underpromotion, demotion and derailing, early retirement, unclear career future and the threat of job loss. More recent sources of stress include voluntary mergers, corporate takeovers, white-knight rescues and so on. In post-industrial society, many a worker experiences the threat of job security (fear of being redundant, early retirement) and status incongruity (frustration at having reached one's career ceiling, under- or overpromotion; Cooper & Marshall, 1978).

Home-work interface A final potential source of occupational stress is managing the interface between work and home, particularly for dual career couples or those experiencing financial crises. By adopting family-friendly employment policies and providing more flexible work arrangements, this source of stress may be ameliorated.

Outcomes of occupational stress

Career stress is associated with multiple negative outcomes (Ivancevich & Matteson, 1987), including: job dissatisfaction and debilitated levels of performance, family problems and poor physical and mental health (Schuler, 1980). The indirect costs of stress are reflected in a variety of indices of social pathology including: levels of substance abuse, high divorce rates, accident statistics and mortality rates. Stress may also result in higher incidences of aggressive behaviours, accidents and thefts in the occupational environment. Furthermore, work stressors may feed into the family and social environment, becoming a potential source of disturbance that subsequently pervades the whole quality of an individual's life.

Research by Cooper and Marshall (1978) suggests that quantitative overload ('too much to do') is indeed a major source of stress with important health implications. At the same time, both qualitative ('task is too difficult') and quantitative overload produce an array of different symptoms of psychological strain, including: tension, low self-esteem, threat, job dissatisfaction, high cholesterol levels and tobacco abuse. More chronic and serious consequences include coronary heart disease, escapist drinking and absenteeism. Over the past two decades a substantial amount of research on job stress has demonstrated the potential adverse consequences of stress on criterion variables, such as job satisfaction, job burnout and mental health, the practice of pro-health behaviours, physical disease, morbidity and mortality (Beehr & Newman, 1978).

Coping with stress

Coping, broadly speaking, involves a person's efforts – cognitive and behavioral – to manage (i.e., reduce, minimize, master, tolerate) both the external and internal demands of a person–environment transaction that is appraised as stressful (Lazarus & Folkman, 1984; Folkman, 1991; Lazarus, 1991). Accordingly, when the demands of a potentially stressful situation (e.g., having to prepare and present an important business plan before the company's board) are perceived as stressful and taxing one's personal resources, efforts are directed at dealing with the problem at hand and/or regulating emotional stress (Folkman & Lazarus, 1986).

Although a wide array of taxonomies of coping strategies are currently available, researchers appear to converge on the following three categories: (i) problem-focused coping, designed to manage or solve the problem by removing or circumventing the stressor (e.g., carefully planning for a major presentation before the company's board); (ii) emotion-focused coping, designed to regulate, reduce, channel, or eliminate the aversive emotions associated with the stressful encounter (e.g., seeking emotional support from co-workers, denying the importance of the event, distancing oneself cognitively from the evaluative threat); and (iii) avoidance-focused coping, referring to strategies designed to circumvent or avoid the stressful situation, either via use of person-oriented strategies (e.g., distracting oneself by socializing with others) or task-oriented strategies (e.g., taking a holiday, as avoidant strategy). Newman and Beehr (1979) identified four strategies people use in coping with occupational stress: (i) changing one's behaviour to accommodate existing work conditions; (ii) changing one's physical conditions (diet, exercise); (iii) changing psychological conditions (planning ahead, managing one's life, and so forth); and when all else fails, (iv) changing one's work environment. Latack (1986) provided empirical evidence for three dimensions of coping with job stress: (i) control (both actions and appraisals); (ii) escape (actions and thoughts); and (iii) symptom management (relaxation and exercise).

A review of the literature suggests that work-related stress and routine daily work hassles elicit more problem- than emotion-focused strategies (Cartwright & Cooper, 1996). This outcome resonates with the findings of Lazarus (1991), who observed that individuals used more problem- than emotion-focused coping when managing stressful events on the job, particularly when the source of stress is controllable. Problem-focused coping may be preferred to emotion-focused coping because opportunities to discharge emotions in the workplace are generally restricted. Overall, the literature suggests that adaptive coping with occupational stress should lead to positive outcomes, such as heightened job satisfaction, fewer psychosomatic symptoms and decreased anxiety (Latack, 1986). Hence, if EI is found to be meaningfully related to coping, high EI individuals should benefit from the satisfaction of coping effectively and positive job outcomes.

La Rocco and Jones (1978) suggest that social support, a major form of coping, bears a direct main effect on job-related strains (such as job dissatisfaction). In addition, social support has a buffering effect on health-related variables, including psychological and somatic outcomes. Furthermore, emotion-focused coping was found to be positively related to the amount of work-related strain. These findings suggest either that those palliative forms of coping may not be adaptive with respect to job stress, or alternatively, that emotion-focused coping is simply a reaction to high levels of job stress (rather than a cause of stress and/or strain). These authors conclude that little is to be gained by exhorting human service professionals to change their ways of coping, because individual coping has little impact on job strain.

A body of research suggests that whereas individual coping efforts may not be particularly effective in organizational settings, group coping, operationalized as social support, might be particularly effective in group settings (Shinn et al., 1984). Thus, in the workplace, where many influential stress factors are beyond an individual's control, individual coping strategies may be less potent than 'higher-level' strategies (involving the support of groups of workers or entire organizations). That is, occupational stressors may be among the problems that are not very amenable to individual solutions, but rather depend on highly organized cooperative efforts that transcend those of the individual – no matter how well developed one's personal resources. Pearlin and Schooler (1978) surveyed the effectiveness of coping in four realms: work, marriage, parenting and household economics. Whereas coping responses had relatively little effect on strain resulting from work, they were successful in reducing the strain in the final three putative domains.

Does EI help in coping with stress?

Research suggests that most people do not cope very well with organizational change and transitions, and consequently suffer long-term adverse mental and physical health. In fact, coping with and managing work stress may be more complex than dealing with stressful events outside work. This results from inherent constraints within the work environment, which restricts the range of acceptable coping responses and the degree of limited individual control. This further emphasizes the importance of emotional competencies in coping with the stresses of current work environments. Accordingly, proponents of EI often see effective coping with stress as central to the EI construct. In fact, current thinking among EI researchers (e.g., Salovey et al., 2000) suggests that the way people identify, understand, regulate, and repair emotions (in self and others) helps determine coping behaviors and consequent adaptive outcomes.

Research devoted to uncovering relations between EI and effective coping strategies has generally touched on two related issues. The first has involved determining how EI measures correlate with established coping scales. The second, more subtle, has involved ascertaining whether coping mediates associations between EI and well-being. There are a variety of explanations for the reported correlations between self-reports of EI and coping outcomes, including the confounding influence of personality traits, self-enhancing response biases, and 'criterion contamination' in that some EI questionnaires contain items assessing well-being (e.g., Zeidner et al., 2001; Matthews et al., 2004). To date, published questionnaire-based studies have failed to test these competing hypotheses. Thus, findings based on objective assessments of EI are arguably more compelling, although in the review that follows, we consider studies that follow both approaches.

Two research strategies have been used in testing whether EI does, in fact, relate to choice of coping strategy (see Zeidner et al., 2006, for a comprehensive review). The first is to relate EI to the person's general style of coping. There are various questionnaires that seek to assess the broad classes of strategy that people use, such as the problem- and emotion-focused strategies previously described. In addition to studying these general preferences, we can also investigate the coping strategies used to manage some specific event or challenge. For example, we might ask workers how they coped with stress after a company merger, instead of how they cope with life in general. When compared with assessing general coping style, this approach may bring us closer to the person's actual coping, in the organizational context.

Several studies have correlated measures of EI with scales assessing coping style in general. These cross-sectional studies, assessed outside of organizational contexts, substantiate associations between EI and various aspects of coping (ibid.). Two recent studies

(Petrides et al., 2007; Saklofske et al., 2007) found that questionnaires for EI related to more use of rational coping, and less use of emotion-focused coping. Goldenberg et al. (2006) reported that the Schutte et al. (1998) EI scale correlated with three coping factors, which they labelled as (i) problem-focus, (ii) cognitive reappraisal and restraint, and (iii) seeking social support and expressing emotion. A recent series of studies conducted by the author (Zeidner & Kaluda, in preparation) also links EI to a preference for problem- over emotion-focused strategies. Fewer studies have attempted to link objective tests for EI to coping, although Goldenberg et al. (2006) found that correlations between the MSCEIT (Mayer–Salovey–Caruso Emotional Intelligence Test) and their coping scales barely exceeded chance levels. Similarly, Burns et al. (2007) found that a maximal performance scale (MSCEIT) was unrelated to coping style, once personality and ability were controlled.

A second research strategy is to assess coping with a specific challenge. Salovey et al. (2002) had their subjects perform difficult cognitive tasks, under high time pressure, and assessed their coping. Most of the correlations between self-report EI scales and situational coping were non-significant, but the study did show that the mood repair scale of the Trait Meta-Mood Scale (TMSS) related to appraising the tasks as less threatening, and to reduced usage of 'passive coping' (e.g., denial and disengagement). Matthews et al. (2006) also tested whether EI predicted coping with task stressors, using the MSCEIT as the measure of EI in the lab. Three elements of stress response – task engagement, distress and worry – were measured using the Dundee Stress State Questionnaire (Matthews et al., 2002). EI was associated modestly with lower distress and worry, and with reduced use of emotion-focus and avoidance coping, strategies likely to be maladaptive in the per- formance context. With the Big Five controlled, EI related only to less worry and avoid- ance coping, providing some support for the MSCEIT as a predictor of stress processes. There is also evidence that the MSCEIT may relate to more effective mood regulation (Ciarrochi et al., 2001, 2002), although these studies did not assess coping directly.

Studies that investigate EI, coping, and mood regulation within specific contexts (e.g., Salovey et al., 2002; Matthews et al., 2006) should be better suited than studies using global coping measures for identifying mediating mechanisms, but this promise has yet to be realized. Research using more narrowly focused mood-regulation questionnaires such as the TMMS appear promising, especially as (i) these measures may be less confounded with personality than are many EI questionnaires (Gohm & Clore, 2002), and (ii) Salovey et al.'s (2002) study showed evidence for meaningful psychophysiological correlates. Objective tests for EI appear to be more modest predictors of both coping and well-being/ stress outcomes; our own work suggests, however, that the MSCEIT has some modest incremental validity with respect to personality and ability (e.g., Matthews et al., 2006; Zeidner & Kaluda, in preparation). The personality and situational factors that moderate the impact of EI on coping remain obscure, and it has yet to be established that the coping styles characteristic of high scorers on tests for EI actually confer any direct benefits in terms of well-being, behavioural adaptation, or health.

Unresolved issues, pitfalls and fissures
The empirical data leave many issues unresolved. First, the few studies looking at the rela- tionship between EI and coping have not been conducted in organizational settings, so the specific role of EI as a factor in adaptive coping with job stress remains an unresolved

issue. If we do extrapolate from existing studies to occupational contexts, a second issue is the extent to which findings are simply a consequence of the well-known confounding of EI scales with personality assessments. On the basis of the overlap between EI and both extroversion and low neuroticism, biases towards positively framed coping strategies, and away from negatively framed strategies, are exactly what might be expected (e.g., Dawda & Hart, 2000). However, although some studies have neglected to control for personality, both Gohm and Clore (2002) and Petrides et al. (2007) showed that a number of associations between EI and coping remain significant with the Big Five personality traits controlled.

A third issue is that both EI and coping scales may actually reflect stress outcomes. Petrides et al.'s EI scale includes items for general mood, and the example item they give for their emotion-focused coping scale is 'Feel worthless and unimportant', which seems more like a symptom of maladaptive coping rather than a strategy that someone would choose to manage emotion. If both EI and coping scales are picking up moods and stress symptoms, it is not surprising that the two measures should correlate – but the data tell us little about the coping process.

A fourth troubling issue is that EI appears to be a considerably more robust predictor of general style of coping than of measures of actual coping in a specific situation. In line with the previous comment, EI scales may simply pick up generic attitudes about self-efficacy and coping, which are not necessarily indicative of the person's choice of strategy for dealing with a specific stressor. It is possible, though, that the weakness of EI as a predictor reflects the task challenges used to induce situational stress. Perhaps EI would relate more strongly to coping with organizational and social stressors.

A fifth issue is that the mechanisms linking EI constructs to coping and stress outcomes remain obscure. A promising mediating mechanism is coping through seeking emotional social support, which has been implicated both in the effects of self-reported (Goldenberg et al., 2006) and performance-based EI (Zeidner & Kaluda, in preparation). However, it is important to differentiate availability of social support from coping by seeking support. Various studies show that EI relates to perceptions of the size and quality of social networks (e.g., Lopes et al., 2003), but availability of social support may be a product of superior social skills rather than coping. The emotionally intelligent person may simply make friends more easily, irrespective of stress. Some evidence in favour of mediation by coping, comes from studies reported by Ciarrochi (e.g., Ciarrochi et al., 2003a/b), that showed that troubled adolescents are less likely to seek help if they are low in emotional competencies, even when social support is potentially available.

A final issue is that it seems ironic that EI should relate to using rational task-focused coping in preference to emotion-focused strategies (e.g., Saklofske et al., 2007). The problem focus of high EI persons appear to be at variance with these individuals being more in touch with their emotions, and better able to manage emotion. One study using the TMMS (Gohm & Clore, 2002) obtained results more consistent with definitions of EI, in showing that the TMMS scales related to strategies including seeking emotional social support and focusing and venting negative emotions, although the clarity scale of the TMSS related to active, coping. Across both types of study, research appears to converge in pointing to a positive association between EI and problem-focused strategies and a negative association between EI and emotion-focused and avoidance strategies.

Management of occupational stress

Different taxonomies have been proposed to categorize organizationally based stress management and training intervention programs. One scheme classifies interventions designed to reduce stress at the worksite by the *target* of intervention, namely: (i) the organization, (ii) the individual, and (iii) the individual–organization interface. Organization-focused interventions involve improving macro-level factors in the organization (improved selection, restructuring, organizational development). Interventions that focus on the individual include stress education activities (identifying sources of stress, manifestations of stress, teaching effective ways of coping with stress, etc.); relaxation programmes (meditation, deep breathing and progressive muscle relaxation); and employee skill training (e.g., assertiveness training, anger management, mood repair). Interventions focusing on the organization–individual interface centre on improving the personal–organizational interface (e.g., improving emotional or practical skills of employee or management to match job descriptions and requirements).

Cartwright and Cooper (1996) have distinguished three levels of intervention for stress at the worksite (see also Murphy, 1988; Cooper et al., 1996). The first level, *primary prevention*, involves stress reduction, including modifying environmental stressors by direct action to eliminate negative impact on the individual (e.g., reducing workload, improving lighting conditions, providing night transportation to workers). *Secondary prevention* involves mainly stress management, designed to teach employees who are high risk for stress to cope with demands at work in a more adaptive manner. The third level, *tertiary prevention*, involves programmes targeting employees who have suffered from high degrees of disabling stress. The programmes are generally 'employee assistance programmes', which focus on dealing with outcomes or consequences of the stressful situation. In any case, the last two levels deal with stress management rather than modifying environmental stresses. Ivancevich and Matteson (1987) provide a slightly different classification scheme. These researchers identify three possible areas for intervention in the workplace: (i) reducing intensity and number of stressors, (ii) helping the individual modify perception or appraisal of potentially stressful situations, and (iii) improving the range of competencies in coping with stress.

Despite a growing volume of studies on occupational stress, relatively few studies have addressed employees' efforts to cope with the stress of the workplace. Indeed, the literature is relatively silent about the ways that employees cope with transitions in the workplace. Furthermore, there is little empirical data bearing on the relationship between EI, coping and adaptive outcomes in specific occupational settings. Thus, we are in need of studies that not only provide richer and more systematic information about how people cope with stressful encounters and events that are important at work, but also research that sheds light on the role of EI in coping with occupational stress.

The EI literature is replete with practical suggestions for coping with occupational stress. In their popular book *Executive EQ*, Cooper and Sawaf (1997) recommended a three-step strategy for managing emotional energy: (i) acknowledge and feel – rather than deny or minimize – the emotion experienced; (ii) listen to the information or feedback the emotion is giving you (e.g., if one experiences anger or sadness, one should ask: what principles, values, assets, resources or goals are at stake); and (iii) guide or channel the emotional energy into an appropriate constructive response. The underlying assumption of these authors is that emotions are an energy that is neither good nor bad. What is important is how you respond to it and employ it to your own ends. Presumably, by applying this three-step strategy, one can learn how to better cope with aversive emotions and stress at the worksite and achieve better adaptive outcomes.

Goleman (1998) believes that emotionally intelligent people handle stress well, often employing a stress management technique they call on when needed (workout in the gym, meditation, taking a hot bath, etc.). According to Goleman, regular daily practice of a relaxation method seems to reset the trigger point for the *amygdala*, making it less easily provoked. The neural resetting gives us the ability to recover more quickly from 'amygdala hijacks' while makes us less prone to them in the first place. Unfortunately, little empirical support is generally offered to back up these ideas.

Concluding remarks

This chapter discussed the theory and evidence supporting the claimed role of EI in coping with stress at the workplace. Overall, EI is currently evaluated as being an important and valuable potential personal resource for *organizational* settings, purportedly related to coping with tasks where there is a clear emotional skill required for successful performance. Recent reviews of the literature show that EI modestly predicts a wide array of organizational outcomes, ranging from job performance to job satisfaction, organizational citizenship and leadership (Zeidner et al., 2009). At present, relatively few studies have addressed employees' efforts to cope with the stress of the workplace, and the literature is relatively silent about the ways that employees cope with transitions in the workplace. Furthermore, there is little data shedding light on the role of EI in coping with occupational stress.

The implications of current research on coping in occupational settings for the role of EI are complex. On the one hand, theory would suggest that individuals high in EI would show a preference for problem-focused over other forms of coping when something can be done to alter the source of stress. However, when little can be done to alter the source, emotion-focused coping should be the most adaptive. Unfortunately, there is little published research that bears this out, and further research is needed to test these hypotheses. On the other hand, given the research that suggests that individual coping efforts are not very effective in making a difference at the workplace, it is highly questionable to what extent coping strategies would be helpful to those emotionally intelligent individuals who apply them. Overall, the role of EI in impacting on the effectiveness of macro-level interventions would be expected to be minimal. Furthermore, there are no peer-reviewed studies in the literature, to our knowledge, that systematically looked at the relationship between EI, coping and adaptive outcomes in specific occupational settings. Thus, we are in urgent need of studies that enable people to report events, or stressful encounters that are important to them in specific occupational sites, how they cope with them, and the role of EI in coping with occupational stress. Research has yet to establish that general EI plays some unique role in the coping process.

Acknowledgements

The preparation of this chapter was supported by a grant from the Israel Foundation's Trustees (2002–04).

This chapter is based, in part, on materials prepared jointly with Professor Gerald Matthews and Dr Richard Roberts. The author thanks these colleagues for their contributions to his thinking on the topic of EI and occupational stress.

References

Ashford, S.J. (1988), 'Individual strategies for coping with stress', *Journal of Applied Behavioral Science*, **24**, 19–36.

Ashforth, B.E. & Humphrey, R.H. (1995), 'Emotion in the workplace: a reappraisal', *Human Relations*, **48**, 97–125.

Ashkanasy, N.M., Hartel, C.E.J. & Daus, C.S. (2002), 'Diversity and emotion: the new frontiers in organizational behavior research', *Journal of Management*, **28**, 307–38.

Ashkanasy, N.M. & Tse, B. (2000), 'Transformational leadership as management of emotions: a conceptual review', in N.M. Ashkanasy, C.E.J. Hartel & W.J. Zerbe (eds), *Emotions in the Workplace: Research, Theory, and Practice*, Westport, CT: Quorum Books/Greenwood, pp. 221–35.

Baron, R.A. & Neuman, J.H. (1996), 'Workplace violence and workplace aggression: evidence on their relative frequency and potential causes', *Aggressive Behavior*, **22**, 161–78.

Beehr, T.A. & Newman, J.E. (1978), 'Job stress, employee health, and organizational effectiveness: a facet analysis, model, and literature review', *Personnel Psychology*, **31**, 665–99.

Boyatzis, R., Goleman, D. & Rhee, K. (2000), 'Clustering competence in emotional intelligence: insights from the emotional competence inventory', in R. Bar-On & J.D.A. Parker (eds), *The Handbook of Emotional Intelligence*, San Francisco, CA: Jossey-Bass, pp. 343–62.

Burns, N.R., Bastian, V.A. & Nettelbeck, T. (2007), 'Emotional intelligence: more than personality and cognitive ability?', in G. Matthews, M. Zeidner & R.D. Roberts (eds), *The Science of Emotional Intelligence: Knowns and Unknowns*, New York: Oxford University Press, pp. 167–96.

Cartwright, S. & Cooper, C.L. (1996), 'Coping in occupational settings', in M. Zeidner & N.S. Endler (eds), *Handbook of Coping*, New York: Wiley, pp. 202–20.

Cherniss, C. & Goleman, D. (2001), 'Training for emotional intelligence: a model', in Cherniss & Goleman (eds), *The Emotionally Intelligent Workplace*, San Francisco, CA: Jossey-Bass, pp. 209–33.

Ciarrochi, J., Chan, A.Y.C. & Bajgar, J. (2001), 'Measuring emotional intelligence in adolescents', *Personality and Individual Differences*, **31**, 1105–19.

Ciarrochi, J., Deane, F.P. & Anderson, S. (2002), 'Emotional intelligence moderates the relationship between stress and mental health', *Personality and Individual Differences*, **32**, 197–209.

Ciarrochi, J., Caputi, P. & Mayer, J.D. (2003a), 'The distinctiveness and utility of a measure of trait emotional awareness', *Personality and Individual Differences*, **34**, 1477–90.

Ciarrochi, J., Wilson, C.J., Deane, F.P. & Rickwood, D. (2003b), 'Do difficulties with emotions inhibit help-seeking in adolescence? The role of age and emotional competence in predicting help-seeking intentions', *Counselling Psychology Quarterly*, **16**, 103–20.

Cooper, C.L., Liukkonen, P. & Cartwright, S. (1996), *Stress Prevention in the Workplace*, Dublin: European Foundation for the Improvement of Living and Working Conditions, Lanham, MD: UNIPUB.

Cooper, C.L. & Marshall, J. (1978), 'Sources of managerial and white collar stress', in C.L. Cooper & R. Payne (eds), *Stress at Work*, Chichester: Wiley, pp. 81–105.

Cooper, R.K. & Sawaf, A. (1997), *Executive EQ: Emotional Intelligence in Leaders and Organizations*, New York: Grosset/Putnam.

Damasio, A.R. (1994), *Descartes' Error: Emotion, Reason, and the Human Brain*, New York: Avon Books.

Dawda, D. & Hart, S.D. (2000), 'Assessing emotional intelligence: reliability and validity of the Bar-On Emotional Quotient Inventory (EQ-i) in university students', *Personality and Individual Differences*, **28**, 797–812.

Elkin, A.J. & Rosch, P.J. (1990), 'Promoting mental health at the workplace: the prevention side of stress management', *Occupational Medicine: State of the Art Review*, **5**, 739–54.

Folkman, S. (1991), 'Coping across the lifespan: theoretical issues', in E.M. Cummings, A.L. Greene & K.H. Karraker (eds), *Life-span Developmental Psychology: Perspectives on Stress and Coping*, Hillsdale, NJ: Lawrence Erlbaum, pp. 3–19.

Folkman, S. & Lazarus, R. (1986), 'Stress process and depressive symptomatology', *Journal of Abnormal Psychology*, **95**, 107–13.

French, J.R.P. & Caplan, R.D. (1973), 'Organizational stress and individual strain', in A.J. Marrow (ed.), *The Failure of Success*, New York: AMAC Com, pp. 30–36.

Gohm, C.L. & Clore, G.L. (2002), 'Four latent traits of emotional experience and their involvement in well-being, coping, and attributional style', *Cognition and Emotion*, **16**, 495–518.

Goldenberg, I., Matheson, K. & Mantler, J. (2006), 'The assessment of emotional intelligence: a comparison of performance-based and self-report methodologies', *Journal of Personality Assessment*, **86**, 33–45.

Goleman, D. (1998), *Working with Emotional Intelligence*, New York: Bantam Books.

Goleman, D. (2001), 'Emotional intelligence: issues in paradigm building', in C. Cherniss & D. Goleman (eds), *The Emotionally Intelligent Workplace*, San Francisco, CA: Jossey-Bass, pp. 13–26.

Hamner, C. & Tosi, D. (1974), 'Relationship of role conflict and role ambiguity to job involvement measures', *Journal of Applied Psychology*, **4**, 497–99.
House, J.S. (1981), *Work Stress and Social Support*, Reading, MA: Addison-Wesley.
Ivancevich, J.M. & Matteson, M.T. (1987), 'Organizational level stress management interventions: a review and recommendations', in J.M. Ivancevich & D.C. Ganster (eds), *Job Stress: From Theory to Suggestion*, New York: John Wiley, pp. 229–48.
Karasek, R. & Theorell, T. (1990), *Healthy Work: Stress Productivity and the Reconstruction of Working Life*, New York: Wiley.
Kottkamp, R.B. & Travlos, A.L. (1986), 'Selected job stressors, emotional exhaustion, job satisfaction, and thrust behavior of the high school principal', *Alberta Journal of Educational Research*, September, 234–48.
La Rocco, J.M. & Jones, A.P. (1978), 'Co-worker and leader support as moderators of stress–strain relationships in work situations', *Journal of Applied Psychology*, **63**, 629–34.
Latack, J.C. (1986), 'Coping with job stress: measures and future directions for scale development', *Journal of Applied Psychology*, **71**, 377–85.
Lazarus, R.S. (1991), *Emotion and Adaptation*, Oxford and New York: Oxford University Press.
Lazarus, R.S. & Folkman, S. (1984), *Stress, Appraisal, and Coping*, New York: Springer.
Lopes, P.N., Salovey, P., Côté, S. &. Beers, M. (2005), 'Emotion regulation abilities and the quality of social interaction', *Emotion*, **5**, 113–18.
Lopes, P.N., Salovey, P. & Straus, R. (2003), 'Emotional intelligence, personality, and the perceived quality of social relationships', *Personality and Individual Differences*, **35**, 641–58.
Mack, D.A., Nelson, D.L. & Quick, J.C. (1998), 'The stress of organisational change: a dynamic process model', *Applied Psychology: An International Review*, **47**, 219–32.
Matthews, G., Campbell, S.E., Falconer, S., Joyner, L., Huggins, J., Gilliland, K., Grier, R. & Warm, J.S. (2002), 'Fundamental dimensions of subjective state in performance settings: task engagement, distress, and worry', *Emotion*, **2**, 315–40.
Matthews, G., Emo, A.K., Funke, G.J., Zeidner, M., Roberts, R.D., Costa, P.T. Jr. & Schulze, R. (2006), 'Emotional intelligence, personality, and task-induced stress', *Journal of Experimental Psychology: Applied*, **12**, 96–107.
Matthews, G., Roberts, R.D. & Zeidner, M. (2004), 'Seven myths about emotional intelligence', *Psychological Inquiry*, **15**, 179–96.
Matthews, G., Zeidner, M. & Roberts, R.D. (2002), *Emotional Intelligence: Science and Myth*, Cambridge, MA: Bradford Book/MIT Press.
McGrath, J.E. (1976), 'Stress and behavior in organizations', in M.D. Dunnette (ed.), *Handbook of Industrial and Organizational Psychology*, 1st edn, Chicago, IL: Rand McNally, pp. 1351–95.
Murphy, L.R. (1988), 'Workplace interventions for stress reduction and prevention', in C.L. Cooper & R. Payne (eds), *Causes, Coping, and Consequences of Stress at Work*, Chichester: Wiley, pp. 301–39.
Newman, J.D. & Beehr, R. (1979), 'Personal and organizational strategies for handling job stress: a review of research and opinion', *Personnel Psychology*, **32**, 1–43.
O'Driscoll, M.P. & Cooper, C.L. (1994), 'Coping with work-related stress: a critique of existing measures and proposal for an alternative methodology', *Journal of Occupational and Organizational Psychology*, **67**, 343–54.
Pearlin, L.I. & Schooler, C. (1978), 'The structure of coping', *Journal of Health and Social Behavior*, **19**, 2–21.
Pekrun, R. & Frese, M. (1992), 'Emotions in work and achievement', *International Review of Industrial and Organizational Psychology*, **7**, 154–200.
Petrides, K.V., Pérez-González, J.C. & Furnham, A. (2007), 'On the criterion and incremental validity of trait emotional intelligence', *Cognition and Emotion*, **21**, 26–55.
Rafaeli, A. & Sutton, R.I. (1989), 'The expression of emotion in organizational life', *Research in Organizational Behavior*, **11**, 1–42.
Saklofske, D.H., Austin, E.J., Galloway, J. & Davidson, K. (2007), 'Individual difference correlates of health-related behaviours: preliminary evidence for links between emotional intelligence and coping', *Personality and Individual Differences*, **42**, 491–502.
Salin, D. (2003), 'Ways of explaining workplace bullying: a review of enabling, motivating, and precipitating structures and processes in the work environment', *Human Relations*, **56**, 1213–32.
Salovey, P., Bedell, B.T., Detweiler, J.B. & Mayer, J.D. (2000), 'Current directions in emotional intelligence research', in M. Lewis & J.M. Haviland-Jones (eds), *Handbook of Emotions*, New York: Guilford Press, pp. 504–20.
Salovey, P., Stroud, L.R., Woolery, A. & Epel, E.S. (2002), 'Perceived emotional intelligence, stress reactivity, and symptom reports: further explorations using the trait meta-mood scale', *Psychology and Health*, **17**, 611–27.
Schaubroeck, J. & Jones, J.R. (2000), 'Antecedents of workplace emotional labor dimensions and moderators of their effects on physical symptoms', *Journal of Organizational Behavior*, **21**, 163–83.

Schmit, M.J. (2006), 'EI in the business world', in K.R. Murphy (ed.), *A Critique of Emotional Intelligence*, Mahwah, NJ: Erlbaum, pp. 211–34.

Schuler, R.S. (1980), 'Definition and conceptualization of stress in organizations', *Organizational Behavior and Human Performance*, **25**, 184–215.

Schutte, N.S., Malouff, J.M., Hall, L.E., Haggerty, D.J., Cooper, J.T., Golden, C.J. & Dornheim, L. (1998), 'Development and validation of a measure of emotional intelligence', *Personality and Individual Differences*, **25**, 167–77.

Shinn, M., Rosario, M., Morch, H. & Chesnut, D.E. (1984), 'Coping with job stress and burnout in the human services', *Journal of Personality and Social Psychology*, **46**, 864–76.

Sy, T., Tram, S. & O'Hara, L.A. (2006), 'Relation of employee and manager emotional intelligence to job satisfaction and performance', *Journal of Vocational Behavior*, **68**, 461–73.

Weisinger, H. (1998), *Emotional Intelligence at Work: The Untapped Edge for Success*, San Francisco, CA: Jossey-Bass.

Zeidner, M. & Kaluda, I. (in preparation), *Emotional Intelligence and Coping with Stress*.

Zeidner, M., Matthews, G. & Roberts, R.D. (2001), 'Slow down, you move too fast: emotional intelligence remains an "elusive" intelligence', *Emotion*, **1**, 265–75.

Zeidner, M., Matthews, G. & Roberts, R.D. (2006), 'Emotional intelligence, coping, and adaptation', in J. Ciarrochi, J. Forgas & J.D. Mayer (eds), *Emotional Intelligence in Everyday Life: A Scientific Inquiry*, 2nd edn, Philadelphia, PA: Psychology Press, pp. 100–125.

Zeidner, M., Matthews, G. & Roberts, R.D. (2009), *The Primer of Emotional Intelligence*, Cambridge, MA: MIT Press.

27 The relationship between the psychological contract and emotional labour at work and the implications for psychological well-being and organizational functioning

Ashley Weinberg

Introduction

There are many considerations which cross our minds when we look ahead to the day at work; these can range from high levels of satisfaction and fulfilment right through to misery and desperation, depending on our situation both inside and outside of work. Ideally work should give rise to positive thoughts and emotions and the occupational psychology literature has made a huge contribution in highlighting the potential sources of both personal gratification and strain in the work environment. Indeed aspects of the workplace have become well documented as predictors for psychological and physical well-being, including levels of control (Sparks et al., 2001) and workload (Michie & Cockcroft, 1996). This is of great benefit where organizations are in a position to design or modify such features of the work environment or job characteristics; however, in a world of work where conditions rarely remain static as the demands of policies and economies shift, the impact of change often represents an extraneous variable which cannot be readily foretold or assessed and alters the reality experienced by employees. The resulting work situation may be most immediately registered in the perceived psychological contract (Conway & Briner, 2002) which reflects the unwritten set of mutual expectations held by workers and their organizations which can in turn play a major role in determining attitudes and behaviour in the workplace (Argyris, 1960).

Whatever the political reality of change, for good or evil, it is always likely to send reverberations through the organizations in which it takes place. Change impacts on employees in a number of ways as it emerges from rumour to become a realistic prospect, and then transforms from firm proposal to implementation and thereafter into real-world consequences for all concerned. For example, research findings have illustrated the positive impact on workers' well-being when they are given some measure of control over their work environment during a period of uncertainty (Bordia et al., 2004). Similarly, change need not be negative where careful management of the process is exercised (Firns et al., 2006).

Partly in response to the acknowledged effects of change on employees, efforts to cajole organizations into adopting good practice in managing change have been transformed into tougher measures across the European Union. A directive now obliges employers to provide advance notice of any major organizational change, for example, a merger (Giga & Cooper, 2003). This suggests the need for a recognized formula for implementing workplace reforms which enhances individual opportunities for adapting to change, rather than jeopardizing them. Given that employees' view of their workplace is filtered through appraisals based on their emotional reactions to it, including how fairly they feel they are being treated at work, the significance of the psychological contract, with its likely impact on emotions and behaviour, cannot be underestimated. Niccolò Machiavelli famously highlighted the difficulties associated with bringing about change, linked as they are to the fears and desires of those affected by change, and it is this emotional reaction to new ways of doing things that deserves further scrutiny. Without assessing emotions, all change risks failure.

The aim of this chapter is to propose a theoretical framework for investigating the impact of job-related changes on employee well-being and job functioning, which takes into account emotion-based appraisals of the workplace, as operationalized through the worker's perception of the psychological contract, and highlights the potentially pivotal role of subsequent emotional investment in the job, that is, through emotional labour, which could be considered a mediator for a range of outcomes, including individual well-being as well as work performance. The context for the proposed model is the UK public sector setting, in which it is assumed that emotional labour is a recognized component of the work. As such, the impact of changing psychological contracts on three public sector jobs and implications for these occupational groups is considered.

The changing psychological contract in the modern public sector

The psychological contract as a concept has attracted much discussion in recent years and not a little disagreement, particularly in relation to how much it is a written or unwritten phenomenon. However, there appears to be consistency over the importance of fairness and trust (Guest et al., 1996) and the 'dynamics of mutuality' (Rousseau, 2003, p. 229) within the relationship between the employee and his/her employer. Indeed where organizational support is perceived to be low it is likely that the psychological contract assumes even greater significance (Coyle-Shapiro & Conway, 2005) and is highly relevant in times of change, such as that experienced by many public sector providers. Scope exists for considering a range of psychological factors likely to influence workers' expectations (Rousseau, 2003) as well as for exploring the impact of violation of the psychological contract on a range of employee behaviours (Turnley & Feldman, 2000). Violations are recognized where the mutual set of obligations fails to be met by one party (in current research contexts this is usually the employer), resulting in a difference between what the employee expects and what he/she actually receives (Coyle-Shapiro & Conway, 2005).

The relevance of the psychological contract has become particularly salient in UK public sector organizations since the 1980s, including health and social care, higher education and legislative government, as heads of industry and policy makers 'set in motion a revolution in the nature of the employment relationship the like of which they never imagined. For they have shattered the old psychological contract and failed to negotiate a new one' (Herriot & Pemberton, 1995, p. 58). Prior to this major shift, mutual expectations in both private and public sectors saw employees prepared to commit to the goals of the organization, displaying conformity and loyalty, while trusting the employer to respect their goodwill and well-being (Herriot & Pemberton, 1995). In return, public organizations were prepared to offer job security, a career path and the necessary training to cement this transaction. Changes fuelled by globalization, technological innovation and government ideology signalled the beginning of a UK public sector that dismantled such assumptions and encouraged an increasing reliance on economic considerations. The new psychological contract shared by employees and their agencies reflects this. In particular, the emphasis on 'managing' the functions offered by the public sector, including health, social care and education, has been perceived by many as a shift away from ensuring professional standards of service delivery. This is not to say that this 'new managerialism' is necessarily motivated by a less customer-focused approach, but that it has produced an increased preoccupation with efficiency and accountability. From the employee's standpoint, success at work tends to mean longer working hours and greater pressure to deliver paper-based targets, along with the ability to withstand change and uncertainty. In return, public sector organizations offer a job which is on average less well paid than private sector roles and which is increasingly subject to performance-related criteria. UK research findings have revealed levels of psychological strain running at very high levels among the affected occupational groups (Taylor et al., 2004), more sick leave than in private sector jobs (8.1 versus 6.0 days per year; CBI/AXA, 2006), as well as increased staff turnover from occupations such as nursing (Scott, 2002) and social work (Huxley et al., 2005), resulting in skill shortages. However, alongside these outcomes policy makers tend to highlight the financial benefits and enhanced efficiencies in organizational functioning, as well as claiming greater choice for the service user, patient and student.

The National Health Service (NHS) and Community Care Act (1990) and the ethos of 'added value' signalled a turning-point in the life and work of UK public sector employees, which includes social care, health and education organizations. Since the Second World War, UK employees' contributions had funded public sector organizations, ensuring that health and social services were free at the point of delivery, thus enshrining the key difference between these public organizations and their private sector counterparts. Prior to 1990, the success stories within these public services had been based on building relationships with the people in receipt of them. The essence of such relationships lay within the individual employee's capacity to invest in gaining the trust of, and empowering, the service user. However, the government-prescribed shift in the expectations of what public sector employees should deliver (as heralded by the 1990 Act), recast this psychological contract in terms which instead emphasized the costing, administration and management of services. Some would argue that this has encouraged a return to the scientific management principles of Taylorism. In other words, those characteristics routinely practised in many private sector environments, including the production line, found a new welcome in the changing priorities of service delivery in public sector organizations. In addition, the current public sector psychological contract draws on elements of the organizational culture model which influenced so much of 1980s corporate strategy. This entailed the winning of employees' 'hearts and minds', such that training and socialization by the organization provided them with knowledge of how to respond in a manner consistent with the 'new' culture of the organization. Within the melding of this curious combination of early and late twentieth-century management styles lies the origin of emotional labour, that is, the exercising of demand on employees to behave, even to think, in a way that will maximize their added value to the organization. Thus an increasing feature of people-oriented occupations, both in the public and commercial sectors, is pressure to deliver the service in a prescribed manner and timescale.

Emotional labour

Occupational psychology research increasingly recognizes the significance of emotions, whereas at one time these were considered of secondary importance (Fineman, 2000;

Ashkenazy et al., 2002). For example, affective events theory (Weiss & Cropanzano, 1996) acknowledges the impact of work events on employee emotions and highlights the role of cognitive appraisal in shaping such reactions. However, while concepts which encompass emotions are a growing feature of the literature, these have yet to be fully integrated into existing approaches to research and intervention. Emotional labour is a case in point. It has been described as the act of 'managing feelings to create an impression that is part of a job' (Smither, 1998, p. 43). It is certainly part of almost any job which involves working with other people, where the employee, in order to maintain standards and therefore achieve success, has to consider not simply the task in hand, but also the manner in which it is accomplished. According to Mann (1997) this is relevant to two-thirds of workplace interactions. The manner in which employees' emotional display is conveyed can depend on their ability to 'act' or 'fake' apparent emotion (verbally or non-verbally), or at a deeper level 'by directly exhorting feeling . . . or by making use of a trained imagination' (Hochschild, 1983, p. 38), such that they really feel the emotion which they perceive the situation demands. Whichever is pertinent to the employee, it is the outcome of convincing others that he/she is experiencing the appropriate emotion that is significant to the service organization, for example, appearing concerned about a complaint or smiling to reassure a client.

However, where the priorities of the organization do not match those of the individual, emotional dissonance is likely to be experienced by the employee. This is where the employee is required to 'express organisationally desired emotions not genuinely felt' (Morris & Feldman, 1996, p. 986). Call centres (Taylor, 1998) represent an extreme example of this type of interaction, reminiscent of early twentieth-century management styles, where employee–client conversations are scripted and often monitored, thus removing individual freedom from the worker to respond as they actually feel. It can be argued that public sector organizational culture is increasingly geared to moulding the observable behaviour of its workers in a comparable way. This may not be at the specific level of following a script, but in a way which directly influences the nature of the interaction. Thus some social service organizations, through changing the job title of social workers to 'care managers' and by outsourcing care services, emphasize the need to 'manage' care packages rather than 'practise' social work, which in reality means insufficient time spent with a service user (Weinberg et al., 2003). Lecturing staff in higher education are increasingly conscious of the erosion of academic freedom, with operational requirements to balance the demands of paying customers (students), prescribed academic standards as well as research demands (Constanti & Gibbs, 2004). These shifting emphases dictate employee interactions indirectly as well as directly, including the amount of time a tutor may be available to see his/her students or the measures to be taken to address individual student needs.

To this end, the setting of objectives by organizations for their employees' exchanges with those in receipt of services in public sector roles, rather than actually scripting interactions has fostered the belief that high quality will be guaranteed, for example, expected length of hospital stay, or hospital bed occupancy. There is an underlying assumption that the imposition of organizational targets will sit easily with individuals' capacity to fulfil their expectations of the job role. For many public sector employees this can result in emotional dissonance, as their knowledge and experience of what works well for users of public services increasingly contradicts organizational prescriptions for practice. The individual user of a public service can have a variety of potential needs that exceed the system's capacity to respond. By strictly adhering to the requirements of the organization, employees – against their own trained judgement – may not feel able to meet these needs. In other words, a working culture which seeks to guarantee quality by ensuring that everyone gets the same treatment in a given set of circumstances can actually represent a direct challenge to providing the best outcome for the individual service user. This parallels the problem of requiring employees to use scripted interactions.

In committed public sector workers, this is likely to produce role conflict between what the organization permits them to do and the actions employees might carry out based on their training and expertise. As such, employees' experienced and expressed emotions are likely to differ. This does not presuppose that organizational practices and prescriptions are wrong, but recognizes the limitations of a 'one size fits all' approach for those involved in its implementation and in receiving the service. In relation to emotional labour, public servants may feel pressured to compromise their personal expectations of quality service delivery, yet are also obliged to present the predetermined line of the organization.

The relationship between the psychological contract, emotional labour and employee well-being and organizational functioning

Research has shown that violations of the psychological contract are frequent and this fits with the levels of cynicism to be found in many of today's workplaces (Turnley & Feldman, 2000). It has been recognized that psychological contract violation represents the emotional response to a perception that the psychological contract has been broken (Morrison & Robinson, 1997), although the possibility that the psychological contract may be exceeded should not be discounted. It is also well documented that where violations have occurred, these have been linked with a range of negative perceptions and behaviours among employees, including decreases in job satisfaction, rises in staff turnover, poorer work performance (Turnley & Feldman, 2000) and increases in job strain (Gakovic & Tetrick, 2003). There is evidence that mediating variables play a significant role in producing such negative outcomes, although the processes involved have yet to be fully explored. The finding that lack of job satisfaction is a mediator between violations of the psychological contract and neglect of in-role job duties (as well as intent to quit and organizational citizenship behaviours) (Turnley & Feldman, 2000), highlights the link between felt emotions and the perceptions of the relationship between employees and their organizations. Logically it can be suggested that where the worker is dissatisfied with the psychological contract, the behavioural outcome which is most congruent with the individual employee's emotions is more likely to be consistent with 'getting out' or 'getting even' (Herriot & Pemberton, 1995), rather than with the organization's definition of success.

In the arena of trading emotions, which arguably most work-based and non-work interactions involve, there is often a need to manage one's communications in order to create a desired impact. At work, such an emotional investment can logically be influenced by the perceived fairness of the psychological contract and would therefore influence the degree of emotional labour demonstrated in a job role. Hence a disgruntled call-centre employee might rebel against his/her manager: 'when I am positive she is not listening, I have been really short [impatient/angry] with customers, it's a great feeling' (Taylor, 1998, p. 95). However, such a negative emotional response is less easily conducted in the face-to-face context of many public sector roles, especially where the potential outcome is likely to be related to the client's health, welfare or educational progress. In a role characterized by the need for demonstrating personal care, involving a professional relationship with a patient, client or student, the recipient relies on the employee to invest levels of emotional labour. Therefore any decision to withdraw or modify this behaviour on the part of the employee can assume a much greater significance for the user of that service. For example, social workers or doctors may not spend as much time as they would wish listening to a client's problem and in turn the patient feels he/she is not being taken seriously.

Many workers facing a conflict between an unsatisfactory psychological contract and the necessity to invest emotional labour will state that they 'just can't walk away from someone needing their help' as this would be against their own moral and professional inclinations. However, the question remains whether or not employees are aware that their perceptions of 'fairness' of the psychological contract will affect their desire and/ or ability to invest emotional labour where it is needed. This has not so far been tested to the knowledge of this author. Certainly, greater role identification signifies that the employee is more likely to experience the required emotions (Ashforth & Humphrey, 1993) and this fits with the notion of satisfaction with the psychological contract, which in turn promotes the likely investment of emotional labour. It is not surprising that those working in human service jobs where caring duties are required report higher levels of personal accomplishment than other occupational groups, indicating intrinsic rewards from carrying out this kind of work (Brotheridge & Grandey, 2002). Notwithstanding such individual responses to a given situation requiring emotional labour, a number of public sector occupations in the UK are actually experiencing high levels of turnover and staff shortages (Scott, 2002; Huxley et al., 2005).

Given the widespread prevalence of emotion work across a range of occupations, it is hard to define certain job roles as requiring significantly more emotional labour than others (Brotheridge & Grandey, 2002). However, levels of burnout and psychological strain are known to be high in a number of public sector occupations (e.g., Wall et al., 1997; Littlewood et al., 2003), and although relatively little is known about how this affects employees' ability to meet emotional labour demands, it is recognized that surface acting and the faking of emotions inherent in so much emotional labour are significantly correlated with emotional exhaustion and depersonalization (Brotheridge & Grandey, 2002). This suggests that emotional effort which is incongruent with felt emotions can in turn promote psychological strain (Brotheridge & Lee, 2003). Indeed, this has been demonstrated in a number of job settings ranging from holiday agents (Guerrier & Adib, 2003) to legal representatives (Harris, 2002). The concept of burnout (Maslach & Jackson, 1986) incorporates the emotional exhaustion which can follow employees' exposure to the demands of many public sector jobs. However, for those who enter a profession after lengthy training and join an organization which is undergoing the types of changes outlined above in the UK, they may find that on a daily basis their expectations are not met or fulfilled, or alternatively they may encounter limited staffing resources such that the emotional strain is considerable, resulting in high rates of psychological distress and burnout (Littlewood et al., 2003).

The proposed model (Figure 27.1) features the key concepts discussed so far in this chapter, that is, employee perceptions of the psychological contract, emotional

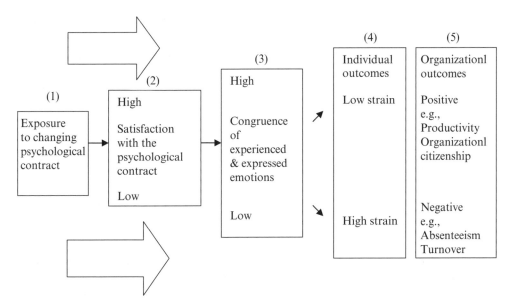

*Figure 27.1   Model showing the relationship between the perceived psychological
contract, the degree of congruence experienced and expressed emotions and
the implications for psychological well-being and organizational functioning*

experiences requiring the expression of emotions which are incongruent with those
actually felt by employees, as well as a range of outcomes for individual well-being and
organizational functioning.

In the context of major organizational changes, such as those witnessed in a number
of UK public sector jobs, it is likely that employees have been exposed to alterations in
the psychological contract shared with their employer, whether the health service, welfare
provider or educational institution (Figure 27.1, box 1). For example those employed
in such jobs expecting to be able to spend time with their patients/clients/students, have
found this time eroded by pressure to complete administrative tasks which satisfy organizational targets. Inherent in this is a mismatch between expectations of what the job
should and actually does entail. Alternatively, an employee hoping to be rewarded for
meeting organizational targets, could expect to be remunerated appropriately and would
welcome the introduction of performance-related pay. Following on from this, and influenced by the employee's own behavioural style and personality factors, such as positive
and negative affect, is the level of satisfaction which the individual has with the resulting
psychological contract (see box 2). This reflects the recognition by workers of the extent
to which they felt the organization is obliged to, and actually does, provide features of the
job, for example, pay, prospects for self-development, appropriate autonomy in carrying
out job tasks, etc. A continuum running from 'positive' to 'negative' indicates satisfaction
levels in relation to the psychological contract.

Given previous research which suggests that some degree of emotional labour is
required in a range of jobs, whether explicitly involving human services, such as caring,
or not, for example, construction (Brotheridge & Grandey, 2002), it is assumed that for

the majority of public service functions, a moderate to high level of emotional labour is required. Therefore what is emphasized in the model is the level of matching between the employee's experience and expression of emotional labour, again illustrated on a continuum from high to low (see box 3). It is proposed that where satisfaction with the psychological contract is positive, this favourable attitude towards the job promotes congruence in the emotions the employee feels and expresses in their work. Following the course of this particular state of working harmony, and allowing for equilibrium in other domains of the employee's life outside of work, one would expect relatively low levels of psychological strain to result (see box 4), as well as improved organizational outcomes in terms of good job performance and higher levels of organizational citizenship behaviour (see box 5). These employee and organizationally oriented effects can in turn be expected to feed back into the level of satisfaction with the psychological contract (box 2). However, where there are low levels of satisfaction with the psychological contract, yet emotional labour is required in order to perform the job, there is likely to be dissonance between the employee's experienced and expressed emotions (box 3). It is proposed that this scenario produces unfavourable outcomes for employee well-being (box 4) and/ or job performance (box 5). Such effects can in turn promote negative responses to the psychological contract, especially where feedback from colleagues and managers reflects their dissatisfaction with the individual's performance.

The model builds on previous work by uniting the relationships so far demonstrated between the psychological contract and its violation (e.g., Turnley & Feldman, 2000) with employees' requirements to display emotional labour within their work, featuring the link between emotional dissonance and emotional exhaustion (Brotheridge & Grandey, 2002). In addition, the model attempts to describe the potential for positive outcomes in a working context where the psychological contract is changing and emotional labour is demanded. The role of individual differences (e.g., negative affect) is also acknowledged, as is the tendency for employees to reassess their satisfaction with the psychological contract, in line with the assumptions about appraisal made by affective events theory (Weiss & Cropanzano, 1996). It is acknowledged that there are more complex models of human emotion at work which attempt to incorporate daily variation in employee mood and workgroup climate (e.g., Hartel et al., 2002), but the aim of the proposed model is to facilitate a clearer understanding for organizations of the dynamics between workplace change and individual/organizational outcomes. Furthermore, there are implications for practice as measures have been introduced in the UK by the Health and Safety Executive to advise employers of management standards for tackling stress at work. Such advice includes appropriate processes for informing employees of organizational change, in addition to ensuring acceptable employee perceptions of demands, control, support systems, relationships and roles at work. Clearly such measures have the potential to impact on the psychological contract between organizations and their employees, yet they remain advisory and there remains a need to explain to employers the potential benefits for organizational performance as well as workers' well-being. It is hoped that the proposed model highlights potential predictors of these key variables, which remain to be confirmed by future research. The following sections attempt to illustrate the relevance of the considerations incorporated in the model to selected public sector occupational roles, namely social work, healthcare professional and lecturer.

The social worker or the care manager?

The use of this occupational title depends on the local perceptions, organization and practice of the job role. In itself the difference in job title illustrates the post-reform debate in the UK influencing workers in this profession: 'the dilemma of increased administrative work is one that features significantly in the analysis of the care manager role' (Gorman, 2000, p. 150). This dilemma derives from the role conflict experienced by employees, many of whom entered a profession expecting to spend a significant proportion of their time working directly with service users. The NHS and Community Care Act (1990) provided them with a new and non-negotiable psychological contract which demanded a quite different set of skills. This pattern of an increasingly bureaucratic system approach has been repeated in other public services too. As Gorman states, 'the cost to the worker and potentially to the user of services in this environment relates to the worker relinquishing control over how the work is to be done' (p. 154). This clearly has implications for reduced satisfaction with the psychological contract.

In relation to care managers' direct role with service users, a reduced percentage of their time is spent talking, counselling and advising than would have been the case prior to the reforms (Weinberg et al., 2003). Furthermore, a proportion of this direct contact is consumed with completing forms, thus changing the nature and emphasis of the interaction between the worker and the individual requiring help. Put simply, it is more difficult to converse and deploy effective listening skills while word processing documentation. If time for interaction is more constrained, as dictated by the administrative approach, limits are being imposed on the emotional investment that the employee can place in the interaction, which contrasts with the 'caring' aspect of the job role as conceived before the reforms. Either way, the impression left with the service user is likely to be of someone who appears more distant and/or preoccupied than they were expecting (Weinberg & Huxley, 2000). From the workers' standpoint, the potential for dissatisfaction with their job is increased as the dissonance between their experienced and expressed emotions develops.

One method for managing employees' emotional investment is to compromise between achieving genuine empathy and attaining organizational targets. Where workers feel that they should be in a position to genuinely 'care', but organizational realities and time dictate otherwise, then the individual engages in emotional labour in order to adequately convince the other person that the employee is attentive and empathic. In effect, this is emotional labour operating counterintuitively to that previously documented in service environments (e.g., Taylor, 1998). In this situation, caring workers may find it necessary to mask their genuine motivation to care in order to achieve organizational goals. However, at the interface between the employee and the service user, commercial employees are culturally encouraged to give the customer positive feedback (Hochschild, 1983), while their public sector counterparts are being similarly discouraged from investing in the type of personal communication which many service users would claim they need.

As the 1990 reforms dictate, the flow of social workers' time is towards managing care. This also has implications for the psychological contract and the use of emotional labour 'in-house'. This is most clearly brought into focus by the approval process for funding for care packages for service users. Due to financial limitations, this can mean individuals waiting for care to be arranged, even though the social worker has assessed the need for it. This can leave the employee with an increased feeling of helplessness and a greater feeling of resentment towards the prevalent culture. A situation such as this represents a violation of the psychological contract in which the social welfare employee expects to arrange care and yet cannot do so. How the individual manages this requires a further investment of emotional labour in order to behave in a way which will be acceptable to the organization. This may be easier within a supportive team and/or with an understanding team leader who may share such frustrations. Yet even within this supportive network, organizational repression of emotion is likely to take a toll in reduced job satisfaction and increased aspects of burnout, such as emotional exhaustion, or the projection of blame on to management levels. Not surprisingly, higher levels of psychological distress have been found among organizational cultures where management were perceived as failing to provide the support care managers expected (Thompson et al., 1996). Evidence already points to greater workload and experiences of stress among social workers (McGrath, 1996) and data indicate that the new approach is affecting the amount of contact with service users (Weinberg et al., 2003). This has led to increased non-statutory service provision in the areas once met by social workers; for example, working with families of sufferers of severe mental health problems (Weinberg & Huxley, 2000). In addition to these negative outcomes for social work employees and a change in the expectations of service users, increased turnover has created staff shortages in the UK among this occupational group of approximately 25% (Huxley et al., 2005).

From the model, it can be hypothesized that the pattern of change has produced dissatisfaction with the psychological contract, and against the backdrop of ongoing emotional labour (promoting increased dissonance) as witnessed in this scenario, has led to poor outcomes for employee well-being and organizational functioning. The model proposed in this chapter describes the relationships between these variables and requires research to test its applicability. Studies which assess the situation before and after major changes would be particularly useful.

Healthcare professions in the UK National Health Service

It is arguable that the major public sector reforms of 1990 impacted most notably on the provision of healthcare in the UK. The changes introduced a marketplace ethos comprising providers and purchasers of healthcare, where previously there had been no such business model. A new emphasis on patient 'throughputs' and bed occupancy heralded an administrative model of patient care. This meant that clinicians became responsible for budgets as well as medical practice, experiencing a new psychological as well as actual contract. One longitudinal study of the introduction of this change among local doctors (general practitioners) noted significantly higher levels of depression and somatic anxiety, as well as significantly lower job satisfaction compared to the pre-change period (Sutherland & Cooper, 1992). Perceived sources of strain for healthcare employees included those related to the state of the psychological contract, including 'doing a different job from the one doctors felt trained to do', 'responsibility without power', 'fear of redundancy' and 'too much administration' (Prosser et al., 1997). Such employee perceptions of a potentially undermining work situation would have created clear dissonance between employee emotions about the organization and the emotional labour necessary to carry out a caring/clinical role successfully. Consistent with the proposed model, decreased career satisfaction was associated with emotional exhaustion and poorer psychological health (ibid.).

The toll on employees and the organization was duly recognized. Eight years after the UK NHS reforms, a review of 178 published research articles on healthcare workers recorded a raised prevalence of psychological ill health among employees (which exceeded that in the general population), as well as identifying very high levels of turnover and decisions by doctors to take early retirement (Williams et al., 1998). For hospital doctors, workplace factors including high workload, were also linked with increased stress during consultations and psychological distress was associated with reduced confidence in conducting clinical work (Williams et al., 1997). Lack of support from line managers featured as a major job factor predicting the incidence of minor psychiatric disorders among healthcare workers including doctors, nurses, administrative and ancillary staff (Weinberg & Creed, 2000). Doctors' working hours and organizational systems have become the focus of changes in the NHS since 2000, but the challenges of staff shortages remain evident (Scott, 2002). More research is needed with healthcare occupations to assess the impact of continuing government reforms.

Lecturing staff in higher education institutions
Recent years have also seen changes in the higher education sector in the UK and elsewhere. Academic careers gained a reputation for moving at a leisurely pace in comparison to many other types of work, with relatively high levels of workplace control and support. However, it is claimed that 'British higher education has undergone a more profound re-orientation than any other system in industrial societies' (Trow, 1994, p. 11). One study has shown that 72% of UK academic staff claim to work longer hours than previously and 52% report lowered levels of job satisfaction (Kinman & Jones, 2004). Half of the respondents to a nationwide survey recorded high levels of symptoms of distress and a quarter of the sample declared a stress-related illness in the previous 12-month period (ibid.). This appears to be a picture that is found elsewhere, with higher levels of psychological strain reported by lecturers in Australian universities than was evident even among prison officers (Winefeld, 2000). The link between high stress levels and intention to leave the profession (Kinman & Jones, 2004) is therefore not surprising.

The unhappy findings cited here coincide with the shift towards a managerial approach to control and standardization in higher education while the sector adopts the 'inherent characteristics of other service-related industries' (Constanti & Gibbs, 2004, p. 243). Thus the academic employee is expected to meet the demands of both the customer (formerly known as the student) and a system of management. The lecturer is expected to deliver an increasingly quantifiable product, which can be defined in terms of learning aims and outcomes and is measured via student achievements and evaluation exercises. Given the psychological nature of the learning and teaching process and the potential impact of many individual variables on its success, this is likely to cause tension for the individual lecturer as well as the student. Traditionally, academic occupations have enjoyed a high level of autonomy, yet the need to fulfil organizational objectives reduces the level of control that the individual employee can exercise. Over a six-year period, Kinman & Jones (2004) identified no shift in the opinion held by academic staff in the UK that management does not seem sensitive to their needs. Furthermore, they found significantly more negative perceptions of workload, quality assurance procedures and of opportunities to carry out their job to a high standard (ibid.). This has resulted in a reappraisal of and dissatisfaction with the psychological contract, wherein academic staff attest to a decline in the status of the job role. In a climate which continues to demand high levels of emotional labour, the negative outcomes for staff well-being and for turnover are as predicted by the proposed model.

The relinquishing of job autonomy in the context of a more managerial model echoes the psychological contract experienced by social workers. This necessitates an increased use of emotional labour, as lecturers attempt to mask a 'sense of helplessness . . . an emotion frequently felt and concealed in the classroom, concealed for the benefit of both the student and the management' (Constanti & Gibbs, 2004, p. 246). Lecturers' ability to optimally deliver their chosen specialism, by keeping abreast of latest developments and carrying out their own research, is likely to be undermined by the need to complete the increasingly prescribed administrative duties. The significant decrease in time that academic staff identify to undertake scholarly work is indicative of this situation (Kinman & Jones, 2004). It may come as little surprise that UK academic and academic-related staff record among the highest levels of psychological strain, compared to other occupational groups. Once again an unsatisfactory psychological contract seems to underpin the need for emotional labour, and the toll is evident in staff strain.

Conclusions

This chapter has proposed a model which marries together salient themes in the context of modern public sector working which is being altered by organizational (including ideologically motivated) change. A mediating role for emotional labour in the relationship between exposure to the reformed psychological contract and employee experiences of psychological strain is proposed. Although the potential use of the model has been exemplified by relevant occupational groups in one country, it is recognized that similar issues are faced by these professions elsewhere. Research studies which assess the relationships between the psychological contract, emotional labour (particularly dissonance) and outcomes including psychological ill health and organizational losses, are therefore encouraged.

Changing psychological contracts across key UK public services have created conditions in which the likelihood of dissonance between employees' experienced and expressed emotions has increased. Emotional labour is a potential component in any interaction and in those jobs which are based on health, welfare or educational interests, careful consideration is needed in altering factors which may contribute to this known predictor of employee strain. This is crucial in times of organizational and job change, where the psychological contract shared by employer and employee is reassessed and can influence the manner in which job roles are carried out. Furthermore, where emotional labour is considered crucial for sound organizational performance, investment in the employee's training and satisfaction is obvious. In establishing the acceptable limits of emotional labour, organizations will need to consider the expectations of front-line workers entering those professions. In the meantime it may be considered perverse that within the UK, private sector organizations which earn the accolades of 'innovative' and 'a pleasure to work for' (*The Sunday Times*, 2006) are those successfully employing the human relations approach so valued in the pre-1990s public sector, while UK public sector organizations have been encouraged to shift towards more Taylorist-led models of operation. Given the growing toll of stress in a range of people-oriented jobs which demand high levels of emotional labour, and where emotional dissonance occurs, the need to recognize the value of individual effort and to engender a climate of trust has never been more compelling!

The basis of this is likely to be a psychological contract which is mutually acceptable to employers and employees alike. In the context of a fairer and more just understanding between public servants and their employers, one would expect that the demands for emotional labour are less likely to result in emotional dissonance and are therefore less likely to promote psychological strain, absenteeism and turnover. By working towards a more explicit understanding of the psychological contract and its relationship with emotional labour, it is hoped that workplaces – particularly in the types of public sector roles discussed here – will become more able to promote well-being among the employees who are needed to help others.

References

Argyris, C. (1960), *Understanding Organisational Behaviour*, Homewood, IL: Dorsey Press.

Ashforth, B.E. & Humphrey, R.H. (1993), 'Emotional labour in service roles: the influence of identity', *Academy of Management Review*, **18**, 88–115.

Ashkanasy, N.M., Zerbe, W.J. & Hartel, C.E.J. (2002), *Managing Emotions in the Workplace*, New York: Sharpe.

Bordia, P., Hobman, E., Jones, E., Gallois, C. & Callan, V.J. (2004), 'Uncertainty during organizational change: types, consequences and management strategies', *Journal of Business and Psychology*, **18**, 507–32.

Brotheridge, C.M. & Grandey, A.A. (2002), 'Emotional labour and burnout: comparing two perspectives of "people work"', *Journal of Vocational Behaviour*, **60**, 17–39.

Brotheridge, C.M. & Lee, R.T. (2003), 'Development and validation of the Emotional Labour Scale', *Journal of Occupational and Organizational Psychology*, **76**, 365–79.

Confederation of British Industry/AXA (2006), 'Cost of UK workplace absence tops £13bn – new CBI survey', http//:www.cbi.org.uk/ndbs/press.nsf on, 15 May 2006.

Constanti, P. & Gibbs, P. (2004), 'Higher education teachers and emotional labour', *International Journal of Educational Management*, **18**, 243–9.

Conway, N. & Briner, R.B. (2002), 'A daily diary of affective responses to psychological contract breach and exceeded promises', *Journal of Organizational Behavior*, **23**, 287–302.

Coyle-Shapiro, J.A.-M. & Conway, N. (2005), 'Exchange relationships: examining psychological contracts and perceived organizational support', *Journal of Applied Psychology*, **90**, 774–81.

Fineman, S. (2000), *Emotions in Organisations*, 2nd edn, London: Sage.

Firns, I., Travaglione, A. & O'Neill, G. (2006), 'Absenteeism in times of rapid organizational change', *Strategic Change*, **15**, 113–28.

Gakovic, A. & Tetrick, L.E. (2003), 'Psychological contract breach as a source of strain for employees', *Journal of Business and Psychology*, **18**, 235–46.

Giga, S.I. & Cooper, C.L. (2003), 'Psychological contracts within the NHS', *Human Givens Journal*, **10**, 38–40.

Gorman, H. (2000), 'Winning hearts and minds? Emotional labour and learning for care management work', *Journal of Social Work Practice*, **14**, 149–58.

Guerrier, Y. & Adib, A. (2003), 'Work at leisure and leisure at work: a study of the emotional labour of tour reps', *Human Relations*, **56**, 1399–418.

Guest, D., Conway, N., Briner, R. & Dickman, M. (1996), *The State of the Psychological Contract in Employment*, London: Institute of Personnel and Development.

Harris, L.C. (2002), 'The emotional labour of barristers: an exploration of emotional labour by status professionals', *Journal of Management Studies*, **39** (4), 553–81.

Hartel, C.E.J., Hsu, A.C.F. & Boyle, M.V. (2002), 'A conceptual examination of the causal sequences of emotional labor, emotional dissonance, and emotional exhaustion: the argument for the role of contextual and provider characteristics', in Ashkanasy et al. (eds), pp. 251–75.

Herriot, P. & Pemberton, C. (1995), *New Deals*, Chichester: Wiley.

Hochschild, A.R. (1983), *The Managed Heart: Commercialization of Human Feeling*, Berkeley, CA: University of California Press.

Huxley, P., Evans, S., Gately, C., Webber, M., Mears, A., Pajak, S., Kendall, T., Medina, J. & Katona, C. (2005), 'Stress and pressures in mental health social work: the worker speaks', *British Journal of Social Work*, **35**, 1063–79.

Kinman, G. & Jones, F. (2004), *Working to the Limit*, London: AUT.

Littlewood, S., Case, R., Gater, R. & Lindsey, C. (2003), 'Recruitment, retention, satisfaction and stress in child and adolescent psychiatrists', *Psychiatric Bulletin*, **27**, 61–7.

Mann, S. (1997), 'Emotional labour in organizations', *Leadership and Organisation Development Journal*, **18**, 4–12.

Maslach, C. & Jackson, S. (1986), *The Maslach Burnout Inventory*, Palo Alto, CA: Consulting Psychologists Press.

McGrath, M. (1996), 'The roles and tasks of care managers in Wales', *Community Care and Planning*, **4**, 6185–94.

Michie, S. & Cockcroft A. (1996), 'Overwork can kill?', *British Medical Journal*, **312**, 921–2.

Morris, J.A. & Feldman, D.C. (1996), 'The dimensions, antecedents, and consequences of emotional labour', *Academy of Management Review*, **21**, 986–1010.

Morrison, E.W. & Robinson, S.L. (1997), 'When employees feel betrayed: a model of how psychological contract violation develops', *Academy of Management Review*, **22**, 226–56.

Prosser, D., Johnson, S., Kuipers, E., Szmukler, G., Bebbington, P. & Thornicroft, G. (1997), 'Perceived sources of work stress and satisfaction among hospital and community mental health staff, and their relation to mental health, burnout and job satisfaction', *Journal of Psychosomatic Research*, **43**, 51–9.

Rousseau, D.M. (2003), 'Extending the psychology of the psychological contract; a reply to "Putting psychology back into psychological contracts"', *Journal of Management Inquiry*, **12**, 224–38.

Scott, H. (2002), 'Nursing profession is finding it harder to retain nurses', *British Journal of Nursing*, **11**, 1052.

Smither, R. (1998), *The Psychology of Work and Human Performance*, New York: Longman.

Sparks, K., Faragher, B. & Cooper, C.L. (2001), 'Well-being and occupational health in the 21st century workplace', *Journal of Occupational and Organizational Psychology*, **74**, 489–509.

Sunday Times, The (2006), 'The 100 best companies to work for', *The Sunday Times*, London.

Sutherland, V.J. & Cooper, C.L. (1992), 'Job stress, satisfaction, and mental health among general practitioners before and after introduction of new contract', *British Medical Journal*, **304**, 1545–8.

Taylor, S. (1998), 'Emotional labour and the new workplace', in P. Thompson & C. Warhurst (eds), *Workplaces of the Future*, Basingstoke: Macmillan, pp. 84–103.

Taylor, M.F., Brice, J., Buck, N. & Prentice-Lane, E. (2004), *British Household Panel Survey User Manual Volume A: Introduction, Technical Report and Appendices*, Colchester: University of Essex.

Thompson, N., Stradling, S., Murphy, M. & O'Neill, P. (1996), 'Stress and organizational culture', *British Journal of Social Work*, **26**, 647–65.

Trow, M. (1994), 'Managerialism and the academic profession: the case of England', *Higher Education Policy*, **7**, 11–18.

Turnley, W.H. & Feldman, D.C. (2000), 'Re-examining the effects of psychological contract violations: unmet expectations and job dissatisfaction as mediators', *Journal of Organizational Behavior*, **21**, 1–25.

Wall, T.D., Bolden, R.I., Borrill, C.S., Golya, D.A., Hardy, G.E., Haynes, G., Rick, J.W., Shapiro, D.A. & West, M.A. (1997), 'Minor psychiatric disorder in NHS Trust staff: occupational and gender differences', *British Journal of Psychiatry*, **171**, 519–23.

Weinberg, A. & Creed, F. (2000), 'Stress and psychiatric disorder in healthcare professionals and hospital staff', *The Lancet*, **355**, 533–7.

Weinberg, A. & Huxley, P. (2000), 'An evaluation of the impact of voluntary sector family support workers on the quality of life of carers of schizophrenia sufferers', *Journal of Mental Health*, **9**, 495–503.

Weinberg, A., Williamson, J., Challis, D. & Hughes, J. (2003), 'What do care managers do? A study of working practices in older people's services', *British Journal of Social Work*, **33**, 901–19.

Weiss, H.M. & Cropanzano, R. (1996), 'Affective events theory: a theoretical discussion of the structure, causes and consequences of affective experiences at work', *Research in Organizational Behavior*, **18**, 1–74.

Williams, S., Dale, J., Glucksman, E. & Wellesley (1997), 'Senior house officers' work related stressors, psychological distress, and confidence in performing clinical tasks in accident and emergency: a questionnaire study', *British Medical Journal*, **314**, 713–18.

Williams, S., Michie, S. & Pattani, S. (1998), 'Improving the health of NHS workforce. Report of the Partnership on the health of the NHS workforce', London: Nuffield.

Winefeld, A.H. (2000), 'Stress in academe: some recent research findings', in D.T. Kenny, J.G. Carlson, F.J. McGuigan & J.L. Sheppard (eds), *Stress and Health Research and Clinical Applications*, Sydney: Harwood.

PART VII

SOCIAL SUPPORT ASPECTS

28 Stress, social support and blood pressure: worktime–downtime distinctions

Brian M. Hughes

Stress, social support, and health: from ordinary life to the workplace

It is widely appreciated that psychological stress exerts a negative impact on physical health. Traditionally, the pathways through which such impacts are transmitted have been categorized as either indirect (i.e., the impact exerted by stress-related behavior, such as smoking) or direct (i.e., the impact exerted by stress-related physiological arousal). Research evidence to support the claim that psychological stress contributes to ill health both indirectly and directly has been accumulating steadily over the history of behavioral epidemiology and health psychology, and the idea that psychosomatic stress mechanisms can underlie the development of disease is now very much part of mainstream medicine. Statistically, the contribution of stress to disease is striking. In one of the largest analyses of its kind, an international project known as the INTERHEART study – which involved over 11,000 myocardial infarction (MI) patients and 13,000 matched controls across 52 countries – high prevalence of psychological stress was associated with a doubling of MI risk even *after* controlling for smoking (Rosengren et al., 2004). The adverse effect of stress on cardiological health was found to be present across genders, ethnic groups, and indeed continents.

That the impact of stress on physical well-being is recognized to be acutely relevant to the consideration of occupational health is reflected in the identification of occupational stress as a major workplace hazard in the World Health Organization's Global Strategy on Occupational Health (WHO, 1994). In fact, some of the most extensive research into stress and health has been conducted in occupational settings. Such research has linked work-related stress to symptoms such as sleep disturbance (Leineweber et al., 2003), vital exhaustion (Kristenson et al., 1998), and headaches (Swan & Cooper, 2005). In the landmark Whitehall studies of British civil servants, having a stressful job (i.e., one where personal control was greatly outweighed by environmental demand) was associated with a variety of indicators of poor health, including depression (Griffin et al., 2002), obesity (Brunner et al., 1997), high blood pressure (Marmot et al., 1991), coronary deaths (Marmot et al., 1997), and the metabolic syndrome (Chandola et al., 2006). When the INTERHEART study assessed data on work stress in isolation (as distinct from stress in general), the researchers found no difference in its impact on MI incidence (Rosengren et al., 2004).

Like psychological stress, low social support has long been implicated in cardiovascular disease (Cohen, 1988; House et al., 1988; Eriksen, 1994). Theoretically, social support boosts health either by conferring generalized benefits irrespective of circumstances (the so-called 'direct model') or by attenuating the damaging effects of stress in the individual's environment (the so-called 'buffering model'). Evidence for a direct effect can be seen in inverse statistical associations between social support and atherosclerosis (Rozanski et al., 1999), incidence of MI (Hedblad et al., 1992), and depression following MI (Frasure-Smith et al., 2000). A buffering effect can be inferred when, statistically, social support and stress are found to influence health synergistically (i.e., where stress–support interactions are found to be significant). For example, in a seven-year follow-up study of over 750 healthy Swedish men aged 50 or over, social support was found to be less protective against mortality among men reporting few recent life stressors than among those reporting many recent life stressors (Rosengren et al., 1993). Statistically, such synergistic effects may represent incidents of either mediation or moderation, which in turn may reflect whether social support itself attenuates stress (by, psychologically, making the environment feel less stressful) or enhances the individual's coping abilities (by, behaviorally, providing resources with which stressors can be ameliorated).

Social support has also been associated with direct effects on well-being in occupational contexts, but statistical evidence for buffering effects on work stress has been less clear (Beehr et al., 2003). In a meta-analysis of 68 studies of social support and work stress, Visweswaran et al. (1999) documented an overall inverse association between support and well-being suggestive of a direct effect. Partialing out the impact of social support did not alter the relationship between stress and well-being, implying that support was not a mediator; but consideration of the relevant cumulated R^2 values across studies suggested that support may have had a small moderating role. It is worth noting, however, that in the literature reviewed by Visweswaran et al., self-report methods were used to measure all the key variables (stress, social support, and well-being) and so it is difficult to assess the degree to which shared method variance may have accounted for the findings.

Aside from their implication in the psychosomatic etiology of disease, physiological measures also offer objective indices of stress and so can be useful in circumventing problems of shared method variance. However, research investigating the association between social support and physiological indices at work has yielded mixed findings. For example, while some researchers have reported an inverse association between work social support and heart rate (e.g., Undén et al., 1991; Evans & Steptoe, 2001), other researchers have reported no association (e.g., Ituarte et al., 1999). Studies using cortisol output as an index of stress have been similarly inconsistent (e.g., Luecken et al., 1997; Evans & Steptoe, 2001). However, with few standardized measures available to researchers, the assessment of work social support has tended to be inconsistent across studies (Evans & Steptoe, 2001), implying that cross-study construct validity differences may underlie the heterogeneity of findings. Notably, the observations of significant associations between work social support and both heart rate (Undén et al., 1991; Evans & Steptoe, 2001) and cortisol (Evans & Steptoe, 2001) were drawn from studies using the same instrument to measure work social support (namely, that described by Undén et al., 1991).

Such findings are indicative of direct effects of work social support on stress responses. The possibility that buffering effects may also operate was suggested by Steptoe (2000), who found stress-related heart rate response at work to be reduced among participants reporting high social support. However, this study focused on generic social support (including that provided by friends and family) as opposed to work social support, and so the generalization of such findings to work social support specifically would require the assumption that the psychosocial ecology of the workplace substantially mirrors that of the home.

In any event, there are a number of complicating methodological aspects to the demonstration of buffering effects, especially in field studies (Morris et al., 1986; McClelland & Judd, 1993). First, relatively larger samples are required for the detection of statistical mediation and/or moderation than for the detection of direct associations (Aiken & West, 1993), which may account for the greater frequency with which direct effects are demonstrated in social support research. Further, the greater likelihood for non-significant findings to be accepted for publication when sample sizes are large than when sample sizes are small (see Schulz et al., 1995) may produce a publication bias that contributes to greater inconsistency in the buffering effects literature. In addition, even when large samples are studied, a number of statistical artifacts need to be accounted for before interactions can be interpreted as incidents of true buffering (Veiel, 1992). Finally, a number of other psychosocial factors could be relevant to the association between social support and the sequelae of stress – such as the congruence of source of support with type of stress (Beehr et al., 2003) and relevant gender roles (Vermeulen & Mustard, 2000; Beehr et al., 2003) – which themselves may moderate and/or mediate aspects of the observed relationships.

Job satisfaction and stress: from the workplace to ordinary life
It stands to reason that work stress is likely to contribute to (low) job satisfaction. Job satisfaction has itself been the subject of thousands of studies (Cranny et al., 1992). While low job satisfaction has been associated with poor mental and physical health (Faragher et al., 2005), it is interesting to note that many of its adverse consequences impinge upon or invoke the relationship between work life and life outside work. For example, low job satisfaction has been found to be a predictor of employee absenteeism (e.g., Wegge et al., 2007), which amounts to a preference for life outside work over that in the workplace. Similarly, in certain contexts low job satisfaction has been found to be associated with increased tardiness (Iverson & Deery, 2001) and employee turnover (Boswell et al., 2005), again perhaps reflecting a motivation to exchange the workplace for life outside work. As such, one consequence of work stress might be to impact upon the individual's perception of the comparative value of work life and of life outside work.

Such perceptions may have important consequences for the question of how the relationship between work and non-work demands might best be maintained, both at individual and societal levels. This matter has frequently been discussed with reference to terms such as 'work–life balance' (Crompton & Lyonette, 2006), 'work–life conflict' (Siegel et al., 2005), or 'work–life integration' (Jones, 2003), although the somewhat profound theoretical implications of the choice between using the terms 'balance', 'conflict', or 'integration' appear seldom acknowledged: a number of authors have noted the tendency for academic treatments of the question of work–life balance to be centered on economic, policy, and political concepts rather than psychosocial ones (Taylor, 2001; Crompton & Lyonette, 2006; Bryson et al., 2007).

In the psychological literature, the precise relationship between job satisfaction and satisfaction with life in general has been the subject of a controversial conceptual debate (Rain et al., 1991; Judge & Watanabe, 1993). Classically, three possible mechanisms have been proposed (Wilensky, 1960): 'spillover' occurs when job satisfaction is positively associated with satisfaction with life; 'compensation' occurs when job satisfaction is inversely associated with satisfaction with life; and 'segmentation' (or 'compartmentalization') occurs when there is no association between job and life satisfaction. In psychological terms, spillover is often described as the inevitable result of the integrative phenomenological link that exists across various domains of life as experienced by the individual: satisfaction or dissatisfaction in one domain will continue to be felt in the other. Compensation is often described as an adaptive defense mechanism, in which the individual seeks to fulfill appetitive needs for satisfaction by cultivating a particular level in one domain in order to offset perceived shortages in the other. Where it occurs, segmentation is also described as adaptive, insofar as it enables the individual to ignore dissatisfaction in one domain when functioning in the other. Given that statistical evidence has been reported for each mechanism, it is likely that each is plausible under particular circumstances.

The stress–support–health relationship: from workplace to ordinary life, and back again

The competing scenarios of spillover, compensation, and segmentation effects need not apply exclusively to job satisfaction. It appears equally plausible that such trends may appear in other contexts. For example, the constructs of work stress and life stress are likely to be strongly (inversely) related to those of job satisfaction and life satisfaction; thus, the relationship between work stress and life stress may also manifest spillover, compensation, or segmentation trends. Without specifically invoking such terminology, such concepts have been the subject of some previous research (e.g., Zuzanek & Mannell, 1983; Patterson et al., 2005).

It is also conceivable that the constructs of work social support and life social support might too manifest spillover-, compensation-, or segmentation-like trends. For example, in a spillover-like situation, a worker may report similar levels of social support at work as in ordinary life. Such a contingency might reflect a genuine spillover, wherein people maintain social relationships with work colleagues outside the workplace. However, a positive association between work social support and life social support may also reflect underlying dispositional factors. For example, it may reflect the fact that people's stable personality traits influence the nature and degree of their social support relationships, to the extent that work and home relationships become similar (Cloninger, 1986). Alternatively, it may be consistent with the suggestion that the reporting of social support reflects less of the objective reality of a respondent's environment than a disposition toward viewing interactions or relationships in a particular way (Kessler et al., 1992). Either way, such a pattern might suggest that the individual's preferences regarding social interaction are being met in both work and life contexts.

In a compensation-like situation, people's social support at work would be inversely related to their social support outside work. If this were genuine compensation then people who had low social support in one domain of life (work or outside work) would make active efforts to obtain high social support in the other. However, alternatively, such a pattern may be said to suggest poor work–life balance, in that it requires people's social behavior to be different in different domains. Given that stable personality traits (e.g., introversion–extraversion) are normally characterized by a *fixed* pattern of preferred social behavior, a so-called 'compensation pattern' may indicate a suboptimal situation where an individual finds one domain of life substantially preferable to the other.

Finally, in a segmentation-like situation, there would be no particular statistical association between work social support and life social support across persons. Such a pattern may reflect genuine segmentation. However, the likelihood of genuine segmentation appears low given that it would require a person's social interactions or relationships at work to bear no similarity at all with those outside work, which in turn would require the absence of any common antecedents to social behavior across domains (such as socially-relevant personality traits). Across a sample of individuals, a segmentation pattern may simply reflect the fact that the sample is composed of a mixture of individuals, some of whom manifest spillover and others of whom manifest compensation. While the overall correlation between work social support and life social support may be close to zero, for some workers it would be positive and for others it would be negative.

Conceptually, the above eventualities might be investigated by examining the correlation between work social support and life social support across a group of workers. If people vary in the extent to which they succeed in establishing balance between work social support and life social support then the correlation between the two should be close to zero. Then, of interest would be the relationship between work social support and life social support on individual bases. Such relationships could be categorized as 'dispositional' (i.e., where both work social support and life social support are high/low – equivalent to a spillover effect) or 'compensational' (i.e., where one is high and one is low). This could be achieved by examining the product of z-transformed work social support and life social support scores: positive products would represent a dispositional pattern, negative products a compensational pattern; the absolute size of the product would reflect the degree to which the individual represents either category. For example, an individual standing well above the sample means for work social support and life social support would have z-scores well above zero for both variables; the product score would also be well above zero (reflecting a strong dispositional effect). At the other extreme of strong disposition, an individual standing well *below* the sample means for both variables would have z-scores well below zero for each; the product of which would again be well *above* zero. (By ensuring a positive product score for *both* high–high *and* low–low combinations of work and life social support scores, the multiplication approach ensures that persons tending toward a dispositional pattern will be scored similarly, whether they have high or low social support in both domains.) On the other hand, persons with a compensational tendency (i.e., high work social support with low life social support, or vice versa) would yield *negative* product scores (the necessary result of multiplying positive z-scores with negative ones). Once again, the absolute size of the product would reflect the extent to which work and non-work social support diverge (i.e., the extent to which the individual is manifesting compensation).

In summary, the product of z-transformed work social support and life social support scores could be used by researchers to represent a continuum ranging from 'compensational' to 'dispositional', against which the nature of an individual's balance between work and life social support could be assessed. This measure could then be used to assess whether such balance is associated with health and well-being. Given that a compensational pattern implies that people's preferences for certain types of social interaction are being met only some of the time, but that a dispositional pattern implies that such preferences are being met most of the time, it can be hypothesized that dispositional patterns will prove to be more healthful.

Illustration

Psychometric measures allow for the assessment of variables such as social support in separate work and non-work domains. In addition, when contemplating the two domains, it is perhaps helpful to consider them as phases of time as much as realms of existence. For example, a suitable conceptualization might be the distinction between worktime (time spent at work, often during daytime and during the week) and downtime (time spent away from work, often in the evenings and at weekends). If so, then measures of stress taken at different times of the day, or on different days, might facilitate the inference of typical levels of work stress and non-work stress (or, at least, the impact on the individual of mental and physical challenges faced during work compared to those faced outside of work).

By way of illustrating the potential benefits of considering worktime–downtime distinctions in social support as well as in variables such as satisfaction, this author examined data collected during a larger study of personality factors and occupational stress (see Hughes, 2006). In this study, 33 male employees (mean age = 40.06 years, SD = 10.59 years; range, 27 to 63 years) of a mid-sized European university completed a battery of psychometric instruments prior to engaging in a five-day cardiovascular measurement regimen. In this regimen, participants self-monitored cardiovascular function throughout three consecutive workdays followed by two consecutive weekend days using a portable automated sphygmomanometer (Omron 637IT). The measurement validity of this sphygmomanometer has been confirmed against international standardization protocols (Eckert et al., 1997; Watson et al., 1998), and the apparatus has been used successfully in previous research in occupational health psychology (Evans & Steptoe, 2001). On each day, participants recorded 10 separate measures of cardiovascular function (including systolic blood pressure: SBP, and heart rate: HR), at various pre-set times from morning to bedtime.

Across the sample, cardiovascular measures taken during worktime were compared with those taken during two types of downtime. First, cardiovascular measures taken at work were compared with those taken during the evening after work of workdays. SBP was observed to decline from mean worktime levels of 121.36 mmHg (SD = 12.30 mmHg) to mean downtime levels of 120.21 mmHg (SD = 12.84 mmHg). Across the sample, the mean change from worktime to downtime was −1.15 mmHg (SD = 8.14 mmHg), although it is notable that individually the observed changes ranged from −14.58 mmHg to +17.00 mmHg, indicating that the changes observed varied considerably. Mean HR was observed to decline from worktime levels of 68.98 bpm (SD = 10.91 bpm) to downtime levels of 67.45 bpm (SD = 9.33 bpm), amounting to a mean change of −1.53 bpm (SD = 6.83 bpm). Again, the range of decline was broad, from −14.75 bpm to +10.50 bpm. As the participants were office workers and academics, it can reasonably be surmised that such patterns reflect the impact of psychological burdens (such as stress or cognitive challenge) rather than physical ones: self-report indices confirmed the assumption that time spent at work was spent tackling psychological, not physical, tasks. Second, cardiovascular measures at work were compared with those taken during equivalent times on weekend days. This comparison also showed SBP to be higher during worktime (mean = 122.45 mmHg, SD = 11.66 mmHg) than during downtime (mean = 120.26 mmHg, SD = 10.65 mmHg; amounting to a mean decline of 2.19 mmHg, SD = 7.48 mmHg). Similarly, HR was higher during worktime (mean = 70.14 bpm, SD = 9.43 bpm) than during downtime (mean = 69.74 bpm, SD = 9.92 bpm; a mean decline of 0.41 bpm, SD = 7.82 bpm). Once again, the observed changes varied considerably, ranging from −16.92 mmHg to +14.80 mmHg for SBP, and from −17.85 bpm to +16.13 bpm for HR. The fact that there was a broad range of changes from worktime to downtime implies that it is reasonable to consider what other variables might account for such individual differences.

Among the psychometric instruments completed by participants were measures of work social support (that described by Undén et al., 1991) and life social support (Sarason et al., 1987). The former comprised five items, requiring participants to rate their agreement with statements representing perceived quality of social support in the workplace. The latter comprised six items, requiring participants to rate their satisfaction with various types of social support available to them in ordinary life. In the present sample, both instruments manifested good internal consistency, with Cronbach's alphas of 0.74 and 0.86, respectively. The (Pearson) correlation between the two was close to zero ($r = +0.03$), suggesting possible segmentation between work social support and non-work social support. To score each participant's balance between work social support and non-work social support in terms of the compensational–dispositional continuum, the method described above was used: both work social support and non-work social support measures were z-transformed, and then each participant's z-transformed scores were multiplied together.

Scrutiny of bivariate cross-correlations revealed that compensational–dispositional scores were significantly and inversely correlated with shifts in HR observed in the evenings of workdays ($r = -0.38$, $p = 0.031$; see Figure 28.1). This pattern suggests that participants whose worktime and downtime social support were congruent (i.e., work social support and non-work social support both high or both low) experienced a decline in HR from worktime to downtime, perhaps indicative of an enhanced ability to relax (or 'unwind') after work (Vrijkotte et al., 2000). Conversely, participants whose worktime and downtime social support were incongruent (i.e., high work social support and low non-work social support, or vice versa) showed inclines in HR following work. This pattern was not observed for SBP. However, both HR and SBP showed similar relationships with compensational–dispositional scores when the worktime–downtime comparison focused on workdays and weekends. Shifts in HR from worktime to downtime were again correlated with compensational–dispositional scores ($r = -0.41$, $p = 0.019$; see Figure 28.2), as were shifts in SBP ($r = -0.42$, $p = 0.015$; see Figure 28.3). Using partial correlation to partial out variance due to age not only confirmed the presence of these relationships, but in the case of SBP appeared to strengthen the relationship statistically. The correlation for same-day worktime–downtime shift in HR became $r = -0.34$ ($p = 0.032$); that for weekend worktime–downtime shift in HR became $r = -0.42$ ($p = 0.018$); and that for weekend worktime–downtime shift in SBP became $r = -0.46$ ($p = 0.008$). Given that changes in cardiovascular parameters may be a function of their initial values (i.e., participants with higher worktime HR may exhibit larger decreases during downtime; see Benjamin, 1967), the correlations were recomputed with worktime values partialled out. The correlation for same-day worktime–downtime shift in HR became marginally non-signficant, $r = -0.34$ ($p = 0.060$), but the significance of other correlations was confirmed: the correlation for weekend worktime–downtime shift in HR became $r = -0.39$ ($p = 0.028$); and that in SBP became $r = -0.44$ ($p = 0.012$).

Conclusions and implications
Although based on a small sample and on few variables, the findings indicate that congruence between social support during work and outside work may be more adaptive than incongruence. Specifically, people whose levels of work social support were similar to their levels of non-work social support (i.e., those with more 'dispositional' associations

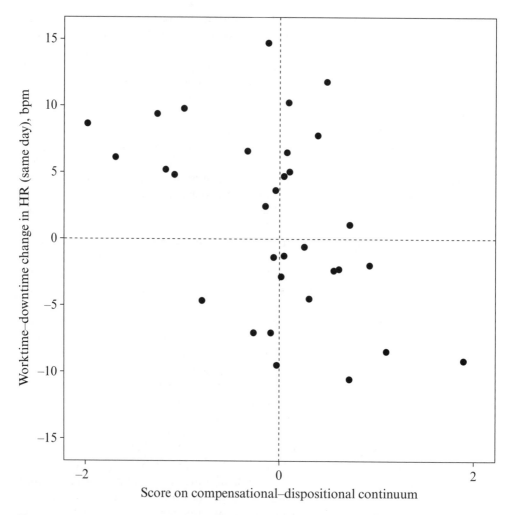

Notes:
1. Daytime-to-evening changes on workdays.
2. Low scores on the continuum reflect a compensational pattern in the association between work social support and non-work social support; high scores a dispositional pattern.
The correlation between the two variables is $r = -0.38$ ($p = 0.031$); after age is partialled out, it becomes $r = -0.34$ ($p = 0.032$).

Figure 28.1   *Scattergram showing worktime–downtime changes in HR[1] as a function of scores on the compensational–dispositional continuum[2]*

between the two) showed greater ability to unwind during downtime, as measured by the decline in two cardiovascular parameters (HR and SBP). On the other hand, people whose levels of work and non-work social support diverged (i.e., those with more 'compensational' associations) showed less ability to unwind, exhibiting increased HR and SBP during downtime. These relationships were observed to be independent of age. They were also observed to hold when initial values were controlled, meaning that the

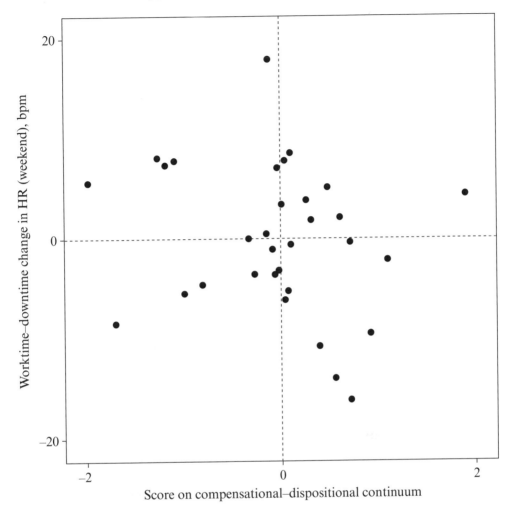

Notes:
1. Changes from workdays to weekend days.
2. Low scores on the continuum reflect a compensational pattern in the association between work social support and non-work social support; high scores a dispositional pattern.
The correlation between the two variables is $r = -0.41$ ($p = 0.019$); after age is partialled out, it becomes $r = -0.42$ ($p = 0.018$).

Figure 28.2   Scattergram showing worktime–downtime changes in HR[1] as a function of scores on the compensational–dispositional continuum[2]

differences pertained to actual changes from worktime to downtime and were not arti-facts of initial worktime levels. In general terms, the ability to unwind following work is of health benefit in that it contributes to lower levels of so-called 'usual' HR and blood pres-sure. On a population-wide basis, it is well established that inflated usual blood pressure represents a computable risk factor for premature death from a variety of causes. James (2004) has computed that a reduction across the general population of just 4 mmHg in

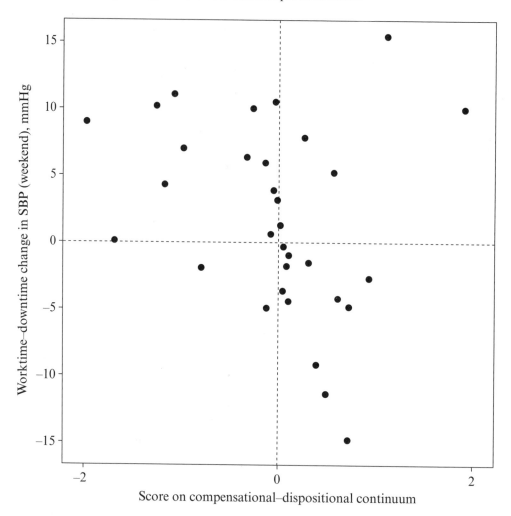

Notes:
1. Changes from workdays to weekend days.
2. Low scores on the continuum reflect a compensational pattern in the association between work social support and non-work social support; high scores a dispositional pattern.
The correlation between the two variables is $r = -0.42$ ($p = 0.015$); after age is partialled out, it becomes $r = -0.46$ ($p = 0.008$).

Figure 28.3   Scattergram showing worktime–downtime changes in SBP[1] as a function of scores on the compensational–dispositional continuum[2]

SBP could be expected to reduce premature death from coronary heart disease by 14% and from stroke by 20% (see also Prospective Studies Collaboration, 2002; Wolf-Maier et al., 2003). As can be seen in Figure 28.3, for most participants the shift in SBP from worktime to downtime was well in excess of 4 mmHg, and so the impact on measures of 'usual' blood pressure would be marked. Overall, therefore, the association in the present data between compensational–dispositional patterns and cardiovascular parameters is of potential epidemiological significance at a population level. The pattern suggested implicates incongruence between work and non-work social support – as distinct from low social support *per se* – in cardiovascular ill health.

The drawing of wide conclusions from the present illustrative dataset is inhibited by a number of conspicuous methodological limitations. First, only men are included and so there may be limited scope for generalizing findings to women: not only would men and women be expected to differ in cardiovascular function, but gender differences in both qualitative and quantitative aspects of social support would be expected (see Hughes, 2007b). Social support was measured by self-report, which may introduce shortcomings in construct validity. Further, although the participants all had sedentary occupations, the extent to which physical (rather than mental) exertion contributed to differences in cardiovascular function is unclear.

Nonetheless, the present data provide some food for thought. Conventionally, research on worktime–downtime distinctions has focused on each domain in isolation, or perhaps the contrast that exists between the two. However, the fact that the two domains might be related in a systemic way, such that differences in one influence the impact of the other, has rarely been studied. Everyday experience shows us that, for most people, work and non-work domains both have strong bearings on our personal identities: the prospect that a symbiotic, or homeostatic, connection between social support networks within and without the workplace might be empirically scrutinized offers exciting possibilities. Indeed, it could be that research that focuses exclusively on either domain might offer an incomplete perspective on the relationship between social support and stress in adults.

A further aspect of note is that the present data confirm the observation that people differ in their need for social support. In other words, the amount of support available to an individual (compared to what is available to others) is potentially less important than whether the amount available matches the individual's need. Having low social support is less of a problem for people who prefer autonomy and seclusion to interdependence and communion. Indeed, such individuals might find it stressful to be in environments where social interaction and supportive intervention are plentiful. The present data suggest that best adjustment is achieved by individuals whose level of workplace social support mirrors that which the individual has nurtured for themselves outside of work. The fact that not all people wish to have lots of social support may be an important consideration when seeking to address instances of workplace stress. Such preferences are likely to be shaped by individual differences in personality traits and types. Dispositions such as social dominance (Hughes & Callinan, 2007), hostility (Hughes, 2007a), and neuroticism (Kennedy & Hughes, 2004) are known to affect cardiovascular function; the fact that each would appear to be important in influencing social interaction and relationships suggests that personal preferences regarding social support may not only influence individuals' appraisal of the stressfulness of environments, but also reflect factors that in turn determine their habitual emotional and physiological responses to such environments.

The likelihood that the impact of social support on adjustment to stress is contingent on individual differences in social support preferences is likely to mean that the direct effect model is oversimplistic in scope. By positing a direct association between support and well-being, the direct effect model does not account for the role of individual differences, and so does not facilitate predictions regarding the interrelationships (if any) between worktime and downtime stress, and between work and non-work social support, in the assistance of coping. Further scrutiny of individual differences and the precise nature of the worktime–downtime nexus will be of continuing importance to occupational health psychologists, and should be considered in future methodological developments in the field.

Acknowledgement

This research was supported by a Government of Ireland Grant awarded by the Irish Research Council for Humanities and Social Sciences.

References

Aiken, L. & West, S.G. (1993), 'Detecting interactions in multiple regression: measurement error, power, and design considerations', *The Score: APA Division 5 Newsletter*, **16**, 7.

Beehr, T.A., Farmer, S.J., Glazer, S., Gudanowki, D.M. & Nair, V.N. (2003), 'The enigma of social support and occupational stress: source congruence and gender role effects', *Journal of Occupational Health Psychology*, **8**, 220–31.

Benjamin, L. (1967), 'Facts and artifacts in using analysis of covariance to "undo" the law of initial values', *Psychophysiology*, **4**, 187–206.

Boswell, W.R., Boudreau, J.W. & Tichy, J. (2005), 'The relationship between employee job change and job satisfaction: the honeymoon–hangover effect', *Journal of Applied Psychology*, **90**, 882–92.

Brunner, E.J., Marmot, M.G., Nanchahal, K., Shipley, M.J., Stansfeld, S.A., Juneja, M. & Alberti, K.G. (1997), 'Social inequality in coronary risk: central obesity and the metabolic syndrome – evidence from the WII study', *Diabetologia*, **40**, 1341–9.

Bryson, L., Warner-Smith, P., Brown, P. & Fray, L. (2007), 'Managing the work–life roller-coaster: private stress or public health issue?', *Social Science and Medicine*, **65**, 1142–53.

Chandola, T., Brunner, E. & Marmot, M. (2006), 'Chronic stress at work and the metabolic syndrome: prospective study', *British Medical Journal*, **332**, 521–5.

Cloninger, C.R. (1986), 'A unified biosocial theory of personality and its role in the development of anxiety states', *Psychiatric Developments*, **3**, 167–226.

Cohen, S. (1988), 'Psychosocial models of the role of social support in the etiology of physical disease', *Health Psychology*, **7**, 269–97.

Cranny, C.L., Smith, P. & Stone, F.F. (1992), *Job Satisfaction: How People Feel about Their Job and How It Affects Their Performance*, New York: Lexington.

Crompton, R. & Lyonette, C. (2006), 'Work–life "balance" in Europe', *Acta Sociologica*, **49**, 379–93.

Eckert, S., Gleichmann, U., Zagorski, O. & Klapp, A. (1997), 'Validation of the Omron R3 blood pressure self-measuring device through simultaneous comparative invasive measurements according to protocol 58130 of the German Institute for Validation', *Blood Pressure Monitoring*, **2**, 189–92.

Eriksen, W. (1994), 'The role of social support in the pathogenesis of coronary heart disease: a literature review', *Family Practice*, **11**, 201–9.

Evans, O. & Steptoe, A. (2001), 'Social support at work, heart rate, and cortisol: a self-monitoring study', *Journal of Occupational Health Psychology*, **6**, 361–70.

Faragher, E.B., Cass, M. & Cooper, C.L. (2005), 'The relationship between job satisfaction and health: a meta-analysis', *Occupational and Environmental Medicine*, **62**, 105–12.

Frasure-Smith, N., Lespérance, F., Gravel, G., Masson, A., Juneau, M., Talajic, M. & Bourassa, M.G. (2000), 'Social support, depression, and mortality during the first year after myocardial infarction', *Circulation*, **101**, 1919–24.

Griffin, J., Fuhrer, R., Stansfeld, S. & Marmot, M. (2002), 'The importance of low control at work and home on depression and anxiety: do these effects vary by gender and social class?', *Social Science and Medicine*, **54**, 783–98.

Hedblad, B., Östergren, P.-O., Hanson, B.S. & Janzon, L. (1992), 'Influence of social support on cardiac event rate in men with ischaemic type ST segment depression during ambulatory 24-h long-term recording: the prospective population study "Men born in 1914", Malmö, Sweden', *European Heart Journal*, **13**, 433–9.

House, J., Landis, S.A. & Umberson, D. (1988), 'Social relationships and health', *Science*, **241**, 540–45.

Hughes, B.M. (2006), 'Workaholism, the work environment, and occupational stress: a biopsychosocial perspective', in P. Buchwald (ed.), *Stress and Anxiety: Application to Health, Work Place, Community, and Education*, Newcastle: Cambridge Scholars Press, pp. 196–211.

Hughes, B.M. (2007a), 'Individual differences in hostility and habituation of cardiovascular reactivity to stress', *Stress and Health*, **23**, 37–42.

Hughes, B.M. (2007b), 'Social support in ordinary life and laboratory measures of cardiovascular reactivity: gender differences in habituation-sensitization', *Annals of Behavioral Medicine*, **34**, 166–76.

Hughes, B.M. & Callinan, S. (2007), 'Trait dominance and cardiovascular reactivity to social and non-social stressors: gender-specific implications', *Psychology and Health*, **22**, 457–72.

Ituarte, P.H., Kamarck, T.W., Thompson, H.S. & Bacanu, S. (1999), 'Psychosocial mediators of racial differences in nighttime blood pressure dipping among normotensive adults', *Health Psychology*, **18**, 393–402.

Iverson, R.D. & Deery, S.J. (2001), 'Understanding the "personological" basis of employee withdrawal: the influence of affective disposition on employee tardiness, early departure, and absenteeism', *Journal of Applied Psychology*, **86**, 856–66.

James, J.E. (2004), 'Critical review of dietary caffeine and blood pressure: a relationship that should be taken more seriously', *Psychosomatic Medicine*, **66**, 63–71.

Jones, A.M. (2003), 'Managing the gap: evolutionary science, work/life integration, and corporate responsibility', *Organizational Dynamics*, **32**, 17–31.

Judge, T.A. & Watanabe, S. (1993), 'Another look at the job–life satisfaction relationship', *Journal of Applied Psychology*, **78**, 939–48.

Kennedy, D.K. & Hughes, B.M. (2004), 'The optimism–neuroticism question: an evaluation based on cardiovascular reactivity in female college students', *Psychological Record*, **54**, 373–86.

Kessler, R.C., Kendler, K.S., Heath, A., Neale, M.C. & Eaves, L.J. (1992), 'Social support, depressed mood, and adjustment to stress: a genetic epidemiologic investigation', *Journal of Personality and Social Psychology*, **62**, 257–72.

Kristenson, M., Kucinskiene, Z., Bergdahl, B., Calkauskas, H., Urmonas, V. & Orth-Gomér, K. (1998), 'Increased psychosocial strain in Lithuanian versus Swedish men: the LiVicordia study', *Psychosomatic Medicine*, **60**, 277–82.

Leineweber, C., Kecklund, G., Jansky, I., Akerstedt, T. & Orth-Gomér, K. (2003), 'Poor sleep increases the prospective risk for recurrent events in middle-aged women with coronary disease: the Stockholm Female Coronary Risk Study', *Journal of Psychosomatic Research*, **54**, 121–7.

Luecken, L.J., Suarez, E.C., Kuhn, C.M., Barefoot, J.C., Blumenthal, J.A., Siegler, I.C. & Williams, R.B. (1997), 'Stress in employed women: impact of marital status and children at home on neurohormone output and home strain', *Psychosomatic Medicine*, **59**, 352–9.

Marmot, M.G., Bosma, H., Hemingway, H., Brunner, E. & Stansfeld, S. (1997), 'Contribution of job control and other risk factors to social variations in coronary heart disease', *Lancet*, **350**, 235–40.

Marmot, M., Davey Smith, G. & Stansfield, S. (1991), 'Health inequalities among British civil servants: the Whitehall II study', *Lancet*, **337**, 1387–93.

McClelland, G.H. & Judd, C.M. (1993), 'Statistical difficulties of detecting interactions and moderator effects', *Psychological Bulletin*, **114**, 376–90.

Morris, J.H., Sherman, J. & Mansfield, E.R. (1986), 'Failures to detect moderating effects with ordinary least squares moderated-regression: some reasons and a remedy', *Psychological Bulletin*, **99**, 282–8.

Patterson, C.R., Bennett, J.B. & Wiitala, W.L. (2005), 'Healthy and unhealthy stress unwinding: promoting health in small businesses', *Journal of Business and Psychology*, **20**, 221–47.

Prospective Studies Collaboration (2002), 'Age-specific relevance of usual blood pressure to vascular mortality: a meta-analysis of individual data for one million adults in 61 prospective studies', *Lancet*, **360**, 1903–13.

Rain, J.S., Lane, I.M. & Steiner, D.D. (1991), 'A current look at the job satisfaction/life satisfaction relationship: review and future considerations', *Human Relations*, **44**, 287–307.

Rosengren, A., Hawken, S., Ôunpuu, S., Sliwa, K., Zubaid, M., Alhahmeed, W.A., Blackett, K.N., Sitthi-Amorn, C., Sato, H. & Yusuf, S. (2004), 'Association of psychosocial risk factors with risk of acute myocardial infarction in 11,119 cases and 13,648 controls from 52 countries (the INTERHEART study): case-control study', *Lancet*, **364**, 953–62.

Rosengren, A., Orth-Gomér, K., Wedel, H. & Wilhelmsen, L. (1993), 'Stressful life events, social support, and mortality in men born in 1933', *British Medical Journal*, **307**, 1102–5.

Rozanski, A., Blumenthal, J.A. & Kaplan, J. (1999), 'Impact of psychological factors on the pathogenesis of cardiovascular disease and implications for therapy', *Circulation*, **99**, 2192–217.

Sarason, B.R., Sarason, I.G., Shearin, E.N. & Pierce, G.R. (1987), 'A brief measure of social support: practical and theoretical implications', *Journal of Social and Personal Relationships*, **4**, 497–510.

Schulz, K.F., Chalmers, I., Hayes, R.J. & Altman, D. (1995), 'Empirical evidence of bias: dimensions of methodological quality associated with estimates of treatment effects in controlled trials', *Journal of the American Medical Association*, **273**, 408–12.

Siegel, P.A., Post, C., Brockner, J., Fishman, A.Y. & Garden, C. (2005), 'The moderating influence of procedural fairness on the relationship between work–life conflict and organizational commitment', *Journal of Applied Psychology*, **90**, 13–24.

Steptoe, A. (2000), 'Stress, social support and cardiovascular activity over the working day', *International Journal of Psychophysiology*, **37**, 299–308.

Swan, J. & Cooper, C.L. (2005), *Time, Health, and the Family: What Working Families Want*, London: Working Families.

Taylor, R. (2001), *The Future of Work–Life Balance*, Swindon, UK: Economic and Social Research Council.

Undén, A.L., Orth-Gomér, K. & Elofsson, S. (1991), 'Cardiovascular effects of social support in the work place: twenty-four-hour ECG monitoring of men and women', *Psychosomatic Medicine*, **53**, 50–60.

Veiel, H.O.F. (1992), 'Some cautionary notes on buffer effects', in Veiel & U. Baumann (eds), *The Meaning and Measurement of Social Support*, New York: Hemisphere, pp. 273–89.

Vermeulen, M. & Mustard, C. (2000), 'Gender differences in job strain, social support at work, and psychological distress', *Journal of Occupational Health Psychology*, **5**, 428–40.

Viswesvaran, C., Sanchez, J.I. & Fisher, J. (1999), 'The role of social support in the process of work stress: a meta-analysis', *Journal of Vocational Behavior*, **54**, 314–34.

Vrijkotte, T.G.M., van Doornen, L.J.P. & de Geus, E.J.C. (2000), 'Effects of work stress on ambulatory blood pressure, heart rate, and heart rate variability', *Hypertension*, **35**, 880–86.

Watson, S., Wenzel, R.R., di Matteo, C., Meier, B. & Luscher, T.F. (1998), 'Accuracy of a new wrist cuff oscillometric blood pressure device: comparisons with intraarterial and mercury manometer measurements', *American Journal of Hypertension*, **11**, 1469–74.

Wegge, J., Schmidt, K.-H., Parkes, C. & van Dick, R. (2007), '"Taking a sickie": job satisfaction and job involvement as interactive predictors of absenteeism in a public organization', *Journal of Occupational and Organizational Psychology*, **80**, 77–89.

Wilensky, H. (1960), 'Work, careers, and social integration', *International Social cience Journal*, **12**, 543–60.

Wolf-Maier, K., Cooper, R.S., Banegas, J.R., Giampaoli, S., Hense, H.-W., Joffres, M., Kastarinen, M., Poulter, N., Primatesta, P., Rodríguez-Artalejo, F., Stegmayr, B., Thamm, M., Tuomilehto, J., Vanuzzo, D. & Vescio, F. (2003), 'Hypertension prevalence and blood pressure levels in 6 European countries, Canada, and the United States', *Journal of the American Medical Association*, **289**, 2363–9.

World Health Organization (WHO) (1994), 'WHO: Declaration on occupational health for all', http://www. who.int/occupational_health/publications/declaration/en/index.html, July 5, 2007.

Zuzanek, J. & Mannell, R. (1983), 'Work–leisure relationships from a sociological and social psychological perspective', *Leisure Studies*, **2**, 327–44.

29 Social support in the work stress context
Roman Cieslak

Introduction

For the last 50 years social support has been one of the most frequently investigated variables in psychology. Social support gained attention not because of theoretical developments addressing the social support concept and its role, but because of practitioners' observations that across a variety of stressful situations, social support has a positive effect on heath and well-being. However, a lack of theoretical background in studying social support was, and sometimes still is, a main problem of the research supporting this area. Years of intensive investigation of the concept finally led to some conclusions, but there is still a field for future development. One of the conclusions that can be drawn from the last decades of research is that the social support concept served as an umbrella term for many researchers: the same term was often used to describe different concepts and phenomena. The second conclusion is that social support is a multidimensional phenomenon, and such aspects of social support as its source (e.g., family, friends, co-workers, and supervisors), type (e.g., emotional, appraisal, instrumental, and informational support), direction (giving or receiving support), reciprocity, and visibility may be related to health, well-being, stress, or other variables in different ways. Finally, social support is a context-sensitive variable. Positive and negative functions ascribed to it depend on matching between social support characteristics (e.g., perceived social support from supervisors) and characteristics of an outcome variable (e.g., work-related well-being). These context-sensitive effects of social support are also extended to individual factors, such as gender and personality. Overall, it means that social support relates to the specific outcome variables, particularly when we control for certain individual characteristics.

According to the context-specific nature of social support, this chapter will focus on one type of social support outcomes, that is, work stress. It will be shown how the relationships between social support and work stress may depend on other variables, such as gender, personality and so on. We shall begin, however, with more basic information about definitions of social support and models of relationships between social support and its outcomes.

Social support definitions and models

The ambiguity in defining social support may be well illustrated by the fact that one of the recent analyses identifies over 30 definitions of social support (Williams et al., 2004). However, only a few of them have been used often by researchers and practitioners. The frequently used definitions are those formulated by Caplan (1974), Cobb (1976), House (1981) and Cohen and Syme (1985). Cobb claimed that social support is 'information leading the subject to believe that he [or she] is cared for and loved, esteemed, and a member of a network of mutual obligation' (1976, p. 300). For Cohen and Syme (1985), social support is the resource, that is, potentially useful information or things, provided by other persons. They also claimed that social support may have both positive and negative impacts on health, and that the relationship between health and social support may vary across life stages (p. 4). Caplan (1974) indicated that social support has different forms: 'the significant others help the individual mobilize his [or her] psychological resources and master his [or her] emotional burdens, they share his [or her] tasks, and they provide him [or her] with extra supplies of money, materials, tools, skill and cognitive guidance to improve his [or her] handling of his [or her] situation' (p. 6). With regard to the scope of this chapter, the definition fitting the work stress context was proposed by House (1981) in his book on social support and work stress. House claimed that social support is 'an interpersonal transaction involving one or more of the following: (1) emotional concern (liking, love, empathy), (2) instrumental aid (goods or services), (3) information (about the environment), or (4) appraisal (information relevant to self evaluation)' (p. 39).

In years of research and methodological analyses, three major facets of social support have been identified: perceived social support, received social support, and social embeddedness (Barrera, 1986). The first facet is related to a belief that social support would be available in times of need. The second refers to a perception of help that is being received at present or has been received in the past. In a nutshell, perceived social support refers to a future, while received social support is a perception of current or past supportive behaviors. Social embeddedness refers to the structural components of relationships, for example, to the types and number of relationships that a person is involved with, duration of contacts and so on. Although all three facets are interrelated, it was shown that they are related to health, well-being, and stress in a different manner or affect health through different mechanisms (Kaniasty & Norris, 1993).

Numerous theoretical models have been proposed to explain mechanisms through which social support is related to stress and health. Although some analyses yielded up to 12 models (Lin, 1986), three of them gained more attention and were tested frequently: the main effect of social support, its moderating (or buffering) effect, and its mediating effect (Viswesvaran et al., 1999). The primary notions of theses models are illustrated in Figure 29.1. The main effect model assumes that social support and stress affect stress outcomes independently. For example, role ambiguity at work has a negative effect on workers' well-being, and independently, low social support from family has a negative effect on well-being. Neither predictor of well-being (i.e., social support from family and role ambiguity at work) has to be interrelated to exert a deteriorating effect on a worker's well-being. The moderating effect of social support assumes that the negative effect of stress on a stress outcome can be reduced if high social support is present. For example, a negative effect of role ambiguity at work on well-being might not be observed if social support from co-workers is high. Finally, the mediational model indicates that stress may operate through social support and, indirectly, influences a person's well-being. For example, role ambiguity at work worsens relationships between workers and their supervisors, and this may result in a lack of social support from supervisors, which in turn has a direct effect on workers' well-being. This indirect effect of stress on health or well-being (via social support) does not, however, exclude the possibility of co-existing direct effects of role ambiguity on well-being. If both the direct and the indirect effects exist, then social support partially mediates the effect of role ambiguity on well-being. If there is only an indirect effect, then it could be considered as a fully mediated model of relationships among stress, its outcomes, and social support (see Baron & Kenny, 1986).

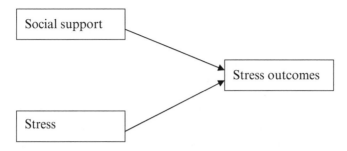

(1) Direct effects of social support and stress on stress outcomes

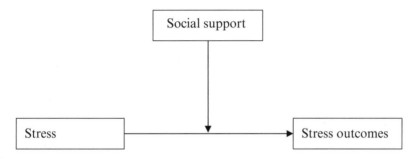

(2) Negative effect of stress on stress outcomes is moderated (buffered) by social support

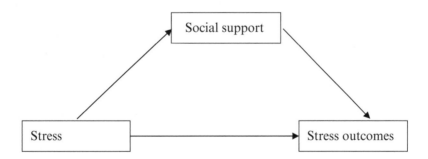

(3) The effect of stress on stress outcomes is mediated by social support

Figure 29.1   *Three basic theoretical models of relationships among social support, stress, and stress outcomes*

Social support and work stress models
Several work stress models consider that social support contributes to processes that lead to work stress and its negative outcomes. These models vary in their assumptions, complexity, and in the degree to which they have been tested. Some of them will be reviewed below, with an emphasis on social support processes.

The demand–control–support model
The demand–control–support (DCS) model is probably one of the most frequently tested models in occupational health psychology. In the earlier version of this model – i.e., the job demands–control model (JD–C) – it was assumed that work strain (i.e., work stress) is the result of working in conditions that may be characterized as high job demands and low latitude of control (Karasek, 1979). In a later development of this model (i.e., in the DCS model), a moderating role has been assigned to social support. It was hypothesized that high job demands and low job control will produce work strain if social support is low. If social support is high, interaction between high job demands and low job control should not lead to work strain (Johnson & Hall, 1988; Karasek & Theorell, 1990).

Although there is limited evidence that interaction of job demands, job control, and social support is predictive of mental health outcomes or well-being, many studies indicated that the main effects of these three work conditions are predictive of well-being, work stress, burnout and so on (e.g., Pelfrene et al., 2002; De Lange et al., 2003; Bakker et al., 2004). Recently, it was also shown that the relationship between these three psychosocial working conditions and mental health is not curvilinear (Rydstedt et al., 2006). The results of a longitudinal study conducted by Rydstedt et al. in a large sample is of particular importance, because one of the major critiques addressing the DCS model stated that relationships between the working conditions and health may be curvilinear (De Jonge & Kompier, 1997). For example, a previous cross-sectional study indicated a possible U-shaped relation between social support and emotional exhaustion as well as social support and depression (De Jonge et al., 2000). The same study also showed that there are direct linear effects of social support on job satisfaction, psychosomatic complaints, and absence due to sickness.

Another critique related to the DCS model is an oversimplification of the relationships among the three working conditions. The DCS model assumes that interaction among job demands, job control, and social support is predictive of work strain and health-related indices. In a longitudinal study involving workers of five occupations, Cieslak et al. (2007) showed, however, that relationships among working conditions need further investigation. They indicated that relationships between social support and work strain characteristics (i.e., job demands and job control) are actually reciprocal and furthermore, the directions of reciprocal relations are moderated by a personality variable: neuroticism. Among workers with a low level of neuroticism, high social support from supervisors was predictive of high job control. However, among workers with high neuroticism, high job demands and low job control predicted low social support from supervisors. In another longitudinal study involving a multinational sample of 542 administrative workers, Rodriguez et al. (2001) demonstrated that the effect of the interaction of job demands, control, and social support on job dissatisfaction is also moderated by a personality variable, that is, locus of control. High social support buffered the effects of work strain (high job demands and low job control) on job dissatisfaction, but only among participants who had internal locus of control. Among participant with external locus of control, social support did not buffer the effects of work strain on job dissatisfaction.

Model of the Pressure Management Indicator
A practice-based and -oriented approach to define work stress was proposed by Williams and Cooper (1998). They developed the Pressure Management Indicator (PMI), a

modified and shortened version of another questionnaire, that is, the Occupational Stress Indicator (OSI, Cooper et al., 1988). The PMI integrates achievements of other theories and studies on occupational stress to present a comprehensive picture of occupational stress dimensions. The authors assumed that the PMI had to be a very practical tool, thus the questionnaire is based on a simple theoretical model. Dimensions of occupational stress were grouped into three major categories: (i) stressors (workload, relationships, recognition, organizational climate, personal responsibility, managerial role, home–work balance, daily hassles); (ii) outcomes (job satisfaction, organizational satisfaction, organizational security, organizational commitment, state of mind, resilience, confidence level, physical symptoms, energy level); and (iii) moderators of relationships between stressors and outcomes (Type A drive, patience/impatience, control, personal influence, problem focus, life–work balance, social support). Results of analyses of data obtained from over 8,500 workers suggested that social support is positively related to job and organizational satisfaction, organizational security, organizational commitment, and resilience. Social support was negatively associated with the state of mind, confidence levels, physical symptoms, and energy levels. All correlation coefficients were, however, rather small (from 0.03 to 0.07, $p < 0.05$) (Williams & Cooper 1998). Moreover, the PMI assessed a specific facet of support: received rather than perceived social support and informational or instrumental rather than emotional or appraisal support.

Using the PMI model, Bellman et al. (2003) tested one of the notions of this model, namely the assumption that social support moderates the effects of stressors on the outcomes. They collected data from 204 Australian managers and showed a different pattern of results for male and female participants. For example, only among male managers did social support moderate the effect of workload on job satisfaction, organizational security, organizational commitment, and energy level. In contrast, only among female managers did social support moderate the effect of organizational climate on job satisfaction, organizational commitment, and state of mind. Although the authors did not discuss whether social support may buffer or enhance the negative effects of stressors on the outcomes, the result indicated that gender is an important contextual variable for investigating the relationship between social support and work stress.

Conservation of resources
Several studies in occupational health psychology applied conservation of resources theory (COR) to investigate predictors of workers' stress, health, well-being, and burnout. COR theory emphasizes that both individual and environmental factors are predictive of stress. According to Hobfoll (2001), stress occurs when at least one of three conditions is met: (i) resources are threatened with loss; (ii) resources are lost; and (iii) there is an insufficient gain of the resources after an investment of resources. Resources, the key term in COR theory, are defined as 'objects, personal characteristics, conditions, or energies that are valued in their own right, or that are valued because they act as conduits to the achievement or protection of valued resources' (p. 339). Hobfoll listed 74 such resources, many of them related to social support, for example, feeling valuable to others, intimacy with one or more family members, support from co-workers, loyalty of friends, help with tasks at home, affection from others, and companionship.

In line with COR theory, results of a meta-analysis of 114 papers suggested that lack of social support is predictive of burnout (Halbesleben, 2006). The meta-analysis also suggested some effects that were not indicated in COR theory. For example, sources of social support differed in predictive power across three dimensions of burnout (i.e., emotional exhaustion, depersonalization, and lack of personal accomplishment). Work-related sources of support were predictive of exhaustion, while non-work-related sources were predictive of depersonalization and a lack of personal accomplishments (ibid.). Freedy and Hobfoll (1994) confirmed some of the assumptions of COR theory in an experimental study. They tested whether two types of intervention aiming at increasing coping resources were effective in stress reduction among nurses: the first aimed at an enhancement of both social support and mastery; the second targeted only the enhancement of mastery (personal control). The results showed that the first intervention was effective, that is, it caused reductions in psychological stress, among participants with low baseline levels of social support or mastery. The other intervention was less effective. This study confirmed that an enhancement of social support resources may be of particular importance in stress reduction among workers.

The Michigan model
To date, many versions of the Michigan model have been developed (see LaRocco et al., 1980; House, 1981; House et al., 1988), however, all of them focused on the relationship among social support, work stress, and health. The most frequently cited version of the model (House, 1981) describes three avenues by which social support affects workers' health: (i) it reduces work stress, thus work stress does not affects workers' health; (ii) it has a direct positive effect on health; and (iii) it moderates or buffers the negative effects of work stress on health.

In a study of male middle-level managers, Luszczynska and Cieslak (2005) found that the effects of social support on work stress and health depend on sources of support. For example, only support from supervisors predicted low work stress. Social support from other sources (i.e., co-workers, friends, and family) predicted positive affect (curiosity) only in the interaction with a personality factor, that is, hardiness. Managers benefited from high social support if their levels of hardiness were low. The buffering hypothesis was also confirmed when hardiness was considered. The negative effect of work stress on curiosity was buffered by social support from co-workers or family, but only when participants had low levels of hardiness. These results support the notion of taking into account personality variables when the role of social support is investigated. Another study that tested the Michigan model also showed that personality factors should be considered. Jones et al. (2005) indicated that among newly hired healthcare professionals, neuroticism contributed to perceptions of managerial social support, work characteristics, and stress outcomes. They also demonstrated that perceptions of managerial social support mediated the effects of neuroticism on work characteristics and stress outcomes. These two studies suggest that personality factors are involved in the relationships between social support and work stress; however, further investigations are needed to learn what personality characteristics are crucial and in which way they influence the relationships assumed in the Michigan model.

Social support as a context-specific variable
The review of models applied to work stress indicates that social support is a crucial factor that may influence workers' health and well-being through various processes. Studies that

tested hypotheses derived from these models suggested, however, that relations among social support, work stress and health are sensitive to contextual variables. Overall, social support is a beneficial resource when the type of social support is relevant for the investigated outcomes, types of stress, and individual characteristics of participants. This contextual approach to investigate the role of social support was supported in a line of research. For example, Bowling et al. (2005) found that giving social support is related to receiving it. Moreover, extraversion and agreeableness were associated with giving and receiving non-job-related social support and with giving and receiving positive work-related support. None of the three investigated personality traits (extraversion, agreeableness, and neuroticism) predicted giving or receiving negative work-related social support. The study also showed that the effect of extraversion on receiving non-job social support and on receiving positive work-related support was mediated by giving non-job support or by giving positive work-related support, respectively. The same pattern of results was found for another personality factor, agreeableness. Overall, these results emphasize the role of reciprocity in social support processes and showed that personality factors play an active role as the antecedents of social support.

Many studies indicated that gender is an important individual variable in investigating the relationship between social support and health or distress (Bellman et al., 2003). Testing for the effects of gender may result in obtaining different results for men and women workers. For example, in a study of men and women managers, Lindorff (2000) showed that a negative effect of perceived social support on distress is observed among both men and women. In contrast, receiving emotional support increased symptoms of distress only among men. Moreover, among men the negative effects of perceived social support on distress were insignificant when men received high social support. This effect was not observed among women.

Another contextual variable that is usually neglected refers to the reciprocity of the relationship between social support and work-related health. Most social support models hypothesize that social support has a positive effect on health. There is evidence for a reverse causation, that is, some research indicated that social support is influenced by health. For example, the cross-lagged data analyses of the data collected among 668 employees confirmed that job satisfaction is positively related to social support from supervisors measured during a follow-up. More importantly, the relationship between social support and emotional exhaustion was reciprocal: emotional exhaustion predicted low social support from supervisors measured during a follow-up. On the other hand, low social support predicted high emotional exhaustion measured during a follow-up (De Lange et al., 2004). Other studies, however, failed to confirm a reciprocal relationship between social support and work-related health (De Jonge et al., 2001; Ter Doest & De Jonge, 2006). Although there might be many explanations of these contradictory results, a time lag between waves of measurement is a primary suspect. As Ter Doest and De Jonge demonstrated in a study with a longer time lag between the waves of data collection (i.e., two years), relationships between social support and work-related well-being was not reciprocal, but unidirectional: high social support predicted high job satisfaction and low emotional exhaustion measured at a follow-up two years later. Overall, these results mean that reciprocal relationships should be considered when social support is investigated in the occupational health context. A time lag between waves of measurement, however, should be carefully considered.

We have demonstrated in this chapter that relationships between social support, work stress, and stress outcomes are complex and sensitive to the contextual variables. Although during recent decades knowledge about social support and its effects has accumulated, there are still many challenges that need to be investigated. The research evidence indicates that a beneficial role of social support does not occur in every circumstance and not for everyone. Work-related social support may affect some areas of well-being, but remain unrelated to others. For example, research indicates a decrease in emotional exhaustion and negative affect and an increase in job satisfaction and positive affect, but very few studies provide evidence for beneficial effects of social support on physical aspects of well-being or somatic symptoms. From the practical point of view this means that social support interventions should be tailored not only to workers' actual situation (e.g., type of employment and organizational structure), and their gender, but also to respondents' personality (e.g., neuroticism, extraversion, agreeableness) which may affect perception of social support and consequently, the effectiveness of social support interventions. Therefore, one way to successfully implement social support interventions in organizations would be to monitor not only working conditions and stress outcomes, but also individual needs for a specific type of social support.

References

Bakker, A.B., Demerouti, E. & Verbeke, W. (2004), 'Using the job demands–resources model to predict burnout and performance', *Human Resource Management*, **43** (1), 83–104.

Baron, R.M. & Kenny, D.A. (1986), 'The moderator–mediator variable distinction in social psychological research: conceptual, strategic and statistical considerations', *Journal of Personality and Social Psychology*, **51** (6), 1173–82.

Barrera, M. (1986), 'Distinctions between social support concepts, measures, and models', *American Journal of Community Psychology*, **14** (4), 413–45.

Bellman, S., Forster, N., Still, L. & Cooper, C.L. (2003), 'Gender differences in the use of social support as a moderator of occupational stress', *Stress and Health*, **19** (1), 45–58.

Bowling, N.A., Beehr, T.A. & Swader, W.M. (2005), 'Giving and receiving social support at work: the roles of personality and reciprocity', *Journal of Vocational Behavior*, **67** (3), 476–89.

Caplan, G. (1974), 'Support systems', in Caplan (ed.), *Support Systems and Community Mental Health*, Behavioral Publications, New York, pp. 1–40.

Cieslak, R., Knoll, N. & Luszczynska, A. (2007), 'Reciprocal relations among job demands, job control and social support are moderated by neuroticism: a crossed-lagged analysis', *Journal of Vocational Behavior*, **71** (1), 84–96.

Cobb, S. (1976), 'Social support as a moderator of life stress', *Psychosomatic Medicine*, **38** (5), 300–314.

Cohen, S. & Syme, S.L. (1985), *Social Support and Health*, Academic Press, Orlando, FL.

Cooper, C.L., Sloan, S.J. & Williams, S. (1988), *Occupational Stress Indicator*, NFERNelson, Windsor, UK.

De Jonge, J., Dormann, C., Janssen, P.P.M., Dollard, M.F., Landeweerd, J.A. & Nijhuis, F.J.N. (2001), 'Testing reciprocal relationships between job characteristics and psychological well-being: a cross-lagged structural equation model', *Journal of Occupational and Organizational Psychology*, **74** (1), 29–46.

De Jonge, J. & Kompier, M.A.J. (1997), 'A critical examination of the demand–control–support model from a work psychological perspective', *International Journal of Stress Management*, **4** (4), 235–58.

De Jonge, J., Reuvers, M.M.E.N., Houtman, I.L.D. & Kompier, M.A. (2000), 'Linear and nonlinear relations between psychosocial job characteristics, subjective outcomes, and sickness absence: baseline result from SMASH', *Journal of Occupational Health Psychology*, **5** (2), 256–68.

De Lange, A.H., Taris, T.W., Houtman, I.L.D., Kompier, M.A.J. & Bongers, P.M. (2003), '"The very best of the Millennium": longitudinal research and the demand–control–(support) model', *Journal of Organizational Health Psychology*, **8** (4), 282–305.

De Lange, A.H., Taris, T.W., Kompier, M.A.J., Houtman, I.L.D. & Bongers, P.M. (2004), 'The relationships between work characteristics and mental health: examining normal, reversed and reciprocal relationships in a 4-way study', *Work and Stress*, **18** (2), 149–66.

Freedy, J.R. & Hobfoll, S.E. (1994), 'Stress inoculation for reduction of burnout: a conservation of resources approach', *Anxiety, Stress, and Coping*, **6** (4), 311–25.

Halbesleben, J.R.B. (2006), 'Sources of social support and burnout: a meta-analytic test of the conservation of resources model', *Journal of Applied Psychology*, **91** (5), 1134–45.

Hobfoll, S.E. (2001), 'The influence of culture, community, and the nested-self in the stress process: advancing conservation of resource theory', *Applied Psychology: An International Journal*, **50** (3), 337–421.

House, J.S. (1981), *Work Stress and Social Support*, Addison-Wesley, Reading, MA.

House, J.S., Umberson, D. & Landis, K.R. (1988), 'Structures and processes of social support', *Annual Review of Sociology*, **14**, 293–318.

Johnson, J.V. & Hall, E.M. (1988), 'Job strain, work place social support and cardiovascular disease: a cross-sectional study of a random sample of the Swedish working population', *American Journal of Public Health*, **78** (10), 1336–42.

Jones, M.C., Smith, K. & Johnston, D.W. (2005), 'Exploring the Michigan model: the relationship of person-ality, managerial support and organizational structure with health outcomes in entrants to the healthcare environment', *Work and Stress*, **19** (1), 1–22.

Kaniasty, K. & Norris, F. (1993), 'A test of the support deterioration model in the context of natural disaster', *Journal of Personality and Social Psychology*, **64** (3), 395–408.

Karasek, R. (1979), 'Job demands, job decision latitude, and mental strain: implications for job redesign', *Administrative Science Quarterly*, **24** (2), 285–308.

Karasek, R. & Theorell, T. (1990), *Healthy Work*, Basic Books, New York.

LaRocco, J.M., House, J.S. & French, J.R.P. (1980), 'Social support, occupational stress, and health', *Journal of Health and Social Behavior*, **21**, 202–18.

Lin, N. (1986), 'Conceptualizing social support', in Lin, A. Dean & W. Ensel (eds), *Social Support, Life Events, and Depression*, Academic Press, Orlando, FL, pp. 17–48.

Lindorff, M. (2000), 'Is it better to perceive than receive? Social support, stress and strain for managers', *Psychology, Health and Medicine*, **5** (3), 271–86.

Luszczynska, A. & Cieslak, R. (2005), 'Protective, promotive, and buffering effects of perceived social support in managerial stress: the moderating role of personality', *Anxiety, Stress, and Coping*, **18** (3), 227–44.

Pelfrene, E., Vlerick, P., Kittel, F., Mak, R., Kornitzer, M. & De Backer, G. (2002), 'Psychosocial work environment and psychological well-being: assessment of the buffering effects in the job demand–control (–support) model in BELSTRESS', *Stress and Health*, **18** (1), 43–56.

Rodriguez, I., Bravo, M.J. & Peiro, J.M. (2001), 'The demands–control–support model, locus of control and job dissatisfaction: a longitudinal study', *Work and Stress*, **15** (2), 97–114.

Rydstedt, L., Ferrie, J. & Head, J. (2006), 'Is there support for curvilinear relationships between psychosocial work characteristics and mental well-being? Cross-sectional and long-term data from the Whitehall II study', *Work and Stress*, **20** (1), 6–20.

Ter Doest, L. & De Jonge, J. (2006), 'Testing causal models of job characteristics and employee well-being: a replication study using cross-lagged structural equation modelling', *Journal of Occupational and Organizational Psychology*, **79**, 499–507.

Visweswaran, C., Sanchez, J.I. & Fisher, J. (1999), 'The role of social support in the process of work stress: A meta-analysis', *Journal of Vocational Behavior*, **54** (2), 314–34.

Williams, P., Barcley, L. & Schmied, V. (2004), 'Defining social support in context: a necessary step in improv-ing research, intervention, and practice', *Qualitative Health Research*, **14** (7), 942–60.

Williams, S. & Cooper, C.L. (1998), 'Measuring occupational stress: development of the Pressure Management Indicator', *Journal of Occupational Health Psychology*, **3** (4), 306–21.

Index